Springer Series on Cultural Computing

More information about this series at http://www.springer.com/series/10481

Tula Giannini · Jonathan P. Bowen
Editors

Museums and Digital Culture

New Perspectives and Research

Springer

Editors
Tula Giannini
Professor
School of Information
Pratt Institute
New York, USA

Jonathan P. Bowen
School of Engineering
London South Bank University
London, UK

Southwest University
Chongqing, China

ISSN 2195-9056 ISSN 2195-9064 (electronic)
Springer Series on Cultural Computing
ISBN 978-3-319-97456-9 ISBN 978-3-319-97457-6 (eBook)
https://doi.org/10.1007/978-3-319-97457-6

Library of Congress Control Number: 2019935154

This Springer imprint is published by the registered company Springer Nature Switzerland AG
The registered company address is: Gewerbestrasse 11, 6330 Cham, Switzerland

Enquire Within by Jill Lauriston (2017), a mixed media work exhibited at the Weston Library, Bodleian Library, Oxford, “From King Alfred to Chaucer: First graphic designers of English texts”. (© Jill Lauriston)

Foreword

Understanding digital culture is critical to the success of a museum professional in the 21st century. The digitization of the world has created a paradigm shift for museums: It is challenging our models of thinking and working. If museums are to retain their relevance, we will need to adapt museum strategies, planning processes, workflows, practices and programs to align with the expectations and behaviors of our digitally enabled audiences.

For our audiences, a digital experience is not inferior, less authentic or a substitute to a physical experience. It is simply a different experience. It is the responsibility of museum professionals to study, analyze, test that difference and determine how best to leverage the opportunities it provides to more impactfully fulfill our institutions' goals. Whether those goals are to scale the museum's mission globally or design a more multisensory exhibition experience or develop a networked collection management practice, there is no one size fits all. Our success in guiding our institutions through the transformative and complex impacts of digitization requires that we continue to cultivate what is unique about our institutions: their collections, audiences, remits and identities. To achieve this, we need to be thinking about digitization on several different levels, and through a depth of different perspectives: This is what this book does.

By exploring digital culture and museums through nine different lenses, this book provides the reader with a foundational framework around which to develop our understanding of digital culture. It looks at the topic from the perspective of educators, curators, artists and audiences, through the lens of history and the future, and from operational and creative perspectives. In so doing, ideas are introduced, explored, re-explored and developed throughout the book, enabling the reader to build a richer understanding of the key issues at hand.

By virtue of living in the 21st century, we are all students of digitization. The next generation of technologies that are reaching mass-markets—artificial intelligence, augmented realities, virtual realities and machine vision—will only accelerate the rate of digitization of our world. Now is the time to ensure we have the tools necessary to make sense of that future.

New York, USA
2019

Loïc Tallon
Chief Digital Officer
The Metropolitan Museum of Art

Preface

This richly illustrated book offers new perspectives and research on how digital culture is transforming museums in the 21st century, as they strive to keep pace with emerging technologies driving cultural and social change, played out not only in today's pervasive networked environment of the Internet and Web, but in everyday life, from home to work and on city streets. In a world where digital culture has redefined human information behavior as life in code and digits, increasingly it dominates human activity and communication. These developments have radically changed the expectations of the museum visitor, real and virtual, the work of museum professionals and, most prominently, the nature of museum exhibitions, while digital art and life in a digitally saturated world is changing our ways of seeing, doing, our senses and aesthetics.

Overall, this book creates a new picture of the 21st-century museum field. As museums become shared spaces with their communities, local, national and global and move from collection-centered to user-/visitor-centered institutions, they are assuming new roles and responsibilities tied to new goals for engaging their audience, conveying meaning through collections, creating learning experiences and importantly, connecting to daily digital life and culture integral to the museum ecosystem. Our studies of recent exhibitions at museums leading change are used to exemplify new directions, while they point to a reimagined vision for museums of the future at the heart of which is the integration of digital culture and visitor experience and participation in real and virtual space.

This volume builds upon the work of the editors, Giannini and Bowen, including co-authored articles published over the past few years, lectures and research-based teaching related to museums and digital culture. Considered holistically, these research forays into museum life and exhibitions shed new light on museums during a period of digital transformation in the context of emerging technologies and dramatic social change both local and global. Increasingly, museums are reaching beyond their walls to engage with their communities and audiences, onsite and online. Through conversations mediated by Web sites, social media and online collections, museums are listening to public voices fostering greater diversity and inclusion. Using this as a starting point, the editors have organized the discussion broadly, while contributors speak from their own experiences and expertise that taken together creates a new view of the field. Recent exhibitions at museums that are leading change are used to exemplify new directions and new vision for museums of the future.

Having surveyed recent books on museums, this book is distinguished by its focus on how museums are interacting with their external environment and the people they serve, set in a digital moment of rapid social and cultural change. We look at how museums are transforming from their 19th century past to reinvent their identity, and the look and feel of museum galleries, seeking new ways of conveying meaningful narratives and messages. So, while other books are considering museums from the inside—administration, management, process and collections—our book considers museums from the vantage point of inside/outside interaction, participation and collaboration. This porous, flexible model enables new ideas and change—breaking out of the established silos of past practice.

We feature case studies through the lens of digital artists, exhibitions, gallery design and architecture, both physical and virtual. The book aims to create a body of new evidence that inspires the reader to consider the new evolving museum landscape and its diverse communities. We show how the digital ecosystem, to which we are all connected and which is spawning the Internet of Things, has laid the foundations of the postdigital world we are now entering, in which physical and digital aspects are integrated seamlessly.

In Part I of the book, we introduce the digital culture background of the book beginning in the 1940s, with the work of Alan Turing, inventor of computer science, and Claude Shannon, inventor of information theory and digital communication, a moment in time which marked the dawn of the digital revolution, one that links to the popular cultural revolution of the 1960s to 1980s. These breakthroughs set the stage for the introduction and development of the Internet, and the defining moment in 1989 when Tim Berners-Lee brought us the World Wide Web. Acting as a catalyst for growing participation online, the Web turned the digital tide toward visual interface, smartphones and personal digital devices that sparked the rapid rise of digital culture. Through observations over time, we document how these developments have touched every aspect of human life. As the space between digital and physical, real and virtual blurs, recasting art, cultural, social life and human behavior into new digital forms, places and spaces, digital life and culture are merging and redefining the way we live, while more and more we think and see digitally. From a foundational view, we look at how museums living in a digital culture are changing and adopting to the digital behavior of visitors who enter the museum with smartphones in hand, looking at a small screen, as the focus of life and their lens on the world. From observations in museums and online, we discuss how museum/audience interaction is altering the expectations of visitors and their sense of what the museum experience should be. At the same time, we explore how digital art shifts our ways of seeing, our senses and aesthetics to the digital realm, while the ubiquitous presence of digital is blurring the lines between pop art and high art, real and virtual, as we enter a postdigital world merging physical and digital reality.

Part II considers philosophical and theoretical aspects of how technology is affecting the artist's sense of being and experience, questioning what in art changes and what is lasting, whether we see through our sense of poetry and nature, or through the lens of a camera that can distance the artist from the thinking and feeling about art. From the vantage point of the 19th and 20th centuries, we look at the question of how technology might change the artist's sensibilities, juxtaposing the theories of art from Hegel, Goethe, Barfield and McLuhan, and moving from past to present, to observe the nature of digital change.

Part III covers digital aspects of art and museum-related temporary exhibitions. We present evidence drawn from experience and data gathered, as well as the literature—books and articles—over the past few years. Exhibitions, considered the centerpiece of the life of the museum, are increasingly tied to the museum's digital life where most of museum work and activities are carried out and where art and information come together to convey content, meaning and narrative. We present a survey of exhibitions over the past few years by leading museums in New York and London to show new trends, innovative use of digital media technology, and an increasing presence of digital, installation and mixed media art. We juxtapose digital works exhibited inside and outside the museum and explore how the use of digital displays across most sectors of society is influencing how the public views art which in turn questions its very nature and meaning.

In Part IV, we consider some digital aspects of museum collections, which may themselves now be digital in nature. An important current issue is how permanent exhibitions in museums are being updated to meet audience expectations. To accomplish these goals, museums are developing a digital strategy applied across the entire museum. Generally, museums in 19th- and early 20th-century buildings are being challenged to find innovative ways to re-conceptualize their galleries and public space for the 21st century.

Part V presents issues with museum audiences and visitors in a digital and virtual context. Real and digital interaction and participation are all important aspects to be considered by museums. Visitors/users empowered by digital technology, especially smartphones, have new expectations for engagement. There is a need for museums to convey meaning, engage visitors and reflect social consciousness and awareness. Museums of any size must have programs for outreach, diversity, inclusion and community interaction. Digital states of being and identity are changing visitor behavior and recasting museums' identity to aid visitors in new ways of thinking about the world, as well as their evolving social and cultural consciousness. As museums build relationships through social media, they can find themselves more vulnerable to audience opinion and its relationship to art on display.

Part VI presents the ideas and work of several digital artists, mostly in the form of interviews with selected digital artists. Digital aesthetics and senses, installation, mixed media, interactive and participatory art, virtual reality, augmented reality, robots and robotics, and the presence of digital artists on the Web, in their own voices, all impact on museums, and especially on art galleries. Increasingly, people are seeing digital as the world they inhabit is saturated with digital media. This immersion in digital media is affecting the human sense of color, light, space and time.

In Part VII, educational aspects are considered. For example, Tula Giannini designed and introduced to Pratt School of Information three museum-related programs, the first of their kind: fall 2015, a new museum master's program, Master of Science in Museums & Digital Culture, that newly defines the knowledge and skill sets for 21st-century museum professionals through its cutting-edge curriculum; fall 2016, a new Advanced Certificate in Digital Curation and Preservation; fall 2016, a dual-master's degree, MS Library & Information Science and MFA Digital Arts, and an Advanced Certificate in Museum Libraries. We address the need to diversify the museum profession, but not only in terms of staff, but equally the knowledge and skills that students acquire, moving from a laser focus on curatorial skills and art history, to an amalgamation of content, curation and communication in the context of the digital ecosystem of 21st-century culture moving to an education that is relevant and speaks to contemporary narratives and values.

Part VIII presents some issues for museum libraries and archives. Among the world's finest libraries are those housed in museums and universities. Examples include the Frick Art Reference Library, part of the Frick Museum, and the Bodleian Library at Oxford University, as covered in this part. Such libraries including special and archival collections, rare books and ephemera constitute a treasure trove of materials on art, design and architecture, and importantly, their collections in general have been developed around subject areas of the museum's object collections. Further, such libraries have conservation laboratories, provide public access and services and support scholarly research on topics relevant to the collections.

Part IX of the book covers aspects of the future of museums with respect to developments in digital culture. We consider the growing forces competing with museums for audience including entertainment, and the many hours people spend each day with digital media. Museums have long identified with their physical space as a specific place in time and space, have now expanded to cyberspace and have a digital identity on the Web. Developments such as smart cities will further affect how museums fit into the digital culture overall.

In summary, we have entered the next wave of the digital revolution as all media has gone digital, a state of being that closely aligns with human creativity and innovation—mainly, art, culture and the humanities, the lifeblood of the museum. The convergence of media as digital, which makes all media equally usable, is fueling the rise of human expression through visual and sound media, as we shift to a post-text-dominated era to life on the Internet, while new technology is introduced regularly such as visual recognition using AI. This trend reveals the power of visual and sound media as digital media language that enables museums to reach larger more diverse audiences. We hope that readers will enjoy this selection of viewpoints on the relationship of museums and the rapidly evolving digital culture in which they find themselves.

New York, USA
London/Oxford, UK
2019

Tula Giannini
Jonathan P. Bowen

Acknowledgements

The annual EVA London Conference on *Electronic Visualisation and the Arts* has been influential on the contents and selection of authors in this volume. Thank you to Jim Hemsley for initiating the EVA conferences in London in 1990, now continuing in several cities around the world. Some of the material in chapters by the editors has been adapted and updated from recent papers in the EVA London Conference. Thank you to all individual photographers who have allowed their work to appear in this book, especially Jill Lauriston for the frontispiece and George Mallen, Co-Founder of the UK Computer Arts Society in 1968. All such photographers are acknowledged individually in figure captions in the book. Organizations that have allowed photographs to be included are also acknowledged in individual figure captions within the book, and we thank these institutions for their generosity, especially the Bodleian Libraries (University of Oxford), InvisibleStudio and Tate Modern. Some photographs and images are from Wikimedia Commons (http://commons.wikimedia.org), and we thank the contributors to this wonderful altruistic facility. Again, such images are individually acknowledged in figure captions. We thank Pratt Institute for their research support of Pratt Professor, Tula Giannini, Co-Editor of this book, during her sabbatical for the academic year 2017–2018. Jonathan Bowen thanks Museophile Limited for financial support.

Contents

Editors and Contributors

About the Editors

Tula Giannini Ph.D., MLS, MM is tenured full Professor in the School of Information at the Pratt Institute, New York, USA, serving as Dean of the School from 2014 to 2017. At Pratt, she has initiated and managed several collaborative digitization projects with leading New York City museums and libraries, supported by the Institute of Museum and Library Services (IMLS), and in 2015 obtained a Master of Science (MS) in museums and digital culture. Since 2016, she has co-organized the EVA London Symposium, associated with the annual EVA London Conference on Electronic Visualisation & the Arts. An interdisciplinary scholar also working in musicology, she served as Curator of Musical Instruments at the Library of Congress. Her publications include 25 entries to The New Grove Dictionary of Music and Musicians, Oxford University Press and the book, *Great Flute Makers of France: the Lot and Godfroy Families*, published by Tony Bingham, London.

Jonathan P. Bowen FBCS FRSA is Emeritus Professor of Computing at London South Bank University in London, UK; Adjunct Professor at Southwest University in Chongqing, China; and Chairman of Museophile Limited, a consultancy company in the area of museums and IT. In 1994, he founded the *Virtual Library museums pages* (VLmp), part of the WWW Virtual Library, later adopted by the International Council of Museums (ICOM). He was invited to be the Honorary Chair of the first *Museums and the Web* conference in 1997 and was a regular contributor subsequently. More recently, he has been Co-Chair of the annual EVA London Conference on *Electronic Visualisation and the Arts*. In 2013, he was Co-Editor of *Electronic Visualisation in Arts and Culture*, published in the Springer Series on Cultural Computing. In 2017, he co-authored *The Turing Guide*, on the life and work of the computing pioneer Alan Turing, published by Oxford University Press. He is Life Fellow of the British Computer Society, Life Fellow of the Royal Society of Arts and Liveryman of the Worshipful Company of Information Technologists.

Contributors

Rachel Ara London, UK

Stefania Boiano InvisibleStudio, London, UK

Ann Borda The University of Melbourne, Melbourne, Australia

Jonathan P. Bowen School of Engineering, London South Bank University, London, UK;
Southwest University, Chongqing, China

Stephen J. Bury The Frick Collection, New York, USA

Seb Chan Australian Centre for the Moving Image, Melbourne, Australia

Catherine Devine Microsoft, Seattle, USA

Sara Devine Brooklyn Museum, New York, USA

Douglas Dodds Victoria and Albert Museum, London, UK

Stuart Dunn King's College London, London, UK

Graeme Earl King's College London, London, UK

Ernest Edmonds De Montfort University, Leicester, UK

Tom Ensom Tate Gallery, London, UK

Patrícia Falcão Tate Gallery, London, UK

Rosanna Flouty New York University, New York, USA

Anna Foka DH Uppsala, Department of Archives, Museums and Libraries, Uppsala University, Uppsala, Sweden;
Humlab, Umeå University, Umeå, Sweden

Francesca Franco University of Exeter, Exeter, UK

Giuliano Gaia InvisibleStudio, London, UK

Carla Gannis Pratt Institute, New York, USA

Tula Giannini School of Information, Pratt Institute, New York, USA

Courtney Johnston Museum of New Zealand Te Papa Tongarewa, Wellington, New Zealand

Nick Lambert Research Office, Ravensbourne University London, London, UK

Andy Lomas Goldsmiths, University of London, London, UK

Ross Parry University of Leicester, Leicester, UK

Gareth Polmeer Royal College of Art, London, UK

Judith Siefring Bodleian Libraries, University of Oxford, Oxford, UK

Matt Tarr American Museum of Natural History, New York, USA

Deborah Turnbull Tillman University of New South Wales & New Media Curation, Sydney, Australia

Bruce Wands MFA Computer Arts, School of Visual Arts, New York, USA

Will Wootton King's College London, London, UK

Abbreviations

3D	Three-dimensional
ACM	Association for Computing Machinery
ACMI	Australian Centre for the Moving Image
ACT UP	AIDS Coalition To Unleash Power
AHRC	Arts and Humanities Research Council
AI	Artificial Intelligence
AIDS	Acquired Immuno Deficiency Syndrome
AIML	Artificial Intelligence Markup Language
AMNH	American Museum of Natural History
ANSI	American National Standards Institute
API	Application Programming Interface
AR	Augmented Reality
ARIES	ARt Image Exploration Space
BBC	British Broadcasting Corporation
BCE	Before Common Era
BCS	British Computer Society
BFA	Bachelor of Fine Arts
BLE	Bluetooth Low Energy
Bodleian	Bodleian Libraries
CAD	Computer-Aided Design
CAS	Computer Arts Society
CC	Creative Commons
CDP	Canadiana Discovery Portal
CMS	Collection Management System
COBOL	COmmon Business Oriented Language
CTG	Computer Technique Group
DAH	Digital Art History
DAHL	Digital Art History Lab
DCMS	Department for Digital, Culture, Media & Sport
DMA	Dallas Museum of Art

DMT	Digital Manuscripts Toolkit
E.A.T.	Experiments in Art and Technology
EC	European Commission
ENoLL	European Network of Living Labs
ERASMUS	EuRopean Community Action Scheme for the Mobility of University Students
EU	European Union
EVA	Electronic Visualisation and the Arts
Fab Lab	Fabrication Laboratory
FBI	Federal Bureau of Investigation
FGM	Female Genital Mutilation
Frick	The Frick Collection
GDPR	General Data Protection Regulation
GIS	Geographic Information System
GLAM	Galleries, Libraries, Archives and Museums
HCI	Human–Computer Interaction
HIV	Human Immunodeficiency Virus
IBM	International Business Machines Corporation
ICA	Institute of Contemporary Arts
ICT	Information and Communications Technology
IEC	International Electrotechnical Commission
IEEE	Institute of Electrical and Electronics Engineers
IIIF	International Image Interoperability Framework
ILS	Integrated Library System
IMLS	Institute of Museum and Library Services
IoL	Internet of Life
IoT	Internet of Things
ISEA	International Symposium on Electronic Art
ISO	International Organization for Standardization
IT	Information Technology
JPEG	Joint Photographic Experts Group
JPL	Jet Propulsion Laboratory
LACMA	Los Angeles County Museum of Art
LGBT	Lesbian, Gay, Bisexual and Transgender
LMS	Learning Management System
LOD	Linked Open Data
LOTI	London Office of Technology and Innovation
MARC	MAchine-Readable Cataloging
MDC	Museums and Digital Culture
Met	Metropolitan Museum of Art
MFA	Master of Fine Arts
MI	Machine Intelligence
MIT	Massachusetts Institute of Technology
MoMA	Museum of Modern Art

MOOC	Massive Open Online Course
MPEG	Moving Picture Experts Group
MR	Mixed Reality
MRes	Master of Research
MS	Master of Science
Mu.SA	Museum Sector Alliance
MVP	Minimum Viable Product
MW	Museums and the Web
NAL	National Art Library
NFC	Near-Field Communication
NLA	National Library of Australia
NLP	Natural Language Processing
NMC	New Media Curation
NYARC	New York Art Resources Consortium
NYC	New York City
OCLC	Online Computer Library Center
OCR	Optical Character Recognition
Pratt	Pratt Institute
QA	Question Answering
RA	Royal Academy of Arts
RCA	Royal College of Art
RFID	Radio-Frequency Identification
RRC	Rapid Response Collecting
SAT	Society for Arts and Technology
SIGGRAPH	Special Interest Group on Computer GRAPHics
SOAS	School of Oriental and African Studies
SVA	School of Visual Arts
TEI	Text Encoding Initiative
TIFF	Tag Image File Format
TMS	The Museum System
UCD	User-Centered Design
UN	United Nations
UNSW	University of New South Wales
URL	Uniform Resource Locator
USB	Universal Serial Bus
UX	User eXperience
V&A	Victoria and Albert Museum
VR	Virtual Reality
VSA	Visitor Service Associate
W3C	World Wide Web Consortium
Watermans	Watermans Art Centre
WAV	WAVeform Audio File Format
Whitney	Whitney Museum of American Art
Wi-Fi	Wireless Networking Technology

WSN	Wireless Sensor Network
WWW	World Wide Web
XML	eXtensible Markup Language
ZKM	Zentrum für Kunst und Medien

Part I
Introduction

Chapter 1
Digital Culture

Tula Giannini and Jonathan P. Bowen

Abstract We trace the foundations of digital culture to Claude Shannon and Alan Turing, pioneers of information theory and computer science including algorithms, machine learning, and artificial intelligence, demonstrating how these developments are shaping our digital life and digital future. We examine life in code and digits in the context of digital ways of doing, knowing, being, and living, covering, for example, digital information behavior and the impacts of the convergence of all digital media, a digital tipping point at the heart of digital culture. This chapter provides the background and context for the rest of the book in the framework of museums and related cultural and heritage institutions.

1.1 Introduction

This book offers new perspectives and research on how digital culture is transforming museums in the 21st century as they strive to keep pace with emerging technologies driving cultural and social change played out not only in today's pervasive networked environment of the Internet and web, but in everyday life, from home to work and on city streets. In a world where digital culture has redefined human information behavior as life in code and digits, increasingly it dominates human activity and communication. These developments have radically changed the expectations of the museum visitor, real and virtual, the work of museum professionals and, most prominently, the nature of the museum exhibition. Museums have become porous interacting with their environments, living beyond their walls in both physical and digital worlds. Taking this as a starting point, the editors frame the discussion broadly while contributors speak from their own experiences, expertise, practice, and research.

T. Giannini (✉)
School of Information, Pratt Institute, New York, USA
e-mail: giannini@pratt.edu

J. P. Bowen
School of Engineering, London South Bank University, London, UK
e-mail: jonathan.bowen@lsbu.ac.uk

Southwest University, Chongqing, China

T. Giannini and J. P. Bowen (eds.), *Museums and Digital Culture*,
Springer Series on Cultural Computing, https://doi.org/10.1007/978-3-319-97457-6_1

Overall, this book creates a new picture of the 21st-century museum field. As museums become shared spaces with their communities, local, national, and global, as they move from collection-centered to user/visitor-centered institutions, they are assuming new roles and responsibilities tied to new goals for engaging their audience, conveying meaning through collections, creating learning experiences and, importantly, connecting to daily digital life and culture, integral to the museum ecosystem.

Our studies of recent exhibitions at museums leading change are used to exemplify new directions while they point to a new vision for the museums of the future at the heart of which is the integration of digital interaction, visitor participation, and the merging of physical and digital space.

1.1.1 A Word on Methods

The book builds upon the work of the editors, Giannini and Bowen, including co-authored articles published over the past few years (Bowen and Giannini 2014, 2016; Bowen et al. 2017; Giannini and Bowen 2016, 2017), lectures, and research-based teaching related to museums and digital culture. Considered holistically, they shed new light on the way museums are transforming as they keep pace with emerging digital technologies, the Internet and web, and the dramatic social changes both local and global—all of which are important for a museum that is porous with its environment, that goes beyond its walls, and lives and creates in both physical and digital worlds that are culturally diverse. Using this as a starting point, the editors will organize the discussion broadly, while contributors will contribute from their own experiences and expertise that taken together creates a new picture of the 21st-century museum field. As museums become shared spaces with their communities, local, national, and global, moving from collection-centered to visitor-centered institutions, they are taking on new roles and responsibilities with the goals of engaging their audience, conveying meaning through their collections, and creating learning experiences. Recent exhibitions at museums that are leading this change are used to exemplify new directions, expressing a new vision for museums of the future.

We use a form of documentary narrative that captures and curates the last few years of museums and digital culture based predominately on experiential evidence and primary source materials which encompass museum visits with observation of museum life, exhibitions and audience, conference papers and discussions, online news from the art world such as Artnet News, Artsy, Hyperallergic, exhibition catalogs, exhibitions online, museum blogs, gallery texts, artist interviews, panel discussions, media such as YouTube, WNYC radio in New York City, TV (BBC, PBS), also consulting scholarly journals, research reports and books. This approach reflects this fast-moving field as it strives to keep pace with advances in digital technology, evolving digital behavior and the expanding reach of the digital culture ecosystem that connects us all through communication, participation and interaction. So, rather than a static more didactic approach, it is our intention that this book will reflect the digital revolution as has played out in museums over the past several years and note that most of the exhibitions discussed were visited by the authors who have drawn upon their research onsite as well as exhibition websites.

1.1.2 Noting Key Features

We offer interdisciplinary approaches across the fields of information, communication, and computer science, featuring case studies and research through the lens of academics, digital artists, exhibitions, gallery space, design and architecture—both physical and virtual creating a body of evidence, so not a didactic approach, but rather one that inspires the reader to reconsider the new and evolving museum landscape.

Having surveyed recent books on museums, this book is distinguished by its focus on how digital culture is changing the relationship of museums to the public they serve, brought together in a digital era of rapid social and cultural change. Although the museum as it is defined today remains essentially a 19th-century institution that embodies 19th-century aesthetics and values, we present new research that shows the impact of how digital life is changing visitor perceptions during this period of rapid societal change. Going beyond the research of museum professionals and curators, what will be fresh and new is that we give voice to a range of professionals across GLAM, the creative industries, IT sector, academia, and digital artists.

While other books on museums generally look at museums from the inside—administration, management, process, collections, etc., in essence, the traditional departments, this book considers museums from inside/outside interactions, participation and collaboration, while also considering key social issues and global contexts that are today highly influential in art and culture. From this approach, emerges a porous, flexible model of the museum of the future that enables new thinking and change, and breaks out of the established silos of past practice.

The book's contributing authors are highly distinguished in their fields while possessing specific expertise and are framing their work from the vantage point of forward-looking, innovative, and creative approaches to contemporary issues around museums in today's evolving digital landscape.

1.2 The Birth of Digital Culture

1.2.1 Setting the Stage for the Digital Revolution—The First Wave

In the 1940s, when Claude Shannon (1916–2001) invented "Information Theory," and Alan Turing (1912–1954) considered computers as thinking machines, they could foresee the universality of computer science and digital information applied across disciplines, including the arts and humanities, which has underpinned the digital convergence of media (Giannini and Bowen 2017). Thus, the once differentiated technologies for sound recording, film, text, and video, have now become part of same digital fabric, and the new digital landscape of the mixed media digital culture that we inhabit. When Shannon connected information and communication in a single theory, the electronic message was born, laying the foundation for the birth of Internet and the invention of the World Wide Web, and the virtual world of cyberspace, a place where digital communication has moved to the heart of real and virtual life.

This development over the past several decades, especially from the 1940s to the 1990s, is often overlooked in terms of its effect on human communication and interaction, not only with information, but life and art as well. Only now, some 75 years since the birth of computer science and information theory, are the dramatic impacts of this marriage of fields being realized. Increasingly, we are experiencing the life-changing impacts of digital convergence as our daily lives are increasingly taken up with digital interactions and the Internet of Things (IoT) (Raine 2017). Human and digital information behavior are forever linked, merging real and digital life and art, while the growing presence of virtual and augmented reality and robotics are becoming intermeshed with every aspect of real life experienced through digital senses and aesthetics that pervade our mind and how we see ourselves in a new ethos of computational culture, a culture that now defines 21st-century digital thinking and aesthetics.

1.2.2 The Second Wave—Coded Art and Life

As digital human interaction becomes integrated in real and virtual space and transforms our states of being (Bowen et al. 2018a) and doing, it becomes causal to a new wave of human evolution powered by digital applications, computations, codes, algorithms and artificial intelligence. This growing phenomenon of the digital enhancement of physical life can be observed and experienced regularly in our daily lives, whereby digital culture mirrors real culture, life and art.

A Pew report (Pew 2017), entitled *The Revolution is Digital*, observes that, "the internet has transformed how people around the globe gather information, invent new products, communicate, and lead their daily lives," and presents statistics on Internet use to show that its use in the US has increased dramatically since the millennium from 52% to 88% in 2016, with students and college graduates accounting for the largest group of users, while the "global median use" has risen to 67%, with South Korea leading at 94% compared to the US at 89% (Pew 2017).

Making connections between digital evolution and human evolution, especially as it impacts human thinking, senses, aesthetics, expression, behavior and communication, is central to understanding how museums will evolve and change alongside our evolving digital culture landscape. And, the digital journey has only begun. Advancing along a digital path that opens up new possibilities for education, participation, innovation and creativity, we enter the museum of the future deeply immersed in a complex and evolving digital landscape, the center of which is human life as it flows through diverse states of physical and digital being, which now intertwined, are increasingly indistinguishable and inseparable. Although we transverse these states of being seamlessly, traveling through cyberspace in real space, interacting in social and cultural space, our states of consciousness are being altered as we engage locally and globally, react to current social states in time and place, and communicate via digital media, while face to face.

The boundaries between physical and digital space are blurring as we engage and communicate in digital terms and move rapidly into an exciting digital future that empowers and amplifies individual voice, speaks to human rights and social issues, and embraces diversity and inclusion, and where digital plus physical is additive—and not a question of either or. We need to expand our senses and creative vision as we open ourselves to new ways of seeing and understanding difference which means breaking out of traditional silos where gatekeepers of all sorts lock up vast areas of cultural heritage. Museums as public institutions provide essential public space, access to collections and rich cultural experiences in ways not before imagined. As we evolve together in these spaces and domains, sharing our stories, our past and present, we progress towards an exciting museum and digital future.

1.2.3 Being Physical, Seeing Digital

Seeing ourselves as digital is embodied in the ever-present selfie, a form of digital capture of the "me" at the center of life's experiences. Selfies (aka "cellfies"), or digital self-portraits, have become ingrained in visitor activities, while equally prominent are the cellphone cameras of visitors taking pictures of works of art, for after the visit reflection. One effect of the selfie obsession, is that artists' self-portraits viewed in the context of the selfie, are gaining greater visitor interest and understanding. For example, two recent exhibitions featuring self-portraits—Portraits by Cézanne at the Musée d'Orsay, June to September 2017, and Edvard Munch at the Met Breuer, November 2017 to February 2018—deeply engaged audiences particularly as they could see the artist evolve in time as they embarked on a chronological journey of his works. Making connections between portraiture, a long-standing traditional art form, and the selfie, an emerging form of digital expression, is but one example of how museums visitors gain insight into the artist's perceptions of self, and by extension their own sense of self as a creative being. This digital dynamic grows out of a long-standing artistic practice of the artist looking at self. Once limited to the artist's hand, now the hands of millions of users holding cell phones can partake in this ritual, part of the me and me-too digital culture. The selfie is but one example of how people are translating physical ways of doing to digital ways.

1.2.4 Digital Art and Expressions of Self

The work of digital artist, Carla Gannis (see Chap. 21) brings contemporary insights to the self-portrait through the "selfie." Her brilliant work in this area, which received a 2017 LumenPrize, delves into concepts of self, identity and gender. Talking about her early family life in North Carolina, she notes that her father was a computer scientist and her mother a performer and notes that "All these things create our identity," adding "I feel like I come from a Southern Gothic culture and now I feel like I'm a part of online gothic culture." Her selfie works show how the process of doing digital art tends to transform the artist's identity through the exploration of new digital representations of self. As artists make art using digital tools viewed through their digital senses, there seems to be no limit to the creative spectrum of digital arts (Bowen et al. 2013; Candy et al. 2018). At the same time, digital capture using a smart phone has become universally adopted for creating selfies with more than a million selfies being uploaded through social media each day (Fig. 1.1).

Fig. 1.1 *Skulls, flowers and dots*, by Carla Gannis, 2016. We see the self in the selfie and the process of identity creation. (With permission of Carla Gannis, https://technical.ly/brooklyn/2016/02/10/carla-gannis-art-selfie/)

1.2.5 A Place for Self-reflection—Enter Museum of the Selfie

Recognizing the adoption of the selfie as a basic mode of communicating the self, the Museum of the Selfie, the first of its kind, opened April 1 2018 for a two month engagement 2018 in Glendale, CA. Museum Co-founders, Tommy Honton and Tair Mamedov, both game designers, in an interview with *Mashable* noted that, "Now people don't want to just be a silent consumer, they want to be a part of the art." And, Honton points out that, "If we didn't have social media, the selfie probably wouldn't have taken off. … You can take a selfie with a Polaroid, but unless you can share it, or upload it quickly, what effect will it have? Selfies are universal—it's culturally represented." The author of the Mashable article, Rachel Kraus, wonders about the effect selfies might be having on audience appreciation of great art, but nonetheless feels, "what better way to acknowledge a fundamental shift in our interactions with art than with a little meta-self-reflection" (Kraus 2017).

1.2.6 Digital Culture: Back to the Future with Shannon and Turing

In order to fully understand the origins of 21st-century digital life and culture, we look to the groundbreaking inventions in the 1940s of two prodigious 20th-century scientists: Alan Turing, considered the father or founder of computer science (Bowen 2017), and Claude Shannon, the father of Information Theory and digital communication, based on his 1937 master's thesis at MIT and his pioneering paper, *A Mathematical Theory of Communication*, published in 1948, we see that their work set the stage for the digital revolution that spawned digital art, life and culture (Shannon 1948).

1.3 Digital Convergence

iFuture-forward, digital developments now drive the convergence of the very disciplines Shannon and Turing introduced—information tied to digital communication and computing, which has brought us to a critical juncture, or the second wave of the digital revolution that is more dramatically transforming digital culture, while blurring the lines between real and virtual life. At the same time, universities are pressing the reset button for education in these merging disciplines as they establish new colleges or schools of information, communication and computing to prepare students as participants in the global digital economy.

Exploring the convergence and impact of the work of Turing and Shannon that set the stage for today's ubiquitous digital culture, we go back to 1943, the year Shannon and Turing met at Bell Labs in New York City to focus on the intersection of their work as a catalyst of the digital revolution and how their shared interests in artificial intelligence, algorithms, and machine-learning could mirror functions of human brain, and digital expressions in the arts and culture. In 1955, Shannon, working with John McCarthy, an Assistant Professor of Mathematics at Dartmouth, played a pivotal role writing a proposal to the Rockefeller Foundation to fund the "Dartmouth Summer Research Project on Artificial Intelligence," which marked the first reference to AI, an area of study increasingly viewed as foundational to the fields of information, communication, and computing. It was predictive of today's most significant technological developments—indeed visionary of our digital future where coded communication, digital seeing and aesthetics alter states of being, as increasingly human activity sits at the intersection of real and virtual life.

1.3.1 Shannon's Dream Comes True—All Media Are Communicated in zeros and ones

Finally, in the 2000s, when all media went digital, from text and photography, to sound recording, film and video, digital convergence recast the domain of art, culture and the humanities in digital contexts, and museums ushered in the virtual museum while establishing the digital life of the physical museum encompassing all museum work, activities and functions. With this gradual rise of digital convergence, the subject areas of information, communication, and computing, fields which had developed separately, become integral and inseparable, while inspiring emerging fields such as digital art, humanities and culture (Bowen et al. 2013).

Significantly, this new integrated state of these disciplines represents far more than the sum of their parts, as it expands into new areas such as AI, virtual and augmented reality, social media, cloud computing, global networks and computational culture. The convergence of media as digital, which makes all media equally usable, is fueling the rise of human expression through visual and sound media, as we shift to a post-text-dominated era where digital life on the Internet is dominated by podcasts, video, and images while emerging technology is being introduced regularly such as Google Lens for smart phone visual recognition using AI. According to SocialPilot statistics, "by 2020 over 75% of the world's mobile data traffic will be video," and DZone statistics show that "YouTube usage more than tripled from 2014–2016 with users uploading 400 h of new video each minute of every day! Now, in 2017, users are watching 4,146,600 videos every minute." These trends breathe new life into the power of art, design and sound as universal tools for learning and communication, and for museums to reach larger more diverse audiences. Indeed, ICC research has become the engine of change as it moves to the heart of innovation and creativity while empowering interaction of individuals and institutions across the globe.

1.3.2 Turing's Life and Work—A Fusion of the Digital and Social Revolutions

Turing was not only groundbreaking in his computer science work, but in the visibility of his gay identify, which influences how we "see" his work and his person, and which brings a new dimensionality, constituting an important aspect of how we interpret information in the digital age, especially since creators/artists can reveal themselves via the Internet (Bowen 2016). In many respects, Turing's life's experiences foreshadow today's social consciousness and human rights struggles, considering what he endured living in a world intolerant of homosexuality (Bowen and Copeland 2017). His honesty and integrity as a human being, also reflected in his computer research, no doubt put him in jeopardy. He was not afraid to be different and to forge his own path. Fast forward, to the Tate Britain exhibition—"Queer Art"—bringing new perspectives on the queer artist (http://www.tate.org.uk/art/queer-british-art-1861-1967) (Fig. 1.2).

Fig. 1.2 Shannon (left), Turing (right). Science Museum, London, on exhibit in the Winton Mathematics Gallery. (Photograph by Tula Giannini, March 8, 2017)

1.3.3 21st-Century Social, Cultural and Digital Revolutions Converge

Social and cultural change, social justice and political movements, are being facilitated by the digital revolution which gives voice to communities and individuals empowered by digital forms of expression as full-fledged digital participants. They share their thoughts and creative works through social media, e-messaging, blogs, websites and YouTube. And by extension, in a digital world where access to information and communication via the web and Internet is available 24/7, museum audiences can enjoy new and powerful ways to engage online. For example, they can explore collections, view exhibitions and video presentations and plan onsite visits. As we take flight into cyberspace, as physical space and human interface is merged with artificial life and the Internet of Things (IoT), we cannot but marvel at the genius of Shannon and Turing (Bowen et al. 2018b) who gave us not only the science and technology of what is now our future, but as well the vision that shapes it.

Drawing upon our research and publications on digital culture and museums over the past few we look at new models of museum exhibitions, and graduate education for the 21st-century's evolving digital landscape, taking for example, the MS in Museums and Digital Culture introduced by Pratt School of Information in fall 2015 (see Chap. 25, Education for Museum Professionals) and explore how new thinking on museums is being impacted by visitors' digital states of being, from digital behavior, seeing and aesthetics, to ways of doing, knowing and communicating, while the museum itself is being organized and managed around digital systems, networks, websites and the Internet.

Uniquely positioned in the digital the life of the museum, that sphere of human activity, where physical and digital, real and virtual interact, converge and integrate, and as such, the first museum book to envision the future of museums from the vantage point of the digital revolution beginning in its first phase developing from the 1940s inventions of Shannon and Turing, including artificial intelligence and machine learning, to the second phase marked by the invention of the Internet by Vint Cerf, and to Paul Barron in the 1970s, to a third phase in the 1990s with the invention of the World Wide Web by British computer scientist Tim Berners-Lee.

1.3.4 Digital Contexts of the 21st-Century Museum—The Rise of Digital Culture

In the 1940s, when Shannon invented information theory, and Turing invented thinking machines, they could foresee the universality of computer science and digital information applied across disciplines, including the arts and humanities which has underpinned the digital convergence of media, so that the once differentiated technologies for sound recording, film, text, video, have now become part of same digital fabric, and the new digital landscape of the mixed media digital culture we inhabit.

When Shannon connected information and communication in a single theory, the electronic message was born, laying the foundation for the birth of Internet and the invention of the World Wide Web, and the virtual world of cyberspace, a place where digital communication has moved to the heart of real and virtual life. This development over the past several decades, especially from the 1940s to the 1990s, is often overlooked in terms of its effect on human communication and interaction, not only with information, but life and art as well. Only now, some seven-five years since the birth of computer science and information theory, are the dramatic impacts of this marriage of fields being realized. More and more, we are experiencing the life-changing impacts of digital convergence as our daily lives are increasingly taken up with digital interactions and the Internet of Things (IoT) (Raine 2017). Human and digital information behavior are forever linked, merging real and digital life and art, while the growing presence of virtual and augmented reality and robotics are becoming intermeshed with every aspect of real life experienced through digital senses and aesthetics that pervade our mind and how we see ourselves in a new ethos of computational culture, a culture that now defines the 21st-century museum.

1.3.5 Artificial Intelligence and Robots—A New Frontier for Museums

Already robots are working alongside humans, or independently doing tasks once reserved for humans, such as driving cars, while the algorithms for artificial intelligence run computer systems and operations that collect data, learn as they go and make decisions that affect our lives (Ross 2017).

Life in Bits and Bots by Tula Giannini (2018)

When robots roam the earth
will a dearth of human activity
cause a proclivity to make love
or war against digital life
strife between real and virtual
will we embrace the eventual
spiritual ritual of the digital
Is there a choice
No singular voice.

Traveling between here and cyberspace
We find our place
in the cosmos of virtual life
Inhabiting physical spaces
real places of the mind
shared with bits and bots
A new human identity
from ones and noughts.

1.3.6 Information, Cultural Computing and States of Being

Today's understanding and use of information and cultural computing stemming from the work of Shannon and Turing, provides the scientific foundations and engine for the next phase of the digital revolution. It is interesting to note, that information seeking, storage and retrieval, which by the 1960s had become the centerpiece of information science (Kline 2004) was in essence not a part of their vision, but rather theirs' was about digital communication through e-messages, receiving and decoding them with a minimal degree of entropy, merging information theory and computing to advance artificial intelligence with the goal of developing an artificial brain capable of machine learning and robotics to enhance human capability while creating artificial life. Over the past 75 years (1943–2018) since Shannon and Turing met and together looked into the future, their work now becomes our reality and the driver of future digital developments. And, in 2018 the Alan Turing Institute and the British Library are partnering to apply AI new to digitized humanities collections, developing new scholarly research methodologies (British Library 2019). With Digital convergence of media and digitization of knowledge (for example Google Books and Scholar), GLAM collections (Galleries, Libraries, Archives, and Museums) intersecting with massive born-digital publications and user generated content on the web, we are now able to use these vast dynamic gatherings of data and new computational methods and analytics from which we can draw meaning while marshalling the past and present, to create new knowledge. We find ourselves at a juncture in which information moves to the foreground and where it manifests in new forms such as virtual reality (VR), augmented reality (AR), and artificial intelligence (AI), and where human digital interaction and communication dominate life itself.

In a virtual world, moving at the speed of light, the moment new content is published on the web, its bits, regardless of media and content, become part of a global network, a limitless sea of digital information that we experience not only via digital media display, but more and more via digital technology embedded in human activity such as wearables, cameras with face recognition in public places and institutional spaces. Bit by bit, word by word, information is aggregated, disaggregated and juxtaposed in new and unforeseen ways.

1.3.7 Making Digital Connections Between Art and Information

Another gallery experience issue is the lack of an apparent narrative and an effective way of communicating it. This points to the challenge of integrating works on exhibition with the extensive trove of information a museum holds about its collections, including the specific information related to an exhibit, and the long tail of information that resides in museum libraries and archives. How can we these materials enhance the gallery experience so that viewers not only receive information but as well create their own personal meanings in addition to what museum curators and designers are conveying? The most prevalent conveyance of information in museum galleries are audio guides and texts on the wall and on plaques. The more important exhibitions usually offer a print catalog for sale in the museum shop which is generally too heavy to carry around. One wonders why a digital exhibition catalog is not offered. Perhaps museums should consider including a catalog designed for the web made available with an exhibition ticket, especially since most museums and are seeking digital solutions to improve audience experience and engagement with art and are experimenting with new and emerging technologies while they explore innovative gallery design especially for exhibitions using new media, installation and digital art.

1.3.8 Digital Art and Artists—The 21st-Century Gallery's Raison-d'être

Still, despite these developments, the use of digital technology in museum exhibitions and galleries of digital, installation and media art, is evolving slowly. Inevitably, it will be the artists themselves that forge new paths and methods for meeting this all-important challenge, while musicians and composers are exploring new ways of working with the visual arts. Responding to contemporary art, museums are re-thinking how and what they define as art, and also how they can best exhibit and communicate their collections. The Pompidou Centre's 40th anniversary celebration of its opening in 1977, was also a celebration of bringing innovation to audience experience. For the museum's evening programs, visitors were both seeing and making art, participating in group projects, interacting with jazz musicians composing and performing in galleries, and seeing signs saying, "touche, touche." Scores of young visitors entered the Pompidou's vast public space with excitement as they were immediately drawn into live music performance. Today's museum landscape is indeed complex, as it assumes multiple identities, real and virtual and maintains traditional roles and responsibilities accumulated over time, while the role of serving the general public has taken center stage. And, because they not only bring their digital information behavior into the museum, but as well their digital senses and contemporary cultural and social views, understanding and responding to these new digital states of being is essential to museums thriving in our evolving digital culture. Emerging digital technology offers new ways of engaging visitors so that museums will not appear dusty and unrelated to their real and virtual lives. With the latest developments in AI, VR, and AR, museums have fresh opportunities to bridge the gap between old school and new school ways of engaging visitors as participants in the exhibition experience, an experience that empowers them with new knowledge of the world and themselves (Figs. 1.3, 1.4 and 1.5).

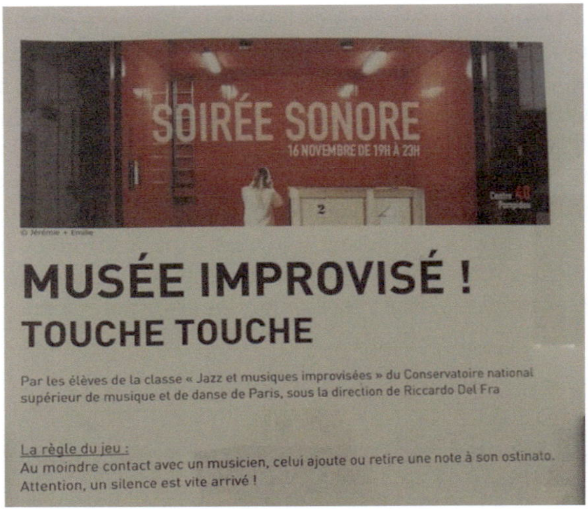

Fig. 1.3 *Soirée Sonore*. The sign posted upon entering the gallery. "Improvised Music—Touch Touch by the students of the class Jazz and Improvised music—of the National Superior Conservatory of music and dance of Paris. The rule of play—at the least, make contact with a musician, to add or remove a note to their ostinato." (Photograph by Tula Giannini, November 16, 2017)

Fig. 1.4 *Soirée Sonore* (an evening of sound) jazz interactions between students from the Paris Conservatoire and museum visitors. Pompidou Centre, Paris, November 16, 2017. (Photograph by Tula Giannini)

Fig. 1.5 Ground-level public space becomes a performance place with jazz. Pompidou Centre, Paris. November 16, 2017. (Photograph by Tula Giannini)

1.3.9 Parallel Revolutions—Digital, Social and Cultural

Developing in parallel to the digital revolution, were the cultural and social revolutions of the 1960s through the 1990s, and then at the dawn of the new millennium, we witnessed their coming together to produce the pervasive digital culture of today's complex museum environment, where people exist between real and virtual worlds, work with digital tools and technology, and with applications that respond to a new social and cultural order. The cultural norms and values that grew out of the 1960s were enabling to the rapid rise of the digital world and the universal adoption of the Internet and web.

1.3.10 A Cultural Collage from the 1960s Revolution to the Digital Age

What is art, a soup can? So thought Andy Warhol, predictor of social media in the 1960s (Kenney 2018) and early adopter of Mac Paint in the 1980s. Looking back in time- the breaking up of physical reality in light as if digits (Seurat)—impressionism (Cezanne)—the reality of the human mind and emotions interplays with physical reality (Munch)—in music, from Debussy's chromaticism and 24-tone scale to Schoenberg's 12 tone music—while John Cage and his aleatoric music and his

1952 composition *4′33″* (4 min and 33 s) of silence reverberated throughout the music and art world—breaking apart the cannon. 1960s artists such as Bob Dylan, the Beatles, and Pink Floyd created original forms of music and poetic expression defining the new rock music movement—just as digital reinvented modes of human communication. Enter the museum into this new cultural and artistic realm. Looking at architecture, the world is amazed as the Pompidou Centre turns things inside out and re-conceptualizes interior spaces and public places—another revolution, (Renzo Piano). From this social re-visioning of form and function in museum space emerges the Tate Modern—again influenced by the revolution of artistic language and a new digital language of communication, the digital self and a new blending of identifies reinventing the cultural self—the power of images in art and cell phone cameras in hand—with everyone posting images on the web, colliding videos and visual narratives through YouTube—cyberspace becomes a new frontier of innovation and creativity, and where virtual museums are attracting millions of visitors.

Looking back at some three decades of the leadership of Nicholas Serota, Director of the Tate (1988–2017), and how Serota redefined the nature of the relationship between museum director and artist was highlighted in a recent article in *The Guardian* newspaper in the UK (Higgins 2017):

> It is this relationship with artists that provides the key to his [Nicolas Serota] vision of Tate: a museum, in his view, should be refracted through the eyes of those who create. As Serota takes up his new position as Chair of the Art Council England, his goal is that the arts become "integral to life; and for everyone, not just the few.

Also writing for *The Guardian*, Adrian Searle, chief art critic of the newspaper, makes insightful observations on the Tate's new Switch House building and how it connects to new trends in coded communication, digital senses and aesthetics, merging art and life (Bowen and Giannini 2016). He notes that "the way we encounter and look at art has changed, and there is an effort here to encourage as well as accommodate live art, the ephemeral and the temporary; art that is as much about people as the things they make" (Searle 2016).

1.3.11 Digital Experience and City Life—From Streets and Stores to Digital Media Display

The digital image whether on a smart phone, a digital media display in a museum, a bigger-than-life screen at Times Square in New York City, at a movie theater, storefront window, rock concert stage, or museum gallery, all contribute to an evolving digital aesthetic where humans see life in digital color for most of their waking hours. This means that we are living in neither a digital or physical world, but a world in which coded life and computational culture is one in the same with the real life. Visitors to a museum enter with their digital devises and aesthetics reflecting their day to day experiences (Fig. 1.6).

Fig. 1.6 Digital media dominates this public square. Crowds gather 24/7 to marvel at its vast digital panorama of commercial "art?" Times Square at Night, New York City. (Photograph by Tula Giannini, February 27, 2018)

Traveling in Digital Reality by Tula Giannini (2018)

I'm going online
taking the onramp to digital life
at the intersection of the web and Internet
don't forget
I see you
but we've never met
Exiting at the museum stop
No more bits and bots
No Google maps or apps
As I travel from digital life
to reality
I enter a gallery
A visitor in a foreign land
Cell phone still in hand

1.3.12 Outside the Museum World, the Diverse Faces of "Art" in the Real World

(See Figs. 1.7, 1.8, 1.9, 1.10, 1.11 and 1.12.)

Fig. 1.7 Holiday window display with digital reflections of city buildings. Macy's 34th Street, New York City. Is this art? (Photograph by Tula Giannini, March 31, 2016)

Fig. 1.8 *Work in progress*—Chalk on cement walls of the FIT building on 7th Avenue in New York City displaying student art for the Senior Art show 2018. Each work displays the artist's URL. The student's art clearly connects with digital culture with each work including the artist's web address, as well as in the subject matter. (Photograph by Tula Giannini, October 10, 2018)

1.4 Conclusion

As the boundaries blur between real and virtual life, between art and commerce in physical and digital spaces and places, interweaving past, present, future, gender, race, and identity, we sense that we are experiencing a tectonic shift that at once enriches and disrupts our lives and our ways of living in a world that is increasingly digital. Across all sectors of work and the workplace and in particular, galleries, libraries, archives, and museums (GLAM) , the rapid advance of digital culture from the latest digital devices and applications dominating human communication, to the infusion of artificial intelligence, algorithms, machine learning, and the seeming digitization of everything tied to Internet of Thing (IoT), now recasts the museum's social contexts, roles and responsibilities, aesthetic principles and cultural milieu. Unlike the cultural institutions of the past, where museums were self-deterministic, in the 21st century, new digital directions, and the very nature of the enterprise have by necessity become a shared endeavor between the museum, its audience, and the general public.

Happily, the recasting of these relationships has strengthened the ties between museums and their communities on-location and online. It continues to redefine the very identity of the museum as it transforms into a 21st-century democratic institution reflective of contemporary life and art, ready to meet the challenges brought on by the digital revolution and the rise of digital culture. Museums are seizing upon the

Fig. 1.9 Street view from Hackney House Gallery, London, where the Lumen Prize event took place showing works by digital artists awarded in 2017. Note the street art on the side of the building picturing a woman wrapped around a man. (Photograph by Tula Giannini, July 11, 2017)

Fig. 1.10 Oakley retail sports store on Fifth Avenue, New York City. The ceiling is designed by Moment Factory as a permanent digital installation. (Photograph by Tula Giannini, March 24, 2017)

Fig. 1.11 Zara retail store on Oxford Street, London. Large digital display of "Shape the Invisible—a collaboration between Zara and new talents emerging from some of the most important design schools." (Photograph by Tula Giannini, September 17, 2017)

Fig. 1.12 Zara retail store, Oxford Street, London—"Shape the Invisible," a digital media display show. (Photograph Tula Giannini, September 17, 2017)

new and exciting opportunities that our digital culture ecosystem is creating, and which in turn enables museums to more effectively make a difference to the lives of their visitors and users in ways not before imaginable. Fasten your seatbelts—as we enter the second wave of the digital revolution in which daily digital life and culture becomes broadly embedded across human activities and interactions real and virtual, online, on the web and Internet, and as human behavior and senses evolve to new states of being and consciousness.

References

Bowen JP (2016) Alan Turing: virtuosity and visualisation. In: Bowen JP, Diprose G, Lambert N (eds) EVA London 2016 conference proceedings, Electronic Workshops in Computing (eWiC), BCS, pp 197–204. https://doi.org/10.14236/ewic/eva2016.40

Bowen JP (2017) Alan Turing: founder of computer science. In: Bowen JP, Liu Z, Zhang Z (eds) SETSS 2016: engineering trustworthy software systems. Lecture Notes in Computer Science, vol 10215, pp 1–15. Springer. https://doi.org/10.1007/978-3-319-56841-6_1

Bowen JP, Copeland BJ (2017) Turing's legacy, chapter 42, pp 463–474. In: Copeland BJ, Bowen JP, Sprevak M, Wilson R, et al (eds) The Turing guide. Oxford University Press

Bowen JP, Giannini T (2014) Digitalism: the new realism. In: Ng K, Bowen JP, McDaid S (eds) EVA London 2014 conference proceedings, Electronic Workshops in Computing (eWiC), BCS, pp 324–331. https://doi.org/10.14236/ewic/eva2014.38

Bowen JP, Giannini T (2016) From analogue to digital in literature and art. In: Bowen JP, Diprose G, Lambert N (eds) EVA London 2016 conference proceedings, Electronic Workshops in Computing (eWiC), BCS, pp 1–4. https://doi.org/10.14236/ewic/eva2016.1

Bowen JP, Keene S, Ng K (eds) (2013) Electronic visualisation in arts and culture. Springer Series on Cultural Computing. https://doi.org/10.1007/978-1-4471-5406-8

Bowen JP, Giannini T, Polmeer G (2017) Coded communication: digital senses and aesthetics, merging art and life. In: Bowen JP, Diprose G, Lambert N (eds) EVA London 2017 conference proceedings, Electronic Workshops in Computing (eWiC), BCS, pp 1–8. https://doi.org/10.14236/ewic/eva2017.1

Bowen JP, Giannini T, Polmeer G, Gannis C, Gardiner J, Kearney J, Wands B, Weinel J (2018) States of being: art and identity in digital space and time. In: Bowen JP, Weinel J, Diprose G, Lambert N (eds.), EVA London 2018 conference proceedings, Electronic Workshops in Computing (eWiC), BCS, pp 1–7. https://doi.org/10.14236/ewic/eva2018.1

Bowen JP, Trickett T, Green JBA, Lomas A (2018) Turing's genius—defining an apt microcosm. In: Bowen JP, Weinel J, Diprose G, Lambert N (eds) EVA London 2018 conference proceedings, Electronic Workshops in Computing (eWiC), BCS, pp 155–162. https://doi.org/10.14236/ewic/eva2018.31

British Library (2018) Living with machines: the Alan Turing Institute and the British Library awarded £9.2 million for a major new project set to revolutionise research. British Library Press Office, 19 Dec 2018. https://www.bl.uk/press-releases/2018/december/living-with-machines

Candy L, Edmonds E, Poltronieri FA (eds) (2018) Explorations in art and technology. Springer Series on Cultural Computing. https://doi.org/10.1007/978-1-4471-7367-0

Giannini T, Bowen JP (2016) Curating digital life and culture: art and information. In: Bowen JP, Diprose G, Lambert N (eds) EVA London 2016 conference proceedings, Electronic Workshops in Computing (eWiC), BCS, pp 237–244. https://doi.org/10.14236/ewic/eva2016.46

Giannini T, Bowen JP (2017) Life in code and digits: when Shannon met Turing. In: Bowen JP, Diprose G, Lambert N (eds) EVA London 2017 conference proceedings, Electronic Workshops in Computing (eWiC), BCS, pp 51–58. https://doi.org/10.14236/ewic/eva2017.9

Higgins C (2017) How Nicholas Serota's Tate changed Britain—over three decades, he transformed a nation's attitude to art. But is his revolution now in danger of being reversed? The Guardian, UK, 22 June 2017. https://www.theguardian.com/artanddesign/2017/jun/22/how-nicholas-serota-tate-changed-britain. Accessed 27 Jan 2019

Kenney N (2018) Andy Warhol for the instagram age: huge retrospective opens at the Whitney in New York. The Art Newspaper, 8 Nov 2018. https://www.theartnewspaper.com/preview/andy-warhol-for-the-instagram-age. Accessed 29 Jan 2019

Kline R. (2004) What is information theory a theory of? Boundary work among information theorists and information scientists in the United States and Britain during the Cold War. In: The history and heritage of scientific and technical information systems: proceedings of the 2002 conference. Chemical Heritage Foundation, Medford, NJ. https://books.google.com/books?hl=en&lr=&id=76OOQannpBgC&oi=fnd&pg=PA15&dq=kline+2004+information+science&ots=ZMOVxDHlyH&sig=qISRcYKDKc0vrLa2pR0vTaA--zc#v=onepage&q=kline%202004%20information%20science&f=false

Kraus R (2017) Here comes the Museum of Selfies to stoke your Instagram-art obsession. Mashable, 21 Dec 2017. https://mashable.com/2017/12/21/museum-of-selfies-instagram-art/#fX3E4B44vOq8. Accessed 27 Jan 2019

Pew (2017) The revolution is digital. Trend, Pew Trusts, 12 June 2017. http://trend.pewtrusts.org/en/archive/summer-2017/crunch-the-revolution-is-digital. Accessed 27 Jan 2019

Raine L (2017) The Internet of Things is the next digital evolution—what will it mean? Trend, Pew Trusts, 12 June 2017. http://trend.pewtrusts.org/en/archive/summer-2017/the-internet-of-things-is-the-next-digital-evolution-what-will-it-mean. Accessed 27 Jan 2019

Ross A (2017) Your next co-worker may be a robot. Trend, Pew Trusts, 12 June 2017. http://trend.pewtrusts.org/en/archive/summer-2017/your-next-co-worker-may-be-a-robot. Accessed 27 Jan 2019

Searle A (2016) Tate Modern's Switch House review—brain-fizzing art to power a pyramid—supersized sculpture, live performance and piles of goo get the airing they deserve in an expansion full of surprise—the 360-degree lookout is art itself. The Guardian, UK, 14 June 2016. https://www.theguardian.com/artanddesign/2016/jun/14/tate-modern-switch-house-review-brain-fizzing-art-pyramid. Accessed 27 Jan 2019

Shannon C (1948) A mathematical theory of communication. Reprinted with corrections from The Bell System Technical Journal 27:379–423, 623–656, July & October 1948. http://affect-reason-utility.com/1301/4/shannon1948.pdf. Accessed 27 Jan 2019

Chapter 2
Museums and Digitalism

Tula Giannini and Jonathan P. Bowen

Abstract The distinguishing characteristic of digitalism is its focus on human behavior in cultural and social contexts. When we think of the developments of computer science and "information theory" that spawned the digital revolution, the focus generally defaults to digital tools and technology, as opposed to its effects on human life and culture and how advances in computing, digital communications and technology are transforming our ways of doing, seeing, knowing, learning, living and loving, to name a few examples. The impact of digitalism is all encompassing, touching all disciplines and human pursuits. How will museums change and transform themselves to connect in authentic ways with their communities while remaining relevant in a world transformed by digital culture that is moving full speed ahead, advancing in a state of constant change and development? While museums have been cautious and relatively slow to challenge traditional ways, they are surely noticing that we are reaching a digital tipping point of sorts that demands digital thinking and strategy to keep pace with evolving states of digital being, aesthetics, seeing and identity in world where everyone is connected to an all-encompassing digital ecosystem of shared networks and platforms. Although museums might argue that this shift to digital culture steeped in a user-centric model might be a costly one, not moving in this direction with a sense of timeliness becomes a far riskier strategy, being one that lacks consonance with museum audiences, and is out of synch with contemporary and digital life. This chapter looks at the relationship between external digital life of museum goers with the internal museum environment aligned more with the pre-digital world than with contemporary culture. How will museums recalibrate the gap between the visitors' digital self and the museums physical identity? And, how will they revision the gallery experience for visitor learning, interaction, and participation? Will museums proceed fearlessly into digital life and art, embracing change, and the digital aesthetics and social milieu of the 21st century?

T. Giannini (✉)
School of Information, Pratt Institute, New York, USA
e-mail: giannini@pratt.edu

J. P. Bowen
School of Engineering, London South Bank University, London, UK
e-mail: jonathan.bowen@lsbu.ac.uk

Southwest University, Chongqing, China

T. Giannini and J. P. Bowen (eds.), *Museums and Digital Culture*,
Springer Series on Cultural Computing, https://doi.org/10.1007/978-3-319-97457-6_2

2.1 Introduction

In 2014, the article, *Digitalism: The new realism*, (Bowen and Giannini 2014) took up the subject of how digital culture was transforming every aspect of human life and fundamentally changing ways of doing, knowing and being. Four year later, looking again at the phenomenon of digital transformation, we see that digital culture has advanced far more quickly than anticipated by digital naysayers, and to the contrary has gone viral across the globe, as digital culture takes its place at the center of human life. Bowen and Giannini (2014) states:

> (All things) × (Digital) = Digitalism. From the digitization of documents to the digitalization of life itself and the birth of the digital self, digitalism demands new ways of doing, knowing, being, and thinking. Digitalism has become a central driver of human activity and sits at the heart of all disciplines from medicine and science to the arts. What most distinguishes digitalism is that is goes beyond people using digital technology and tools to a new realm of digital behaviors so that people might spend more time being digital via their computers, smartphones, and tablets, compared to other life activities – whether in school, at home, at work, or on holiday – the digital aspect is present and part of one's daily interactions.

For museums, what began as a digital nuisance, and forbidden digital zone, visitors' use of smartphones is now welcomed and considered an asset to audience building and relationships. The "digital divide" of have and have nots has faded, as the divide between physical and digital life has merged seamlessly into what is increasingly referred to as the postdigital age. Visitors and users are digital and wear their digital culture to the museum, which means their new sense of contemporary and global awareness, cultural identity and social milieus become one with their vision of the world, and their expectations for relevance and participation. Digital culture crosses social and cultural boundaries, breaks down silos pushing against elitism and privilege. Given this digital new state of being, museums are listening to their audiences and rethinking collection narratives as they adopt more complex conceptual ways of thinking that challenge the alter of traditional ways of doing that build on the strengths of digital culture—sharing, transparency, inclusiveness, diversity, communication, access to information and knowledge. What not long ago seemed dreamlike is now a daily reality ushering in new opportunities for museums to be at the forefront of digital culture (Giannini 2017), as they welcome digital art and life, and move beyond their walls to become one with their audience and communities.

Digital Speak [Reality is Digital] by Tula Giannini (2014)

Looking at you
You text me
My cell phone sounds
An email found
Click –
I hear your digital voice
On YouTube

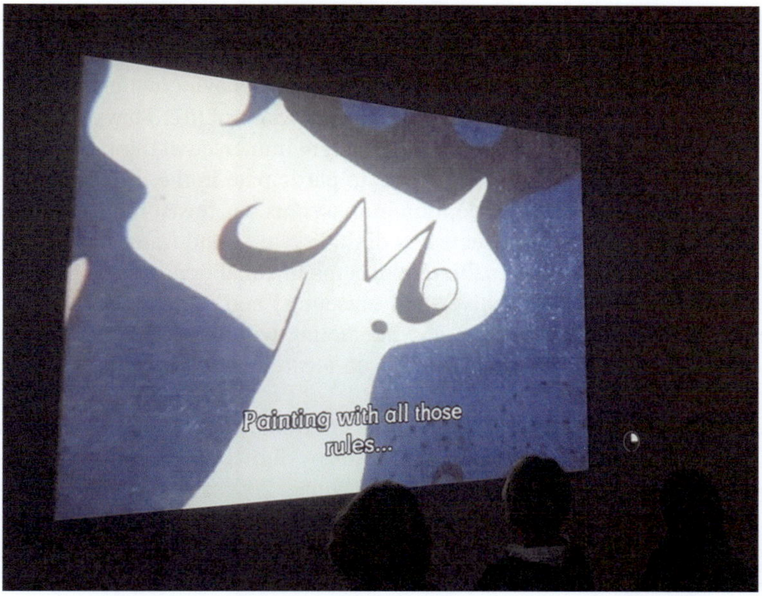

Fig. 2.1 Visitors watching a video interview at the Joan Miró exhibition at the Grand Palais, Paris. In the video frame, Miró says, "Painting with all those rules," making reference to his early period of following the masters that came before him, and from whom he liberated himself finding his true identity as an artist of great originality and imagination. To this we add in reference to museums-liberate yourself from old ways of doing and embrace digital culture, bringing new creativity and innovation to the life of the museum. (Photograph by Tula Giannini, December 17, 2018)

Your digital self speaks
Your analogue voice
I can't remember
Holding my cell I can't let go
What's next - I don't know
Digital suspense
Losing my sense of reality (Fig. 2.1).

2.2 Digital Contexts of the 21st-Century Museum

2.2.1 Museums in Real and Virtual Space and Time

21st-century life is increasingly becoming digital life as all aspects of human existence are being impacted by digital culture from human interaction with information, communication and computing, to ways of doing, knowing, being, thinking and seeing. These digital states of being (Bowen et al. 2018) cut across all disciplines and fields sharing commonalities in their use of digital tools and technologies. At the heart of digital culture is the rapid transformation of human behavior, which is increasingly defined by the digital behavior of people across all walks of life. They are the visitors, audience and users of museums who, increasingly immersed in digital activity, enter the museum with heightened expectations to participate in the life of the museum, while at the same time, digital adoption in museums has recast modes of operation across all departments interconnected by digital systems and frameworks. It is these digital developments that are enabling museums to collaborate across GLAM institutions (galleries, libraries, archives and museums) and to advance from showing and telling their public, to serving, and interacting with them, reaching beyond the walls of the museum to engage with users on location, online and in public spaces, real and virtual.

In essence, museums, like other cultural institutions, are shifting from a collection-centered to a visitor/user-centered model driven by digital culture, not only by emerging digital technologies and tools (Tallon and Walker 2008), but equally by the impact of the ubiquitous nature of digital adoption and use. New constructs of cultural and social life have grown around a core of digital activities, most broadly, modes of communication and new media. Importantly, the digital life of the museum, in physical place and cyberspace, is at the heart of museums' communication and interaction with their visitors and communities, whether meeting in real space or cyberspace, they find common ground in the realm of digital culture.

2.2.2 Digital and Museum Culture Merge—Some Key Points

The following are some key issues for museums with respect to digital culture:

- New museum architecture—public and museum spaces are being redefined as more porous with the outside environment;
- Digital art, installation art, new media art, performance art, video and net art—will be drivers of change in the traditional museum;
- New audience expectations for participation and interaction will rapidly emerge as a product of digital identity;
- Social, cultural and political perspectives on contemporary life will pervade contemporary art museums such as the Whitney, Tate, and MoMA;
- Seeing digital—changing audience perceptions of new and old, of color and light, static and dynamic states of being are shifting as digital becomes embedded in the body and soul of human existence;
- Human digital states of being present major issues for traditional approaches to exhibitions, gallery design, space and architecture;
- The conceptual shift of museum vision and values from collection-centered, to an audience/user centered institution will accelerate;

- Process—the making of art and exhibitions, works in progress and generally the process of the becoming, exposing this process to the public and engaging them in "critical and digital thinking";
- Conveying information, meaning and message to the audiences via their digital devices—smartphones, tablets and laptops, and deepening audience experience using AR, AI, VR, and MR;
- The roles and responsibilities of curators and curatorial staff extend beyond the silos of their departments to achieve greater inclusion and diversity, embrace digital in galleries, dialogue and converse with communities and audiences in order to reflect contemporary culture, values and perspectives;
- Museum narratives for permanent collections and special exhibitions will seek relevancy to contemporary culture;
- Digital ephemera will take on new meaning as it is captured in the cloud.

2.2.3 Expanding the Domain of Museum Exhibitions

Driven by today's computational culture, museums are conveying meaning to visitors onsite, online and beyond their walls facilitated by a rapidly growing community of digital, installation and mixed media artists who are transforming the museum gallery and changing the way museums engage audiences.

Over the past few years, we have been collecting data on-location in museums, gathered from our experiences at exhibitions, observing visitor behavior, reading curatorial commentaries and exhibition narratives and analyzing this data in the context of our research in information and computer science as well as published studies by a range of leaders in the field of digital culture.

Looking at recent exhibitions at world-leading museums in New York, London and Paris, we see that they have featured a group of iconic artists who have had enormous influence on new trends and ways of thinking about art and artists today, and whose work delves into most prominently themes of social and cultural matters, social consciousness, activism, everyday life, and real people, demonstrating how these art and exhibitions have remained transformational as the digital world has evolved from the 1960s to present.

2.2.4 Beyond the Walls—Reaching Audiences Inside, Outside and Online

As museums redefine and redesign their space, they are seizing the opportunity to strengthen their relationship with their audience and strive to make connection with the values, social and cultural behaviors and identities of the general public. Museums find themselves working within complex notions of public space, real and virtual, and how the spaces and identifies they create motivates and inspires the public to engage and participate, to visit, and return, to retain a space in their hearts, minds and imagination that keeps them connected to the life of the museum. To accomplish this, museums are creating new ways to go beyond their walls by making them porous with the dynamic and diverse states of contemporary life in order to grow and thrive and to meet the cultural, social and educational needs of life in the digital world.

2.2.5 Tate Modern—"It's Bigger Than Its Four Walls"

Tate Modern, perhaps more than any other museum, has sought to create "a museum of the 21st century." A wonderful narrative about the process of building a new museum for the public, is told through a series of interviews in a book edited by Chris Decron and Nicholas Serota. In an interview with Decron, Ian Cartlidge, founder of the London-based design studio, Cartlidge Levene (http://cartlidgelevene.co.uk/), talks about some of his central design principles pointing out that "We specialise in the creation of identity and visual language across all points of communication: printed, digital and environmental." Speaking with Cartlidge, Decron notes that in contrast to 20th-century practice, "They [museums] embrace visitors. And people flock to museums, not to shut off from their life, but to feel closer to it." In his response, Cartlidge observes that, "Tate Modern has helped to regenerate a whole urban district in London. It's bigger than its four walls. You don't necessarily say, I'm going to Tate Modern today to see a specific artist or show; you can still do that, but it is now enough to say I'm going to the Tate Modern today—where a whole set of experiences and possibilities will unfold." (Decron and Serota 2016) (Fig. 2.2).

Beyond the Walls by Tula Giannini (2018)

The writing is on the wall
Texts rise and fall
Art hangs on the wall
No interaction at all

Standing close to read
Far to see
Pacing to and fro
in a circular flow
What's this all about
I don't know

The writing is on the wall
Text is too small
Can't see beyond the wall
I'm inside the gallery

Fig. 2.2 Crossing the Millennium Bridge to the Tate Modern. Constructed in 2000 as part of the opening of the new Tate Modern Museum on London's South Bank, it has since become a major driver of change and development achieving the goals set out by Decron and Serota (2016). (Photograph by Tula Giannini, July 20, 2018)

in digital reality
No one is looking
just at themselves
tells me they're alone
looking at their phone

Seeing is not believing
I'll be leaving
Going beyond the walls
Leave no graffiti
Gone without a trace
Just my sweetie
And virtual space.

This poem is about the connection between real and virtual space inside the museum and galleries, and beyond, and building relationships with the public in the gallery, which extends to collaboration and outreach, social engagement with the community inside and outside the museum.

2.2.6 Rethinking Museum space

Digital and virtual space, digital life and culture is radically changing real space in the physical museum as it merges and becomes part of a new digital culture ecosystem–one that embraces diversity, inclusion, complexity and contemporary art and culture.

The notion of walls is omnipresent in the minds of visitors, from the walls of the museum to the walls of galleries. People experience gallery walls as impenetrable two-dimensional space defined by barriers, lines on the floor or rope between visitors and art on the walls, while the 3D space inside in the center of the gallery is the place they inhabit. Thus, in terms of the central space of most exhibition galleries, the gallery can seem empty. Happily, there is an emerging trend in the museum and art world to reconsider gallery design in ways that enhance visitor experience and their connections to works on exhibit. A key challenge is how can this be done effectively given the complex organization of the museum and its staff which tends to create isolated departments. We see that museums are responding by seeking new ways of engagement using emerging digital technologies with exciting results and thus meeting this challenge by creating new ways to communicate an exhibition's meaning and message without focusing audience attention to text on walls or non interactive apps on cellphones, both distracting viewers away from the main menu of visually exploring the art. The Cooper-Hewitt Museum in New York tackled this issue in new digital ways that were highly successful and importantly were organic, intuitive and individual to the visitor's gallery experience (Fig. 2.3). Most notable were tables with touch interaction and the "pen" supplied by the museum to all visitors enabling them to digitally capture art and information on their own museum-generated website.

2.3 Digital Information Behavior Driving Museum Transformation

2.3.1 Galleries Designed for People and Art Interaction

Ian Cartlidge's Perspectives on the relationship of a museum to the street and to its surrounding environment discussed above, speaks to the work of architect, Renzo Piano, most recently seen in his design of the new Whitney Museum in the Chelsea district of New York City. Piano will now extend his museum vision and architectural philosophy to create a new art gallery also in Chelsea at 540 West 21st Street, New York, City, for David Zwirner, a leading figure in New York's gallery scene with the goal of establishing "a visual psychological connection between the building and the street." Piano underscores that a key distinguishing feature of the Whitney is that, "There is a porosity (Fig 2.4). In this building [the Zwirner Gallery], it will be the same thing. It's very important." Thinking about the visitor's experience of art, he

Fig. 2.3 Visitors reading text on the wall at the David Hockney exhibition at the Metropolitan Museum, New York City. (Photograph by Tula Giannini, January 9, 2018)

theorizes that, "You kill art by making just white boxes, so you need to integrate emotion in some way," adding that "You cannot be neutral, because otherwise you disappear." (Pogrebin 2018).

Not only is a grand gallery being constructed, but it promises to be a gallery that challenges how we think about the relationship between galleries and museums, which in a sense harks back to the Uffizi Gallery in Florence, begun in 1560 with Giorgio Vasari, painter and architect, and Cosimo de'Medici, Grand Duke of Tuscany. Fast forward to Piano and Zwirner, we see that their project in many ways blurs the boundaries between galleries and museums. According to *Architectural Record*, the new Piano building will have five stories, with the upper two occupied by offices ("uffizi"). The gallery adjoins a 20-story residential building (à la MoMA), and in terms of gallery space, the Zwirner building will have 50,000 square feet, about the same as the Whitney's. The Whitney's website is well branded and communicates in-depth information on the full range of its activities while demonstrating the close ties it cultivates with its local and global community. Will the Zwirner Gallery develop in comparable directions? Given that Zwirner also has a gallery in London and in Hong Kong (à la Guggenheim outreach), this seems likely (Klimoski 2018).

Fig. 2.4 *Young Girl Escaping*, sculpture by Joan Miró (1967), painted bronze, included in the Joan Miró exhibition in Paris, December 2018. The digital capture and curation of works of art in public places magnifies their presence on the web and social media, as their images are shared across time and space, giving these public works both physical and digital life. (Photograph by Pere Lopez, 2012, Wikimedia Commons, https://commons.wikimedia.org/wiki/File:Fundaci%C3%B3_Mir%C3%B3_P1370077.JPG)

2.3.2 Digital Journeys of Art and Artifacts in Public Space

The life of art and artifacts across real and virtual space is a critical part of documenting an object's provenance and identity, including public reception revealed through social media, museum and gallery exhibitions as well as online journals and blogs. This data also plays a key role in determining an object's value, both monetary and artistic, as images on the web increase public awareness and can reach global audiences in the millions (Waller and Waller 2018). A new and unintended consequence of museums sharing detailed object records online ties to the emerging repatriation movement, making documenting the life of the object even more important (see Chap. 5, Contested Space). Tied to the unstoppable force of digital capture and curation by anyone with a smartphone, this digital development has transformed isolated lives of museum objects siloed in place, merging them with their born-digital life in cyberspace. Photographs of art objects permanently in public spaces, such as a park, are generally not subject to copyright, which allows contemporary works to be shared on the web (Fig. 2.3).

2.3.3 Digitized Collections and Museum Website Trends and Strategies

Over the past 20 years or so, museums, libraries and archives have been digitizing their collections and increasingly making them available online. From the early 2000s, museums have been redesigning their websites in ways that reflect new digital strategies (Stein 2017) at the heart of which is the connection between the onsite and online museum experience with focus on exhibitions and collections. For example, visitors experience the real objects onsite and learn about them online via videos by curators talking about how an exhibition was put together and explaining its values, while artists speak to their work on exhibit, how it was made and the ideas it conveys, it conveys. Further, virtual gallery tours virtual gallery tours allow users to explore works through installation views, and study individual works photographed in high resolution in 2D and 3D.

High profile exhibitions at three New York museums exemplify this approach: *Heavenly Bodies* at the Metropolitan Museum of Art, *Thinking Machines*, Stephen Shore at the Museum of Modern Art and Andy Warhol at the Whitney Museum (Kenney 2018). Interactions and connections between the physical museum and its website thread across most museum activities, while exhibitions take center stage in the life of the museum as they engage administration, curators, and staff of all curatorial departments, exhibit related lectures, workshops and special events, while museum shops onsite and online offer themed merchandize, and use social media, mostly Twitter and Instagram, to strengthen their relationship with audiences. A striking example was the star-studded Met Gala around the *Heavenly Bodies* exhibition

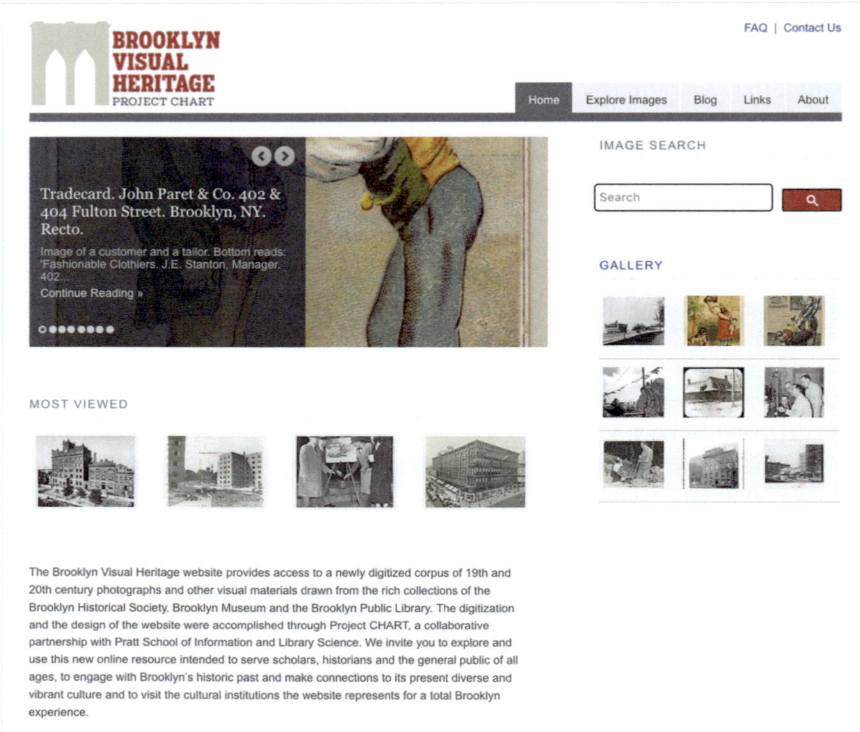

Fig. 2.5 Screenshot of the Brooklyn Visual Heritage website (http://www.brooklynvisualheritage.org). Project led by Tula Giannini, Pratt Institute, in partnership with the Brooklyn Museum, Brooklyn Historical Society, and Brooklyn Public Library (Giannini and Bowen 2014). (Image by Tula Giannini)

at the Met that grabbed global attention while setting the stage for record-breaking exhibition attendance of some 1.6 million visitors (Passy 2018).

The Brooklyn Visual Heritage website (see Fig. 2.5) is the result of a three-year IMLS grant, 2010–2013 that also provided Pratt students two-semester internships with stipends. It stands as one of the first examples of a project in which three different types of cultural institutions working in partnership, digitized about 14,000 historic photographs of Brooklyn, and where images are searched seamlessly across the collections of the Brooklyn Museum, Brooklyn Public Library and Brooklyn Historical Society using API technology for interoperability. In the context of open source museum collections online, many major museums are forming partnerships, for example, with the Internet Archive and Wikimedia Commons, a trend that promises to dramatically increase free access to the public. Despite this progress, issues around copyright, intellectual property and cases where copyright is applied to 2D reproductions of public domain works, present challenges to open access and use, but progress is being made (Giannini and Bowen 2015).

By adopting a digital strategy that by design integrates the onsite and online experience and reflects a user-centered strategy, museum goers planning to attend an exhibition can familiarize themselves with the works on display, learn about the artists, gain curatorial perspective and view gallery installations. Taken together, museum websites are increasingly providing in-depth information that make the visitor experience of the museum more meaningful and memorable.

Besides museums digitizing their object collections and exhibitions, museum libraries and archives have been digitizing their primary source materials critical to the knowledge and understanding of museum objects. We note especially three New York City museum libraries of world renown, the Watson Library, Met Museum, the Frick Art Reference Library and the Morgan Museum and Library. This ties to another trend we see in museum exhibitions, which is the gallery display of archival materials used to add greater context to an exhibition, or in some cases, for example the Stephen Shore and the Adrian Piper exhibitions at MoMA, where art and the archives are merged, both receiving high marks from the critics.

With the rapid growth of museum and archive collections on the web, combined with massive born-digital materials across all media, a new digital scholarship tied to digital culture is transforming and merging the arts and humanities fields of digital art, digital art history and digital humanities, integrating their once siloed existences into a vibrant field of study that uses both digital and traditional methods of humanities research, and this portends growing demand and increasing use of digital museum and archives collections by researchers, and the general public. Without use, online collections become digital dust, so as these new trends transform the scope and use of digital research materials, we will also see art and humanities narratives move from a linear approach, to one that is more complex, inclusive, while less exclusively Western and chronological going beyond academic resources, including new voices, media, and formats, including blogs, videos, popular born-digital publications, interviews, and material gathered using digital capture and curation (Fig. 2.6).

2.4 Integrating Digital Across the Museum

2.4.1 Digital Work Behind the Scenes

Digitization of museum collections, exhibitions, and a vast array of related scholarly materials, studies and reports, is underway across the world. A great deal of digital activity in museums is not visible to visitors. It is the work associated with managing and preserving collections, digitizing collections and making them accessible online and the digital management software and systems that describe and provide digital services such as TMS Collections by Gallery Systems (The Management Software). A major aspect of this work includes web design, website usability, audience eval-

Fig. 2.6 Whitney Museum outside "gallery" space overlooking New York City. (Photograph by Tula Giannini, February 29, 2016)

uation, and communications. In fact, most of the work of museum departments is done with digital tools, involved with digital asset management and digital labs for research and development of digital devices used for visitor engagement, and when digital culture is physical—digital tools are making physical works of art using for example 3D printing.

2.4.2 *Digital Video in Exhibitions Adds Relevance and Reality*

One digital technology in museum galleries that is gaining considerable traction, is the use of video. Two 2018 exhibitions that come to mind for making effective use of video are the Joan Miró retrospective exhibition at the Grand Palais, Paris, and *I am Ashurbanipal—king of the world, king of Assyria* (ruled 669–c.631 BCE) at the British Museum, London. The Miró show included video interviews with the artist working in his studio and talking about his process of thinking about and making art. Visitors crowded in the room, all seats were taken with many people standing, and intensely focused on the images and words of Joan Miró. The videos brought important insight into Miró's style of expression adding an important component to the exhibition.

The use of video for the *I am Ashurbanipal* exhibition served as the exhibit's finale. Two videos were presented each having a separate area with seating. The final one, proved extremely informative as it establishes contemporary context, relevance, and emotional connections. The video featured conversations between former curators of the Mosul Museum and Gareth Brereton, British Museum curator of the exhibition discussing plans and dreams to work together to rebuild the Mosul Museum destroyed during the Iraq War, to undertake new excavations in order to find as yet undiscovered Assyrian art.

> Mosul, together with the nearby Nineveh plains, is one of the historic centers for the Assyrian people, and their churches; the Chaldean Catholic Church, the Syriac Orthodox Church, and the Assyrian Church of the East, containing the tombs of several Old Testament prophets such as Jonah, some of which were destroyed by ISIL in July 2014. (Wikipedia, https://en.wikipedia.org/wiki/Mosul, accessed January 29, 2019)

The press release for the exhibition details these collaborative plans between Iraq and the British Museum.

> Many of the objects featured in the exhibition come from archaeological sites in Iraq such as Nineveh and Nimrud that have been systematically targeted and destroyed by Daesh (IS). The final section of the exhibition will highlight the challenges faced in protecting Iraqi cultural heritage under threat and will showcase the work of the 'Iraq Emergency Heritage Management Training Scheme'. In response to the destruction of heritage sites in Iraq, the British Museum developed this scheme to train Iraqi archaeologists in rescue archaeology and emergency heritage management. An overview of the project's training and research will be presented to visitors through film footage of the excavations and exclusive interviews with participants. (British Museum 2018) (Fig. 2.7)

2.4.3 Visitor Engagement

The Victoria and Albert Museum (V&A) in London has taken a leadership position in exhibition innovation and design with an eye to visitor engagement in content, meaning and personal connection. Among their exhibitions over the past few years are several standout ones, notable for their highly immersive design that speaks to creating and communicating the exhibition narrative. One example is the 2017 Pink Floyd V&A exhibition, *Their Mortal Remains* (the band made their debut in 1965). It represents current thinking on exhibition design particularly in how it brings together diverse objects and documentation including archives, musical instruments, music recordings and videos, all recreating a moment in time, as the museum narrates the band's musical journey in full technicolor. Entering the show's final gallery, the audience sitting on the gallery floor, sees and hears the band performing the "Wall," as if inside a total Pink Floyd world. Through the exhibition, the audience experiences the band's music composition and performance, and delves into their thoughts and feelings, images, imagination, art works, travels, and recordings, a culmination of

Fig. 2.7 Ashurbanipal, King of Assyria, from the exhibition, I am Ashurbanipal at the British Museum. An exhibition that moves from past to present, from the magnificent art of Assyria to the destruction of the Mosul Museum in 2015 by ISIL. (Photograph by Tula Giannini, December 22, 2018)

sorts of everything the audience has experienced and learned. The 360-degrees of the *Wall*—one of Pink Floyd's most revered albums, draws on the symbolism of walls as central to their social commentary which makes interesting analogies to museum walls.

2.4.4 Expanding the Domain of Museum Exhibitions

Driven by today's computational culture, digital tools and technology, museums are communicating message and meaning to visitors onsite, online and beyond their walls facilitated by a rapidly growing community of digital, installation and mixed media artists who are transforming the museum gallery and changing the way museums engage audiences.

Over the past few years, we have been collecting data on-location in museums, gathered from our experiences at exhibitions, observing of visitor behavior, reading curatorial commentaries and exhibition narratives and analyzing this data in the context of our research in information and computer science as well as published studies by a range of leaders in the field of digital culture.

Considering major exhibitions at world-leading museums in New York, London, and Paris, we see that they have featured a group of iconic artists who have had enormous influence on new trends and ways of thinking about art and artists today, and whose work delves into most prominently themes of social and cultural matters, social consciousness, activism, everyday life, real people and things demonstrating how these art and exhibitions have remained transformational as the digital world has evolved from the 1960s to the present.

Looking at recent exhibitions at world-leading museums in New York, London and Paris, we see that they have featured a group of iconic artists who have had enormous influence on new trends and ways of thinking about art and artists today, and whose work delves into most prominently themes of social and cultural matters, social consciousness, activism, everyday life, real people and things demonstrating how these art and exhibitions have remained transformational as the digital world has evolved from the 1960s to present.

2.5 Museums Collaborate Internationally on Major Exhibitions

Museums collaborating on exhibitions demonstrate how resource sharing can have enormous benefits that extend beyond exhibitions to digital resources such as shared collection catalogs, shared platforms for museum education and art information and history, and a range of a museum's digitized materials. For example, in 2018, two major exhibitions mounted by the V&A were on show at the Brooklyn Museum, *David Bowie Is*, March 2–July 15, 2018, and *Soul of a Nation: Art in the Age of Black Power*, September 14, 2018–February 3, 2019. The Bowie exhibition set attendance records for the museum, about 180,000 visitors, and the exhibition on black power contributed to the appreciation and understanding of African American art for the Brooklyn community and beyond.

2.5.1 Featured Collaboration 2016–2018

During 2016–2018, audiences reveled in two major Rauschenberg exhibitions, one mounted by the Tate Modern and the other by MoMA. This was a time in which Rauschenberg was once again an international celebrity, with major shows that attracted large audiences.

Writing about the Rauschenberg exhibition at MoMA, art critic, Leah Dickerman, Curator of Painting and Sculpture at MoMA, quotes Rauschenberg in the Museum's 2016 press release on his artistic vision, "Painting relates to both art and life. Neither can be made. (I try to act in that gap between the two.)" (Dickerman 2016). In a similar sense, artists today find themselves working "in that gap between" digital art and life. The exhibition at MoMA, "Rauschenberg: Among Friends" brings into focus the influence he exerted on his contemporaries, and how he used ordinary things to create extraordinary art that reflects both his life and the popular culture surrounding it (Dickerman 2016).

Major museums also collaborated on the 2017 Cezanne Portraits exhibition. Organized by the National Portrait Gallery in London, it opened in Paris at the Musée d'Orsay, and was followed by shows in London and the National Gallery in Washington D.C. (Boucher 2016).

The David Hockney exhibition was shared by three museums—Tate Britain, the Pompidou Centre, and the Metropolitan Museum of Art. Each framed their show with distinct emphasis. Hockney's work provides a wonderful example of a contemporary artist doing both paint on canvas and more recently, digital art on the iPad. His works of art form a personal narrative while depicting his social milieu of the 1960s revolution from homosexuality, Hollywood aesthetic values and a new bright color palette, which in retrospect, almost looks digital.

During 2016–2017, Georgia O'Keefe was the subject of a major retrospective exhibition of her work at Tate Modern, and later at the Brooklyn Museum, when they mounted a major O'Keefe show with the theme "The Living Modern," illuminating O'Keefe's herself as a work of art. Since 2017, sharing and collaboration among museums is strengthening along with the rise global communication networks intrinsic to digital culture.

2.6 Conclusion

As museums redefine and redesign their space, they find themselves dealing with complex notions of public space, both real and virtual, and how the design of public space that serves diverse public identities can be marshalled to motivate and inspire people to engage and participate, to visit, and return, to retain a place in their hearts, minds and imagination that keeps them connected to the life of the museum. To accomplish this, museums are exploring new ways to be more porous with their environment and the dynamic nature of contemporary life and digital culture in order to grow and thrive in the digital world.

As boundaries blur between real and virtual life, between art and commerce in physical and digital spaces and places, interweaving past, present, future, gender, race, and identity, we sense that we are experiencing a tectonic shift that at once enriches and disrupts our lives and our ways of living in a world that is increasingly digital. Across all sectors of work and the workplace and in particular, galleries, libraries, archives, and museums (GLAM), the rapid advance of digital culture from the latest digital devices and applications dominating human communication, to the infusion of artificial intelligence, algorithms, machine learning and the seeming digitization of everything tied to Internet of Things (IoT) (Rainie 2017), now recasts the museum's social contexts, roles and responsibilities, aesthetic principles and cultural milieu.

Unlike cultural institutions of the past, where museums were self-deterministic, in the 21st century, new digital directions, and the very nature of the enterprise have by necessity become a shared endeavor between the museum and its audience, and the general public. Happily, the recasting of these relationships has strengthened the ties between museums and their communities on-location and online and continue to redefine the very identity of the museum as it transforms into a 21st-century democratic institution reflective of contemporary life and art, ready to meet the challenges brought on by the digital revolution and the rise of digital culture (Giannini 2017). Museums are seizing upon the new and exciting opportunities that our digital culture ecosystem is creating, and which in turn enables museums to more effectively make a difference to lives of their visitors and users in ways not before imaginable.

Fasten your seatbelts—as we enter the second wave of the digital revolution in which daily digital life and culture becomes broadly embedded across human activities and interactions real and virtual, online, on the web and Internet, and as human behavior and senses evolve to new states of being and consciousness. Overall there are many issues for museums to consider as they adapt to the rapidly changing digital culture that surrounds them. The rest of this book covers some of these aspects from different perspectives.

References

Boucher B (2016) First-ever exhibition of Cézanne Portraits to tour London, Washington, and Paris. Artnet News, 8 Dec 2016. https://news.artnet.com/exhibitions/paul-cezanne-portraits-tour-2017-776921. Accessed 27 Jan 2019

Bowen JP, Giannini T (2014) Digitalism: the new realism. In: Ng K, Bowen JP, McDaid S (eds) EVA London 2014 conference proceedings, Electronic Workshops in Computing (eWiC), BCS, pp 324–331. https://doi.org/10.14236/ewic/eva2014.38

Bowen JP, Giannini T, Polmeer G, Gannis C, Gardiner J, Kearney J, Wands B, Weinel J (2018) States of being: art and identity in digital space and time. In Bowen JP, Weinel J, Diprose G, Lambert N (eds) EVA London 2018 conference proceedings, Electronic Workshops in Computing (eWiC), BCS, pp 1–7. https://doi.org/10.14236/ewic/eva2018.1

British Museum (2018) The BP exhibition—I am Ashurbanipal: king of the world, king of Assyria. Press release, The British Museum, UK, Nov 2018. https://www.britishmuseum.org/docs/Ashurbanipal_Final_PR.docx. Accessed 29 Jan 2019

Decron C, Serota N (2016) Tate Modern building a museum for the 21st century. Tate Publishing, p 169

Dickerman L (2016) Robert Rauschenberg: among friends. MoMA Press, Museum of Modern Art, New York. http://press.moma.org/2016/01/robert-rauschenberg/. Accessed 27 Jan 2019

Giannini T (2017) Museums and the evolving digital landscape: opportunities and challenges. In: MATCON conference, Craiova, Romania, Sept 2017. https://www.researchgate.net/publication/320065551. Accessed 27 Jan 2019

Giannini T, Bowen JP (2014) The Brooklyn visual heritage website: Brooklyn's museum and libraries collaborate for project CHART. In: Museums and the Web, Baltimore, MD, USA, conference proceedings, 2–5 Apr 2014. https://mw2014.museumsandtheweb.com/paper/the-brooklyn-visual-heritage-website/. Accessed 31 Dec 2018

Giannini T, Bowen JP (2015) A New York museums and Pratt partnership: building web collections and preparing museum professionals for the digital world. In: MW2015: Museums and the

Web 2015, Chicago, USA, 8–11 Apr 2015. https://mw2015.museumsandtheweb.com/paper/a-new-york-museums-and-pratt-partnership-building-web-collections-and-preparing-museum-professionals-for-the-digital-world/. Accessed 26 Jan 2019

Kenny N (2018). Andy Warhol for the instagram age: huge retrospective opens at the Whitney in New York. The Art Newspaper, 8 Nov 2018. https://www.theartnewspaper.com/preview/andy-warhol-for-the-instagram-age. Accessed 29 Jan 2019

Klimoski A (2018) Renzo Piano to design new David Zwirner Gallery in Chelsea. Architectural Record, News, Jan 2018. https://www.architecturalrecord.com/articles/13196-renzo-piano-to-design-new-david-zwirner-gallery-in-chelsea. Accessed 27 Jan 2019

Passy C (2018) Met museum's Catholicism-inspired fashion exhibit draws record crowds. Wall Street J, 11 Oct 2018. https://www.wsj.com/articles/met-museums-catholicism-inspired-fashion-exhibit-draws-record-crowds-1539293434. Accessed 29 Jan 2019

Pogrebin R (2018) Mega-dealers taking over the world: David Zwirner plans a new $50 m art gallery. The Independent, UK, 10 Jan. http://www.independent.co.uk/arts-entertainment/art/features/david-zwirner-bridget-riley-renzo-piano-a8150181.html. Accessed 31 Dec 2018

Rainie L (2017) The Internet of Things is the next digital evolution—what will it mean? Trend, The Pew Charitable Trusts, 12 June 2017. http://trend.pewtrusts.org/en/archive/summer-2017/the-internet-of-things-is-the-next-digital-evolution-what-will-it-mean. Accessed 31 Dec 2018

Stein R (2017) Museums and digital strategy today. Alliance Labs, 10 July 2017. http://labs.aam-us.org/blog/museums-and-digital-strategy-today/. Accessed 27 Jan 2019

Tallon L, Walker K (eds) (2008) Digital technologies and the museum experience: handheld guides and other media. AltaMira Press

Waller HJ, Waller DS (2018) Opera costumes and the value of object biographies. J Documentation 74(6):1162–1174 (2018). https://doi.org/10.1108/jd-02-2018-0032

Part II
Philosophy and Theory

Chapter 3
Historical Questions on Being and Digital Culture

Gareth Polmeer

Abstract This chapter discusses poetic and imaginative experience in relation to being, aesthetics and technology. It considers ways in which art's past and future in the gallery and museum is connected to the language and ideas of technological development, and questions of technology and the loss of meaning. The technological focus of discussions of digital art limits the possibility of understanding it. What art communicates about meaning is lost, and with it the poetic dimension of experience. The discussion draws upon selected writings of Marshall McLuhan and Owen Barfield in the historical questions of art, science, philosophy and the imagination. The aim is to examine art, technology and meaning within questions of art's meaning amidst its technological developments, and creativity and the imagination. If art is to be evaluated increasingly alongside its technological properties, then its meaningfulness can be understood poetically as well as technically. The historical development of technical understanding in philosophy and the sciences, of which art and technology are largely a continuation, will be considered within the poetical and spiritual questions of experience towards different perspectives on the idea of art and the museum.

3.1 Introduction

Reason, said Goethe, in his conversations with Eckermann of 1829, 'with its tendency towards the divine, has only to do with the becoming, the living; but understanding with the become, the already fixed, that it may make use of it.' (Goethe 1850, p. 132). These remarks highlight a difference in the understanding of knowledge and reason, in what might be termed the poetical and technical senses, and in what one might call the life or being of nature, as opposed to the way in which it is studied. Such a difference is attributable to what Stanley Rosen has called 'an age of anxiety, where optimism is defined as the belief that man is a machine, and where the spirit exists only in the dread of nothingness.' This, Rosen states, is the 'root of contemporary nihilism

G. Polmeer (✉)
Royal College of Art, London, UK
e-mail: gareth.polmeer@network.rca.ac.uk

T. Giannini and J. P. Bowen (eds.), *Museums and Digital Culture*,
Springer Series on Cultural Computing, https://doi.org/10.1007/978-3-319-97457-6_3

[which] lies in the origins of the modern epoch' (Rosen 1969, outside cover). This partly concerns the historical developments of reason and positivism, and Rosen's analyses of nihilism, and on the nature of reason and the poetical and the mathematical (Rosen 1980), to which further details will be given, are connected with those of a number of thinkers directly concerned with media, technology and an imaginative participation of creativity, of which particular ontological questions on the nature of being and meaning in the context of art and technology are relevant.

Owen Barfield, for whom Goethe is a central figure in the historical dialectic of the quantitative and the qualitative (Barfield 2013, pp. 27–28), or the understanding and 'becoming' reason—a question framed in his comparisons of the harp and the camera (Barfield 2013, pp. 94–114)—saw nihilism, or the problem of meaning and its 'rediscovery' (Barfield 2013, pp. 13–29) to be at the center of questions of human nature and modernity, and it is to Goethe's 'becoming' that he refers when he critiques something comparable to the 'understanding' when he writes of 'positivist limitations' that

> By detaching himself more and more from the world of nature – as he has been doing ever since the Scientific Revolution – man has gradually developed the exact quantitative approach which has given him, over such a wide area, his marvelous powers of manipulative control. But in doing so he has necessarily lost for the time being that felt union with the inner origin of outward forms which constitutes perception of their meaning. (Barfield 2013, p. 29)

The perception of meaning and its relation to technology and to nature in the digital world reflect the story of the current age into the future of the arts. The following discussion will therefore expound an understanding of the historical nature of the questions with which Barfield or Rosen are concerned, how they can be seen to hold particular meaning to the concerns of technological development, and the ways that a technologically driven, quantitative culture can better understand its qualities. The first section of the chapter will address some of the immediate questions about art and technology in the present, locating the idea of technology and art, and their interrelationship in the historical idea of understanding and meaning. This is followed by an exposition of the idea of modernity and knowledge, explaining the idea of reason in its poetical and technical senses, with reference to Rosen. These contextual sections establish the bases for a discussion of technology and perception in McLuhan's writing, and the question of meaning in Barfield's work, and ways that poetic experience can inform an understanding of art and the future of art and the museum.

3.2 Experience, Technology and Culture

To define the qualities of a technological world seems at once to be met by the nature of its insubstantiality. It is a place in which the past disappears and the future approaches in the progressive aspiration of technological development, and in which its central questions are held to be both largely attributable to technology, and resolvable by the promises of the technologized future. As Marshall McLuhan put it, 'There is no more "past" under electric culture: every "past" is now. And there is no future: it is already here.' (McLuhan 2010, p. 80).

Technological advance is the latest development of a broader historical movement, the pattern of which emerges in other events in the history of ideas in the ontological shift away from the relation to being, to the relation to things; from the evolution of the sciences and philosophy, the secularizing changes of the Enlightenment, the developments of rationalism, the shifts of the relation of subject and object after Immanuel Kant's philosophy in the 18th century, and the decisive historical changes in attitudes to knowledge and meaning.

The 'digital' in digital technology can be understood synonymously with 'technological', which itself is synonymous with 'modern' and 'progress'. In this respect, the continued predominance of a technical worldview, manifested contemporarily in digital/electronic media. This is therefore an historical idea that has been developed alongside rationalist, materialist or positivist ones. Such a sense of the progress described is driven by technological developments in knowledge. One major consequence of this is a loss of consciousness, where elements of human thinking fail to act reflexively on the nature of its condition. This is in part, because of the loss of human autonomy, and in particular that of the artist. Because art has itself become connected with the idea of technology and development, certain key questions it has historically framed have been obscured. If art is subsumed under technical aims, its purpose, transcendence, or ability to be a 'pure appearance' that 'points through and beyond itself' (Hegel 1975, p. 9), to be 'an end and aim in itself' (Hegel 1975, p. 25) as G. W. F. Hegel put it, are lost. This is related to art's increasingly technical development within a particular theory of knowledge, and the purpose and meaning of art as its own end is closely connected to the human ability to create in the world in a sensuous realization of form in art, reflecting the dynamic, spiritual nature of being, 'the inner origin of outward forms' (Barfield 2013, p. 29), that would be otherwise lost in the technological ideas of the future, and of the reduction of humans to technicality.

There is a contrast between the technical understanding of the world and the poetic dimension of imagination. McLuhan wrote in *Counterblast* that 'The age of co-presence of all individuals is the age of communication—the age of instant humans. Computer data-banks dissolve the human image.' (McLuhan 1969, p. 35). And, as he notes in *Understanding Media*, with 'these extensions of ourselves' and the 'displacement of perception that follows automatically', we become alienated to the 'images of ourselves.' (McLuhan 2001, p. 51).

The contemporary questions that surround technology have variously precipitated the concerns of which McLuhan spoke, and this reflects on the nature of self-understanding in a world in which the technical development of knowledge in the rationalist and materialist modes, or scientism, has become distant from the poetic dimension of experience. It is of great importance to say that to address these questions is not to develop irrationalism and postmodern relativism, nor to reject science. On the contrary, to the extent that this has important consequences for various forms of understanding the world, such as the spiritual and poetical, such questions illuminate perspectives outside of the predominant ones associated to technological development, such that this technological development can be better understood. Neither is the aim to reject technological development or progress as such, but rather to examine certain ideas in what this has come to mean to the arts. The point is to explore the possibilities of technology more broadly from the point of view of an historical reconsideration of the imagination, which is to bring to bear various discussions on how to understand the digital world. This, it might be added, has applications to the imaginative dimensions of the sciences and technical disciplines, and to the variety of experience that constitutes human nature.

Whilst the language of spirit is profoundly absent in contemporary discourse on media, this has been replaced by promises of a future of technological transcendence. Where the spiritual language of being and meaning in the world has been replaced by technical understanding, the language of eternity, truth and transcendence reemerges in science fiction utopias of human-machine connections and artificial intelligence. A reflection of the historical dimensions of these ideas—of the relation of art, humanity and spirit to what is transcendent—is therefore an important factor in the understanding of technology and art. In referring to spirit and to the works of Barfield or McLuhan, one might reflect upon various themes relative to art and technology and consider some of the depth of their insights, and of the nature of knowledge and history. Whatever conclusions one wants to draw from the question of spirit—be they religious or areligious—the question of being and the imagination is frequently lost in technological worldviews, and it is just such imagination that can bring about a deeper sense of what human reason and knowledge is, and what Barfield calls the 'rediscovery of meaning' (2013, pp. 13–29), which might be conducive to a better sense of understanding art and technology.

3.3 Modernity and Knowledge

The ideas of meaning in Barfield's concerns, is one connected with the loss of the spiritual, mythical and poetical. The postmodern era of the latter 20th century did much to repudiate these things, the legacies of which have influenced the emergent media philosophies of the internet age, and the theorization of technology and human interaction. Such theories have frequently led to forms of nihilism or meaninglessness, and an abandonment of the human in a technological sense of artificial intelligence and the possibilities of some future body-mind-machine utopia. In this latter respect, the repudiation of metaphysics, and philosophy more broadly by scientism, has also contributed to the situation of nihilism described by Rosen, the negation of the spiritual or mythical aspects of being, and a move away from human nature to that of technology.

Barfield writes, 'How is it that the more able man becomes to manipulate the world to his advantage, the less he can perceive any meaning in it?' (Barfield 2013, p. 13). These are comparable to Rosen's comments that 'contemporary man is in immediate danger of losing all capacity to understand himself, and this, as it were, in the midst of scientific plenty' (1980, p. 221). Rosen's works such as *Nihilism* (Rosen 1969) and *The Limits of Analysis* (Rosen 1980) have developed a significant critique of modernity, and the question of what reason is, and how it is to be understood in the relations of contemporary and ancient thought. The question of meaninglessness, or nihilism in Rosen's terms, is connected to the balance of the poetical and mathematical (Rosen 1980, p. 128), and this might be likened to what Leszek Kolakowski calls the 'technological core' and 'mythical core' of human life, the first developed in the sciences, and the second in metaphysics. The technological repudiates the metaphysical or mythical, insofar it tends to 'reject from the area of valid knowledge whatever has no chance of technological application' (Kolakowski 1989, p. 1). In Rosen's terms, 'The soul, spirit, or intellect is not a mathematical relation' (Rosen 1980, p. 236), such that the predominance of the technical systemization of knowledge in positivistic philosophy and scientism, or the consideration of philosophy as only analytical, rather than also synthetic, and intuitive (Rosen 1999, p. 247), means that in a comparable manner to what Barfield will also call 'nothingness' (Barfield 2010, p. 23) or nihilism, we are led to the sense that 'The context of analysis is a dream, not an analytical discourse' (Rosen 1980, p. 121).

What Rosen terms the poetical and mathematical 'seem to be two discontinuous levels of human spiritual activity', these 'are what they are, and both are necessary' says Rosen 'However, the common ground from which they spring is neither a poem nor a set of axioms.' In seeing the differences, there is a sense in which we wish to 'bring the picture into focus' but he suggests rather, that we '*leave the picture blurred*' (1980, p. 128). The discontinuity between the elements is the nature of human activity, and of reason, and losing sight of this in the aspiration for technical completion in understanding the world, happens at the expense of understanding human nature. Where Rosen speaks of 'dreaming reasonable dreams' (Rosen 1980, p. 260) and of keeping the distinction between poetry and mathematics blurred (Rosen 1980, p. 128), this is connected with what Kolakowski calls the 'mythological and the rationalized orders of culture' or the 'mythical or the phenomenal', which are coexistent, which is to say that 'culture thrives both on a desire for ultimate synthesis between these two conflicting elements and on being organically unable to ensure that synthesis.' (Kolakowski 1989, p. 135).

3.4 McLuhan, Technology, and Perception

The work of Marshall McLuhan contains many important questions on being and meaningfulness in relation to media, technology and culture. Insofar as McLuhan's foresights on media have reflected into contemporary culture, these are connected with historical, spiritual and ontological questions of technology. In *Understanding Media* McLuhan cites William Blake's *Jerusalem: The Emanation of the Giant Albion*, of 'the Reasoning Power in Man…separated From Imagination and closing itself as in steel' (Blake 1972, p. 714; McLuhan 2001, p. 50). Blake, writes McLuhan '…sees man as fragmented by his technologies' and he cites *Jerusalem* further:

> If Perceptive Organs vary, Objects of Perception seem to vary:
> If the Perceptive Organs close, their Objects seem to close also. (Blake 1972, p. 661; McLuhan 2001, p. 50)

McLuhan writes that 'To behold, use or perceive any extension of ourselves in technological form is necessarily to embrace it…to undergo the "closure" or displacement of perception that follows automatically.' (2001, p. 50), and this relates to the great technological shifts and messages of media and the emergence of the modern mind. This is a consideration that one can connect with Barfield's thoughts on the detachment from things with the methods of the empirical measures of positivism, absent the creative activity of a perceiving subject, of a scientific measurability that denies the reality of things. He comments that a 'scientism—which has reached the stage of abolishing the 'thing', will go on to abolish the mind…when it turns inward to the mind of the Knower, [it] finds there a nothingness within, to match the nothingness without' (Barfield 2010, pp. 22–23). The importance of a broader consideration of the relation to a world of being, one might say, rather than that of things, and the different sense of engagement one has, can be understood further by remarks made by Barfield elsewhere, that:

> The meaning of a process is the inner being which the process expresses. The denial of any such inner being to the process of nature leads inevitably to the denial of it to man himself. For if physical objects and physical causes and effects are all that we can know, it follows that man himself can be known only to the extent that he is a physical object among physical objects. (Barfield 2013, p. 14)

The 'inner being to the process of nature' of which Barfield speaks is of particular importance to considering the way in which one understands technology, and the metaphors for being or knowledge that derive from it. As Barfield suggests, the reduction of nature to measurability is also a loss of understanding of human nature, and, it could be added, the loss of the poetical interpretation or mythology of being which is manifest in the creation of art. If such art represents only the externalization of materially determined nature, then its meaning is lost, and with it the meaning of the self, for it can have no 'inner process' or meaning. This process is a central part of perception, and of a different kind of engagement with the world. McLuhan commented in the 1954 lecture 'Catholic Humanism and Modern Letters' that:

> In ordinary perception men perform the miracle of recreating within themselves – in their interior faculties – the exterior world. This miracle is the work of the *nous poietikos* or of the agent intellect – that is, the poetic or creative process. The exterior world in every instant of perception is interiorized and recreated in a new matter. Ourselves. And in this creative work that is perception and cognition, we experience immediately that dance of Being within our faculties which provides the incessant intuition of Being. (McLuhan 2010, p. 165)

This active, creative role might be seen against the "closure" or displacement of perception' (2001, p. 50), and it is one that must adapt to an awareness of the historical development of culture and technology. For, as McLuhan continues in the same lecture:

> as we trace the rise of successive communication channels or links, from writing to movies and TV, it is borne in on us that in order for their exterior artifice to be effective it must

> partake of the character of that interior artifice by which in ordinary perception we incarnate the exterior world. Because human perception is literally incarnation. So that each of us must *poet* the world or fashion it within us as our primary and constant mode of awareness. (McLuhan 2010, p. 169)

Such words are echoed in Barfield's writing, for he says that 'Great poetry is the progressive incarnation of life in consciousness' (2010, p. 179), and what McLuhan has to say here on the interior/exterior and the 'dance of Being' connects significantly to other areas of Barfield's thought. It is to Barfield's considerations on the imagination and knowledge, and on the 'camera civilization' (Barfield 2013, p. 110) and of what 'sweeps the music into being' (Barfield 2013, p. 111), that the following considerations develop, for both Barfield and McLuhan's ideas share some sense of how the historical worldview that has come to predominate is lacking in several key aspects, aspects that are essential for meaning and the questions of poetic experience and art.

3.5 Barfield, Meaning, and the Imagination

Barfield was a noted figure in the Oxford literary group known as the Inklings, whose members included C. S. Lewis and J. R. R. Tolkien. It is partly within this context that one might further reflect upon the aforementioned relation of the poetical and mathematical, or the mythical and technical in culture, for it is a central aspect of this group to have variously explored the spiritual and mythical dimension of the human condition in response to modernity. In the 1961 essay 'The Rediscovery of Meaning', Barfield examines the historical developments from the scientific revolution to positivism in the 19th century, and logical positivism in the 20th century. He critiques science's claim to be the principle form of understanding, insofar as its attention to the mechanisms of cause and effect and empirical study give only certain perspectives on the meaning of things, and that the language and method of scientism has been responsible for the development of a 'general sense of meaninglessness' (Barfield 2013, p. 17), insofar as it excludes any interpretation of phenomena outside the view of scientific methodology. Much of this problem for Barfield, concerns the use of language, and the manner in which the 'symbolic significance…inherent in the forms of the outer world themselves' (Barfield 2013, p. 19) is a fundamental part of the representation or symbolic form of conceptualization, such that any meaningfulness of language must correspond to the meaningfulness of nature (Barfield 2013, p. 20).

It is, Barfield suggests, that the concern for language in the positivist sense, by which words do not refer to anything essential, or to being as such, has been brought about by the forgetting of a '*common origin*' (Barfield 2013, p. 21) of the inner and outer world. Humankind has had to 'wrestle…subjectivity out of the world…gradually into a duality' which has become a detachment from the world of nature (Barfield 2013, pp. 21–22). Thus, the '"common origin" of man's outer and his inner worlds' (Barfield 2013, p. 24) is denied in the present as the traces of a mythical past from which humankind has developed to modernity. This development however, is also a 'detachment' that has allowed humans to 'describe, weigh, and measure the processes of nature and to a large extent to control them', for which there has also been a correspondent 'loss…of any meaning' in both nature and the self (Barfield 2013, p. 24). Barfield's work does not propose that one abandon such knowledge and approaches in the sciences, and indeed he suggests that this duality is a consequence of the movement of subjectivity and objectivity, but rather that the imagination again take a more active place in human perception, that we 'read' as well as 'observe and describe' nature (Barfield 2013, p. 25), and instead of 'merely copying and describing' such observation, begin 'to apprehend it as a series of images symbolizing concepts' (Barfield 2013, p. 25), thus to 'begin once more to experience nature as image' (Barfield 2013, p. 26), and to reconnect in that world that the quantifiable, technical view has so successfully observed, whilst also finding its meaningfulness outside of the utility to which it has been put.

The word 'rediscovery' suggests that there are intrinsically worthwhile things which have been forgotten in the progressive technological drive, that has in part led to the contemporary conditions between art, culture, and technology, things which have their roots in an origin of which the duality of modern consciousness has created a greater detachment. And it is the sense of the active imagination where such a duality is overcome, insofar as imagination 'signifies that very faculty of apprehending the outward form as the image or symbol of an inner meaning' (Barfield 2013, p. 25).

Barfield's 1977 essay 'The Harp and the Camera' presents an examination of the use of metaphor and of the way in which an 'historical event may be a symbol of the historical process of which it is a part.' (Barfield 2013, p. 100). It is also related to the historical relations of nature and image, positivism and imagination, meaninglessness and meaning articulated in his other writing. Barfield examines the variety of references to the Aeolian harp or wind-harp in the poetry of the Romantics of the 18th and 19th centuries, alongside the development of what he terms the 'camera sequence' (Barfield 2013, p. 99), which is set in motion by the invention of the camera obscura. This, he suggests, has led to a 'Copernican Revolution in the human psyche…formulated rather than initiated by Immanuel Kant, whereby the human mind more or less reversed its conception of its own relation to its environment.' (Barfield 2013, p. 100). The camera obscura is '*instrumental* in actually bringing about the change' of the historical relation between mind and being, or the world, writes Barfield (2013, p. 100). Barfield traces the development of the camera sequence from camera obscura, and the change in the 'art of imitating…reduced to the technique of copying', and thus the ancient and modern conceptions of the aesthetic relation to nature (Barfield 2013, p. 102). This moves historically to the photograph, and back to the magic lantern as the antecedent of the projected image of film, and the element of printing 'in the technique of television.' (Barfield 2013, p. 104).

Barfield speaks of the 'enormous contrast between the camera and the wind-harp, taken as typifying the process of perception' (Barfield 2013, p. 104), and this relates to an understanding of the contemporary circumstances concerning art, experience and technology, of which one might say the screen-based media of computers and mobile devices extends the camera sequence into a new manifestation of projection and printing, as the unification of the camera and the image created into a single medium. The contrast explained by Barfield is articulated in the sensorial differentiation of the harp and camera, whose different media—wind and light—convey different senses of inwardness and outwardness, and of the activity of perception. Wind or air is taken into the body, and thus the harp is an 'emblem of *inspiration*', a term related to air or breath, whereas light is 'stopped short at the surface of the eye'. (Barfield 2013, 104). That the harp becomes an 'inside', a 'modulated voice for [the air] to speak with' (Barfield 2013, p. 105), differs in manner of perspective, and the eye projects a view, a 'punctiliar nothingness' (Barfield 2013, p. 106). In this respect, he argues, the camera is an 'emblem, or perhaps…caricature, of *imagination*', this being derived from the relation to the word 'image' (Barfield 2013, p. 105), and insofar as the camera is a 'true emblem of perspective', it 'looks always at and never into what it sees.' (Barfield 2013, p. 106).

Thus, the camera comes to represent a process comparable to a loss of meaning and might be associated with the lost 'union with the inner origin of outward forms which constitutes perception of their meaning', as Barfield expresses it elsewhere (Barfield 2013, p. 29). Barfield develops further associations in the idea of 'projection' to the changed relation to things in philosophy and science, that is the separation of humans from being, and from nature, in the divided relation between perception and reality (Barfield 2013, p. 108). This division, or the nature of projection as the distance from things is exemplary of the predominance of a 'ruling metaphor' (Barfield 2013, p. 108), and one might extend this into the contemporary philosophy of mind and the theorization of technology, where it concerns computational metaphors, and the discussion of the mind or brain as machine or computer-like. If we are to imagine ourselves in comparable terms to a technology, then the metaphor will strongly determine the way we understand our relation to the world, and to meaning, and this is a sense in which Barfield's ideas converge with the technological extension of McLuhan's notions.

The 'camera civilization' (Barfield 2013, p. 210) has brought us to a particular projective attitude, a distance or externality to things, of a surface of things. But, Barfield asks, in reflecting on the metaphor of the harp, where 'has the music gone? Where has the wind gone that sweeps the music into being'? (Barfield 2013, p. 111). Barfield examines the prevalence of the image of the wind harp in the poetry of the Romantics, and this connects with his views on the question of meaning, as this can be understood in the modern mode of the projective, or in respect of an 'archetypal substance' and the 'archetypal element in myth' (Barfield 2013, p. 110) as a kind of movement of being, or creative activity. Barfield discusses how the means to understand the perceptive differences of these media is to understand that inasmuch as we require projection, and it has an historical development in the nature of human history and culture, neither is the mind a harp (Barfield 2013, p. 112). Instead, he sees a combination of the two as the path to a new understanding, imagining 'a sort of mini-harp stretched across the window of the eye' an 'image for the joy of looking with imagination' (2013, p. 113).

We can discern from Barfield's analyses of these metaphors for perception, and of McLuhan's to '*poet* the world or fashion it within us as our primary and constant mode of awareness.' (McLuhan 2010, p. 169), that culture has a means for its understanding in the tools developed within it and to create it, and in the imaginative dimensions of experience where the prevalent technologies of the day become the language of a way to understand it. Thus, one might think about the meaning of the digital, of data and media, and reflect upon the ways that they might allow something inward in connection to the meaning of things, rather than being a continuation of quantification, technical thinking, or the measure and distance of things, and the ideas with which digital art are concerned are one such area where this imaginative engagement can occur.

3.6 Art and Technology—Recurring Questions

The questions developed by thinkers such as Barfield and McLuhan towards an idea of active or poetic perception, and an imaginative engagement with the world, are ideas with which artistic and digital practices can be considered relating to both the recurrent questions which art frames about being and experience, and of the progressive ideas which technological developments in art suggest. This is the question of what is changing and what is lasting, and the means by which art creates meaning as the dynamic of these relations.

As has been suggested in the foregoing discussion, senses of change and impermanence have been emphasized by many of the aspects of technical knowledge attributable to modernity, and this has developed a certain sense in which the technological capacities of digital art could be said to emphasize a kind of detachment, which to recall in Barfield's sense of the 'camera civilization' (Barfield 2013, p. 210) is a form of distance or externality to things, of which digital media and art, as was noted, has become an extension of Barfield's camera sequence notion. A result of this has been a certain limitation in the understanding of what digital art, or art made within the concerns of technological ideas can say, when such art is affected by its technological properties, and when its meaning is attributed to the technical approach to knowledge.

One instance of this might be the sense in which the abstract sense of digital art as ephemeral or insubstantial, that is as merely code, or as lacking the physical presence or materiality of other arts, is reflected into the idea that it cannot convey anything meaningful, or that such meaninglessness or insubstantiality is the actuality of the world in art. Such views, developed further in relation to postmodern thought, have tended to emphasize a technologically deterministic idea of art, and also of a more broadly deterministic picture of human experience, wherein the active aspects in Barfield's sense are precluded by the worldview that has been encompassed by the detachment of technical thinking. Whilst technology does indeed have such impacts, one can also understand approaches to digital art in much the same way as Barfield or McLuhan propose to engage poetic experience, and this is to view the relation in which humans '*poet* the world' (McLuhan 2010, p. 169) or further consider the 'joy of looking with imagination' (Barfield 2013, p. 113). That is, to engage the technical and the poetical together in the form of the work of art, and its imaginative possibilities.

The 'universal need for art' said Hegel, is a 'rational need to lift the inner and outer world into…spiritual consciousness' (Hegel 1975, p. 31), and this sense of the artwork as a relation between the outer and inner might be seen within the context of the lost 'union with the inner origin of outward forms which constitutes perception of their meaning', as Barfield (2013, p. 29) put it. Thus, the sense in which a digital work of art might bring about a new union or interrelation of these aspects, or reconnect human poetic creation, with an understanding and meaningfulness of the world, might be thought of in the way that the form of representation determined by the technological properties of the digital work of art can be reflected into the process and possibilities of its making.

Video works and abstract color/light projections that have been developed between 2011 and 2017 under the ongoing series titles of *Variations* and *Distance* respectively, might be evaluated as one example of an attempt to consider this relation, for they set out variously to engage with a creative, poetic visual experience, in which the sense of the surface of the image, or of the ordinary detachment established in the technical separation of the viewing of natural phenomena with a camera, or of the framed image more generally—in the terms of perspectival position and depth between image and object—is brought into a dialectic of inner perception and outward form through the nature of the image, and of the temporal realization of shifting phenomena such as light or natural forms within the temporal complexities of shifting pixels, and the perception of motion and color in the digital image (Polmeer 2015b).

Interpreted in Barfield's sense of the camera, as that which 'looks always at and never into what it sees.' (Barfield 2013, p. 106), works such as this that engage the ontological questions of the image attempt to create a kind of interrelation between the process by which natural phenomena are seen and experienced, and the way in which the digital camera, digital images, and subsequently digital video encoding etcetera, relate to seeing the image. One might say that it is a kind of making of an inwardness to the digital image, beyond its surface, and the idea of distance engages this in terms of a seeing beyond or into the image in greater depth, a depth that is also reflected back into the contemplative viewing of the work and the inner experience and perception of the work.

The digital image in time is a kind of fluctuation in which millions of pixels and lines of resolution constitute an ephemeral form whose appearance is both there and not there, or as Hegel put it, 'Something moves, not because at one moment it is here and at another there, but because at one and the same moment it is here and not here, because in this 'here', it at once is and is not… motion is existent contradiction itself.' (Hegel 1969, p. 440). In the *Variations* and *Distance* series works (Fig. 3.1), this is reflected in the manner in which multiple video recordings, layers of images or blocks of digital color are layered into one thousand and eighty layers, each one pixel in width and one thousand nine hundred and twenty pixels wide in correspondence to the high definition (1920 × 1080) digital video image. Each of the layers act as narrow frames in which animated sequences of images move across different times and motion. The resulting image creates an abstract space, that is 'there', as it were,

Fig. 3.1 *Sea Variations* (2011–2015) by Polmeer (2015a)

but that is also only a possibility of the processual nature of the progressive scan video image, and the means by which the technology renders movements of pixels into a realistic appearance.

The works are abstract fields of color and depth. Thus, the interconnection between 'real' phenomena, and digitally processed color develop a movement of perception between the creative representation of natural phenomena, and the imaginative perception involved in the viewing of the work, and this has as its basis a means to develop a relation between the outward form of nature, and the inner perceptive mode in which it is creatively apprehended through the specificity of digital processes, and of the image moving in time. The works are both transitory and a series of temporal depths, such that they provide a contemplative experience of the beauty of nature, through a form intrinsic to the nature of technology and the changing ideas of a technical culture. The technology, or the work of art, and the phenomena represented by it, are set into a relation of form, and this balance is that dynamic through which art, in its reflections of its time, frames meaning.

3.7 Conclusion

Culture is connected to the works of art and creative possibilities that have been developed within it, and to the frames that are established by the imagination in how technologies allow us to interact with the world. These can however alienate human nature and the human spirit. If in McLuhan's ideas, a closure exists in technological extensions, then the humanness found in the objects of the future archive and museum may reflect a profound emptiness created by the aims of technological development. This is an extension of the outwardness and distance of the camera civilization of which Barfield spoke. If the history of objects in the museum, or the work of art in the gallery, is viewed as the progressive development towards technical understanding, absent the sense of our creative or poetic being, then the recent artifacts of the digital age might be viewed in the future as moves towards a technological determinism that wrongly separated the poetical from the technical. As Barfield wrote, 'Only by imagination therefore can the world be known. And what is needed is, not only that larger and larger telescopes and more and more sensitive calipers should be constructed, but that the human mind should become increasingly aware of its own creative activity.' (Barfield 2010, p. 19).

To recall, Barfield imagined a connection between the harp and the camera, to be found in the 'joy of looking with imagination', with the image of a 'mini-harp stretched across the window of the eye' (Barfield 2013, p. 113), in which the inwardness of being is met with the outwardness of the self in nature, in a new sense of creative relation, and the role of the mythic and poetic, of the 'archetypal substance' (Barfield 2013, p. 110). It is not science or mathematics, nor indeed technology itself, but rather an over determination of technical approaches to knowledge that puts us at a distance from meaning. This should therefore be seen to be continuous with science and technological progress, insofar as a renewed sense of perspective and the relation of human experience to technology and imagination is a way to view such developments anew, and to see the poetry of our relation to things and to being, as essential to understanding the world and self.

Art creates a particular meaningfulness and a different imaginative engagement with the world. McLuhan and Barfield were interested in different ways to understand the historical development of the technical understanding of nature and of media and technological development, without a loss of meaning. Seeing this is a balance between past and future, in which art in Hegel's terms 'points through and beyond itself' (Hegel 1975, p. 9) in a way that creates something meaningful in the relation of the poetical and imaginative, and of technological ideas of understanding.

References

Barfield O (2010) Poetic diction: a study in meaning. Barfield Press, Oxford
Barfield O (2013) The rediscovery of meaning, and other essays. Barfield Press, Oxford
Blake W (1972) Blake: complete writings. In: Keynes G (ed). Oxford University Press, Oxford

Goethe JWV (1850) Conversations of Goethe with Eckermann and Soret, vol 2. Smith, Elder and Co., London
Hegel GWF (1969) Hegel's science of logic (trans: Miller AV). Humanity Books, Amherst
Hegel GWF (1975) Hegel's aesthetics: lectures on fine art, vol 1 (trans: Knox TM). Oxford University Press, Oxford
Kolakowski L (1989) The presence of myth (trans: Czerniawski A). University of Chicago Press, Chicago
McLuhan M (1969) Counterblast. Harcourt-Brace, London
McLuhan M (2001) Understanding media: the extensions of man. Routledge, Oxford
McLuhan M (2010) The medium and the light: reflections on religion and media. In: McLuhan E, Szklarek J (eds). Wipf and Stock Publishers, Eugene
Polmeer G (2015a) Processes and variations in digital landscapes. In: Ng K, Bowen JP, Lambert N (eds) EVA London 2015 conference proceedings, Electronic Workshops in Computing (eWiC), BCS, pp 218–219. https://ewic.bcs.org/content/ConWebDoc/54907. Accessed 20 Jan 2019
Polmeer G (2015b) Motion to becoming: nature and the image in time. Ph.D. thesis, Royal College of Art, London, UK
Rosen S (1969) Nihilism. Yale University Press, New Haven
Rosen S (1980) The limits of analysis. Yale University Press, New Haven
Rosen S (1999) Metaphysics in ordinary language. Yale University Press, New Haven

Chapter 4
Museums, Art, Identity, and the Digital Ecosystem: A Paradigm Shift

Tula Giannini and Jonathan P. Bowen

Abstract A defining moment in the development of digital culture, when communication went digital, can be traced to the paper, *A Mathematical Theory of Communication* by Shannon (Bell Syst Tech J 27:379–423, 1948), the inventor of the "bit" and a new digital model of communication that he referred to as *Information Theory* which postulates that "all data could be reduced to zeros and ones, easily measured, processed, and copied – and that's now the basic architecture that underlies large chunks of our everyday lives. In fact, Shannon's master's thesis a decade before had already explored the idea of processing binary information with electronic circuits." (Morris 2016). Looking through our 21st-century lens, we see that Shannon's work set the stage for the paradigm shift from analog to digital communication across the Internet where people and digital things connect using a variety of devices and modalities from smart phones, tablets, laptops, streaming video, film and TV to embedded media. Living in a media saturated society, we find ourselves part of an expanding digital ecosystem that connects human activity, the arts and science. Now enter museums, as they transform from their siloed existence in a world dominated by experts and glitterati focused on cultural heritage preservation, conservation and curation, to wearing a new social identity made real by digital communication and media, which in turn is driving a new social order in place and cyberspace where people and cultural institutions meet and converse.

4.1 Introduction

The digital shift is causing museums to rethink traditional values and roles in ways that elevate the quality of visitor experience, and the museum and visitor relationship.

T. Giannini (✉)
School of Information, Pratt Institute, New York, USA
e-mail: giannini@pratt.edu

J. P. Bowen
School of Engineering, London South Bank University, London, UK
e-mail: jonathan.bowen@lsbu.ac.uk

Southwest University, Chongqing, China

T. Giannini and J. P. Bowen (eds.), *Museums and Digital Culture*,
Springer Series on Cultural Computing, https://doi.org/10.1007/978-3-319-97457-6_4

As museum life becomes an integral part of digital life, diverse voices from outside the museum, from professionals, academics, artists and writers to the general public, students and families, are being heard and included. The museum now finds itself in dynamic real-time communications with its communities and audiences. Digital devices in hand and on body, visitors use emails, texts, tweets, Facebook, blogs, YouTube, video, photographs, online petitions, social organizing tools and more to convey their thoughts and feelings and their museum experience. From these digital interactions, museums gather data from websites, social media and in-museum activities using digital devices by which they can gain deeper understanding of their local and global impact, while discovering new ways to communicate message, meaning and narrative. These activities signal a paradigm shift by which museums are becoming an integral part of the emerging digital ecosystem where states of being are encoded into the Internet of Things (IoT) and Internet of Life (IoL). At the heart of this transformation, museums are moving from a collection centered model to one that is visitor/user centered and responsive to the digital human behavior, identity and culture.

4.2 Digital Identity in Real Life

I'm real therefore I'm digital

As life increasingly plays out on the Internet, human states of being (Bowen et al. 2018), both conscious and unconscious are being recast in digital incarnations of self and identity. The Internet, and especially the web as a global creative platform and public space of communication and interaction brings together and juxtaposes diverse identities, places and spaces that more than ever, cause us to question who we are in real and virtual life as we seek to evolve towards an integrated self that is at once physical and digital. This chapter considers the impact of these changes in what is often described as a paradigm shift by which human existence is becoming part of today's digital ecosystem in which life itself is encoded and integral to the Internet of Life (IoL)—of sorts. We focus on how this emerging state of living on the Internet is changing art and culture. As we enter the next wave of the digital revolution marked by the digital convergence of all media, which closely aligns with 21st-century human creativity and innovation, we explore these questions from diverse perspectives which seem to indicate that we have reached a digital point of no return. There's no going back to pre-digital life, the question is who we will be in our digital future.

4.2.1 States of Digital Being and Art on the Internet

The future is now—GRAMMATRON (http://grammatron.com), a futuristic work created in a public domain narrative environment "depicts a near-future world where stories are no longer conceived for book production but are instead created for a more immersive networked-narrative environment that, taking place on the Net, calls into question how a narrative is composed, published and distributed in the age of digital dissemination" (Amerika 1997).

Looking back to 1997, eight years after Tim Berners-Lee invented the World Wide Web, Mark Amerika created the groundbreaking work, GRAMMATRON, introducing the notion of *The Virtual Artist in Cyberspace* foreshadowing 21st-century developments that today have made the Internet a central platform for seeing, creating and communicating art. The exhibition, *Art in the Age of the Internet, 1989 to Today*, which opened in 2018 at the Institute of Contemporary Art in Boston (ICA 2018) is one of the first major exhibitions to focus on the revolutionary changes to art brought about by the web (Dafoe 2018). According to the show's curator, Eva Respini, "It's a show about how the internet has affected art, noting that, "The internet has introduced a new way of seeing and being – It's affected how we shop, eat, date, travel, our social behaviors, our political machines, and how we create and consider art" (Sayel 2018). The show is organized around several themes including new ways of thinking about the human body and its enhancement, how the Internet is being used for surveillance and social causes, access to information and images, virtual communities, virtual worlds, social media and performing the self. The latter theme delves into how we create and perceive our digital selves in art and on the web as the selfie takes center stage in terms of the relationship between art and identity.

Almost twenty years of Internet development precede the 1989 point of departure of the ICA Boston show. Yet, it was during this time that the Internet evolved, leading to the invention of the web, doing so concurrently with the social and cultural revolutions that began in the 1960s when artists like Andy Warhol and Robert Rauschenberg, changed the way we look at the artist's role in society and how artists frame their identity influenced by the growing internationalization and democratization of art. The art and life of John Lennon, an iconic figure of this period, captures its essence in ways that speak to the themes of the ICA show. His musical compositions, performances, recordings, TV and radio appearances and anti-Vietnam war protests, mobilized world opinion and participation. Songs such as "Give Peace a Chance" (1969) and "Imagine" (1971) were being sung by millions of people across the globe, so that in effect his person, using the analog technologies of those years, created a human network of social change. He suffered under relentless FBI surveillance for his anti-war activities, a precursor of today's growing Internet surveillance crisis. Importantly, Lennon, as have artists of the 60s forward, created a new vision of popular culture and art that continues to develop in digital translation (Fig. 4.1).

The Whitney Museum of American Art in New York City also took up the surveillance theme which was featured in the 2016 exhibition, "Astro Noise" by the artist and journalist, Laura Poitras. The show, which used the entire 8th floor of

Fig. 4.1 Commemorative graffiti to John Lennon, photographed by Scarton. John Lennon Park in Callao, Péru. 2008. This graffiti art is a telling symbol of political protest that sits beyond museum walls in public space. Wikimedia Commons, https://commons.wikimedia.org/wiki/File:ParqueJohnLennon.jpg

the museum, was narrated through the artist's personal archive of film, video and FBI documents and conveyed her experiences in Russia where she interviewed and filmed Edward Snowden, and victims of the Iraq war to convey her story of being constantly surveilled by the FBI. This brings to light social contexts of contemporary culture and constructs of human identity. Just before exiting the exhibit, visitors were drawn to read a prominent sign with the following message, "Dear Visitor, your attendance at Astro Noise has been permanently recorded – think privacy."

4.2.2 The Internet as a Creative Platform for Art and Artists

The Met's Open Access Initiative makes some 406,000 works of art from its collections available online adding substantially to the vast art collections on the web that are being used to support scholarship and creative endeavors inspiring works to be reimagined. For example, Simone Seagle, a web and educational software developer, has used this open access collection to create several animations of master paintings that literally breathe digital life into the painting creating new ways of seeing these

Fig. 4.2 Cat Watching a Spider, c.1888–92, by Ōide Tōkō, (Japanese, 1841–1905). Charles Stewart Smith Collection, Metropolitan Museum of Art. Met Collection, Open Access, Public Domain, https://www.metmuseum.org/art/collection/search/50826

works. Seagle's animated GIFs of Kandinsky's *Violett*, 1923, Claude Monet's *Bridge Over a Pond of Lilies*, 1889, and Ōide Tōkō's *Cat Watching a Spider*, c. 1888–92 (see Fig. 4.2), can viewed on the Met's website (Seagle 2018).

Large-scale digitization of art works is making possible the use and reuse of works in ways not before imagined. Although we have no way of knowing how these artists would view their works reimagined as animated GIFs, this would seem beside the point, which is to encourage new ways of looking at old works, using new digital technologies, now made possible thanks to open access museum initiatives like that of the Met Museum.

4.2.3 David Hockney and the Allure of Digital

Over the past few years, the artist David Hockney has created a body of digital art works with wonderful results. Along digital lines, it seems that his recent paintings which were on view at his 2016 show at the Tate Modern and in 2017 at the Met, show that his use of a brighter and more intense color palette seems to be influenced by digital color, again pointing to the interaction between physical and digital aesthetics. At his exhibition at the Met, January 2018, three of his digital works created on an iPad were on display in a darkish gallery that emphasized the digital light being emitted by the works. Digital Hockney was decidedly popular with the audience, especially children. An engaging feature was that the viewer was able to see Hockney's process of creating these digital works. A crowd gathered around them, in part because of the works' time-based nature seen as a perpetual work in progress (Fig. 4.3).

Hockney's digits look back to the dots and dashes in luminous colors of van Gogh's 1887 self-portrait which is more than a selfie, as his representation of self is interpreted through his style of painting, here conveying his inner self and state of being with all the fantasy and imagination that implies (Fig. 4.4). His visible brush strokes create a digital-like impression of seeing the colors of his palette separate into patterns likened to ones and zeros. The portrait is real but the image Van Gogh paints of himself compared to how he would have appeared in his "real" person, is quite different—but not fake, but rather a projection of his real inner self.

4.2.4 From the "Age of Anxiety" to the Age of Artificial Intelligence, 1940s to Present

Just after World War II in 1947, W. H. Auden's wrote his monumental book length poem, *The Age of Anxiety* in New York City. The poem's title, *Age of Anxiety*, mirrored the deep sense of anxiety felt by millions of people in the aftermath of war. Significantly, this was the very time that the groundbreaking work of Alan Turing in computer science, and of Claude Shannon in digital communication led to their inventions of artificial intelligence and machine learning which foreshadowed its emergence in the 21st century and its implications for art and identity. It is important to realize, that both Turing and Shannon were involved in the war effort, both working in the area of cryptology which brought them together in 1943 at Bell Labs in New York City at 463 West Street in New York. Their post war efforts in AI and machine learning produced historic results in 1950, the year each saw the publication of their seminal research papers, a defining moment for AI, machine learning,

Fig. 4.3 Three digital works by David Hockney on view at the Met Museum's Hockney exhibition, 2018. Three small children watching Hockney's digital iPad works come to life were very engaged and expressed delight. They loved the vivid colors and images appearing and changing. (Photograph by Tula Giannini, January 9, 2018)

and programming. Shannon's paper, "Programming a computer for playing chess" (Shannon 1950) Turing's paper, "Computing Machinery and Intelligence" (Turing 1950) were foundational to establishing a scientific and conceptual model for future development. Tragically, on March 31, 1952, Alan Turing went on trial for homosexuality, then illegal in the UK and was convicted. He died two years later in 1954 at the age of just 41.

Concurrently, and also, borne out of the conflicting emotions of the 1940s post war era, Auden's poem and the works it inspired portray the period's conflicting emotions of exuberance and despair, which seems to have continued as an unbroken progression from the 1950s to the dawn of the digital age, challenging human states of being, seeing, feeling and doing. As we seek to meet these challenges we grow and discover new ways of being human and welcome the many positive aspects of digital life such as free access to knowledge, communication, interaction and sharing; advancing democracy and equality, and the freedom to choose, create and

Fig. 4.4 *Self-Portrait with a Straw Hat* (obverse: *The Potato Peeler*) Vincent van Gogh (Dutch, Zundert 1853–1890 Auvers-sur-Oise) Date: 1887/Medium: Oil on canvas Accession Number: 67.187.70a. A selfie of sorts. Wikimedia Commons, https://commons.wikimedia.org/wiki/File:Self-Portrait_with_a_Straw_Hat_(obverse-_The_Potato_Peeler)_MET_DT1502_cropped2.jpg

innovate, while we are fearful about the negative impacts such as fake identity, loss of privacy, omnipresent surveillance, isolation, depression, addiction, metal health issues, loneliness and physical decline (Fig. 4.5).

In 1948, the year Auden won the Pulitzer Prize for poetry, the American composer, Leonard Bernstein (1918–1990), who said that he was deeply moved by Auden's poem, composed his *Age of Anxiety Symphony No. 2 for Piano and Orchestra*, a composition of two themes each having several variations. In 1950, Bernstein conducted the New York Philharmonic for the work's first recording with Lucas Foss (d. 2009) at the piano. Also in 1950, Jerome Robbins (1918–1998) choreographed

Fig. 4.5 *Do you dare to show your real face*. Screen shot by Teo Spiller's net.art. December 1, 2017. Wikimedia Commons, https://commons.wikimedia.org/wiki/File:Teo_Spiller_Do_You_Dare_to_show_your_Real_Face%3F_(net.art).jpg

Bernstein's *Symphony No. 2* for the New York City Ballet, and in 2014, Liam Scarlett choreographed Bernstein's *Age of Anxiety* for the Royal Ballet London with great public success, which was again featured in their 2018 season.

> I sit in one of the dives
> On Fifty-second Street
> Uncertain and afraid
> As the clever hopes expire
> Of a low dishonest decade…
> The unmentionable odour of death
> Offends the September night…
>
> (from *Age of Anxiety* by W. H. Auden)

Auden's work continues to symbolize conflicting states of human existence and emotions, similar to those between digital exuberance and the dark side of digital. This dichotomy was still present when Bernstein was interviewed in 1986 just before he conducted *Age of Anxiety Symphony No. 2* with the London Philharmonic, and David Zimmerman at the piano, although listening to Bernstein speak about the work

Fig. 4.6 Detail from *Nighthawks*, 1942, by Edward Hopper, Art Institute of Chicago. Wikimedia Commons, https://commons.wikimedia.org/wiki/File:Nighthawks_by_Edward_Hopper_1942.jpg

26 years after its premier, it seems clear that his emotions of the post-war era were still being felt.

> Finally – Age of Anxiety – I intend to use the painting by Edward Hopper called Nighthawks as a kind of frontispiece for the performance – [is the mood of the piece] yes people sitting in the bar – yes it is certainly the mood of the opening where these four characters get to know one another and through the friendship and the circumstances which are at the beginning of the war – the war news coming out of the radio – and abetted by liquor – there's an awful lot of wine in this program – and between Plato symposium where everyone's drinking all the time – and the age of anxiety where wine turns them on or liquor whatever – they become very close these four characters and in fact when the bar closes – they are invited by the girl to come up to her apartment for a nightcap – so they go on drinking – and that's where this Jazz thing happens – their party up there – this is all fake of course because it's fake hilarity and comes to grief – but not grief but to nobility – I mean they pass out and somewhere in the aftermath of that false hilarity- during the war trying to be what they think might constitute happiness or being happy during miserable times – at least one of the characters does find the core of faith which is what one is after – and what I'm after I guess, in every work I write.
>
> (Transcription of Bernstein speaking, YouTube, https://www.youtube.com/watch?v=Q-aU2Se1RHw)

Bernstein's use of Hopper's 1942 iconic work, Nighthawks as the "frontispiece" for the Symphony seems a perfect match for Hopper's painting that uncannily depicts the very setting Auden imagined for his *Age of Anxiety* poem, namely, three men and a girl having drinks at a bar in Chelsea, a scene that evokes isolation and its dichotomy, human interaction (Fig. 4.6).

As the duality of what we experience between the physical world, and the virtual world of the Internet merges as one, and human information behavior, art and aesthetics are being transformed, buoyed by our digital ecosystem connecting all things and beings, we find ourselves in a "postdigital" world, not knowing where this journey between Earth and cyberspace is headed. Thinking about this, Omar Kholeif, in his chapter for the exhibition catalog, *Art in the Age of the Internet, 1989 to Today,* writes, "It is this context [the duality of the Internet] that returns me to the condition of art after the invention of the internet, an art – and an art world – that embodies a relentless state of anxiety" (Respini 2018, pp. 96–97), and questions whether we are becoming "one with machines, symbiotic creatures?" He sees a key issue arising from this anxiety as we posit whether "the world after the rise of digital culture is: are we happy? Do we actually believe that any such 'technological symbiosis' leads us to any real and lasting contentment?" This perspective highlights how digital culture is causing humans to make fundamental shifts in the way they see themselves in the world, the way they think and seek information, which now morphs to into nonlinear and nonhierarchical models capable of handling complexity, dichotomy, diversity and dimensionality. Rather than opposing these dichotomies, new multifaceted states of being have become part of an evolving state of human complexity that we more readily accept and even celebrate, from art and identity, to gender and aesthetics.

In 2018, the Whitney Museum mounted the exhibition, *Programmed: Rules, Codes, and Choreographies in Art, 1965–2018* (Smith 2018). Expertly curated by Christiane Paul, it offered a rare opportunity to see digital art over half a century through the lens of many of the artists who have led the field. A featured standout work in the show, *Fin du Siècle II* was created by the Korean artist Nam June Paik in 1989, the year it debuted at the Whitney Museum's exhibition, *Image World: Art and Media Culture*—the same year the Internet was invented. Forcefully delivering a burst of multimedia video art experience, the work saturates the senses with programmed TV screens and choreographed image patterns drawing on 1980s TV programs, video and music messaging political and social images that monopolize and mesmerize the minds of the viewers. As a video artwork of great complexity, Paik includes the music video *Musique Non Stop*, filling the gallery with riveting electronic sounds and images of virtual mannequins and David Bowie coded by facial animation software repeats the text, "Boring, Bum, Tschak"—is this saying that time in front of the TV is boring? The total effect of work's seven-channel video installation (partially restored) is experienced through 207 operating period model TV sets and sound tracks that realize a physical grandeur of 14 ft high × 40 ft wide × 5 ft deep. The TV sets mix and mash 1980s main stream media TV shows programmed and choreographed in patterns controlled by codes and algorithms.

The allure of *Programmed*, reveals how artists use programming as a means to structure their work while achieving high levels of artistic expression that produce original and disparate results. Viewing works in the show by Joseph Alpers from 1967 in the form of theme and variations on coded color, their beauty and simplicity sits in sharp contrast to Paik's images on TV screens forming patterns, that vividly illustrate the artistic range of programmed art, experienced by viewers as they move from Alpers' color squares to Paik's square video screens showing mainstream media content that engages audiences in questions of identity and cultural memory. In *Fin de Siècle*, we see the image of a nude female model, her near-perfect body walking as if on the runway, her many duplicate images inhabiting the periphery of the work, contrast the images of males taking powerful poses set front and center. This dichotomy of masculine and feminine identity seems striking and begs the question of why a stereotypical female is juxtaposed with a male identity of complexity and creativity. The work presents strong visual messages on identity as it does on the

Fig. 4.7 Installation view—right, partial view of Fin du Siècle by Nam June Paik, 1989, and left, works by Josef Albers (1888–1976), set of four works, Homage to the Square, 1967, and a set of six works, Ten Variants, 1966 (Whitney Museum Collections). These works are programmed to produce variations of color combinations, similar to the musical concept of theme and variations and convey a purity of color and shape often associated with Piet Mondrian. (Photograph by Tula Giannini, October 18, 2018)

state of 1980s TV and mainstream media, which seems to be captured by the many repetitions of the lyric, "Boring" (Fig. 4.7).

4.2.5 Warhol—An Icon of Pop Culture and Mass Media Identity

The Andy Warhol 2018 exhibition at the Whitney, *Andy Warhol—From A to B and Back Again*, stands as the first retrospective since the 1989 Warhol exhibition at MoMA and coincidentally marks thirty years since the emergence of the web, a moment that is seared into human consciousness in ways that affect seeing digital images and the self, and yet, since Warhol's death in 1987, his iconic portraits have remained fresh and of the moment. As the web ushered in a new visual and communications landscape, the time people once spent talking on the phone and face to face, is now time spent looking at a screen, sharing digital images and information, and it's all about the projection of self in a land where no one is anonymous and billions of people are broadcasting their identity on Facebook, sharing thoughts on Twitter and images on Instagram. And, this shift has transpired over a relatively short period of time, when the mass media landscape dominated by TV and film personas crafted by Hollywood studios was overtaken by the masses, while Warhol's appropriation of the most iconic of Hollywood stars as an expression of American identity still holds sway on the global stage of human identity.

In every sense, Warhol's life as an artist seems to embody his personification of self (his selfie) as an icon of pop culture, whose Campbell soup can, Coca Cola bottle, and dollar bill framed by his portraits of Hollywood "stars" shine bright in the American imagination. Hewn from the analog methods of photography, silkscreen and painting, from these simple means, Warhol invents pop culture in mass media terms opening the gates of the art world to a new way of seeing, where Hollywood and television are not denigrated as low culture but elevated to a new form of American high art embraced by the average American. The strong public identification with the personalities of Warhol portraits have become emblazoned images of the idealized self in the public imagination that re-contextualize identity and culture from the 1960s to the 1980s.

Warhol recalibrated the framework of social class and art opening it to new images and ideas of American identity from Liz Taylor, Marilyn Monroe and Elvis Presley, to Nixon and Mao, while religious images by da Vinci in his *Last Supper* are remixed in his 1986 work, *Camouflage Last Supper*. Painted one year before his death, he uses a technique whereby a green camouflage overlays the image to new effect and meaning, seeming to foretell the rise of augmented reality. From this, we can posit that this technique applies as well to his abundant production of portraits, where photographic images become paintings of power tied to the expression American mass media culture. His images thus transformed, Warhol moves them from the silver screen and supermarket to the art gallery and museum, while his revolutionary art practice and love of new media parallel and intersect with the social and cultural movements of his time from gay culture, the AIDS crisis and Vietnam antiwar to human rights. In doing so, he sets the stage for the 21st-century digital culture of global communication and participation. Warhol's death at the dawn of the world wide web remains a stunning loss jolting the development of art in the age of media and identity. Importantly, Warhol was a keen observer of daily life capturing its subtle changes that he recorded to portray the ebb and flow of his art and social commentary that have become intrinsic to the American fabric of identity (Figs. 4.8 and 4.9).

4.2.6 Warhol Embraces America's Love Affair with Mass Media and Screens

Warhol's prodigious output in filmmaking during the 1960s of some 500 films coincides with the rise of film and TV as a dominant force in American life. By 1970, 95% of US homes owned at least one TV set had the effect of homogenizing culture into a shared national experience delivered over cable networks (Ganzel 2007). By the dawn of the 21st century, Americans were watching almost nine hours of TV per day, compared to about six hours in 1970 and just under eight in 2017 (Fig. 4.10).

Fig. 4.8 Installation view, Warhol Exhibition, Whitney Museum, 2018, including Warhol's iconic bigger-than-life portrait of Mau, 1972, in acrylic, silkscreen ink, and graphite on linen (Art Institute of Chicago), and his 1972 portrait of Nixon, the year the US President visited China. (Photograph by Tula Giannini, November 15, 2018)

Fig. 4.9 Gallery installation view, Ads. 1985. Eight ads from a portfolio the ten screen-prints, 38 × 38 in. Note "Life Savers (top, 3rd. from left) which appeared on the cover of the March 1985 issue of Artforum. (Photograph by Tula Giannini, November 15, 2018)

Fig. 4.10 Installation view, visitors watching videos by Warhol from the 1970s, *½ and ¾ in. reel to reel* videotape with audio transferred to digital video with sound. (Photograph by Tula Giannini, October 2018)

> The thing that Americans do most often with their free time is not cooking or exercising or hiking or any other seemingly salutary activity. No, Americans watch TV. That's the default the current move to even tinier screens has to be measured against… Americans still watch as much TV as they did before the creation of Facebook, YouTube, and Netflix. (Madrigal 2018)

In tandem with the ascent of the global digital ecosystem, screen time continues to grow having reached about 12 hours per day in 2018, and not only occupies viewing, but as well communication, social media, and digital capture and curation, a mix of digital activity that flows across all media and screen sizes. From the silver screen to the smartphone, Warhol's imagery of American pop culture remains relevant, and can be seen in its symbiotic relationship to the screen culture of the 1960s, a period characterized by American mass media culture, and one that has laid the foundation for digital culture which is on view in daily human information behavior, popular art, aesthetics and narratives, so that by the time Steve Jobs announced the iPhone in 2007, it burst onto the digital stage at a moment when Americans, followed by the rest of the world, were ready to wholeheartedly adopt this new technology, its look, feel and function. But far more than a matter of screen size, users addicted to media gazing could take their screens with them and never let go, as if their smartphone, tablet or laptop was an extension of their physical being (Specktor 2018) (Fig. 4.11).

4.2.7 The Digital Path of Art and Culture

The 2018 digital art exhibitions, *Art in the Age of the Internet, 1989 to Present,* at the ICA Boston, and *Programmed: Rules, Codes, and Choreographies in Art, 1965–2018* at the Whitney Museum, situate Paik's *Fin du siècle* at a moment in time

Fig. 4.11 Statue of Andy Warhol in Bratislava. (Photograph by Peter Zelizňák, 2009, Wikimedia Commons, https://commons.wikimedia.org/wiki/File:Bratislava_Venturska_ulica1.jpg)

just before Berners-Lee invents the web some 20 years after Vint Cerf invents the Internet, and some 40 years after Shannon and Turing (Giannini and Bowen 2017) gave us computer science, programming, AI and machine learning. In the almost 30 years since the web's introduction, life as we knew it, has changed dramatically as we have gradually moved the many facets of our lives to cyberspace, a place at the end of the mind, the new frontier of human knowledge, information, learning, communication, interaction, creativity and art—the place where digital culture integrates real and virtual life and where humans and objects are coded and connected.

Human information behavior is redefined as it shifts to forms of digital behaviors most notably those associated with smartphones. The result being that Google search has become the first destination for search, the place where the lion's share of human inquiry begins (Giannini 2000). In our postdigital age, a new information infrastructure emerges as a virtual place built on the Internet and web that has also spawned a new social and cultural framework for creating, accessing and using information tied to communication. One key result is that the gates of the gate-keepers have been crashed—people are free to search for the information they need, the art they like, and to publish and communicate their thoughts. The web has ushered in a new era of individual expression and participation which has dramatically broadened the scope, diversity and inclusiveness of its inhabitants and the cultures they represent. With users traveling across the digital ecosystem through time and space at the speed of light, we dare not underestimate this monumental digital shift in communication, and the culture of sharing and being connected, as it continues to grow, deepen and evolve at an unprecedented rate, fueled by AI and machine learning, advancing in digital network and platform technology.

4.2.8 The Dark-Side of Digital—Digital Addiction

Just as digital life (Richter 2013) has led to fake news (Warzel 2018), so we see the emergence of what might be perceived as "fake life" (Herrick 2015) leading to questions about human identify and digital sates of being sometimes associated with isolation from lack of face-to-face interactions. In 2017, Americans were spending on average 12 hours per day on screen time and new evidence seems to indicate that young people are choosing to live in digital space rejecting even family relationships or time with real humans. Is this state of digital existence predisposing them to living with robots?

4.2.9 Blurring Boundaries Between the Real and Virtual Self

In an era of digital uncertainty and volatility, where boundaries between real and virtual states are blurred, the struggle for identity, from gender and sexuality to living the authentic sense of self in a time of digital deluge, one's being adrift in a sea of computation and digital dreams, where location of place and time is unknown (Fig. 4.12).

Fig. 4.12 Photograph by Darius Bashar on Unsplash, 2018. https://unsplash.com/@dariusbashar

Blurred by Tula Giannini (2018)

My image blurred
in high resolution
Life deferred
no solution
no detail
male – female

My image blurred
photoshop perfected
unprotected
from cyber intrusion
identity confusion
Life pixelated
Unanticipated
simulated state
Can't escape

Out on the edge
fading fast
Just a blur
no contrast

Focus click
What's the trick
Want to see
who I want to be

Check my phone
Find a place
in cyberspace
going there
alone.

In an era of digital uncertainty and volatility, where boundaries between real and virtual states of being are blurred, the struggle for identity, from gender and sexuality to living the authentic sense of self in a time of digital deluge, one's being adrift in a sea of computation and digital dreams, where location of place and time is unknown.

In January 2018, two major investors in Apple Inc. sounded alarms about the iPhone and "digital addiction" among young people. Their solution was to give parents more control to block and limit usage (Specktor 2018). In France, Emanuel Macron called for the banning of smart phones in primary schools. Parents and teachers are sensing that they are losing their children to "digital addiction," but ignore the fact that they too are living a digital life (Twenge 2017). Studies of addictive behavior tells us that banning and prohibiting, and other such tactics, simply does not work. As parents try to deal with questions of their children's identity, there is growing concern that young people are becoming attached to their digital identity on the Internet, one that is manufactured, wishful and perhaps narcissistic, which can be described as "fake life" that appears to be evolving from the media frenzy about "fake news" (Gray et al. 2017). So, if your life is mostly virtual (not real), is it fake? It seems that everyone is to some extent addicted to things digital, as more time is spent working and living digital. If digital reality is the new normal, it seems likely that digital art and culture will continue to experience rapid growth.

4.2.10 From Fake News to Fake Life

Social media, now at the center of "fake news" can also be seen in the way people create manufactured cosmetically altered identities by which they distance themselves from the messiness of everyday life. This seems to incentivize spending more time online than in real life and conversely, people are increasingly altering their physical state of being as a reflection of their imagined digital being, through makeup, plastic surgery, fashion, and other manifestations.

The theme of "fake life" is seen in the work, *Take a Selfie/Fake a Life, 2015,* by Columbian artist, Camilo Matiz which has been on view at the Avant Gallery—"Art is Life," in Miami, Florida (Matiz 2015). It is made from a neon framed black mirror on which the work's title is scrawled. The self-image of people who spend the lion's

Fig. 4.13 Mirror image selfie. (Photograph by Tula Giannini, January 26, 2018)

share of their life on the Internet seems to be morphing into new digital states that manifest visually and are often translated to their physical appearance in so-called real life. This phenomenon was on view at the Exhibition Art in the Age of the Internet at ICA discussed above, in that most works were not digital, but rather, it shows that the aesthetic perceptions of the artists and their works on view were admittedly influenced by seeing digital and aesthetics.

Humans are drawn to living on the Internet: looking through a screen to find themselves—their mirror on the world, causing digital addiction and fear of the real world—anxiety and depression from fake news (Figs. 4.13 and 4.14).

My Fake Life by Tula Giannini (2018)

My fake life
in digital reality
is all about me
a matter of singularity
A fake space
No trace
of real encounter
Just me
hearing fake news
I can't refuse
the digital banter.

My life is fake
For heaven's sake
Exit now
Don't take digital devices
Avert the crisis
Make real love.

My digital lifeline
disconnected
My fake life
Unprotected

Can't go back
I've been hacked
My fake life
like the digital abyss
Got your message
cease and desist
Give it up
for a kiss
Me too
I miss
You.

Fig. 4.14 "Gray crewneck unisex sweatshirt" ties to gender and sexual identity—real or fake? Photograph and sweatshirt by Fakelife, with permission, https://www.fakelife.org

4.2.11 Customizing the Digital Environment

From smart phones to smart wearables and smart homes, people are living in their customized digital environment wherever they are and wherever they go. At home, on the train, at work, on the street, at a show, gallery and museum. They are in communication with self, the world around them and across the globe. In many ways, this behavior can become as isolating as it is controlling what one hears and sees, as they take their personal digital environment with them.

Just as individuals surround themselves by their digital reality, institutions also create their version of digital museum life which often leads to competing visions or conflicting digital bubbles, each communicating that self on social media and each hoping to meet up in the physical museum place, both inhabiting and interacting with micro (the self) and macro (the universe) digital platforms making for complex relationships from the perspective of the individual to that of the museum.

As more humans live in smart networked homes, which have for example, Rokus and Apple TVs, music by Spotify and a wireless network controlled by voice with Control4 and Amazon Alexa, wear smart digital devices and spend most of their waking hours on their smart phone or laptop, one wonders—what remains that is not smart—the humans in the room? This desire and need for augmenting our lives and our states of being is growing exponentially as the Internet becomes an extension of our brain. Without our smart phones—do we feel dumb when we're disconnected. The symbiotic relationship between digital and physical states puts communication and information at the core of human existence. Digital devices "talk" to us and vice versa, and to themselves, others, the crowd, and the world so that, "within a decade, many of us will live in "smart homes" that will feature an intelligent and coordinated ecosystem of software and devices, or "homebots," which will manage and perform household tasks and even establish emotional connections with us." Will we see the emergence of the "smart" museum? (Coumau et al. 2017).

4.2.12 *Museums in a Mixed Reality World—New Opportunities*

The digital ecosystem connects people, organizations, things, physical and digital to a system of communication via the Internet encompassing disparate identities and conversations so that we now live and share a mixed reality, and "contextual computing, where digital information seamlessly blends into our physical reality as active parts of our environment—a world where computers can understand our surroundings and where technology feels unbound from the human experience" (Rizzotto 2016). Clearly, contextual computing would greatly enhance the museum experience and go a long way to add meaning. Further, through virtual reality, museums will be able to provide public access to major exhibitions extending the show indefinitely (Alton 2016). Doing so, serves to memorialize and preserve the exhibit. Preservation of major exhibitions in a way that captures its full experience, is surely a worthwhile goal, and more so considering the high cost of mounting which is labor and resource intensive, can be considered in of itself, a work of art and VR exhibitions could be viewed around the world.

4.2.13 *Arbiters of Digital Life*

Are the arbiters of our digital life—Google, Apple, Facebook, Twitter and Instagram? Are we living in an illusory autonomy bound by our personal digital bubble being filtered, hacked and spied upon, or are we creating our own customized digital views?

> "In the past, the information that was disseminated by media contained a wide, comprehensive range of content that viewers could use to obtain a full view of the news. Today, that is no longer the case and consumers now demand (and customize) content to match their world view. The results are a new world where opinion is fact and the truth is debatable." As Sanjay Nazerali of Dentsu Aegis Network said, "I don't need to believe in anything anymore because it has a user rating of 4.6. So, the whole notion of trust is now earned largely by collective experience rather than the symbols of faith." (Eyre 2017)

This raises significant questions about the quality and value of the information we receive, the influence of the "crowd"—and our ability to think independently and form measured options in an ecosystem infused with for example, Google filters, analytics, personal and corporate data—a Google that knows what we do when and where we are and much more. Is this an existential dilemma for human identity juxtaposing real and fake identities and bots, with individual desire to assert free will unencumbered.

Museums too are being impacted by the rough and tumble of digital of life playing out in a sea of diverse cultures and identities, as they seek to assert their voice with authenticity and authority, while the influence of the crowd on social media is growing and is more stridently expressing its voice. Exhibitions are becoming the battleground of social and cultural issues.

4.2.14 Creating Digital Identity—One Click at a Time

We see through the lens of the eye, the mind and the camera—we see ourselves in multiple views and places. What is this allure of the lens—the search for self, for identity and connection? Entering a museum, digital capture is paramount—without it, does our experience exist? Was it real? Leaving the museum, we check our images—where was I, what did I see? The lens is a reflection of self through which we tell and document our lives. Yes, I did exist, here are the pictures on Instagram and Facebook. I'm real because I'm digital.

Life through the Digital Lens by Tula Giannini

Who am I online
In digital space and time
Feeling free
of reality
Looking into the lens
Click
My digital self appears
Sharing myself with friends
Press send
Entering the digital ecosphere

4.2.15 Installation Art in the Public Square

Times Square, a public space in the heart of New York City, is known for its enormous digital display screens and millions of visitors flocking to experience America in neon light and commercial images almost as if they were at a museum exhibition. This year, 2018, Times Square marked the 10th anniversary of its Valentine's Day competition. The art installation, *Window to the Heart,* a 12-foot lens, said to be the largest lens in the world was the prize winner. (Xu 2018). Tim Tompkins, president of the Times Square Alliance insightfully noted, "I'm reminded every year of the extraordinary creativity of the design community of New York." He described *Window to the Heart*

Fig. 4.15 Window to the Heart, art installation of a 12 ft. lens by Aranda\Lasch + Marcelo Coelho. Winner of the Times Square Valentine's Day Prize. (Photograph by Tula Giannini, February 27, 2018)

as a "reflection on the culture of selfies and narcissism, and all the pictures taken here—there are 17,000 social posts *a day* in Times Square."

The work was designed by the firm ArandaLasch (http://arandalasch.com) and architect Marcelo Coelho (http://www.cmarcelo.com). Formlabs (https://formlabs.com), a 3-D-printing manufacturer did the 3-D rendering of this gigantic lens installation, graced by a cutout in the shape a heart. The designers observed, "Times Square is a symbol for how we experience our world. It is a physical manifestation of our culture, one dispersed and absorbed through cameras and screens. And in this culture, to fall in love you must first fall through a lens," said Aranda\Lasch + Marcelo Coelho about the piece (Fig. 4.15).

A sign near the lens installation work says that "optically bending light towards its center, the sculpture will focus our attention on love with its window to the heart." Passers-by taking selfies are invited to "Share your photos and love on Instagram and Twitter at #HeartTSq", which is followed by a quote from the artists, "Times Square is a symbol for how we experience our world. It is a physical manifestation of our culture, one dispersed and absorbed through cameras and screens. And in this culture, to fall in love you must first fall through a lens."

This art installation provides a wonderful example of how digital art, aesthetics, behavior and the digital self, have entered deep into the consciousness and imagination of the public, affecting people's ways of expression, feelings, and imagining themselves in the world. It brings attention to this iconic place that is at once commercial and yet invites the sort of public interaction and enjoyment we associate with the museum experience, raising questions about museum identity.

Fig. 4.16 *A Curated Mix of Fashion*. Macy's 34th Street, digital media display with timed images. (Photograph by Tula Giannini, February 27, 2018)

4.2.16 Seeing Life and Self Through the Digital Lens

Each day some 95 million photographs are uploaded and by 2020, more than 75% of the world's mobile data traffic will be video, as a once text-dominated world continues to fade (SocialPilot 2018). People of all ages digitally capture and curate their lives, sending their data to the cloud where companies like Google are collecting it to create big data sets which they can mine and analyze and get to know who we are. Although this big data scenario conjures up negative overtones around privacy, security and surveillance, the digital ocean of productive and creative activities empowered by individual expression far outweighs these issues that can and are being addressed. As we become more deeply immersed in digital culture, our creative self is evolving through digital capture that gives everyone the ability to curate their life through images, video and sound, as they form their digital identity connected to the global digital ecosystem (Fig. 4.16).

4.3 Conclusion

As never before museums are caught up in the ebb and flow of life's interactions across our shared digital ecosystem, at once local, national and global. Rather than existing in the illusion of parallel universes divided by physical and digital reality, cultural institutions, especially public museums now live in a world of shared space and time. As we inhabit the spaces between physical and digital being and identity, our life on the Internet highway seems to be merging into a third space of mixed reality, where real and digital life blend seamlessly. Are we not surprised that digital technology not only makes apps and programs, but as well is being used to create hybrid identities that are evolving into new states of being human.

We have entered the next wave of the digital revolution, which most closely aligns with human creativity and innovation in art, culture and technology, the lifeblood of the museum. This digital shift will perhaps be the greatest challenge to museums as they move into the future especially because museums are so much about the projection of human identify expressed through art and science—a place where artists, curators and designers create narratives about life's many states of being and existence that educate, inspire, enlighten and bring meaning to life itself.

Acknowledgements Parts of this chapter are based on material from Giannini and Bowen (2018).

References

Alton E (2016) How virtual reality could give new life to museum exhibits. Entertainment Designer, 10 Oct 2016. http://entertainmentdesigner.com/news/museum-design-news/how-virtual-reality-could-give-new-life-to-museum-exhibits/. Accessed 31 Jan 2019

Amerika M (1997) GRAMMATRON. https://www.grammatron.com/about.html. Accessed 31 Jan 2019

Bowen JP, Giannini T, Polmeer G, Gannis C, Gardiner J, Kearney J, Wands B, Weinel J (2018) States of being: art and identity in digital space and time. In: Bowen JP, Weinel J, Diprose G, Lambert N (eds) EVA London 2018 conference proceedings, Electronic Workshops in Computing (eWiC), BCS, pp 1–7. https://doi.org/10.14236/ewic/eva2018.1

Coumau JB, Furuhashi H, Sarrazin H (2017) A smart home is where the bot is. McKinsey Quarterly, January. https://www.mckinsey.com/business-functions/digital-mckinsey/our-insights/a-smart-home-is-where-the-bot-is. Accessed 31 Jan 2019

Dafoe T (2018) The internet totally changed what it means to make art today. A new show explains how. Artnet News, 2 Feb, https://news.artnet.com/exhibitions/ica-boston-art-and-the-internet-preview-1212620. Accessed 31 Jan 2019

Eyre M (2017) Leading in a digital world. Forbes, 14 Feb 2018, https://www.forbes.com/sites/ciocentral/2017/02/14/leading-in-a-digital-world/#6b0389ab5fa9. Accessed 31 Jan 2019

Ganzel B (2007) Television. Farming in the 1950s & 60s, Living History Farm, https://livinghistoryfarm.org/farminginthe50s/life_17.html. Accessed 31 Jan 2019

Giannini T (2000) Web information communities, gatekeepers, gurus and users, defining new relationships. In: Proceedings of the 21st national online meeting. Information Today, Medford, pp 119–128

Giannini T, Bowen JP (2017) Life in code and digits: when Shannon met Turing. In: Bowen JP, Diprose G, Lambert N (eds) EVA London 2017 conference proceedings, Electronic Workshops in Computing (eWiC). BCS, pp 51–58. https://doi.org/10.14236/ewic/eva2017.9

Giannini T, Bowen JP (2018) Of museums and digital culture: a landscape view. In: Bowen JP, Diprose G, Lambert N (eds) EVA London 2018 conference proceedings, Electronic Workshops in Computing (eWiC). BCS, pp 172–179. https://doi.org/10.14236/ewic/eva2018.34

Gray J, Bounegru L, Venturini T (2017) What does fake news tell us about life in the digital age? Not what you might expect. NeimanLab, 6 Apr 2017, http://www.niemanlab.org/2017/04/what-does-fake-news-tell-us-about-life-in-the-digital-age-not-what-you-might-expect/. Accessed 31 Jan 2019

Herrick L (2015) 11 things we fake in our social media lives. The Blog, Huffington Post, 30 June 2015, https://www.huffingtonpost.com/lexi-herrick/11-things-we-fake-in-our-social-media-lives_b_7693182.html. Accessed 31 Jan 2019

ICA (2018) Art in the age of the internet, 1989 to Today. The Institute of Contemporary Art, Boston, USA, 7 Feb–20 May 2018, https://www.icaboston.org/exhibitions/art-age-internet-1989-today. Accessed 31 Jan 2019

Madrigal AC (2018) When did TV watching peak?—It's probably later than you think, and long after the internet became widespread. The Atlantic, 30 May 2018, https://www.theatlantic.com/technology/archive/2018/05/when-did-tv-watching-peak/561464/. Accessed 31 Jan 2019

Matiz C (2015) Take a selfie/fake a life. Avant Gallery, USA, http://avantgallery.com/new_build/collection/camilo-matiz/take-a-selfie-fake-a-life/. Accessed 31 Jan 2019

Morris D (2016) Google celebrates 100th birthday of Claude Shannon, the inventor of the bit. Fortune, 30 Apr 2016, http://fortune.com/2016/04/30/google-claude-shannon-bit-inventor/. Accessed 31 Jan 2019

Respini E (2018) Art in the age of the internet, 1989 to Today. Yale University Press

Richter F (2013) The digital life of American teens. Statistica, 25 Nov 2013, https://www.statista.com/chart/1655/the-digital-life-of-american-teens/. Accessed 31 Jan 2019

Rizzotto L (2016) The mixed reality revolution is here, and it'll change your world forever. Medium, 29 Nov 2016, https://medium.com/futurepi/the-mixed-reality-revolution-is-here-and-itll-change-your-world-forever-177b06dac792. Accessed 31 Jan 2019

Sayel S (2018) Creativity in the digital age: how has the internet affected the art world? The Guardian, UK, 2 Feb 2018, https://www.theguardian.com/artanddesign/2018/feb/02/art-in-the-age-of-the-internet-exhibition-boston. Accessed 31 Jan 2019

Seagle S (2018) Open access at the met: animating artworks in the collection. Metropolitan Museum of Art, USA, 30 Jan 2018, https://www.metmuseum.org/blogs/collection-insights/2018/open-access-artwork-animations. Accessed 31 Jan 2019

Shannon CE (1948) A mathematical theory of communication. Bell Syst Tech J 27:379–423, 623–656. https://doi.org/10.1002/j.1538-7305.1948.tb01338.x

Shannon CE (1950) Programming a computer for playing chess. Philos Mag 41:256–275

Smith M (2018) The Whitney, "Programmed". Sotheby's, Museum Network, 12 Oct 2018, https://museumnetwork.sothebys.com/en/articles/the-whitney-programmed. Accessed 31 Jan 2019

SocialPilot (2018) Why live videos must be a part of your marketing campaign? SocialPilot, 2 Feb 2018, https://www.socialpilot.co/blog/live-video-for-marketing. Accessed 31 Jan 2019

Specktor B (2018) Are iPhones bad for kids? Two investors are urging apple to investigate, LiveScience, 8 Jan, https://www.livescience.com/61367-apple-smartphone-addiction-letter.html. Accessed 31 Jan 2019

Turing AM (1950) Computing machinery and intelligence. Mind 59(236):433–460. https://doi.org/10.1093/mind/lix.236.433

Twenge JM (2017) Have smartphones destroyed a generation? The Atlantic, Sept 2017, https://www.theatlantic.com/magazine/archive/2017/09/has-the-smartphone-destroyed-a-generation/534198/. Accessed 31 Jan 2019

Warzel C (2018) He predicted the 2016 fake news crisis. Now he's worried about an information apocalypse. BuzzFeed News, 12 Feb 2018, https://www.buzzfeed.com/charliewarzel/the-terrifying-future-of-fake-news. Accessed 31 Jan 2019

Xu S (2018) Giant, reflective lens now on view at NYC's Times Square for Valentine's Day. Untapped Cities, 14 Feb 2018, https://untappedcities.com/2018/02/12/giant-reflective-lens-now-on-view-at-nycs-times-square-for-valentines-day/. Accessed 31 Jan 2019

Chapter 5
Contested Space: Activism and Protest

Tula Giannini

Abstract Fueled by social media and activism, the museum world, onsite, online, in galleries and public spaces is being held to account by social movements and causes such as MeToo, the opioid crisis, climate change, environmentalism, women's rights and LGBT. Museum space has become contested space as increasingly the public more than ever is paying attention to the meaning and impact of the message museums are sending, embedded in collections, exhibitions and programs from education to performances. Museum audiences are envisioning a new type of museum for the 21st century, one that now goes beyond participation and interaction, to having impact and representation in museum identity, and importantly one that demands a new social order of museum values that break down past hierarchies creating a more level playing field, where diverse cultures and media of artistic expression are respected and included. This speaks to the very nature of museum space, experience, and meanings. At the heart of this new phenomena of contested public space, a seeming battleground of ideologies, is the Internet, a new social frontier of rapidly expanding space and number of users. A place we describe as a digital ecosystem connecting physical and digital life, and where a new social order is emerging that is changing human relationships, behaviors and values and where everybody is a player, from large corporations, such as Facebook and Google, to cultural institutions and individuals.

5.1 Introduction

As museums increasingly become immersed in the global digital ecosystem, where disparate narratives of history, art and culture live side by side, cultural institutions find themselves riding the waves of daily social media posts by activist groups who marshal their following and crowd to demonstrate and protest to make their voices heard and count on social and cultural issues of concern. With information laden websites that present the latest exhibition information and links to digitized collec-

T. Giannini (✉)
School of Information, Pratt Institute, New York, USA
e-mail: giannini@pratt.edu

T. Giannini and J. P. Bowen (eds.), *Museums and Digital Culture*,
Springer Series on Cultural Computing, https://doi.org/10.1007/978-3-319-97457-6_5

tions, museums are part of daily digital conversations of billions of social media users that also find their way to established publications of the art community such as *Artnet News* and *Hyperallergic* bringing to light the views of writers, historians, academics, critics and bloggers (Gonzalez 2017). In this digital sea of collections and conversations where present and past are juxtaposed and on view, history takes on new life while museum visitors gain greater awareness of their own history, cultural heritage and identity which forms the backdrop to digital seeing, thinking and experience.

This heightened sense of awareness is resulting in increased visitor expectations for being a member the museum community, both real and virtual, while it also motivates visitors to contest museum space in terms of its content, message and meaning. Importantly, museums are listening, and carefully considering visitor and community arguments and demands. This is leading to significant changes in exhibitions, gallery design and the repurposing of public spaces, offering visitors a range of new ways to experience the museum—from lofty and educational, to the more practical, such as having a place to relax and refresh between exhibition viewings. Negotiating, collaborating and sharing are embedded in the notion of contested space in both mind and heart, which challenges museums to think in digital ways emblematic of the postdigital world that thrives on diversity and inclusion.

With growing intensity, cyberspace is evolving as contested space especially as social media companies such as Facebook are using algorithms and machine learning as a means to control what can and cannot be seen online and with nefarious outcomes including banning works by Picasso and Rubens, labeling them pornographic (CBS News 2018), while museum visitors contest gallery space demanding that paintings that run counter to their views on art history, social justice and morality be removed from museum walls (Saltz 2017). These actions can take on a form of censorship potentially challenging constitutional rights to freedom of speech and expression, both onsite and online.

Another form of contested space brings focus to contested works of art based with respect to object histories and cultural identities in support of ownership and cultural heritage claims, and repatriation demands. Works in public spaces are also being contested based on social and political views for example those associated with the American Civil War, such as statues of confederate generals and paintings of slave holders that bring to the fore highly charged emotional subject conjuring historical memories and images of social injustice, so that contested space is also that space in mind and consciousness, both physical and virtual, where we interpret and personalize museum collections.

5.2 Staging Protests in Museum Galleries

New York City, home to some 1,500 art galleries, has an established and major presence in the exhibition world, especially in the fast-growing neighborhoods of Soho, Tribeca and Chelsea, while continuing to expand gallery numbers and square footage, growing its audience of art enthusiasts. Shows at large galleries, such as Werner and Gagosian, seem to blur the lines between galleries and museums, while admission at galleries is free. Relationships between gallery and museum staff, especially curators and dealers are becoming more fluid and collaborative to positive affect as we see greater interaction, real and virtual, in ways that strengthen community connections, diversity and inclusion. Museum and gallery audiences are redefining their roles as participatory, critically engaged and crossing boundaries into the realm of performance art, especially for political expression, which plays out on streets, public squares, galleries and also museums.

A well-organized protest in March 2018 led by the renowned photographer, Nan Goldin, brought together over 100 anti-opioid activists to stage a performance in the Metropolitan Museum's Temple of Dendur in the Sackler Gallery wing named after the Sackler brothers, Arthur, Mortimer and Raymond for their 3.5 million-dollar donation. They called for the Met to cut ties with the Sackler family because of their association with the opioid crisis as founders of Purdue Pharma, a leading manufacturer of opioid drugs. Protests like these for "les cause célèbre" are inspiring performance art on the museum stage attracting the attention of news media, and effectively using social media to advance their causes globally. For example, the many performance protests at the British Museum in the name of climate change stage to protest against sponsorship of exhibitions by British Petroleum. As the number of protest rises, museums are seeing the critical need to develop digital strategies by which museum life onsite and online are merged, and occupies a real place on the digital stage of the Internet and web, where everyone's connected, to converse and interact with their audiences.

5.2.1 #MeToo, Time's Up and Other Social Issues: Challenging Museum and Visitor Identity

Visitors entering a museum bring their digital behavior and senses, and their expectations for participation, conversation and being heard, rather than being part of a herd. Smartphones in hand, they are empowered by global platforms, digital capture of what they see and experience, and can give voice to their views and demands through social media and sites such as change.org. Onsite, museums are directly challenged by demonstrations, and especially so, in cases where the protest itself takes the form of an art installation or performance, begging the question of what constitutes art. The MeToo movement has sparked new conversations beyond sexual abuse, to female identity, self-image and the digital self. With its roots in workplace abuse, the movement has moved quickly to the arts and cultural scene, and most prominently to museums. Protests in the form of installation and performance art now appear without notice in galleries challenging identity as expressed in art with particular art works being singled out by protestors to remove or even destroy a work, or to add texts to wall labels that point out what is objectionable.

The year 2017 will stand out for the significant impact that the "#MeToo, Time's Up" movement continues to exert pressure on museums as protesters demand that museums take seriously their objections to art and artists who they deem to be part of the culture of abuse of women, and we see that protest actions have sparked exhibition closings and cancellations and even removal of art works. Protests by performance artists, most prominently by Emma Sulkowicz's have attracted worldwide media coverage whose work is seen as central to igniting the MeToo movement. When as a student at Columbia University she reported being raped, her claim was met with indifference. Her response was to carry her mattress across campus as a protest to this injustice which "went viral" on the Internet. Her performance art at the Metropolitan Museum prompted the Met's chairman for modern and contemporary art to state. "If we only see abuse when looking at a work of art, then we have created a reductive situation in which art is stripped of its intrinsic worth – and which in turn provokes the fundamental question of what the museum's role in the world should be." (Cascone 2018a). Sulkovicz's protest performance was also on view at the Museum of Modern Art which she staged in front of a Chuck Close painting, and Pablo Picasso's *Les Demoiselles d'Avignon*. In these case instances, her protest focuses on the artists' themselves as abuser of women which challenges the long-held distinction between artists and their word, by which artists are unaccountable for the abuse of women.

These protests indeed speak to both the role and identity of museums facing a new social order, and invoke the need for re-envisioning public space and the space between museum and audience as it develops into a creative participatory space of conversations, relationships and interdependent roles that equally reflect the expectations and identities of both sides of the institutional equation.

Recent protests show how the MeToo movement has sought to challenge institutional judgment, and social and cultural values around art and female identity and how it influences audience perceptions of self. We see that visitor engagement is no longer just a museum activity, but one in which audiences are sharing the stage and exerting growing influence on museums in search of new roles and identity for the 21st century. What these protests make clear, is that the museum whether or not by choice, are participants in the digital ecosystem and as such are porous with the external environment, a 21st century reality from the IoT (Internet of Things) to the IoL (Internet of Life), inevitably, we share the digital platform where life is staged.

In many respects, the MeToo movement clashes with pop culture, its stories, music and images. In her article for *The Atlantic*, Beck (2018) looks at the portrayal of love in film, radio and television (media in the foreground of digital culture) from the 1980s to present and finds demeaning stereotypes of female identity being reinforced. She points out that,

> "Allegations of sexual harassment have been pouring out of the entertainment industry, among others, in recent months. But while predatory male behavior has been condoned and covered up behind the scenes, it's also been glorified on screen and on the page and on the radio ... "It's worth beginning with the more shocking examples of how pop culture condones and redeems violating behavior: In a number of cases, sexual assault is treated as the start of a love story."

Further, Megan Garber's article in *The Atlantic* touches upon the complexity of living in a post patriarchal society, which also is concerned with gender identity in digital culture and how it influences the portrayal of gender in art and museums. Garber (2016) identifies competing states of being, describing "a culture that is living in the aftermath of patriarchy—during a time in which feminism and Puritanism and sex positivity and sex-shaming and progress and its absence have mingled to make everything, to borrow Facebook's pleasant euphemism, Complicated."

Increasingly, we see differences in museum and audience sensibilities around sexual identity. In December 2017, Mia Merill, visited the Metropolitan Museum of Art and claimed that she was shocked upon viewing a 1938 painting by Balthus, *Thérese Dreaming*, so much so, that she used the *Care2 Petitions* website, collecting almost 12,000 signatures for her demand that the Met remove the painting (Kinsella 2017). The Metropolitan Museum's response was published quickly by the *New York Times* with the headline, "Met defends suggestive painting of girl after petition calls for its removal" (McGrath 2017). A statement from the Metropolitan Museum's chief communications officer, Ken Weine, focused on the museum/audience conversation saying that, "Moments such as this provide an opportunity for conversation, and visual art is one of the most significant means we have for reflecting on both the past and the present and encouraging the continuing evolution of existing culture through informed discussion and respect for creative expression" (McGrath 2017).

The Manchester Art Gallery suffered a similar attack on its collections with the result being quite dramatic when the celebrated pre-Raphaelite painting by J. W. Waterhouse, *Hylas and the Nymphs*, was removed from the walls of the gallery housing Manchester's Pursuit of Beauty Collection, being declared by the curator of contemporary art, Clare Gannaway "a cause for embarrassment", in an act, the museum says, aims to "challenge this Victorian fantasy" of "the female body as either a 'passive decorative form' or a 'femme fatale'" (Telegraph 2018; Childs 2018; Keeling 2018). Clearly the MeToo movement had gone viral, as women around the world were looking at social media and reading articles in the news (Fig. 5.1).

Performance art was on public view in front of the Met Breuer Museum as a means to protest against an exhibition of photographs by the Indian artist, Raghubir Singh. The event, organized by Jaishri Abichandani, a Brooklyn artist born in Mumbai, who claimed that she was a "survivor" of sexual abuse by Singh while working as his assistant in India. She gathered supporter saying, "with your help, I would like us to put on a silent performance/protest to ensure that historians cannot erase this part of [Singh's] legacy, to hold institutions responsible for their choices" (Frank 2017). The performance gained immediate social media presence followed by an article in the *Huffington Post*.

These examples demonstrate the power of social media's impact as it translates the US "MeToo" movement to the UK and beyond. What art works will be next in the public court of political correctness going viral? Will it be an Amedeo Modigliani painting of a nude female body? His painting pictured in Fig. 5.2, sold for $170,405,000 at Christie's New York auction on November 2015, with the headline, "Modigliani's Nu couché (Reclining Nude) leads a night of records in New York – five world auction records for an artist set in *The Artist's Muse* sale, as modernist masterpiece

Fig. 5.1 *Hylas and the Nymphs*, by John William Waterhouse, 1849–1917. Wikimedia Commons, https://commons.wikimedia.org/wiki/File:Waterhouse_Hylas_and_the_Nymphs_Manchester_Art_Gallery_1896.15.jpg

sells for second highest price ever paid at auction" (Christie's 2015). If this work were publicly exhibited in the US, what would be the public's reaction? In 1917, when Modigliani's paintings of nudes were first exhibited in Paris, they caused such a scandal that the show was forcefully closed by the police (Wullschlager 2017). There examples show that the female nude does not disappoint in attracting attention and charged emotional response while posing a dilemma of sorts for museums and galleries as social contexts invade their space.

In the UK, a major exhibition of the 2018 art season is Tate Modern's comprehensive retrospective of Modigliani's work, including a whole gallery of nude paintings (Tate 2018). The exhibition has also drawn attention for its innovative use of virtual reality (VR) which recreates the artist's Paris studio in Montparnasse located at 8 rue de la Grande Chaumière where he worked for a year until his death in 1920. Visitors wearing a VR headset feel transported to his studio as if experiencing it in real time, and more deeply immersed in his art making and way of life. This was accomplished using photographs and the studio itself. Through the interpretation of this evidence, the Tate has created a compelling narrative about the artist's practice.

Fig. 5.2 *Nu couché*, by Amadeo Modigliani, 1917. Wikimedia Commons, https://commons.wikimedia.org/wiki/File:Modigliani_-_Nu_couché.jpg

5.2.2 *Judy Chicago—From Brooklyn with Love, NY to Belen, New Mexico Protest*

When Judy Chicago, famed feminist artist, proposed to her hometown of Belen, where she has lived since 1996, to build a museum to house her work, her dream of a museum was met with protests by Belen residents who took issue with what they called the "pornographic" quality of her work. "Some resident protested the museum idea and said Chicago's artistic focus on female genitalia would be "inappropriate" for children. For Chicago, "it brought back memories of 1979, when The *Dinner Party*, a triangular banquet table with plates featuring vulvar and butterfly motifs, was first displayed and generated controversy" and responded by saying that, "she had realized that the museum proposal had 'become a lightning rod for many other issues that have nothing to do with art.'" (Lopez 2018). This story shows that the location of a space or a work of art can change its status from being contested to being accepted. When the *Dinner Party*, Chicago's iconic work, moved to the Brooklyn Museum, it found a permanent home in a space where it has been loved by its community and considered a masterwork of the Museum's collections. Given the negative reception in Belen, Chicago has put the new museum on hold, although the Belen Mayor Jerah Cordova has announced he would give some $10,000 to support the building of the museum (Republic 2018) (Fig. 5.3).

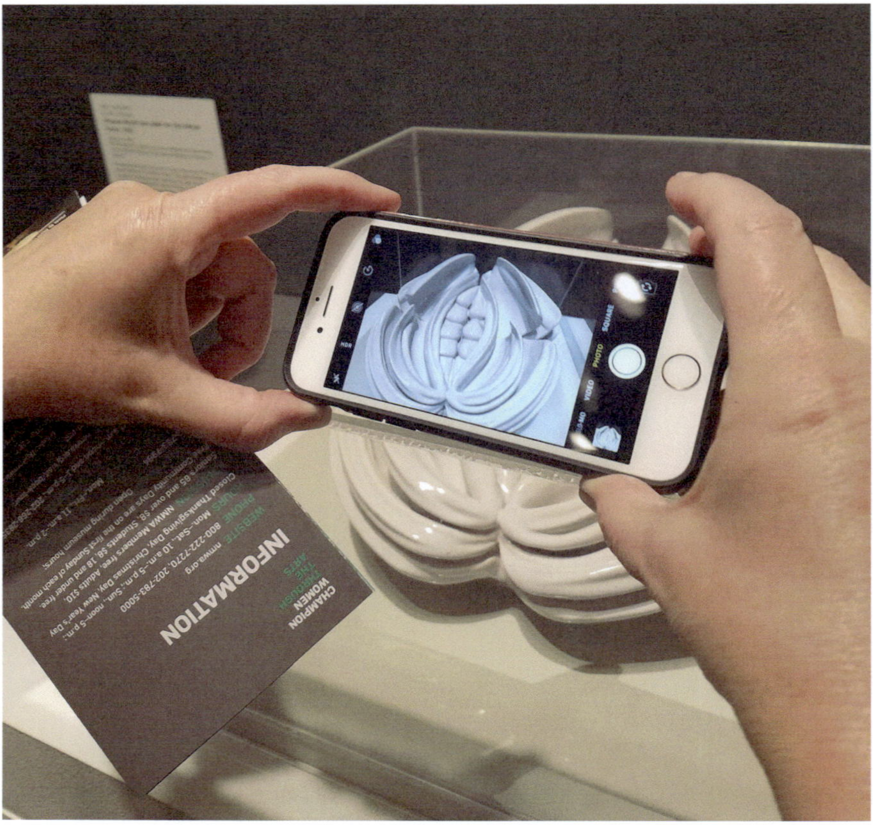

Fig. 5.3 A patron taking a photo of Judy Chicago's Virginia Woolf place setting from *The Dinner Party*, by Judy Chicago, 1979, Brooklyn Museum. (Photograph by Thebrycepeake, March 2018. Wikimedia Commons, https://commons.wikimedia.org/wiki/File:Photo_of_a_patron_taking_a_photo_of_Judy_Chicago%27s_%22Virginia_Woolf%22.jpg).

5.2.3 Gallery Texts and Wall Labels Contested—Changing the Narrative

Wall texts are mostly anonymous presenting vanilla information and perspectives, and for Western art, they rarely challenge the canon, while object labels offer minimal information, reduced to title, author, date and ownership while ignoring pertinent information that might change standard narratives.

> While museum wall labels were once used to explain the "title, artist, date" status of an artwork, they're quickly becoming a place to spark debate, rewrite history and acknowledge untold stories. In light of the #MeToo movement, wall labels are finally starting to include the controversial information that surrounds an artwork or artist. It could soon become the expectation. (Sayej 2018)

Fig. 5.4 Visitors at the David Wajnarowicz Exhibiiton at the Whitney Museum, New York City, read the wall text for the work on view, right, Untitled (ACT UP) 1990, screenprint, two-parts. The text was expanded by the Whitney in response to protests by ACT UP who felt that the AIDS was still in a state crisis in 2018, which had been overlooked in exhibition texts. (Photograph by Tula Giannini, September 6, 2018)

A central responsibility of the museum is to make the collections and experience relevant to the lives of visitors, and in the case of permanent collections, where labels can remain static for decades, that apparent lack of relevance is becoming a critical raison for protests. And yet, why are museums insisting on writing dusty texts on walls when in fact visitors are seeking new meanings and new digital solutions that can be solved by using digital wall text devices that can instantly update texts, and that can also be viewed on one's smartphone? With the growing imperative to create new and relevant narratives for permanent collections, dynamic approaches that use digital are essential to engaging visitors.

Owing to this old-school practice of object labels, a new wave of protests is emerging whereby performance artists take matters into their own hands. For example, Chicago artist and activist, Michelle Hartney staged protest performances at the Met and the Art Institute of Chicago, adding labels to works by Picasso, Gaugin, and Balthus to bring attention to the dark side of these artists' sexual abuse young girls, which penetrates the tension between the artist's persona and their art. Hartley elaborated on this to Artnet News commenting:

> Museums almost infantilize viewers by thinking they can't handle having this biographical information. What's wrong with having an aesthetic opinion about a piece of artwork and other feelings about the artist himself? I look at Gauguin's painting on a aesthetic level, and they are amazing and beautiful. But I also think he was pretty horrible to take three teenage brides. I can have those two feelings about it. (Cascone 2018c)

In the pre-Internet, pre-social media days, museums could ignore what is now regarded an abusive behavior but given the mass of freely available information on the web that invades personal life, this option seems no longer feasible and returns us to the point that everyone is connected to the digital ecosystem, and living in a complex, nonhierarchical digital landscape. At the Met, Hartley's label installation, *Performance Call to Action*, was placed next to the Met's label for Picasso's 1932 painting, the *Dreamer*, of nude Marie-Thérèse Walter, who met Picasso when she was 17 and he was 45; according to Hartley, their difference in age and status was in of itself a sign of sexual abuse (Cascone 2018c). Posting a video to Instagram of her performance and label text, her message notes the museum's role in education was being undermined by inadequate artist information saying, "Many people learn about Picasso and other artists solely through museums. I enacted a performance/call to action to separate the art from the artist." Via her Instagram, she gained immediate attention, responses and "likes," so that her "Call to Action" can be seen to exemplify the digital culture framework of her thoughts and actions by which she could instantly connect to the global conversation amplified by her performance connection with the Met. This set of complex relationships are proving to have powerful social implications that the simply cannot be ignored, and this is but one instance of burgeoning social movements around museums globally, across a range of causes from sexism and abuse to racism and colonialism.

5.2.4 Protests at the Whitney Museum, July 2018

The David Wojnarowicz exhibition, History Keeps Me Awake at Night at the Whitney opened on July 13, 2018 to great acclaim by art critics and in news publications. It came as somewhat of a shock when on July 27 a protest was staged by ACT UP NYC who felt that the exhibition text failed to recognize that the AIDS crisis never ended—it was not history. On the group's website (http://actupny.com), they expressed their concerns and reasons for the protest.

> The first goal of this action was to draw attention to the fact that the Whitney has a featured exhibition by a well-known member of ACT UP — who addresses AIDS in much of his art, who died of AIDS — that does not make explicit connections to the present AIDS crisis within the exhibit. In an otherwise excellent exhibit, this is an oversight that falls into a pattern of arts institutions historicizing the activism of the past even when there are almost identical contemporary struggles.
>
> When arts institutions do not connect historical activism to the present activism being done on the same issue, they are missing an opportunity to reach an interested and sympathetic audience who might then become activists themselves, or who might at least be inspired to read up on the state of the world.

The Whitney Museum listened and took ACT UP's objections to heart, promptly taking action by adding text to the show's iconic first work displayed, and also entering into conversation with the group. The end of the second paragraph of the new wall text for *Untitled* reads:

> On the evening of Friday, July 27, 2018, members of ACT UP New York stages an action in the Whitney's galleries to reassert that AIDS is not history. Members carried placards with articles and information pertaining to the ongoing HIV and AIDS pandemic. To find a selection of those articles as well as exhibition-related videos, interviews and writings, please visit whitney.org/Perspectives.

These examples show that people are reading and thinking about the message and the meaning museums convey about their objects and the contexts in which they are displayed. Overall, there seems to be a consensus that there is a lack of information, and that the information presented is often incomplete and not reflective of contemporary views, thus lacking relevance to visitor perspectives (Cascone 2018b). This becomes more critical, as museums put their collection databases online and are use the same label texts onsite and online, and thus is viewed and critically analyzed across the globe sparking conversations and protests too! This convergence can be an opportunity for museums to engage and grow their audience, or to retreat into the past clinging to old narratives (Fig. 5.4).

5.3 Contested—Restitution of Museum Objects

5.3.1 Online Collection Databases Grows Public Awareness

The British Museum views its online collections database as "an inventory of the Museum's collection and aims to record what is known about it. It is primarily designed to support curatorial and research work, and much of the text is specialized in nature and terminology." And yet, this treasure trove of information is designed as open access and is an ongoing project. In the spirit of crowd sourcing the Museum notes that, "Users are invited to use the feedback link on each record to help us improve the information… and that, "New images are being added to the database and made available here at the rate of about 2,000 each week. Images of some objects have been withheld for copyright reasons."

Bringing context to the making of the database, the Museum points out that "the database is the result of 35-years" work but is still in its early stages," and remains a work in progress using the latest technology and adding new object research and newly digitized object images making this a critical resource for curators, scholars and the general public (British Museum 2017a).

The digitization of museum collections has become a top priority shared by the museum community. An ongoing global project with the goal of making cultural heritage visible and accessible, especially since many collections held by museums for decades, have often lacked public visibility and awareness of their histories and itineraries, that collection databases are now providing, and which museums continue to develop with new research. An unexpected consequence of online public access to in-depth collection information and high-resolution images, is on the one hand, there is a growing sense of appreciation for cultural heritage and its value to a country's

Fig. 5.5 Installation view from David Wojnarowicz Exhibition at the Whitney Museum, features work on right, *Fuck You Faggot Fucker*, 1984 which includes four black-and-white photographs, acrylic, and collaged paper on Masonite, 48 × 48 in. (121.9 × 121.9 cm). Collection of Barry Blinderman. (Photograph by Tula Giannini, September 6, 2018)

standing in the world community, while on the other hand, virtual museums and collections have stage for renewed calls for repatriation and restitution of museum objects, for example, from Africa and the Middle East.

For the first time in the 150 years, British Museum officials agreed to meet with a delegation from Rapa Nui of the Easter Islands, to open discussions on the repatriation of a large statue held by the department of Africa, Oceania and the Americas collections, and on exhibition. A museum spokesperson said the monumental sculpture is one of the most popular and most photographed exhibits among its six million annual visitors (Rea 2018b). The British Museum also welcomed Chile's minister for national property, Felipe Ward, joined by UK's Chilean ambassador David Gallagher to discuss the matter of repatriation.

The towering eight-foot tall Moai sculpture, Hoa Hakananai'a (see Figs. 5.5 and 5.6) is a case in point. Hoa Hakananai'a and a smaller figure, Moai Hava, both statues were carved by the Rapa Nui people the Easter Islands, since 1888 under Chilean rule, were taken by the crew of the HMS Topaze in 1868. The following year, the ship's captain Commodore Richard Powell presented these ancestral figures to Queen Victoria who donated them to the British Museum.

Fig. 5.6 *Hoa Hakananai'a*, photograph taken at the British Museum, August 8, 2009. The database record for *Hoa Hakananai'a* (British Museum 2017b) goes far beyond the standard information and includes new object research, conservation reports and exhibition history. Wikimedia Commons, https://commons.wikimedia.org/wiki/File:SNC11003.JPG

5.3.2 From Africa to France and Back Again

When French Prime Minister Emanuel Macron met with the President of Benin, Patrice Talon at the Elysée Palace in Paris, March 2018, he came face to face with calls for the restitution of art from Benin now in the collections of the Musée du quai de Branly in Paris (Adams 2018). To confront the cultural crisis this represented,

Macron commissioned the Senagalese writer and economist, Felwine Sarr, and the French economist, Bénédicte Savoy, to research the issue of restitution of art, and to write an in-depth report with recommendations and new vision (Sarr and Savoy 2018; Brown 2018). The result was, *The Restitution of African Cultural Heritage—Toward a New Relational Ethics*, in 2018. In it, the authors state, "The report comes at a time when the subject of colonial restitution has been catapulted from an insider topic within museum communities to a worldwide public issue." Some would say it has "gone viral." Indeed, the report sent shockwaves across the museum world, so that major museums of so-called "colonial collections" are finding themselves part of a far-reaching digital debate buoyed by museum collection databases with detailed object information by which the unknown becomes known and accessible to all with a smartphone and Wi-Fi.

Stéphane Martin, President of the Musée du quai Branly for African Art, identifies the "main problem" with the report stating, "it sidelines museums in favor of specialists in historical reparations" who characterize "all that was collected and bought during the colonial period" with "the impurity of colonial crime." From the perspective of the artists and that of museums and collectors, the biography and itinerary of each objects represents specific circumstances across time and space. The journey and life of each work needs to be traced through study and documentation (Rea 2018c) (Fig. 5.7).

The unflinching manner of the report in favor of restitution set the stage for far reaching discussion and debate, new historical interpretations and provenance research, and new way to collaborate and share across borders (Small 2018a, b). Hartmut Dorgerloh, General Director, Humboldt Forum, Berlin, sharing perspectives in an article jointly written with his colleagues, Nicholas Thomas, director of the Museum of Archaeology and Anthropology in Cambridge, and Tristram Hunt, director of the V&A, recognized the impact of cultural issues in a digital world of connectedness (Hunt et al. 2018):

> Finding a suitable approach for dealing with cultural assets from colonial contexts is a pressing and complex political issue—in Germany as well as in France. The debate about how to treat this important aspect of the colonial heritage is as challenging as it is overdue. Essentially the question is: what is our relationship to people, countries, religions and cultures in America, Africa or Asia, in a world where everything is becoming ever more connected—economically, socially and politically?

Overall, the French Report supports restitution with specific qualifications, but French law would need to be changed which requires approval by the Parliament (Small 2018b). By all estimations, these initial meetings and the Report have ushered in a period of discussion and working together to deal with long-standing issues defined by the history of colonialism and empire, but in ways that increase the value of museums in a postdigital world. What is especially significant, is that the movement already has spurred plans for new museums and cultural centers as the Ivory Coast and South Africa (Rea 2018a; Cascone 2018d, e). No doubt this is only the beginning of a journey that ties to reassessing history, but that also plays to the phenomenon of new states of connectedness in the digital culture ecosystem (Fig. 5.8).

Fig. 5.7 Sculpture, *Gardien de reliquaire*, Central Africa, Gabon, Hust-Ogooué, Ondumbo, before 1886, wood, Inv: 71.1886.79.6. Collection, Musée du quai Branly. Paris, France. Wikimedia Commons, https://commons.wikimedia.org/wiki/File:Figure_de_gardien_de_reliquaire,_Mus%C3%A9e_du_quai_Branly.jpg

Fig. 5.8 Three royal statues from the Palaces of Abomey in Benin, on display at the Musée du quai Branly, Paris. They are works selected to be returned to Benin (Toodehfallen, 2018). (Photograph by T. Giannini, December 19, 2018)

5.3.3 Restitution Goes Global

The restitution movement traveled from Paris to New Jersey, when the Eastern Orthodox Church filed a federal lawsuit against the Princeton University Library seeking the return of "stolen" manuscripts that had been taken during World War I from a monastery in Kormista, a village in northern Greece, and were now held by the Princeton University Library. They are described in the book, *Greek Manuscripts at Princeton, 6th to 19th Century: A Descriptive* Catalogue by Sofia Kotzabassi and Nancy Patterson Ševčenko, with the collaboration of Don C. Skemer. This lavishly illustrated book published by Princeton University Press in 2010 no doubt drew attention to Princeton's Greek manuscript collection especially since the book is listed in the Library's online catalog.

> Among the manuscripts are some spectacularly illustrated works, key monuments in the history of Byzantine illumination: an 11th-century codex of John Klimax's Heavenly Ladder with vivid and unusual depictions of monastic life; evangelist portraits from a number of artistic periods and centers; extraordinary pages of pure ornament; and fine examples of post-Byzantine liturgical illustration of the 16th and 17th centuries. (Moynihan 2018)

> The plaintiffs in the federal suit filed in New Jersey, including Ecumenical Patriarch Bartholomew I of Constantinople, say that Bulgarian guerrilla forces stormed the Theotokos Eikosiphoinissa Monastery in 1917, assaulted the monks who lived there and made off with a trove of ancient texts.

The Church cited the Princeton 2010 catalog, as a key source of evidence to substantiate their claim, which provides another example of the power of online information to bring to light materials hidden in collection, be they museums or libraries. Speaking about the stolen manuscripts, a representative of the Easter Orthodox Church stressed their importance saying, "They're part of sacred history, and that's our spiritual and cultural identity,"—adding that the loss of the manuscripts and the efforts to recover them had been "very painful." The lawsuit also claims that manuscripts in the Morgan Library in New York, and the Duke University Library were stolen.

The lawsuit also claims that Duke University and the Morgan Library and Museum in New York City hold manuscripts stolen from the monastery and "renews its call to these institutions to recognize that the Ecumenical Patriarchate is indeed the rightful owner of these precious and irreplaceable documents, and to return them immediately" (Moynihan 2018).

5.3.4 Rapid Response Collecting

The concept of Rapid Response Collecting (RRC) was introduced by the Victoria and Albert Museum in London (V&A 2014). RRC provides a strategy by which museums can keep pace with change and social movements by collecting materials and ephemera, such as—posters, hats, signs, objects and buttons to convey the narrative of social movements telling their stories in their own words, images and contexts (Marshall 2018). Digital capture and curation is a key technique for gathering images of social movements from Black Lives Matter, the Women's Rights, Gay Rights to museum protests and demonstrations. The key concept of RRC is capturing history as it happens (Bowley 2017). Increasingly curators are using this strategy to build new collections documenting important social movements over time (Johnson 2018). Archive-it (https://archive-it.org)—is a subscription service under the Internet Archive (https://archive.org) that works with some 400 institutions including museums and art libraries that is devoted to helping institutions build online archival collections freely available on the web (Fig. 5.9).

Fig. 5.9 2018 Women's March in New York City on 6th Avenue, between 49th Street and 50th Street, at Radio City Music Hall, January 20, 2018—a good march for RRC. (Photograph by Rhododendrites, Wikimedia Commons, https://commons.wikimedia.org/wiki/File:2018_Women%27s_March_NYC_(00331).jpg)

5.4 Conclusion

The concept of contested space is grounded in social and political notions of space in time and place, on history and provenance, what stories are told, the beliefs they represent and who is privileged by them. For museums, this represents a new struggle, as under-represented groups seek to assert their rights through protest and digital speak. The stakes are high and challenge museums to rethink their values and goals. At the heart of this battleground is the digital culture ecosystem which connects dueling parties communicating via social media, email and online publications. What happens in New York and Brooklyn is heard in London and Paris and around the world. A new state of transparency with nowhere to hide fuels viral movement such as *de-colonize* and MeToo; it adds urgency to calls for diversity and inclusion supported by digital networks and platforms. This new social state of being informed and connected across the globe is unprecedented in human history as anyone with a smartphone can be a participant.

The notion of contested space is born from the outside in and pierces the walls of museum silos where all seemed fine in the inherited state of doing and being. The space of curators too is being challenged as we see from the Brooklyn Museum protests when they hired a white female scholar to curate the African collections begging the question—was there not one African American worthy of that post. Equally important, protestors wondered, is not the post in need of black perspectives?—a question that arises increasingly across the museum field. Contested space is the space occupied by texts on walls and labels of art works that most often anonymously describe works and their authors while circumscribing the limits of the story they tell. In this case, contested space is that which is excluded as we see with the actions of the MeToo movement who post alternative texts in museums about sexual abuse by artists, and who organize protests using social media and digital publications.

Contested space is the digital space of museums online, with authorized versions of texts coexisting with the unauthorized texts, juxtaposing a vanilla world, undisputed and uncontested, versus the real world of the open web, where ideas are debated and challenged. Bringing these two worlds together presents new challenges to museums, as they bridge digital space and the physical space inside their walls and seek to reconcile internal and external voices into a cohesive state of being in contemporary digital culture of the fast-evolving postdigital world.

References

Adams GK (2018) Macron report advocates permanent return of colonial-era African objects. Museum Association, News, 11 Nov 2018. https://www.museumsassociation.org/museums-journal/news/28112018-macron-report-repatriation. Accessed 29 Jan 2019

Beck J (2018) When pop culture sells dangerous myths about romance. The Atlantic, 17 Jan 2018, https://www.theatlantic.com/entertainment/archive/2018/01/when-pop-culture-sells-dangerous-myths-about-romance/549749/. Accessed 3 Jan 2019

British Museum (2017a) About the collection database online. The British Museum, UK, https://www.britishmuseum.org/research/collection_online/about_the_database.aspx. Accessed 3 Jan 2019

British Museum (2017b) Hoa Hakananai'a ('lost or stolen friend')/Moai (ancestor figure). Collection online, The British Museum, https://www.britishmuseum.org/research/collection_online/collection_object_details.aspx?assetId=12842001&objectId=512302&partId=1. Accessed 3 Jan 2019

Bowley G (2017) In an era of strife, museums collect history as it happens. The New York Times, 1 Oct 2017, https://www.nytimes.com/2017/10/01/arts/design/african-american-museum-collects-charlottesville-artifacts.html. Accessed 29 Jan 2019

Brown K (2018) In a groundbreaking report, experts advise French president Macron to begin the 'restitution' of looted African Art. Artnet News, 20 Nov 2018, https://news.artnet.com/art-world/french-restitution-policy-macron-1399429. Accessed 3 Jan 2019

Christie's (2015) Modigliani's Nu couché (reclining nude) leads a night of records in New York. Christie's Daily, 10 Nov 2015, http://www.christies.com/features/Modigliani-Nu-couche-Reclining-Nude-leads-a-night-of-records-in-New-York-6782-3.aspx. Accessed 3 Jan 2019

Cascone S (2018a) Artist Emma Sulkowicz Wore Asterisks—and little else—to protest chuck close at the met (and Picasso at MoMA). Artnet News, 2 Feb 2018, https://news.artnet.com/art-world/emma-sulkowicz-performance-protest-1214429. Accessed 3 Jan 2019

Cascone S (2018b) Following ACT UP Protest, the Whitney draws attention to the ongoing AIDS Epidemic with a New David Wojnarowicz Wall Text. Artnet News, 6 Aug 2018, https://news.artnet.com/art-world/david-wojnarowicz-wall-text-whitney-act-up-aids-1329068. Accessed 3 Jan 2019

Cascone S (2018c) ‘Museums almost infantilize viewers’: a guerrilla artist puts up her own wall labels at the met to expose male artists’ bad. Artnet News, 7 Nov 2018, https://news.artnet.com/art-world/michelle-hartney-met-protest-picasso-gauguin-wall-labels-1387801. Accessed 3 Jan 2019

Cascone S (2018d) ‘It still belongs to Africa’: Trevor Noah of ‘the daily show’ says colonial-era art should be returned—with interest. Artnet News, 18 Dec 2018, https://news.artnet.com/art-world/daily-show-restitution-african-art-1423081. Accessed 3 Jan 2019

Cascone S (2018e) The ivory coast drafts a long list of the colonial-era works it wants back from France as support for repatriation grows, the ivory coast is asking France to return 148 works. Artnet News, 20 Dec 2018, https://news.artnet.com/art-world/ivory-coast-148-works-from-france-1426252. Accessed 3 Jan 2019

CBS News (2018) ‘It's ridiculous. It's Picasso’: Facebook reviewing anti-nudity policy after blocking Montreal museum ad. CBC News, Canada, 2 Aug 2018, https://www.cbc.ca/news/canada/montreal/mmfa-nudity-facebook-picasso-1.4771464. Accessed 3 Jan 2019

Childs K (2018) With a Manchester gallery removing an ‘objectifying’ painting, why are we in such a hurry to erase the past? The Independent UK, 3 Feb 2018, https://www.independent.co.uk/voices/manchester-gallery-john-william-waterhouse-hylas-metoo-removal-art-objectification-a8192666.html. Accessed 3 Jan 2019

Frank P (2017) Artist stages protest at Met Breuer, where her alleged abuser's work is on View. Huffington Post, UK, 4 Dec 2017, https://www.huffingtonpost.com/entry/raghubir-singh-protest-me-too_us_5a21dce3e4b03350e0b6d61f. Accessed 3 Jan 2019

Garber M (2016) How Rom-Coms undermine women. The Atlantic, 1 Nov 2016. https://www.theatlantic.com/entertainment/archive/2016/11/its-rom-coms-fault-too/505928/. Accessed 3 Jan 2019

Gonzalez R (2017) Keep the conversation going: how museums use social media to engage the public. The Museum Scholar, 1(1), 2017. http://articles.themuseumscholar.org/vol1no1gonzalez. Accessed 3 Jan 2019

Hunt T, Dorgerloh H, Thomas N (2018) Restitution report: museum directors respond. The Art Newspaper, 27 Nov 2018, https://www.theartnewspaper.com/comment/restitution-report-museums-directors-respond. Accessed 3 Jan 2019

Johnson C (2018) Museums and rise of rapid response collecting. Radio New Zealand (RNZ), https://www.radionz.co.nz/national/programmes/ninetonoon/audio/2018652117/museums-and-rise-of-rapid-response-collecting. Accessed 3 Jan 2019

Keeling N (2018) Naked water nymphs painting back on show at Manchester Art Gallery after backlash from the public. Manchester Evening News, 3 Feb 2018, https://www.manchestereveningnews.co.uk/news/naked-water-nymphs-painting-back-14241791. Accessed 3 Jan 2019

Kinsella E (2017) The Met Says ‘suggestive’ Balthus painting will stay after petition for its removal is signed by thousands. Artnet News, 5 Dec 2017, https://news.artnet.com/art-world/met-museum-responds-to-petition-calling-for-removal-of-balthus-painting-1169105. Accessed 3 Jan 2019

Lopez R (2018) Proposal for a Judy Chicago museum divides a New Mexico town. The Art Newspaper, 28 Nov 2018, https://www.theartnewspaper.com/news/proposal-for-a-judy-chicago-museum-divides-a-new-mexico-town. Accessed 3 Jan 2019

McGrath K (2017) Why new yorkers are petitioning - The met over adolescent sexual exploitation, outrage over a 1938 painting has sparked a petition that has garnered thousands of signatures. Architectural Digest, 5 Dec 2017, https://www.architecturaldigest.com/story/balthus-therese-dreaming-met-museum-adolescent-sexual-exploitation

Marshall A (2018) Posters, banners, boarding passes: museums try to get a head start on history. The New York Times, 18 June 2018, https://www.nytimes.com/2018/06/18/arts/design/rapid-response-collecting-ireland-berlin.html. Accessed 3 Jan 2019

Moynihan C (2018) Church leaders sue Princeton over ‘Stolen’ manuscripts. The New York Times, 14 Dec 2018, https://www.nytimes.com/2018/12/14/arts/design/princeton-eastern-orthodox-church.html. Accessed 4 Jan 2019

Rea N (2018a) France's president has promised to return Africa's Heritage—now Macron's Pledge is being put to the test. Artnet News, 8 Mar 2018, https://news.artnet.com/art-world/macron-repatriate-african-heritage-1238219. Accessed 4 Jan 2019

Rea N (2018b) Delegates from Easter Island meet with the top brass at the British Museum to demand the return of a monumental head sculpture. Artnet News, 20 Nov 2018, https://news.artnet.com/art-world/easter-island-british-museum-1399990. Accessed 4 Jan 2019

Rea N (2018c) A French museum director pushes back against a radical report calling on macron to return looted African art. Artnet News, 28 Nov 2018, https://news.artnet.com/art-world/quai-branly-president-macron-africa-restitution-report-1404364. Accessed 4 Jan 2019

Republic (2018) New Mexico mayor to donate $10 K for eyed Judy Chicago museum. The Republic, 10 Dec 2018, http://www.therepublic.com/2018/12/10/nm-feminist-artist-museum-flap/. Accessed 4 Jan 2019

Saltz J (2017) 11,000 people have demanded the met remove this painting. They Aren't going to. Nor should they. Vulture, 15 Dec 2017, https://www.vulture.com/2017/12/11-000-demanded-the-met-remove-this-painting-they-wont.html. Accessed 4 Jan 2019

Sarr F, Savoy B (2018) The restitution of African cultural Heritage—toward a new relational ethics, Nov 2018, http://restitutionreport2018.com. Accessed 4 Jan 2019

Sayej N (2018) 'The art world tolerates abuse'—the fight to change museum wall labels. The Guardian, 28 Nov 2018, https://www.theguardian.com/artanddesign/2018/nov/28/the-art-world-tolerates-abuse-the-fight-to-change-museum-wall-labels. Accessed 4 Jan 2019

Small Z (2018a) President of France will recommend full restitution of looted African works. Hyperallergic, 20 Nov 2018, https://hyperallergic.com/472215/president-of-france-will-recommend-full-restitution-of-looted-african-works/. Accessed 4 Jan 2019

Small Z (2018b) French president wants to return Benin's artifacts, but will French law allow him? Hyperallergic, 28 Nov 2018, https://hyperallergic.com/473075/french-president-wants-to-return-benins-artifacts-but-will-french-law-allow-him/. Accessed 4 Jan 2019

Tate (2018) Modigliani exhibition, Tate Modern, 23 Nov 2017 – 2 April 2018. Tate website https://www.tate.org.uk/whats-on/tate-modern/exhibition/modigliani

Telegraph (2018) Manchester art gallery's #MeToo-inspired removal of nude Nymphs painting branded a 'pathetic stunt'. The Telegraph, UK, 1 Feb 2018, https://www.telegraph.co.uk/art/what-to-see/manchester-art-gallerys-metoo-inspired-removal-nude-nymphs-painting/. Accessed 4 Jan 2019

Toodehfallen A (2018) A French report on repatriating African cultural Heritage stirs the pot. Hyperallergic, 7 Dec 2018, https://hyperallergic.com/474573/a-french-report-on-repatriating-african-cultural-heritage-stirs-the-pot/. Accessed 4 Jan 2019

V&A (2014) Rapid response collecting—Room 74a. Victoria and Albert Museum, UK. https://www.vam.ac.uk/collections/rapid-response-collecting. Accessed 4 Jan 2019

Wullschlager J (2017) The shock factor: Modigliani at Tate Modern. Financial Times, 24 Nov 2017, https://www.ft.com/content/02b1de80-cf7a-11e7-b781-794ce08b24dc. Accessed 4 Jan 2019

Part III
Exhibitions

Chapter 6
Past the Museum Floor: Criteria for Curating Experience

Deborah Turnbull Tillman

Abstract This chapter examines exhibition design methodologies explored by the research platform, New Media Curation. From University Labs, to Museum floors to Festivals, the chapter outlines how adopting disruptive methodology resituates the curator as a specialist carer of objects to a collaborative producer of experience mediated by technology. It considers experiential learning and the affect it has on practitioners. It traces the legacy of Beta_space and its impact on practice-based research and reflective practice in contemporary curatorship. It extends these modalities of practice past the educational platforms of the University Lab and the Museum and into the public and experimental platform of the Festival. Three case studies will be examined: (1) *Denouément*, as part of VIVIDMusic 2015; (2) *ISEA2015: disruption*, and (3) *Re/Pair*, as part of the Big Anxiety Festival based at UNSW Art & Design. The aim of these case studies is to examine and expose criteria for curating interactive art, gleaned through in situ audience evaluation, with data collection in the form of surveys and specialist interviews.

6.1 Introduction

This study is about curating interactive art in new ways by examining the tension between my creative and professional practice as recorded and analyzed in the research platform New Media Curation (Turnbull Tillman 2008). I will cite several frameworks to support analysis of the practical and theoretical aspects of my curatorial methods—namely practice-based and practice-led research utilizing public in situ Living Laboratories, disruptive design, and collaborative partnerships. As the study progressed, I came to utilize festivals as the main public space and took up a Bricolage Research approach as Case Study projects evolved from one to the next. The action research involved takes the interdisciplinary design of interactive art systems out of labs and studios and into public spaces in the form of prototype exhibitions with emerging, mid-career and established practitioners in three Case

D. T. Tillman (✉)
University of New South Wales & New Media Curation, Sydney, Australia
e-mail: deborah@newmediacuration.com

T. Giannini and J. P. Bowen (eds.), *Museums and Digital Culture*,
Springer Series on Cultural Computing, https://doi.org/10.1007/978-3-319-97457-6_6

Studies: (1) *Denouément*; (2) *ISEA2015: disruption*; and (3) *Re/Pair*. The artworks and exhibitions in which they sit become part of a designed set of methodologies offered for evaluation through the medium of audience engagement.

6.2 The Curatorial Research

This research is artist-led and responds to a call for change in current curatorial processes involving new media and interactive art (Graham and Cook 2010). The application of design thinking methodologies, such as prototyping, iterative making and audience evaluation, shares much with HCI methodologies (Hutchinson et al. 2003). In creating interventions disruptive to ordered processes, these approaches first focus on gauging the audience's ability to identify and enjoy interactive art (a humanities definition of authenticity) (Dutton 2003; Turkle 2007; Greer 2013) before extending past a surface engagement to better understand how one might then describe those experiences in discursive language resulting in criteria gleaned through experiential learning (Lachapelle 1997; Edmonds 2010). As such, the study focuses on disrupting the usual flow of exhibition experience for an audience, and then explores a humanities definition of authenticity. In terms of stepping through the process, I will first define parameters for authenticity within fine arts and responsive systems before examining—through the application of evaluative frameworks to iterative exhibition processes—how one might capture and utilize criteria for curating interactive art as informed by artists, creative practitioners and, finally, curators.

From 2004 to 2008, Dr. Lizzie Muller researched integrating "the exhibition" into the design/making aspect of the artists by developing Beta_space, a public lab for prototyping interactive artworks in league with the Creativity and Cognition Studios and the Powerhouse Museum. This research culminated in her 2008 Ph.D. thesis, *The Experience of Interactive Art: a curatorial study*. I inherited Beta_space from Muller, and from her learned to integrate the audience and their experience and engagement with the work as materials for consideration in art making and exhibiting. Muller has continued to engage the audience as a kind of design material for her interactive exhibitions, her teaching, her research and her publications. She has an iterative and collaborative approach to exhibition design that starts with the artists, involves an experiential workshop, an exhibition, and an audience evaluation (see http://www.lizziemuller.com). In the conclusion of her doctoral thesis, she cites the public realm as an ideal testing space for Living Laboratories evaluating the process of curating interactive art (Muller 2008). It is this idea that I respond to in bringing the Living Laboratories ethos outside gallery spaces and into festivals, to test whether the audiences have authentic experiences of the scenarios presented featuring prototype artworks (Fig. 6.1).

Fig. 6.1 Beta_space in the Cyberworlds Exhibition, Powerhouse Museum, Sydney, 2007. (Image courtesy of Julien Phalip)

I also became interested in the way that experiential learning can factor into transformative behaviors. In 2010, Dr. Sarah Cook and Dr. Beryl Graham published the book *Rethinking Curating: Art after New Media*. They speak to a terminology of behaviors when discussing new media art, in regard to the artwork and the people that engage it. They are interested in "the processes and methods of curating … that might be useful to other curators". Collaboration and sharing knowledge then become modalities of curating. Interestingly, they introduce the way they speak about new media art as one of "common-language terminologies" as a way of "avoiding a static model" for curating. They also review different "types" of curators and models for curating, namely Embedded, Adjunct and Independent curators and Iterative, Modular and Distributed exhibitions. These approaches will be considered in the collation of data and analysis of discursive language when formulating my own criteria (Fig. 6.2).

Beryl Graham is also the founder of CRUMB (the Curatorial Resource for Upstart Media Bliss) which is an online repository for new media curating tools, videos, links, interviews and avenues for exploration that fall outside the normative linear curatorial task (see http://www.crumbweb.org). Here I answer the call to be an "upstart" and experiment with new ways to exhibit new media art.

Fig. 6.2 Sarah Cook speaking about Distributed Art with an image of Beryl Graham (2010) at the first Theory Talk at The Temporary Stedelijk in Amsterdam in 2013. Graham is engaging with artist TaeYoon Choi's robotic duck, Camerautomata Charlie. (Projected image courtesy of Sarah Cook; image courtesy of Ernst van Deursen)

6.3 The Research Question and Significant Contributions

Through an examination of design thinking and HCI methods as applied to interactive art making, artists, curators and audience members will be led through critical and creative spaces by speculative design, engagement and evaluation, and analysis of data collected. These spaces become public Living Laboratories existing outside the traditional walls of galleries or museums and become in situ studies of art/science behavior on the part of audiences, creative practitioners and curators.

The main research question is:

> How can contemporary curators apply design thinking techniques to exhibitions comprised of digital interactive art at various stages of art practice to reveal new criteria for curating digital interactive art?

The statement of contribution and significance is:

> This research demonstrates how, via Disruptive Design Methods and the provision of authentic experiences for audiences through the Living Laboratories model, a space is created for curators to work reflectively with creative practitioners and audiences to collaborate on public prototype exhibitions. From the dialogue around these creative collaborations, critical language in the form of criteria have emerged and been recorded, along with a new model of curating. Combined, the two contributions provide the next generation of new media curators with a novel approach to experiment with.

In working through a reflection-in-action practice-based research methodology, this study will reflect on the way my appreciative system has developed over a 10-year period of curating both under the NMC banner (as an independent curator) and at the Powerhouse Museum (as both an embedded and adjunct curator). The methodologies for presentation are well suited to the research Environment of the Creative Robotics Lab at UNSW Art & Design (Velonaki 2011), where my studies are based on responsive systems and human interaction rather than traditional engineering or robotics.

6.4 The Problem with Traditional Versus Experience Curating

Central to this enquiry are the problems associated with digital interactive art, including its immateriality and repositioning of time and space, which thus make the act of evaluating one's interaction with it problematic. As discussed in Graham and Cook (2010), these problems place a particular responsibility on the curator to revise traditional practice.

6.4.1 Traditional Curatorial Practice

Traditional curatorial practice usually involves the care of a collection of objects, the cultural significance of which has been determined by a museum expert or fine arts connoisseur. I performed the role of Assistant Curator in Design and Technology embedded within the Powerhouse Museum (PHM) between 2012 and 2014. Here, I assisted in collecting and caring for objects, which were then closely monitored with a concern for preservation, conservation, and the registration of their movements—practices aimed at keeping their significance relevant in historical and social contexts (Russell and Winkworth 2009). Technology has played a role in making these tasks easier, from heaters to air conditioners and dehumidifiers to the maintenance of complex databases to monitor exhibition cycles and movement of objects (Fig. 6.3).

While working here, I noticed how the traditional approach to caring for static physical objects has proven difficult for new media artworks. The lifecycles are different, existing more so in the elegant code shown through projectors or on huge data screens, or in the specifically timed animation of engineering or robotics. In fact, I was not permitted to collect digital art or design objects when on staff simply because we could not permanently care for digital artefacts due to the obsolescence of technology and the aim of the museum to collect objects forever. Matthew Connell (a mentor and then my direct supervisor at the PHM) comments that "the stuff of computers programs, data, [and] operating systems … are perhaps only really

Fig. 6.3 Deborah Turnbull Tillman performing a curatorial interview during DesignTech 2014. (Image c/o Deborah Turnbull Tillman and taken by Kathleen Phillips 24 January 2014)

meaningful when being used by a person" (Turnbull and Connell 2011). As such, the code and software—realized as images, sound, or vibrations—that drives interactive artwork only comes to life when the audience engages with them. As stated above, the works themselves move; they are not static, and as such are constantly changing. New media curators then necessarily concern themselves with how the work is experienced in the moment, the same way a traditional curator might worry about the paint fading on a Ming vase if it's on exhibition too long, or about someone bumping it and damaging it; there are slightly different concerns for each medium. The discursive language in experiencing a curated engagement with an interactive artwork would then also be different, as would the language used when organizing or structuring that engagement and the ensuing actions one might take.

6.4.2 Extending Independent Curating

In 2014, I concluded my role as a traditional curator within an institution and became interested in how I might extend NMC as a research platform. How could I take what I had learned in curating objects and experience and use this to contribute to and grow the field of curating new media and interactive art? The ability to do this formally was made available to me through the Creative Robotics Lab and UNSW's Art & Design Campus. Initially led by artists Mari Velonaki and Petra Gemeinboeck, this is a lab that investigates the effects of computational systems—namely cultural robotics and

Fig. 6.4 The studio space at the Creative Robotics Lab, UNSW Art & Design. The image features Director Mari Velonaki (right) speaking about her kinetic sculpture *Diamandini* (2011–13) and *Fish_Bird* (2004) to lab visitors. (Image c/o Deborah Turnbull Tillman)

engineering—on humans through an artistic context, so that aesthetics and artistic concerns lead the inquiry. This interdisciplinary approach appealed to me, as did the potential to identify an NMC Methodology through reflecting on past case studies. As such, a mixed practice-based and practice-led research approach to curating emerged, as did the opportunity to test it in an experimental arts environment (Fig. 6.4).

These research questions were first addressed by the staging of *Denouément*, an in situ intervention into a larger exhibition called *Musify+Gamify* (Bown and Loke 2015) for the VIVID Music Festival in June 2015. In utilizing prototype works of emerging practitioners, I created a temporary exhibition for audiences to experience before entering the formal exhibition space. This disruption created the opportunity for them to pause and reflect on the works at hand, then express feedback on their experience via on-the-spot surveys. This quantitative data was collected and collated to determine whether they could recognize the experience as interactive and if they enjoyed it enough to participate again (Turnbull Tillman et al. 2017). This qualitative data was then utilized to design a more focused approach: the resulting research questions have been tested in the exhibition *Re/Pair*, which sets up a similar scenario as an intervention into *The Big Anxiety Festival*, this time with more established artists in a more finished space with more sophisticated prototypes (https://www.thebiganxiety.org/events/repair/). This opportunity provides audiences with more time to think through their experiences via semi-structured interviews in a festival which examines mental health, namely anxiety due to existing social phenomena being addressed in the arts. In between the two case studies, I performed a reflective practice Case Study as exhibition production manager for *ISEA2015*: *disruption* (Turnbull Tillman and Velonaki 2016). In this role, I was also able to utilize the knowledge from *Denouément* to execute a larger scale exhibition of in situ prototype works for another major festival, this time the International Symposium on Electronic Art (ISEA). This process honed my appreciative system, again preparing me for *Re/Pair*. The iterative nature of this experiential curatorial learning yields criterion for curating this new medium, one filled with discursive language and working methodologies that is/are flexible and adaptable for audiences, creative practitioners and curators.

6.5 The Contexts for Experiential Learning

Experiential Learning is a key consideration for the methodologies being tested. Richard Lachapelle's work on experiential learning and Discipline-based Art Education articulates the importance of marrying the experience of art making with the theory of how it is made. The two characteristics of experiential learning are: "(1) the emphasis that is placed on a direct contact between learner and the subject of the study and (2) the learner's involvement in actively investigating that subject" (Lachapelle 1997). In relation to Lizzie Muller's work on exhibiting using interaction design considerations, setting experiential goals with the artists interested in exhibiting was the first step to her iterative process. As a practice-based researcher, the curator becomes the learner in Lachapelle's scenario, with the artists and their making activities the subject of the study. The application of the learner (the curator) then actively investigating that subject (the artists and their making) requires direct contact.

Along with the Creative Robotics Lab, relevant foundational work in this field includes that of Ernest Edmonds and Linda Candy's research group, the Creativity and Cognition Studios (CCS, http://www.creativityandcognition.com). Prior to starting NMC and working in traditional curating at the Powerhouse Museum, I was a research assistant to Edmonds, and central to my own research is the initial work done in Beta_space—a publicly housed laboratory at the Powerhouse Museum, Sydney. Here CCS set up an infrastructure and a methodology for measuring experience and emotion in digital interactive art between 2006 and 2013. Their influence and the writings about this work form an important basis for the Ph.D. research. Reports on the curatorial practice of Lizzie Muller, Matthew Connell and myself all detail the making and evaluating of interactive art at various iterative phases in a public laboratory. Lizzie Muller's Ph.D. and related writings report the core research that forms the background to this study (Muller 2008). The significance of the Creativity and Cognition Studios' work was innovation in:

1. bringing the work out of a university lab and into a public institution before it was finished (Edmonds et al. 2006);
2. establishing a set of criteria for measuring audience experience (Bilda et al. 2007; Costello 2007);
3. offering this process to the public as an exhibition on display for public consumption (Turnbull and Connell 2011);
4. taking these processes out of the realm of culture and into the community as creative practice for corporations and institutions as well as artists and curators (Edmonds et al. 2009; Turnbull and Connell 2014);
5. producing three models for curating digital interactive art, two of which hold preliminary criteria for exhibiting digital and interactive art that artists and creative practitioners needed to meet in order to be considered for commission (Turnbull and Connell 2014).

These are different then the criteria I have established in this Ph.D. study for audiences, creative practitioners and curators to better execute exhibitions.

These activities were first captured en masse in the book *Interacting: art, research and the creative practitioner* (Candy and Edmonds 2011) and later in the book *Interactive Experience in the Digital Age* (Candy and Ferguson 2014). The former publication reviews the methodologies followed during the seven years Beta_space was actively programmed in the Powerhouse Museum, but provides a history of digital interactive art in which Candy and Edmonds outline the current categories, aesthetics, influences, paradigms, creative spaces, and cultural shifts in relation to the artist and audience—the producers and consumers of art. The latter looks at the effects of technology based interactive art has on the audience, changing them from a viewer or attendee to a participant and thereby changing the nature of creative engagement from passive to active. The key component across ever-expanding platforms for public arts engagement is the feedback from audience evaluation (Candy and Ferguson 2014). This is a key contributor to my Ph.D. research in that, through utilizing a Living Labs model in the public sphere, I was able to begin to design a test for my working methodology with a mediating factor of foundational knowledge.

In the midst of changing jobs from a museum professional to an academic, and in starting to reflect on NMC more closely, I noticed a tension in my practice. It is worth mentioning at this stage that there is a clear distinction between professional and creative work for most practice-based researchers. It seems so especially for curators, who are often administrators as well as specialists, authors, editors, archival resources and event planners. In situating myself within Donald Schön's reflection-in-action method as a function of practice-based research after Schön and Muller (Muller 2011), I was actively engaged in a tension between creating and producing, where one practice starts, and the other intervenes, or even encroaches to create disharmony. Similar to the metaphor of technology as a living organism as posited by Gassmann (2006), John Dewey tracks the experience of the "live creature" as follows:

> Life overcomes and transforms factors of opposition to achieve higher significance. Harmony and equilibrium are the results not of mechanical processes but of rhythmic resolution of tension. The rhythmic alternation within the live creature between disunity and unity becomes conscious in humans. Emotion signifies breaks in experience which are then resolved through reflective action. Objects become interesting as conditions for realising harmony. Thought is then incorporated into them as their meaning. (Leddy 2013)

Where the tension and resolution of creation versus/production could likely be articulated by any contemporary curator, in the NMC Case Studies for analysis I am examining exhibitions that I both conceived and supported others in realizing. As a curator, representing institutions and funding bodies, while also working quite closely with artists and technologists, disruptions come in different forms associated with observing, recording and analyzing the intentions, actions, and reactions of artists, technologists and audience members. This part of the study proposes to reflect on a series of NMC exhibitions, treating them as curatorial prototypes for analysis in order to form the foundation of a larger iterative cycle involving practice-based research and curatorship. This cycle will be analyzed by way of audience evaluation with consideration to disruptive design methods and authentic experiences within public Living Labs. The methodology then explores the research question: once intentionally distracted from their intended visitation by a situated activity, will the audience member take time to reflect on the prototype work(s), recognize them as art, and then enjoy them enough to return to them repeatedly? How can we encourage this through best practice models or standards? In pondering a solution to what context might be ideal for pursuing this line of enquiry; I began thinking about the festival in general as a place for experimental practice.

6.6 The Methods for Establishing a Practice-Based and Led Research Curatorial Platform

Where I have always considered myself a practice-based researcher within the field of interactive art, Candy and Edmonds (2018) recently published on the differences between practice-based and practice-led research and how misunderstandings are diminishing the quality of Ph.D. research. Their article has made me re-think my approaches and outcomes and I now find my research approach to be practice-based, with the outcomes being practice-led. As such I identify somewhere in between the two definitions.

In taking an approach to curating experiences rather than objects, there are a few historical examples of the development processes that support and analyse audience engagement through experiential or in situ learning. Stringer's approach of LOOK → THINK → ACT is based in social reform and draws on Lewin's "spiral of steps" that attempt to depict "comparative research on the conditions and effects of various forms of social action, and research leading to social action" (Smith 2007). Johnson, a social scientist from the 1970s, has revised Lewin's spiral utilizing words such as UNFREEZING → CHANGING → REFREEZING. A more contemporary, and specifically curatorial, take on these approaches is outlined in Lizzie Muller's close reading and application of Donald Schön's reflection-in-action. Muller (2008) quotes Schön's endorsement of "on the spot experiments" as a way of framing the lived experience of interactivity. In learning to curate under Muller at the Beta_space public laboratory, I am a product of her own experiential approach to curating interactive art via her documented process of experimenting → prototyping → reflecting → iterating → publishing. This cycle results in three layers of accountability on the curator, that of "the real situation in which [she] conducts [her] experiments, … [her] own underlying appreciative system, … and the actual experience of the audience". These are the approaches I aim to harness, expand on, and then extend past the gallery and into public spaces.

Overall, I appropriate a Bricolage Research approach to the methodologies I select based on the project itself. Each Case Study stands on its own, testing the NMC Methodology with a framework supporting the data collection and analysis. Bricolage is an artistic term that denotes making use of leftover materials to create new and unexpected artwork. Bricoleurs use only the tools and materials available or on-hand to them. Bricolage Research exists as a metaphor "within the domain of qualitative research" with its methodologies based on "eclecticism, emergent design, flexibility, and plurality". It can apply to examining competing (or supporting) 'phenomena' or 'sites,' theories and even methodological perspectives (Rogers 2012). This approach is extremely useful to the nature of my independent practice, the distributed and unique festival sites where I perform my Case Studies, and the way in which data is collected and analyzed for the study. It is important to the methodologies I work through that I am using a hybrid bricoleur approach amidst five types. They are defined in Table 6.1 in a post-structuralist way. As with finding Edmonds and Candy, Muller and Connell, and Graham and Cook influential in establishing, moving through and then situating myself in my practice, I find the definitions that Rogers explores below as apt descriptors for the methodologies I was moving through, but had not yet found language for. Where the NMC Methodology as enacted through the three Case Studies most closely follows the interpretive and methodological bricoleur approaches, there are necessarily elements of the theoretical and narrative bricoleur in presenting practice-based and—practice-led research.

6.6.1 Living Laboratories: Experimenting with Disruption and Authenticity in Denouément

For *Denouément*, I took a quantitative approach to data collection and analysis, presenting and publishing the results at a Human-Computer Interaction conference (see Fig. 6.5). This data specifically gauged the audience's experience of the prototype interactive artworks by emerging practitioners in a disruptive setting, querying whether they had an authentic experience or not. This suited the exploratory and experimental nature of a preliminary case study, the resulting data of which formed

Table 6.1 Norman Denzin and Yvonna Lincoln's categories of bricoleur practice (Rogers 2012)

Type of bricoleur	Definition and characteristics
The interpretive bricoleur	This practitioner understands that research is an interactive process that is social and inclusive of their own demographic. They do not just examine any one thing (object or idea) but they do so in relation to their own relationship to the research process. They are usually qualitative and reflexive researchers and allow other media or specialities to be explored in line with their research
The methodological bricoleur	This researcher combines multiple tools to accomplish a meaning-making task. They are generally fluid, eclectic and creative in their approaches and respect the complexity of making meaning in allowing the context to dictate the approaches to data collection and analysis, rather than imposing one that may not work as well. They generally use the tools "at hand" to accomplish their work, and choices tend to take shape as other aspects of the process unravel. Decisions are not necessarily made in advance
The theoretical bricoleur	This type of researcher reads A LOT. They can apply many different theories to any given theoretical problem which provides different theoretical contexts in which an object or idea can be interpreted. This gives multiple perspectives and a plurality of influences for any given phenomenon
The political bricoleur	These researchers are clear on how knowledge and power are connected, and often use this to fight hegemony, social injustice and disenfranchisement that is rampant within white patriarchal society
The narrative bricoleur	This practitioner understands the context in which things are perceived, understood and recorded. They do not take the ideologies and discourses in which narratives emerge for granted, rather they reject any single voice narrative in favour of multiple perspectives, voices and sources

the criteria for audiences engaging authentically with interactive art. Living laboratories have a history quite devoid of artistic experimentation, concerned as they are with technical innovation based on user feedback. Where there are now many different definitions of what a Living Lab is, it is most important to my research in that the outcomes of these Living Lab experiments are linked to experiential learning. It is generally agreed that there are four key components to a Living Lab: (1) co-creation; (2) exploration; (3) experimentation; and (4) evaluation (Pallot et al. 2010).

In the creation of Beta_space as a Living Laboratory inside an institution, there was room left in Muller's relevant research to explore a Living Lab outside of the espoused spaces of galleries and museums. Festivals such as *La Nuit Blanche* (Paris, FR), *Ars Electronica* (Linz, AU), *ISEA* (Brighton, UK), *Experimenta* (Melbourne, AUS), *ANAT* (Adelaide, AUS) and other international platforms for art and technology research have a long-standing history of exhibiting interactive art, and even of supporting such exhibitions with research residencies. What they often miss, being

Fig. 6.5 A presentation slide depicting images of *Denouément*, *Musify+Gamify*, VIVIDMusic, 2015. (Individual images courtesy of Lucy Tillman)

festivals, is the carrying over of tacit or experiential knowledge to the next iterative cycle, thus not making full use of the audience as a tool for co-creation.

In Case Study #1—*Denouément*, I explore the four key components of the Living Lab expressed in Table 6.2. This exhibition marked the first and exploratory leg of my thesis study. In following my NMC Methodology, I worked closely with the curators to produce the exhibition component of *Musify+Gamify* for *VIVID Music* in June of 2015. As part of the exhibition and launch, I intervened as a planned disruption to the order of the project by inserting *Denouément* as my exhibition piece. In the lead up to this, I worked with students in their studios and along with their tutor, Tom Ellard, I provided them with a brief in line with the *Musify+Gamify* theme and visited the class on a few occasions to check the progress of those interested. Of the 30 or so students, two maintained an interest in exhibiting prototype works. As such, realizing I had material to work with, I liaised with the Seymour Theatre Centre staff to ensure ethical standards were maintained for their staff and audience during my study, and once we appropriated the screen adjacent to the square in front of the Theatre, I was ready to evaluate the works with the audience and for the emergent practitioners in interactive media art. (A UNSW HREA Panel B: Arts, Humanities & Law Ethics Application was applied for and modified twice over the three Case Studies—policy number is HC15109).

Table 6.2 Living Lab components as utilized in public space

Pallot (2010)	Turnbull Tillman et al. (2017)
1. Co-creation	1. Working with the students in SOMA3412 in Semester 1 of the 2015 school year to bring viable ideation to a set of working prototypes suitable for exhibition Co-creators: Tom Ellard, Laura Wenham, Seunghyun Kim
2. Exploration	2. Securing partners, exhibition space, and ethics approval to promote and support a study that disrupts the audience's experience of interactive art in a public space. Worked with curators Oliver Bown and Lian Loke and the Seymour Centre Theatre
3. Experimentation	3. Staging the exhibition on a reclaimed (hacked) screen prior to the proper exhibition site, thereby waylaying participants to the scheduled exhibition and performances
4. Evaluation	4. Utilizing questionnaires to perform evaluation on 95+ willing audience participants over 5 nights

In performing the exploratory study by following aspects of both practice-based and -led methodologies, I had a path to follow. This first event set up and tested partnerships within one of the parameters of my practice (working with emergent practitioners), involved the audience, set up my ethics, allowed me to produce to an international festival standard, and connected me to my next study. It was rich and fertile ground and allowed an effective platform for me to set up and begin my further research methodologies.

6.6.2 *Autoethnography and Reflective Practice—ISEA2015: Disruption*

For *ISEA2015: disruption*, I took an auto-ethnographical and reflective approach to data collection and analysis, publishing in this same Springer book series on Cultural Computing. This data revealed reflective practice models for moving through the production phases of a festival over distributed sites (Fig. 6.6). The criteria that emerge advises creative practitioners, both artists and technologists, on what they potentially need to provide for their collaborators—who are namely clients and audiences. There is a branch of auto-ethnographic research (the study of reflexively writing about oneself) that explores a divergence from traditionally discipline-based qualitative methods based on the research of others. Social scientist Carolyn Ellis (2004), credited with being the originator and a key developer of "autoethnography" (Wikipedia, n.d.) within her study of qualitative research, has noted several "traditional criteria" for "good autoethnography". Her approach is in keeping with the bricolage theme of my own methodology in that rather than applying a dictionary definition to her own experience, she instead collates the work of several other authors in her book *The Ethnographic I: A Methodological Novel about Autoethnography* (Ellis 2004).

Fig. 6.6 A presentation slide for *ISEA2015: disruption* showing the Curator-as-Producer activities I analyzed for the Reflective Practice Case Study. Images c/o Deborah Turnbull Tillman

Sufficing as a definition for this section, Ellis first borrows from Laurel Richardson who approaches any social experiment in terms of:

(a) **Substantive contribution**: Does the piece contribute to our understanding of social life?
(b) **Aesthetic merit**: Does this piece succeed aesthetically? Is the text artistically shaped, satisfyingly complex, and not boring?
(c) **Reflexivity**: How did the author come to write this text? How has the author's subjectivity been both a producer and a product of this text?
(d) **Impactfulness**: Does this affect me emotionally and/or intellectually? Does it generate new questions or move me to action? and
(e) **Expresses a reality**: Does this text embody a fleshed-out sense of lived experience? (Richardson 2000).

Eleven years later, Ellis, in collaboration with Adams et al. (2015), nutted out a four-stage process for the evaluation of auto-ethnographic work that encompasses "descriptive, prescriptive, practical and theoretical goals". Any good auto-ethnographical study should:

1. Make contributions to knowledge;
2. Value the personal and experiential;

3. Demonstrate the power, craft, and responsibilities of stories and storytelling;
4. Take a relationally responsible approach to research practice and representation.

Where there is space within practice-based research to encompass autoethnography, it differs slightly in that there is an emphasis on iterative process and evaluation of data within practice-based research. The iterative process allows for testing similar methods more than once, and the evaluation of data is usually more interpretive and analytical then merely tallied or opinion-based. In fact, autoethnography takes into account the metrics of many professions—namely those where first-person accounts are valued, like the humanities disciplines of performance studies, education, English literature, history and arts education (2018); human sciences like social work, sociology, psychology, and anthropology; and more human-centered studies like physiotherapy, communication studies, marketing, business and educational administration (Bochner 2014). As such, it needs to be flexible and adaptive in its approach to analysis.

In setting up Case Study #2—*ISEA 2015: disruption*, both reflexivity and autoethnography became useful in living, recording, recalling and re-iterating my experience for learning and publication. Echoing my first study in a Curator-as-Producer role for *Musify+Gamify*, I began working with the organizers of the symposium, which was to take place during the *New Forms Festival* and the Vancouver Art Gallery's *FUSE Festival*. I had also previously produced an *ISEA 2013: Resistance is futile* exhibition in my role as Assistant Curator at the Powerhouse Museum. Both these roles informed my decision-making in the lead up to the realization of this case study. Where one can read the full account of this reflective practice case study in my co-authored book chapter with Mari Velonaki entitled *Disruption and Reflection: A curatorial case study* (Turnbull Tillman and Velonaki 2016), one of the key takeaway ideas for me from this project was a curator-as-producer model adapted from Schön (1983), Killion and Todnem (1991), and Hampe (2013). Hampe utilized terminology and process from Schön (1983) and Killion and Todnem (1991) to create her own map for reflective practice, which I then used for curatorial production (see both models in Figs. 6.7 and 6.8). In an email exchange, Hampe explained how her process is more reflective practice then practice-based research:

> When I made my diagram I intended for it to start at the top (as in the written outline in my document below the diagram) so it goes Reflection-on (what you've done), to reflection–in (what you're doing), to reflection-for (what you'll do next time), which then cycles back to thinking about what was done. Whereby "reflection-for-action is the desired outcome of both previous types of reflection. We undertake reflection not so much to revisit the past or to become aware of the metacognitive process one is experiencing … but to guide future action … while examining our past actions and our present actions, we generate knowledge that will inform our future actions" (Killion and Todnem 1991, p. 15). So you need to have gone through the processes of after and during in order to move into before, otherwise I think you are merely planning not undertaking reflective practice. (Turnbull Tillman 2019)

Although Hampe and I differ slightly at the starting point of the cycle, reflecting on past experience to move through a process is something that we share. Once I had decided on the relevant terminology to describe the stages through which I would pass during the reflection cycle, I was able to break down the experience into linear

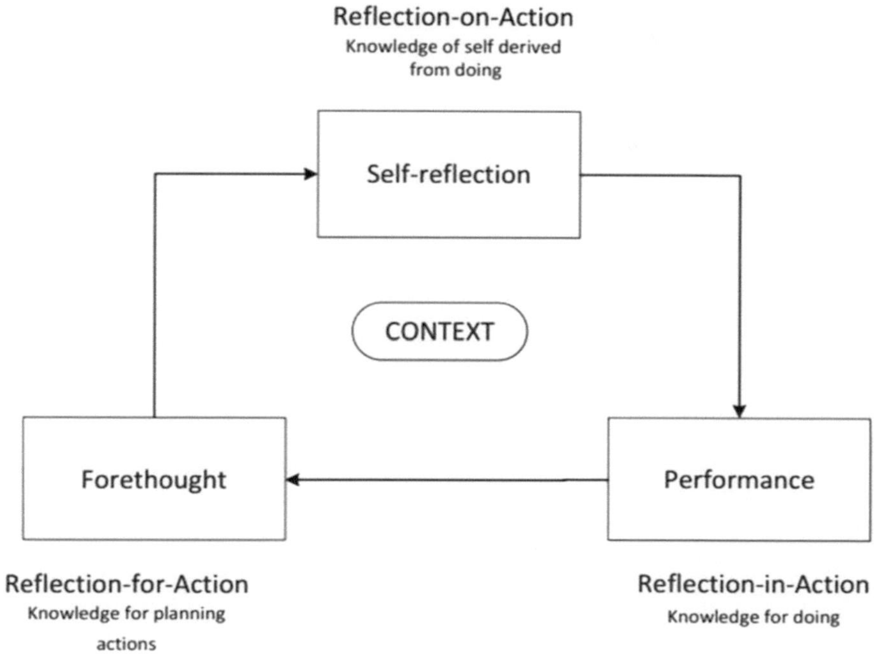

Fig. 6.7 Reflective cycle model (Hampe 2013)

timeframes (Pre, During and Post-Production), but as attached to an analytical type of reflection relating to experiential learning that reveals meaning in otherwise relatively mundane administrative tasks attached to exciting outcomes. This is because the situation in which I was Reflecting for, in and on Action was a series of high quality pop-ups over five nights at five different locations involving 85 interactive artists at varying stages of their academic and creative careers. As such, I was able to group my experiences into the chapter headings as in Table 6.3.

Another way of tracking this learned experience is presented in Table 6.4:

In the closing section of *Disruption and Reflection: A curatorial case study*, I speak to what I learned from performing the role of Curator-As-Producer for *ISEA2015: disruption*:

> In every way, treating this contract as a reflective practice case study allowed me to step back and observe, as well as perform within, the study. Surprisingly, this conscious disconnect minimized my stress levels, and eased my usual need to control the outcome of exhibitions I am involved with. This acceptance of my place as observer and social scientist allowed me room to really stop, think, and look at what was happening at any given time. In this way, I could quite quickly come to accept any situation as either solvable or irrelevant. (Turnbull Tillman and Velonaki 2016)

Table 6.3 Chapter headings and synopses for reflection processes (Turnbull Tillman and Velonaki 2016)

Chapter headings	Synopses
12.5.2 Pre-Production: Reflection-for-Action|Knowledge for planning actions (p. 190)	This section describes setting up the contract, setting the parameters for work, what the key production problems might be and countering with knowledge from previous experience
12.5.3 Production: Reflection-in-Action|Knowledge for Doing (p. 193)	This section describes the situated experience of producing away from your normal networks and in challenging and ever-changing environs. The key challenge here was managing up, down and across to maintain relationships through production being a large part of this in situ experience. Staff availability, artist expectation and budgetary and curatorial requirements from upper management were constant constraints
12.5.4 Post-Production: Reflection-on-Action|Knowledge of Self, Derived from Doing (p. 196)	This section highlights the tasks and challenges of closing a festival over multiple sites and platforms and returning both national and international artworks to participants

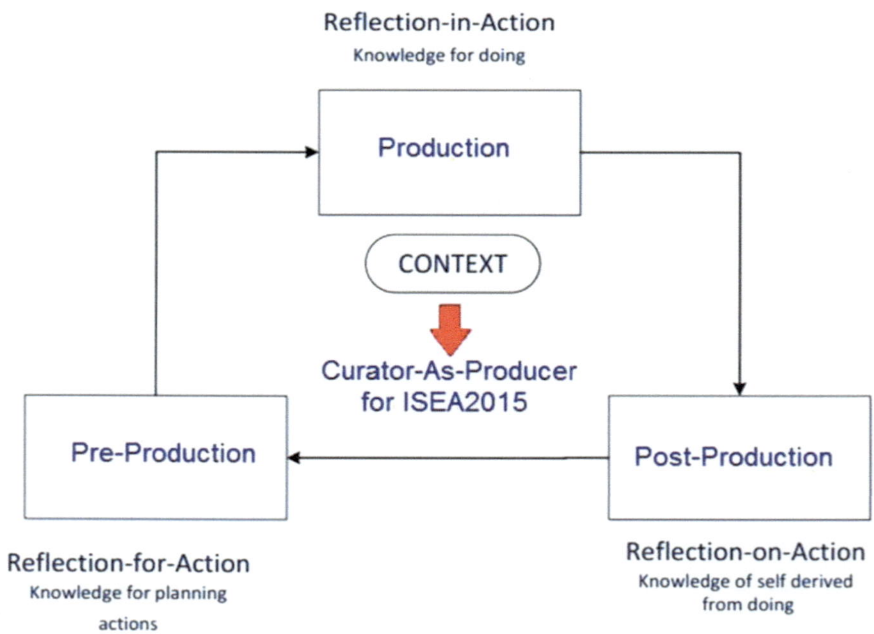

Fig. 6.8 My reflection cycle for curator-as-producer developed in 2016. Image reworked from Hampe (2013). c/o Deborah Turnbull Tillman

Table 6.4 Tracking my experiential curatorial learning from theory to practice

Schön (1983)	Killion and Todnem (1991)	Hampe (2013)	Turnbull Tillman and Velonaki (2016)
	Reflection-for-Action	Knowledge for Planning Actions	Pre-Production—Thoughtfully learning to collaborate and plan an exhibition; meeting people, gauging personalities, opening and securing lines of communication across all platforms
Reflection-in-Action		Knowledge for Doing	Production—Thoughtfully operating while inside the happening of the exhibition; failures, problem solving, and successes happen here
Reflection-on-Action		Knowledge of Self Derived from Doing	Post-Production—Thoughtfully reflecting on the final stages and wrap-up of the exhibition; articulating the lessons and communicating them to relevant parties

6.6.3 Discourse Analysis: The Big Anxiety Festival and Re/Pair

In the final Case Study, *Re/Pair*, I initiated an artist-led workshop on experiential learning in order to establish relevant content for analysis. Based on the results, I then designed a survey and semi-structured interview for data collection. I interviewed 11 curators as part of the *Re/Pair* exhibition and 3 international curators to enrich and add to the exhibition data, giving the work both a practice-based and -led angle. The data from this Case Study was analyzed pragmatically through a talking-in-interaction conversational analysis covering Action, Structure and Inter-Subjectivity. The criteria that emerged from this Case Study informs the preliminary best-practice standards for curating new media and interactive art from curators, for curators (Fig. 6.9).

The process began in my thinking about possible opportunities available for financial and venue collaboration. It began to make more and more sense to collaborate with my host institution, UNSW Art & Design. I researched and visited the galleries and spaces available to me as a student on campus, namely Kudos Gallery, UNSW Galleries and the Black Box Theatre. There are also public spaces, like the concrete stage in the campus courtyard, that are "bookable" by members of the student body. Once I had a solid plan in place, I approached my supervisor, Mari Velonaki, and pitched my idea to her. I proposed an exhibition featuring artists affiliated with the Creative Robotics Lab. She was very supportive of the idea, even agreeing to exhibit a prototype work of hers in the exhibition. Upon consultation, Velonaki's preference for venue was the UNSW Galleries, as it was the highest profile for everyone involved in the final Case Study and did not relegate it to being merely a 'student show'. I had worked with emergent practitioners, I had worked with mid-range practitioners, and now I was set to work with established practitioners.

Fig. 6.9 *Machine Movement Lab 1: Becoming Body* by Petra Gemeinboeck and Rob Saunders, *Re/Pair*, 2017. Image courtesy of Petra Gemeinboeck

In terms of a methodology, I wanted to apply elements of Discourse Analysis, particularly in light of Baxandall's take on signs, signifiers and what is signified in making, and the influence it had on the NMC Exhibition *Image Ecologies* (Baxandall 1985; Turnbull 2009). I also wanted an evaluation method that allowed for an exhibition on interactive art and the propositions made within that context (arguably a communication event), to be considered a type of text for analysis. In adapting Foucault's approach of a moving and changeable text based on a given situation (and enforced by patterns within connections of knowledge and power) (Foucault 2002), I wanted to be able to utilize the institution of the University in a festival setting; the early ideation of the prototype works of the established artists associated with the Creative Robotics Lab (CRL); and the language of an audience participating in the exhibition as a communication event. I want to capture this data pragmatically, through a conversation-in-interaction approach to observing and then interviewing participants. The three contexts in which I planned to capture and analyze data are:

1. **Action**—Organization of actions distinct from outside of a conversation. This could include openings and closings of conversations, assessments, storytelling, and complaints.
2. **Structure**—All human social action is structured and has rules, conversation is no different. In order to participate in a conversation, the participants must abide by these rules and structures to be an active participant.

3. **Intersubjectivity**—talk and interaction are examined as a site where intersubjective understanding concerning the participants' intentions, their state of knowledge, their relation, and their stance towards the talked-about objects is created, maintained, and negotiated (Peräkylä 2007).

I felt this method had a strong philosophical base but also allowed me to work within the spaces and with the artists I had available to me through creatively collaborating with my host institution. I was hoping to reveal characteristics in the artists and the way they worked that I, as a curator, could fit in with, to ease the transition from making to exhibiting.

From here I began to infiltrate my NMC Methodology with Discourse Analysis. I approached the artists associated with the lab, pitched my idea via a group email, collected responses and began to plan a project whereby an exhibition initially titled *Prototype to Process* was the platform for testing works made in collaboration with the CRL studio space. From there, we would secure a venue and exhibit the works in prototype phase for audience evaluation, preferably during a festival of sorts. Upon application to the UNSW Galleries and some local and international follow up with then Galleries Director Felicity Fenner, I was told it was a strong idea with good artists but that all the spots were already booked for 2017 due to *The Big Anxiety Festival* running from September to December (directed by Jill Bennett). It was then that a colleague from CRL suggested I book the Black Box, which I then did for the opening week of the festival. It was too late to apply to be in the festival or perform a Curator-as-Producer role as I had in my two previous case studies, but perhaps I could collaborate with the festival in some way or at least make use of the festival audiences during either the opening or closing week.

Where there is a lot of data regarding the processes I went through to secure and begin to work with the CRL artists, it is much more easily digested in Tables 6.5 and 6.6:

In thinking through my original request to each of the artists, there were variations to the methods I requested. Namely the methodology I was following was not going to be straightforward for each artist as most of them were collaborating with other

Table 6.5 Preliminary tasks, events and timelines for artists agreeing to be a part of *Prototype to Process* (which became *Re/Pair*)

Key communication events (attendance required)	Communication event requirements	Dates
Interviews	Minimum of six interviews requested	First half of 2017
Experiential Workshop	1 morning of artwork/exhibition planning	22 March 2017
Exhibition during the BAF	1 week of install, launch, evaluation, bump out	Initially 18–22 September 2017 Switched to 6–11 November 2017

Table 6.6 Tracking invitation replies to CRL affiliated artists for *Prototype to Process* (which became *Re/Pair*)

Date	Communication events	Artist(s)	Result
29 July 2016	Supervisor Meetings, Skype Interviews, Experiential Workshop	Mari Velonaki	Approved idea for Case Study #3 and agreement to participate as an artist, then met with me nine times and participated in the Experiential Workshop
14 October 2016	Group Email, Interviews, Experiential Workshop	Alex Davies	Replied "yes" and met me for two artist interviews and participated in the Experiential Workshop
14 October 2016	Group Email, Interviews, Experiential Workshop	Petra Gemeinboeck and Rob Saunders	Replied "yes" for herself and Rob Saunders, performed 1 artist interview and participated in the Experiential Workshop
14 October 2016	Group Email, Private Emails, Interviews	Wade Marynowsky	Replied "yes", met with me three times, offered me an evaluation slot on his tour of Robot Opera to Taiwan, later offered me a paid writing role to produce the catalogue essay for his launch of the work he would iterate for my Case Study #3
14 October 2016	Group Email, Interviews, Experiential Workshop and Grant Support	Rochelle Haley	Replied "yes" and made her notes with MIT collaborator Sang-won Leigh available to me as well as meeting with me eight times. She also supported a NAVA grant to travel with her to MIT, but it was not successful. She attended the Experiential Workshop and also performed the closing interview with me

(continued)

Table 6.6 (continued)

Date	Communication events	Artist(s)	Result
4 May 2017	Private emails, Interviews, Meetings	Tricia Flanagan	Replied "yes", met with me two times for curatorial and two times for evaluation, did not attend the Experiential Workshop as she was O/S
14 October 2016	Group Email (too busy)	Kate Dunn	No reply after initial chat regarding participation

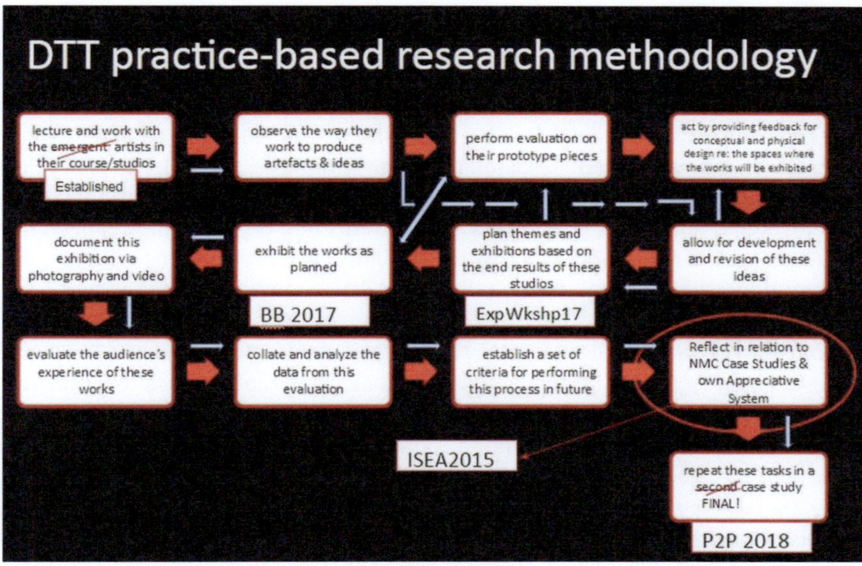

Fig. 6.10 Deborah Turnbull Tillman's Methodology, 2017—the blue arrows indicate iterative cycles during the planning sessions for the final case study exhibition of the Ph.D. and touring exhibition plans afterwards

parties and so required consultation with their partners. The key modifications to the methodology can be found in Fig. 6.10.

Much of the early work of New Media Curation was moving past the work performed at Beta_space and making new and novel work in exciting ways. This was mostly done by invitation from fellow researchers who required someone outside the university, corporate or museum spaces with a different locus of control. In looking to forge collaborations outside the university, corporate or museum/gallery space, these researchers provided me the opportunity to extend my practice, change the parameters of who my audience might be, and thereby generate curatorial work in new ways. The interdisciplinary nature of this work is articulated in Ben Shneiderman's *The New ABCs of Research: Achieving Breakthrough Collaborations* (2016). This text is a collection of traditionally disparate practitioners (designers) and academics (scientists, engineers) working together to produce meaningful results from carefully designed experiments more quickly and with more impactful results than if they pursued the topic only within their specialized disciplines.

There are "five research life cycle strategies" Shneiderman (2016) believes necessary to this process across "combining both applied and basic research" (The ABC Principle) and "blending methods of science, engineering and design" (The SED Principle) to produce "higher-impact results" on all disciplines involved. The five strategies cover addressing problems with meaningful and contemporary solutions; utilizing observation, interventions and controlled experiments no matter the discipline; creating diverse research teams with equally diverse skillsets to tackle all aspects of a complex problem in a meaningful way; testing ideas and prototypes, both experimentally and in controlled environments, while combining both qualitative and quantitative data to do so; and promoting adoption through refined strategies that assess impact. In his introduction to this book, Shneiderman calls on diverse groups of "highly motivated" research teams to "embrace … and deftly apply" the ABC and SED principles "to deal with the challenges of our time while inspiring their colleagues and future researchers". Upon reflection on this call, I realized that I have spent my career working across art, design, science and engineering and that in submitting a practice-based research Ph.D., I am combining applied and basic research.

From 2009 to now, Australian activist, designer, environmentalist and "provocateur" Dr. Leyla Acaroglu has created exhibitions, handbooks, educational devices and toolkits around the Disruptive Design Method—an approach that rings true with the way I operated New Media Curation. While she runs the UnSchool in New York City where she teaches and publishes on her methodology, it is in her TED Talk titled *Paper beats plastic? How to rethink environmental folklore* (Acaroglu 2013) that distributed her intuitive framework, her focus on experiential knowledge or gut feeling, and her acceptance of oral histories that draws the attention of experimental practitioners. The amalgamation of these ideas leads to Life Cycle Thinking (planning) and Assessment (scientific testing and analysis) and the behavior changing systems that develop because of her Disruptive Design Methodology. Here she calls for pioneers in the cause of design-led systems change for sustainable practice (Acaroglu 2017). Acaroglu later honed this process into reflective three-dimensional cycles involving Mining, Landscaping and Building research in closed and iterative cycles rather than in a linear fashion (Acaroglu 2018). These cycles frame this doctoral thesis, as she too looks to intervene in known processes to make change. The exhibitions I submit as part of this doctoral thesis were interventions and reflections on larger festival scenarios. In this way, I have fashioned the experiments to test my methodologies in a disruptive way. From my practice-led research, I contribute a model and the preliminary criteria for curating interactive art.

6.7 Outcomes and Results

The outcomes of this study are a posited set of criteria and novel model for curating digital interactive artworks that better evoke an authentic experience in the audience. The main aim is to understand the benefits/drawbacks of the disruptions of iterating, evaluating and modifying within a practice-based research framework while reflecting and refining my own curatorial dichotomy (professional practice ↔ creative practice) through my appreciative system. This section presents the analyzed data gathered from the three Case Studies performed during this Ph.D. It also presents a new model for curating interactive art that can begin at any stage, and malleable criteria for curating interactive art for creative practitioners—namely curators.

The first Case Study (*Denouément*) took a close, or micro-, study of emerging practitioners in their studios as they made interactive works following a brief and exhibiting as part of the VIVID Music festival in 2015. The data collection was quantitatively designed as a poll for the audience to respond to, giving us the criteria for what they required to return to the work, experience it again and enjoy it more than the first time—in keeping with the previously mentioned humanities definition of authenticity, while disrupting the design, making and exhibition aspects of the artworks the artists created. From Case Study #1—*Denouément* came the criteria for what the audience requires of interactive art to enjoy and return to it. They are listed below:

1. ***Fun/Enjoyable/Interesting***—words used to describe the experience by those that understood it and felt confident speaking about it;
2. ***Curious/New/Different***—an articulation of the above positive experience;
3. ***Games/Art/Sound***—what it made the audience think of in relation to the work;
4. ***Art Galleries/in Music/in Media/Anywhere***—where the audience might see this work being displayed in another scenario.

However, there was also qualitative data generated in *Denouément,* the observation and analysis on the part of a curator-as-producer, feeding into my appreciative system for the next Case Study for analysis, *ISEA2015: disruption* in Vancouver, Canada. This was a larger, or macro-, study of how mid-career, interactive practitioners were creating, writing about and experimenting with projects around interactive and electronic art. I engaged as a Curator-As-Producer, creating criteria through my reflections of the experience. The data was qualitative; the methodologies of its collection are discussed earlier in this chapter. From Case Study #2—*ISEA2015: disruption* came the criteria for creative practitioners to arm themselves with for their collaborators, namely their clients, practitioners and audiences. These criteria are listed below:

1. ***Accessibility and Inclusivity***: In order for the artwork to be available to most people who approach it, whether it be the point of engagement or the content they are engaging, it would be best practice to have a legible and easy-to-use or

intuitive interface, while not simplifying the story/message/other communication in order to do so.
2. ***Plurality of voices and mediums for diversity in stories and storytellers*** is important in navigating an interdisciplinary medium with practitioners from different fields coming together on one or a series of related projects.
3. ***Authoritative and Contributory***: For those in Directorial, Managerial, or even Marketing positions (including the generation of social media content), you want to be sure the information you are grouping together and how you communicate it is strong and contributes to an existing dialogue.
4. ***Relational and Representative***: A context and core message/critique/communication is important, especially when showing prototypes or Works-in-Progress.
5. ***Absent Presence and Present Absence***: This refers to the ability of the Curator-as Producer to be present but removed as work unfolds around them, accepting that they are unable to control outcomes of experimental practice, while also observing, reflecting and documenting the process analytically.
6. ***Tacit and Physical Knowledge***: These are knowledges internalized and accessible to a practitioner from having performed and thought through the process previous.

The final Case Study—*Re/Pair* was specifically focused on a collaborative artist-led curatorial method and involved a close look at who was working in close proximity to me and how, and in what ways that might be harnessed for exhibition. The exhibition research had a Bricolage approach, and the elements leading up to it held aspects of interaction design for human-computer interaction and reflective curatorial practice. The data was designed to be collected both qualitatively and quantitatively, the artists taking their data, and the curator keeping theirs. From that rich data fortified by 11 in situ evaluations including a survey and semi-structured interviews and two independent interviews with three lead international curators, came the criteria for curators (traditional and independent, institutional and experimental) working in new media and interactive art. These criteria contain personality characteristics, structural or organizational thinking, and scaffolding to gather and present the works around and through. They are listed below within the subtexts of Conversation Analysis; Action, Structure and Inter-Subjectivity:

I. **Action**

1. ***Curiosity***: Investigat[ive]
2. ***Confluence/Hybridity***: Cohesion
3. ***Entertain[ing]***: Emotional Reaction
4. ***Cultural Thinking***: Thematic/unfinished/questioning/futuring/understanding how art practice is extended
5. ***Curating-As-Action (discursive words for what curators "do")***: Collaborate/language and mapping work/Authorship and Authority/Communicating/Reflecting/Mirroring/Transposing different communities and demographics

II. **Structure**

1. ***Curator (as a title—a power in communicating what you do to others)***: thematic/didactics/signs/props/cues/prompts/language mapping work/constraints/narrative/communication/pragmatism/diverse outcomes/clever/balance and imbalance/interesting/worthy/authorship
2. ***Artist (as a title—a power in communicating what you do to others)***: humanization/embodiment/chaotic/disruptive/unsure/clever/embedding/balance versus imbalance/control/interesting/worthy
3. ***Social Practice and the Cultural Producer***: emotional reaction/language mapping work/intrigue/futuring/authorship/trust/investigat[ive]
4. ***Impact***: cohesive/fluid/ubiquitous/positive
5. ***Longer and Shorter work experience in collaborators***: balance versus imbalance
6. ***Collaborative Decision Making***: process over outcomes/useful ways of understanding/capable/inclusive
7. ***Moveable***: boundary-free/bleed (no barriers between works)/works as border line objects, but instead mirror and reflect societies ideas/programmed/anthropomorphism

III. **Inter-subjectivity**

1. ***Audience-as-Platform***: interrogation/extending your own body/identifying mechanisms for oneself as a site for internal discussions/reflecting and mirroring our own human behaviors
2. ***Festival as Proving Ground (as with Ars Electronica)***: history-making/change-making/interacting/improvising/transposing experience/diverse outcomes/investigat[ive]/companionship
3. ***Tribe and Collaborators (Community and Evangelists)***: change-making/interacting/improvising/companionship/industry assistance/robot [art] as a template for thinking about and facing human flaws
4. ***Platforms and Contexts, Situations and Vehicles***: history-making/change-making/interrogation/extending our own bodies/identifying mechanisms for oneself as a site for internal discussions/reflecting and mirroring/transposing experience/achieving diverse outcomes

After the execution, analysis and grouping of criteria in relation to the three Case Studies, the NMC Methodology can now be depicted as in Fig. 6.11.

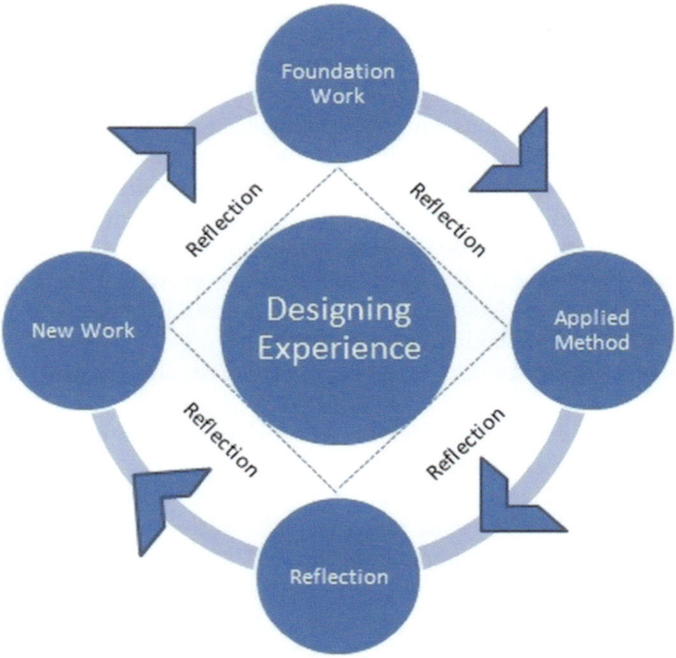

Fig. 6.11 My NMC curatorial model for designing interactive engagement, 2017

6.8 Conclusion

Consider this comment by Gérard Artaud in relation to experiential learning:

> [Use of] the word integration [to designate this new knowledge] means precisely that this new knowledge can only take form by integrating itself to the very structure of personality and, thereby, modifying it … The learner, who has thus acquired a new vision of his world, who has attained a more profound understanding of the phenomena that, before, were hidden from him or her, can no longer remain as before: his or her attitude has changed. There is every reason to believe that he or she will not be able to behave in the usual way. The goals of learning have been reached: by its interaction with scientific knowledge, experiential knowledge has not only broadened and consolidated itself, it has been transformed into a whole new way of being[.]. (Artaud 1989, p. 141)

Here, Artaud speaks of learning through experience as a situated and personality-modifying experience resulting in "a new vision of the world", one that provides "a more profound understanding of phenomena that before were hidden" (Artaud 1989, p. 141). Not only is one's attitude changed, but, as such, their behavior is changed, making their traditional movements or known ways of doing things difficult. They now struggle to behave as they did before. In Artaud's opinion, when experiential learning and scientific knowledge intersect, not only have the goals of learning been reached, but they have broadened and consolidated the experience underway, transforming the learner and their process into a new way of being (Artaud 1989; Lachapelle 1997).

In applying this idea with a Disruptive Design Methodology to elicit a more authentic experience for audiences of interactive art, I posited three Case Studies that, when evaluated and analyzed, would yield flexible criteria to guide this transition from one known space to another through experiential learning. This process of transitioning is where the experiential learning takes place and language begins to develop describing the experience. In my study, New Media Curation is the research platform and my own practice-based research as a reflective practice curator is the subject.

This chapter has largely covered the design of the Case Studies as informed by my foundational practice at New Media Curation (NMC) working as an independent curator, but embedded and adjunct in my roles with Festival settings. It has shown phases of the work that honed my appreciative system as a reflective practice-based researcher, most notably beyond the Museum floor. The final parts of the chapter focused on what the Case Studies yielded in terms of a working NMC Methodology and criteria across three types of exhibitions (a curated set of film clips that disrupted a music festival exhibition, a distributed digital and electronic art festival, and a living laboratory workshop on mental health and the arts) with three types of practitioners (audiences, exhibition partners, and curators as creative practitioners). This new work forms my significant contribution to knowledge: a novel model and flexible criteria for curating interactive art.

Acknowledgements Much of the text presented for publication in this chapter has previously been submitted in April 2018 for a Ph.D. Study through the Creative Robotics Lab at the University of NSW, Faculty of Art and Design under Tillman, Deborah Jane Turnbull (2018). *New Media Curation: a novel methodology with preliminary criteria for curating new media and interactive art*. University of New South Wales, Art & Design; Sydney, Australia (170 pages). It was awarded in September 2018.

References

Acaroglu L (2013) Paper beats plastic? How to rethink environmental folklore. TED Talks, YouTube, 18:07

Acaroglu L (2017) Disruptive design: a method for activating positive social change. Disrupt Design LLC, New York

Acaroglu L (2018) Talks and workshops. Leyla Acaroglu. https://www.leylaacaroglu.com/talks/. Accessed 4 Jan 2019

Adams TE, Jones SH, Ellis C (2015) Autoethnography: understanding qualitative research. Oxford University Press, New York

Artaud G (1989) L'intervention educative, Ottawa, CA, Les Presses de I'Universite d'Ottawa

Baxandall M (1985) Patters of intention: on the historical explanations of pictures. Yale University Press

Bilda Z, Candy L, Edmonds E (2007) An embodied cognition framework for interactive experience. CoDesign: Int J CoCreation Design Arts 3(2):123–127

Bochner AP (2014) Coming to narrative: a personal history of paradigm change in the human sciences. Left Coast Press, Walnut Creek, CA

Bown O, Loke L (2015) Musify+Gamify. http://www.musifygamify.info. Accessed 4 Jan 2019

Candy L, Edmonds E (2011) Interacting: art, research and the creative practitioner. Libri Publishing, Farringdon

Candy L, Edmonds E (2018) Practice-based research in the creative arts: foundations and futures from the front line. Leonardo 51(1):63–69

Candy L, Ferguson S (eds) (2014) Interactive experience in the digital age: evaluating new art practice. Springer series on cultural computing, Springer International

Costello B (2007) A pleasure framework. Leonardo 40(4):370–371

Dutton D (2003) Authenticity in art. In: Levinson J (ed) The Oxford handbook of aesthestics. Oxford University Press

Edmonds E (2010) The art of interaction. Digital Creativity 21(4):257–264

Edmonds E, Muller L, Connell M (2006) On creative engagement. Visual Commun. 5(3):307–322

Edmonds E, Bilda Z, Candy L (2009) Artist, evaluator, and curator: three viewpoints on art, evaluation and audience experience. Digital Creativity 20(3):141–151

Ellis C (2004) The ethnographic I: a methodological novel about autoethnography. Altamira Press, Rowman & Littlefield, Walnut Creek

Foucault M (2002) Archaeology of knowledge. Tavistock & Routledge, London

Gassmann O (2006) Opening up the innovation process: towards an agenda. R&D Manage 36(3):223–228

Graham B, Cook S (2010) Rethinking curating: art after new media. MIT Press, Cambridge

Greer J (2013) Affective connections: performance studies, videogames and digital characters. PhD, University of Texas, USA

Hampe N (2013) Reflective practice and writing: a guide to getting started. Australian Library and Information Association. http://www.alia.org.au/sites/default/files/documents/Reflective.Practice.Writing.Guide20130409JB.pdf. Accessed 27 Jan 2019

Hutchinson H, Mackay W, Westerlund B, Bederson BB, Druin A, Plaisant C, Beaudouin-Lafon M, Conversy S, Evans H, Hansen H, Roussel N, Eiderbäck B (2003) Technology probes: inspiring design for and with families. In: Proceedings of the SIGCHI conference on human factors in computing systems CHI'03, Ft. Lauderdale, FL, USA. ACM, pp 17–24

Killion JP, Todnem GR (1991) A process for personal theory building. Educ. Leadership 48(6):14–17

Lachapelle R (1997) Experiential learning and discipline-based art education. Visual Arts Res. 23:135–144

Leddy T (2013) Dewey's aesthetics. Stanford Encyclopedia of Philosophy. Stanford University, Stanford, CA, pp 5–7

Muller E (2008) The experience of interactive art: a curatorial case study. PhD, University of Technology Sydney, Australia

Muller L (2011) Learning from experience—a reflective curatorial practice. In: Candy L, Edmonds E (eds) Interacting: art, research and the creative practitioner. Libri Publishing, pp 94–106

Pallot M, Trousse B, Senach B, Scapin D (2010) Living lab research landscape: from user centred design and user experience towards user cocreation. First European Summer School "Living Labs". HAL-Inria, Paris

Peräkylä A (2007) Conversation analysis. In: Ritzer G (ed) The Blackwell Encyclopedia of sociology. Blackwell Publishing, Malden, MA, pp 791–794

Richardson L (2000) Evaluating ethnography. Qual Inq 6(2):253–255

Rogers M (2012) Contextualising theories and practices of bricolage research. Qual Rep 17(48):1–17

Russell R, Winkworth K (2009) Significance 2.0: a guide to assessing the significance of collections. Collections Council of Australia Ltd.

Schön DA (1983) The reflective practitioner: how professionals think in action. Basic Books, New York

Shneiderman B (2016) The new ABCs of research: achieving breakthrough collaborations. Oxford University Press, Oxford

Smith MK (2007) Action research. The Encyclopedia of informal education. Infed. http://infed.org/mobi/action-research/. Accessed 4 Jan 2019

Turkle S (2007) Authenticity in the age of digital companions. Interact Stud 8(3):501–517

Turnbull D (2009) Image ecologies. DAB DOCS, University of Technology, Sydney, Australia

Turnbull D, Connell M (2011) Prototyping place: the museum. In: Candy L, Edmonds E (eds) Interacting: art, research and the creative practitioner. Libri Publishing, Faringdon, pp 79–93

Turnbull D, Connell M (2014) Curating digital public art. In: Candy L, Ferguson S (eds) Interactive experience in the digital age: evaluating new art practice. Springer International, pp 221–242

Turnbull Tillman D (2008) New Media Curation. http://www.newmediacuration.com. Accessed 4 Jan 2019

Turnbull Tillman D (2019) Personal email communication between N. Hampe and D. Turnbull Tillman, 22 Jan 2019

Turnbull Tillman D, Velonaki M (2016) Disruption and reflection: a curatorial case study. In: England D, Schiphorst T, Bryan-Kinns N (eds) Curating the digital: space for art and interaction. Springer International, pp 181–202

Turnbull Tillman D, Forseck J, Velonaki M (2017) An exploratory case study into curatorial intervention within the context of HCI. In: Marcus A, Wang W (eds) Design, user experience, and usability: understanding users and contexts. Springer International, pp 540–555

Velonaki M (2011) Creative robotics lab. University of New South Wales, Australia. http://www.crl.niea.unsw.edu.au. Accessed 4 Jan 2019

Wikipedia (n.d.) Autoethnography. Wikipedia, Wikimedia. https://en.wikipedia.org/wiki/Autoethnography. Accessed 4 Jan 2019

Chapter 7
Digital Road Trips: The Shifting Landscape of Digital Art Shows

Nick Lambert

Abstract Digital art exhibitions have been held since the early 1960s. Over fifty years, they have stimulated artists using computational media to develop their work. Several key exhibitions helped to define the area of "digital art"—insofar as it exists as a separate area of art practice and have assisted this developing medium by favoring certain aesthetic and critical preferences. This chapter considers selected exhibitions and prizes, together with their influence and impact. Key questions include: issues of scale, the perception of digital art, the development of the forms within it and the expectations of artists involved; and promotion of this medium to the general public.

7.1 Introduction

Art made with computers has been shown in a variety of settings since the mid-1960s when the first digitally-mediated works were shown in Stuttgart and New York. At that time, there was a broader interest in art created using various forms of high technology, and groups such as Experiments in Art and Technology were founded. Beyond this, the emergence of kinetic art and video/TV art demonstrated that new artistic media gained some acceptance in the post-World War II art world. In the decades since then, video art has been largely accepted as a gallery medium and kinetic art has a place within the wider area of installations, but computer-mediated art (i.e., both created and shown using digital systems) has only attracted sporadic interest in the mainstream. According to art historian Christiane Paul:

> The term "digital art" has become an umbrella for a broad range of artistic practices and does not describe one specific aesthetic. Artists have used digital technologies as a tool for creating an art object, such as a sculpture created through rapid prototyping, a print, or a digital photo and video. In some cases, these works display distinctive characteristics of the digital. In others, it is not easy to tell whether the work has been created by means of digital or analog technologies. (Paul 2002, p. 472)

N. Lambert (✉)
Research Office, Ravensbourne University London, London, UK
e-mail: n.lambert@rave.ac.uk

T. Giannini and J. P. Bowen (eds.), *Museums and Digital Culture*,
Springer Series on Cultural Computing, https://doi.org/10.1007/978-3-319-97457-6_7

Therefore, there are degrees of "digitalness" evident in these works that rather determines their reception as obviously computational or not. Certainly, the general public has become used to reading images as "digital" due to obvious characteristics such as pixelated edges; however, the diversity of digital artworks does not depend on the presence of these forms. However, the philosopher of aesthetics Dominic McIver Lopes distinguishes between "digital art" in the general sense and a more specific class of "computer art". Whereas digital technologies can be used to extend earlier artforms—viz digital filmmaking, digital photography or digital music—McIver Lopes looks for a more fundamental difference between computer art and other areas. He comes up with a theory of computer art that hinges on interactivity as a key characteristic of the new art form:

> an item is a computer art work just in case (1) it's art, (2) it's run on a computer, (3) it's interactive, and (4) it's interactive because it's run on a computer. (McIver Lopes 2010, p. 27)

On this basis, McIver Lopes identifies aspects of the interactive experience that engages the viewer in a more direct way than previous artworks. He also extends the "art" boundary to include video games, connecting to work that usually sits outside the typical art gallery but has risen to become a new area of creative endeavor to rival the film industry. Certainly, many interactive art works partake of a game-like experience, and some games have been exhibited as works of art.

In my own thesis, I proposed an additional aspect: the impact on the artist of the intrinsic qualities of the digital medium. The immaterial yet quasi-physical aspects of the computer image make it malleable, ephemeral and yet an expression of mathematical processes; in other words, the medium itself is significant. Without this, the interactive aspects would be impossible.

> [There] is a twofold rupture between Computer Art and all traditional art because:
>
> i. the artist manipulates information directly, without the limitations that are intrinsic to a physical medium;
> ii. the computer can respond to the artist during production and the viewer after production, or even act as a creative agent in its own right if programmed to do so.
>
> I propose that artworks must satisfy both points in order to qualify as Computer Art, which is distinguished from other artforms because these two qualities occur in combination. (Lambert 2003)

With this in mind, it is appropriate that the term "computer art" existed in distinction to "digital art" and is not merely historically defined as belonging to the early period of experimentation with computers (as Christiane Paul suggests). Rather, computer art points towards something new. It was this fact that led to the foundation of the Computer Arts Society in the UK in 1968 with a manifesto that focused on the computational aspects of the arts (in plural, and not merely the visual). It is also significant that the first artistic project by the CAS was in fact an interactive work called *Ecogame* (1970).

In terms of its history, the earliest computer art arose in the climate of general experimentation with advanced technologies in the arts and undoubtedly benefited from the attention given to Art and Technology. This resulted in some large and well-funded exhibitions such as "Nine Evenings", organized by Experiments in Art and Technology (EAT) at the New York Armory in 1966. Until the early 1970s, these shows tended to receive funding and support from museums and patrons, but a changing social and economic climate consigned the large-scale art and technology movement to the utopian aspirations of the 1960s.

Despite this changing context, computer-based works of art were shown in smaller galleries, some museums and non-art venues such as computer trade shows. Organizations like CAS fostered an art scene that continued in spite of official indifference to this new art form. Following the emergence of Net Art and New Media art from the mid-1990s onwards, computer-based art has attained a higher profile, but exhibitions at large venues remain comparatively scarce. The typical venue for much digital art remains festivals, conferences, and small art galleries. These require flexible approaches to display and presentation that utilize the advantages of digital formats but also require a high level of technological support that is rarely found in the domain of art galleries. Thus, traveling exhibitions of computer art should provide their own expertise and understanding to meet the needs of these smaller venues while showing the work to its best advantage.

Over the past six decades, computer artists have innovated in significant ways but many of the concepts they explored were never taken to conclusion due to primitive technologies and changing art practices, which consigned many of these ideas to obscurity. An initial burst of enthusiasm for "Art & Technology" in the 1960s was followed by several decades of widespread disinterest in the mainstream art world for computational art.

A conference I co-organized in 2010 at the British Computer Society was inspired by this suggestion in Brian Reffin Smith's chapter in *White Heat, Cold Logic*:

> There is a mine, a treasure trove, a hoard – I cannot emphasize this too strongly – of art ideas that emerged in the early decades of computer art that still have not remotely been explored. We know how this happens. The next big thing comes along and the Zeitgeist has its demands: things get left behind… (Smith 2008, p. 388)

In response to this, I gathered together computer art pioneers, theorists and historians under the title "Ideas Before their Time" to discuss areas in which computer arts had emerged in the period 1960–2000. I well remember the splenetic reaction of Alan Sutcliffe, one of the three original founders of the Computer Arts Society, who attacked the very title of the conference. "They were not ideas *before* their time," he declared, "they were ideas *of* their time.!"

This stuck with me and I have since looked for the continuities between the early computer artists and their precursors, instead of simply emphasizing the break between previous artforms and the digital; though this *rupture* formed the basis for differentiating computer art. From Jack Burnham onwards, theorists of the digital medium have often emphasized its radically disjunct nature, its unprecedented arrival and the division between the *virtual* and the *real.* Yet there is also a case for seeing it as the organic evolution of a desire for externalizing the human visual imagination onto a new surface, be it the walls of the cave, canvas, silver nitrate paper or a CRT screen.

For artists who grew up since the 1980s and might be considered "born digital", computer imagery is ubiquitous and therefore part of a widespread culture. To utilize computational processes in creating art does not suggest subscribing to a set of shared values. Whereas the pioneer computer artists were strongly influenced by High Modernism and also the first wave of Conceptual Art, the disparate range of influences on modern digital artists is much larger and often drawn from digital culture in the widest sense.

Obviously, there are artists who work with data and whose aesthetic is based on their source material. Ryoji Ikeda's 'Test Pattern' series is one such example, and the recent staging of *test pattern* [*N°12*] in September 2017 at the Store X on the Strand in London showed the impact of large-scale digital works on the public. [Spice 2017] Visitors' responses to being immersed in a room-sized projection of live AV data visualized as monochrome bars demonstrated a growing familiarity with the tropes of digital imagery that suggests a broader appreciation for computer-based art. Ikeda's work was projected in a large dark space and the audience was fully contained within the projections, an experience that could seem hypnotic and disorienting at the same time. It was dynamic and sculptural, an all-encompassing work with a suitably driving soundtrack.

In some respects, the linear data-driven imagery of Ikeda connects back to the classic works of nascent "computer art" from the 1960s. These generally followed a Constructivist schema and was mostly highly abstract, as much a consequence of the technology of the time as the aesthetic preferences of its main exponents. Except for early animations by Ed Zajec and Tony Pritchett, and robotic and cybernetic sculptures, the majority of computer-based art was experienced as prints on paper because this was the primary graphical output from computers of the era. Early interactive computer systems were rare and staggeringly expensive, attached to mainframes and therefore unavailable for public access. However, the promise of computer-mediated art was already drawing significant interest by the time of "Cybernetic Serendipity" at the ICA in 1968, and as will be described below, a series of very large art shows drew attention to the creative potentials of computers and allied visual technologies.

This paper will contrast the scale and budget for these early exhibitions with the "grassroots" efforts that kept promoting computer-based art after the significant reaction against the "Art and Technology" paradigm in the 1970s. This curtailed the availability of large venues with significant technical budgets until the re-emergence of digital art as "Net Art" and "New Media Art" in the late 1990s. In this interim period, organizations such as the Computer Arts Society and later SIGGRAPH and Digital Salon promoted computational creativity through smaller exhibitions.

Fortunately, this period also witnessed the rise of desktop and home computers with significant graphical and multimedia capabilities, and the development of increasingly high fidelity display systems that made the public display of born-digital art feasible. It is still rare for galleries to be fully equipped with sufficient hardware to mount large digital art shows, but computer artists and curators have faced this challenge by developing their own technical expertise. The examples of the New York

Digital Salon and the more recent Lumen Prize for Art and Technology demonstrate the significant technological overheads that need to be overcome in order to exhibit computer art works in their own medium.

As well as works that are wholly computer-based, there are new kinds of "electronic art" where the computer is merely part of the infrastructure of the work. However the digital aspect brings with it a significant overhead in terms of installation, electrical power, mounting and positioning of screens, projectors and digital interfaces, and the overall presentation of the work in a traditional gallery setting. Having spent much time installing and presenting computer art, as well as writing on it, I would like to reflect on these aspects in the course of this essay.

7.2 EAT and Cybernetic Serendipity

Billy Kluver and Robert Rauschenberg first conceived of Experiments in Art and Technology (EAT) , the progenitor of much of the technological arts activity that followed, in 1966 following Kluver's earlier work with Tinguely on behalf of MOMA in 1960. EAT intended that artists should be able to utilize the latest in contemporary electronic equipment. With the support of Bell Labs and later other corporate sponsors, they commanded budgets in excess of $100,000 and significant technical support as well. A series of performances was held in October 1966 at the New York Armory by artists and performers including John Cage, Lucinda Childs, Robert Rauschenberg, David Tudor, and Robert Whitman. They collaborated with over 40 engineers and scientists from Bell Telephone Laboratories using specialist equipment that was used as an integral part of the event (Vasulka 1998). This was due to Bell Labs' support for Kluver's ideas and the perceived benefits for their corporate image.

The scale and availability of expertise meant that the first EAT show was produced on a scale associated with theatrical events rather than an art exhibition. Given its 'live' nature and the complexity of the setup, it is hardly surprising that the failure rate was high, and it was lambasted for its numerous technical issues. However, its scale of ambition certainly inspired other similar events.

When Jasia Reichardt assembled the funding for 'Cybernetic Serendipity' in 1968, on a model inspired directly by EAT's activities, the Institute of Contemporary Arts (ICA) in London managed to raise £20,000 including £5,000 from the Arts Council. This was about a third of the cost of the contemporary Matisse show at the Hayward Gallery (at £60,000) and the equivalent amount in 2018 would be around £330,000 (MacGregor 2008, p. 86).

By comparison the ICA spent a total of £604,585 on its exhibitions in 2017, which provides some idea of the scale of Cybernetic Serendipity (Institute of Contemporary Arts 2017). When costs of UK traveling art shows were assessed in a 2016 survey by the Touring Exhibitions Group, it found that the average cost of a touring exhibition is £62,500 although many groups are producing them with budgets of £5,000 or less (Dew 2016). Even today, then, Cybernetic Serendipity would rank as a very significant art exhibition.

Despite its subsequent success in terms of visitor numbers, Cybernetic Serendipity never gained as much corporate support as intended. Brent MacGregor records the results of the ICA's fundraising which started in December 1966:

> The ICA held a press conference in December of 1966, announcing the planned exhibition and commencing the process of fundraising [...] letters went out to over two hundred firms seeking support. This eventually futile search for sponsors led to some of the tight-fisted corporations being named and shamed at the exhibition press launch. (MacGregor 2008, p. 85)

Cybernetic Serendipity joins the somewhat ignominious list of large 1960s Art and Technology ventures begun by Experiments in Art and Technology's 'Nine Evenings' show in 1966 that Jack Burnham lists in his doleful article "Art and Technology: The Panacea That Failed" (Burnham 1980). He estimates the cost of 'Nine Evenings' at around $100,000 plus a further $150,000 of donated time and equipment; its Pepsi Pavilion at Osaka in 1970 at $405,000 (which caused Pepsi Co to pull out funding the event); 'Software' at the Jewish Museum NYC in 1970 at around $75,000; and Maurice Tuchmann's five-year 'Art & Technology' programme at the Los Angeles County Museum of Art at 'between $500,000 and $1,000,000' (Burnham 1980). For comparison, $100,000 in 1968 is worth around $700,000 in 2018.

One of Burnham's principal lines of attack on these "mega projects" was the paucity of their artistic results versus the cost and complexity of staging them, in which he includes his own Software exhibition. Even so, Cybernetic Serendipity's reputation has survived the years rather better than the others and was measurably more successful at the time, in terms of visitor numbers and positive press coverage.

Whatever the outcomes of individual shows, the phase of large technological art exhibitions of the 1960s was never again repeated and the largesse given to these exhibitions resulted in the mythology surrounding them later.

7.3 The Computer Arts Society

By contrast, the low-key model of small exhibitions practiced by groups such as the Computer Arts Society was more durable and as the availability of computers increased through the mid-1980s onwards, it became possible to show various kinds of digital outputs in a variety of venues. Although cost remained a key factor, the other constraints around technology became somewhat less problematic as display devices multiplied.

The first Computer Arts Society exhibition, 'Event One' was staged at the Royal College of Art in 29–30th March 1969 following the Society's foundation in 1968. The show was intended to showcase the range of artistic outputs that were being developed using computational means at the time, hence the "Arts" in the Society's title rather than "Art". This resulted in different media including sculpture, a DEC

PDP-7 minicomputer, performances and computer-generated films, as well as the pen plotter drawings that came to characterize this era of computer-based art.

As with other art and technology exhibitions that were located in educational establishments, 'Event One' benefitted from the collaborations that existed between the RCA and nearby Imperial College:

> The Royal College of Art was chosen as a venue because a number of CAS committee members had associations there. This included the architect Ian Pickering who was teaching there. In addition Lansdown knew Patrick Purcell, an advocate of interdisciplinary work at the RCA since 1964 [...] Purcell persuaded Professor Bill Elliott at Imperial to loan the PDP-7. (Mason 2009)

Thus, the cost and complexity of mounting such a technically challenging exhibition were mitigated by the expertise available to the organizers. As a launch for the new Society it was a considerable success with over 700 visitors; however, its range of media meant it required significant ongoing technical support for the duration of the show (Mason 2008, p. 121).

For this reason, many later CAS exhibitions were on a much more modest scale and consisted solely of prints and some films, which toured as a collection to various galleries in the UK and internationally. When the Society's collections were archived in the early 2000s there was little digital material amongst them, in terms of magnetic media and other formats. Ironically this facilitated their preservation by the Victoria and Albert Museum where CAS provided the original bequest to their Computer Art Collections. The V&A were able to use their considerable expertise in conserving prints and drawings to preserve the paper-based archive from CAS and the two-dimensional works are now regularly exhibited in various venues. It would seem that CAS's "low tech" approach to exhibitions paid dividends in terms of creating a future legacy.

The later Computer Arts Society exhibition "Interact: Man, Society, Machine" (1973), was part of the Edinburg Festival Fringe. This typified another venue where computer-based art was often represented: arts festivals. With a total budget of £3,000 from the Scottish Arts Council (worth around £30,000 in 2018) (Mason 2009), CAS commissioned four artworks: Edward Ihnatowicz's *The Bandit*, John Lifton's *Green Music*, Anna Valentina Murch's *Tent* and Stephen Willats's *Edinburgh Social Model Construction Project*; in addition to prints of graphic output by Manfred Mohr, Herbert Brun and others; and various live events. With the scope afforded by this grant, CAS was able to curate and present another technically complex exhibition (Computer Arts Society 1973).

CAS continued to stage various exhibitions until it was effectively suspended in 1985, returning in 2006 as part of the CACHe Project to reflect on the history of computer art. Since 2006, CAS's funding model has consisted mainly of charitable support from its parent body, the British Computer Society plus additional funding from the Arts Council England for specific projects, such as "Null Object: Gustav Metzger Thinks About Nothing" with London Fieldworks, Gustav Metzger and Black Dog Gallery in 2013 (Gilchrist and Joelson 2012).

In my capacity as Chair of CAS, I have helped to stage and curate exhibitions in conjunction with Kinetica, the Lighthouse in Brighton, the Phoenix in Leicester and numerous other organizations. These are all collaborative events with larger arts organizations and typically involve around 12–20 artists' work. The majority of the exhibits are shown on screens, though printed and 3-dimensional works of various kinds are often shown. The budget for these shows is usually around £2,000 and rarely exceeds £5,000 but we benefit from contributions of time, space and effort from our collaborators. Obviously, the artists themselves often provide equipment and expertise in setting up their work. Such exhibitions continue the CAS tradition of small grassroots computer art shows (Fig. 7.1).

From the 1970s onwards, in the face of limited interest from large cultural institutions concerning the area of computer-based art (as opposed to, say, video art in the same period), there was an increased tendency towards small exhibitions within conferences and trade shows. This route was praised by Jonathan Benthall in 1970 when he reviewed the Computer Arts Society's seminal contribution to the Computer 70 trade show, the *Ecogame*:

> The Computer 70 exhibition at Olympia in October was not the first trade exhibition to have included an art contribution as the centrepiece. The idea seems a good one, and could become a traditional medium of patronage. Such occasions involve the exchange of large sums of money, so that the costs of financing the art contribution (whatever it may be) can be absorbed. (Benthall 1970, pp. 229–230)

The *Ecogame* was itself a significant piece of early computer-driven interactive art that received sponsorship from Computer 70 and was later presented at the inaugural European Management Forum at Davos in 1971 (Fig. 7.2).

Fig. 7.1 CAS50: fifty years of the Computer Arts Society exhibition at the LCB Lightbox Gallery in Leicester, May 23, 2018. (Photograph by Nick Lambert)

Fig. 7.2 Computer Arts Society *Ecogame* at Davos European Management Forum in 1971. (Courtesy of George Mallen)

7.4 The SIGGRAPH Art Show

Benthall's prediction also proved quite prophetic in terms of the development of the computer art exhibition at the SIGGRAPH computer graphics trade show in the USA. SIGGRAPH had run since 1974 as a Special Interest Group within the Association for Computer Machinery (ACM), which had shown occasional exhibitions of computer art at conferences, such as that in New York in 1970. In 1980 that the artist Darcy Gerbarg proposed a dedicated art show, Computer Culture Art, at SIGGRAPH 81. Though its scope was initially limited, Gerbarg made use of an existing exhibition, High Art Technology, that had been shown at the Library of Congress in April 1981. The works themselves were two-dimensional prints that could be mounted and displayed in a traditional gallery setting and were a cross-section of contemporary American digital artists (Prince 1989, pp. 3–5).

By 1985 the SIGGRAPH Art Show had considerably enlarged and diversified into new media, including early examples of networked artworks. Patric D. Prince, who chaired later SIGGRAPH art shows and extensively documented this period, notes the scope of the 1985 show:

> The SIGGRAPH '85 Art Show was based at the Moscone Convention Center in San Francisco, but held events at several San Francisco locations. Over 100 works were exhibited at the Moscone Center. These included environmental, interactive, on-line, and traditional [printed] works. The Student Poster Animation Competition and Exhibition (SPACE) took place at the Academy of Art College Gallery. A computer graphics festival entitled "In-

> put/Output" was held in the North Gallery of the San Francisco Museum of Modern Art. Two installations were mounted at the Exploratorium, and a performance was staged at the Palace of Fine Arts. (Prince 1989, p. 5)

Given position as part of the preeminent computer industry tradeshow for graphics and digital media, the SIGGRAPH Art Show was probably the main locus for computer artists for nearly two decades from the early 1980s to the early 2000s. In this role, it displayed the work of many of the most significant exponents of computer-based art and continues to have an important position despite the emergence of other annual venues such as Ars Electronica.

Copper Giloth's useful Chronology of Computer Art details the major exhibitions up to 1990, and though not entirely comprehensive captures the occasional nature of computer art shows (Giloth and Pocock-Williams 1990, p. 283). One of the more significant ones was "Computers and Art" in 1988 at New York: IBM Gallery of Science and Art, curated by Cynthia Goodman who also published the influential and useful catalogue *Digital Visions* that documented the exhibition. It drew together many works, as noted by this contemporary report in the Christian Science Monitor:

> There are 141 works in all, including several collaborative pieces, by more than 150 painters, sculptors, architects, and video artists, all of whom have utilized computers at some point in the creative process. These works represent almost every stylistic approach, from traditional oil paintings to "high-tech" video and 3-D "synthetic" images, and include examples by, among others, Andy Warhol, Philip Pearlstein, Robert Rauschenberg, Larry Rivers, and Kenneth Noland. (Wolff 1988)

7.5 The New York Digital Salon

In 1993, another long-lasting series of annual computer art exhibitions was inaugurated by Bruce Wands, who was until recently Chair of the MFA Computer Art Department and the Director of Computer Education at the School of Visual Arts in New York. For over twenty years, the New York Digital Salon provided a venue for digital arts in New York City.

While running Digital Salon, Wands encountered a series of technical hurdles as well as issues of acceptance despite the growing maturity of the digital art field. As the founder of the course at the SVA, which itself demonstrated the acceptance of digital art within an established visual arts college, Wands had a significant insight into the most recent developments in this area, and the rising profile of the digital creative industries. This combined with his location in New York provided the backdrop to the development of the Digital Salon.

The first venue for Digital Salon was the Art Directors Club in Manhattan and only consisted of prints. There were over 600 entries and Wands and his judges rigorously reviewed the submissions. Many of the rejected images lacked aesthetic content, good use of color and composition and were essentially experiments on what the software was capable of. The curatorial decisions were not based on purely technological issues but took into account the way the computer was used in some during the creative process. The aesthetic aspects were paramount: for prints, it was the visual uniqueness, creativity, composition, color and content. Installations were chosen based on the quality and unique nature of the interaction, as well as user friendliness. Works that needed extensive instructions on how to operate them and maintenance were not curated into the exhibition. Video and animation were judged on the same criteria as the prints.

As the Salon evolved, the organizers required artists to supply all of their technology. One of the challenges was to get the work into operating condition and have a gallery assistant turn everything on and off each day. Surprisingly only a few artists attended the installation of the exhibition, therefore the installers asked for clearly written instructions. The complexities of the technology required frequent phone calls to the artists and other technical support to cope with breakdowns, software glitches and similar failures. Wands was able to employ a systems administrator to do the troubleshooting when needed.

As the Digital Salons toured abroad, the costs of shipping the equipment and art was considerable, especially for venues in Spain, Italy, Portugal and elsewhere in Europe. The Salon organizers relied on the venues and corporate sponsors to support these costs.

Wands evolved a formula for exhibitions of 40–50 prints, an hour each of digital video art and computer animation, 5–10 websites and 8–12 installations. This enabled a proportion of the work to be presented in a live digital format while minimizing the overall technical overhead. In his role as curator, he would train the gallery staff in the operation and troubleshooting of the installations, in order to overcome the issues caused by breakdowns as far as possible.

By the late 1990s, most venues had video equipment and hanging the show was a standard procedure. However, for web-based works internet access was difficult even at that time, which was just when broadband was beginning to displace modem-based access over phonelines. Wands recalls in one venue that he had to hack a public phone line to get it. As for wireless access, this was quite rare until after 2000.

In terms of current interest in exhibiting computer-based art, Wands said:

> Early gallery interest was mainly a result of the gallerists' interest in this art form. Very few of them had the technology needed. As time passed, many galleries did start to acquire laptop computers, monitors and have WiFi access. However, for any exhibition with complex technical requirements, a gallery assistant with knowledge of the works was needed. We would often have students act as docents in the gallery. Today, this is still the norm: even museum curators are still relatively new to digital art. While they do incorporate public demand as a criterion for putting on these types of shows, very few have an extensive knowledge of digital art.
>
> (From author's interview with Bruce Wands, June 20, 2018)

Wands stated that one "outstanding exception to the rule" is Christiane Paul, who was early on an Adjunct New Media Curator at the Whitney Museum of American Art and now oversees the galleries at Parsons—The New School in New York City. Another American curator Wands sees as an active promoter of digital art is Steve Dietz, who started as a New Art Curator at the Walker Art Center and is still actively curating digital art exhibitions.

7.6 Carla Rapoport and the Lumen Prize

While the Digital Salon benefitted from strong institutional support in New York and built an international reputation through its strong connections to the digital arts community, another approach was developed in Cardiff, Wales by interdisciplinary arts entrepreneur Carla Rapoport. A financial journalist by training, she was intrigued by the possibilities suggested by David Hockney's 2012 exhibition "A Bigger Picture" at the Royal Academy that featured Hockney's work on his iPad. Rapoport swiftly realized there was a significant amount of born-digital art and decided to launch an art prize to both celebrate and recognise together an art prize to recognize this area. She was not under any illusions about the acceptability of digital art in the mainstream art world, however:

> The contemporary art scene has a love/hate relationship with work created digitally. Curators are afraid it won't work, museums worry that the equipment will become obsolete and galleries aren't comfortable with art that can't be framed, shipped and sold. (Niio 2017)

The purpose of the Lumen Prize for Art and Technology was to enable artists who engage with technology to gain more recognition and also gather together a cross-section of the best art created with technology around. From the year of the first Call in 2012, Lumen had little support from larger entities. However, the City of Cardiff gave around £10K over 3 years and Cardiff City Hall was therefore the first venue for the awards ceremony. Therefore, Lumen benefited from opportunities available in this small capital city, which although somewhat removed from the art scene of London was attractive to new creative ventures in the early 2010s. A small space was made available in the digital industry hub Cardiff & Co and after this shut down, Lumen's office was located in the Cardiff Business and Technology Centre at the university.

Through an introduction to Professor Gaynor Cavanagh of Cardiff School of Art & Design, Lumen forged a relationship with this arts institution, and Cavanagh then got the lecturers involved in the first exhibitions in this space. Around this time Rapoport hired her first assistant, Alex Miller, who was followed by James Britton. These assistants were directly responsible for setting up and running all the technologies used by the exhibiting artists, as well as maintaining the Lumen presence on social media and promoting the prize (Fig. 7.3).

The Prize was also able to secure some key figures from the art world as judges, not least Bruce Wands (see Chap. 21) and Douglas Dodds (see Chap. 10) of the Victoria and Albert Museum, who brought together the national collection of Computer Art at the museum and was Senior Curator in this area. Awarding prizes in several areas of endeavor such as Still Image, 3D animation, Interactive, and Virtual Reality, the major prize each year has gone to artists who typify new approaches to digital art.

Carla Rapoport underwrote the Prize from the start and acted as the main promoter, finding venues for the travelling exhibition across the globe. Lumen shows have appeared in Athens, Riga, Shanghai, Amsterdam and New York as part of Creative Tech Week. While it recoups money through the entry fees to the Prize and receives

Fig. 7.3 The Lumen Prize at Caerphilly Castle, South Wales, in November 2016. (Photograph by Nick Lambert)

commissions from festivals and other venues where the show is exhibited, it operates on the small to medium scale with a lean organizational structure.

Throughout this period, Rapoport and her fellow organizers were keen to provide art and technology experiences to existing arts groups, for enlarging audiences and widening participation. She discovered that digital festivals were often key to this area and participated in several festivals. This brought the prize to the attention of the Onassis Cultural Centre in Athens that staged a major show in November 2014, perhaps the point at which Lumen "broke out" into the wider cultural arena. Since then, the prize has attracted hundreds of applicants each year and provides a good cross-section of the creative works in this area.

Nevertheless, Rapoport remains closely involved, both on a personal and financial level, because she knows it is necessary in order to direct Lumen's evolution and cannot yet step back because it is at a crucial phase. Between her and Lumen's assistants, the pressures of assembling and delivering a series of travelling exhibitions is a year-long activity that involves significant investments of time and finance. At present, some of the major outcomes are specific exhibitions in larger museums, rather than selling artwork as with other areas in the art market.

Artist Jack Addis, a graduate of the MA in Fine Art Digital programme under Jonathan Kearney at Camberwell College of Art, became involved with Lumen in 2015. It was in fact through this connection that he helped to produce a Lumen Prize exhibition and Carla Rapoport realized he had a strong skill set in installing the artworks. This skill set came about due to the fact that he had been a gallery technician for various galleries since 2010.

As a technician, the focus of Addis's work was coordinating the artists and artworks to arrive on time to and to make sure that the exhibition was finished to the best standard it could be. Through his work with Lumen, his role has now developed with a focus on curating and partnership management. In putting on exhibitions of digital art, Addis's main goal is to create exhibitions or events that are able to reach and inspire wide and diverse audiences, who would not typically go to museums or galleries; all the while trying to set and keep standards of paying artists a fair fee for the labor. He works closely with Lumen's partners to get the best results for our artists in terms of paid opportunities alongside providing skillsets in installing and curating digital art, that in-house teams lack.

The recent exhibition at Eureka! The Children's Museum in Halifax (UK) provides a good case study. As Addis notes:

> Lumen presented a wide range of interactive artworks and the young visitors really engaged for a long time learning the quirks or mastering the controls of the artworks on display, spending I would say more time than an adult would interacting with individual artworks. However, if an audience is able to get over the wow factor present in many digital works engagement is usually very strong, and people are keen to learn more. Something I notice is that visitors like to touch and use interactive artworks and if they are not able to 'get' a reaction or interaction immediately they move on to something else. Meaning that the artwork has to 'work', and ideally be robust enough for 100 s of users to enjoy. Not that I advocate the dumbing down of an artist's practice to meet an audience – I think it can be a fine balance.
>
> (Email interview with Jack Addis, conducted in June 2018)

In terms of the issues of transporting and setting up digital artworks across the globe, Addis believes the main issue is that of time differences between venues in different countries. Global coordination is possible, even for a small team of exhibitors, provided they work together using social media. Applications like Team Viewer or Skype mean that an artist who is not able to be physically at the exhibition can still be telepresent from their studio, as their artwork is being installed on the other side of the world.

Addis avers the most important skill is good project management with setting up digital works around the world and bringing a big bag of adapters! Transporting artworks is again not a huge issue as long as there is time for customs processes, or a local version of an artwork to be made to the artist's specification.

From his point of view, Lumen is aiming to do more for artists and audiences; to provide a lot more than just gallery or museum-style exhibitions. The organization achieved commissions with major cultural institutions in 2018, such as the Barbican Performing Arts Centre in London, large site-specific outdoor public artwork in China, and is hoping to set up residencies aimed at working with local communities, all with the twin goals of bringing art and technology to new audiences and supporting the artists making this work.

7.7 Conclusion

In the 52 years since "Nine Evenings" launched 'Art and Technology' into the public sphere, the area of computer art exhibitions has gone through some significant upswings in fortune as well as periods of near-decline. Had the model for technological art remained that of the corporate-funded blockbuster then the area might have faded into obscurity with the changing cultural climate of the 1970s. However, the emergence of artists and organizers with considerable technical proficiency and an adaptable approach to small venues and new technologies meant that computer-based art shows continued in a variety of settings.

Now there are several organizations at different levels actively promoting digital artists, the area seems more sustainable than previously and as the skills and outputs diversify in a population that is increasingly "born digital" the role of computer-based artworks is gradually entering the mainstream art world. Although the transition will not be sudden, nor as revolutionary as the original pioneers of digital art hoped, it is gradually changing expectations of the way that art is presented in galleries and museums. Interactive and dynamic works are rapidly becoming an accepted medium and this can only bolster the visibility of computer art.

In this regard, it is notable that the Lumen Prize dropped the phrase digital art in 2018 but rather has the strapline "The Global Award for Art and Technology" (see https://lumenprize.com). The organizers now believe that the ubiquity of digital devices means that merely referring to "digital art" is no longer sufficient and a more general approach to technology should be highlighted. In this respect, Lumen is returning to the origins of this area with EAT and other groups in the 1960s. This approach is to be welcomed so long as the special characteristics of "computer art" are still recognized.

References

Benthall J (1970) Technology and art 20. Studio Int 180(928) (December)

Brown P, Gere C, Lambert N, Mason C (eds) (2008) White heat cold logic: British computer art 1960–1980. MIT Press, Cambridge

Burnham J (1980) Art and technology: the panacea that failed. In: Woodward K (ed) The myths of information. Coda Press

Computer Arts Society (1973) Computers in the arts conference/event/exhibition, Edinburgh, 27–31 Aug 1973. Computer Art Society, British Computer Society Specialist Group. Birkbeck College, University of London, UK. http://www.bbk.ac.uk/hosted/cache/archive/CAS/Interact%20Documents%201973.pdf. Accessed 1 Jan 2019

Dew C (2016) An analysis of touring exhibitions practice in the UK. Economics of touring exhibitions survey report, Touring Exhibitions Group (TEG)

Gilchrist B, Joelson J (2012) NULL OBJECT: Gustav Metzger thinks about nothing. London Fieldworks.https://londonfieldworks.com/Project-2-NULL-OBJECT%3A-Gustav-Metzger-thinks-about-nothing. Accessed 1 Jan 2019

Giloth C, Pocock-Williams L (1990) A selected chronology of computer art: exhibitions, publications, and technology. Art J 49(3) (Autumn. Computers and art: issues of content)

Institute of Contemporary Arts (2017) Report and financial statements for the year ended 31 March 2017. Charity Commission, UK. http://apps.charitycommission.gov.uk/Accounts/Ends48/0000236848_AC_20170331_E_C.PDF. Accessed 20 Jan 2019

Lambert N (2003) A critical examination of 'computer art'. Unpublished thesis, submitted to University of Oxford, UK. http://computer-arts-society.com/static/cas/computerartsthesis/index.html. Accessed 20 Jan 2019

MacGregor B (2008) In: Brown P et al (eds) Cybernetic serendipity revisited, Chapter 7, pp 83–93

Mason C (2008) Interview with Colin Emmett, a computer in the art room. JJG Publishing, Hindringham

Mason C (2009) The fortieth anniversary of event one at the Royal College of Art. In Seal A, Keene S, Bowen JP (eds) EVA London 2009: electronic visualisation and the arts. BCS, London, UK, 6–8 July 2009, pp 117–128. http://www.catherinemason.co.uk/pdf/TheFortiethAnniversaryofEventOneEVA09.pdf. Accessed 20 Jan 2019

McIver Lopes D (2010) A philosophy of computer art. Routledge, UK

Niio (2017) The lumen prize: a conversation with founder/director Carla Rapoport. Niio blog. https://www.niio.com/blog/the-lumen-prize-a-conversation-with-founderdirector-carla-rapoport/. Accessed 20 Jan 2019

Paul C (2002) Renderings of digital art. Leonardo 35(5):471–474, 476–484 (Tenth Anniversary New York Digital Salon)

Prince PD (1989) A brief history of SIGGRAPH art exhibitions: brave new worlds. Leonardo (Computer art in context supplemental issue)

Smith BR (2008) In: Brown P et al (eds) From 0 to 1: art made between the times of having and not having a computer, Chapter 27, pp 377–388

Spice A (2017) Ryoji Ikeda premieres mind-bending new A/V artwork test pattern [N°12] at The Store X, Sept 10 2017. https://thevinylfactory.com/news/ryoji-ikeda-new-test-pattern-n12-store-studios/. Accessed 20 Jan 2019

Vasulka W (1998) Experiments in art an technology. A brief history and summary of major projects 1966–1998. Experiments in Art and Technology, Berkeley Heights

Wolff TF (1988) The computer as artistic collaborator. Shows at IBM Gallery feature computer art and John Sloan works. Christian Science Monitor, May 16 1988

Chapter 8
Rethinking Museum Exhibitions: Merging Physical and Digital Culture—Past to Present

Tula Giannini and Jonathan P. Bowen

Abstract This chapter brings focus to museum exhibitions and how they are evolving in the digital landscape while connecting past and present, mixing physical and digital media. Taking an evidence based approach and writing from experience, we note that most of the exhibitions discussed here were attended by the authors, mainly in London, New York and Paris during the past few years and studied in the context of digital life and art in these world-leading cultural capitals We draw on observation, published reviews, research materials and multimedia sources with the goal of creating a rich tapestry that merges art, information and experience, which taken together offer new perspectives on how museums are transforming in the digital ecosystem in ways that bring together museums, people and communities, locally, globally, onsite and online. We explore these developments in depth and with attention to the context of the social, cultural and digital forces driving them.

8.1 Introduction

At the heart of the museum enterprise and visitor experience, is the exhibition. Exhibitions are where visitors go to see a "show" that many have previewed online, and for which creative works are curated, stories told and narrated, and where ideas and their expression come to life, being documented by the exhibition catalog. Usually installed across several galleries, exhibitions marshal the efforts of museum departments from curatorial, conservation and digital to audience development and virtual exhibitions. Visitors enter the museum with the excitement and anticipation of the physical experience, of being there in real time and space, and hoping to be inspired, surprised and challenged by new ways of thinking and seeing (Giannini and Bowen

T. Giannini (✉)
School of Information, Pratt Institute, New York, USA
e-mail: giannini@pratt.edu

J. P. Bowen
School of Engineering, London South Bank University, London, UK
e-mail: jonathan.bowen@lsbu.ac.uk

Southwest University, Chongqing, China

T. Giannini and J. P. Bowen (eds.), *Museums and Digital Culture*,
Springer Series on Cultural Computing, https://doi.org/10.1007/978-3-319-97457-6_8

2016). They view and communicate, share thoughts and feelings, message, tweet, photograph, and become part of a global conversation. The museum gallery, like the stage of a theatre, is where audiences gather for the main attraction. Increasingly, museums are using their public stage as a space shared with visitors designed for participation and interaction facilitated by digital intermediaries from the common audio-guide to video, virtual reality, robots, visualization and sound, a model which is being extended for staging shows online. And still, in the midst of remaking exhibitions for 21st-century digital culture, artists and their works remain the stars of the show, while new technologies are deepening audience experience and changing current thinking about museum space as exhibitions are designed to be immersive while new trends in museum architecture redefine public space for participation. Contemporary works using digital, media, installation and performance art are broadening our notion of what is art, and how we define the relationships between art, information, technology and human consciousness (Bowen and Giannini 2014). These new approaches serve to create exhibitions and audience experiences with the power to transform lives, real and virtual.

8.2 Conceptual Models

8.2.1 Digital Frameworks and New Curatorial Roles

The roles of curators and artists are changing as museums shed the formalistic and formulaic 20th-century exhibition structure. As digital art and culture become more dominant in the 21st century, we see museums seeking new ways of thinking about exhibitions and audiences. This emerging trend comes with the growing recognition that museum life is embedded in the public life of our digital ecosystem expanding the scope of curatorial roles from the solo curator to a curatorial team, including digital curators necessitated by digital technologies that offer exciting ways of amplifying visitor experience including virtual and augmented reality, mixed media, and digital media displays, to gallery and experience designers for onsite and online exhibition experience, and curators of contemporary contexts and related archival and documentary materials. For exhibitions of works by living artists, especially for digital, installation and mixed media art, artists are assuming key curatorial roles. Significantly, the broader vision that comes with a curatorial team, fosters a creative process inclusive of new and diverse perspectives that reach beyond the museum. As curators take full advantage of the ways in which digital technologies can mediate visitor interactions, and education, tell stories and convey meaning, they will find that exhibitions will have greater impact in society. An expanded curatorial production process serves to integrate the physical works of art and information into a digital framework designed to engage audiences as participants. As this new conceptual model of the exhibition is embraced, one of partnership between the museum, audience and the general public, museums will find new success in building their community locally and globally.

For digital, installation and mixed media art, the curator's role is more complex given the technical aspects of exhibiting works, lighting challenges for video, and digital art, and figuring out space and time elements of visitor experience. When video is shown as part of a larger exhibition, viewing it in a separate dark room can be seen as a work isolated from the larger show. Since these works tend to be time-based, and often occupy an entire gallery, gallery design and set-up is critical from where visitors enter and to where they exit, almost as if exhibitions are being choreographed (see the role of the curator, http://www2.tate.org.uk/nauman/themes_4.htm).

8.3 Immersive Exhibitions at the V&A

8.3.1 Pink Floyd-Their Mortal Remains

The Victoria and Albert Museum exhibition, *Pink Floyd-Their Mortal Remains* drew heavily on the Pink Floyd archives. Stereo headphones for visitors served to immerse the audience of this mixed media exhibition in Pink Floyd's music, that guides them as they walk through the galleries. Use of documentary material from film, and video to the band's musical instruments and electronic equipment such as sound mixers, take visitors beyond the expected in the use of highly creative means that suggest a new conceptual exhibition model. Documentation in the arts can be very broad—from the essential, the work of art, to the supplementary non-essential. Nonetheless, the more ephemeral material can significantly increase the audience's emotional and intellectual reception of the works—as with documentation of the artist's studio, his house, clothing, instruments, family, photographs, letters, legal documents, notebooks—all are part of conveying the artist's work and life, so that two dimensional objects (paintings) appear alongside digital and 3D physical things (Figs. 8.1 and 8.2).

The Pink Floyd exhibition redefines what user experience can mean. From the headphones that provide a musical journey, the gallery lighting that focuses visitor attention of the objects displayed, the bands musical instruments, recordings, videos, personal messages, from films to iconic Pink Floyd objects handing from the ceiling, and the final gallery of surround sound and image of the bands final concert, in a gallery where visitors occupy the floor, sitting down or reclining—as they listen intently and look at the walls showing a video display of "The Wall".

Museums generally offer a scant view of their exhibitions online, perhaps a couple of images and a few paragraphs of text which means that visitors have limited knowledge about the show prior to their visit. Once at the museum, the exhibition itself provides minimal information—some wall text and object identification plaques. The relationship of onsite and online exhibitions seems to be in the early stages of devel-

Fig. 8.1 Two views of Nick Mason's Ludwig double bass drum kit with hand-painted images of *The Great Wave* by Hukusai, on view at the Pink Floyd Exhibition, Victoria and Albert Museum (Photographs by Tula Giannini, July 26, 2018)

Fig. 8.2 The Great Wave by Katsushika Hokusai (Japanese, 1760–1849). Polychrome woodblock print; ink and color on paper. Metropolitan Museum of Art. This work was featured at the British Museum exhibition, Hukusai: Beyond the Great Wave, 2017 (Public Domain, https://www.metmuseum.org/art/collection/search/45434)

opment. With a paucity of information being offered online to inform visitors—why not provide an online digital exhibition catalog.

The Pink Floyd exhibition catalog, in contrast to established catalog form of a subject essay followed by object description, reads like an exciting story narrated by friends and colleagues of the band drawing upon the objects and archival materials of the exhibition. In terms of reader engagement, it reflects the conceptual model of the exhibition while enhancing its total experience. This brings into question how museums are thinking about the role of the catalog for onsite and online visitors. In light of its value to visitor education and engagement, two key areas of concern to museums, it seems a missed opportunity to only make available the print publication, when a digital catalog would offer new digital ways of conveying the meaning and message of an exhibition allowing museums to replace text on walls and plaques, in favor of in-depth digital information that museums and visitors could customize to use and purpose, employing digital devices, tools, applications, virtual, augmented and mixed reality. People need to be able to "search" the catalog, which by definition goes beyond being a "book" but rather it is more a database of in-depth knowledge that can be drawn upon in response to a myriad of visitor queries.

8.3.2 Opera: Passion, Power and Politics

The exhibition, *Opera: Passion, Power and Politics*, mounted in collaboration with the Royal Opera House, was staged in the V&A's Sainsbury Gallery that opened summer 2017. In ways similar to the Pink Floyd exhibition, this exploration of opera is designed to be immersive and uses a broad range of mixed media materials including sound recordings, musical scores, iconographic paintings, musical instruments, artists' portraits, opera posters, stage sets and costumes, which combine to create musical and social contexts that show the connections between opera, art and politics. Before entering the exhibition, visitors are given high quality earphones to listen to musical selections corresponding to gallery objects and narratives programmed to follow the visitor's journey through space and time beginning in 1643 with Monteverdi's *L'incoronazione di Poppea*.

Gathering exhibition materials from various collections at the Tate and from other museum and library collections, the materials are brought together seamlessly at the service of the exhibition's theme. Traversing the galleries, visitors travel chronologically to European cities starting with Venice, then London, Vienna, Milan, Paris, Dresden and Leningrad by which they explore seven opera premiers and ending their adventure with "Opera-Today and Tomorrow." Musically rich and thought provoking, the exhibition conveys the themes convincingly while creating a compelling opera experience in the context of passion, power and politics. Tim Ashley, classical and opera critic of *The Guardian UK* in his enthusiastic review of the exhibition comments on its connections with feminism and women's rights, "Eroticism tips into expressionist violence in the sixth opera, Strauss's Salome, the 1905 Dresden premiere which took place against the background of the emergence of the psychoanalytic movement and the growing consolidation of feminism." He also notes "A poster for International Women's Day in 1925 closes the section and leads us towards Shostakovich's heroine and her sympathetically observed, if catastrophic, revolt against the male world in which she finds herself trapped." (Ashley 2017).

Looking at the 1905 production of Salome through photographs and posters and comparing it to the 2017 production of Royal Opera House, the one featured in the exhibition, the differences between interpretations are quite striking, as early 20th-century social sensibilities and aesthetics give way to 21st-century interpretations that often shock audiences with their raw emotions and stark realism. Importantly, these mixed media, immersive exhibitions demonstrate that social awareness of past and present contexts form a bridge by which visitors traverse personal states of being and find points of connection and identification to the Salome a narrative—crossing time past to present, with each remix bringing a new interpretation of the biblical story of Salomé, as we see with the 1891 book of Oscar Wilde inspiring the 1905 opera of Ricard Strauss reinterpreted in the 2017 performance by the Royal Opera setting the story in contemporary context (Bucknell 1993). In an interview for Artnet News, Max Hollhein, Director of Metropolitan Museum of Art talked about how he plans to redefine contemporary art at the Met given the museums plans to expand the footprint of its modern and contemporary collections. His response focuses on "contemporary perspectives" and he points out the significance of painters such as Gustave Moreau, his Salomé is pictured in Fig. 8.3.

> I think it's a question of contemporary art, but also contemporary perspectives, and finding the contemporary in some places around the museum where you might not expect it. I once did a show with the art historian Raphael Rosenberg that was called "Abstraction," and it showed work by Victor Hugo, Gustave Moreau, and late J.M.W. Turner. So it showed you abstraction before anyone was even talking about abstraction (Goldstein 2018)

8.3.3 Visitors Set Sail—Ocean Liners: Speed and Style

The exhibition *Ocean Liners: Speed and Style* that opened in March 2018 at the V&A beckons museum goers to, "Experience a unique journey through the design stories of the world's greatest ocean liners, including the Titanic, Normandie, the Queen Mary and the Canberra, and find out how these impressive vessels helped shape the modern world." And indeed, the exhibition captures the imagination with its focus on industrial design combined with high fashion and night life. Special effects, many using digital, create the illusion of ocean liner travel by recreating with impeccable detail an ocean liner hyperreality of sorts.

Together, these V&A exhibitions advance the establishment of a new mixed media exhibition genre of immersive experiences that touch audience emotions and sen-

Fig. 8.3 Salomé through time, three interpretations (1925, 1907 and c.1876), each more risqué, tie to the V&A Opera exhibition showing the Royal Operas 2017 production with Salomé mostly nude and bloody. **Left**: Salomé, painting by Gaston Bussière, 1925. French symbolist painter and illustrator (1862–1928). He illustrated Oscar Wilde's Salomé written in Paris, 1891. The artist captures the seductive quality of Salomé's Dance of the Seven Veils as heard in the Richard Straus opera featured in the V&A exhibition. Comparing this personage of Salomé to the Royal Opera production, 2017, we can see her sexual identity morphing into a 21st-century femme fatale. Wikimedia Commons, https://commons.wikimedia.org/wiki/File:Gaston_Bussi%C3%A8re_-_Dance_of_the_Seven_Veils_(1925).jpg **Center**: Maud Allen as Salomé in her dance costume, 1907. Her Salomé dance of the seven veils "went viral" through a postcard campaign—an early form of social media (Childs 2018). Her popularity in the US and France contrasts her reception in England where she was derided for being sexually inappropriate and a lesbian (Messy and Nessy 2018). She sued for libel and lost in what was a ruinous trial, May 1918. Wikimedia Commons, https://commons.wikimedia.org/wiki/File:Maude_Allan_LCCN2014696602.tif **Right**: *Salomé Dancing Before the Head of St. John the Baptist.* Painting by French artist, Gustave Moreau (1826–1898), Paris, c. 1876, Oil on wood. Metropolitan Museum of Art, Gift of the Eugene V. and Clare E. Thaw Charitable Trust, 2018. Wikimedia Commons, https://commons.wikimedia.org/wiki/File:Salome_Carrying_the_Head_of_John_the_Baptist_on_a_Platter_by_Gustave_Moreau.jpg

sibilities, making for memorable experiences through art. Comparing the Salomé production, premiered in 1905, and its many iterations over time, to the Covent Garden performance represented in the V&A exhibition, the differences are dramatic and seen vividly in the nude bodies of Salomé and Jokanaan soaked in blood, clinging to each other on a stage designed in a minimalist fashion. Flora Wilson headlines in her *Guardian* review, "McVicar revives his provocative production for a third time with more nudity, a severed head and a heroine who acts like a petulant pseudo-teen." Wilson attributes social awareness of contemporary issues in the 2017 Salomé production observing that, "we've gradually come around to all manner of once-outrageous ideas, from onstage nudity and performers who stand with their backs to the audience to voting women and same-sex marriage" (Wilson 2018). The high voltage emotions conveyed in McVicar's production and also seen in the V&A's Pink Floyd exhibition, that seem to make connections with contemporary social movements that dominate social media and the Internet (Figs. 8.3 and 8.4).

Fig. 8.4 *Gallery view from the Ocean liner exhibition at the V&A.* The realism of the scene is achieved by employing digital media and real objects creating an immersive *mise-en-scène* that transcends the gallery. (Photograph by Tula Giannini, March 21, 2018)

8.3.4 Museums, Digitization, and Online Access—Charles I: King and Collector

Museums generally are striving to digitize their collections, and by so doing, are playing a key role in providing online open access on their website that make important contributions to strengthening visitor interest in the collections and exhibitions. Further, a large number of museum images are now available on Wikimedia Commons and are linked to a Wikipedia page providing information on the work and the artist. This allows scholars and students to illustrate their commentary and criticism, and share images and comments on blogs, Twitter or Instagram.

The exhibition, *Charles I: King and Collector*, at the Royal Academy of Art, March 2018, featured the works of great European artists, most prominently Anthony van Dyck, official court painter, Titian, Caravaggio, Rubens, and Artemisia Gentileschi, the sole woman painter among them. The final gallery of the show features the larger than life van Dyck work, *Cupid and Psyche*, painted 1639–1640 is a celebration of love. Visitors were not permitted to take photographs, although this paintings and others viewed in the exhibition have been digitized by the Royal Collection Trust and can be viewed on their website (https://www.royalcollection.org.uk). In addition, many of the van Dyck paintings can be found on Wikimedia Commons with relevant links to Wikipedia. This linkage of works from the exhibition to the web has enormous potential for scholarship and education, and for deepening the connection between art and information, by which users/visitors can create new narratives and connect historical works to the present and to their own lives. For example, the exhibition shows that Charles I was international in his tastes, who as a collector had a predilection for Dutch and Italian artists. The most prevalent genre of painting in the show was the portrait, including a stunning self-portrait (selfie) by Artemisia Gentileschi as the *Allegory of Painting*, the only female artist in the show, whose artistic talent was well appreciated with Charles I. The vast number of public-domain works of art now available online through museum websites, wiki commons, and other Internet open access sources, is growing exponentially and has become an integral part of important new fields of study such as digital art history and digital humanities. With modern and contemporary art, copyright and intellectual property rights present challenges and barriers to access and use to varying degrees depending on rights and permissions of creators, collectors and institutions (Fig. 8.5).

A review by Will Gompertz for the BBC focuses on Charles I's passion for art and collecting but points out the great loss to Britain, when the Royal collection he had amassed, was sold at his death by execution in 1649 mainly to the Prado and Louvre. He notes that the exhibition presented a first and unique opportunity

Fig. 8.5 *Cupid and Psyche* by Anthony van Dyck, 1639–1640, oil on canvas, painted for Charles I, depicts a mythological theme also used for a cycle of paintings by Jacob Jordaens commissioned for Queen Henrietta Maria's residence in Greenwich. Wikimedia Commons, https://commons.wikimedia.org/wiki/File:Anthonis_van_Dyck_001.jpg

for the public to see the best of this royal collection. Thus, although the story of this exhibition celebrating 250 years of the Royal Academy of Art seems to convey a bitter sweet message, at the same time, it reminds us that digital culture offers wonderful opportunities for global access to many of these works as well as the possibility of creating a digital version of the exhibition for the web that could also convey its story, a compelling and emotional history of art and politics (Gompertz 2018) (Fig. 8.6).

From the collection inventory volume displayed, visitors could view two pages of entries. Here a digital copy of the complete inventory viewed on a digital media display screen allowing for a page by page viewing, would have added greatly to understanding the collection's scope and size and almost 2,000 works. The exhibit brought together a breathtaking selection of works collected by Charles I (Jones 2018). To fully engage the audience, rather than the minimal labels and text on walls, the use of interactive digital could have been used to bring to life the exhibition narrative and create an immersive environment whereby the visitor was at once at the RA and the court of Charles I. One way to advance this goal would have been visitors hearing the music of William Lawes (1602–1645) who Charles I appointed as court composer, "musician in ordinary for lutes and voices." At Lawes' death, he honored him with the title, "Father of Musick." Lawes exquisite lute compositions

Fig. 8.6 Entrance to the Royal Academy of Arts, for the exhibition, *Charles I: King and Collector*. (Photograph by Tula Giannini, March 29, 2018)

make connection to the self-portrait with lute by Artemisia Gentileschi that was on view at the exhibition, a painter that stands on equal footing with works of the male artists surrounding her and in recognition of her talent, Charles I invited her to serve at court (Fig. 8.7).

What is so striking about this exhibition, and which has gone unnoticed—is that the Royal collection of art stands in striking contrast to English art of the 17th century. High necklines, no nudity nor lovers, but rather starched and stiff appearances, formalistic without sensuality and little imagination. Charles I's collection was one that brought startling beauty to the English court, a clash of cultures that possibly evoked its treacheries influencing the disfavor of Charles I. Just as the digital self is a revolution today, so the nude human form seemed radical in 17th-century England. This raises questions about the English court of Charlies I and his artistic vision of what constituted great art, which would seem to be a relevant theme of the exhibition which with digital applications could have been explored and intriguing to the audience. This speaks to contemporary contexts on globalism, since with the Internet, users can easily explore cultural differences and conflict, and importantly have access to vast cultural resources. Besides cultural contexts, the art critic, Jonathan Jones, in his review in the Guardian is critical of "the exhibition's refusal to engage with the civil war not so much a political failing as a historical one. It robs us of the art's proper context," (Jones 2018) while the art critic, Martin Kettle in his Guardian

Fig. 8.7 *Self-Portrait as a Lute Player* by Artemesia Gentileschi, painting, 1615–1617. Female painter at the court of Charles I. Wikimedia Commons, https://commons.wikimedia.org/wiki/File:Artemisia_Gentileschi_-_Self_Portrait_as_a_Lute_Player.JPG

review, goes beyond the lack of 17th-century historical contexts to its political implications, noting that, "the resonances of these 17th-century conflicts – which had deep roots in Scotland, Ireland and Wales as well as England – are still there, and not far below the surface." (Kettle 2018). Without conveying cultural, historical and political contexts while showing their connections to contemporary 21st-century life, audience engagement and understanding of the art and its connections with self and daily life is impeded. The issues raised by these reviews could have been addressed using digital media and communication both in the galleries and online. Indeed, more thought, innovation and creativity are needed to bring the promise of audience engagement and participation to fruition.

8.4 Using Digital Mediation—Degrees of Digital

8.4.1 Victorian Greats: The Birth of Art Photography

The exhibition, *Victorian Greats: The Birth of Art Photography* at the National Portrait Gallery, London, March 2018, used video to engage visitors in learning about the photographic process used to produce the 19th century images on exhibition, and using digital touch screen, visitors could view all of the pages of two large volumes of photographs on exhibition, each open to specific pages. Turning the pages on the touchscreen—each page contained one photographic portrait, and allowed visitors to view a large number of photographs by the artists featured in the show which would not have been possible otherwise.

8.4.2 Modigliani and Picasso Exhibitions at Tate Modern, 2018—Research Meets Digital

Digital culture and exhibitions are converging in both visible and unseen ways that more and more influence how exhibitions are created and how they are received by the public. The making of the exhibition draws on digital communication, digital copies of objects to be displayed and used for study. Research on exhibitions, its objects and themes, draw heavily on digital art history and resources including documents, photographs and other archival materials, much of which is represented in the printed exhibition catalog. It is in this process of creating context and narrative that relationships between objects and primary source materials are established, a process which often draws on web-based resources, and by which social and cultural contexts can be explored, and ways of using digital technology are considered to enhance the communication of meaning and engagement with visitors.

The Modigliani exhibition at the Tate Modern, November 2017 to April 2019, covers his work during the last 14 years of his life, from 1906 the year he came to

Paris to his death there in 1920 at the age of 36, while the Picasso exhibition Love, Fame, Tragedy at the Tate, March to September 2018, covers a single year, 1932, of the artists life and works in Paris, his adopted home from 1904. The photograph below shows the two artists, together in 1916 in front of the Café de la Ronde on the Boulevard Montparnasse where both as painters and immigrants, found a welcoming community on the left bank. The photograph in many respects captures the narrative of these exhibitions that convey the excitement and passion of the international art scene in Paris in the early years of the 20th century (Fig. 8.8).

In terms of digital, what visitors see in the Modigliani show is the Tate's first foray into virtual reality as part of a major exhibition. As discussed earlier, VR is used to bring his studio in Paris to life, so that visitors experience being there in time and space creating strong visceral and emotional audience connections to Modigliani's identity and art. The exhibition conveys a strong sense of authenticity which in great measure grows out of new research and documentation by Tate curators led by Nancy Ireson whose Ph.D. thesis was on Modigliani. The exhibition website provides background information, some views of paintings, and videos of interviews with curators. While the catalog stands as an important scholarly work, but not as a replacement for the onsite viewing experience. Ideally, rather than being mutually exclusive, with a digital catalog, both could come together in service of the same critical objectives, audience immersion in the narrative, the meaning, the works,

Fig. 8.8 Modigliani (1884–1920), Italian painter of Jewish descent, and Picasso (1881–1973) with André Salmon (1881–1969, French poet and art critic) in front the Café de la Rotonde, Paris. Image by Jean Cocteau in Montparnasse, Paris, 1916. Wikimedia Commons, https://commons.wikimedia.org/wiki/File:Modigliani,_Picasso_and_Andr%C3%A9_Salmon.jpg

Fig. 8.9 Virtual reality experience of Modigliani's Studio. (Photograph by Tula Giannini, March 19, 2018)

the scholarship, all being part of an intense learning experience that viewers could continue to review, study and relive in their digital life (Fig. 8.9).

The Picasso exhibition at the Tate Modern, *Picasso 1932: Love, Fame, Tragedy*, is like a journey through time, month-by-month, week by week, his paintings narrate not—painting narrates the story of his love affair with Marie Thérèse Walter. The show draws on extensive research and documentation, some of which adds to the reality of the narrative, but visible digital elements are lacking save the digital images on a screen to the right of the exhibition entrance (see below). Art critic, Mark Hudson, captures the sense of intimacy the exhibition creates with the audience in the title of his review, "The artist as you've never seen him before." The device of focusing on one year-in-the life taking a chronological approach provides a framework for understanding Picasso's artistic and personal life and relationships, where art and life become intertwined as one.

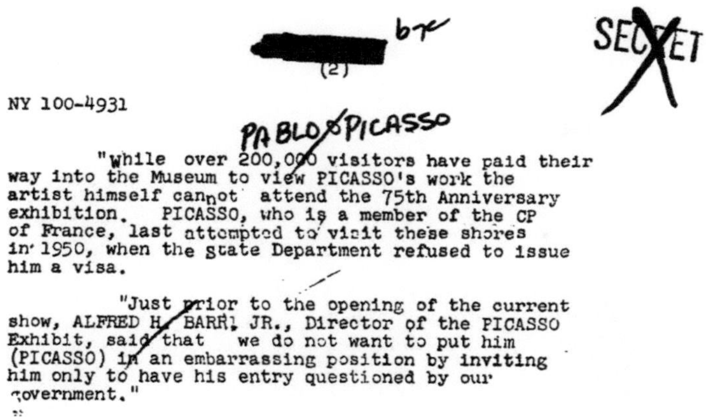

[redacted] b7c

(2)

SECRET

NY 100-4931

PABLO PICASSO

"While over 200,000 visitors have paid their way into the Museum to view PICASSO's work the artist himself cannot attend the 75th Anniversary exhibition. PICASSO, who is a member of the CP of France, last attempted to visit these shores in 1950, when the State Department refused to issue him a visa.

"Just prior to the opening of the current show, ALFRED H. BARR, JR., Director of the PICASSO Exhibit, said that we do not want to put him (PICASSO) in an embarrassing position by inviting him only to have his entry questioned by our government."

Fig. 8.10 Picasso FBI file, October 18, 1957 (Public Domain, Internet Archive, https://archive.org/details/PabloPicassoFBI/page/n51)

> By focusing on works from one short period, the show allows you to step into that world with an intensity I've encountered in few exhibitions on any artist. If Picasso's ruthless monomania prevents the exhibition from being an entirely comfortable experience, comfort isn't really what you want from the most challenging artist of the 20th century. (Hudson 2018)

The Tate's Picasso exhibition pays tribute to the artist's first retrospective exhibition which took place in Paris during June and July of 1932 at the Galleries Georges Petit located at 8, rue de Sèze. Celebrating Picasso's 50th anniversary, the catalog lists some 228 paintings, as well as pastels, works on paper, seven sculptures and six illustrated books. Twenty-five years later in 1957, the Museum of Modern Art in New York honored Picasso's 75th anniversary with a grand retrospective show. Picasso was not in attendance for this splendid occasion because he was unable obtain a visa to the US as an artist under investigation by the FBI (Figs. 8.10 and 8.11).

On April 14, 2018, members of the Independent Workers' Union of Great Britain staged a demonstration at the entrance to the Picasso exhibition to protest the exhibition's sponsor, Ernest & Young (EY) for low pay and layoffs. Protests at exhibitions of corporate sponsorship by EY over workers' rights and British Petroleum (BP) on climate change, have occurred with some regularity (Voon 2018).

Fig. 8.11 Visitors waiting in line at the entrance of the Picasso exhibition, Tate Modern. Note the video on the back wall to the left, showing Picasso. (Photograph by Tula Giannini, March 2018)

8.4.3 A Mixed Media Performance Spectacular Takes the Tate

The work of performance artist, Joan Jonas, was on view at the Tate in gallery spaces across the museum. Thus, on any one day from March 13 to April 2, 2018, visitors to the Tate Modern had the opportunity of seeing three major exhibitions and in terms of degrees of digital in the gallery from least to most, are Picasso, Modigliani and Jonas (Fig. 8.12). However, considering digital beyond the gallery, there is much to applaud. The exhibition websites including essays and video interviews mostly by curators and importantly vast online resources relevant to the exhibitions including reviews in newspapers and other publications, archival materials, Wikimedia Commons images, and researching these artists more deeply, digital resources provide a treasure trove of materials. Most museums including their libraries and archives, for example, the Metropolitan, Frick, MoMA, Guggenheim and Whitney, the Getty, Tate, Louvre, Prado and many more, have or are in the process of digitizing their collections, archives, photographs, ephemera and other collection materials. These projects, as well as those of private foundations, are transforming the way of doing museum, and art and humanities research. Using new digital tools and methods researchers are finding new relationships, creating new narratives, interpretations and meanings, and connecting past and present in digital time and space, cultures and places which in turn, is changing the way we see and view art and exhibitions.

In essence, the challenge curators face is the imagining of how to use digital to heighten the experience of an exhibition that would uniquely add new layers to ways of seeing and understanding present to past and future. As a continuum that interjects

Fig. 8.12 *Reanimation*, a work that combines sculpture and digital art. Crystal sculpture and digital light projection by Joan Jonas, Tate Modern exhibition. (Photograph by Tula Giannini, March 19, 2018)

contemporary perspectives revealing to viewers ways of relating art to self and one's world, real and virtual.

8.5 Design Museum in London, *Ferrari: Under the Skin*

The Ferrari exhibition at the Design Museum in London, *Ferrari: Under the Skin*, explores the history the Ferrari, an automobile of dreams, and its many iterations over the past 70 years, as more than a beautiful car, but rather as a work of art sculpted by hand and assigned human-like attributes, as the title suggests, that make reference to the human form and the engine under the hood, sex-appeal, and the power and animal force of maleness symbolized by the "prancing horse". The exhibition concentrates on Ferrari race cars from the earliest to present. Working collaboratively with the Ferrari museum and factory in Maranello, and the Enzo Ferrari Museum in Modena, the design museum could devote one gallery to historic documentation, while the

Fig. 8.13 *Ferrari form and design*, Design Museum, London. Large gallery with four Ferraris in various states of production and four video displays. (Photograph by Tula Giannini, March 25, 2018)

largest gallery showed Ferraris in various stages of production combined with the effective use of videos on the process of making a Ferrari racing car (Fig. 8.13).

8.6 Political Narrative and Art

8.6.1 Tania Bruguera: Untitled—Art and Politics

Political and social contexts dominate three 2018 exhibitions at MoMA that explore life in the 20th century but are best understood viewed through a 21st-century digital lens. The exhibition, *Tania Bruguera: Untitled (Havana 2000)*, is an installation piece by Tonia Bruguera, an artist-activist born 1968 in Cuba and now living in the United States. It transforms gallery space into what seems to be a pitch-dark cave that feels prison-like and evokes a sub-human experience. The work was created for the Havana Biennial in 2000 where it was censored, and later purchased by MoMA. The gallery walls are rough, and its floors covered with straw are uneven. Walking towards the back of the cave, rays of light emanate from a video screen on the ceiling showing film of Fidel Castro, while the light reveals four nude males described as dancers. Although barely moving, they reinforce the sense of a prison environment.

The exhibition is all about the experiencing of the human emotions of fear, dread, doubt and the oppressive political power of the Cuban state over the lives of its citizens. Bruguera, the winner of the Tate Modern's Turbine Hall 2018 Hyundai Commission, states that "the challenge of the artist today is to redefine public space," as a place for performance art, political and social commentary and action. "Best known for her politically-engaged projects and activism, Bruguera makes work that addresses institutional power, borders and migration. She has established a unique concept for her political approach to art – Arte Util (useful art)" One wonders how this work will be preserved and possibly exhibited in the future. Given its performance and ephemeral aspects, it takes on characteristics of a musical score which is interpreted anew with each performance and a way to reimagine the work in a new context (Tate 2018).

8.6.2 Tarsila do Amaral: Inventing, Modern Art in Brazil Raises Questions

In contrast to these exhibitions that speak to the social consciousness and aesthetics of the audience, MoMA's exhibition, *Tarsila do Amaral: Inventing, Modern Art in Brazil* presenting works and documents mostly from the 1920s, frames them in a seemingly static context as though time had stopped c.1930. Lacking the interpretation that would make connections between Tarsila's art and 21st-century life, viewers were left somewhat baffled. Artnet critic, Sara Roffino in her review, "Why MoMA's Exhibition of Towering Brazilian Modernist Tarsila do Amaral Misses the Mark" headlines, "The museum's overly formalist approach that misses out on an opportunity to delve into the politics of Brazilian Modernism." and makes the insightful observation that, "this exhibition seems to have been planned in a bubble. Racial tensions may be dealt with differently in Brazil and the United States, but isn't an exhibition of this sort the perfect opportunity to look at how and why they are different and what that has meant for their respective art histories?" (Roffino 2018).

The speed and immediacy by which political messaging and social movements travel across the globe, has changed the way the museums communicate and interact with the art world, artists, with each other, with their visitors. The global art community has a heightened sense of awareness of what is trending, of museum protests and social commentary in art itself. We see this with the MeToo movement, and charged social issues as social justice, equality and democracy. This also extends to information issues such as privacy, surveillance, illegal drugs, copyright and public domain, opensource which ties to online sharing of museum experiences and people are watching how museums address these societal concerns. Visitor expectations for sensitivity, respect, inclusion and participation are rising putting more pressure on museums to reflect these human values and in the design of their visitor experience.

8.6.3 Emerging Digital Directions

The exhibitions featured here, all have digital elements from a website to in-gallery media, and the level and extent of this digital use is fast accelerating and it is easy to imagine that visitors will use smartphones to not only capture images on their camera, but to use it to see digital for 3D, augmented and virtual reality. As new digital devices that magnify our senses are created and more frequently worn, this will affect both the way exhibitions are designed and communicated as it will human behavior. Although museums are challenged to commit to new digital directions, not doing so risks being left behind and perceived as a conservative institution adrift in calm isolation from the digital ecosystem. On the other hand, emerging directions in museum exhibitions already demonstrate that the mixing of digital, virtual and physical reality as it plays out on network platforms and in museum spaces, and we see that to this strategy draws a more culturally diverse and engaged audience. They are making connections between themselves and the museum through the art, the stories and the message—capturing their experience digitally to view and review at home, while performance art increasingly takes its place in museums (Fig. 8.14).

8.7 Computer Art Looks Back for Inspiration—Two 2018 Exhibitions

8.7.1 Thinking Machines: Art and Design in the Computer Age, 1959–1989 at MoMA

The March 2018 exhibition at MoMA, *Thinking Machines: Art and Design in the Computer Age, 1959–1989* makes connections to early abstract art seen in two works by Vera Molnar entitled, *A la recherche de Paul Klee*, one is in felt-tip pen and paper and the other an ink on paper, plotter drawing. The influence of painting techniques used by impressionist artists, most notably George Seurat to break up light, color and image, is interpreted in new ways in digital works on display combing computing and technology. The artist Tamiki Thiel and his design team produced a supercomputer, CM2, a hypercube, or cube of cubes with sixteen printed computer boards and exterior LED lights. The show also takes up issues of gender associated with the "computer age" including photographs by Lee Friedlander showing women working at computers doing for example, data input. Based on works primarily from MoMA's collections, the exhibition traces computer art in its early years and shows how it influenced music and dance in the compositions of John Cage and Merce Cunningham created at the intersection of computing and technology (Fig. 8.15).

An exhibition "drawn primarily from MoMA's collection, *Thinking Machines: Art and Design in the Computer Age, 1959–1989* brings into focus artworks produced using computers and computational thinking together with notable examples

Fig. 8.14 *Activism* performance art protest for Cannabis Rights on Independence Day in San Francisco, July 2, 2016. Wikimedia Commons, https://commons.wikimedia.org/wiki/File:FREE_CANNABIS_on_INDEPENDENCE_DAY._.jpg (See Chap. 5, Contested Space: Activism and Protest, takes up this topic in detail.)

of computer and component design. The exhibition reveals how artists, architects, and designers operating at the vanguard of art and technology deployed computing as a means to reconsider artistic production." (*Thinking Machines* exhibition website—https://www.moma.org/calendar/exhibitions/3863).

Divided into three themes, "Experimentation: 1960–1969", "Transformation: 1970–1979", and "Proliferation: 1980–1989", the exhibitions focuses on computer art and its technology, for example, on display there is a circuit board from IBM's first commercial computers, the CM-2 Supercomputer, Apple's 1980s Macintosh series. A review of the exhibition by Banyi Huang concludes with the following observation:

> We perceive through machines, think like machines, and expand our horizons by reflecting on social hierarchies and limitations through them. As Korot [Beryl Kort, video artists, b. 1945] has so eloquently put in an interview, that she was struck by "the encoding of information in lines and patterns throughout human history", our task would be the decoding of buried connections within this short yet very complex history. (Huang 2017)

A centerpiece of the exhibition was the CM-2 super computer produced by the Thinking Machine Corporation in the 1980s called a "connection machine." Its design, led by Tomiko Thiel, created a "hypercube" network of eight smaller cubes. A powerful computer for its time, it was used for "large-scale commercial purposes including artificial intelligence" (quoted from exhibition label text). The CM-2's geometric shapes with flashing red lights, project decorative design qualities making the supercomputer into a work of art, of sorts (Fig. 8.16).

Vera Molnar's A la recherche de Paul Klee in the context of her computer art focuses attention on Klee's works featuring graphic type designs, dots, and squares, which brings deep insight into both artists' aesthetic vision. Klee's artistic vision, intuiting computer art, was far ahead of his time, while he was influenced by the pointillism of Seurat, born a generation earlier.

Fig. 8.15 *Model Standing*, by George Seurat, c.1887. Pointillism as a precursor of digital art and the digital self. Wikimedia Commons, https://commons.wikimedia.org/wiki/File:Georges_Seurat_058.jpg

Molnar's work (see detail in Fig. 8.17), featuring shapes and patterns, as the work's dedication notes, takes inspiration from Paul Klee's paintings such *Variations (Progressive Motif)*, 1927 (Met Collection, https://www.metmuseum.org/art/collection/search/483167) and his 1932 painting *Clarification* using dots that almost appear as a digital screen with lines and squares that form patterns from geometric shapes (also in the Met Collection, https://www.metmuseum.org/art/collection/search/483174) (Gotthardt 2016).

The Tate Modern's fall 2013 season featured the *EY Exhibition, Paul Klee—Making Visible* (Tate 2013). According to its curator, Matthew Gales, the show "begins with the artist's breakthrough during the First World War, when he first developed his individual abstract patchworks of color that later became characteristic of his 'magic square' paintings," a series of work reflecting his travels to Tunisia in 1914. Gales notes that the show's title was inspired by a remark of Klee, "art does not reproduce the visible, rather it makes visible," which can be interpreted to mean the vision and emotions of the inner self. Gales, "hoped that the design of the exhibition would at times enable visitors to feel that they could 'transgress'—stepping out of time and into Klee's studio." The Tate's fall 2017 Modigliani exhibition does just this with wonderful results using VR (Tate 2013).

Fig. 8.16 *Connection Machine, CM-2 Super Computer*, MoMA exhibition—*Thinking Machines*. (Photograph by Tula Giannini, February 27, 2018)

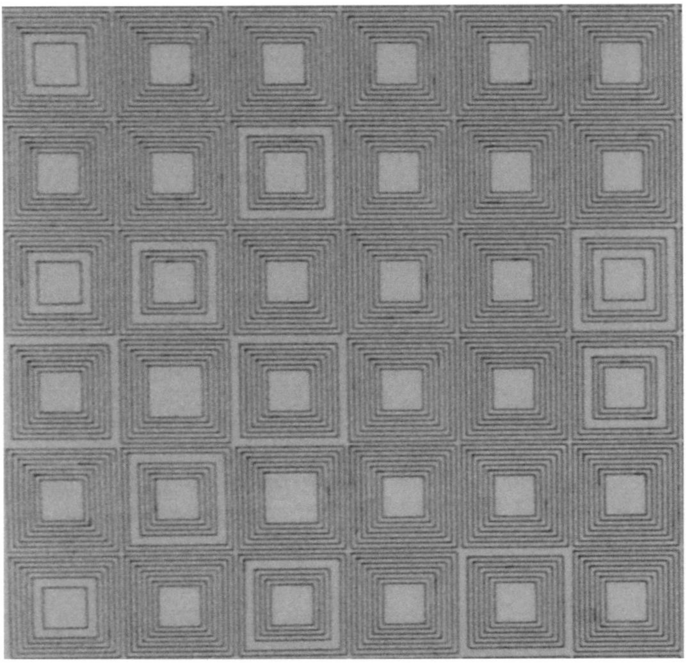

Fig. 8.17 Detail of *A la recherche de Paul Klee*, 1971, by Vera Molnar (b. 1924, Budapest, Hungary). Ink on paper, plotter drawing. Her work was, "concerned with the intersections of abstract aesthetics with information and technology" quoted from wall text, *Thinking Machines* exhibition at MoMA. (Photograph by Tula Giannini, February 27, 2018)

8.8 Remix—Photography and Archives Capture Life as Art

8.8.1 Shape of Light at the Tate—Inspired Connections, Abstract Painting, Photography, and Digital Art

The 2018 exhibition at the Tate Modern, *Shape of Light: 100 Years of Photography and Abstract Art* was not only a visually eye-popping experience, but as well a show designed to inspire viewers to compare abstract painting and abstract photography and to consider the role of media and technology in art, and to observe how these become inseparable qualities of the works themselves. The gallery view below (Fig. 8.18) is an example of such comparisons and an entree into the world of a genre of photography that continues to develop as shown in the *Shape of Light* exhibition.

The exhibition focuses on elements that connect the abstract paintings with the abstract black and white art photography, so that the artistic expression in one media, painting, is transferred to another, photography, with fresh, original visual effects. With the entrance of computer art in the 1960s, we can observe a predilection for geometric shapes and patterns again influenced by the earlier 20th-century masters of painting and photography, as seen in Fig. 8.18.

The *Shape of Light* exhibition draws on the groundbreaking 1960 exhibition, *The Sense of Abstraction*, mounted by MoMA and features works by Man Ray from that show titled, *Unconcerned Photographs* taken with a polaroid camera, referred to as an "instant camera" that within seconds printed a developed photograph, makes connections with smartphone photography today—in terms of the immediacy of producing an image, but one that is digital and can be shared, posted on online, and photoshopped. This ties to the discussion that follows on the Stephen Shore 2018 retrospective exhibition at MoMA, where the show ends with a photograph of taken with his smartphone which he used to take "instant" photographs to be posted on Instagram (Figs. 8.19 and 8.20).

The two works by Stan Douglas in Fig. 8.21 seem to bridge abstract art and digital photography, their artistic strength and striking beauty employs one of the many modes of expression used by digital artists to great effect. Using software and a mixing deck, Douglas produces "bands of color and kaleidoscopic shapes. In the process of turning the infinite possibilities of digital information into a single photograph, the artist's role takes on a particular significance." (quoted from gallery wall plaque).

Tate's Senior Curator of Photography, Simon Baker, in a video interview with Caroline Von Courten, posted on the Museum's Exhibition website (https://www.tate.org.uk/whats-on/tate-modern/exhibition/shape-light), discusses the development of

Fig. 8.18 Gallery installation view, left to right, Wassily Kandinsky (1866–1944) *Swinging*, 1925, oil paint on board (Tate Purchase in 1979); Marta Hoepffner (1912–2000) *Hommage to Kandinsky* and *Hommage to de Falla*, both 1937, Stadtmuseum Hofheim am Taunus; Piet Mondrian (1872–1944) *Composition C (No. III) with Red, Yellow and Blue*, 1935, Private Collection; German Lorca (b. 1922) *Mondrian Window*, 1960. (Photograph by Tula Giannini, July 20, 2018)

Fig. 8.19 Installation view, Shape of Light, on the far wall, note the work by Jacques Mahé de Villeglé (French artist, b. 1926, associated with nouveau realism of the 1960s,) *Jazzman*, 1961, printed papers on canvas. A stunning work that lights up the gallery, it creates a vivid color abstraction from found materials as posters, from his observation of "the actions of passers-by who had torn and stripped the posters, a process that he regarded as a spontaneous art of the street." (Quoted from wall text, gallery 8, Surface and Texture) (Photograph by Tula Giannini, July 20, 2018)

Fig. 8.20 *Unconcerned Photographs*, Gallery installation of seven photographs by Man Ray, Tate *Shape of Light* exhibition, 2018. (Photograph by Tula Giannini, July 20, 2018)

photography as represented by the show's some 350 works and 100 artists, spanning more than a century of artistic expression. At the end of interview, Baker notes:

> In the last hundred years the relationship between photography and painting is transformed – the show in the end feels a little bit like the way the museum has tried to take photography into itself – maybe at the beginning of the show there's painting and there's photography – and then by the end of the show you have just art. We could do it again with just pictures of people.

One wonders, how will we consider pictures of people, especially those millions of selfies, a growing archive of human identity across time and cyberspace, and

Fig. 8.21 Installation view from *Shape of Light* exhibition at the Tate Modern. Right: Two works by Stan Douglas (b. 1960). Lacquered UV ink on two gessoed panels, made 2016. (Photograph by Tula Giannini, July 20, 2018)

what these images say about human identity, digital aesthetics and seeing. As art photography from its inception to present is viewed through a digital lens, we see that artists finding new digital techniques to create art photography that although often derives from earlier works, for example of abstract art, is infused with innovative forms of digital expression that open our eyes and minds to new ways of digital seeing and feeling.

8.8.2 Stephen Shore at MoMA: From a Black and White 1960s Camera to the iPhone and Instagram

The Stephen Shore exhibition at MoMA, May 2018, the first New York survey of the work of this iconic American photographer, provided a wonderful opportunity to view his photographic production over his career spanning five decades. It was as if the visitor traveled with Shore through time and space, from the 1970s to present experiencing the seeing of his work "with conscious attention" from his teenage days working in black and white to his pioneering color photographs of the 1970s to present, with the iPhone and Instagram forming the body of his work since 2014. By viewing a series of videos on the exhibition presented on MoMA's website, one can listen to Shore speak about his work, and follow him through the galleries as he extemporizes on his thoughts and the memories his works on view evoke, as an actor speaking through photography. An artist of deep conscious thought and decision making, his identity as a photographer melds with his experiences of seeing and capturing the image, while his work constantly would take new directions and adopt new techniques, such as using a Studio Realist 3D camera in the 70s. Here is the artist in his own words as transcribed from videos posted on the MoMA website for the Stephen Shore exhibition, about 19 in all, in which Shore traces his career over some 50 years as beautifully presented in the show, in talk and photographs (https://www.moma.org/calendar/exhibitions/3769):

> Whenever I find that I begin to repeat myself I looked ahead to a new direction. This series began as a road trip – the idea was to keep a visual diary of meals I ate, people I met, motel rooms I slept in, and I wanted pictures that felt as natural as speaking. Here I'm using an 8 × 10 camera, in this picture I'm thinking about how three-dimensional space is rendered in two Dimensions … when I encountered Instagram I could try an idea for a day (Fig. 8.22).

Here, Shore talks about the exhibit and recalls how he met Andy Warhol and his time at the Factory, the epicenter of American 1960s art and culture:

> I'm Stephen Shore. I'm a photographer and this is an exhibition of my work at the Museum of Modern Art. It covers about 50 years of my work and career. This is a room of black and white work I did when I was a teenager. When I was seventeen, I met Andy Warhol and asked if I could come to his Studio to photograph – and as soon as I went there realized that was more interesting than going to high school so this is what I did instead of going to college. I spent three years on and off photographing at The Factory.

Pointing to a black and white photograph of himself and Andy Warhol, Shore comments:

Fig. 8.22 Shore exhibition—gallery of mixed media works viewed with digital projector and print-on-demand books made 2003 hanging from the ceiling contain thematic photographs from Shore's travels. (Photograph by Tula Giannini, May 11, 2018)

Fig. 8.23 Installation view of *A Rock is a River*, by Maya Rochat, 2018, in *Shape of Light* exhibition, Tate Modern. (Photograph by Tula Giannini, July 20, 2018)

> This picture was made probably within the first week or two of my going to The Factory, and it's a picture of me and Andy, and I guess this will go down in history as being my first selfie.

With both the *Shape of Light* and Stephen Shore exhibitions, visitors embark on a journey through photography experiencing both its development and that of the artists' works and techniques across time and space, arriving in the digital present. The Tate show ends with Maya Rochat's *A Rock is a River*, described in the wall text as "layered, multi-dimensional installations [that] feature photographs, painted surfaces and projections," for which the digital light adds a sense of dynamic experience for the visitor, a large-scale work, executed in a brilliant array of colors favoring blues and greens, the work occupies an entire wall of the gallery. As digital photography continues to develop, it simulates modernist techniques such as blurring, as new techniques are introduced, including 3D, mixed-media and mixed reality (Fig. 8.23).

8.9 Conclusion

This chapter draws on the authors' experiences, observations and information gathered at major museum exhibitions. Viewing many of these exhibitions, one might ask—so where's there digital—to that, we answer—it is in the hands of the visitors, in their tweets and Instagram, the photos they take, which they bring home and digitally curate. It is on the museum website for the exhibition, the online collections database, where visitors can learn about provenance, history and the physical properties of the objects they have viewed.

This journey to exhibitions in New York, London, and Paris, is a journey through art from oil painting to mixed digital media, while the Modigliani exhibition at the Tate stands out for its use of virtual reality. Alongside the emerging uses of digital in art, we see new sensibilities expressed in the narratives of exhibitions that reveal more socially conscious themes and dare to portray hidden intimate and honest representations of the artist as a real person, as museums abandon their reticence to explore controversial topics.

Museum websites have made significant advances that tie to better visitor experiences, such as videos of artists and curators talking about the show, panel discussions, and 3D rendering of galleries online, all designed to enhance user knowledge and engagement. Museums are sharing images and information through their online collections, and the Met has a digitization program that provides free access to about 569 past exhibition catalogs (MetPublications 2018), while curators and staff post blogs that provide important insights on their work. With more and more museums aiming to fully digitize their collections and make them accessible online, we are now able to see objects of art not on display.

Over the past several years, an enormous amount of work has been done in these areas, particularly the digitization, description and research on collection objects, and on their curation in support of exhibition narratives, and these areas will not doubt continue to advance. Looking ahead, we will see both exhibitions onsite and online take fuller advantage of advanced technologies, and venture into their all-important use in galleries connecting the in-gallery and online exhibition experiences. With this developing relationship, as the real and virtual visitor experience connects, the impact and sustainability of an exhibition after it closes, can have a new life online, so that its content and message are not just a memory prone to fade, but a digital reality that continues through time. With 3D photography, an online exhibition tour can feel almost real, and with these technologies, the past is propelled into the future. Past exhibitions available on museum websites provide important material for research, and as part of the digital ecosystem we all share, as we document past to present.

References

Ashley T (2017) Opera: passion, power and politics review—a game-changing spectacular show. The Guardian, 27 Sept 2017. https://www.theguardian.com/music/2017/sep/27/opera-passion-power-and-politics-victoria-and-albert-museum-review. Accessed on 26 Jan 2019

Bowen JP, Giannini T (2014). Digitalism: the new realism. In: Ng K, Bowen JP, McDaid S (eds) EVA London 2014 conference proceedings, Electronic Workshops in Computing (eWiC), BCS, pp 324–331. https://doi.org/10.14236/ewic/eva2014.38

Bucknell B (1993) On "Seeing" Salome. ELH 60(2):503–526, Summer 1993. JSTOR. http://www.jstor.org/stable/2873388. Accessed on 26 Jan 2019

Childs K (2018) A hundred years on from the 'cult of the clitoris' libel trial, let's remember that fake news is nothing new. The Independent, UK, 31 May 2018. https://www.independent.co.uk/news/long_reads/oscar-wilde-maud-allan-cult-of-the-clitoris-black-book-first-world-war-a8369811.html. Accessed 26 Jan 2019

EY Tate Arts Partnership (2013) The EY exhibition: Paul Klee. Press launch, 14 Oct 2013. https://www.ey.com/gl/en/about-us/our-sponsorships-and-programs/our-partnership-with-tate---making-visible--press-launch

Goldstein A (2018) Max Hollein on how the met will redefine the entire way we think about contemporary art. The freshly installed met director spoke to Andrew Goldstein about his plans for new art, new technology, and new funding at the museum. Artnet news, 25 Sept 2018. https://news.artnet.com/art-world/met-director-max-hollein-interview-part-2-1355749

Giannini T, Bowen JP (2016) Curating digital life and culture: art and information. In: Bowen JP, Diprose G, Lambert N (eds) EVA London 2016 conference proceedings, Electronic Workshops in Computing (eWiC), BCS, pp 237–244. https://doi.org/10.14236/ewic/eva2016.46

Gompertz W (2018) Will Gompertz reviews Charles I: King and Collector. BBC News, 27 Jan 2018. http://www.bbc.com/news/entertainment-arts-42830544. Accessed on 2 Jan 2019

Gotthardt A (2016) A brief history of Bauhaus Master and Father of Abstraction Paul Klee. Artsy, 25 Apr 2016. https://www.artsy.net/article/artsy-editorial-what-you-need-to-know-about-paul-klee. Accessed on 2 Jan 2019

Huang B (2017) Thinking through machines at MoMA. CoBo Social, Nov 2017. https://www.cobosocial.com/dossiers/thinking-through-machines-moma/. Accessed on 3 Jan 2019

Hudson M (2018) Picasso 1932, Tate Modern, review: the artist as you've never seen him before. The Telegraph, 6 Mar 2018. https://www.telegraph.co.uk/art/what-to-see/picasso-1932-tate-modern-review-artist-never-seen/. Accessed on 2 Jan 2019

Jones J (2018) Charles I: King and Collector review—majestic collection fit for an unfit king. The Guardian, 22 Jan 2018. https://www.theguardian.com/artanddesign/2018/jan/22/charles-i-king-and-collector-review-royal-academy-london. Accessed on 2 Jan 2019

Kettle M (2018) Don't mention the civil war: the English are still fighting it. The Guardian, 25 Jan 2018. https://www.theguardian.com/commentisfree/2018/jan/25/dont-mention-civil-war-english-still-fighting-charles-1-exhibition-royal-academy. Accessed on 2 Jan 2019

Messy Nessy (2018) Maud & the cult of the clitoris. Messy Nessy Chic, 29 June 2018. http://www.messynessychic.com/2018/06/29/maud-the-cult-of-the-clitoris/. Accessed on 2 Jan 2019

MetPublications (2018) Book titles with full-text online (569). MetPublications, Metropolitan Museum of Art, USA. https://www.metmuseum.org/art/metpublications/titles-with-full-text-online?searchtype=F. Accessed 21 Jan 2018

MoMA (n.d.) Picasso: forty years of his art. The Museum of Modern Art, USA, 15 Nov 1939–7 Jan 1940. https://www.moma.org/calendar/exhibitions/2843. Accessed on 2 Jan 2019

MoMA (2017) Club 57: film, performance, and art in the east village, 1978–1983. Museum of Modern Art, USA, 31 Oct 2017–8 Apr 2018. https://www.moma.org/calendar/exhibitions/3824. Accessed on 2 Jan 2019

Roffino S (2018) Why MoMA's exhibition of towering Brazilian modernist Tarsila do Amaral Misses the Mark. Artnet News, 1 Mar 2018. https://news.artnet.com/opinion/moma-tarsila-amaral-review-1234778. Accessed on 2 Jan 2019

Tate (2013) Paul Klee—making visible. The EY Exhibition, Tate Modern, 16 Oct 2013–9 Mar 2014. https://www.tate.org.uk/whats-on/tate-modern/exhibition/paul-klee-making-visible. Accessed 27 Jan 2019

Tate (2018) Tania Bruguera to undertake 2018 Hyundai Commission for the Turbine Hall. Tate, Press Release, 21 Feb 2018. http://www.tate.org.uk/press/press-releases/tania-bruguera-undertake-2018-hyundai-commission-turbine-hall. Accessed on 2 Jan 2019

Voon C (2018) Union workers rally at Tate Modern, Protesting Corporate Sponsor. Hyperallergic, 14 Apr 2018. https://hyperallergic.com/438279/union-worker-protest-tate-modern-corporate-sponsor/. Accessed on 2 Jan 2019

Wilson F (2018) Salome review—an injection of fresh blood for chilling, Gory Strauss. The Guardian, 9 Jan 2018. https://www.theguardian.com/music/2018/jan/09/salome-review-david-mcvicar-strauss-royal-opera-house. Accessed on 2 Jan 2019

Chapter 9
Rethinking Museum Exhibitions: Merging Physical and Digital Culture—Present to Future

Tula Giannini and Jonathan P. Bowen

Abstract As we move into the future, more than ever, museum exhibitions will ride the wave of rapidly advancing technologies, intrinsic to development across all fields and disciplines. We are entering the next wave of the digital revolution, having traveled from the 1940s at the dawn of computing and digital communication, to the 1960s' introduction of the Internet leading to the World Wide Web in the 1990s; we arrive at the present where all media has gone digital. We take a deep breath, as we travel into new territory where digital technologies and computing intrude into real life, capable of mimicking human expression and behavior. New digital devices talk to us in human sounding voices, and robots look and act like humans. Digital has become real, as it takes on human affordances which in turn deepens our relationship with virtual life. Increasingly, we live in altered states of being as we see art through a digital lens. Creating art with our digital tools, we use artificial intelligence, machine learning, augmented and virtual reality, while our sense of self morphs and imitates digital reality. Looking into the future, exhibitions will increasingly feature digital art capable of molding digital media into real-life immersive experiences, so that digital beings will become more real. What will be the effect on the human psyche? Will we love art more causing museums to attract larger audiences. Surely, radical change is upon us, as the unstoppable force of digital progression makes its way to the heart of the museum.

9.1 Introduction

This chapter traces digital and social developments through recent exhibitions focusing on those that the authors have viewed. We present new trends in museum exhibitions and some of the challenges tied to advances in computing that are

T. Giannini (✉)
School of Information, Pratt Institute, New York, USA
e-mail: giannini@pratt.edu

J. P. Bowen
School of Engineering, London South Bank University, London, UK
e-mail: jonathan.bowen@lsbu.ac.uk

Southwest University, Chongqing, China

T. Giannini and J. P. Bowen (eds.), *Museums and Digital Culture*,
Springer Series on Cultural Computing, https://doi.org/10.1007/978-3-319-97457-6_9

growing exponentially and concurrently with social activism, which taken together is driving change at an unparalleled pace. We explore exhibitions using mixed media to those that are fully digital, and show how digital art in museums, to digital media displays in public places are challenging the notion of what is art. From mixed media and 3D video animation at the Whitney to digital remix of Klimt and Michelangelo at new museum venues in Paris and the Vatican respectively, artists are creating new digital experiences, and the self, a born-digital selfie. With exhibitions expanding into new places, audiences have more choices than ever in how they wish to experience art, and with the rise of populism, the need to attract larger, more divers audiences, museums feel compelled to find new strategies to remain relevant to contemporary culture—and our research shows that museums are beginning to do just that. The results of their efforts are becoming more visible as we see exhibitions featuring women artists, artists of color, and gender diversity, while seeing digital in exhibition galleries still awaits a clarion call to fully embracing the digital world, inside and outside the museum.

9.2 Mixed Media, Archives, and Performance

The Whitney exhibition, *Transmissions* 2018, features mixed media works by Nick Mauss that encompass aspects of installation, performance, experience art and archival collections. Taking up a large gallery at the Whitney Museum, it stages and reinterprets a 30-year period of American modernist ballet by creating a mixed-media space that is at once a dance performance and an art show of 2D and 3D real and digital materials that museum visitors view. Together this forms a 360-degree dance experience that both informs and challenges assumptions about ballet while engaging and delighting the visitors. Artist, choreographer Nick Mauss talks about his work in a video produced for the exhibition and seen on the Whitney's website.

> My name is Nick Mauss. We're in rehearsal for my exhibition *Transmissions*. The exhibition is conceived in many layers – you'll see photographs, films, dancers, museum visitors, projections and sculptures – together with a group of dancers I've been collaborating with on a new sequence. The focus of the show is a moment in the history of New York where ballet and the avant-garde reacted very intensely with one another, roughly in the 1930s to 1950s. A lot of people have associations of rigidity and purity when they think about ballet, but in fact it's something that is constantly scraping against itself and breaking open and reinventing itself. Most of the works in this show are images of bodies – then there is also a few buildings, you have these shifts in scale, these kind of doll-sized objects and miniaturized skyscrapers that then stand in relation to the viewers body, the dancers body…
>
> What you'll see is a performance that doesn't really have a beginning or an end – you might arrive at a moment where the dancers are just warming up.

A database of some 826 photographs by Carl Van Vechten of star ballet dancers have been reformatted into a digital slide-show using large-scale projections with timed changes of images. This digital show is seen on the wall opposite the dance floor area making an especially effective juxtaposition of time and space. Transmission

Fig. 9.1 *Transmissions*, Gallery view of exhibition at the Whitney Museum by Nick Mauss, a multi-dimensional exploration of the American modernist ballet, 1930s to 50s featuring live performance, film projections, photography and a range of archival materials. (Photograph by Tula Giannini, May 10, 2018)

reimagines use of gallery space so that visitors are at once viewers, participants and audience of this immersive dance experience (Fig. 9.1).

9.2.1 Art and Archives Recreates East Village Life

The East Village of the 1970s and 1980s comes alive in MoMA's 2018 exhibition "*Club 57: Film, Performance, and Art in the East Village, 1978–1983*" which the museum describes as, "the first major exhibition to fully examine the scene-changing, interdisciplinary life of this seminal downtown New York." Drawing on the archives of Club 57, the exhibition is designed to recreate the its ambiance and milieu, so that visitors entering the galleries feel the sense at the club. The richness of the film collections on view, made possible through the digitization of film and sound recordings, are in this case and generally, invaluable as a means to recapture and document important art movements. At this exhibition, the audience has an inside view of a moment in the New York art scene and as well sheds light on the LGBT movement and digital culture.

9.2.2 Restoration on View

In 2016, in celebration of the Musée d'Orsay's 30th anniversary, the museum inaugurated a program to restore works in its collection that had not been displayed since the museum opened in 1986 as works are not generally exhibited that are fragile and damaged in ways that detract from their artistic and aesthetic value. The program's goals were to restore several large and medium sized paintings not seen before expanding the range of collections and to exhibit the restored paining to coincide with the opening of new galleries in 2018. To bring attention to this project, the museum created a restoration space on public view so that visitors could see painting restoration in process, watching conservators at work.

The conservation or restoration of museum objects generally takes place in conjunction with mounting an exhibition as museums avoid displaying works in poor condition. Thus, before works are displayed they are analyzed for condition. Allowing the public to view and understand this process, which increasingly involves digital instruments to identify which treatments will be most appropriate and allow for the least invasive techniques and ideally, are reversible. Digital techniques and principles for the conservation and preservation of digital art is addressed in depth in Chap. 11 (Fig. 9.2).

9.3 Exhibitions Across Digital Space and Time

9.3.1 Interactive Digital Art—Art and Audience Connect

The Glass Room London (https://theglassroom.org) is an innovative type of "gallery" popup exhibition space that attracted thousands of visitors to participate in an exhibition co-sponsored by Mozilla and Tactical Technology Collective focusing on individual users, the Internet and social media looking at questions of privacy and identity, posing the question:

> What is personal data in an age where data is everything but personal? The Glass Room is a space for reflection, experimentation and play that provides different ways of understanding how technologies and data are changing our lives. Here you can find content divided in the thematic exhibition areas. … The projects displayed here present more speculative and playful ways of visualizing the uses and misuses of our data. You are invited to experiment and reconsider the idea that even if we think we might have nothing to hide, we should at least understand what we're not hiding.

In the jam-packed gallery, with people waiting in line on the street, visitors participated in a wide range of activities, games and workshops that sharpened their awareness of their digital surroundings (Fig. 9.3).

Fig. 9.2 Restoration in process of a large painting by Adolf Schreyer (German, 1928–1899), Musée d'Orsay, Paris, *Charge of the Artillery of the Imperial Guard* in Traktir, Crimea, August 16, 1855. (Photograph by Tula Giannini, July 23, 2016)

9.4 Digital Installation Connects Fashion to Master Art Works

The Gucci fashion house is marketing its 2018 collection drawing inspiration from master art works through the use of "massive digital installations in stores across the world". Gucci's flagship boutique on via Montenapoleone in Milan has large digital screens in its windows designed to delight and engage passers-by as they view Gucci's remake of Ophelia by John Everett Millais (c. 1852). Other works in the remix series is the "Garden of Earthly Delights" by Hieronymus Bosch (1480–1490). Gucci describes his concept saying, "A large screen will show an animated digital illustration, as if it were an artwork in a gallery. On most windows, this impression is reinforced by the presence of a bench facing the screen on which colored velvet-covered mannequins will sit, as if looking at the art hung on a gallery wall" (Bateman 2018). The conceptual model of mixing past and present inspired by digital thinking invites new interpretations and meanings conveying new meaning and greater relevance.

Fig. 9.3 Street view of the Glass Room from its Charring Cross gallery window. (Photograph by Tula Giannini, November 11, 2017)

9.4.1 From the Internet to the Museum Gallery

Although much progress has been made in bringing digital into the gallery, the relationship between museums, digital artists and the public remains a work in progress that is challenging traditional exhibition practices that hark back to traditional collection-centered principals along with the preservation and curation of digital art while at the very time digital art had entered a period of intense creativity, innovation and the rapid adoption of emerging technologies across all forms of communication, information and experience. Living within the digital ecosystem, museums are being swept into a digital tide that encompasses museum life onsite and online so that seeing and being digital in museums is shared by both artist and audience who increasingly are using digital and mixed media art to communicate their message.

9.4.2 *Augmented Reality Meets MoMA's Pollack Gallery*

A group of eight Internet artists working as an art collective, under the name MoMAR organized an unauthorized augmented reality (AR) show in MoMA's Jacksons Pollack gallery, called, "Hello, we're from the Internet" (DeGuerin 2018).

MoMAR created a smartphone AR application with specific images for each Pollack paintings on view in the gallery so that anyone with a smartphone could experience MoMAR's art superimposed over Pollack's paintings (Ollinger 2018). The gallery was abuzz with visitors intensely engaged in a highly animated visual experience, which provides a good example of what might be described as digital art "performances" at MoMA, where AR is used to transform the gallery experience.

> Museums have long dealt with unauthorized augmentations of their exhibitions, such as unofficial tours, but technology has opened up new possibilities for activists and art enthusiasts eager to have a part in shaping the museum-going experience. (Katz 2018)

9.4.3 *Digital Remix from Klimt to Michelangelo*

Digital infusion of galleries in the likes of AR, VR and IA will not doubt grow and develop creating new types of immersive and ways to communicate meaning and message of works of art, taking the concept of digitizing art into new territory, one in which masterworks are remixed and interpreted through digital media experiences. Two striking examples of recreating masterworks using digital techniques are experience by visitors at the Atelier des Lumières in Paris and the 2018 theatrical mixed reality production in Rome with *Universal Judgment: Michelangelo and the Secrets of the Sistine Chapel*.

9.4.4 *A New Type of Digital Museum in Paris—Seeing Art Through Light*

On April 13, 2018, Atelier des Lumières opened in Paris at 38 Rue Saint-Maur in the eleventh arrondissement featuring an inaugural exhibition on Gustav Klimt (Fig. 9.4).

As the term *lumières* suggests, the exhibition, produced by Culturespaces, a private company that manages museums and cultural heritage sites, constitutes a laser light show of grand proportions using visual space with surround sound, where visitors immerse themselves in the art of Klimt viewed as digital light renderings of his paintings (Digy 2018). Thus, through innovative digital thinking, Culturespaces has re-imagined their vision of the exhibition creating two museums referred to as

Fig. 9.4 *The Kiss*, by Gustav Klimt (1862–1918). Painted 1907–1908, this work is featured in the Klimt exhibition at the Atelier des Lumières, Paris, opened April 13, 2018, and marks 100 years since the painter's death. Wikimedia Commons, https://commons.wikimedia.org/wiki/File:Gustav_Klimt_017.jpg

"digital art centres"—the first, Carrières de Lumières in Les Baux-de-Provence, and the second, the Atelier des Lumières in Paris. Occupying a former foundry with 30,000 m^2 of gallery space, it is billed as the first Parisian museum created around digital light and music to achieve what the Atelier calls "a complete immersive experience" described as "more than a mere exhibition – it is a unique show, a feast for the senses mixing space, paintings and music."

A review of the Atelier and the exhibition by Artnet critic Kate Brown poses a key question in its title. "Is This the Future—or the End—of Art? A Selfie-Centric Art Space Opens in Paris With a Show of Klimt Projections." This makes connections with Culturespaces' president Bruno Monnier who "said in a statement that sensory-based, digital art experiences represent the future of art exhibitions: 'The passive observation of works of art is no longer relevant.'" (Brown 2018).

This begs the question, is this an art exhibition or art à la Disneyland? Described as an "Immersive Digital Exhibition," it was created by Gianfranco Iannuzzi, Renato Gatto, Massimiliano Siccardi with Luca Longobardi, a musical artist, composer of the exhibition's soundtrack drawn from compositions of Beethoven, Chopin and Wagner. A bigger than life show, it was produced using 140 light projectors that interpret the art of Klimt taking the viewer on a chronological journey by way of his best-known paintings. Michael Couzigou, Director of the Atelier, points out, "This is an entirely different type of experience from what you would get in a museum… It provokes a strong emotional response. As such, the Atélier has great potential as an educational space. Our priority is to open culture to everyone, and digital art allows this." Couzigou has future plans for an exhibition on street art saying that "It works really well when it's projected…We want to show art that captures the attention. And street art…it doesn't leave you indifferent." (Warde-Aldam 2018).

9.4.5 Digitizing the Sistine Chapel

With the blessings of the Pope, a Michelangelo digital extravaganza opened in March 2018 in Rome's Auditorium Conciliazione, a large 1,763-seat theater located close to the Vatican. The multimedia production directed by Marco Balich is known for his closing ceremony spectaculars for the Olympic games in Turin and Tokyo. With the collaboration of the Vatican providing high resolution scans of the Sistine Chapel, the music of Sting, a theater group and dancers, the digital Michelangelo takes on all the bells and whistles of a Disney-like experience. Although the show riled the rather conservative art critics in Rome, Balich responded noting that the work respected the artistic and historic authenticity, and the religious values of the Vatican in a manner that met with their approval and tried to dispel their fears that people would go to the show and not the Sistine Chapel in the real. According to the *National Catholic Register*, "The show is translated into nine languages and has sold more than 100,000 tickets. An agreement with the Vatican Museums is being discussed to include a joint ticket to visit the real Sistine Chapel, which continues to welcome 6 million visitors every year"—and in this instance, the close proximity of the digital to the real would make this coupling a convenient option for visitors—but will it succeed—or will play as does a Broadway show? (Cascone 2018) (Fig. 9.5).

9.5 Museum Directors and Artists Think Digital

When Art Leaders Network met in Berlin, April featured 2018 they featured a panel of museum directors in conversation with Hilarie Sheets of the New York Times. The lively discussion between Glen Lowry, Director of MoMA, Dr. Marcus Hilgert, Director of the Berlin Museum of the Ancient Near East Museum and Gary Tinterow, Director of the Museum of Fine arts Houston, brought insights into how museums of the future are evolving. A lively discussion presented by a distinguished panel of museum directors featuring Glenn Lowry, Director of the Museum of Modern Art in New York City, who spoke convincingly about the need "to learn to think digitally … and fundamentally rethink how we think."

Fig. 9.5 *Creation of Adam*, fresco painted by Michelangelo (1475–1564), Sistine Chapel ceiling (1508–1512), The Vatican, Rome, Italy. (Photograph by Jörg Bittner Unna, 2011, Wikimedia Commons, https://commons.wikimedia.org/wiki/File:%27Adam%27s_Creation_Sistine_Chapel_ceiling%27_by_Michelangelo_JBU33cut.jpg)

> I would just add, I think it's more than just content, I think the real issue for all of us in the museum world is to learn to think digitally so that what we're talking about is not simply the transformation of certain kinds of stories into different formats or the use of new technologies to deliver those stories, but the fundamentally rethink how we think, to move away from the kind of analog art history that we were all taught, hierarchical, sequential, to a more networked reconsidered manner of actually presenting works of art, so that we begin to move into a realm where the way in which we look at art, the way in which we display art, actually is no longer so analog and I think one of the great advents of digital technology is that it has begun to teach us how to imagine different relationships between objects and between viewers and objects and technology is simply the glue or the conduit by which those relationships can be developed, but we have to actually start thinking about the kinds of exhibitions we're doing in new and different ways. (Art Leaders Network 2018)

As the notion of thinking and speaking digitally in multi-dimensions is emerging rapidly, and in contrast to analog or linear thinking and storytelling—our once prevalent mode of messaging, we begin to open our minds to the richness and complexity of experiencing digital life as it plays out in our mixed-media digital ecosystem. Moving seamlessly through real and virtual space and time, human communication deeply engages with a post-text culture, dominated by visual and sound media. Public expression on Facebook, Twitter, YouTube and Instagram are common platforms for artistic expression reaching out to millions of subscribers so that digital expression becomes commonplace replacing written communication, as we speak to our computers, mobile phones and robots.

9.6 Digital Art Experienced in 2D, 3D, Augmented and Virtual Reality

9.6.1 Contemporary Art—New Voices and New Stories

Contemporary art brings new perspectives and ways of seeing art and by extension world, giving us the opportunity to hear artists speaking about their own work. One way this is being facilitated is with video recordings made specifically for an exhibition and that can be accessed via the museum's website. The authentic voice of the artist is invaluable to visitor understanding and experience of the works on view and helps them establish personal connections. Further, museums continue to expand the range of exhibited works that can be studied online. Virtual tours of exhibition galleries also promote learning, and taking that a step further, video that provides virtual tours by artists speaking impromptu about how they create and think about their work, methods and techniques, gives visitors a framework for their onsite experience.

9.6.2 When Art Morphs into Alternative Realities—From a Fantasy World to the Art World

Vince Kadlubeck, CEO of Meow Wolf, an artist collective and for-profit production company, is the creator of the House of Eternal Return, a grand Victorian house for large-scale shows in Sante Fe, New Mexico that can be described as a Disney-like museum that serves up "a unique art experience featuring an astonishing new form of non-linear storytelling that unfolds through exploration, discovery and 21st-century interactivity" (quoted from Meow Wolf website, https://santafe.meowwolf.com/). The mention of, "non-linear storytelling" makes connection with Glen Lowry's statement quoted above contrasting thinking analog to thinking digital and juxtaposing works in unexplored ways to infuse them with fresh ideas that reveal new ways of seeing. This venue will no doubt appeal to digital natives who seek innovative ways to experience art and new art to experience. "Kadlubeck envisions a future where the lines between things like art, theme parks, role-playing games, and augmented reality will be blurred. The emerging term, he explains, is 'alternative reality'. For Meow Wolf, this will mean providing a multitude of alternative reality experiences that are, for the audience, spontaneous and unpredictable." In the words of

> Kadlubeck 'I think that Museum of Ice Cream, Meow Wolf, and immersive theater are all just precursors to what is about to really pop-off for everyone, I don't even know if it's art anymore. There's a whole way of being that's going to be shifting soon.' (Lesser 2018)

9.6.3 Artificial Intelligence

The exhibition, *Artists and Robots* at the Grand Palais, Paris, 5 April 2018–9 July 2018, is described as "an opportunity to experience works of art produced with the help of increasingly sophisticated robots. Featuring works by some forty artists, it offers a gateway to an immersive and interactive digital world – an augmented body sensory experience that subverts our notions of space and time." Covering the period 1956 to 2018, the show illuminates 60 years of artists' research that delve into creative ways to use AI applications to make programmed robotic art works across all media including photography, painting, video, installation, architecture and design (Quoted from the exhibition website, https://www.grandpalais.fr/en/event/artists-robots).

For science author, Laura Spinney, the exhibition poses the question, "can a robot create a work of visual art?" (Spinney 2018). Taking a chronological approach, the exhibition guides visitors on a journey from the 1950s to present. A 60-year period, it parallels that of the digital revolution sparked by the introduction of artificial intelligence and machine learning invented by Shannon and Turing in the 1940s, to development of the Internet and web, while the exhibition culminates with the theme, "The robot emancipates itself," a premise challenged by Spinney's question about robots and creativity (Giannini and Bowen 2017). An example of programmed process art is seen in the work of artist, Joan Fontcuberta. Using algorithms, she creates a computer-generated 3D painting from a 2D landscape painting by the French impressionist, André Derain under the title, *Orogenesis: Derain* (2004), referring to the process of mountain formation and its impact on patterns of the Earth's crust, bringing to mind Alan Turing's theory of morphogenesis in the context of chemistry, cell formation and patterns. Increasingly digital artists are channeling great artists of the past to reinvent works using new and exciting digital forms that imbue them with contemporary identities and contexts.

Digital Dimensionality and Reality by Tula Giannini

Screens are flat
not fat
A 2D experience
not much variance
Moving into another dimension
not to mention
3D—that's you and me
Step out of the screen
into space
Digital reality
alternative and augmented
not cemented
but invented
digital experience
not subversive or coercive

but a mash-up
of artificial intelligence
with machine learning
and relevance
concerning
the shape of digital culture
Art as digital sculpture
Digital life soon to be
the new reality.

9.6.4 A 3D Video Animation by Olivares at the Whitney, a Teddy Bear in Conversation with the Audience

The 3D video animation, Moléculas, a 2017 work created by Juan Antonio Olivares, a young Puerto Rican artist, born 1988, was on view at the Kaufman Gallery, the featured work of the Olivares exhibition at the Whitney Museum during spring 2018. The video, made using the animation software Cinema 4D, brings a stuffed teddy bear to life as a reincarnation of his beloved father. Casting overtones of a Disney-like character, the teddy bear speaks in his father's voice, which the artist digitally captured during an interview. The work's predominately black and white palette punctuated with splashes of color used for heightened emotion, reflect the somber mood of the approaching moment of this father's death. The Moléculas exhibition on the Whitney's website presents an audio recording of Olivares speaking about the making of the video in which reveals his thinking on why he chose 3D digital animation to represent his artistic vision.

> I was interested in animation in this way and delving so deeply into it was because of that freedom that I felt in the digital space of these programs you don't have material constraints you just basically have your imagination and your commitment to realizing that side of your imagination I also really like that everything in its usual space or an animation space is intentional…
>
> I felt that the story was basically asking for how much more imaginative approach to images from me I thought the story was asking of me to delve deeper into making these images from a somewhat more visceral place and animation was the way to create that for me.

Using 3D animation allows the audience to enter into video space, a place Olivares digitally replicates, taking inspiration from a Le Corbusier image of an apartment by which he captures a moment in time at once past and present, as the teddy bear speaks personally to the audience and himself.

9.7 Alternative Spaces

9.7.1 Turning Times Square into a Digital Art Exhibition Space

Since 2012, Times Square Arts has presented *Midnight Moment* billed as "the world's largest, longest-running digital art exhibition, synchronized on electronic billboards throughout Times Square nightly from 11:57 pm to midnight. Presented by the Times Square Advertising Coalition… it has an estimated annual viewership of 2.5 million."

The Times Square Streaming Museum (http://streamingmuseum.org), a networked museum, produces and presents contemporary-themed exhibitions of international multi-media arts, innovative ideas and related programs to a global audience via mobile devices, a network of big screens worldwide, and at cultural and public centers. Since its launch on January 29, 2008, exhibitions have been viewed on big screens in over 55 cities on seven continents. Programs are generated in collaboration with a variety of cultural and educational organizations, prominent and emerging visual and performing artists, curators, and visionaries across fields.

The digital artwork of Carla Gannis (see also Chap. 19), *Portraits in Landscape* was showcased for Midnight Moment during August 2018, creating fantastical moving portraits that reach back to the painting of Giuseppe Arcimboldo, a 16th-century mannerist painter unique for creating portraits formed from collages of fruits, vegetables, fish, animals and books. Gannis then travels through time and space to connect with the groundbreaking work of Ada Lovelace, the 18th-century female computer scientist, returning to 21st-century digital life as Ava. Gannis writes, "Times Square's history and present are saturated with technology and communication. We see it in the spectacular electronic billboards that compose our digital landscape, and in the hands of the millions of people who make it the second-most Instagrammed place in the world." (Times Square Arts 2018). "Carla Gannis is an artist who is thinking deeply and playfully about the relationship between our smartphone culture and our nature. Exhibiting this work as a part of Midnight Moment closes the loop between the people on our plazas and our unique environment." (Times Square Arts 2018).

Writing about her art, Gannis explains her thinking and process wrought from digital art and life using 3D models, avatars and selfies, while referencing 16th-century painting. Here, we gleam the artist's perspectives firsthand.

> *Portraits in Landscape*, a single-channel video from my "After Arcimboldo" series, is a continuation of my focus on combining eccentric art-historical references with visual smartphone language. Through this process I reflect on the constructions and perceptions of identity in contemporary culture. Unlike the subjects of Arcimboldo's paintings, the portraits in this series are not of aristocrats and wealthy patrons. Instead they began as 3D models, the avatars of our age, that I digitally shaped into selfie poses. I then overlaid the models with hundreds of emoji, similar to Arcimboldo's process of using everyday objects to sculpt uncanny human likenesses. Bringing the portraits to life in a hyper landscape teeming with "digital nature" expresses my fascination with how virtual and physical embodiments intersect in our networked communication age. (Times Square Arts 2018) (Fig. 9.6)

Fig. 9.6 *Portraits in Landscape* by Carla Gannis, on view for *Midnight Moment*, Times Square, August 2018. (Photograph by Carla Gannis, with artist's permission)

9.7.2 New York Street and Stores Become a Gallery Experience

Virtual Reality (VR) can turn any place into a personal gallery experience since it exists in digital space (see Fig. 9.8), while digital display screens can transform public spaces into gallery-like space (see Fig. 9.8) (Fig. 9.7).

9.7.3 From the Street to the Gallery—Welcoming Smartphone Data for Exhibition Planning

Museums once reluctant to allow Wi-Fi and cellphones in galleries, now welcome this digital intrusion as it can provide useful data for gauging audience behavior. For example, by gathering data on Wi-Fi use in galleries, the Chicago Art Institute was able to more customize its exhibition programming. The data revealed that offering small scale exhibitions over a short time period not only increased visitor numbers significantly and but also showed that overall, visitors spent more gallery time at new installations. Jacqueline Terrassa, woman's board endowed chair of learning and public engagement noted that the Institute is "focused on building something new for you to do each time you walk through the doors of the Art Institute," adding that, "It's a whole experience of engagement, interpretations and education – a menu of experiences." (Bertagnoli 2018). This also speaks to visitor expectations for things new to discover and explore and providing this more dynamic environment mounting small rotating exhibitions à la gallery style. This also creates opportunities for digital art exhibitions and the in-gallery use of virtual and augmented reality, interactive active art, robotic art, and other emerging technologies used for art and visitor experience (Fig. 9.9).

Fig. 9.7 Street view of a Virtual Reality (VR) demonstration at the Microsoft store on 5th avenue, New York. On the left is a large digital media screen. From the store front window, passers-by can see a three-story digital display. The VR experience is gradually coming to a museum near you—"Discover a new way to go beyond." (Photograph by Tula Giannini, March 24, 2017)

Going to Exhibitions by Tula Giannini

Going to exhibitions
immersed in a super-reality
three dimensionality
At once real and virtual
Traveling through time and space
from past to present
speeding into the future
On a V&A ocean liner
from New York to London
to hear Opera and Pink Floyd

Fig. 9.8 Digital media display installation at Macy's 34th St., New York City. The height of the digital light columns changes every few seconds, sometimes also having fashion images. Digital media displays are interwoven throughout Macy's ground floor with entrance on 6th avenue and 7th avenue. Visitors/customers respond to these as though they were in a museum—viewing and capturing displays with their smartphones. Incorporating digital into the customer experience seems to be creating a festive mood for buying. (Photograph by Tula Giannini, February 27, 2018)

Seeing Picasso and
Modigliani at the Tate
Can't wait for
Paris and Miro
Don't know
what's next.
Exhibitions permeate
visions and views
Seeing art
on streets and walls,
in parks and stores
Can't stop seeing
Digital screens
Streaming images and stories
Living in art
Is living life
and its glories.

Fig. 9.9 *Galleries, Musée*—Pompidou Center, Paris. Lights, action, crowds of people going to exhibitions. (Photograph by Tula Giannini, November 16, 2017)

9.8 Conclusion

With the proliferation of digital media displays and installations embedded in everyday places, people are experiencing gallery-like environments as if department stores and other public spaces were imitating museums as life imitates art. Life in the fast lane of digital culture immerses people in visual environments soaked in digital color, sound and moving images. Increasingly these are mirrored in the real space of city streets and places, that are connected to the shared platforms of our digital ecosystem to which museums too are connected.

Museums need not only acknowledge these connections but use them to advantage for building communities and social networks with the goal of reaching-out to broader more diverse audiences, exchanging information and increasing awareness of exhibitions and the activities surrounding them. Pursing these goals, museums will be able to touch the inner being of visitors in inspiring and life-changing ways. Already, museums have exited the elitist models of the past, and have entered into the realm of digital culture—now it is a question of how to create exhibitions, that whether historical or contemporary, see through the digital lens of the 21st-century to fully engage and find commonalities with their audiences and ways for them to participate as partners in a shared cultural enterprise (Fig. 9.10).

Fig. 9.10 *"Explore art from the Tate collection – touch any moving word or image on the screen to begin."* From children to teenagers and adults, this digital interactive display screen attracts crowds of visitors who learn about the collections. (Photograph by Tula Giannini, March 19, 2018)

References

Art Leaders Network (2018) The future of art museums. 2018 panel discussions. The New York Times, Art Leaders Network. https://www.nytartleadersnetwork.com/aln2018/gallery. Accessed 2 Jan 2019

Atelier des Lumières (n.d.) Immersive exhibition: Gustav Klimt. http://www.atelier-lumieres.com/en/gustav-klimt. Accessed on 2 Jan 2019

Bateman K (2018) Hieronymous Bosch and Ophelia Drowning get a Gucci remix. Hyperallergenic, 8 Mar 2018. https://hyperallergic.com/431448/gucci-ophelia-millais/. Accessed on 2 Jan 2018

Bertagnoli L (2018) Art institute uses data to give visitors what they want. Crain's Chicago Business, 18 May 2018. Chicago Business. http://www.chicagobusiness.com/article/20180518/issue01/180519840

Bowen JP, Giannini T, Polmeer G (2017) Coded communication: digital senses and aesthetics, merging art and life. In: Bowen JP, Diprose G, Lambert N (eds) EVA London 2017 conference proceedings, Electronic Workshops in Computing (eWiC), BCS, pp 1–8. https://doi.org/10.14236/ewic/eva2017.1

Brown K (2018) Is this the future—or the end—of art? A selfie-centric art space opens in Paris with a show of Klimt projections. The new Atelier des Lumières opens with light installations inspired by Klimt and Schiele. Artnet News, 13 Apr 2018. https://news.artnet.com/exhibitions/atelier-des-lumieres-1264601. Accessed on 2 Jan 2019

Cascone S (2018) Sistine Chapel, the ride? See inside Michelangelo's Masterpieces in Rome's high-tech theatrical production. Artnet News, 3 Oct 2018. https://news.artnet.com/art-world/giudizio-universale-michelangelo-sistine-chapel-1360087. Accessed on 26 Jan 2019

DeGeurin M (2018) Internet artists invaded the MoMA with a guerrilla augmented reality exhibit. Motherboard, 5 Mar 2018. https://motherboard.vice.com/en_us/article/8xd3mg/moma-augmented-reality-exhibit-jackson-pollock-were-from-the-internet. Accessed on 2 Jan 2019

Digby WA (2018) A new immersive installation in Paris lets you step inside Klimt's Masterpieces. Artsy, 23 Apr 2018. https://www.artsy.net/article/artsy-editorial-new-immersive-installation-paris-step-inside-klimts-masterpieces. Accessed on 26 Jan 2019

Giannini T, Bowen JP (2017) Life in code and digits: when Shannon met Turing. In: Bowen JP, Diprose G, Lambert N (eds) EVA London 2017 conference proceedings, Electronic Workshops in Computing (eWiC), BCS, pp 51–58. https://doi.org/10.14236/ewic/eva2017.9

Katz M (2018) Augmented reality is transforming museums. Wired Magazine, Apr 2018. https://www.wired.com/story/augmented-reality-art-museums/. Accessed on 26 Jan 2019

Lesser C (2018) A new breed of immersive art experiences offers a gateway to alternative realities. Artsy, 21 May 2018. https://www.artsy.net/article/artsy-editorial-new-breed-immersive-art-experiences-offers-gateway-alternative-realities. Accessed on 26 Jan 2019

Ollinger C (2018) Augmented reality 'Gallery' at MoMA allows viewers to virtually alter art—a non-profit artist group developed an AR app that allows the public to interact with Jackson Pollock's paintings. PSFK, 8 Mar 2018. https://www.psfk.com/2018/03/momar-augmented-reality-gallery-moma.html. Accessed on 2 Jan 2019

Spinney L (2018) Can robots make art? Nature 557:490–491, 27 Apr 2018. https://doi.org/10.1038/d41586-018-04989-2

Times Square Arts (2018) Portraits in landscape, 1 Aug 2018 – 31 Aug 2018. Times Square, USA. http://arts.timessquarenyc.org/times-square-arts/projects/midnight-moment/portraits-in-landscape/index.aspx. Accessed 2 Jan 2019

Warde-Aldam D (2018) A new immersive installation in Paris lets you step inside Klimt's masterpieces. Artsy, 23 Apr 2018. https://www.artsy.net/article/artsy-editorial-new-immersive-installation-paris-step-inside-klimts-masterpieces. Accessed on 2 Jan 2019

Part IV
Collections

Chapter 10
Collecting, Documenting, and Exhibiting the Histories of Digital Art: A V&A Perspective

Douglas Dodds

Abstract The Victoria and Albert Museum (V&A) is the UK's national museum of art and design. In its early years as the South Kensington Museum, the institution was involved with various initiatives that bridged art and science. The modern V&A acquired its first computer-generated images as long ago as 1969. Following the acquisition of the archives of the Computer Arts Society (CAS) and the Patric Prince Collection in the mid-2000s, the Museum now holds the UK's national collection of early digital art. The V&A's computational art collection includes some 2,000 prints, drawings, photographs and born-digital works, created from the 1960s to the present day (Dodds and Beddard 2010). Pioneering computer artists include Georg Nees, Frieder Nake, A. Michael Noll, Vera Molnár, Manfred Mohr, Colette and Charles Bangert, Harold Cohen and Paul Brown, who were followed by Roman Verostko, Mark Wilson, Barbara Nessim, William Latham and others. The Museum also holds recent born-digital artworks by artists such as Casey Reas, Aaron Koblin, Daniel Brown and Andy Lomas. V&A exhibitions and displays include *Decode* and *Digital Pioneers* (both 2009/10), plus *Chance and Control: Art in the Age of Computers* (2018). This chapter outlines some of the issues involved in acquiring, maintaining, documenting and exhibiting a diverse range of physical and digital artworks created with code.

10.1 Introduction

The Victoria and Albert Museum (V&A) is the UK's national museum of art, design and performance. Established after the Great Exhibition of 1851, the Museum of Manufactures soon changed its name to the South Kensington Museum. In its early years the institution was involved with various initiatives that bridged art and science, and it was also one of the first museums to embrace new technologies such as photography and electrotyping.

D. Dodds (✉)
Victoria and Albert Museum, London, UK
e-mail: d.dodds@vam.ac.uk

T. Giannini and J. P. Bowen (eds.), *Museums and Digital Culture*,
Springer Series on Cultural Computing, https://doi.org/10.1007/978-3-319-97457-6_10

The V&A's Word and Image Department (WID) was established in the early 2000s, with the merger of the National Art Library (NAL) and the Prints, Drawings, Paintings and Photographs Department (PDP). Word and Image now holds more than a million artworks, including an increasing range of computer-generated works from the early 1960s to the present day. Nowadays, WID is responsible for collecting digital art, while the Museum's Design, Architecture and Digital Design Department (DAD) collects examples of digital design.

In practice though, the boundaries of digital art are quite hard to define, not least because of the overlapping concepts, formats and specialisms that exist. The new medium is also beset with a bewildering range of terms to describe particular genres, styles or movements. In brief, I use the term "computer art" to refer to early works made with the help of computer hardware or software, from the late 1950s to the 1970s or thereabouts. The same term is often applied to more recent works too, if they exhibit some of the same characteristics. In practice though, computer art and computer graphics overlap considerably, especially in the early period before different specialisms and professions emerged. More recently, the term "digital art" tends to be applied to born-digital works that don't have a specific practical function. Somewhat confusingly, it can also be used to indicate the whole field of computer-generated art, from early computer art to contemporary interactive pieces that explore recent developments in digital technologies. In contrast, "digital design" focusses on the practical use of these technologies in real-world applications.

10.2 Collecting

The V&A collected its first computer-generated images as long ago as 1969, when it bought a portfolio of seven prints published in association with a landmark exhibition, *Cybernetic Serendipity*, held at London's Institute of Contemporary Arts in 1968. The set included two works by the Computer Technique Group (CTG), plus individual works by Charles Csuri, William Fetter, Maughan S. Mason, Donald Robbins and Kerry Strand. However, the V&A's acquisition records reveal that there had been some reluctance to buy them at all. Indeed, one curator even described the computer artworks as a "characteristic aberration". In the end, though, the Museum paid a grand total of £5 for the complete set (Dodds 2015a, b). One of the prints by CTG, Running Cola is Africa (V&A CIRC.770-1969), is now on semi-permanent display in the Museum's Toshiba Gallery of Japanese art and design, while others have been lent to exhibitions throughout Europe in recent years. As described in more detail below, the *Cybernetic Serendipity* prints have also featured in various V&A exhibitions and displays, including *Digital Pioneers* (2009–10) and *Chance and Control* (2018).

After the initial burst of activity in 1969, the Museum's computer-generated holdings grew slowly in subsequent years. In 1978, the V&A acquired two prints by Manfred Mohr (born 1938), from the artist's *Scratch Code* series. A few years later, the V&A obtained its first computer-generated artwork created by a woman—*Homage à Béla Bartók*, a screenprint after a plotter drawing by Vera Molnár (born 1929).

The print by Molnár (E.528-1981) was in a portfolio of works by various artists, published to celebrate the life of the Hungarian composer. Molnár had also been born in Hungary but settled in Paris and started to use computers in the late 1960s, at much the same time as Manfred Mohr (Lenz 2017; Taylor 2014).

Very few computer-generated artworks were acquired by the V&A in the following decade or two, and the collection grew very slowly until the early years of the 21st century. At that point, a mixture of institutional, managerial and personal factors contributed to a significant shift in emphasis. The Museum's new Director, Mark Jones, decided to merge various curatorial departments, including the Prints, Drawings and Paintings collection and the National Art Library. After more than a decade in a senior role in the NAL, I found myself in the newly created Word and Image Department. I had previously been responsible for automating the Library's activities, establishing an online catalogue of the collection and launching the first website in the Museum. I had also worked in art colleges and universities in the past, managing large computer systems and working alongside academics who were introducing computer graphics into the curriculum. In parallel, I had also developed an interest in the impact of new technology on art and design.

At much the same time, the Computer Art Context History Etc project (CACHe) had started at Birkbeck, University of London, funded by the Arts and Humanities Research Board. CACHe's main focus was the archives of the Computer Arts Society (CAS), which had been established following the *Cybernetic Serendipity* exhibition of 1968. According to a CAS leaflet published at the time, the organization was founded to "promote the creative use of computers in the arts, and to encourage the interchange of information in this area." With this in mind, the Society published an influential newsletter called *PAGE*, the first editor of which was the German artist Gustav Metzger. CAS went on to organize various exhibitions, conferences and events, including *Event One* (1969) at the Royal College of Art and *Interact: Machine, Man, Society* (1973) at Edinburgh Festival. Along the way, the Society accumulated an important collection of artworks created by visiting artists, scientists and computer programmers. Although CAS's prominence waned in the 1980s, the collection was stored in the offices of System Simulation Limited for many years, until it was assessed by the CACHe project. The Society was reinvigorated, thanks to the work of Paul Brown, George Mallen and others. I became increasingly aware of CAS and its significance. The bulk of the collection was then donated to the V&A in 2008.

In parallel, the Museum also acquired another collection of some 250 artworks from Patric Prince, an American historian of digital art. Patric was responsible for organizing several key computer art exhibitions, including the SIGGRAPH Art Show retrospective in 1986. She has also written and lectured extensively on the subject (Prince 2003). Her husband, Bob Holzman, worked at the Jet Propulsion Laboratory in Pasadena, where he encouraged artists-in-residence such as David Em to use JPL's computer graphics facilities in the 1970s. Thanks to Paul Brown, I became aware of Patric's impressive collection in 2003 or thereabouts, and subsequently visited her home and lock-up storage facility in California. Patric had tried to interest other museums in the material she had accumulated, but none of them had been prepared to accept the collection in its entirety. As it happened, the creation of the V&A's Word and Image Department meant that we were uniquely placed to deal with such a diverse range of objects, including prints, drawings, photographs, books, manuscripts, ephemera and born-digital material. The Patric Prince Collection was donated to the American Friends of the V&A in 2005, and subsequently transferred to the Museum. Patric donated her extensive library and archive directly to the V&A too.

Following these two major acquisitions, the Museum suddenly held one of the world's largest and broadest collections of computer-generated art. Although other institutions had impressive holdings relating to particular artists or geographical areas, the broad coverage of the V&A's collection was—and probably still is—almost unique. In Europe, the nearest comparable collection is held at the Bremen Kunsthalle, which acquired the archive of Herbert Franke . The Zentrum für Kunst und Medien (ZKM) in Karlsruhe also has a significant collection that includes works by Nake, Nees and Kawano, among others. In practice, most of the earliest computer-generated artworks in the V&A collection (and indeed, the one in Bremen) are actually works on paper—in particular, prints, plotter drawings or photographs—rather than digital files (Fig. 10.1). However, we do have some computer programs too, including a set of FORTRAN punch cards (E.1459-2011) for Manfred Mohr's P-032 Matrix Elements, a print of which is also in the collection (E.245-2008). The Patric Prince Collection also contains a range of early born-digital works, such as the American artist Sonya Rapoport's *Shoe Field* installation on floppy disk (E.1012-2008).

The V&A's Collections Development Policy gives more information about the Department's holdings and acquisition priorities:

Fig. 10.1 *Pathway Series, Bird 2* (1990) and *Cyberflower, Sunshine Version I* (2008) by Roman Verostko (© Douglas Dodds)

> Until recently, the Museum held relatively few works that illustrate the early years of computer generated art and design. However, the Department now holds one of the world's largest collections of computer art, created from the 1950s onwards… We also collect born-digital artworks selectively, by artists such as Daniel Brown, Aaron Koblin and Casey Reas. The technological and logistical problems of preservation and display lead us to focus on works that require little or no active maintenance. Priority is given to digital works, or applications of digital technology, which extend our holdings in other media… (V&A 2015, pp. 59–60)

In 2011, the Museum acquired a generative digital artwork by Ernest Edmonds, entitled *Shaping Form 14/5/2007*. The work includes a Mac Mini, a square screen, a small camera, a bespoke Perspex frame created by the artist, and software that utilizes MaxMSP with Jitter. The artwork evolves in response to its environment; any movement detected by the camera produces changes in the program over time. The ways in which people move around the piece determine how the images are constructed, shaping the pattern, colors, and timing.

In 2016 the Museum acquired a group of artworks by Andy Lomas, who had featured in a one-person show at London's Watermans Gallery earlier that year. Lomas had also been the winner of the Lumen Prize in 2014, when the present author was one of the judges. V&A curators had thus been aware of Lomas's work for some time. The works in the V&A collection include large-format digital prints and video pieces, plus a stereoscopic version of the artist's Hybrid Forms. Lomas even supplied his own 3D-printed viewer, designed to work with a smartphone. As Lomas explains in more detail in Chap. 17, the acquisition process included detailed discussions about the practicalities of what works to collect, and how.

Increasingly, other V&A curatorial departments also collect born-digital material. The East Asia collection, for example, holds a range of projection mapping created by Korean artist Yiyun Kang, who undertook a residency at the Museum in 2015–16 (Kang 2018). The V&A's recently-established Design, Architecture and Digital Design Department has accumulated a diverse range of designed objects that also include a hardware and software element (Shannon 2014). Examples include Cody Wilson's infamous 3D-printed gun (2013) and the Flappy Bird mobile app (2014), both of which have been shown in the Museum's Rapid Response Collecting gallery.

10.3 Research

In collaboration with Birkbeck, we undertook a major research project entitled Computer Art and Technocultures, funded by the UK's Arts and Humanities Research Council (Dodds 2007; Lenz 2014). The project ran from 2007 to 2010, enabling the Museum to appoint a dedicated curator, Honor Beddard. The prime focus of the research was the recently-acquired Patric Prince collection, but the project also built upon the work of the earlier CACHe project undertaken by Birkbeck. One of the outputs was the *Digital Pioneers* show (2009/10), timed to coincide with *Decode: Digital Design Sensations* and described in more detail below. Another outcome was

Fig. 10.2 Artists attending the V&A's decoding the digital conference included (l to r): Karsten Schmidt, Casey Reas, James Faure Walker, Mark Wilson, Manfred Mohr, Roman Verostko and Frieder Nake (© Douglas Dodds)

a well-attended conference, *Decoding the Digital*, organized by Douglas Dodds and Honor Beddard in conjunction with the curators of the V&A's *Decode* exhibition, Louise Shannon and Shane Walter. Other speakers included Frieder Nake, Paul and Daniel Brown, Casey Reas, Karsten Schmidt, Beryl Graham, Hannah Redler, Bruce Wands, Roman Verostko, collectors Anne and Michael Spalter, and Patric Prince herself (Fig. 10.2).

Nearly a decade after *Digital Pioneers* and *Decoding the Digital*, I also organized a V&A symposium timed to coincide with *Chance and Control: Art in the Age of Computers*. Speakers in the first session included the curator of the original Cybernetic Serendipity exhibition, Jasia Reichardt, plus Frieder Nake (again) and myself. The second session started with Aaron Marcus, who worked at Bell Labs in the 1960s and went on to have a high-profile career as an information designer. Two artists who featured in the *Chance and Control* show, Andy Lomas and Esther Rolinson, each spoke about their art practice, while Charlie Gere explored the reasons why there seemed to be little or no information about early computer artists in China.

10.4 Documenting and Preserving

The V&A's Collection Management System (CMS), supplied by System Simulation Ltd, is used to record information about all newly-acquired objects. The Museum has recently installed a new Digital Asset Management System (DAMS) supplied by Aetopia, replacing the earlier VADAR software. All the digital artworks acquired by the Word and Image Department are catalogued in CMS, whilst the images and various other digital files are held in the Museum's new DAMS. The catalogue records and digital images are exported to the Museum's public catalogue, Search the Collections, which is updated daily (Fig. 10.3).

The Department's archival holdings—including the Patric Prince archive and the Computer Arts Society archive—are also recorded on the Collections Management System and made accessible to the public via a similar web service to Search the Collections, known as Search the Archives. Printed books and periodicals—including those acquired from Patric Prince—are listed in the National Art Library's online catalogue, which now utilizes OCLC's library management system.

Of course, acquiring, displaying and preserving a diverse range of digital artworks presents many challenges for museums. The V&A's Research Institute (VARI) recently embarked upon a project entitled Content/Data/Object, the aim of which is to "articulate ways in which museum practice and international cultural property law could adapt to accommodate and enable meaningful access to conceptual, ephemeral and immaterial digital artworks." Work started in 2017 with a finish date of 2020. As the project's web page (V&A, 2019) states:

> The V&A collects digital works in a wider variety of forms than any other cultural institution in the UK. Such collections and the challenge they present have been the subject of debate internationally, though solutions for cataloging and preserving them are still somewhat exper-

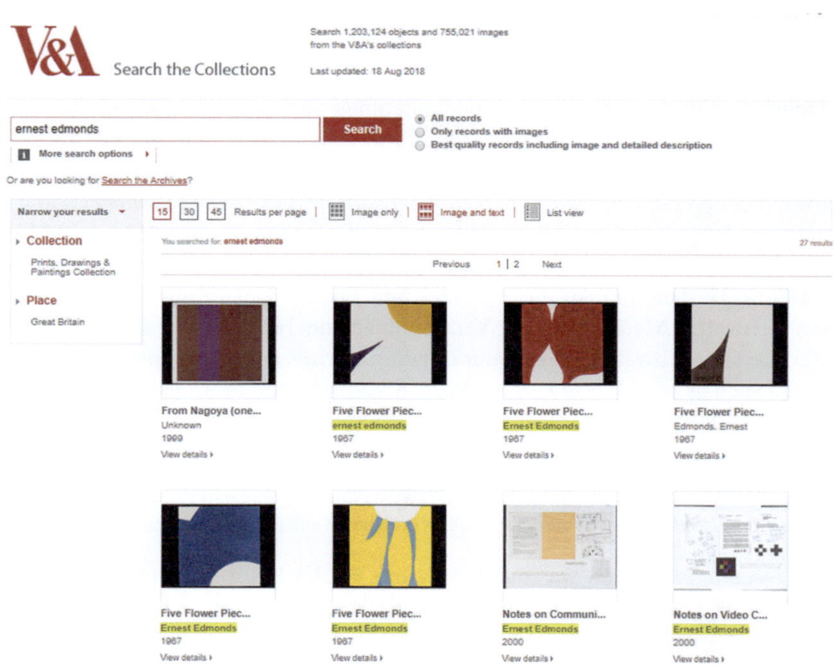

Fig. 10.3 V&A Search the Collections entries for Ernest Edmonds (Douglas Dodds/V&A)

Fig. 10.4 *Digital Pioneers* installation showing works from the 1960s and early 1970s, 2009–10 (© Douglas Dodds)

imental. Looking closely at the production and reception of such works, this project aims to find descriptive forms appropriate to collections management for the multiple dimensions, including time and experience, that they encompass.

10.5 Exhibiting

As mentioned above, one of the major outcomes of the AHRC-funded Computer Art and Technocultures project was *Digital Pioneers*, a display in the V&A's Prints and Drawings galleries during 2009/10. Timed to coincide with a contemporary exhibition called *Decode: Digital Design Sensations*, the *Digital Pioneers* show set out to provide an overview of the early years of computer-generated art (Beddard and Dodds 2009). Pioneering artists who featured included Ben Laposky, Desmond Paul Henry, Herbert Franke, Georg Nees and Frieder Nake, plus Ken Knowlton, Lillian Schwartz, Manfred Mohr, Vera Molnár and Harold Cohen (Dodds 2011, 2012). The show also included plotter drawings, prints and digital prints by leading Algorists such as Jean-Pierre Hébert, Roman Verostko and Mark Wilson (Fig. 10.4). It was particularly well-received and even generated a favourable review by Alice Rawsthorn in *The New York Times*:

> Compellingly simple and made with rudimentary technology, much of the work in "Digital Pioneers" is astonishingly beautiful and seems both brave and prescient… (Rawsthorn 2009)

The *Decode* exhibition was curated by the V&A's Louise Shannon, along with the creative director of onedotzero, Shane Walter. It provided a highly interactive showcase for works by Rafael Lozano-Hemmer, Golan Levin, John Maeda, Casey Reas, Troika (Eva Rucki, Conny Freyer and Sebastien Noel) and many others. At the end of the show's international tour, several artworks were acquired for the V&A's

Fig. 10.5 Transformations: digital prints from the V&A Collection, Great Western Hospital, Swindon 2012 (© Douglas Dodds)

permanent collection, including Daniel Brown's *On Growth and Form* (2009), Aaron Koblin's *Flight Patterns* (2009) and an updated version of Random International's *Study for a Mirror* (2009–10). We also acquired another piece by Casey Reas, *Process 18* (*Software 3*) (2010). This is currently on view in the foyer to the V&A's Sackler Centre, close to the Learning Department's digital studio. In practice, Reas's artwork also acts as a signpost to the Museum's digital art collection. Similarly, Aaron Koblin's *Flight Patterns* was previously shown in the entrance to the Learning Centre. Individual works are also shown at various locations throughout the Museum from time to time. *Shaping Form 14/5/2007* by Ernest Edmonds, for example, was exhibited in the V&A's new acquisitions gallery in 2012–13.

The V&A has also collaborated with Paintings in Hospitals, a charity that loans artworks to hospitals across the UK. *Transformations: Digital Prints from the V&A Collection*, was installed at the Great Western Hospital in Swindon in 2012, then a revised version was shown at the Royal Brompton Hospital in London in 2013 (Fig. 10.5). Artists who featured in one or both shows included Paul Brown, Ernest Edmonds, James Faure Walker and Mark Wilson. The V&A's Learning Department also organized various digital art activities for patients at the Royal Brompton, which is located quite close to the Museum.

One of the digital artists who features in the V&A's Patric Prince Collection is Barbara Nessim, an eminent American fine artist and illustrator. Some years after we acquired Patric's collection, I was introduced to Barbara when she visited the Museum to view some of the artworks. As a result, I became more aware of the impressive range of her activity as a digital artist from the early 1980s onwards. Barbara subsequently donated many more examples of her analogue and digital work, from the 1960s to the present day. The digital artworks include a range of photographs of computer-generated faces such as Ode to the Statue of Liberty, made at Time Inc. in the early 1980s, plus recent computer-manipulated collages for The Model Project. We marked the artist's generous donation with an unprecedented one-person show in the V&A's 20th century gallery, entitled *Barbara Nessim: An Artful*

Life (February–May 2013). I also curated a revised and much-expanded version, at the Bard Graduate Center in New York City (September 2014–January 2015) (Dodds 2013).

Opening in July 2018, an exhibition in the V&A's Prints and Drawings Galleries marked the 50th anniversary of Cybernetic Serendipity and the foundation of the Computer Arts Society. *Chance and Control: Art in the Age of Computers* featured several artists who contributed to the original ICA show—such as A. Michael Noll, Frieder Nake and Georg Nees—plus artworks and ephemera from the V&A's Computer Arts Society collection. It also offered an opportunity to show some of the wide range of significant artworks acquired in the decade since *Digital Pioneers*, by North American artists such as Colette and Jeff Bangert, Katharine Nash, Frederick Hammersley and Aaron Marcus, plus South Americans such as Miguel Ángel Vidal, Waldemar Cordeiro and his daughter, Analivia Cordeiro (Lenz 2014). British artists active in the 1970s and 1980s included Clive Richards, Darrell Viner, Dominic Boreham, Paul Brown and William Latham.

Chance and Control also provided a showcase for a range of recent works that complement, or were inspired by, the earlier generation of artists, scientists and computer programmers. Examples included plotter drawings, photographs and digital prints by artists such as Damien Borowik, Andy Lomas, Fabrizio Poltronieri and Esther Rolinson (Fig. 10.6). The show was scheduled to overlap with two major V&A exhibitions—*The Future Starts Here* (May–November 2018) and *Videogames: Design/Play/Disrupt* (September 2018–February 2019)—both of which explore significant aspects of digital art and design. Like the earlier *Digital Pioneers*, *Chance and Control* was surprisingly well-received for a relatively modest exhibition. It attracted a great deal of positive feedback on social media and one review, by Catherine Mason for Studio International, was particularly complimentary:

> Organised in-house and taken from the museum's own computer art holdings, Chance and Control: Art in the Age of Computers is a beautifully curated display of "artists and programmers [who] have used computers to create prints, drawings, paintings, photographs and digital artworks that explore aspects of chance and control". What is immediately apparent is the remarkable diversity of this collection and how it has grown from early beginnings in just 10 years. (Mason 2018)

The show closed in November 2018, with a UK tour during 2019–20. However, some of the plotter drawings in the original version are quite fragile or light-sensitive and will have to be replaced with more robust prints or photographs by the same artists.

Of course, the museum is clearly unable to collect everything. Instead, we continue to undertake an ambitious range of events and temporary installations that present aspects of digital art and craft to new and existing audiences. The V&A's Digital Design Weekend brings together artists, designers, engineers, technologists and the public to celebrate and share contemporary digital art and design, engage in conversations, and learn about processes. Established in 2012, Digital Futures is a series of innovative events, some of which are held at the V&A and others are located elsewhere. Irini Papadimitriou has explained that the programme was initiated as "an open platform for displaying and discussing work by researchers, artists, designers,

Fig. 10.6 *Chance and Control* installation, showing works by Mark Wilson, Damien Borowik, Andy Lomas and Fabrizio Poltronieri, 2018 (© Douglas Dodds)

companies and other professionals working with art, technology, design, science and beyond" (Papadimitriou 2015). One of the most recent temporary exhibitions is *Artificially Intelligent* (V&A, September 7–December 31, 2018), which explored our complex relationships with technology and AI. Curated by Irini Papadimitriou, it included works by Katriona Beales, Kate Crawford, Vladan Joler, Fabio Lattanzi Antinori, Maral Pourkazemi, Anna Ridler, Caroline Sinders, Nye Thompson and Cecilie Waagner Falkenstrøm.

For many years, the Museum has also commissioned temporary exhibitions and displays of digital art and design—in the garden, throughout the buildings, or online. In many cases, the artworks selected could not be added to the permanent collection, principally because of the range of complex issues that they might manifest. Indeed, some of the Museum's most successful born-digital exhibitions have been ephemeral, with video or other documentation as the principal legacy. Other artworks with an analogue or digital element have been commissioned for the building itself, but not accessioned into the permanent collection. Examples include Random International's Swarm chandelier installed on the staircase leading to the Ceramics and Glass Galleries, or Troika's animated V&A logo, displayed in the Museum's tunnel entrance for some years.

Now that the V&A is known for its digital art collection, individual works are also in great demand for loans to other major institutions in the UK and abroad. The Whitechapel Gallery's *Electronic Superhighway* exhibition (2016), for example, featured early pieces by Frieder Nake, Vera Molnár and Hiroshi Kawano. Other borrowers include the Centre Georges Pompidou in Paris, the Grand Palais in Brussels and the new Museum of Art, Architecture and Technology in Lisbon. The Pompidou's *Coder le Monde* exhibition (2018), featured eleven works from the V&A collection, including works by artists who were active in Paris in the 1960s and 1970s.

10.6 Conclusion

In the last fifteen years or so, the Museum has made a concerted effort to develop its digital art collection, expanding the range, depth and geographical coverage of this important new medium. As a result, the V&A now holds the UK's national collection of early computer art, plus an increasing number of recent born-digital works. The Museum remains one of the few public institutions in Europe with extensive holdings of early computer-generated artworks, all of which are readily accessible online. Much remains to be done—particularly in areas relating to collecting, documenting and preserving contemporary digital works—but we hope to make more progress in the coming years.

References

Beddard H, Dodds D (2009) Digital pioneers. V&A Publishing, London, p 2009
Dodds D (2007) Computer art then and now: evaluating the V&A's collections in the digital age. In: Digital archive fever, CHArt 23rd annual conference, Birkbeck, London, 8–9 Nov 2007
Dodds D (2011) Response. In: Desmond Paul Henry: Manchester pioneer of computer art. MOSI, Manchester
Dodds D (2012) Mark Wilson: code matrix 1985–2012. Galerie [DAM], Cologne
Dodds D (2013) Random access memories and digital publishing. In: Galloway D (ed) Barbara Nessim: an artful life. Abrams/V&A
Dodds D (2015a) Collecting fifty years of computer-generated art at the V&A. In: Aesthetica: 50 years of computer generated art. DAM Gallery, Berlin
Dodds D (2015b) By appointment to Victoria and Albert. In: Art that makes itself: Brown & Son: purveyors of digital images since 1968. pp 54–61
Dodds D, Beddard H (2010) Codifying history: the CAT project examines the international trajectory of computer art 1975–2000. In: ISEA conference proceedings, 2010
Dodds D, Lenz M (2014) A history of digital art. Arts & Humanities Research Council, UK. http://www.ahrc.ac.uk/research/readwatchlisten/imagegallery/2014galleries/ahistoryofdigitalart/. Accessed 4 Jan 2019
Kang Y (2018) Casting: site-specific projection mapping installation. Leonardo 51(4):399–404
Lenz M (2014) Cataloguing change: women, art and technology. V&A Online J 6 (Summer)
Lenz M (2017) Early Argentine computer art at the Victoria & Albert Museum. J Des Hist. https://doi.org/10.1093/jdh/epx035
Mason C (2018) Chance and control: art in the age of computers [Review]. Studio International, 25 July 2018. http://www.studiointernational.com/index.php/chance-and-control-art-in-the-age-of-computers-review-victoria-albert-museum. Accessed 27 July 2018
Papadimitriou I (2015) A report from Digital Futures and rebooting the digital commons. V&A Blog. Victoria and Albert Museum, UK, 14 May 2015. https://www.vam.ac.uk/blog/museum-life/a-report-from-digital-futures-and-rebooting-the-digital-commons. Accessed 4 Jan 2019
Prince P (2003) Women and the search for visual intelligence. In: Malloy J (ed) Women, art & technology. MIT Press, Cambridge, pp 2–15
Rawsthorn A (2009) London portrays the past and future of digital art. The New York Times, 13 Dec 2009. https://www.nytimes.com/2009/12/14/arts/design/14iht-design14.html. Accessed 4 Jan 2019
Shannon L (2014) Curating emerging art and design at the Victoria and Albert Museum. In: Graham B (ed) New collecting: exhibiting and audiences after new media art. Ashgate, UK

Taylor GD (2014) When the machine made art: the troubled history of computer art. Bloomsbury, UK

V&A (2015) V&A collections development policy. Victoria and Albert Museum, UK. https://www.vam.ac.uk/info/reports-strategic-plans-and-policies. Accessed 17 Aug 2018

V&A (2019) Content data object—articulating and enabling meaningful access to digital artworks. Victoria and Albert Museum, UK. https://www.vam.ac.uk/research/projects/content-data-object. Accessed 4 Jan 2019

Chapter 11
Conserving Digital Art

Patrícia Falcão and Tom Ensom

Abstract The emergence of digital technologies has impacted not only the nature of museums as institutions, but also the practice of artists. Consequently, artworks which employ digital media (such as video and software) in their access or display are making their way into permanent collections in increasing numbers. These digital media can pose considerable challenges in terms of long-term access and display, due to a changing technological environment and resulting risk of obsolescence. Contemporary art museums are among those leading the way in developing approaches to collecting and caring for these types of object. This accompanies a general shift in conservation theory and practice, from a traditional object-centric approach to one which allows the continued evolution of the work through time. The presence of digital media in collections is also forcing the art museum to look beyond its walls and engage with experts from formerly unfamiliar domains. In this chapter, we will introduce the imperatives driving digital preservation and discuss the state of the art in the field of conserving and preserving digital art. We will then focus on recent research relating to specific digital media types and present a number of case studies from the Tate collection.

11.1 Introduction

In this chapter we will introduce the field of digital art conservation within the art museum, including its primary goals and methods, and recent insights from research and practice at Tate and elsewhere. Research efforts in the conservation and preservation of digital media have been gaining momentum over the past few decades. Through new collaborations between disciplines and international partners, considerable progress has been made toward addressing many of the theoretical and technological challenges faced. We will first introduce the fields of digital preservation and art conservation, which while increasingly interconnected in the context of digital art conservation, have distinct origins and patterns of discourse. For each, we will also

P. Falcão (✉) · T. Ensom
Tate Gallery, London, UK
e-mail: Patricia.Falcao@tate.org.uk

T. Giannini and J. P. Bowen (eds.), *Museums and Digital Culture*,
Springer Series on Cultural Computing, https://doi.org/10.1007/978-3-319-97457-6_11

highlight recent research and its implications for the conservation of digital art. We will then discuss in detail two digital media types—digital video and software—including the preservation challenges they present (illustrated using a number of case studies from the Tate collection) and recent research that has sought to address them.

Much of the content of this chapter builds from our experiences in Tate's Time-based Media Conservation team, a section of the Conservation Department. Tate's mission includes the care of the artworks in the collection and to ensure these can be exhibited to the public in the long-term. Over the last 20 years we have seen wide changes in the technologies used by artists, and the Time-based Media Conservation team's remit has grown from roots in technologies like film, to include digital video, software-based and performance artworks. Tate was the first contemporary art museum to have a time-based media conservation department and has led in building the expertise required to care for these artworks. These works are mostly technology dependent and can be installed in variable ways. Preserving them requires a continued engagement with the new forms of media being used by artists and with the emerging field of digital preservation. While this new expertise has built on existing experience with conservation of contemporary art, it has also required bringing in technical knowledge from outside the museum to help deal with challenges ranging from cathode ray tube maintenance to digital preservation storage; from analog video playback to hardware emulation. This has proved to be, like the artist's practice that drives it, an ever-evolving process.

11.2 Digital Preservation

Digital Preservation is defined by the Digital Preservation Coalition as "(…) the series of managed activities necessary to ensure continued access to digital materials for as long as necessary" (DPC 2015). (The Digital Preservation Coalition is a UK-based non-profit organization which advocates for digital preservation and supports its members in ensuring long-term access to digital content and services.) In this section, we will consider what this means in the context of the museum and introduce the ideas from digital preservation which are shaping the way museums care for digital artworks. Following in the footsteps of archives and libraries, museums have begun adopting (and where necessary adapting) standards, best practices, tools and infrastructures developed by the digital preservation community (Fino-Radin 2018). Digital preservation initiatives must extend across the whole organization. Planning and implementing digital preservation infrastructure therefore requires close collaboration between departments, including those working with the art collection, the archives, photography and records. The development of infrastructure that meets the varied needs of different teams and media types remains an active area of exploration for museums.

The so-called "three-legged stool" model, developed at Cornell University for the Digital Preservation Management training course (Kenney et al. 2003), conceives of digital preservation as supported by three "legs". The "organization" legs represent organizational concerns: what the organization is collecting, the policies in place, and the processes and procedures that support digital preservation. The "technology" leg refers to technological infrastructure: the hardware, software, and skills required to implement the policies and procedures. This also includes the monitoring of the constantly evolving technologies of artwork production and preservation. Finally, the "resources" leg refers the resources that support digital preservation: funding for development, training of staff and perhaps most importantly the operational costs of maintaining preservation activities and infrastructure (McGovern 2007). The balancing of the stool in relation to these three legs is one way of understanding what constitutes a "fully-implemented and viable long-term preservation strategy" (Kenney et al. 2003). This is not a one-time activity but demands ongoing engagement and advocacy. It is essential that digital preservation infrastructure receives sustained support at all levels, to ensure that digital objects are preserved, even in the face of significant changes in the technological environment. Fortunately, many years of research in the digital preservation community has resulted in knowledge and tools which offer a head start to organizations approaching digital preservation for the first time.

The formative times in the development of digital preservation were the early 1970s (Day 2000), when the need to preserve electronic records started to become apparent. As early as 1982, the major international space agencies created the Consultative Committee for Space Data Systems (CCSDS) to provide a forum for discussion of common problems in the development and operation of space data systems (CCSDS 2017). This collaboration led to the development of the reference model for an Open Archival Information System in 2003 with the last update published in 2012 (Consultative Committee for Space Data Systems 2012). This model is much debated and critiqued in the digital preservation community but remains an important de facto standard and baseline for discussions within the field. The OAIS model does not specify technological solutions; rather it identifies the "functions" required to ensure the preservation of digital records. It places digital preservation at the core of an archive or institution and makes explicit the importance of the context under which this occurs; the systems and processes needed to preserve the data for the long-term do not exist in isolation but are intrinsically linked to the *producers* and *users* of the data that the archive holds. Digital preservation is therefore intrinsically cross-disciplinary, offering an overarching set of technical frameworks, with the individual negotiation of what precisely counts as preservation occurring within the sub-field relating to the type of materials to be preserved (Owens 2018). The field has several other well-established standards worth considering, from the relatively simple and pragmatic NDSA Levels of Digital Preservation (Phillips et al. 2013) to the gold-standard Trustworthy Repositories Audit and Certification (Ambacher et al. 2014). These standards can provide useful targets for institutions to work towards when developing their own systems and policies.

In working towards any of these standards, it is necessary to understand the risks faced by digital materials, and appropriate responses to these risks. We will now introduce the two primary risks (see Rosenthal et al. 2005 for a more complete examination): the loss of the bits of digital information; and the loss of the means to access information because of a changing technological environment. The first of these is perhaps the most apparent risk faced by digital materials, and the failure or loss of storage media will be something very familiar to any computer user. By storage media, we mean the physical carrier for the bits (be it magnetic tape, a hard drive or a USB flash drive)—the fundamental unit of digital storage—which encode the digital materials. Failure can occur for a multitude of reasons and at different rates depending on the type of media–the principle of "inherent vice", or the tendency for all materials to deteriorate over time (AIC 2017), applies just as much to digital storage media as to any other. Fortunately, approaches to dealing with this risk have advanced dramatically since it was identified, and we are approaching a situation in which it is possible to mitigate it—providing the resources are available to implement a solution at the required scale.

At its core, a digital object can be understood as a bitstream: a specific sequence of bits (that is, values of 0 or 1). Bit-level preservation concerns ensuring that the exact sequence of bits that constitute a digital object is maintained through time. By storing identical copies in multiple locations (such as a magnetic LTO tape or a hard disk drive in a data center) and applying fixity checks, the integrity of a bitstream can be verified and monitored. Fixity checks are automated methods which use an algorithm to generate a digital fingerprint from the bitstream, often referred to as a checksum. If any bit within the bitstream is altered, the resulting checksum will change. These checksums can be stored alongside a digital object and used to verify the integrity of the bits whenever they are copied (NDSA Infrastructure and Standards Working Groups 2014). Various steps can be taken to minimize risks to bit integrity when storage media is accessed and archived. Tools and techniques from the field of digital forensics, which has emerged around the requirement for demonstrable bit integrity in criminal investigations, are increasingly being used in the capture of digital materials in museums (Kirschenbaum et al. 2013). For example, the use of write-blocked disk imaging (shown in progress in Fig. 11.1) allows the capture of a complete bit-for-bit representation of the contents of a hard drive, while mitigating the risk of writing any data back onto the source storage media. At Tate, we have used the free and open-source BitCurator toolset to help us implement digital forensics in our workflows (BitCurator n.d.).

While frameworks for bit-level preservation are now well established and widely agreed upon, ensuring the long-term usability and accessibility of born-digital materials is a tougher challenge. This problem is caused by technological obsolescence, which can be understood as the decrease in use and availability of a specific technology. A classic example of hardware obsolescence is the 3½″ floppy disk. Once a popular storage medium for which reader devices were ubiquitous, as more efficient forms of storage such as the compact disc became available, interest in the floppy disk declined and production slowed, rendering it obsolete. Software and file formats may also become obsolete, sometimes as a trickledown effect from hardware obsolescence (for example, when a processor architecture becomes obsolete, so too does the software which runs on it), and sometimes independently (for example, where development ceases on a software program which is required to access a specific file format). A considerable amount of research over the past few decades has focused on

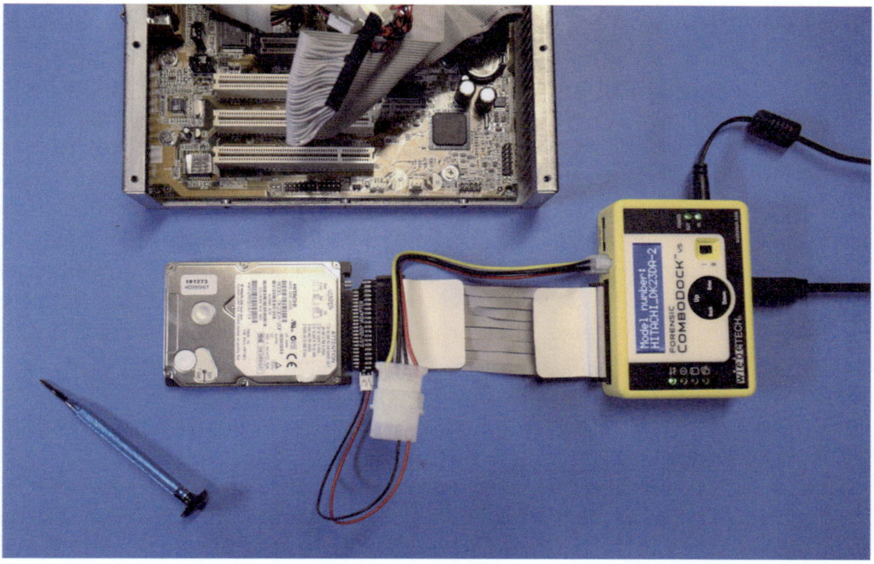

Fig. 11.1 Using forensic write-blocking hardware to acquire a disk image of a hard drive extracted from a PC. (Photograph by Tom Ensom)

how we might respond to these problems, and has resulted in several distinct strands of thought, which we characterize as *content-centric* and *object-centric*.

Content-centric strategies seek to alter the technical structure of digital objects to meet the requirements of a changing technical environment, while ensuring the original content is maintained. For example, data stored in an obsolete file format might be converted to a more stable one. The primary drawback of this approach is that important characteristics of the content may be lost in the migration process, particularly if the new format does not support all the features that the original did. Object-centric strategies seek to maintain a suitable technical environment using emulation (and related technologies), allowing continued access to the original unaltered object. Recent advances in emulation technology and the tools to apply it mean that object-centric digital preservation has become more common and usable at scale (von Suchodoletz et al. 2013; Cochrane et al. 2017). However, such an approach can still not be used successfully in all circumstances; it is contingent on a suitable emulator having been developed to support the required technical environment. Both strategy types introduced here are returned to in subsequent sections of this chapter—Conserving Digital Video and Conserving Software-based Art respectively—where specific examples of their application are discussed.

Both strategy types demand a degree of change, either in the digital object itself or its environment, and as a result frameworks have been developed to ensure that the important characteristics of a digital object can be maintained through time. In doing so, we aim to ensure that the digital materials preserved can be considered authentic.

This idea is widely understood in digital preservation as preserving "significant properties" (Wilson 2007). Although significant properties can be problematically vague as a term and hard to implement consistently in practice (Dappert and Farquhar 2009; Yeo 2010), it remains a useful way of thinking about the potential appropriateness of a particular preservation strategy and measuring its success if applied. Beyond documentation to support an understanding of significant properties, documentation standards within digital preservation are linked primarily to the metadata which accompanies a particular object in archival storage. There are established standards for this, ranging from the baseline Dublin Core specification (Dublin Core Metadata Initiative 2012), primarily supporting access, to the specialized PREMIS standard (PREMIS Editorial Committee 2015), which enables sophisticated machine-driven management of digital objects. Off-the-shelf storage and management systems have also been developed, that provide digital object management, access and information services for collections, such as the free and open-source Archivematica (Artefactual Systems Inc. 2019).

As digital preservation matures, there are a number of challenges on the horizon. One is the sustainability of the field, and its tool and technologies. With this in mind, we are increasingly seeing the favoring of open-source tools to meet digital preservation requirements (Gengenbach et al. 2016). While this may not always be practical, when it can be achieved it helps ensure that development is transparent, can be picked up easily by others and carried out collaboratively. In this chapter we have tried to highlight open-source options where possible. Another emerging challenge is the increasingly common blurring of the boundaries of what we have typically understood as digital objects. The increasing use of software that is cloud-based and dependent on the web for access poses challenges to digital preservation, such as the widespread use of Google Docs (Mitcham 2017). As a result, there is increasing interest in capturing a record of the subjects' history and context as documentation, as means to extend, augment or event act in place of object-centric and content-centric preservation efforts. This may be particularly important in cases where the subject of digital preservation is inextricable from the networks it occupies—for example, virtual worlds (McDonough et al. 2010) and Internet art (Dekker 2018).

11.3 Art Conservation

Conservation "encompasses actions taken toward the long-term preservation of cultural property" (AIC, n.d.). The principles and theories that support it as a discipline were shaped over the 20th century, evolving from the in-depth knowledge of production processes and constituent materials of objects to concerns about authenticity and the ability to study original materials. Principles that have resulted from this evolution include: making any treatment or intervention clearly identifiable and reversible; introducing the least possible change to original materials; and an emphasis on thorough and accurate documentation of actions taken (AIC 1994). Paraphrasing Jill Sterrett, Director of Collections at the San Francisco Museum of Modern Art, one of the roles of contemporary art conservators is to create finds for future researchers (personal communication in 2016).

Traditionally there has been a strong focus on the materiality of the preservation object, but different specialties in the field—from ethnographic objects to industrial heritage to contemporary art—have widened the scope of conservation to include considerations about the context of objects and their use, that influence or sometimes determine how an object is preserved (Muñoz-Viñas 2012). Contemporary art—including art with digital components—has, because of its dependency on complex industrial technology, widened the focus of conservation from the physical object to include the artist's intent and the public's experience of an artwork. The principles developed for the preservation of traditional materials still apply, but the outlook of conservation has changed from avoiding change to managing inevitable change (Depocas et al. 2003; Laurenson 2006; Phillips 2007).

An important aspect of time-based media art (art involving technology and a durational element) is its often spatial and performative nature, meaning that an artwork only exists if its equipment is running and properly set-up within a space that meets certain requirements. Conservators of time-based media work with artists, technicians, galleries and curators to define what the artwork is, how it should be displayed and how an artist may want to see it preserved. The concept of work-defining properties (similar to the significant properties concept introduced in the Digital Preservation section) provides a framework to support decisions around changes to an artwork. This can vary from changing a specific piece of equipment (for instance, swapping projectors from a technology like LCD to DLP) to migrating to a new medium. While this technical evolution of the artwork is a necessary component of contemporary conservation, the extent to which an artwork may change varies considerably, and conservators and curators are responsible for overseeing these processes within the museum. Negotiating change involves maintaining a balance between changing a work to be able to display it and wanting to be respectful of its technical art history. A strategy to keep that balance is to create thorough documentation of original systems and the changes made to them. If art historians in 20 years' time are to understand a specific artwork, its context, how it has evolved over time, then the focus on documentation is essential, and the effort put into it by teams of conservators fully justified.

A time-based media conservator needs very specific knowledge of the technologies involved in production, but also on the strategies and tools being developed for preservation. Training in this field was first available in 1999, when the first specialization was launched at the University of the Arts in Bern, Switzerland. In the US the degree in Moving Image Archiving and Preservation started in 2005 at the Tisch School of the Arts at NYU, with a broader focus in moving image. The need for further expertise in this field has been acknowledged in the US in the last 5 years, with new positions and fellowships in time-based media conservation in museums like the Denver Art Museum, the Metropolitan Museum of Art, Hirshhorn Museum and the Smithsonian Institution. The National Digital Stewardship Residency has also supported fellows in institutions working with time-based media art collections. There is currently no similar training in the UK, as far as the authors are aware.

Artists working with video or software are also confronted with the need to maintain their works, and often they must support collectors and institutions in their preservation measures. This has happened with video from the beginning, with artists migrating video tapes as needed, and the same trends apply to artists who are asked to show now obsolete works. Many artists are interested in approaches to the aging or evolution of their artworks. One accessible introduction has been written by the artist Rafael Lozano-Hemmer, whose "Best Practices" document serves as a guide to other artists interested in the longevity of their work (Lozano-Hemmer 2015). In this document, among his other recommendations for artists, he suggests that artists trust conservators—and that is good advice if artists are interested in keeping their work alive.

11.4 Conserving Digital Video Art

The medium most frequently found in Tate's collection of time-based media art is video. This includes single-channel video works, video as part of sculptural or installed works and as complex multi-channel video installations. It is fair to say that any video work-of-art is the result of four elements: the media, the playback system, the display equipment, and for video installations, the exhibition space and all its elements. Conservators must understand the specificity and relevance of all these elements to maintain the identity of a work. This understanding is a key part of any acquisition process even before a work is fully brought into the collection. It must be kept in mind that this understanding is also likely to change, at least partially, over the life of the work. The initial questions of conservators pertain to the production process and the media of an artwork, along with its display parameters and equipment. Following Tate's usual workflow, we will start by addressing the files themselves and processes around them, and then focus on the display parameters and equipment.

The media is usually the core of a work, and also the object of most of the conservation actions taken. These actions include tape to file migration for obsolete formats, quality control of any files supplied or produced from migration and sometimes file transcoding. It is also essential to have archival digital storage in which to keep them. A good example is In the Bush (1970), by Gilbert and George, which together with Gordon's Makes Us Drunk (1972b) and A Portrait of the Artists as Young Men (1972), are the earliest video works in the collection, being acquired in 1972, shortly after their production.

In the Bush was produced and stored in analog open-reel tape, then transferred to digital tape formats in 1998, and in 2010 transferred to a file format. By then it was clear that all the tape-based video media would need to become file-based both for preservation and display purposes. At that point it was also clear that more and more artists were working in a fully digital environment and that the production of video art moved from being dependent on hardware and technical facilities to be available on every laptop. This is reflected in the media formats supplied by artists for archiving

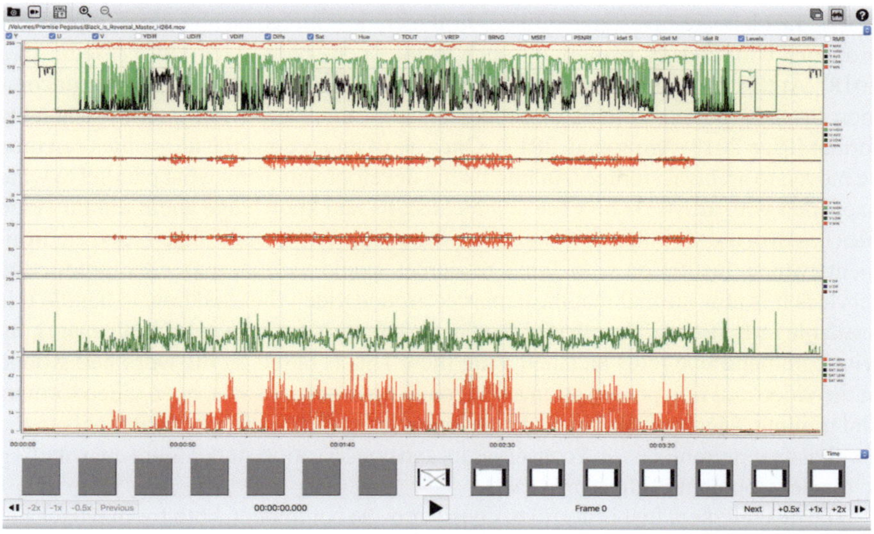

Fig. 11.2 Graphical interface for QCTools (MediaArea 2017), an open-source software tool used to analyze and understand video files, developed by MediaArea.net. Screenshot by Patrícia Falcão

and display purposes, which ranged from Digital Betacam and DVD in the early 2000s to the multiple flavors of Apple ProRes and H264 currently used as master and display formats, respectively. Following the evolution in the entertainment and broadcasting industries, we have seen a shift in resolutions from Standard Definition video to High Definition and more recently 4K, as well as in aspect ratio from 4:3 to 16:9 and now 16:10. It is only a matter of time until we collect our first 3D and Virtual Reality works.

In relation to the media the aim is to preserve both the production format used by an artist and be able to create formats appropriate for display over time, adapting to new playback and display technologies. To decide which formats to preserve it is essential to understand the production process of a video. Did it start as an analog tape? Maybe the video was made from a low quality Mpeg4 file downloaded from YouTube? The image quality may look terrible to some audiences, but that can be part of the artist's intent and certainly part of the production history of a work. The handling, storage and care of these files must be as careful as for any other artwork. At Tate checksums (introduced in the digital preservation section) are calculated as soon as a file comes into ensure any issues with file integrity can be easily detected and any unwanted change corrected. Thorough quality control is done when a work is first received, each video is viewed in its entirety, for content and errors that may have been overlooked. Specialized quality control tools for digital video tools, for instance the QCTools software (MediaArea 2017), are also used to help in this process (Fig. 11.2).

File headers are investigated to confirm technical metadata and identify possible problems with codecs, using tools such as the open-source MediaInfo (MediaArea 2018). At this point risks for preservation are identified, and so files that use uncommon or unsupported formats or codecs must be transcoded to a more sustainable format (Rice 2018; Arms et al. 2017). Once all of this is done the file or files can then be moved to archival storage. An interesting development, somewhat parallel to what happened with artists, is how the technical skills and knowledge about digital video files has evolved with this new digital environment. While in the tape-based environment even an institution with Tate's resources would use external video production services it is now normal that the expertise around video files and how to handle it is available in-house and time-based media conservators are now comfortable working with command line tools and analyzing files. This is based on the work being done in the video and film preservation area around open source tools, open video formats and training. Media archivists and developers are collaborating to create tools to the archivist's requirements, and conservators and conservation students are contributing to the development of their own tools.

The next element that is useful to consider is the equipment, both for playback but mostly the display. Whether an artwork is shown on a monitor or as a projection is usually a very deliberate decision from the artist or possibly curators. Obsolescence of display equipment is the most easily identifiable issue around preserving time-based media—the demise of CRT monitors being a familiar example. This obsolescence process has been very visible and can strongly impact the look of a specific artwork, most clearly when the equipment is meant to have a sculptural effect, as in the work *Joints 4tet Ensemble* (1971–2010) by Charles Atlas, where the CRT monitors are almost like actors in a stage.

We have seen that often the decline of a technology will drive interest from artists in using it. An example is the use of CRT projectors, which have been discontinued in the early 2000s, but were recently used by Mark Leckey in his work *Dream English Kid, 1964–1999 AD* (2015).

The use of obsolete technology means that conservators and technicians are having to develop networks of experts on the different types of equipment. These experts are helpful not only in maintaining existing equipment but also often in sourcing replacement equipment or parts and most of all in training the conservation team on maintenance and repairs. It is also clear that both new and obsolete technology require conservation teams to acquire new skills.

As mentioned at the beginning of this section, videos can also be part of much larger installations including many different components, such as sculptural elements, photographs or even live performances. Commonly these works will be video installations for which video projections have a relationship with the space where they are being shown. For example, William Kentridge's *I am not me, the horse is not mine* (2008) when installed in the space of the South Tank at Tate Modern in 2012/13 (Fig. 11.3), created a different impression to the same work as shown at Inhotim in 2015/16. Information about the exhibition space, the size of the projection, whether the space should be dark and more cinema-like or lighter and whether the work can be shown with other artworks, are all questions that help define the

Fig. 11.3 *I am not me, the horse is not mine*, 2008, William Kentridge. Artwork installed in Tate Modern's South Tank. (©Tate, London 2018)

artwork and the requirements for its display. Often it will also highlight the need for specific playback, display or audio equipment.

Some artists will simply request that a work is projected or shown on a monitor (with varying levels of specificity), where others may require that a particular space is built. To ensure that this happens according to their requirements, artists will often create extensive drawings and plans, provide precise dimensions and specify the type of equipment to be used. Conservation teams will usually collect and keep this information, track it over time and highlight changes and the reasons for them. These are likely to be the finds for many later researchers.

11.5 Conserving Software-Based Art

The term software-based art has emerged from museum conservation practice over the past decade to describe a group of artworks for which software forms the primary artistic medium. For these artworks, software is not only employed in the display of the artwork in a functional sense (that is, software is being executed when the artwork is displayed) but is also utilized by the artist as a means of expressing an artistic statement. Software has been used in such a way by artists since the early days of the technology. The cybernetic sculptures of Nicolas Schöffer (Dreher 2014) and Edward Ihnatowicz (Mundy 2012) for example, both utilized computers developed by the Phillips Company to control a set of sensors and motors which allowed these works to respond to their environment. While these early experiments stemmed from collaboration with industry, the increase in access to computers over the following 50 years, culminating in the personal computer, saw software becoming more accessible to artists (Taylor 2014). Since the early 2000s, software-based art has begun to enter the collections of museums of contemporary art, with Tate acquiring its first—Michael Craig-Martin's *Becoming*—in 2003 (Fig. 11.4). The collection remains relatively small today but shows signs of an increased rate of growth in the last few years. Frances Morris, Director of Tate Modern, said in 2016 that, "for the collection, the next big challenge is going to be digital. In the 19th century we didn't buy photography. It took us over 100 years to catch up. Let's not be in that position again" (Higgins 2016). As a result, identifying strategies for preserving these works has become a pressing concern for conservators of time-based media.

The materials acquired for software-based artworks can vary considerably, ranging from portable storage media (such as external hard drives and USB sticks), to complete computer systems, to digital downloads (for example, from an artist web server). In all cases however, some kind of executable code is at the core of the work, the execution of which results in the experiential qualities of the artwork. Much like digital video, the display of software-based art is often contingent on hardware components which may become increasingly difficult to replace as they become obsolete. These problems are often magnified for software-based artworks, which may employ many interrelated components, including both bespoke and off-the-shelf software, to achieve particular behaviors and characteristics. It can therefore be difficult to predict how change will affect these complex systems without regularly revisiting the work in question (Falcão 2010). Furthermore, software-based art is often diffuse (Laurenson 2013)—that is, it extends into its technical environment. Most commonly this is observed in linkages between the software and the computer system which supports it, but in some cases the connections may extend beyond the gallery walls and into networks and the Internet. These make for some of the most challenging cases for conservators, as the longevity of the artwork involves responding to unpredictable forms of change in external resources—a challenge we will return to later in this section.

For contained software-based artworks (i.e. those for which the technical system does not extend beyond the gallery walls), content-centric and object-centric approaches to digital preservation outlined in an earlier section (see Digital Preservation) can still be applied successfully, although their application may be challenged by certain characteristics of software-based art. Unlike digital video, software is hard to understand simply by examining the digital object which is acquired. This is usually a package of executable software (or 'binaries'), a compiled form of software, the internal data structure of which is designed to be understood by a machine rather than a person. Therefore, gathering information about what it does and how it does it becomes much more challenging using this object alone. This has led to new collaborations with experts from the fields of computer science and software engineering, and work to incorporate this new knowledge into the existing frameworks of conservation. In this section we will highlight research and case studies relating to several complementary approaches to software-based art conservation.

Fig. 11.4 *Becoming*, 2003, Michael Craig-Martin. This was the first software-based artwork to enter Tate's collection. (©Tate, London 2018)

The first is to focus on ensuring that a suitable technical environment is maintained in the long-term. In these cases, the emphasis is on preserving the digital object as-is (without altering the bits) and understanding its links with other components to ensure these links can be maintained. As a starting point, digital forensics tools can be used to capture a complete bit-for-bit copy of the storage device acquired as part of a computer system. This encapsulates all of the software contained, without impacting its internal structure. This can be examined as a virtual device, or if paired with information about the hardware configuration, can be used as the basis of emulation or virtualization strategies. The latter are powerful techniques for preservation, which allow one operating system (i.e., the one encapsulated within the disk image) to be

Fig. 11.5 *Sow Farm (near Libbey, Oklahoma) 2009*, 2009, John Gerrard. Work installed at Tate Britain in 2016. (©Tate, London 2018)

executed on another of a potentially completely different architecture. In this way, the content of a Windows 95 PC hard disk drive could be booted on a contemporary Linux host. The utility of this approach has been explored in recent research at Tate (Falcão et al. 2014; Rechert et al. 2016) and elsewhere (Lurk 2008; Rechert et al. 2013). There remain issues in the legality of approaches which rely on archiving third-party commercial software—a problem affecting software preservation broadly. Recent developments in the United States, including an exemption to the Digital Millennium Copyright Act (Albert 2018) and work toward a Code of Best Practices (Association of Research Libraries 2018), are promising signs of progress.

One example we will briefly highlight is the application of virtualization to John Gerrard's *Sow Farm (near Libbey, Oklahoma) 2009* (2009), an example which demonstrates some of the considerations involved when taking this kind of approach. Gerrard is an Irish artist who works in a medium he calls real-time 3D. This involves the use of technology more familiar from video games and architectural visualization to render 3D imagery from a collection of data assets (including meshes and textures) in a scene dynamically controlled by a simulation model. In this work, a camera orbits a complex of buildings modelled on a real pig farm in the Great Plains of the USA. This scene was painstakingly reconstructed in 3D, based on extensive on-site photography. As the camera slowly orbits the buildings, day and night cycles unfold in real time over the course of 365 days. Once every 156 days, a truck drives up to the buildings and waits for one hour, symbolizing the moment of exchange as the mature pigs are collected for slaughter (Fig. 11.5).

In this case, the software is much more than just functional—and the nuances of the lighting and processing of the rendering engine make the work-defining characteristics of this work difficult to separate from specific software binaries acquired. Furthermore, the engine on which the software is based is no longer commercially available. Moving the simulation to a new 3D engine would be a high-risk option, and the precise qualities of the rendered image specified by Gerrard could be lost. As long as existing hardware supports the specific Microsoft DirectX API employed, the work can be migrated to new hardware. In the longer term, using emulation or virtualization would be a suitable way to recreate this specific technical environment, a process which was tested at Tate in 2015 with promising results (Falcão and Dekker 2015).

For this work, the graphical fidelity of the rendered image is paramount, and the artist has specified particular performance and quality parameters to be maintained when it is displayed. This includes the requirement of smooth camera movement (measured in respect to the frames generated by the host system) and the application of specific rendering effects using the graphics card driver. In this case it was found that when running in a virtualized environment, these characteristics were lost (Ensom 2018), which thus prevents the use of the strategy until the technology allows them to be applied. This example demonstrates the caution required in applying emulation and virtualization, and how problems may emerge where issues of performance are not completely identified. Such strategies must be carefully applied to ensure that the characteristics of the original 'performance' are maintained. This idea of integrity of performance runs through all software preservation work and achieving this could be considered one of the conservator's main goals.

Another approach is to focus on the code—the set of instructions on which the computer system acts when the artwork is realized. Here emphasis shifts from understanding technical environment, to understanding what the software *does* and how this might be changed or reimplemented to avoid obsolescence. The utility of source code in conservation and technical art history has been championed by Professor of Computer Science at NYU Deena Engel, in several collaborations with Glenn Wharton from New York's Museum of Modern Art (Engel and Wharton 2014, 2015) and Joanna Phillips from the Solomon R. Guggenheim Museum (Dover 2016). While many museums had already been seeking to acquire source code with accessioned artworks, this research has demonstrated the value of source code as a key tool in the conservation of software-based artworks, providing a complete description of the functionality of the work, which can then serve as documentation, and allow troubleshooting when applying preservation strategies. The latest strand of this research, conducted by Engel in collaboration with time-based media conservator Joanna Phillips, applied an approach that reframes ideas of minimal intervention for software, by leaving the original code of a website intact (as code comments) while adding new lines to reimplemented original functionality in newer frameworks (Engel and Phillips 2018). Further collaborations of this kind are likely to be very important in continuing to keep museums at pace with fast moving technology.

José Carlos Martinat Mendoza's *Brutalism: Stereo Reality Environment 3* (2007) (Fig. 11.6) is an installed software-based artwork, the formal focus of which is a scale

Fig. 11.6 *Brutalism: Stereo Reality Environment 3*, 2007, José Carlos Martinat Mendoza. Work installed at Tate Modern in 2012. (©Tate, London 2018)

replica of the 'Pentagonito', a building in Peru that housed the secret service during the Fujimori presidency. Sitting on the surface of this sculptural element are a set of thermal printers, connected to a computer by visible cables which sprawl across the gallery floor. This computer is connected to the Internet, and behind the scenes is searching the Internet for terms relating to the word 'brutalism' (or 'brutalismo' when exhibited in Spanish-speaking countries), forging serendipitous connections between the various meanings of the word. Fragments of these search results are printed out, falling onto the gallery floor and accumulating during the time the work is active.

For Brutalism, we can understand many of the artwork's work-defining characteristics as residing in the underlying concept and the instructions that were encoded in its binaries when the source code was compiled. In this case, the source project files (which contain the human authored representation of the code, pre-compilation) acquired with the work might be used, altered or even reimplemented in another language should Java become obsolete. Reworking of the code has already happened once for Brutalism, as the artist and programmer worked remotely on a development machine to update the code to add support for the USB communication protocol, replacing the obsolete parallel port module used in the original version to connect to the printers.

However, the connection with the Internet results in a vulnerability that extends beyond what can be understood simply through functionality expressed as code. The artist and programmer originally utilized the Google Search API, the ubiquitous search engine of the time, through which to harvest Internet search results. Changes to the Google Search API are likely to render this component of the work non-functional in the short term as the API changes, requiring continued work on the code (this has already occurred once in preparation for display at Tate Modern) . What happens if search engines close off their public APIs? What if search engines as we know them cease to exist? In these easily imagined futures, the artwork is not something which can be fixed in terms of digital object or code—rather, it must continue to evolve for it live. The museum therefore faces difficult decisions in the long-term care of this work. Does the work become static, the live link to web severed and the database remaining a historical artifact? Or should the work be reinterpreted in some way to meet the changing world in which it is situated? In this case, future conservation treatments may need to be more drastic in its departure from earlier versions. There are no easy answers to these questions, and museums are having to negotiate them on a case by case basis as they arise.

What we can do however, is document the rich technical history of these works, their variable installation and their shifting relationship with a broader socio-technical context. Forms of documentation that support this may engage directly with process and change. Documentation best practices for software-based artworks now include video recordings of the functioning work and interactions with visitors, acknowledging the limitations of text and still image to document dynamic works. For Internet art, tools like Rhizome's Webrecoder have been developed to capture website documentation (crucially including traces of user interaction with the site) in contained archival file formats which can be replayed in the future (Kreymer n.d.). Museums are now experimenting with forms of process documentation such as the use of version control systems to capture changes in source code as software-based artworks evolve (Haidvogl 2015; Paul and Mancusi-Ungaro 2018). This provides a rich record of the development history of the software, which as we know from research into source code analysis can provide considerable insight into an artist's working practice (Engel and Wharton 2015). Looking beyond technical approaches, the notion of 'artwork biography' has been developed by a group of scholars based in the Netherlands (van de Vall et al. 2011). This philosophical perspective on conservation posits the idea that artworks be considered biographical subjects. We might therefore want to generate rich accounts of their life histories, through an "interweaving [of] partial biographies with different beginnings, itineraries, dynamics and endings" (p. 6). How this desire might mesh with the pragmatism demanded in conservation practice remains an open question, and one that museums may seek to answer in the years to come if they are to help ensure a historical record for this rapidly evolving medium.

11.6 Conclusion

In this chapter, we have introduced the fields of digital preservation and art conservation, and their intersection in the long-term care of digital art. We have examined some of the primary challenges in the conservation of digital art and highlighted some of the recent research (at Tate and further afield) that is being undertaken to meet them. Among the insights gained, it is evident that there is no silver bullet solution nor any one-size-fits-all method for conserving digital art. The process of conserving digital art is driven by the characteristics of the artwork and its relationship with the specific technologies employed in its realization, resulting in a variable set of considerations in each case. Even within a particular digital media type there may be considerable variation in approach taken: an Internet artwork experienced through a web browser, for instance, demands very different considerations to an interactive installation realized in a gallery environment—despite both being dependent on computer systems running software.

As illustrated in the examples discussed in this chapter, developments in preservation technology are also shaping how we approach the preservation of digital art. For example, the growing maturity of emulation and virtualization tools has resulted in a growing interest in their application to digital artworks, particularly as they become more feasibly applied at scale. Collaboration is also proving to be essential in addressing the challenges presented by digital technologies as they enter museum care. Having already helped museums meet the requirements of digital video and its display, we are now seeing new connections forged between conservation practice and expertise in computer science, leading to pioneering new research. Nowhere is this clearer than in preserving software-based artworks, which have required the conservator to engage with expertise outside the museum to understand the role of code and programming in the care of such works.

Looking more broadly, it is evident that the practice of art conservation has evolved from object-centric origins towards an acceptance of the evolution of the artwork over time. Thus, a significant part of the conservator's role becomes managing this process, documenting its phases and brokering collaborations. Within this model for conservation practice, the artwork is not simply collected and stored, but enters a phase in its life of custodianship, in which the museum negotiates its continued placement within an evolving socio-technical environment. For institutions starting out with the conservation of digital art, we recommend an engagement with the established communities who have been involved in the field as it has developed. While the field is always developing to meet the new challenges posed by technologically-engaged artistic practice, many of the common problems faced are surmountable with existing approaches.

References

Albert K (2018) A victory for software preservation: DMCA exemption granted for SPN. Cyberlaw Clinic. https://clinic.cyber.harvard.edu/2018/10/26/a-victory-for-software-preservation-dmca-exemption-granted-for-spn/. Accessed 21 Jan 2019

Ambacher B, Ashley K, Berry J, Brooks C, Dale RL, Flecker D, Giaretta D, Hamidzadeh B, Johnson K, Jones M (2014) Trustworthy repositories audit and certification: criteria and checklist (TRAC). Center for Research Libraries, Chicago

AIC (1994) Code of ethics and guidelines for practice. American Institute for Conservation of Historic and Artistic Works. http://www.conservation-us.org/docs/default-source/governance/code-of-ethics-and-guidelines-for-practice.pdf?sfvrsn=9. Accessed on 21 Jan 2019

AIC (2017) Inherent vice. AIC Wiki, American institute for conservation of historic and artistic works. http://www.conservation-wiki.com/wiki/Inherent_vice. Accessed on 21 Jan 2019

AIC (n.d.) What is conservation? American Institute for Conservation of Historic and Artistic Works. http://www.conservation-us.org/about-conservation. Accessed 13 July 2018

Arms CR, Fleischhauer C, Murray K (2017) Sustainability of digital formats: planning for library of congress collections. Library of congress. https://www.loc.gov/preservation/digital/formats/. Accessed 21 Jan 2019

Artefactual Systems Inc. (2019) Archivematica: open-source digital preservation system. Archivematica. https://www.archivematica.org/en/. Accessed on 21 Jan 2019

Association of Research Libraries (2018) Code of best practices in fair use for software preservation. Association of research libraries. https://www.arl.org/focus-areas/copyright-ip/fair-use/code-of-best-practices-in-fair-use-for-software-preservation. Accessed on 21 Jan 2019

Atlas C (1971) Joints 4tet Ensemble. Tate, UK. https://www.tate.org.uk/art/artworks/atlas-joints-4tet-ensemble-t13849. Accessed on 19 Mar 2019

BitCurator (n.d.) BitCurator. https://bitcurator.net/bitcurator/. Accessed on 21 Jan 2019

CCSDS (2012) Reference model for an Open Archival Information System (OAIS): Magenta Book (No. CCSDS 650.0-M-2). Washington, DC, USA

Cochrane E, Tilbury J, Stobbe O (2017) Adding emulation functionality to existing digital preservation infrastructure. Presented at the iPRES 2018, Koyoto, Japan

Consultative Committee for Space Data Systems (2017) About CCSDS. CCSDS.org. URL https://public.ccsds.org/about/default.aspx. Accessed on 21 Jan 2019

Craig-Martin M (2003) Becoming. Tate, UK. http://www.tate.org.uk/art/artworks/craig-martin-becoming-t11812. Accessed on 20 Jan 2019

Dappert A, Farquhar A (2009) Significance is in the eye of the stakeholder. In: International conference on theory and practice of digital libraries. Springer, pp 297–308

Day MW (2000) Preservation of electronic information: a bibliography. https://www.webarchive.org.uk/wayback/en/archive/20170705065345/, http://homes.ukoln.ac.uk/~lismd/preservation.html. Accessed on 21 Jan 2019

Dekker A (2018) Collecting and conserving net art: moving beyond conventional methods. Routledge

Depocas A, Ippolito J, Jones C (eds) (2003) Permanence through change: the variable media approach. Guggenheim museum publications and the daniel langlois foundation for art, science, and technology, New York, USA and Montreal, Canada

Digital Preservation Coalition (2015) Digital preservation handbook, 2nd Edn. http://handbook.dpconline.org/. Accessed on 21 June 2017

Dover C (2016) How the Guggenheim and NYU are conserving computer-based art. Guggenheim

Dreher T (2014) History of computer art, 1st Update (Sept 2015). (ed) IASL online, Online

Dublin Core Metadata Initiative (2012) DCMI metadata terms. Dublin core metadata initiative. http://dublincore.org/documents/dcmi-terms/. Accessed on 13 July 2018

Engel D, Phillips J (2018) Introducing 'Code Resituation': applying the concept of minimal intervention to the conservation treatment of software-based art. In: Presented at the AIC 46th annual meeting, Houston, TX, USA

Engel D, Wharton G (2014) Reading between the lines: source code documentation as a conservation strategy for software-based art. Stud Conserv 59:404–415. https://doi.org/10.1179/2047058413Y.0000000115
Engel D, Wharton G (2015) Source code analysis as technical art history. J Amer Inst Conserv 54:91–101
Ensom T (2018) Revealing hidden processes: instrumentation and reverse engineering in the conservation of software-based art. In: Presented at the AIC 46th annual meeting, Houston, Texas, USA
Falcão P (2010) Developing a risk assessment tool for the conservation of software-based artworks. MA thesis. Berne, Switzerland
Falcão P, Alistair A, Jones B (2014) Virtualisation as a tool for the conservation of software-based artworks. In: Presented at the iPRES 2014, Melbourne, Australia
Falcão P, Dekker A (2015) Virtualizing John Gerrard's "Sow Farm" (2009), or not?
Fino-Radin B (2018) Digital art storage: what every conservator needs to know. AIC News 43
Gengenbach M, Peltzman S, Meister S, Graham B, Waugh D, Moran J, Seifert J, Dowding H, Carleton J (2016) OSS4EVA: using open-source tools to fulfill digital preservation requirements. Code4Lib J vol 34
Gerrard (2009) Sow Farm (near Libbey, Oklahoma) 2009. Tate, UK. https://www.tate.org.uk/art/artworks/gerrardsow-farm-near-libbeyoklahoma-2009-t14279. Accessed on 19 March 2019
Gilbert and George (1970) A portrait of the artists as young men. Tate, UK. https://www.tate.org.uk/art/artworks/gilbert-georgea-portrait-of-the-artists-as-youngmen-t01704. Accessed on 19 Mar 2019
Gilbert and George (1972a) In the Bush. Tate, UK. https://www.tate.org.uk/art/artworks/gilbert-georgein-the-bush-t01702. Accessed on 19 Mar 2019
Gilbert and George (1972b) Gordon's makes us drunk. Tate, UK. https://www.tate.org.uk/art/artworks/gilbert-georgegordons-makes-us-drunk-t01703. Accessed on 19 Mar 2019
Haidvogl M (2015) Acquiring and documenting Jürg Lehni's "Viktor" (2006). Vimeo. https://vimeo.com/146980154. Accessed on 21 Jan 2019
Higgins C (2016) Saturday interview: Frances Morris. The Guardian, UK
Kenney AR, McGovern NY, Entlich R, Kehoe WR, Olsen E, Buckley E (2003) Digital preservation management workshops and tutorial. digital preservation management: implementing short-term strategies for long-term problems. http://www.dpworkshop.org. Accessed on 20 Jan 2019
Kentridge W (2008) I am not me, the horse is not mine. Tate, UK. http://www.tate.org.uk/art/artworks/kentridge-i-am-not-me-the-horse-is-not-mine-t14213. Accessed on 20 Jan 2019
Kirschenbaum M, Lee CA, Woods K, Chassanoff A et al (2013) From bitstreams to heritage: putting digital forensics into practice in collecting institutions. https://drum.lib.umd.edu/bitstream/handle/1903/14736/bitstreamsto-heritage.pdf. Accessed on 19 Mar 2019
Kreymer I (n.d.) Webrecorder. http://webrecorder.io. Accessed on 16 July 2018
Laurenson P (2013) Old media, new media? significant difference and the conservation of software-based art, In: Preserving and exhibiting media art. Challenges and perspectives. Amsterdam University Press, Amsterdam, pp 73–96
Laurenson P (2006) Authenticity, change and loss in the conservation of time-based media installations. Tate Papers. Tate, UK. https://www.tate.org.uk/research/publications/tate-papers/06/authenticity-change-and-loss-conservation-of-time-based-media-installations. Accessed on 20 Jan 2019
Leckey M (2015) Dream english kid, 1964–1999 AD. Tate, UK. https://www.tate.org.uk/art/artworks/leckey-dream-english-kid-1964-1999-ad-t14666
Library of Congress (n.d.) About—digital preservation (Library of Congress). Library of Congress—digital preservation, USA. http://www.digitalpreservation.gov/about/. Accessed on 23 Jan 2018
Lozano-Hemmer R (2015) Best practices for conservation of media art from an artist's perspective
Lurk T (2008) Virtualisation as conservation measure. In: Archiving conference. society for imaging science and technology, pp 221–225

Martinat Mendoza JC (2007) Brutalism: stereo reality environment 3. Tate, UK. https://www.tate.org.uk/art/artworks/gilbert-georgegordons-makes-us-drunk-t01703. Accessed on 19 Mar 2019
McDonough JP, Olendorf R, Kirschenbaum M, Kraus K, Reside D, Donahue R, Phelps A, Egert C, Lowood H, Rojo S (2010) Preserving virtual worlds final report. Library of congress, USA
McGovern N (2007) A digital decade: where have we been and where are we going in digital preservation? RLG DigiNews
MediaArea (2017) QCTools. http://mediaarea.net/QCTools. Accessed on 20 Jan 2019
MediaArea (2018) MediaInfo https://mediaarea.net/en/MediaInfo. Accessed on 21 Jan 2019
Mitcham J (2017) How can we preserve Google Documents? Digital archiving, University of York, UK. http://digital-archiving.blogspot.com/2017/04/how-can-we-preserve-google-documents.html. Accessed on 20 Jan 2019
Mundy J (2012) Lost art: Edward Ihnatowicz. Tate, UK. https://www.tate.org.uk/context-comment/articles/gallery-lost-art-edward-inhatowicz. Accessed on 16 July 2018
Muñoz-Viñas S (2012) Contemporary theory of conservation. Routledge
Stefano, PD, Fleischhauer, C, Goethals, A, Kjörling, M, Krabbenhoeft, N, Lacinak, C, Mandelbaum, J, McCarthy, K, Murray, K, Navale, V, Rice, D, Ruggaber, R, Owens, T, Zwaard, K (2014) Checking your digital content. http://www.digitalpreservation.gov/documents/NDSA-Fixity-Guidance-Report-final100214.pdf. Accessed on 19 Mar 2019
Owens T (2018) The theory and craft of digital preservation. Johns Hopkins University Press
Paul C, Mancusi-Ungaro C (2018) Programmed: conserving concepts. The institute of fine arts, New York University. https://vimeo.com/310817190. Accessed on 21 Jan 2019
Phillips J (2007) Reporting iterations: a documentation model for time-based media art. Revista de História da Arte, Perform Documentation Conserv Contemporary Art 4:168–179
Phillips M, Bailey J, Goethals A, Owens T (2013) The NDSA levels of digital preservation: explanation and uses. In: Archiving conference. Society for imaging science and technology, pp 216–222
PREMIS Editorial Committee (2015) PREMIS data dictionary for preservation metadata, version 3.0. OCLC, Washington
Rechert K, Espenschied D, Valizada I, Liebetraut T, Russler N, von Suchodoletz D (2013) An architecture for community-based curation and presentation of complex digital objects. In: Urs SR, Na JC, Buchanan G (eds) Digital libraries: social media and community networks. Lecture notes in computer science, Springer, pp 103–112. https://doi.org/10.1007/978-3-319-03599-4_12
Rechert K, Falcão P, Ensom T (2016) Introduction to an emulation-based preservation strategy for software-based artworks
Rice D (2018) Sustaining consistent video presentation. Tate. http://www.tate.org.uk/about-us/projects/pericles/sustaining-consistent-video-presentation. Accessed on 21 Jan 2019
Rosenthal DSH, Robertson T, Lipkis T, Reich V, Morabito S (2005) Requirements for digital preservation systems: a bottom-up approach. D-Lib Magazine 11. https://doi.org/10.1045/november2005-rosenthal
Taylor GD (2014) When the machine made art: the troubled history of computer art. Bloomsbury Publishing USA
van de Vall R, Hölling H, Scholte T, Stigter S (2011) Reflections on a biographical approach to contemporary art conservation. In: Presented at the 16th triennial conference Lisbon, Almada: Critério. DOI: 11245/1.344546
von Suchodoletz D, Rechert K, Valizada I (2013) Towards emulation-as-a-service: cloud services for versatile digital object access. Int J Dig Curation 8:131–142. https://doi.org/10.2218/ijdc.v8i1.250
Wilson A (2007) Significant properties report. InSPECT work package 2.2 No. Version 2
Yeo G (2010) "Nothing is the same as something else": significant properties and notions of identity and originality. Arch Sci 10:85–116. https://doi.org/10.1007/s10502-010-9119-9

Chapter 12
Spatial Narratives in Museums and Online: The Birth of the Digital Object Itinerary

Stuart Dunn, Graeme Earl, Anna Foka and Will Wootton

Abstract Museums represent complex layers of place. From carefully managed curatorial spaces, to exhibition environments, to the layout of display cases, to the representation of distant parts embodied in the collections of the great encyclopedic collections, the negotiation, representation and presentation of place has always been central to the mission of any museum. This chapter will examine the history of how museums (especially museum catalogues) present place, from early origins to the Internet. A set of case studies will be examined as a means of exploring how, where and in what form art objects and artefacts first began to be transported from non-Western to Western nations for display in the museums of Western capitals, thus representing the origins of what Cuno has called our "basic and inevitable cultural interrelatedness"; and what others have called "object itineraries" or "object biographies". A comparison will be made of the same museums' online representation of the same places today. It will thus be possible to present a framework for considering object itineraries—historic and modern—as a subject of both history and historiography.

S. Dunn (✉) · G. Earl · W. Wootton
King's College London, London, UK
e-mail: stuart.dunn@kcl.ac.uk

G. Earl
e-mail: graeme.earl@kcl.ac.uk

W. Wootton
e-mail: will.wootton@kcl.ac.uk

A. Foka
DH Uppsala, Department of Archives, Museums and Libraries,
Uppsala University, Uppsala, Sweden
e-mail: anna.foka@abm.uu.se

Humlab, Umeå University, Umeå, Sweden

T. Giannini and J. P. Bowen (eds.), *Museums and Digital Culture*,
Springer Series on Cultural Computing, https://doi.org/10.1007/978-3-319-97457-6_12

12.1 Introduction

Historical and archaeological museums are physical sites of narrative, telling the stories of diverse pasts of different regions of the world, contextualizing material culture in its tangible forms and at the same time acting as venues of research and conservation. These stories are conveyed in a number of ways, including the selection and classification of objects for display, the ways in which artefacts are categorized and organized into groups, and how information is formatted and communicated in labels and catalogues. These methods of narrative creation form systems of interaction between humans, artefacts, and information in a contained physical space; and they are dependent on several socio-material factors such as the museum's legacy of the past, its location, the artefacts themselves, curatorial input and guidance from educators in the museum. At the same time, the *digital* realm, whose currency is information and binary data rather than physical objects, has adopted the vocabularies of the museum space. The prefix "digital" places terms such as "curation", "preservation", "catalogue" and even "object" alongside terms such as web "page" and web "site" in a liminal vocabulary which links the physical and virtual in one single interface. Similarly, the digital has penetrated the physical and conceptual space of the museum, and in the process revolutionized accessibility and our ability to understand the artefacts they contain.

In the context of these shared lexical spaces, the World Wide Web (WWW) can also act as a medium of narrative creation, but one whose narratives are constructed in an *unphysical* and *unlocated* manner. Rather than establishing sited narratives about cultural heritage (or indeed anything else), the WWW facilitates structures of both power and description by creating unconstrained, multidirectional insubstantial networks enabled by web standards and technologies (Castells 2011). In the last ten years or so, museums and their curators have increasingly appreciated the possibilities of telling the stories of their collections through digital media. "Digital storytelling", which frequently crosses platforms and formats, is entering museum discourses (Wyman et al. 2011), employing different platforms and media, and taking advantage of (now) widely available infrastructures such as Wi-Fi and RFID. As well as providing a means of driving and developing excellent visitor experiences in an age when, in their daily lives, such visitors are constantly interacting with digital culture, these allow curators to tell entirely new kinds of stories (Kahr-Højland 2010). This chapter offers a brief literature and concept review of how we might approach the trajectories of objects through time and space in the digital world, and how the idea of the "object itinerary" drives narrative creation in both physical and virtual space.

12.2 Museums and Spatial Narrative

It can be argued that digital narrative in museums is, first and foremost, a *geospatial* concept. Physical objects and digital data have very different relationships with place and space: the former is tied to a specific location at any one time, the latter exists as a constellation of electrons which, while located in the global physical infrastructure of cables and servers, is theoretically locatable, readable and viewable anywhere, at any time. For example, a south Pacific culture represented in a Central European museum as a collection of artefacts produced by that society, is far removed from the geographical location of the museum, as well as being removed in time, meaning that the objects in their collections have undergone an itinerary, with a start, intermediate waypoints, and an end. This, in itself, invites an obvious invocation of narrative structure. In such cases the focus of the narrative is not a plot, or a character, but the travels and handling of the object itself. The concept of the "end" of the narrative is rather problematic. Does this refer to the end of the object's use in its original context, its discovery or re-discovery (and by whom), its acquisition by, or arrival in the museum, and so forth. For these reasons, some have preferred the term "object itinerary" to "object biography" (see below) which, with the metaphorical allusion to the object having a life, equates its end with death (Gillespie 2015).

Narratives can also be primarily spatial in character (Bodenhamer et al. 2015). Caquard (2011) a notion that develops this theme, distinguishing between physical and nonphysical interaction via "grid maps" and "story maps", where the former describes objects, persons and events in terms of their geographical (physical) location, and the latter are discursive events which take place in space, but are not "mappable" in a physical sense. In this context, maps (especially widely available digital maps, such as Google Earth) are both stimulators of narratives, in that they encourage people to think spatially, but at the same time they limit them due to the restrictions imposed by the base map (Caquard 2011, p. 6). And, of course, these maps themselves are constructed, often following a Western tradition of representing space that might be different from lived experience (especially in non-Western communities and societies). Telling the spatial stories of cultural objects in museums, and thus understanding their shifting biographical significance as they travel through time and space, depends on their literal history (where they are now, where they have been), and the unphysical historical and curatorial context available for them. The aspatial WWW has the potential for transformative impact here.

The first part of this chapter reviews debates around the geographical patterns of communities, the objects they create, and cultural institutions which house collections which include those objects. The second part examines digital approaches to place, and how these approaches inform the kinds of developments in digital storytelling referenced above. The third and concluding part suggests a set of high-level discussion points for future research into the relationship between "the digital" and "the physical" in museums, which makes use of the connective powers of the WWW, especially through methods of Linked Open Data (LOD), which will help scholars, curators and the wider public (including museum visitor) better understand

and develop the idea of the spatial narratives and cultural geographies of the "object itinerary".

12.3 Museums and Physical (Spatial) Narrative

The physical transfer of an object or artefact from one geo-cultural context to another is a significant attribute of that object's historical and spatial narrative, promoting the establishment of extrinsic statements about its history and context (which may or may not have colonial undertones). One key feature of the "Wunderkammer" ("Cabinet of Curiosities") collections of the early modern period was that they provided discreet, sterile environments in a physical place in which visitors—usually members of the educated elite—could be presented with object narratives, and create new, interpretive ones of their own. In the Wunderkammer, the "polyhistor", or polymathic, scholar with expertise in multiple subjects, philosophies and regions, was the main audience, and the main type of visitor (Westerhoff 2001; see also discussions of the Museum of Jurassic Technology in Weschler (1995) for a modern, constructed and destabilizing version in Los Angeles). The position of such a scholar as the author and promulgator of narratives which told "truth" about the regions represented in the collection conferred upon them intellectual and cultural authority, and status and cultural power on the collection itself. This was only enabled because the collection was located and curated in such a way as to facilitate interaction with the objects' culture as a process of detached critical research in the polyhistor's "home" environment, rather than any process of immersive engagement with the culture in question. This inevitably reflected economic, social and political power imbalances at both global and regional scales (Ajana 2015).

Major national institutions with "encyclopedic" collections, i.e. those which deal with the material of many cultures, present collections of material organized geographically and represent especially complex examples of such networks. The early history of large, national Western museums of this type is thus inevitably bound up with the cultural preoccupations of what such societies consider to be important in relation to their own history. In many of the major museums of Northern and Western Europe for example, this preoccupation manifests itself with a great emphasis (in national-level collections) on the history and archaeology of Greece and Rome (Elsner et al. 1996). Historically, the stories of such museums are closely bound up with colonial and postcolonial narratives, and the commodification of "otherness" for domestic consumption (Coombes 1988). Edward Said's famous analysis in *Orientalism* characterized this in terms of critical separation between the student and the studied, where "the Orient" and the material cultures of non-Western countries was characterized as an abstraction, which are intellectually subject to the "Western corporate institution for dealing with the Orient" (Said 1978 p. 3). Such a "reduced status" was, at least in part, legitimized by the physical separation of the artefacts from the geographical context in which they were produced, and the reproduction, or at least the remediation, of that context elsewhere, under the host institution's curatorial direction. For Said, this is cultural appropriation and or oppression; but for others it is a legitimate part of the presentation, understanding and valorization of heritage in a world which is more globally connected than ever before. Making this point, James Cuno, argues that the present-day location of a museum collection, as "the result of collective, national intelligence", is at best irrelevant because all culture is global and interconnected, and at worst calls to "repatriate" artefacts of major significance to their regions of origin represents "an attempt to deny the truth of our basic and inevitable cultural interrelatedness" (Cuno 2010, p. 161).

This debate is more muted in the context of museums which are situated in local communities and display culture that is specific to that group. These are by definition not "encyclopedic" collections. Rather than the detached organizing of the culture of "other" societies according to parameters that make sense to their visitors, and thus perpetuating the processes of cultural separation that implies, such museums can act as hubs of inclusivity and agents of the construction of local identities (Hoobler 2006). They stand in contrast to the "phenomenologically detached" status of Western encyclopedic museums, as described by Said. This distinction, and possible tension between the roles of different kinds of museums revolves around the situatedness they have in relation to the region(s) from which their collections are drawn. This in turn highlights the fact that all museums represent complex multilayered and multi-scalar geographies. More obviously, it highlights the fact that in order to be presented in a museum, an object has to *travel.* How far, over what cultural boundaries, and as a result of what (im)balances of power between cultures determines the character of the museum. It is for this reason that the idea of the "biography" or "itinerary" of the artefact has garnered so much interest, especially in the post-processual discussions of archaeology and museum studies (Gosden and Marshall 1999). The artefact emerges as a material manifestation of cultural and geographical interaction.

An even more fundamental debate is the epistemological nature of the object itself, and the significance it gains when transported to, and displayed in, a specific geographical location. This then shapes the kind of knowledge that is/can be created about collections of objects by third parties, such as visitors and scholars. The Wunderkammer-like, and indeed the colonial-era museum, model assumes that artefacts of far-removed cultures are static and unsympathetic "things" to be analyzed from a standpoint of critical detachment and scientific empiricism. Such empiricism provided the background for the creation of "scientific" typology, and structural categorization of material culture, both contemporary and from the distant past.

19th century Britain, a period of significant economic and cultural success, as well as colonial expansion and consolidation, saw archaeologists such as Augustus Lane Fox Pitt-Rivers developing "scientific" typologies for cultural artefacts based on precepts of Darwinian evolution, where one "class" of object can be seen to evolve inevitably into another. The processes by which this happened were observable, repeatable and predictable; a viewpoint which laid the way for uniformitarian, or processual approaches to archaeology which were widely accepted until the mid-20th century (Hamilakis 2007). This approach assumes a heavy rationalist and materialist basis for the evolution of human culture. Indeed, many saw the curation and presentation of artefacts according to rigid structural logic to be an essential palliative to "irrational" thought in contemporary politics and society—which was perceived as being dangerous to prevailing social order. "There is no use in exhibiting, if we do not educate", wrote Pitt-Rivers in 1857. In 1891, he pressed his case even more forcefully: "The masses are ignorant … The knowledge they lack is the knowledge of history. This lays them open to the designs of demagogues and agitators who strive to make them break with the past, and seek … drastic changes that have not the sanction of experience." (Pitt Rivers 1891). A scientific, Wunderkammer-like commodification of the past into a rational series of sequences and predictable processes, progressing from an unsophisticated state to a sophisticated one, unevolved to evolved, barbarism to civilization, acted as a model for order and enlightened reason in the contemporary world of the 19th century.

Physical geographical situatedness was therefore important to the emergence of the Western museum as a means of creating narratives about histories of "otherness". This is hardly a new observation, and it forms a key part of discussions about the relationship between museums and colonial histories, and the story of their adaptation to the postcolonial present (Aldrich 2009)—and it must be acknowledged that most such museums take active steps to help their visitors access and understands those histories. In more recent history, museology—and, of course, museums themselves—has pushed back against such empiricist and ultra-rationalist views of the past and sought to engage more empathetically with their artefacts and audiences, and with the cultures behind them. Such views recognize that the geographical and cultural diversity which make up their nuanced histories are, in themselves, desirable subjects for discussion and sharing. Among the most notable of the ideas embracing this post-processual approach—a movement in archaeological theory that emphasizes the subjectivity of archaeological interpretations—to objects to emerge is that of "object biography", a label which imbues an archaeological artifact or a museum object with the characteristics of a living thing, which garners experience of the world as it travels across cultural and social boundaries. As Gosden and Marshall state in their introduction to a special issue of *World Archaeology* introducing the idea:

> The notion of biography is one that leads us to think comparatively about the accumulation of meaning in objects and the changing effects these have on people and events. This central thread of comparison, however, makes the variety of relationships between people and things in different cultural contexts even more apparent. Ultimately, the utility of the metaphor of biography will depend upon on its role in revealing this variety. (Gosden and Marshall 1999, p. 173)

The emergence of "biographical" approaches to objects, of which this volume was a key milestone, had much to do with the development of object studies in the social sciences, and an increasing, post-processual concern with the contextual importance of physicality, and the stories that physical objects contain and express, in society more generally. Object biography is directly related to the study of museums and narrative. Narrative is, after all, the process of telling of stories; and the concept of narrative has frequently been used as a vehicle for forming and conveying the historical and archeological events as a sequence of processes (Hodder 1993; Pluciennik 1999). Indeed, the concept of an "event", an occurrence that is bounded and causes change, is central to the idea of narrative itself.

Recognizing the importance of the story behind the object means understanding that an ontological separation between human actors and objects, and the assumption that the former has agency, but the latter has not, is a product of rationalist/materialist traditions (see relevant discussions in Westin et al. 2018): the kind of material rationalism exemplified by Pitt-Rivers. The distinction becomes even more important for an empathetic view of the place of objects in societies *outside* of the post-Enlightenment West with its approaches to materiality. Wallis points out, for example, that aboriginal Australian rock art cannot be understood with reference to Western assumptions about the distinction between human and non-human actors, such as animals and objects: "[t]his reluctance to step beyond a rational materialist standpoint positions indigenous 'animic' ontologies as incorrect; material objects are dynamic ('participate') only insofar as they 'affect us'" (Wallis 2009 p. 51). It is worth restating here therefore that the empiricist nature of the contemporary museum environment, by default, privileges the physicality of the object, and potentially obscures stories which are narratives in a non-Western sense.

Any attempt to address this must, of course, focus on the non-physical attributes of the objects in a collection. Here, the (nonphysical) background to an object that a museum (a) has and (b) displays to its audience is essential. The availability of contextual information attached to objects varies greatly according to a number of factors. These include the date of the object, the amount of provenance gathered at the time of its discovery and/or acquisition, the amount of relevant historical research and documentation available, and so on. Some engaged with the field of object biography research draw a distinction, for example, between objects produced by prehistoric societies and those of literate cultures. In the former, there is be no historical information to provide context about either the object or the society which produced it. In the latter, however, it is possible to access information about processes, rituals, activities and so on that object was involved with (Joy 2009). To take one example, the Parthenon Sculptures in the British Museum are imbued with the complex historical contexts of the 5th century BCE in Athens (and a controversial contemporary one), but this background can only be fully appreciated and analyzed with an understanding of the historical texts (mainly those of Herodotus) which describe the rationale for their commissioning in Athenian military victories against Persia earlier in the 5th century.

There is also the religious context for the mythological scenes on the pediments, the cultic significance of the civic procession, and so on. One could add to this scenes from the sculptures' later biographies, for example the explosion in the Parthenon of 1687, which wrought major damage to them; the conditions of geographical transportation of the these marbles; and the circumstances of their appropriation by the Earl of Elgin from the occupying Ottoman authorities in 1801 (St. Clair 1998); their reception in the 1819 painting by Archibald Archer that depicts the exhibition of the marbles in their first, temporary space in the British Museum; their role in constructing and sustaining National/European narratives (Hamilakis 2007). In contrast, again for example, the faience "Snake Goddess" from Neopalatial Crete, discovered by Sir Arthur Evans in 1903, and now in the Heraklion Museum, is an iconic material cultural representation of Late Bronze Age Crete in the present day; yet very little is known of its history or original significance. Indeed, it has been a subject for debate as to whether it in fact represents a goddess, or a priestess. The lack of any cognitive or historical context renders the process of explicating its biographical narrative one of interpretation and, in many cases, informed guesswork (Herschman and Lapatin 2017).

Other museum, particularly those at sites of historical importance, explicitly seek to mediate between the materiality of the objects and intangible significance of the site itself. The museum at Delos (see Fig. 12.1), for example, curatorially presents the site of the Delian Treasury, whose removal to Athens in 454 BC symbolizes the start of Athenian hegemony in the northern Aegean, and the train of event which led to the Peloponnesian War. Upon entrance to the island, there are visitors' tangible, foldable paper guides designed by the archaeologist P. I. Chatzidakis, in Greek, English and French. The guide, entitled 'A Tour of the Archaeological Sites of Delos' includes maps of the island, narrative and pictures of artefacts and temples on site (such as that in Fig. 12.2).

The first picture one sees when acquiring the guide is a Romantic reconstruction of the sanctuary, made by H. P. Néno in 1882. This guide displays the space of the site and the museum as an encultured entity, presenting a variety of routes to visit the site with annotations of landmarks, and art (mosaics, frescos, sculptures). If one unfolds the whole guide, on the one side there is a 2D pathfinding sketch of the site, with three 'itineraries', and on the other there is an explicit 3D reconstruction of the Sanctuary and the ancient town by Francesco Comi (1995, as seen in Bell' Europa) that is annotated with about a hundred landmarks on site. There are also two smaller 3D reconstructions on the same side of the leaflet: (1) the reconstruction of the sanctuary by the French School of Athens (1996) and (2) the reconstruction of a block of Delian houses by Peter Fister, (1970). The guide has also instructions on how to use it as an 'itinerary' to navigate. It is itself a mini model (prototype) study of town planning, an annotated town map, and it offers several different types of visualizations as it includes pictures of temples and artefacts and a number of annotated maps and reconstructions of the site (such as in Fig. 12.3).

A key part of Gosden and Marshall's biographical approach to objects is that they are deeply embedded in social networks. Social networks are, inevitably, nonphysical in character, yet they are integral to the spatial narrative of objects. In many cases, the biographies of objects and the biography of persons—i.e. a more traditional sense of the word—become intertwined. Mostly however, these are as invisible to the present-day museum visitor (or museum-based scholar) as the original central context of the object, whether it is historic or prehistoric. However, they *can* be traced where we have primary materials relating to the formation of collections, particularly connections that are closely associated with prominent individuals.

One good example of this is the University of Reading's Ure Museum of Greek Archaeology, which is a major collection of artefacts (mainly) from Greece, with materials gathered from various sources from the early 20th century onwards, driven by the work of Percy Ure (1879–1950) and his wife Annie (1893–1976). As well as the objects, the museum contains an extensive archive of paperwork related to the establishment and development of the collection, and from this, insights into the

Fig. 12.1 Papposelenos from the temple of dionysus in the museum of Delos, Cyclades (2nd BCE). (© Anna Foka. Publishing permission granted by the archaeological ephorate of the Cyclades 11/2018)

narratives of the objects, and those who came into contact with them, can be traced. In an account of the museum's founding, written as a foreword to a catalogue of the collection in, Annie Ure notes that the exact date of the museum's inception is difficult to pinpoint, beginning as it did with some Egyptian antiquities given by Flinders Petrie in 1909; with some further objects given by the British School of Archaeology in Egypt a little later. Later, when Percy Ure moved to Reading in 1911, he brought:

Fig. 12.2 Vestibule with copy of the mosaic of the goddess Tanit, House of the Dolphins, signed by Phoenician Asclepiades of in Delos, Cyclades. Original mosaic is preserved in the museum of Delos, Cyclades. (© Anna Foka. Publishing permission granted by the archaeological ephorate of the Cyclades 11/2018)

> a small collection of sherds and fragmentary vases, most of them purchased or picked up in Greece on various sites, a number of them from Rhitsona [in Boeotia], not from the excavations, but actually from the bushes where they had been thrown away by tomb-robbers, who thought they were not worth the trouble of taking into Thebes or Athens to sell. (Ure 1924)

Annie Ure's account illustrates that, unlike an object, a museum is, itself, not necessarily a narratively complete object with a clear beginning, but that the spatial narratives of the objects that make up collections are oftentimes fuzzy, un-grid like, undocumented (and un-documentable), and subject to the vagaries of human estimations of what is worth preserving and what is not. Further examination of the Ure archive shows that the object-person metaphor is made explicit in a letter dated July 10, 1958 from F. Smuts to Mrs. Ure, from the RMS *Praetoria Castle*, thanking her for the meeting they had and for the present of a "Corinthian aryballos". This flask, Smuts writes, "will always be a highly valued possession, and I only hope it will not remain too lonely, but gather some friends of its own kind around it" (Smuts 1958). The formal provenance of this aryballos is not recorded, but the metaphor of it acquiring "friends", itself in the context of an informal social communication between one individual closely associated with a physical museum, and another whom they came into contact with through abstract and immaterial social networks, illustrates perfectly the blending of physical and material histories. It also shows that objects of cultural value will, almost inevitably, pass between social networks through the agencies of gifting, ritual and commerce.

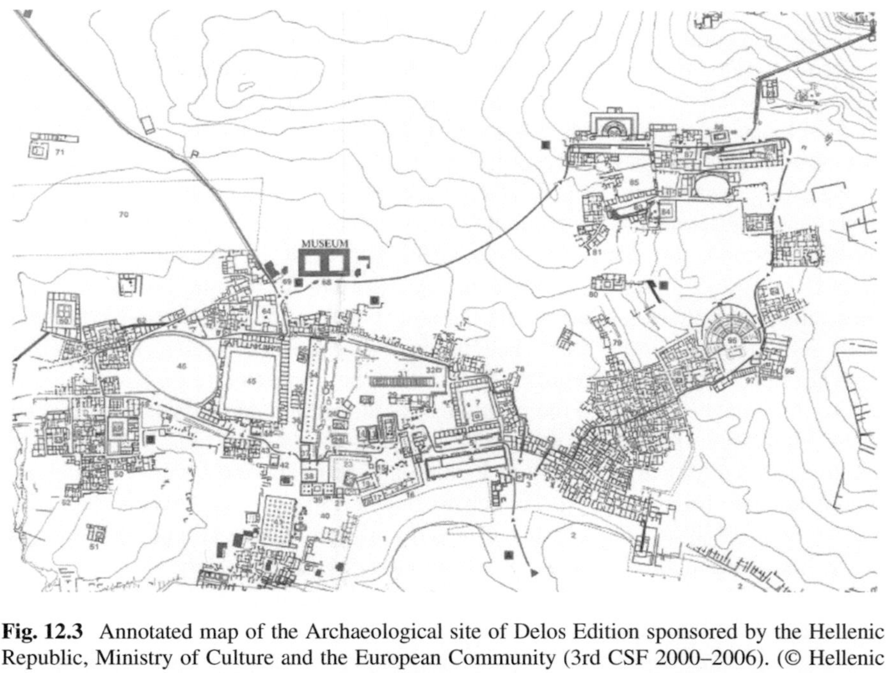

Fig. 12.3 Annotated map of the Archaeological site of Delos Edition sponsored by the Hellenic Republic, Ministry of Culture and the European Community (3rd CSF 2000–2006). (© Hellenic Republic, Ministry of Culture and the European Community, 3rd CSF 2000–2006. Publishing permission granted by the archaeological ephorate of the Cyclades 11/2018)

12.4 Object Itineraries and Digital Narratives

The preceding sections sought to provide a brief summary of the significance of materiality in the trajectories of museum objects and cultural artefacts through time and space, and of how narratives emerge from the processes of transfer. Such narratives emerge from objects, whether they are the empiricist structures of Pitt-Rivers, using classification and typology to tell the story of evolution from one class to the next (thus legitimizing larger narratives of progression from an uncivilized state to a civilized on), or the historical narratives around the Parthenon Sculptures, or the personal narratives read in the records of the Ure Museum. What, however, is the role of the WWW in generating and conveying these narratives?

Connected data, digital objects, virtual museums, linked databases and digitally mediated ways of interacting with objects have bought new ways of exploring and telling object itineraries under what might be called the banners of digital museology, or digital art history. Yet these remain far less problematized or researched than (say) the influence of physical (museum or gallery) environments on the conditioning of object narratives (e.g., Coombes 1988; Moser 2010), or the impact of social media on visitor and curator practices. In the latter case, while great potential was foreseen in the mid-2000s of the "democratizing" effect of social media in museums, at a time when social media and the interactive Internet were becoming widespread in the developed world (see, e.g., Russo et al. 2008; Richardson 2012), the reality is that most museum social media profiles are largely unidirectional, with museum staff broadcasting content with little two-way engagement (Fletcher and Lee 2012). And while many museums are experimenting with digital strategies in order to increase accessibility and promoted user engagement, bar some experimentation with the Internet of Things in museums contexts (e.g. Hudson-Smith et al. 2012), there has been relatively little engagement with the object biographies literature. And finally, while some museums have drawn heavily on digital practices such as Linked Open Data (LOD) in the management of their cataloguing systems (e.g., Szekely et al. 2013), these have focused on the problems of collection management and, in some cases, integration through various "hub" datasets on the Semantic Web. There is therefore a need for a more deeply theorized understanding of the ways in which the spatial and curatorial narratives that convey object itineraries are formed, theorized, and conveyed digitally. There is also a need for greater consideration of the possibilities of semantic encoding of elements of narrative ontologies (Hargood et al. 2012), which would in turn allow for more responsive, contextual generative narratives that better reflect the biographies of the objects described.

A credible starting point for such a theorization is efforts to un-pick colonial and postcolonial entanglements of the type described above. Most obviously perhaps, some have promoted the idea of "digital repatriation", whereby digital material such as scans, images, 3D point clouds and so on (see, for example, Hess et al. 2009) are provided to the objects' originating communities. However, while such initiatives have been known to inspire dialogue and communication between regionally-sited communities and cultural institutions containing objects they created, there are obvious objections to the concept of digital repatriation, mostly framed by the relative value of the physical and the digital object itself. The idea that the latter is necessarily a substitute for the former was perhaps most eloquently critiqued by Jim Enote who, quoted by Bell et al. in their report of their workshop at which he was keynote *Storytelling in a digital age: digital storytelling as an emerging narrative method for preserving and promoting indigenous oral wisdom,* asks "[i]f the digital is so good, why don't you keep it?" (Bell et al. 2007). Others, likewise, have questioned whether transferring a digital surrogate of an object from a museum to a community is in fact either "virtual" or "repatriation" in the accepted sense of either term (Boast and Enote 2013) New media, on the other hand (and as acknowledged by Enote in this Willcox et al.), has a co-creative power which can operate across spatial distance. In particular, this has been leveraged in the curation of oral histories of tribal communities, and in the preservation of those histories in digital media (Cunsolo Willox et al. 2013).

Such questions of digital repatriation also raise wider concerns over the ownership of digital assets, and the other media they may replicate or draw inspiration from. Such ownership need no longer be restricted to that of the digital asset itself but rather to any component of it, and ownership might be defined in such a way that access could be relinquished at any time. This presents both legal and methodological challenges. For example, in the case of crowd-sourced datasets used to derive secondary digital products such as photogrammetric models, the single digital asset that is the outcome of alignment and processing of many thousands of inputs is of far less significance than the whole collection and potentially of a small subset of input data that had most influence on the creation of the final model. In this case the ability precisely to define ownership at a highly granular level for each input image, perhaps through smart contracts of some kind, would enable this level of control. However, even then one must also consider the need to represent contested ownership or contextual access.

The main objection therefore to processes such as digital repatriation is the *placelessness* of the digital world. It is at points such as this—a key one for the cultural and political situatedness of artefacts, as well as their literal/physical situatedness—that any posited equivalence between digital object and physical object breaks down. One key reason for this is that, by and large, digital "objects" relate to only one, or at most two, of the sensory functions, most often vision (Kleege 2018). After all, the literal meaning of the term *visualization* is one of rendering information, or objects, into a medium that can be seen, usually through the agency of an electronic screen. There are various ways and methods of ensuring that the processes by which the 3D visualization of an object is true to the evidence that the visualization work is drawing on—on example being the London Charter initiative, which sets out six principles for ensuring transparency in the construction of 3D models (Beacham et al. 2006). However, while this provides an essential starting point for good curation and model-building practice, neither this, nor most screen-based means for providing access to 3D models, are designed to capture the relationship between formally structured information and the object being visualized.

Considering the limitations of digital repatriation in this way highlights the deficiencies of any model which does (/can)not capture the sensory phenomenologies of sound, smell or touch (although experiments in haptic technology have made some headway with the latter). To dig deeper into an object's spatiality and physicality using formal digital methods, one needs a mechanism of linking data, whether in the form of catalogue entries, or crowd/visitor-generated tags, to the representation of the object. One intriguing solution provided to this is the Harvesting and Aggregating Networked Annotations (HarvANA) system, which allows users to attach tags to 3D scans of museum objects, then allowing those tags to be represented as linkable as RDF datasets (Hunter and Gerber 2010). This enables those "objects" to be represented and integrated into distributed and linkable datasets, rather than just visualized and transmitted visually.

This takes discussion of the "digital object biography" into the realms of web and Internet narrative creation; and the latter has an altogether different set of political and cultural implications for objects and their emplacement. (Digital) data and place have a more complex relationship, formed at bewildering speeds over the past forty years or so with the development of the Internet and, more recently, the WWW itself (Abbate 2000). In particular, since the mid-2000s, the development of major web mapping platforms such as OpenStreetMap (established 2004) and the launch of Google Earth (established 2005) has ushered in a new phase of human interaction with place, through the lenses of web mapping and, more recently, GPS (Haklay et al. 2008). By creating billions of georeferenced data points, a significant proportion of which is generated within cultural sites such as museums, a new disruption to the concept of place itself has emerged. Zook and Graham labelled this "Digiplace", a "fluid and complex state of being, in which agents and structures are interminably enabling and shaping one another" (Zook and Graham 2007). The idea of Digiplace situates place as an entity co-created by billions of Internet interactions as a set of uncontained (and uncontainable) narratives. Just as physical museums, as described above, can be shown to be situated and sited places of the creation of narrative, the "placelessness", or ubiquity of the WWW enables the curation of cultural power-narratives of a different kind. The feminist geographer Monica Stephens, for example, has shown that supposedly neutral and open geographic data platforms such as OpenStreetMap are, in fact heavily gendered and racially skewed "places", whose data, practices, rules and philosophies reflect closely the preoccupations and world-views of those who make up the majority of their user bases—overwhelmingly white, male, Western and relatively well-educated (Stephens 2013). As such, one might think of the worldwide digital maps that have resulted from over a decade of collective web mapping as *uncurated* spatial narratives.

It follows logically from this discussion that distinction between curated and uncurated narratives is useful when considering the overlap between museums and the web. This is furthermore born out when we consider ways in which structured information about objects is presented and managed *without* the physical museum at all. The *Arachne* project for example, provides an online dataset which brings together records of collections held at the German Archaeological Institute (DAI) and the Cologne Digital Archaeology Laboratory (CoDArchLab) at the Archaeological Institute of the University of Cologne (see https://arachne.uni-koeln.de/drupal). This resource promotes the idea that making connections between objects based on a shared understanding and/or interpretation of their physical attributes must always supersede any local project-based implementation. As the explanatory background information on the Arachne website puts it: "[t]he database design reflects a world model based on two very simple assumptions in archaeology or art history: all objects in the "real world" should be comparable on a very general level, and all objects have a context" (https://arachne.uni-koeln.de/drupal). This can also allow "deep digital object" information to be linked to other kinds of web data.

This relates to efforts by digital scholars of the ancient world to federate information which does *not* derive from a physical object, such as attestations of places in texts. These have shown that the same principles apply there. Examples of ways in which such attestations are treated as *digital* objects, to be connected and federated online, include the Pelagios project (Isaksen et al. 2014), which uses canonical URIs for places provided by the Pleiades gazetteer, to link those places with other places, and with databases of objects, (Elliott and Gillies 2009); including the Arachne dataset itself. Such Linked Open Data (LOD) structures are thus able to maintain trails of scholarly authority back to original source material, and this form of authoritative connected narratives transcend individual datasets and sources; while at the same time have the web-like capacity to grow organically. The presence of authoritative sources within object and non-object derived sets of LOD allows different forms of structured knowledge to emerge. These are very distinct from the top-down, super-curated type of knowledge structures that stemmed from the Wunderkammer, and that was presented to the world by Pitt-Rivers in the 1880s. A key reason for this is that such knowledge develops and persists in cyberspace. It could not develop in the same way in the physical world. This raises the question of how it relates to the "fluid and complex" world of "Digiplace" (Zook and Graham 2007). For the LOD and the WWW do not exist in isolation from one another. As Isaksen et al. put it: "Linked Data is sometimes discussed as though it exists as its own parallel Web, unpolluted by the Web of Documents. This is highly detrimental to its adoption" (Isaksen et al. 2014, p. 200).

Finally, some museums have embraced the physical/digital narrative very explicitly. In the physical context of the museum, these can take the form of interactive exhibits and/or installations, which make use of physical and digital infrastructure, such as RFID tags or Wi-Fi. For example, the "EGO-TRAP" installation at the Experimentarium in Copenhagen is a game-like installation facilitated through interaction with visitors' cell phones, which guide them through the exhibits and provide interactive tests at each one, eventually inverting the visitor's assumptions about what they are and are not in control of (Kahr-Højland 2010). Such instances illustrate how disruptive to the physicality of the museum digital narrative can be.

12.5 Conclusion

This brief discussion of the nexus between physically- and digitally-framed narratives highlights a fundamental paradox that lies at the heart of digital museology: as a concept, beginning with the Wunderkammer, the museum is a point of discrete, sited, site-specific creation of narratives deriving from physical objects and their unphysical context. It is culturally and intellectually given to rationalist narratives which structure collections-based knowledge according to positivist frameworks. Conversely, the Web is incorporeal and exists to connect objects together. Such informational context, its history of movement through space as well as time, frames that object's cultural significance. An object can thus be encultured with social and/or political significance which it might not otherwise enjoy—as, for example, with the Parthenon Sculptures in the British Museum, which are up to this day indirectly claimed by the government of modern Greece, after the media campaign for their repatriation in 1984 (New York Times 1984). Museums may thus be seen as nodes in networks formed by the trajectories of their objects, and it is from this that the paradox weakens, and idea of the "digital object biography" emerges.

One of the most obvious problems with both the term "biography" and "itinerary" is that these are both terms which imply narratives describing agency, whereas objects, by themselves, have no agency. They are thus subordinate to the human processes which are typically the concern of anthropology and social history. Gosden and Marshall (1999, pp. 169–178) set out to address this by highlighting relations between people and objects. These relationships, they argue, mean that "objects become invested with meaning through the social interactions they are caught up in" This present chapter has sought to update this premise.

A vision of a "digital object itinerary" which addresses the complexities highlighted by Gosden and Marshall, which navigates the ethical polarities of the debate exemplified by the positions of Said and Cuno, and which positions itself successfully in the post-processual world which came after Pitt-Rivers and the kind of museum he envisaged, must have certain attributes. Firstly, and most obviously, it must contain more than simply visual data. The kind of metadata structures which now routinely capture other sensory attributes need to be integrated. Secondly, any collection or scholar seeking to express object itineraries using the LOD web must acknowledge that in Digiplace, many voices may describe that object. As Isaksen et al. note, LOD and the wider Web do not exist in isolation, and indeed further informational contexts from other, un-curated sources, might enrich our knowledge of that itinerary. These might come from other LOD datasets, from open webpages, or capture the experiences of visitors. Above all, it prompts us to re-think what is meant by "creation" itself. Curation of a digital object itinerary probably cannot be carried out by one person, most likely it will cross spatial, institutional and cultural barriers, and most importantly it demands a new kind of critical analysis which draws not only on the discourses of museum scholarship, but also on the wider questions of digital culture and society.

Acknowledgements We thank the staff of the Ure Museum in Reading for their help with this work—Prof. Amy C. Smith for permission to examine the archives and quote the unpublished material therein; Prof. Jane F. Gardner for further background information, and Jayne Holly-Wait and Claudina Romero Mayorga for practical support.

References

Abbate J (2000) Inventing the Internet, MIT Press
Ajana B (2015) Branding, legitimation and the power of museums: the case of the Louvre Abu Dhabi. Museum Soc 13(3):316–335. https://journals.le.ac.uk/ojs1/index.php/mas/article/view/333
Aldrich R (2009) Colonial museums in a postcolonial Europe. African Black Diaspora Int J 2(2):137–156. https://doi.org/10.1080/17528630902981118
Beacham R, Denard H, Niccolucci F (2006) An introduction to the London charter. In: The E-volution of ICTechnology in cultural heritage, Papers from the Joint Event CIPA/VAST/EG/EuroMed Event, 2006
Bell JA, Christen K, Turin M (2007) Introduction: after the return. Museum Anthropology Review, 7. Indiana University Bloomington Libraries. https://scholarworks.iu.edu/journals/index.php/mar/article/view/3184
Boast R, Enote J (2013) Virtual repatriation: it is neither virtual nor repatriation. In: Biehl PF, Prescott C (eds) Heritage in the context of globalization—Europe and the Americas. Springer, New York, pp 103–113. https://doi.org/10.1007/978-1-4614-6077-0_13
Bodenhamer DJ, Corrigan J, Harris TM (eds) (2015) Deep maps and spatial narratives. Indiana University Press
Caquard S (2011) Cartography I: Mapping narrative cartography. Prog Hum Geogr 37(1):135–144. https://doi.org/10.1177/0309132511423796
Castells, M. (2011). A Network Theory of Power. International Journal of Communication, 5(0), pp. 773–787. http://ijoc.org/index.php/ijoc/article/view/1136
Coombes AE (1988) Museums and the formation of national and cultural identities. Oxford Art J 11(2):57–68. Oxford University Press. http://www.jstor.org/stable/1360462
Cuno J (2010) Who owns antiquity?: Museums and the battle over our ancient heritage. Princeton University Press
Cunsolo Willox A, Harper SL, Edge VL. (2013) "My Word": storytelling and digital media, and Government, R. I. C. Storytelling in a digital age: digital storytelling as an emerging narrative method for preserving and promoting indigenous oral wisdom. Qual Res 13(2):127–147. https://doi.org/10.1177/1468794112446105
Elliott T, Gillies S (2009) Digital geography and classics. Dig Humanities Q 3(1):20
Elsner J, MacGregor A, Bann S, Pearce SM, Bennett T, Pointon M, Messenger PM (1996) The "New Museology" and classical art. Am J Archaeology 100(4):769. https://doi.org/10.2307/506677
Fletcher A, Lee MJ (2012) Current social media uses and evaluations in American museums. Museum Manag Curatorship 27(5):505–521. https://doi.org/10.1080/09647775.2012.738136
Gillespie S (2015) Things in motion: object itineraries in anthropological practice. School for Advanced Research Press, Santa Fe
Gosden C, Marshall Y (1999) The cultural biography of objects. World Archaeology 31(2):169–178. https://doi.org/10.1080/00438243.1999.9980439
Haklay M, Weber P (2008) OpenStreetMap: user-generated street maps. Pervasive Comput IEEE 7:12–18. http://discovery.ucl.ac.uk/13849/1/13849.pdf
Hamilakis Y (2007) Nation and its ruins: antiquity, archaeology, and national imagination in greece (classical presences). Oxford University Press
Hargood C, Jewell MO, Millard DE (2012) The narrative braid: a model for tackling the narrative paradox in adaptive documentaries. In: Proceedings of the 2nd Workshop on Narrative and Hypertext, pp 13–18
Herschman R, Lapatin K (2017) Restoring the minoans: Elizabeth Price and Sir Arthur Evans, Princeton University Press
Hess M, Robson S, Millar FS, Were G, Hviding E, Berg AC (2009) Niabara—the western solomon islands war canoe at the British Museum—3D documentation, virtual reconstruction and digital repatriation. In: 15th International Conference on Virtual Systems and Multimedia, IEEE, pp 41–46. https://doi.org/10.1109/vsmm.2009.12

Hodder I (1993) The narrative and rhetoric of material culture sequences. World Archaelogy 25(2):268–282. https://doi.org/10.1080/00438243.1993.9980243
Hoobler E (2006) To take their heritage in their hands: indigenous self-representation and decolonization in the community museums of Oaxaca, Mexico. Am Indian Q 30(3):441–460. https://doi.org/10.1353/aiq.2006.0024
Hudson-Smith A, Gray S, Ross C, Barthel R, de Jode M, Warwick C, Terras M (2012) Experiments with the Internet of Things in museum space. UbiComp 2012:1183. https://doi.org/10.1145/2370216.2370469
Hunter J, Gerber A (2010) Harvesting community annotations on 3D models of museum artefacts to enhance knowledge, discovery and re-use. J Cultural Heritage 11(1):81–90. https://doi.org/10.1016/j.culher.2009.04.004
Isaksen L, Simon R, Barker ETE, de Soto Cañamares P (2014) Pelagios and the emerging graph of ancient world data. In: Proceedings of the 2014 ACM Conference on Web Science—WebSci'14, pp 197–201. https://doi.org/10.1145/2615569.2615693
Joy J (2009) Reinvigorating object biography: reproducing the drama of object lives. World Archaeology 41(4):540–556. https://doi.org/10.1080/00438240903345530
Kahr-Højland A (2010) EGO-TRAP: a mobile augmented reality tool for science learning in a semi-formal setting. Curator: The Museum J 53(4):501–509. https://doi.org/10.1111/j.2151-6952.2010.00050.x
Kleege G (2018) More than meets the eye: what blindness brings to art, Oxford University Press
Moser S (2010) The devil is in the detail: museum displays and the creation of knowledge. Museum Anthropology 33(1):22–32. https://doi.org/10.1111/j.1548-1379.2010.01072.x
New York Times (1984) Q and A: Melina Mercourt; greece's claim to the elgin marbles. The New York Times, March 4, 1984. https://www.nytimes.com/1984/03/04/weekinreview/q-a-melina-mercourt-greece-s-claim-to-the-elgin-marbles.html. Accessed on 25 Nov 2018
Pitt Rivers AHLF (1891) Typological museums. J Soc Arts pp 115–116
Pluciennik M (1999) Archaeological narratives and other ways of telling. Current Anthropology 40(5):653–678. http://www.ncbi.nlm.nih.gov/pubmed/10539944
Richardson L (2012) Twitter and archaeology: an archaeological network in 140 characters or less. In: Bonacchi C (ed) Archaeology and digital communication. Archetype Publications, London, pp 15–24
Russo A, Watkins J, Kelly L, Chan S (2008) Participatory Commun Social Media. Curator 51(1):21–31
Said E (1978) Orientalism. Pantheon, New York
Smuts F (1958) Unpublished letter to Annie Ure, 1958
St. Clair W (1998) Lord elgin and the marbles, Oxford University Press
Stephens M (2013) Gender and the GeoWeb: divisions in the production of user-generated geographic information. GeoJ 78(6):981–996, Special issue on theorizing the GeoWeb. Springer. https://www.jstor.org/stable/24432638
Szekely P, Knoblock CA, Yang F, Zhu X, Fink EE, Allen R, Goodlander G (2013) Connecting the Smithsonian American art museum to the linked data cloud. In: Cimiano P, Corcho O, Presutti V, Hollink L, Rudolph S (eds) The semantic web: semantics and big data. Springer, pp 593–607. DOI:https://doi.org/10.1007/978-3-642-38288-8_40
Ure AD (1924) Unpublished manucript, Ure Museum Archive, University of Reading, UK
Wallis RJ (2009) Re-enchanting rock art landscapes: animic ontologies, nonhuman agency and rhizomic personhood. Time Mind 2(1):47–69. https://doi.org/10.2752/175169709X374272
Weschler L (1995) Mr. Wilson's Cabinet of Wonder: Pronged Ants, Horned Humans, Mice on Toast, and Other Marvels of Jurassic Technology. Random House. ISBN 978-0-679-76489-2
Westerhoff JC (2001) A world of signs: baroque pansemioticism, the polyhistor and the early modern Wunderkammer. J History Ideas 62(4):633–650. https://doi.org/10.1353/jhi.2001.0041
Westin J, Foka A, Chapman A (2018) Humanising places: exposing histories of the disenfranchised through augmented reality. Int J Heritage Stud 24(3):283–286

Wyman B, Smith S, Meyers D, Godfrey M (2011) Digital storytelling in museums: observations and best practices. Curator: The Museum J 54(4):461–468. https://doi.org/10.1111/j.2151-6952.2011.00110.x

Zook MA, Graham M (2007) Mapping Digiplace: Geocoded Internet data and the representation of place. Environ Plan 34(3):466–482. https://doi.org/10.1068/b3311

Part V
Audiences

Chapter 13
How Museums Made (and Re-made) Their Digital User

Ross Parry

Abstract Surveying archival material from across fifty years of practice, and leveraging multi-disciplinary theoretical perspectives from digital studies, design studies and disability studies, this chapter uses a form of ideational history, to evidence shifting linguistic habits and frames of reference around the construct of the 'digital user', at once both sequential and enduring: from the user as 'operator' (set within a system-orientated context of organizational efficiency); to the user as 'individual' (amidst priorities of usability and experience design); to—emerging today—the user as 'actant' (against which social value and agency are the new indices of success). In these different constructions, the 'digital user' moves from being part of the system, to outside system, to in the world, whilst its principal capability shifts from automation, to personalization to empowerment. Crucially, it is proposed here that it has been the role of accessible design (in particular, the design of digital with disability in mind) that has acted both as a key informant and agitator of this change, but also the practice through which this development can most usefully be seen.

13.1 Introduction

Museums have been talking about computers for over fifty years. And as they have talked, so their specialist vocabularies have become 'registers of experience' (Agnew 2014, p. 312), collecting their own heritage. 'Interactive', 'audio-guide', 'virtual tour', 'online collection', 'digital engagement': these terms (and many like them) all carry forward assumptions regarding technology, the museum and their audiences. Consequently, to look at this lexicon used by the museum profession over time, is to trace a history of digital practice. Indeed, terms such as 'user' and 'digital user' may at first seem perfunctory. And yet, by looking back—deeply and carefully—at how these words and concepts have been constructed and deployed by the museum (and commentators on the museum), we can bring into focus changing priorities, values

R. Parry (✉)
University of Leicester, Leicester, UK
e-mail: ross.parry@leicester.ac.uk

T. Giannini and J. P. Bowen (eds.), *Museums and Digital Culture*,
Springer Series on Cultural Computing, https://doi.org/10.1007/978-3-319-97457-6_13

and intellectual informants. We can, in short, through an ideation history such as this, start to see a sector revealed through its re-making of a word.

Surveying half a century of practice from archival material of three institutional collections (a national museum institution, a sector support agency and an advocating cultural charity), and leveraging multi-disciplinary theoretical perspectives from digital studies, design studies and disability studies, this chapter analyses what Klein (2011) would call the 'linguistic habits' of the museum computing community—specifically around the use of the terms 'user' and 'digital user'. In general terms, the aim here is to animate the value of an ideational approach to the history of digital cultural heritage and to demonstrate the potential of a more expansive criticality around the relationship between 'museum' and 'digital'. More specifically, the objective here is to evidence an evolving frame of reference around the construct of the 'digital user'. It is through this critical long view, that we can witness the user positioned initially as 'operator' (part of the system); to then a user constructed as 'individual' (outside of the system); to—emerging today—the user acknowledged as 'actant' (active 'in the world'). Concurrently, in these different constructions, we notice the principal capability of the 'digital user' shifting from 'automation' (set within a 1970s–80s system-orientated context of organizational efficiency); to 'personalization' (amidst 1990s–2000s priorities of usability and experience design); to finally 'empowerment' (against which social value and agency are the new indices of success).

What emerges is a usage of the term 'user', at the 'semantic core' (Froeyman 2014) of digital practice in the sector, shaped in part by technological change, but also from a growing professional ethic of reflective practice and accessible provision. Crucially, it is proposed here that accessible design (particularly the design of digital with disability in mind) has acted both as a key informant and agitator of this change, but also the practice through which this development can most usefully be seen. The discussion here proposes not just how the concept of the museum's 'digital user' has remained in motion, but, moreover, that this motion (this making, and re-making of the term) serves witness to changing and evolving conceptualizations around accessible digital design, and, indeed, around the very idea of the museum itself. We are left, ultimately with an original modelling of 'user' (and 'use') that is not only a means through which to understand the sector's past but is also—in the era of the "postdigital" (Parry 2013), 'medialization' (Drotner et al. 2019) and 'digital purposefulness' (Parry 2018b)—a means to articulate on-going practice.

13.2 Tracing a 'History of Use'

Fittingly, for a study that intends to leverage a historical long view, it is towards the archive (rather than to, say, modern design and use) that this investigation looks. Specifically, the research here draws upon the collections of the Smithsonian Institution Archives (in the USA), as well as the organizational archives of the Collections Trust (in the UK) and the UK-based charity for accessible digital culture—the Jodi

Mattes Trust. Within the Smithsonian Institution Archives it is, specifically, the extensive holdings relating to the organization's 'automation' and computerization that provide some of the most significant insights into changing language and terminology around digital use.

In contrast, the Collections Trust archive holds over 3,000 documents spanning four decades—including the organization's earlier incarnations as 'mda', then before that 'The Museum Documentation Association', and back to its origins as the 'Information Retrieval Group of the Museums Association'. With the remit of the Trust (and its earlier formations) centering on supporting standards (and skills around those standards) in collections and information management (Collections Trust 2019), its archive of manuals, reports and guides, helps expose a story of shifting assumptions around 'use' and 'user'. From the Jodi Mattes Trust, it is the archive relating specifically to the charity's running (since 2005) of the 'Jodi Awards' that is of particular import here. The archive of nominations and the careful, evidenced, structured cases that each make for distinctive and innovative technological practice warranting recognition, can all be seen as a 'prism' (Parry 2018a) through which to see an evolving relationship within the museum sector, between design, digital and disability. In the language of the winners, their citations and their reflections on practice, we hear assumptions around the digital user, consciously set against the Trust's ambition for a world in which 'disabled people hold both equal access to information and cultural experience through and within digital media, and equal opportunity as participants, creators, co-creators, artists and employees in the cultural sector' (Jodi Mattes Trust 2018).

As a triptych, these three collections complete not only a useful chronology (the Smithsonian Institution Archives reaching back to the 1960s; the Collections Trust strongly focused on the 1980s and 1990s; the Jodi Mattes Trust Archive exclusively relating to 2000s and 2010s onwards), but they also build for us a horizon of both published and unpublished material—evidencing both public-facing and internal discourse around the 'digital user'. It is from their various minutes, applications, project briefs, reports and manuals, that we can hear the authentic voices of both practitioners and policy makers alike, the day-to-day language of work alongside the rhetoric of outward communication.

As we handle these collections, and this evidence, we do so mindful of a wider critical context. Specifically, we recognize here how other disciplines continue to attempt their own anatomies of the 'user' and the 'digital user'. Outside of museology, we note how this terminology has, for instance, undergone considerable scrutiny in media and communication studies. This includes highly self-reflective discourse on what Schrøder (2013, p. 49), at least, sees as the complementary methods and paradigms for understanding 'audiences and users'; as well as scholarship that has tracked the turn towards a more 'user-centric rather than a technology-centric perspective' on the practice of design—the shift to thinking more expansively about 'contexts of user and user goals' (Kunert 2009, p. vii). These methodological and the practical perspectives on 'use' and 'user', have also extended to more philosophical questioning of the relationship between media and the human, in a world in which, according to Lagerkvist (2017, p. 97) '[q]uestions concerning digital technologies are

[...] challenges about human existence'. This is scholarship that emphasizes 'situated use' and the larger 'socio-cultural context' of digital design—such as Participatory Design and its commitment to enhancing users' 'autonomy' and 'power of decision', enabling users to 'understand the systems they are part of' (Stuedahl et al. 2010, pp. 3, 6). Within this community of research that continues to follow the characteristics and consequences of changing digital users and uses of digital design, it is John Hartley's visionary eye that, most notably, chooses to register 'the emergence [...] of the 'user', as opposed to the consumer', in the list of timely motives for rethinking the 'underlying model of communication'. Confidently and circumspectly, Hartley (2012 pp. 2–3) surveys the transformation in the intellectual framework of media and cultural studies 'from a linear to a dialogic mode; from producer to consumer; from powerful corporation and charismatic celebrity to everybody in the population; from representation to productivity; from structural opposition to dynamic systems; from cultural studies to cultural science'. Hartley's declaration (and challenge) to his subject is to turn from what he calls a 'provider' perspective to a 'user' one; for him 'the audience' has transmogrified into 'the user' (Hartley 2012, pp. 8, 114).

Looking up from museum studies, and away from media and communication studies, we are struck by the multiple parallel conversations that continue in other parts of the academy around the 'user' and the 'digital user'. We see computer science plotting the 'evolution' of user-centered design through to UX, and the common centering in each of the 'user', 'usability' and 'prototype use' (Knight 2011, p. 10)—what Noyes and Baber (1999, p. x) powerfully brand as 'the stance [...] to design systems with the focus primarily on the user'. In the context of data visualization, we see GIS articulating a shift in emphasis to a more 'user centred perspective for map design' (Jones 2010, p. 42). And we see critical management studies calling out their own 'turning point' in the use of IT, specifically the alignment of business success with the requirement of 'putting the human perspective—the digital user—at the very heart of the new digitized service-led economy' (Brenner et al. 2014); this is a new orthodoxy of (re-)designing corporate processes 'from the ground up, starting with the user's perspective, thus putting usage experience and utility of the individual center stage' (Brenner et al. 2014).

As ever for the museum, it is perhaps developments within library and information studies (as a cognate discipline and an adjacent profession) that provide particularly resonant inspiration and orientation. We notice, for instance, that as a discipline library science has already framed its own 'history of the "user-centered paradigm"' and been prepared to classify the shift from the 'system' to the 'user' point of view as a 'revolution' (Bowler et al. 2011). As the library sector attempts to understand its role when, according to some of its commentators and practitioners, 'the traditional information environment is breaking down', so the focus turns to understanding who their users are and what their new expectations might now be (Baker and Evans 2013, pp. 2–3). Notably for the discussion here (and its thesis around the contemporary museum user as socially engaged 'actant') we hear a language in this library studies research that foregrounds a 'predominance', 'power' and 'control' of the information user (Baker and Evans 2013, pp. 5–6). Theirs is a user with 'prerogatives' (Frosio 2012, p. 5) and 'privileges' (Guibault 2012, pp. 91, 105).

From the methodological, practical and philosophical recasting of the 'user' in media and communication studies, through to the centering of the user's point of view in computer science and business studies, and the rise of the empowered user in information studies, we see multiple disciplines sustaining their own conversations around the definition, the experience and the role of the 'user' and the 'digital user'. However, whilst sensitive to this context (and, indeed, partly inspired and guided by it) the discussion here, nonetheless, attempts to contribute something different. The outcomes of this study may contribute to a shared sensibility to the significances of the term 'user' in a way that will inform wider practice and scholarship alike. It is also intended to provide an example—dare one say, a 'use case'—to communication and media studies (and other disciplines) on how these core concepts and discussions have played out in the unique mediatized space of the museum. In other words, the intention here is both to draw from, but then in turn to feed respectively back into (and inform) the media scholarship around the 'user', using this discrete museological perspective. This means back into these other academic conversations and sub-fields of 'user, use and utility research' (Brenner et al. 2014); into those live discussions around 'discretionary use' (Knight 2011, p. 10) and the freedom and choice users have; as well as challenging the HCI and UCD orthodoxy that the user is subject to other 'influences', be that 'workplace' or 'environment' (Noyes and Babar 1999), and instead suggest that the user, rather, has agency in the world. Similarly, the 'actant' identified here (another persona for the user, alongside their earlier, but persisting, identities as 'operator' and 'individual') belongs with more recent calls within media studies for what Lagerkvist (2017, p. 107) enthralling calls a 'change of casting' and a greater sensibility to the sociality and the fundamental humanness of the 'principal inhabitant' of the media terrain.

To trace this 'history of use', one final other element of analytical equipment is needed to put alongside the reliable substantive *archive* and this wider critical *context*—and this relates to the *assumptions* being made here around scholarly and professional language. After all, the argument set out here is predicated upon the idea that language (terms such as 'user' and 'digital user') communicates cultural information. Thinking fundamentally about language, theoretical evolutionary biology shows us how language comes from 'shared attention, shared intentionality', and evolves in a 'highly social, potentially cooperative context' (Szathmáry and Számadó 2008). Moreover, historical linguistics provides the framework to allow for historicity within our reflection of professional and specialist terms (Vennemann 2002, p. 245), as well as a precedent for tracing the evolution of linguistic features. Ethnolinguistically, Görlach (2002, p. 83) gives us ways of assembling histories of terms in other sectors and industries—such as advertising. Likewise, we see writers such as Klein (2011), tracing the development of terms such as 'theory', 'memory' and 'historiography' within the discipline of history—what later readers have seen as 'a book about words [...] those words that have formed the semantic core of our thinking about history' (Froeymans 2014).

Similarly, in the area of human geography, writers such as John Agnew (2014), have 'decoded' some of his subject's 'important geographical concepts [...] according to the norms of the history of ideas, broadly construed'. In his case, Agnew helps us specifically to see a tension within what he terms an 'idealist epistemology', namely the idea that the formal meaning ascribed to a word in a discipline or area of practice cannot be presumed to be the limit on how that word is used in all circumstances by that subject. His warning—*for those within his subject and for those of us outside*—is of a 'naive realist empiricism' that uses these specialist and professional terms without thought to their genealogy (Agnew 2014, p. 311). As if speaking directly to the project here, Agnew advises how '[t]racing the meanings of such words historically is valuable insofar as it can alert us to how some, often highly selective, meanings have changed' (Agnew 2014). Most importantly for Agnew, however, are the practices and behaviors that sit around the use of these words. As useful as a 'history of ideas' might be, his concern is the risk of becoming 'obsessed with tracing the intellectual genealogies', detached from the 'practical lives' of those that might be related to them (Agnew 2014, p. 318). With this caution held close to us, we therefore approach our own 'history of ideas' here on the 'digital user', mindful of the need to resist abstraction, and to ground this reading and this analysis firmly within professional practice and evidence.

We see a similar tracing of language and terminology taking place in the field of design and design history, not least as the term 'design' itself has expanded to 'include almost any type of transformative activity' (Huppatz 2011, p. 262). Indeed, almost overwhelmed by what some commentators have seen as the 'vastness and ubiquity of design culture' (Willis 2008, p. 162), and a 'a sprawling and saturating phenomenon' (Highmore 2009), the task of compiling a dictionary of design risks becoming 'an impossible task, one of an infinite regression of terms [...] liable to dissolve into babbling incoherence' (Willis 2008, p. 162). And so, it is here, confronted with such a challenge around academic terms, that the intellectual influence of Raymond Williams is perhaps most important to recognize—in particular, his reflections on specialist language, and his analysis of specialist language within academia.

First published in 1976, Williams' canonical 'Keywords: A Vocabulary of Culture and Society', is self-fashioned as 'the record of an inquiry into a vocabulary: a shared body of words and meanings concerned' in this specific case with 'the practices and institutions described as 'culture' and 'society' (Williams 2013, p. 13). The work was revisited in 2005 by sociologist and cultural theorist Tony Bennett, along with Lawrence Grossberg, and Meaghan Morris, introducing multiple authors and a new overtly international perspective (Bennett et al. 2005). Williams inspires the approach here to trace the history of the museum's 'digital user', in several ways. First, Williams attempted to set out the meanings associated with the common words used within his subject areas, but not owned and contained solely within these disciplines; a helpful, and encouraging, context in which to reflect on 'user'. Second, he sees these meanings as 'developing' and that the connections around them for the community of use was both 'explicit' and 'implicit'. And, thirdly, he approaches these words (and shares the histories of their changing meaning and use) as both a way of showing how these concepts were both discussed and seen:

> I began to see this experience as a problem of vocabulary, in two senses: the available and developing meanings of known words, which needed to be set down; and the explicit but as often implicit connections which people were making, in what seemed to me, again and

again, particular formations of meaning—ways not only of discussing but of seeing many of our central experiences. (Williams 2013, p. 13)

In short, Williams helps us to find a 'a history and complexity of meanings' as he calls it, that sits beyond the dictionary definition (Williams 2013, p. 15). Finally, the sense that he writes at a point 'where several disciplines converge but in general do not meet' (Williams 2013) is recognizable not just to those of us that work in the precinct of digital cultural heritage and museum computing, but to anyone within the wider field of museum studies—a subject area characterized by its concurrent, catholic, multiplicity of disciplinary perspectives.

To summarize, the analytical approach here is to take a diachronic (rather than synchronic) approach to the study of the terms 'user' and 'digital user'—choosing to plot changing usages and consequences of these terms. Underpinning this approach is an 'ideational theory of meaning'—that the meanings of words are subjective ideas. And, consequently, we consider the terms here as potential 'registers of experience' (Agnew 2014, p. 312; Wickberg 2001, p. 384). But as we do, and as we recognize that these words and terms are also a piece of 'shared intentionality' and 'shared attention', we also assume a stance of 'dynamic nominalism'—acknowledging that these changing contexts may also only partly explain the things they describe (Szathmáry and Számadó 2008). It is this socio-linguistic perspective (not usual, it should be stressed, for digital cultural heritage as a subject) that, as Froeyman (2014) so beautifully puts it, 'increases our sensibility to the implications of seemingly innocent words'.

13.3 The User as 'Operator'

The first set of linguistic habits we notice from the professional archive is around the 'user' constructed as an 'operator' of a machine, within a defined and closed system. This is the 'user' type (and use of the term) that particularly characterizes the early years of computerization within the sector—a time when computers were first being noticed as an 'extremely useful tool' for museums (McCormick 1960, p. 281). Carefully briefing the Board of Regents of the Smithsonian Institution with a primer on this emerging technology, an annual report from 1965 records with measured excitement how 'computers are acquiring much faster operating speeds and that their storage capacity is increasing while at the same time their physical size is decreasing [...] Many more thousands of people in the next few years will find that digital computers will play an essential part in their activities' (McCormick 1960, p. 298). For these early adopters and these early constructions of the computer 'user', this 'use' related specifically to designing new systems, new forms of programming and identifying requirements for data processing for making collections information more accessible, in ways hitherto unseen in the industry (Squires 1969, pp. 3–6). In these contexts, we see the 'user' (not yet termed a 'digital user') typically located within what are seen as institution-wide (if not sector-wide) technological challenges.

Moreover, the ‘user’ referred to is often (if not always) generic; the new wave of recommendations for novel information resources that marked these first two decades of museum computing are distinctive in the way they identify ‘users’ in general terms. Whilst there may be references to broad categories of ‘scientists/curators’, ‘specialists’ or ‘other scholars’ (Lytle 1981, pp. 2, 11), the generalization is—more often—sustained at the level of ‘a staff function’ (Lytle 1981, p. 11) or simply ‘human factors’, largely seen in terms of other systems (Smithsonian Institution 1982, p. 2). As well as generic, this ‘operator’ is also largely anonymous.

‘The computer does not know’, one early professional report reads, ‘whether the sequence of instructions which it performs were written by an accountant, linguist, philosopher, librarian, theologian, social scientist, physical scientist, engineer, or mathematician’ (McCormick 1960, p. 299). The operations of the system are, as this report puts it, ‘unified’ into a single set of uses by a single set of users. Most strikingly, this is a ‘user’ that is defined entirely in terms of the system of which they are considered part—be that the ‘collections information system’, ‘catalog information system’, ‘inventory system’, ‘scheduling system’, or the ‘mailing system’ (Smithsonian Institution 1982, pp. 4–7). The utility of the system is measured in how the ‘user’ and machine operate together; one recommendation from an early ‘automation’ report captures this characteristic, suggesting that planned ‘user experience trials’ ought to identify ‘present and projected types of request for information’ (Squires 1969, p. 32). Here the ‘user of the system’ (Squires 1969) is a component of that system, the test being of the operation of operator and machine together.

Notably, this generic, anonymous ‘user’ (part of the system) is presented as operating within a culture of efficiency and operational effectiveness. This is the ‘cost effective use of technology to support defined program needs’ (Smithsonian Institution 1982, p. 1), using technology as a ’tool that would permit doing a large number of operations to solve a problem’ (McCormick 1960, 298), of the museum’s computer user using technology to identifying collections information ‘more precisely’ or by ‘discerning more accurately their relationship to human society’ (Lytle 1981, p. 1). The effectiveness of these new technologies (and users of technology) are, in this context of ‘use’, gauged around their ‘utility’ (Squires 1969, p. 30) for specific functions within defined systems: project management software ‘is used to control the status of the [museum’s] internal projects’; ‘[i]nventory control is used in various ways to keep updated lists of various collections’; ‘a financial control database is used by the administrative services office to keep tabs on museum federal and trust funds’; ‘word processing software […] used to support certain collections registration functions’ (Smithsonian Institution 1984, p. 17). Recurrently, we see this early discourse of ‘use’ centered on the machine and its functionality.

13.4 The User as ‘Individual’

By the early 1980s, museums were over a decade into their move to computerization, and—with it—came other (alternative) linguistic formulations around ‘use’. As they began to review and reiterate their policies around data processing and information resource management, and as they started to develop more audience-facing interfaces for the technology, we hear in the professional discourse new nuances around the construction of the 'user'—particularly with respect to *context*. One key policy and planning report from this time, for example, refers to how: 'Curators would like to be able to sit at their terminals to plan an exhibit, key in several concepts which define the scope and purpose of the planned exhibit, and retrieve a listing and pictures of objects' (Bearman 1982, p. 3). Compared to the discourse of the 'operator' from a decade (or more) before, here, crucially, the 'digital user' has gained *situation*. Here the museum is attempting to construct the 'user' empathetically, considering the curator's perspective and the curator's place (both influentially and physically) in the institution. Significantly, in this alternative construction of the 'user' (distinct from the systems operator) there is now an acknowledgement of a space beyond of the system—and, importantly, that the user can occupy a place within that space. For instance, in its choice of language we see the profession actively attempting to acknowledge the situated 'needs' of varied users, and aiming 'to solicit comments from interested parties', be that inside or outside of the organization (Smithsonian Institution 1984, p. 1). 'The environment must permit controlled access to outside resources', one internal discussion suggests, as well as providing access to the museum's information 'by outside users' (Smithsonian Institution 1982, Appendix B).

We also notice in this alternative construction of 'digital users' that they are no longer generic and anonymous (like the 'operator'), but instead they are identified as 'individuals'—who might have their own varied propositions on use and design that the museum 'has not considered or acquisition options it has not anticipated' (Smithsonian Institution 1984, p. 27). Here is a user now articulated as an 'individual, at any terminal in the Institution [who] should be able to access any information in the Institution which he or she has the right to see, and update any data which he or she has the right to alter' (Smithsonian Institution 1982, p. 2). In contrast to the 'operator', here the discourse is characterized by an empathy and sensibility to how the system might be experienced by the user—be they museum employee, specialist or member of the public; 'The Trust is aware that each individual is unique', explains later one institution's Policy on Access, appended to its description of a new piece of digital design, 'both in terms of how he or she learns and in their access needs' (York Archaeological Trust 2009). This is a language of 'user' that acknowledges not only that there are other systems outside that of the museum that may 'be in use amongst users' (Windsor and Maidenhead 2005), but that these diverse users have themselves different behaviors with these said systems. Here, for instance, the museum begins to recognize the importance of so-called 'user agents'—that online users bring their own software that customizes content for that individual's context, be that their choice of browser, their device, their preferred interface settings, or the assistive technology that will be mediating content to the user (Thackray 2008; Tyne and Wear 2005). And it is here that the we see the museum working from the assumption that, in these new digital settings, 'users are able to choose' (IWM 2009; Jodi Awards 2017b).

With individual preferences and diverse behaviors, as well as an acknowledged existence outside of the museum's system, the 'digital user' is now not just articulated within a context of operational effectiveness (as it was for the user as 'operator'), but now, also, within a new vivid context of 'user experiences' (Wakefield Library 2006). Consequently, rather than to the operation of the *system*, we hear this discourse of the 'individual' user looking instead to the *interface*. These are interfaces that differentiate between (and re-assemble for) the 'screenreader user', 'keyboard only user' and 'voice recognition software user' (British Museum 2008), and that offer 'a number of display options [...] which enable users' (Tate 2006). It is design that foregrounds an 'interface to accommodate the needs of people' (The National Trust 2008). In this more individualized formation of the 'digital user', the emphasis shifts to how the system will work for the user rather than the organization, with the dominant discourse now on 'usability' rather than process. In this usage, we see the language of the museum underscoring 'consultation with users', and how a 'great deal of work has been undertaken on usability' (Tyne and Wear 2005). With the 'user' central to the offer, digital provision is presented as something that 'allows users to search', 'allows users to browse', 'allows users to zoom in on any part of an image'; the aim is 'to provide opportunities to users', 'users can find out more', 'users can explore a theme', and 'users can have fun' (Tyne and Wear 2005).

Significantly, in this construction, we also see this 'digital user' expressed as part of an on-going evaluative relationship and dialogue; 'a reciprocal relationship', as the Canadian Museum for Human Rights puts it, 'whereby the Museum and the visitor mutually inform each other' (Jodi Awards 2015). 'Going forward', another explains, 'we will continue to encourage feedback and consider the views of our users to re-evaluate any aspects that could improve accessibility and usability on this and future online resources' (National Archives 2007). This is the museum involving 'users at each stage' (Wolverhampton Arts and Museum Service 2007). This is 'the needs of the user now driving the design' Thackray Museum (2008). Indeed, in this discourse, 'usability' (and the user at centre of the design) is so significant that it can become the authenticating measure of digital provision; '[t]he app has already been updated and continues to be improved and expanded regularly', one award-winning application explains, 'with continued input from user groups to ensure the integrity of the project is upheld' (Jodi Awards 2017a). Here we hear the 'integrity' of the museum's digital provision reliant upon the involvement (and endorsement) of its digital user—no longer just an operator, but now an individual, with individual needs, and an individual point-of-view.

13.5 The User as 'Actant'

The MDA archive contains a copy of an 'Open Letter' written in 2008 by museum access consultant Marcus Weisen setting out a (Roosevelt-inspired) 'New Deal' for cultural equality for the UK. The letter formed the basis of a keynote address—delivered two weeks later—to a gathering at the British Museum of prominent accessibility and disability practitioners, policy-makers and academics—including the National Trust, English Heritage, British Library, National Archives, University of Cambridge,

National Museums Scotland, and the Wellcome Trust. In the wider history of cultural access and rights, and the role of UK public institutions within this domain, Weisen's rallying cry for 'a complete sea-change to let the creative wind of opportunity freely blow', stands as a key moment of challenge and collective self-reflection (Weisen 2008, Sect. 4). However, for tracing our own ideation history here, Weisen's letter also encapsulates the re-making of the 'user' that was taking place at that time within the museum sector. One significance of the letter and its impassioned call by an individual with experience both with policy (in central government) and with practice (with the Royal National Institution of Blind People), was the extent to which the 'user' was relocated into a context of social purposefulness and redefined as an individual with 'cultural freedoms' and agency in the world. The subject of disability had provided the means to develop a much wider re-imagining of the 'user', and the 'digital user'. What Weisen was calling out (shared at a national event that was reflecting on digital media in the context of disability) was what we might style as a shift in the usage of the word 'user' from 'individual' to 'actant'.

Just five years earlier, in her landmark report to the UK museum sector, we can see Delin (2003, pp. 6, 14) identifying a comparable transition: in her case, from the doctrine of equal opportunities (positioning disabled people as a group 'not to discriminate' against), to the 'notion of disability rights (defining disabled people—-varied and non-homogenous—as 'people with something to contribute'). What Delin described in the context of the 'user', and that Weisen had later located in the context of the 'digital user', was a 'view of disabled people as valuable citizens with equal rights, who make their own life decision and choices', of 'disabled people as part of society and influential on its progress' (Delin 2003, p. 7). This was a view of 'users' not just relevant to disabled people, but with universal application. It was, in other words, a language of 'use' (of agency, of empowerment, of affect) that came to characterize a new discourse on the museum's 'user' and 'digital user'. It was a language of agency (of acknowledging the 'digital user' as an empowered person in the world) that we start to see influencing a values-led approach to a universal design ethic within the museum sector from around the turn of the century (Petrie et al. 2005, p. 10). These are the actants—such as the bloggers identified in the Editorial Policy of arts organization 'Disability Arts Online'—who profile their own work '[w]ithin a global context' and produce their own 'quality writing' on Deaf and Disabled-led arts and culture on their own pages within the organization (DAO 2009a, b). These are the actants, in the 'Speaking for Ourselves' project, whose volunteered 'life-stories' heard in 240 h of recorded testimony on 'living with cerebral palsy' (Scope 2009). And these are the actants, people with learning disabilities and with agency, who in the case of the Outside In Pathways (2008) worked with the V&A (London), producing their own 'digital artefacts', using the museum 'as a base for the creative activity'. In this more recent construction of the 'digital user', the driver crucially is no longer *efficiency* (of the 'operator'), or *accessibility* (of the 'individual'). Instead it is *agency* that defines the 'user'—a socially active user, within a wider world.

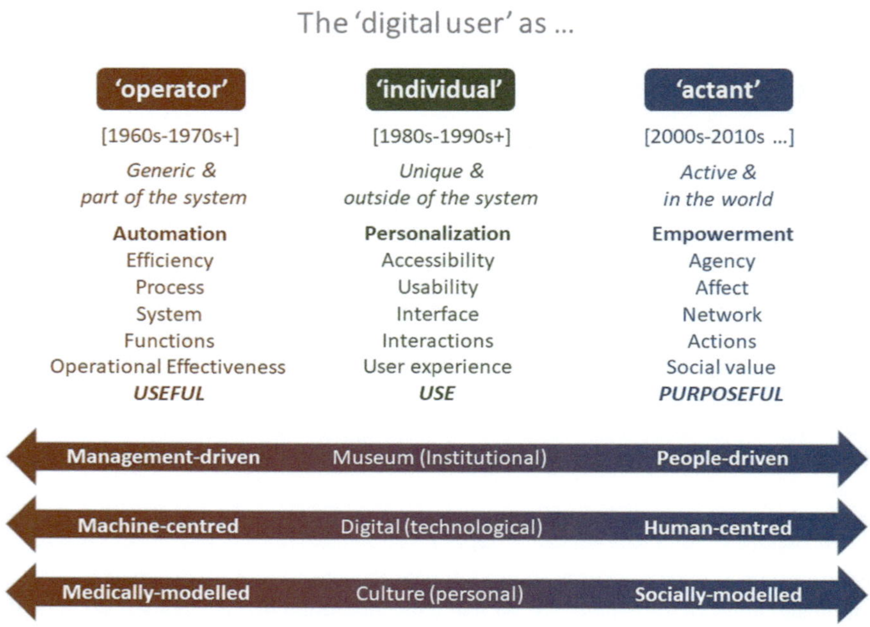

Fig. 13.1 An evolution of the museum's 'Digital User'

13.6 Seeing the Museum Through Its 'Digital User'

These three users (the 'operator', the 'individual' and the 'actant'), evidenced through these key archives of professional practice over the last fifty years, help us to understand a shifting frame of reference around museums and digital (see Fig. 13.1). In the 'operator' (from the 1960s–70s onwards) we see a generic user seen anonymously as part of the efficiency of the 'designed physical system' (Bai and Lindberg 1999, p. 794)—set within new standards around operational effectiveness. In the 'individual' (from the 1980s–90s onwards) we see a unique user acknowledged as being outside of the designed physical system with their own personal accessibility needs—amidst new priorities around user experience. And in the 'actant' (from the 2000s–10s) we see the user accepted as socially active and with agency in the wider world—cast within new emphases around social value.

Across these different constructions of the 'digital user', we can also track a change in emphasis in the profession's dominant discourse: from automation and process; to personalization and usability; to empowerment and affect. And as we do, what we also note is the museum at each point reframing its proposition for this user: for the 'operator', raising questions of *how* the system will work; for the 'individual', questions of by *whom* the interface will be used; and for the 'actant' questions of *why* and *where* on the network there will be effect. It is an evolving construction, from functions, to interactions to actions. And a moving center—from *usefulness*, to *use*, to *purposefulness*.

However, there are wider implications of this evolutionary map. This genealogy of terms also helps us to trace deeper influences that are at play in the museum's construction of its 'digital user'. For behind and within these roles of 'operator', 'individual' and 'actant', we can also hear more profound shifts in the assumptions being made about *machine*, *body* and *organization*—and the relationship between each. After all, the discourse of the 'operator' is one built around machine-centred language of technology, a medically-modelled philosophy of the body, and a management-driven approach to the organization. Whereas, in contrast, the discourse of the 'actant' is one emerging from human-centered language of technology, a socially-modelled (Ellis and Kent 2011, p. 3) and affirmative (Cameron 2014, p. 29) philosophy of the body, and a people-driven approach to the organization. In other words, reflected in the evolving construction of this 'digital user' we can find an analogue not just of an evolving museum (and museology), but an evolving society (and sociology). The shift from 'operator', to 'individual', to 'actant' can be understood as a story of growing institutional maturity and confidence around digital, but—more meaningfully perhaps—it is also the story of: design practice becoming more user-centered; of an inclusive society respecting human rights; and of the institution of the museum becoming more socially purposeful. Plainly put, in the making and re-making of the museum's 'digital user', we see a familiar transition uniquely negotiated by this sector—from the system at the center, to the person at the center.

If this model of 'user' and 'use' is to serve us as a critical framework (here and forwards), there are perhaps other important characteristics of it to be noted in our conclusions, specifically concerning: the chronology and sequencing of these 'user' terms; the importance of context in using this as a term in motion; the specificity of these 'user' constructions to the museum in particular; and the catalytic role for critical disability studies (and museums' experience of disability) within our on-going understanding of the 'digital user'. First, it is important to recognize that whilst these three (re-)makings of the 'digital user' evidenced here are largely *sequential*, they are also *enduring*. In other words, though the prevalence of each can be located in particular moments in museums' recent history (be that the 1960s–1970s *era of automation*, the 1980s–1990s *era of personalization*, or modern *era of empowerment*), and though each may resonate within particular generations of practice, each of them did not supplant and supersede the former. In short, rather than replacing each other, these constructions have multiplied and co-existed alongside each other. Today the museum's digital user is still constructed at times as 'operator' and as 'individual', as well as styled more contemporaneously as 'actant'. And, as a concept, we suspect the 'digital user' will remain—in this way—in motion.

Second, as we look back and continue to write (and learn from) histories of digital cultural heritage, we can no longer assume that the term 'user' is a constant. We cannot project back on to earlier uses of the word the modern inferences and referents associated with it. Similarly, as well as a changing meaning through time, there are clearly different contexts of use—technologically, managerially and curatorially. By building an ideation history, as we have here, we are now sensitized to the importance of sustaining a precision in our professional and scholarly lexicon and retaining this awareness to these complex and overlaying (media, business and design) contexts for 'user' and 'use'.

Third, although there are many features of this ideation history of 'the user' that other disciplines and professions may recognize and share (the origins within operational efficiency; the shift to a user-centered perspective; the rise of the user 'in the world'), the genealogy mapped here, and the user 'types' patterned here, ought to be seen to belong specifically to a *museum* context. Owing to museums' unique history, and because of the specific nature of the sector and the particular formations of the museology over the last fifty years, there are nuances and subtleties here (curatorial, managerial, societal) that belong to museums alone. This particular (re-)making of the digital user speaks, therefore, specifically to the museum. Consequently, this reminds us of the situated nature of media and digital studies, and that whilst we may learn from other related subjects and disciplines, so we also ground their ideas within our own professional and scholarly context. Whilst this account of digital practice would not in itself purport to being 'ethnographic' in a disciplined sense (see Geismar 2012), it does nonetheless stand to demonstrate the importance of reflecting on the 'digital user' critically, historically and in a culturally situated way.

Fourth, and finally, we note here that just as 'museum' has helped us to think about 'digital user' (as a unique stage on which ideas of medialization can be explored), and 'digital' has helped us to think about the 'museum' (and its changing constructions of its audiences and users), so we also notice how 'disability' has helped us here to think about 'digital'. After all, as the archive of the Jodi Mattes Trust has shown so vividly, the place to follow the story of the 'digital user' in the museum, is in the museum's provision for the disabled user. Through this archive of aspiring accessible digital design, we can see the experience of the disabled visitor animating, magnifying and amplifying the evolution of the 'user' from 'operator', to 'individual', to 'actant'. The history of accessible digital design in the museum is where this history of the 'digital user' is most clearly seen. Furthermore, in the museum's maturing views and values around disability (as manifest in the growing confidence, insight and creativity of the archive's 'nominations'), we witness not just a *consequence* but also a *cause* of the evolving construction of the 'digital 'user'. In other words, just as the emergence of the user as 'individual' and then as 'actant' drives a more affirmational and accessible approach to digital design ('sensitised to the manifold complexities of the body' (Imrie 2014, p. 288)), so then also the museum's growing experience of disability drives (*and expects*) the construction of the user as a socially active, empowered agent in the world. In short, as we look through the Jodi Mattes Trust archive we are not only seeing the *results* of the museum constructing the user as 'individual' and then as 'actant'—but also the *causes* of it. It was its experience of that helped the museum see the user as 'actant'.

In this way, this ideation history of the 'digital user' leaves us perhaps with an even more profound outcome—one in which disability provides a powerful frame through which the 'user' and 'digital user' might be re-approached. This is a perspective from which disability is not merely something to be understood, provided for, and studied (e.g.: French and Swain 2014), but is instead an experiential and intellectual way of framing analysis on 'user' and 'use'. This can be a frame informed by the counterdiscourse reasoning of critical disability studies. Faye Ginsburg, for instance, shows us how, within the study of disability, digital technology can be seen to provide 'unanticipated and powerful platforms' for alternative self-representation, but it can do so 'in ways that expand our collective sense of personhood and publics' (Ginsburg 2012, pp. 102–103). This is a critical perspective from which the disabled experience offers ways of constructing the world, challenging particular assumptions about citizenship, and not accepting assigned responsibilities. This is not just about seeking to 'rehabilitate the relevance of impairment to a social, cultural, and political investigation of disability, particularly within the context of digital technologies' (Ellis and Kent 2011, p. 4), but it is about disability (not just for those of us with impairment) as a critical frame, not as an object of gaze, but as affirmative lived experience from which to be activist (Sheldon 2014, p. 331). But, moreover, crucially, compellingly, this is the museum's essential conceptualization of the 'digital user', animated, agitated and activated by insights and experiences of disability.

13.7 Conclusion

As a subject and as practice, 'museum computing' tends (still) to center technology. It is technology, after all, that has driven institutional and sectoral change, that has redefined roles and relationships between organization and audience, and that has enabled the re-assembling (sometimes dramatically so) of multiple concepts, processes and practices of 'museum'. The attraction—perhaps understandably with so much in transition, so much at stake, and so much to say—has been to call out the next big inventive step in systems and device, and to spotlight the next audacious leap in practice and platform. However, amidst this orientation around technology, the *practice of digital* risks eclipsing the *meaning of digital*.

And yet today—especially with fifty years of digital practice now behind us on which to reflect—there is an opportunity for other ways of looking at digital in the context of the museum, and other ways of formulating equations in which digital might function. There are alternative framings to our subject that do not necessarily have to accept the orthodox focus on the functionality of the technology, or changes to business processes, or even the characteristics of digitally-enabled experience. We can, in short, choose to decline the technocratic and techno-centric, and instead allow digital to become a means for other shapes of conversation, other lines of enquiry, and (even) allow other roles for digital in our discourse. This is digital not just as an object to be understood in itself, but as a critical lens and proxy through which to understand other (non-digital) things. This is digital not just within the frisson of the present and emerging future but set in a longer historical view. This is digital not just as a technology, but as an idea.

Acknowledgements I am grateful to several international events that kindly allowed me to share and review early versions of all (or part) of this paper within supportive settings, specifically:

the 11th European e-Accessibility Forum, Cité des sciences et de l'industrie, Paris (June 2017); 'Museum 2017: New Technology in Museums', the Chinese Association of Museums, Taipei City, Taiwan (October 2017), and 'Researching Digital Cultural Heritage—International Conference', Manchester (November 2017). Thanks also go to the staff at the Smithsonian Institution Archives (Washington DC) for their help, particularly Pamela Henson (Historian, Institutional History).

References

Agnew J (2014) By words alone shall we know: is the history of ideas enough to understand the world to which our concepts refer? Dialogues Hum Geogr 4(3):311–319

Bai G, Lindberg L (1999) A sociocybernetic approach to information systems development. Kybernetes 28(67):792–809

Baker D, Evans W (2013) The future of digital information provision. In: Baker D, Evans W (eds) Trends, discovery, and people in the digital age. Chandos Publishing, Oxford, pp 1–12

Bearman D (1982) Policy and Planning Issues for Information Resource Management in the Smithsonian Institution. Smithsonian Institution, Office of Information Resource Management, December 10, 1982. Record Unit 88–173

Bennett T, Grossberg L, Morris M (2005) New keywords a revised vocabulary of culture and society. Blackwell Publishing, Hoboken

Bowler L, Koshman S, Oh JS, He D, Callery BG, Bowker G, Cox RJ (2011) Issues in user-centered design. LIS Libr Trends 59(4):721–752

Brenner W, Karagiannis D, Kolbe L et al (2014) User, use and utility research: the digital user as new design perspective. Bus Inf Syst Eng 6(1):55–66. https://doi.org/10.1007/s12599-013-0302-4

The British Museum (2008) Jodi Awards 2008 for excellence in accessible cultural web sites and digital media: nomination form. Archive of the Jodi Mattes Trust

Cameron C (2014) Developing an affirmative model of disability and impairment. In: Swain J, French S, Barnes C, Thomas C (eds) Disabling barriers, enabling environment. Sage, Los Angeles, London & New Delhi, pp 24–30

Collections Trust (2019) Our aims. https://collectionstrust.org.uk/what-we-do/strategic-aims-2017-22/. Accessed 20 March 2019

Delin A (2003) Disability in context. Resource disability portfolio, Guide 1. Resource

Disability Arts Online (2009a) Jodi awards 2009 for accessible digital media—nomination form. Archive of the Jodi Mattes Trust

Disability Arts Online (2009b). Editorial policy. Archive of the Jodi Mattes Trust

Drotner K, Dziekan V, Parry R, Schrøder KC (2019) Media, mediatization and Museums: a new ensemble. In: Drotner K, Dziekan V, Parry R, Schrøder KC (eds) The routledge handbook of Museums, media and communication. Routledge, Abingdon and New York, pp 1–12

Ellis K, Kent M (2011) Disability and new media. Routledge, New York

French S, Swain J (2014) Disability and social inclusion in the information society. In: Swain J, French S, Barnes C, Thomas C (eds) Disabling barriers, enabling environment. Sage, Los Angeles, London & New Delhi, pp 279–28

Froeyman A (2014) The words of history. Hist Theor 53(2):244–252

Frosio G (2012) Communia and the European public domain project: a politics of the public domain. In: De Rosnay MD, De Martin JC (eds) Digital public domain: foundations for an open culture. Open books, pp 3–45

Geismar H (2012) Museum + Digital = ? In: Miller D, Horst H (eds) Digital anthropology. Bloomsbury Publishing, London, pp 266–287

Ginsburg F (2012) Disability in the digital age. In: Miller D, Horst H (eds) Digital anthropology. Bloomsbury Publishing, London, pp 101–126

Görlach M (2002) A linguistic history of advertising, 1700–1890. In: Fanego T et al (eds) Sounds, words, texts and change: selected papers from 11 ICEHL, vol 2. John Benjamins Publishing Company, Santiago de Compostela. 7–11 Sept 2000
Guibault L (2012) Evaluating directive 2001/29/EC in the light of the digital public domain. In: De Rosnay MD, De Martin JC (eds) Digital public domain: foundations for an open culture. Open Books, pp 61–80
Hartley J (2012) Digital futures for cultural and media studies. Wiley-Blackwell, Chichester
Highmore B (ed) (2009) The design culture reader. Routledge, London
Huppatz DJ (2011) the design history reader by Grace Lees-Maffei and Rebecca Houze (eds) design history: understanding theory and method by Kjetil Fallan. Des Cult 3(2):259–263
Imperial War Museum Duxford (2009) Jodi Awards 2009 for accessible digital media: nomination form. Audio guide to AirSpace for blind and partially sighted visitors. Archive of the Jodi Mattes Trust
Imrie R (2014) Designing inclusive environments and the significance of Universal design. In: Swain J, French S, Barnes C, Thomas C (eds) Disabling barriers, enabling environment. Sage, Los Angeles, London & New Delhi, pp 287–296
Jodi Awards (2015) Canadian Museum for human rights. http://jodiawards.org.uk/winners/canadian-museum-for-human-rights/. Accessed 5 Jan 2019
Jodi Awards (2017a) National Museums liverpool house of memories. http://jodiawards.org.uk/winners/national-museums-liverpool-house-of-memories/. Accessed 5 Jan 2019
Jodi Awards (2017b) Signly: winner 2017 Jodi awards. http://jodiawards.org.uk/winners/signly-winner-2017-jodi-awards/. Accessed 5 Jan 2019
Jodi Mattes Trust (2018) Jodi awards: about us. http://jodiawards.org.uk/about/. Accessed 5 Jan 2019
Jones CE (2010) Cartographic theory and principles. In: Haklay M (ed) Interacting with geospatial technologies, Wiley-Blackwell, pp 37–66
Klein KL (2011) From History to theory. University of California Press, Berkeley, Calif., & London
Knight J (2011) User centred design. ITNOW 53(5):10–11. https://academic.oup.com/itnow/article-abstract/53/5/10/474463. Accessed 5 Jan 2019
Kunert T (2009) User-centered interaction design patterns for interactive digital television applications. Springer-Verlag, London
Lagerkvist A (2017) Existential media: toward a theorization of digital thrownness. New Media Soc 19(1):96–110
Lytle R (1981) Recommendations for development of information resources at the Smithsonian Institution. Unpublished internal report. Smithsonian Institution, USA, June 1981. SI Archives, pp 88–173
McCormick EM (1960) Digital computers: their history, operation and use. In: Annual report of the Board of Regents of the Smithsonian Institution. US Government Printing Office, Washington DC, pp 281–299
The National Archives (2007) Jodi Awards 2007 for excellence in accessible Museum, library and archive technology–nomination form. Prisoner 4099. Archive of the Jodi Mattes Trust
The National Trust (2008) Jodi Awards 2008 for excellence in accessible cultural web sites and digital media: nomination form. The Virtual Tour Project. Archive of the Jodi Mattes Trust
Noyes J, Baber C (1999) User-centred design of systems. Springer, London
Outside In Pathways (2008) Jodi Awards 2008 for accessible digital media: nomination form. Archive of the Jodi Mattes Trust
Parry R (2013) The end of the beginning: normativity in the postdigital Museum. Mus Worlds 1:24–39
Parry R (2018a) The Jodi Awards as a prism of accessible digital culture. In: E-accessible culture, G3ict (Global Initiative for Inclusive Information and Communications Technologies) Business Case White Paper Series. G3ict. http://www.braillenet.org/wp-content/uploads/white_paper_braillenet_2018.pdf. Accessed 5 Jan 2019

Parry R (2018b) Socially purposeful digital skills. In: Malde S, Kennedy A (eds) Connecting digital practice with social purpose. Let's get real 6. Culture24, Brighton, pp 34–35

Petrie H, King N, Hamilton F (2005) Accessibility of Museum library and archive websites: the MLA Audit. City University

Schrøder KC (2013) From dogmatism to open-mindedness? historical reflections on methods in audience reception research. Commun Rev, 16(1):40–50. https://doi.org/10.1080/10714421.2013.757485

Scope (2009) Jodi Awards 2009 for accessible digital media: nomination form. Archive of the Jodi Mattes Trust

Sheldon A (2014) The future of disability studies. In: Swain J, French S, Barnes C Thomas C (eds) Disabling barriers, enabling environment. Sage, Los Angeles, London , pp 326–333

Smithsonian Institution (1982) Automatic Data Processing: planning, ordination and implementation, Internal Planning Report (7 December 1982), SI Archive Accession A88-173 Box 1

Smithsonian Institution (1984) Request for comment on the Smithsonian Collection Information System (1984). SI Archives Accession 01-132, Box 2, Folder 25

Squires DP (1969) An information storage and retrieval system for biological and geological data: the first 19 months. Smithsonian Institution Interim Report submitted to US Department of Health, Education and Welfare, Office of Education, Bureau of Research (January 1969), project no. 7-1159

Stuedahl D, Morrison A, Mörtberg C, Bratteteig T (2010) Researching digital design. In: Wagner I, Bratteteig T, Stuedahl D (eds) Exploring digital design: multi-disciplinary design practice. London, Dordrecht, Heidelberg, New York, Springer

Szathmáry E, Számadó S (2008) Being human: language: a social history of words. Nature 456(7218):40–41

Thackray Museum (2008) Jodi Awards 2008 for excellence in accessible cultural web sites and digital media—nomination form. Archive of the Jodi Mattes Trust

Tate (2006) Jodi Awards 2006 for the most accessible Museum, library and archive websites–nomination form. i-Map: The everyday transformed. Archive of the Jodi Mattes Trust

Tyne and Wear (2005) Jodi Mattes Web Accessibility Awards 2005 for Museums, libraries, archives and heritage sites: nomination form. Discovery Museum, 'Imagine' website. Archive of the Jodi Mattes Trust. Tyne and Wear Museums, UK

Vennemann T (2002) Key issues in English etymology. In: Fanego T et al (eds) Sounds, words, texts and change: selected papers from 11 ICEHL, vol. 2. John Benjamins Publishing Company, Santiago de Compostela. 7–11 Sept 2000

Wakefield Library and Information Service (2006) Jodi Awards 2006 for the most accessible Museum, library and archive websites: nomination form. Archive of the Jodi Mattes Trust

Weisen M (2008) Putting cultural equality of disabled people back on the agenda: Open letter to government, government agencies, disabled people, disability organisations and cultural organisations. Presented to designing for disability: digital media in context. British Museum, London. 5 Dec 2008

Wickberg D (2001) Intellectual history vs. the social history of intellectuals. Rethinking Hist 5:383–395

Williams R (2013) Keywords: a vocabulary of culture and society. Routledge Revivals, Abingdon, Oxon

Willis A (2008) Design Unlimited—Reviews of The Design Culture Reader (ed. Ben Highmore) and Design Dictionary: Perspectives on Design Terminology (eds. Michael Erloff and Tim Marshall). Design Philosophy Papers, 6(2), pp. 157–162

Windsor and Maidenhead (2005) Jodi mattes web accessibility awards 2005 for Museums, libraries, archives and heritage sites: nomination form. 'Webwords' project. Library and Information Services. The Royal Borough of Windsor and Maidenhead. Archive of the Jodi Mattes Trust

Wolverhampton Arts and Museum Service (2007) Jodi Awards 2007 for excellence in accessible Museum, library and archive technology—nomination form. Bantock House project, Archive of the Jodi Mattes Trust

York Archaeological Trust (2009) Jodi Awards 2009 for accessible digital media: nomination Form. Policy on access. Archive of the Jodi Mattes Trust

Chapter 14
The Digital Layer in the Museum Experience

Catherine Devine and Matt Tarr

Abstract The role of digital technologies within the museum context continues to evolve. We have moved from ensuring a digital presence in exhibits to considering digital spaces equal to physical spaces. Now, content and message are driven by most appropriate presentation method. Sometimes, that method is either digital but often, the physical and digital method ologies can be tightly integrated to create a seamless experience. The "digital" is in service of a seamless museum experience. We refer to this as "the digital layer," a digital experience that both sits independently of the physical experience and is designed to work along with the physical experience. It leverages many digital technologies (some seen by visitors while others unseen by visitors) that add to the visitor experience in a way that physical exhibits cannot. It tells a story, connects themes across the Museum, allows visitors to see what they could not otherwise see, all in service of a more impactful Museum experience that contributes to the Museum's mission. This chapter explores how the American Museum of Natural History both thinks about the digital layer and practical applications in all areas of the museum experience and goal to communicating science.

14.1 Introduction

The American Museum of Natural History (AMNH), based in New York City, is one of the world's pre-eminent scientific and cultural institutions. Since its founding in 1869, the Museum has advanced its global mission to discover, interpret, and

C. Devine (✉)
Microsoft, Seattle, USA
e-mail: Catherine.Devine@microsoft.com

M. Tarr
American Museum of Natural History, New York, USA
e-mail: mtarr@amnh.org

T. Giannini and J. P. Bowen (eds.), *Museums and Digital Culture*,
Springer Series on Cultural Computing, https://doi.org/10.1007/978-3-319-97457-6_14

Fig. 14.1 Allosaurus skeleton cast in the Theodore Roosevelt Rotunda of the AMNH. (Photograph by Thomas Quine, May 2015. Wikimedia Commons, https://commons.wikimedia.org/wiki/File:Allosaurus_AMNH_lobby.jpg)

disseminate information about human cultures, the natural world, and the universe through a wide-ranging program of scientific research, education, and exhibition. The Museum is renowned for its 45 permanent halls and exhibitions and scientific collections, which serve as a field guide to the entire planet and present a panorama of the world's cultures.

From dinosaurs to Tibetan sculpture, the AMNH houses a treasure-trove of collections that expand conventional notions of natural history including rich ethnographic collections of Asia and China, and native cultures of the Americas, as seen in the Hall of Plains Indians. Visitors can discover collections using the Museum's *Explorer* app, which is freely available to users for download on their smartphones. Guiding visitors through the museum, it offers easy-to-use navigation and information about the objects they are viewing. With Explorer in hand, visitors can experience exciting displays from dinosaurs to Tibetan sculpture as the example pictured here from the Whitney collection of Tibetan religious objects, or see Chinese jades and lacquerware in the Drummond collection (Figs. 14.1 and 14.2).

Fig. 14.2 *Mahākāla*, a male deity, protector of the Temple, from the Whitney collection of Tibetan religious objects, part of the Asian Ethnographic collections. (Photograph by Daderot, June 2012. Wikimedia Commons, https://commons.wikimedia.org/wiki/File:Mah%C4%81k%C4%81la_-_AMNH_-_DSC06234.JPG)

14.2 The Digital Layer Concept

At the American Museum of Natural History, we have thought strategically about the role of the digital layer in the organization to further progressing the Museum's mission. We do not consider there to be a material distinction between the digital layer and physical experiences, but rather only a categorical distinction. That is, these experiences leverage different categories of tools, of which some are physical in nature and some are digital. These tools represent an array of mechanisms to deliver on the experience, comprising of various characteristics and requiring different skillsets, but essentially remaining building blocks of the experience.

When we reference a digital and physical toolkit of the experience—what do we mean? We mean that the building blocks of an experience could be a physical case exhibiting a collection object, a physical label referencing that item, an interactive that allows a visitor to learn more about the concepts surrounding the item, an app that explains the connecting concepts that reference the collection item or translates to other languages, a voice-based technology that answers visitor questions and a myriad of other existing and emerging technology examples.

As in creating any experience, the pieces of the toolkit are each designed to work together to enhance the experience and further the mission of the Museum. The physical and digital toolsets are just categories of tools that are not developed in isolation, but rather developed to work together.

Digital tools have unique characteristics that make them perfect to solve certain issues in the experience and deliver experiences in a new way that physical tools cannot. For example, digital tools allow a visitor to see what cannot be seen, to communicate concepts across the Museum beyond a single hall, to present different lenses for different audiences, and to regularly update interpretive content to reflect current science.

14.2.1 Properties of Digital Technologies Enhance Human Abilities

The ability to see what you cannot otherwise see: The human eye is limited in what it can see. If we compound that limitation with the physical distance a visitor may be from a collection object (based on the display or exhibition case) then, for some collection items on display we limit the experience. For example, the digital layer allows us to 'zoom in' on objects such as a tiny gem or to rotate a fossil to see it from multiple perspectives.

The ability to communicate concepts beyond a single hall: In a physical space, it is not easy to rearrange the exhibits to allow side-by-side comparisons using items from various collections. But, digital tools allow the museum to do that virtually. For example, to compare how all depicted mammals are displayed in the museum, or to compare the display of Indian elephants with the display of African elephants, then the digital layer is ideal for drawing these connections.

The ability to present multiple lenses: the digital layer can present multiple points of view and narratives without the physical clutter, enabling people to see only what they need at a given time. Audiences and their interests vary widely. They differ in age and life experience, cultural backgrounds, language, and interest level in the content. For example, some audiences will want to dive deeply into the exhibition, while others will want to focus on the bigger picture or the main takeaway. Some audiences will be children and others are adults. Digital as a medium is ideal for presenting content differently to different audiences in a way that a physical space cannot easily meet those needs. The ability to regularly update content: A physical space such as a permanent exhibition hall can be challenging to update. Digital technologies are ideal for presenting a current face on an older physical space through regular updates.

Acknowledging that digital and physical tools can work together in a physical space, we summarize this thinking with the concept of the "digital layer". The digital layer is a concept that represents the leveraging of digital technologies to do what cannot be done with physical tools and an objective of furthering the overall experience. Digital technology leverages the rapidly developing suite of technology and works together with the physical space. This is necessary in order to meet the needs of diverse audiences and when communicating science. This means that we have shifted from delivering a single Museum experience in one way to all audiences to delivering the Museum in many ways to many audiences. It adds complexity of delivery but also increases visitor satisfaction while it furthers the mission of disseminating science.

14.3 Seamless, Connected Experience

Following the concept of the digital layer, we recognize that a visitor's experience does not begin and end in the physical Museum but instead extends beyond their time in the Museum to before, during, and after a visit. This can be an extended experience that exists starting from when a visitor first thinks about coming to the Museum through research they do about ticket prices, opening hours, and working through the logistics of arriving at a later time. This pre-visit experience continues into the actual Museum and further extends after their visit to any follow-up research they may do on a topic they learned about, or any interest they express in furthering their relationship with the Museum, through a membership for example. We term the entirety of the visit 'the seamless, connected experience'.

As we think about this seamless, connected experience, we also recognize that the experience does not exist in a single channel, neither physical nor digital. A visitor may start in one of many ways, on social media, discussing with family and friends, or with Museum advertising. Their experience may extend through Google Maps, the Museum's website, the Museum's apps, follow up on Google search or the Museum's email newsletters.

Visitors do not divide their experience into each of the individual channels that they use, rather they see a visit as a single and cumulative Museum experience. They're not thinking separately of apps, Google, or the website but rather all elements of a larger experience or journey. This is key as the Museum thinks about the entire visitor experience and how to ensure that the entire experience flows and makes sense as visitors move from one physical or digital channel to another. This could be as simple as ensuring a cohesive overall look and feel in design across physical and digital channels, or that tickets bought in one channel are also available on another channel. A more complex example could include ensuring that upon a return visit, people see things that they haven't seen on previous visits, or offering additional content based on collections that they visited when they were here.

This seamless, connected experience approach adds a significant layer of complexity to developing experiences. It requires shifting thinking. Instead of conversations about what features should be on the website or in an app and what content should be on social and in exhibit halls, the conversation becomes a whole new set of never-considered-before requirements. Those are requirements about what visitors need in the experience to connect the experience together. Where do they need to handoff from one channel to another? For example, if a visitor sees something really interesting in the Museum, how can we help them find out more about their interest later?

As museum professionals, we tend to default our thinking to seeing each channel as independent. This is exacerbated since members of the teams that work on these channels also frequently work independently due to the different technical or content skills required for each. For example, very distinct skillsets are needed to develop an app, to design an email campaign, to develop a database, or to plan the infrastructure that persists across these experiences to facilitate handoff from one to another.

The final concept in creating a seamless, connected experience is context. Visitors only require what is needed to have an experience in a particular moment or context, though these needs shift through the stages of their visitor journey. In any single moment, they never need everything. If we expand that logic to our entire audience of multiple visitor segments, then we are significantly increasingly the complexity of developing experiences. Think about a family planning a visit. When deciding which subway to ride to the Museum, they have no need be told what exhibitions are on display at the Museum. Conversely, as the family is planning what exhibits they want to see, they have no need to see ticket prices. The art of creating a seamless, connected experience is to give visitors only what they need when they need it throughout their journey.

Connecting these disparate moments mean that all channels (or visitor-facing 'touch points') need to be connected, through infrastructure sharing core capabilities such as user identity and authentication services or content management systems. These channels need to work together to 'hand off' from one to the other. The experience needs to meet visitors' contextual needs, in the moment, as appropriate for the device, the individual, and the context. This requires a substantial shift in thinking. Digital teams habitually think about all of the content and features available on all touchpoints, but it would be more effective for the visitors if we thought instead about what the visitor needs in that moment and how their experience flows from one touchpoint to the next.

That is how AMNH thought about ticketing—as a part of the seamless, connected experience. Here, ticketing was *designed* as a multi-channel, connected experience with the principle of "buy in any channel, pick up in any channel". Tickets are available to visitors at the physical point of sale (POS) channel, as well as multiple digital channels, including on-site kiosks, web, mobile web and the Explorer app, the Museum's mobile guide. This spectrum of flexibility was intentionally developed as we thought about how visitors really experience the Museum.

14.3.1 Improving Visitor-Museum Interaction

Consider the following examples. The visitor visits the website looking for opening hours and ticket prices; how can the museum then make it easy for this visitor to open their smartphone and buy a ticket when they come onsite? We even have the opportunity to personalize their web experience. We can detect if this individual was, at some point prior, looking at ticket prices on our website and is now in New York City, near our Museum. With this understanding, we can prompt this visitor into the digital ticket path. Or, if this visitor elected to purchase a ticket the same day on the website, we can offer a way to make the ticket quickly available in a physical channel should they prefer (e.g., kiosk pickup).

There are countless other combinations. Visitors can buy at point-of-sale and then see their tickets online or in the app. They can buy a ticket via the web and pick up their tickets on mobile web, app, or at point-of-sale. They may buy ahead on the desktop web, and when they're physically onsite access the pre-purchased tickets on their app or mobile web browser. They may buy at admission-only ticket at the point-of-sale but want to use the mobile web to upgrade their tickets to see a paid exhibition while walking through the museum. The experience, as we have learned, is rarely contained in a single channel and the flexibility in functionality that our visitors need only occurs by thinking about the experience holistically, handing off the right information at the right time in the right channel.

From a contextual angle, we thought specifically about what a visitor needs in the moment that they are trying to find a special exhibition, such as the Space Show in the Museum's planetarium. The Space Show is a timed and specially ticketed event that visitors purchase. Visitors can have their smartphone notify them fifteen minutes before their scheduled show with information including the reminder of the upcoming show, as well as turn-by turn directions to the theater from their current location. This is an example of the combination of contextual needs—what a visitor needs in that moment based on their itinerary—and where that individual is in the Museum. We are leveraging digital technologies to do something that physically could not be done otherwise and providing continuity between channels, from purchasing the ticket through to the app.

14.3.2 Physical and Digital Touchpoints Respond to Interpretive and Logistical Needs

Now that we've discussed how the physical and digital layers need to work together to create a connected experience, we can move onto the realization that from a visitor's perspective interpretive needs are not separate from the logistical needs. For the visitor, how they move through the building or find the cafeteria is a critical part of the experience that also includes learning about the exhibits.

As we blur the experience into a series of physical and digital touchpoints that are connected, a trend emerges: as the distinction between physical and digital channels fade, so does the distinction between logistical and interpretive aspects of a museum visit. By taking a visitor experience point of view, we recognize that the interpretive and the logistical nature of a Museum visit is intertwined from the visitor's perception. Visitors do not see the distinction between the logistical (activities of purchasing tickets, finding their way, finding food, restrooms, exits, etc.) and the interpretive (communicating the exhibit content and its significance). A "great day at the Museum" is finding their way to the dinosaurs, understanding the significance of the exhibition directly in front of them and being able to sit down and enjoy lunch when the time is right. Therefore, it is important that we create connected solutions to meet these different categories of need and intertwine each individual solution into a single, all-encompassing design which blends physical, digital, logistical, and interpretive.

The all-encompassing, blended solution was the core thinking driving Explorer, the Museum's app for the visitor experience. While it is designed for the in-museum experience in its current release, as well as having some connections to other channels for the pre-visit phase of the experience, there are plans to connect it to the post-visit experience in future phases. As we developed Explorer, we integrated the ability to find the amenities and use turn-by-turn navigation to help visitors find the shortest route to cafés, shops, and restrooms and even exits—and receive reminders when a movie, Space Show, or ticketed exhibition is about to start, along with the ability to understand more about the exhibit objects and content immediately in front of the visitor.

We analyzed how visitors experience the Museum and discovered that, while some visitors may plan specific exhibits to see, they often became distracted by seeing interesting exhibits along the way. We wanted to support this serendipitous experience of finding something interesting about immediate surroundings, while also supporting the intentional aspects of a visit with turn-by-turn directions to specific exhibits. For instance, if one walks by the Alaskan Brown Bears, they can use Explorer's Avatour, an augmented reality quiz, which lets users "Be the Bear" exploring the Bernard Family Hall of North American Mammals by unlocking the animal's ursine "superpowers" and answering questions based on the dioramas. Similarly, visitors can also be a "Dino Detective" as they tour the fossil halls. Explorer also allows you to understand larger concepts in the Museum that extend beyond a specific hall, such as the relatedness of all living organisms. Tree of Life, a quiz-based game that connects visitors to the institution's scientific mission by helping them discover how all life, from house cats to *Homo sapiens*, is related as they build their own mammalian tree of life. By meeting the logistical needs of visitors, we enable the science to be experienced. Together, the logistical and the interpretive aspects of Explorer further the mission of the Museum and leverage the digital layer potential to augment the physical experience.

14.3.3 Personalization: Different Experiences for Different Audiences

One of the unique opportunities of the digital layer is in presenting the experience through multiple lenses by presenting the same experience differently to different groups of people. While a physical museum can only offer a single lens, the digital layer affords us the potential to offer the same physical space to everyone with digital overlays for people of varying needs, such as children, or those who want to explore the topic deeply, or those who speak different languages.

The concept of different feeds for different people was mainstreamed by social networking companies. People are comfortable with content that reflects what they engage in, their contacts, and their interests. Increasingly, the capabilities to do personalization are also becoming available in other digital channels. Following their lead, we wanted the Explorer app and the Museum's website to provide experiences that matches each individual user.

Explorer provides different application experiences based on where the user is physically located within the Museum and the interests they have indicated on the introductory page of the app. For example, a user may have indicated more interest in fossils than space and as a result, will be presented with a personalized list of exhibits, prioritizing the fossils and sequencing based on where the visitors is currently standing in the Museum. We aspire to increase the sophistication of personalization by inferring interests based on past behavior not just expressed interests, as well as in additional dimensions. In addition to technical ways to personalize, Explorer also can be personalized for content; it contains many different perspectives on the exhibits so that a visitor interested in seeing 'behind the scenes' or more detail (like the whales' belly button!) can find that in the app.

We are also introducing personalization in the website, which has historically been the same experience for everyone, but it does not need to remain so. As previously discussed, audience segments have varying needs depending on the moment: some visitors are trying to buy a ticket, research topics, or determine what they should see. Rather than presenting all this information to everyone, with the burden of navigation falling on the user, we can predict, using various cues, what each audience segment needs and provide the offering up front.

With careful analysis, our website can identify people who exhibit specific characteristics of an audience. In one example, we identified those who are visiting our website and are likely to be trying to buy a digital ticket. We selected these characteristics based on data that said most mobile ticket purchases are for same-day visits. Their qualities were: (1) using a mobile phone, (2) visiting the website during the morning, and (3) in the vicinity of the Museum. We can validate these assumptions by looking at some other qualities of our web visitors historically. Those in Europe on a mobile phone, for instance would be much less likely to be buying a ticket for the museum that very same day.

Identifying these patterns, we can then segment the audiences and create differentiated and specific web experience for those we predict are trying to buy tickets. Here we can place ticketing options at the center of the experience rather than requiring one to navigate to ticketing, as would be done for the non-local audience. The ability to reduce the number of clicks or steps on a web experience is key, especially on a mobile experience.

14.3.4 Role of Data in Experience

While data is available for both physical and digital tools in the experience, it is both more prolific and available in real-time for digital elements of the experience. Museums previously needed to fall back on our understanding of visitor behavior to drive priorities, but today, both access to data and computing power provide the availability and richness of data which allows us to "drill down" and be more informed about actual visitor behavior and engagement. This knowledge allows us to both pivot as visitor behaviors and expectations change and prioritize the Museum's investments in the experience.

We examine data by dividing it in two categories: behavioral/journey data and optimization data. Behavioral/journey data represents an understanding of how visitors behave in each channel and how they move between channels. For example, how do visitors transition from the web to an app? Are there patterns that can be identified looking at visitor engagement in each channel? We then apply the results to understand what resonates and predict what visitors need in a given moment. The second category is optimization data, which is information about which experience, or messaging resonates best with different types of visitors in different channels. It frequently takes the form of "A/B testing", which isolates and tests variables to confirm which option resonates best with an audience. It is often in the form of messaging, layout, or content. Data via A/B testing provides insights as to what works or doesn't and represents that insights are not static but shift over time.

We have also developed a practice of continuously iterating on the design of experiences, informed by data, as well as continuously monitoring patterns and trends within digital channels emerging and dying off. With the rapid change and evolution in digital channels, specific channels may have a very short life. An example of this is Snapchat, which emerged very quickly as a channel, persisted for several years and is now rapidly dying off while Instagram has emerged as a dominant channel to replace it.

14.3.5 Emerging Technology and Experimentation

It can be difficult to keep up with the ever-emerging pace at which technology changes. In 2018, key channels include, but are not limited to: websites, mobile websites, social media, podcasts, video, email, interactives, apps, chat/text, wearables and voice assistants, some of which have only emerged in the last two years. Constant research and prototyping is necessary to understand the effect these technologies are having or will have on the work we do.

Going forward, we can expect a series of paradigm shifts. First, the development of digital experiences through artificial intelligence and machine learning. While this will be less visible to a visitor, it becomes the engine that allows us to rapidly scale and deploy personalized, data-driven experiences. This emergence presents new opportunities for engaging with the Museum. The second paradigm shift will likely be to the experience through virtual, augmented and mixed reality.

Not all technologies will be equally adopted by a mainstream audience, not all technologies will be effective in communicating the Museum's mission, and not all technologies will survive for the long term. It is difficult to prepare for these new methods of engaging with audiences, balancing the benefits to be had with adopting them without over investing or being too early. The Museum has established practices to prototype emerging technologies long before they are in the mainstream to understand the opportunities they present as well as develop in house expertise about what works, what does not work and what needs to evolve before something new is ready for primetime.

14.4 Conclusion

The core message is that digital methods are not a technological opportunity but rather an experiential opportunity. Digital tools expand the toolkit that can be used in developing permanent exhibition halls. They are not only the tools that are available today (such as web and mobile web), but there will always be emerging technologies which provide new opportunities for the visitor experience. Their rapid emergence continually provides new opportunities to communicate and engage with museum visitors. Additionally, the Museum as an experience is extended and connected. The "before and after" phases of the visitor experience are distinctly different to the in-museum experience, with multiple contexts, audiences and levels of engagement. The digital layer, with its digital tools, allow us to knit together and extend that experience.

We believe strongly that the digital layer experience, as evidenced by Explorer, does and should extend beyond the walls of the physical museum. From the time when a visitor is considering coming to visit, to planning their visit, the time spent at the museum, and the period extending long after they leave, some visitors' interests will be piqued by what they have seen at the museum. Context is key, as we understand where the visitor is and what they need right in that moment. Explorer focused on what visitors' need when they need it within the museum and can extend that concept outside of the museum. As an example, anticipating visitors who are coming to the museum today, prompting them with exhibits they would be interested in seeing, directions for how to get home, and exploring popular topics in greater depths, such as dinosaurs. This experience can extend across several different channels and devices including social, web, app, virtual reality and other technologies as they emerge.

References

Ask J et al (2017) Mobile mind shift maturity framework. Forrester Research, 20 Nov 2017. https://www.forrester.com/Mobile+Mind+Shift+Maturity+Framework/fulltext/-/E-RES115850. Accessed 25 Jan 2019

Braddock KA (2016) Deeper layer of digital. Made by Mant, 25 Oct 2016. https://www.madebymany.com/stories/a-deeper-layer-of-digital. Accessed 25 Jan 2019

Brice K (2018) How your behaviour has changed the way we make digital exhibition labels. Te Papa Blog, 9 May 2018. https://blog.tepapa.govt.nz/2018/05/09/how-your-behavior-has-changed-the-way-we-make-digital-exhibition-labels/. Accessed 25 Jan 2019

Dawson B, Edmundson D (2018) Building a smart museum: tackling in-gallery challenges with digital experience at scale. Museums and the Web, Vancouver, April 2018. https://mw18.mwconf.org/paper/building-a-smart-museum-tackling-in-gallery-challenges-with-digital-experience-at-scale/. Accessed 25 Jan 2019

Douaihy M (2018). Interactive tech tells important story at the museum of natural history. AVNetwork, 30 Nov 2018. https://www.avnetwork.com/features/interactive-tech-tells-important-story-at-the-museum-of-natural-history. Accessed 25 Jan 2019

Erlick N (2017) 20,000-year-old artifacts, 21st-century technology—museums are turning to virtual reality, apps, and interactive experiences to keep tech-savvy visitors engaged. The Verge, 6 May 2017. https://www.theverge.com/2017/5/6/15563922/museums-vr-ar-apps-digital-technology. Accessed 25 Jan 2019

Fenton W (2016) Hands on: the natural history museum's revamped 'Explorer' app. PC Magazine, 5 May 2016. https://mw2016.museumsandtheweb.com/paper/service-design-thinking-for-museums-technology-in-contexts/. Accessed 25 Jan 2019

French A (2016) Service design thinking for museums: technology in contexts. Museums and the Web, Los Angeles, 2016. https://mw2016.museumsandtheweb.com/paper/service-design-thinking-for-museums-technology-in-contexts/. Accessed 25 Jan 2019

Fung K (2013) Numbersense: how to use big data to your advantage. McGraw Hill Education

Herbert L (2017) Digital transformation: build your organization's future for the innovation age. Bloomsbury Business

Kelly K (2017) Digital strategy vs. digital transformation: what's the difference? Digitalist Magazine, 3 May 2017. https://www.digitalistmag.com/digital-economy/2017/05/03/digital-strategy-vs-digital-transformation-whats-the-difference-05048352. Accessed 25 Jan 2019

Leber J (2018) The future of museums is reaching way beyond their walls. fast company, 17 April 2015. https://www.fastcompany.com/3044731/the-future-of-museums-is-reaching-way-beyond-their-walls. Accessed 25 Jan 2019

Murphy A (2018) Technology in Museums, introducing new ways to see the cultural world. Advisor, Museums + Heritage, 30 Jan 2018. https://advisor.museumsandheritage.com/features/technology-museums-introducing-new-ways-see-cultural-world/. Accessed 25 Jan 2019

Price K, James D, Cymru A (2018) Structuring for digital success: a global survey of how museums and other cultural organizations resource, fund, and structure their digital teams and activity.

Museums and the Web, Vancouver, 2018. https://mw18.mwconf.org/paper/structuring-for-digital-success-a-global-survey-of-how-museums-and-other-cultural-organisations-resource-fund-and-structure-their-digital-teams-and-activity/. Accessed 25 Jan 2019
Rowles D, Brown T (2017) Building digital culture: a practical guide to successful digital transformation. Kogan Page
Schadler T, Bernoff J, Ask J (2014) The mobile mind shift: engineer your business to win in the mobile moment. Forrester Research, Groundswell Press
Siggers J (2018) Reinventing Museums for the digital generation. Interview and podcast. Knowledge@Warton, 6 Sept 2018. http://knowledge.wharton.upenn.edu/article/reinventing-museums-for-the-digital-generation/. Accessed 25 Jan 2019

Chapter 15
Engaging Museum Visitors with AI: The Case of Chatbots

Giuliano Gaia, Stefania Boiano and Ann Borda

Abstract This chapter explores the application of artificial intelligence (AI) in museums and galleries in engaging their audiences, specifically through the development and use of chatbot technologies. Through a case study approach, the chapter further provides a practical focus on the design and implementation of an audience development pilot in Milan involving four historic house museums (*Case Museo di Milano*). The pilot aimed to find new and interesting ways to engage teenagers in visiting these museums through visualizing narrative using a convergence of chatbot and gamification platforms.

15.1 Early Speaking Machines

Early speaking machines can be traced to an analogue (as compared to the more recent *digital*) age of technology—i.e., the early "automata" of the late 18th and 19th centuries. The first historically *documented* speaking machine was made by the Hungarian author and inventor, Wolfgang von Kempelen (1734–1804). Kempelen is particularly known for the creation of the mechanical "Turk": a chess-playing automaton that enclosed a human person manipulating the apparent Turk machine through a series of levers.

For the purposes of this chapter, Kempelen is legitimately associated with a "speaking machine" which was originally submitted to a competition set by the St. Petersburg Academy of Science in 1779 to create a machine that could utter the five vowel sounds a, e, i, o, u in the most natural manner. In his book *Mechanismus der menschlichen Sprache nebst Beschreibung einer sprechenden Maschine* (1791)

G. Gaia (✉) · S. Boiano
InvisibleStudio, London, UK
e-mail: giuliano.gaia@invisiblestudio.net

S. Boiano
e-mail: stefania.boiano@invisiblestudio.net

A. Borda
The University of Melbourne, Melbourne, Australia
e-mail: aborda@unimelb.edu.au

T. Giannini and J. P. Bowen (eds.), *Museums and Digital Culture*,
Springer Series on Cultural Computing, https://doi.org/10.1007/978-3-319-97457-6_15

Fig. 15.1 Faber's machine-to-speech "Euphonia" as demonstrated in London, 1846. By Unknown, *illustrazione dell"epoca*. Wikimedia Commons https://commons.wikimedia.org/wiki/File:Euphoniafaber.jpg

Kempelen included a detailed description of his speaking machine. Resembling a miniature organ complete with wind-box and voice-pipe, Kempelen worked on his device for two decades. Kempelen's machine was the first that allowed to produce not only a set of speech sounds, but some whole words and short sentences.

Perhaps the most realistic speaking automaton and first mechanical speech synthesizer was Professor Joseph Faber's *Euphonia* machine (see Fig. 15.1) (Dalakov 2018). The Austrian inventor Joseph Faber (1786–1850) exhibited the Euphonia in 1845 in Philadelphia and in 1846 in London. Faber reportedly spent over twenty-five years developing, the Euphonia which was constructed of several different mechanisms and instruments such as a piano, bellows, and a mechanical replica of the human throat and vocal organs (Inglis 2008; Rossbach 2011; Dalakov 2018). The *Illustrated London News in 1846* reported that the machine could produce French, English, Latin, Greek and German sounds, whisper, laugh and even sing, implying that the machine was sufficiently versatile to truly replicate human vocal performance, depending "upon the agility of the director in manipulating the keys" (Anon 1846). The Euphonia machine was eventually purchased by P. T. Barnum after taking Faber to London to exhibit at the famed Egyptian Hall in Piccadilly (Altick 1978). Barnum showed the device at his American Museum of curiosities in New York City, c. 1860, and later in his touring circus (Inglis 2008; Rossbach 2011).

At the beginning of the 20th century, the progress in electrical engineering made it possible to synthesize speech sounds by electrical means. Homer Dudley (1896–1980), inventor at The Bell Telephone Laboratory in the USA, developed the Voder (from *Voice Operating Demonstrator*) between 1937–38. The Voder attracted the attention of a wider public when it was presented at the World's Fair in New York in 1939. Trained operators were necessary to operate the device, since it was relatively complex to synthesize recognizable speech, and this may have contributed to its discontinuation (Mills 2012).

15.2 Computing Machines and Artificial Intelligence

What we know as "chatbots", also known as "talkbots", "chatterbots", "bots", or conversational agents, have largely evolved in the computer age as computer programs that can mimic conversation using auditory or textual methods. More specifically the functionality of chatbots is predicated on natural language processing (NLP) and a history rooted in artificial intelligence (AI) (Corti et al. 2015; Dale 2016). NLP can be defined as the ability of a machine to analyze, understand, and generate human speech. In simulating human speech, it bridges the gap between human communication and computer understanding.

The concept of chatbots as a form of AI can be traced to Alan Turing's seminal publication *Computing Machinery and Intelligence* in which Turing addresses an overarching question: *Can machines think*? (Turing 1950; Dennett 2004; Hill et al. 2015; Copeland et al. 2017). The parameters of this question would shape the so-called Turing test. In its most simple application, the test is carried out as an imitation game. The test has a human interrogator speaking to several computers and humans through an interface. If the interrogator cannot distinguish between the computers and the humans then the Turing Test has been passed (Dennett 2004; Hill et al. 2015; Warwick and Shah 2016; Proudfoot 2017).

Among the possible influences on Turing's formulation of his test, was the seminal work of Ada Lovelace (1815–1852), the Victorian-era mathematician daughter of poet Lord Byron, and famous for her collaboration with Charles Babbage on the Analytical Engine (Fuegi and Francis 2003; Swade 2017). Celebrated as the first computer programmer, Lovelace envisioned that machines would be incapable of autonomous thinking. Nearly a century later, Turing made objection to this limitation, and assessed the possibility of building machines commonly accepted as "thinking machines" by the end of the 20th century. Thus, the idea of a Machine Intelligence (MI) soon came into the mainstream (Proudfoot 2017; Swade 2017).

One of the earliest natural language applications which might be closest to our notion of an AI-enabled chatbot was called ELIZA developed from 1964 to 1966 at the MIT Computer Science and Artificial Intelligence Laboratory by computer scientist Weizenbaum (1966). ELIZA originally was created to use simple pattern matching and a template-based response (prewritten scripts) to emulate the conversational style of a Rogerian psychotherapist.

ELIZA generated global fascination in creating a natural language bot that might pass the Turing Test. The Loebner Prize launched in 1990 by Hugh Loebner in conjunction with the Cambridge Center for Behavioral Studies in Massachusetts (USA) is an example of a competition expressly designed to implement the Turing Test and builds on both the progressive interest and advances in AI developments (Loebner 2008). The chatbot term itself was coined by Michael Mauldin, inventor of the Lycos web search engine, and the Verbot chatbot program, which was submitted as a Turing test competitor in the 1994 Loebner prize in which it was placed fourth (Mauldin 2009).

Extending the pattern-matching techniques used in ELIZA and advancing NLP capabilities, American scientist Richard Wallace developed A.L.I.C.E. (Artificial Linguistic Internet Computer Entity) in the late 1990s. A.L.I.C.E., also known as Alicebot, is acknowledged for its pioneering programming using Artificial Intelligence Markup Language (AIML) which is an XML schema for creating natural language software agents. Wallace released the first version of AIML in July 2001, subsequently published the Pandora API on which A.L.I.C.E. is based (Wallace 2008). A.L.I.C.E. became a three-time Loebner winner in 2000, 2001, and 2004.

Concurrent to A.L.I.C.E. developments, "Jabberwacky" was being conceived by British programmer, Rollo Carpenter. Jabberwacky was intended to simulate "natural human chat in an interesting, entertaining and humorous manner" (Shah and Warwick 2017). The emergence of the Internet provided Jabberwacky with a dynamic database of thousands of online human interactions from which to process responses. Jabberwacky under the guise of "George" and "Joan" won the Loebner Prize in 2005 and 2006 respectively.

In 2008, Jabberwacky launched a new iteration rebranded as "Cleverbot". Like Jabberwacky, Cleverbot is designed to learn from its conversations with humans (more than 150 million to date according to Wikipedia) . It draws on past interactions to determine future questions and answers (Gehl 2014).

In the endeavor to extend question answering (QA) capabilities posed in natural language, IBM Watson was conceived in 2006 as a QA computing system with the goal of outperforming human contestants on the USA television game show *Jeopardy!* IBM Watson was developed as part of IBM's DeepQA project (Ferrucci et al. 2010). Watson became the first computer to defeat contestants on the TV game show *Jeopardy!*, notably in a special match between Watson and Jeopardy! champions, Ken Jennings and Brad Rutter in 2011 (Best, n.d.).

Chatbots in general are reaching milestones in artificial intelligence capability, as well as their pervasiveness in consumer facing products and services. For example, in 2014, a chatbot called Eugene Goostman, portrayed as a 13-year-old Ukrainian boy, won an AI contest marking the 60th anniversary of Turing's death. In the *Turing Test 2014* organized by the University of Reading, 33% of the interrogators thought that Goostman was human (You 2015; Proudfoot 2017).

Created from AIML technology by programmer, Steve Worswick, "Mitsuku" is a web-based chatbot available on the freeware instant messaging mobile app Kik Messenger and the Pandorabots website (https://www.pandorabots.com/). It is among a growing number of sophisticated bots that can answer questions, play games, and is capable of basic reasoning in QA (Corti et al. 2015; Hill et al. 2015). Mitsuku is a three-time winner of the Loebner prize in 2013, 2016, and 2017.

Generally, the term "chatbot" has referred to a software application that engages in a dialogue with a human using natural language. Most early advances have been associated with written language, but with advances in speech recognition, there is a narrowing of these associations. The IBM Shoebox is one such example. The Shoebox was presented in public during the 1962 Seattle World's Fair after its initial market launch in 1961. This early computer was developed nearly 20 years before the introduction of the first IBM Personal Computer in 1981; it was able to recognize 16 spoken words and the digits 0– 9 (IBM n.d.).

Another early example is *Dragon*, a simple speech understanding system developed in 1975 by Dr. James Baker from Carnegie Mellon University. Other advances in the speech recognition sector have been made possible by VoiceXML which has been published in a series of standards since the first release in the year 2000. The World Wide Web Consortium (W3C) has established a W3C Community Group on Voice Interaction (http://www.w3.org/community/voiceinteraction) in 2017, which aims to explore the future of system-initiated directed dialogs of VoiceXML applications, such as voice assistants.

In just a few years, there has been an exponential rise of voice assistants such as Apple *Siri* launched in 2010, *Google Now* in 2012, Amazon's *Alexa* and Microsoft's *Cortana* in 2015, and *Google Assistant* in 2016. Using NLP and Internet of Things (IoT) platforms, these assistants connect to web services to answer questions and respond to user requests (Hoy 2018; Fast et al. 2018). Social media platforms are similarly incorporating chatbot functionality. Facebook opened its Messenger platform and API to developers in 2017, providing a means to build a simple chatbot on Facebook. Twitter opened its direct messaging channel to chatbots in the previous year that began a hype cycle in "twitterbots" (Alarifi et al. 2016) and other messenger services are rapidly making open APIs more widely available (Hoy 2018; Mool 2018).

15.3 Museums and Chatbots

Museums have been piloting AI and NLP enabled demonstrators for more than a decade (Boiano et al. 2003, 2018, Bickmore 2013; Borda and Bowen 2017; Bordoni et al. 2016; Robinson et al. 2008; Swartout 2010; Vassos et al. 2016). Emerging free chatbot-creating platforms—e.g., Chatfuel, Chatterbot Eliza, among others—and the availability of open APIs, for instance, can offer both large and smaller museums the opportunity of experimenting with chatbots with relatively low effort while keeping costs and staff resources at a low level (Bordoni et al. 2016; Boiano et al. 2003) and potentially less impact on existing infrastructure (Dale 2016).

The exponential growth in the use of chatbots by marketers and online businesses in enhancing customer experiences, often as messaging applications that can personalize the interaction (e.g., recommender systems), is providing further comparable opportunities in the cultural sector (Swartout 2010; Vassos et al. 2016). There are in fact a growing number of museums following this route and using bots as part of their audience engagement programming. For instance, the Heinz Nixdorf MuseumsForum in Paderborn Germany (http://www.hnf.de/en/) has an early experience of using an avatar bot introduced as *MAX*. Developed in 2004, *MAX* is a conversational agent that directly engages with visitors through a screen as a virtual museum guide (Kopp et al. 2005).

The Cooper-Hewitt Smithsonian Design Museum in New York City has been a pioneer in chatbot technologies with the creation of the Object Phone in 2013 in which a visitor can text or call to ask for more information about a museum object in the collection. In 2016, Object Phone became a subscription service so that a visitor can receive a daily update (http://objectphone.cooperhewitt.org). In the words of Micah Walter, Director of Digital & Emerging Media:

> I think institutions like museums have a great opportunity in the chatbot space. If anything it represents a new way to broaden our reach and connect with people on the platforms they are already using. What's more interesting to me is that chatbots themselves represent a way to interact with people that is by its very nature, bi-directional. (Walter 2016)

The San Francisco Museum of Modern Art (SFMOMA) has developed *Send Me SFMOMA* (http://www.sfmoma.org/send-me-sfmoma/), an SMS service that provides an approachable method of sharing the breadth of SFMOMA's collection with the public of which only 5% is seen in the Galleries at any one time (Mollica 2017). Using the service and texting the words "send me" followed by a keyword, a color, or an emoji, a visitor will receive a related artwork image and caption via text message.

In March 2017, the Anne Frank House museum (http://www.annefrank.org/en/) in Amsterdam launched a Facebook Messenger chatbot that allows users to discover the personal history of Anne Frank and practical visitor information. Not simply a collections discovery bot, this application offers various conversation pathways, allowing users to follow different paths in the Anne Frank story with concise information and links to additional content, for example, excerpts from her diary to the context of World War II at the time. Also in 2017, the Museum of Australian Democracy in Canberra (http://www.moadoph.gov.au) marked the 50th anniversary of a landmark

1967 referendum in which Australians voted overwhelmingly to amend the Constitution to include Aboriginal people in the census and to allow the Commonwealth government to create laws for them. The museum launched a referendum chatbot that allows visitors to learn about the historic and present impacts of this vote through chatting with it on Facebook Messenger. Directed towards children and accessible to adults, it uses simple gamification and responses, including emojis.

> It acts like history in your pocket and is helping MoAD spark a conversation about the significance of the 1967 referendum. We"re hoping it will be an effective way for people to get the facts, hear Indigenous perspectives on the referendum and reflect on its continuing relevance today. Marni Pilgrim, Digital Engagement Manager, MOAD. (O"Mallon 2017)

The Carnegie Museums of Pittsburgh Innovation Studio collaborated with Carnegie Museums of Pittsburgh Summer Adventure initiative to create a gamified museum experience with a digital chatbot component (Merrett 2018). The Summer Adventure, which has been an event held in Pittsburgh since 2013, introduced a digital guide, *AndyBot!* in 2018, a Facebook Messenger bot that is assisting participants through on and off-site experiences, finding activities, and collecting stamps at all four of the Carnegie museums. Another digital tour guide which appeared in 2018 is "Dot" at the Akron Art Museum in Ohio. Funded by the John S. and James L. Knight Foundation, Dot is the culmination of more than 18 months of planning and prototyping to create a chatbot that museum visitors can connect with via Facebook Messenger. Like *AndyBot!*, Dot represents an evolving chatbot application, designed to facilitate conversations about the art collections and deeper connections with small groups of friends or family members who take one of her tours (Litt 2018).

The use of chatbots is becoming part of an increasing suite of advancing AI-enabled components, driven by deep learning that is accelerating the ways in which a chatbot can learn to understand an user's intent and context to predict and/or provide more personalized content, information, or engagement (Fast et al. 2018). An example of a museum piloting aspects of deep learning is Museu do Amanhã (Museum of Tomorrow) in Rio de Janeiro, Brazil. The Museum of Tomorrow is one of a small group of museums experimenting with chatbots powered using IBM Watson Services. The IRIS + project is a pioneering use of Watson Services directed to ask open-ended questions and to accept unconstrained answers (Morena 2018). Watson programmers also trained Watson on Portuguese in conversation with hundreds of volunteers and expanded its vocabulary. IRIS + is an innovative application that can engage in interaction with visitors. For example, after a brief introduction, it begins with a question: "After everything you learned in the main exhibition, what are your concerns in today's world?" (Morena 2018). This question can spark a conversation in which visitors are able to talk about their thoughts. In a similar initiative, an AI chatbot is interacting with visitors to the Pinacoteca de São Paulo Museum. IBM Brazil has developed the "A Voz da Arte" (Voice of Art) chatbot project which draws on data from the museum archives, news files, and the Internet to answer visitors' questions about art in the galleries. Visitors can converse with historical figures or with the art itself (Natividad 2017).

15.4 The House Museums of Milan—A Case Study

The House Museums of Milan (Case Museo di Milano) is a group of four historical homes in Milan: Poldi Pezzoli Museum, Bagatti Valsecchi Museum, Necchi Campiglio Villa and Boschi Di Stefano House Museum (https://casemuseo.it/en/). Although each is different in style and historical period, ranging from 19th-century palaces (Poldi Pezzoli and Bagatti Valsecchi) to a 20th-century urban villa with garden (Necchi Campiglio) and a 20th-century apartment (Boschi Di Stefano), these four House Museums share several common features, as follows.

They each hold a large proportion of delicate objects from their collections which are on public exhibition. This has conservation and viewing challenges. Such collections also tend to be static displays. Characteristic of historic house museums, the objects on show are often on display reflecting the original collector's aesthetics. These collections are quite personalized in taste and media, including paintings, furniture, crafts and everyday life objects. Objects are loosely grouped together in ways not readily categorized as in purpose-built museums.

The standard set-up for historic house museums are "rooms full of every kind of object", curated by the original collectors/house occupants and the positions of objects usually remain unchanged through the years. Smaller objects tend to be overlooked due to the abundance of visual stimuli. Additionally, there is little or no dedicated space for interpretation and curatorial placards. For example, three out of four of the House Museums in Milan have no captions for their exhibitions, and visitors are provided with leaflets as a self-guided option. The intention is to lessen interference with the original house layout and owner's collection sensibilities. By default, this preservation of the status quo can create interpretation and outreach challenges. The House Museums of Milan have addressed the problem in different ways, through dedicated guided tours (Necchi Campiglio) or with very proactive volunteer facilitators (Boschi Di Stefano and Bagatti Valsecchi), and with audio guides and apps (Poldi Pezzoli and Bagatti Valsecchi).

Due to these limitations, there is a real problem in attracting returning visitors, and the House Museums have not been able to successfully engage certain visitor groups (e.g. teenagers). Constrained in space for temporary exhibitions or events, and with few possibilities of introducing into their galleries such contemporary enhancements as videos or digital interactives, the House Museums can easily fall into the stereotypical notion of another "museum stuck in the past".

However, House Museums have features which can be attractive for their audiences, including younger ones. The sense of a "lived-in" house can be more emotionally redolent and accessible than the "white-box model" of exhibitions in purpose-built museums and galleries. The architecture tends to support the collections in theme and time-period, and the personality of the collector/founder resonates within the galleries, creating a stronger emotional connection with the visitor. The sheer wealth and variety of objects can be overwhelming, but also compelling, and the labyrinthine structure of nearly all the House Museums can provide avenues for exploration.

15.5 The Chatbot Game Project

With all these factors in mind, the House Museums Network launched a strategic initiative in 2016 aimed at motivating people to visit the four museums. Funded by *Fondazione Cariplo*, a well-known Italian charity fund, the project had many goals, including the experimentation of new digital ways to involve younger audiences in exploring the House Museums.

A London-based cultural innovation company, InvisibleStudio (http://www.invisiblestudio.net), was approached to study this digital part of the project, which came with some requirements: it had to be innovative, aimed at attracting teenager audiences and feasible in three months with a limited budget and a limited consumption of museum staff time. Teenagers are a notoriously difficult public to engage in museums and often far more interested in social interactions between themselves than in cultural content—and this was proven to be even more challenging if that content is associated with a 19th-century historic house. In general, teenagers visiting museums are identified with high levels of distraction and highly adapted to the use of social media (Kelly and Russo 2008; Endo 2016; Fors 2016). Research in the USA, for example, shows that online chatting is one of the highest forms of social interaction of teenagers (Statista 2017).

The InvisibleStudio team had already experimented with earlier chatbot technology in 2002, while working at the Museum of Science and Technology Leonardo da Vinci in Milan (Boiano et al. 2016; Boiano and Gaia 2017a). The process provided important lessons in the development of a chatbot application. This early chatbot was developed to mimic a Leonardo da Vinci character with whom the user would interact. This set high expectations for the user experience and led to frustrations when the chatbot was not able to understand the user beyond simple introductory chat (Hill et al. 2015). Consequently, user issues occurred quite soon in the conversation. (Boiano and Gaia 2017a).

As an initial step in the process of addressing these past issues, InvisibleStudio applied Design Thinking as a strategic methodology to bring together stakeholders to think about a suitable solution for teenagers. Design Thinking is a problem-solving method developed at the D-School of Stanford University based on five iterative phases (https://dschool.stanford.edu):

1. Empathy with the user to understand their needs;
2. Definition of the problem;
3. Ideation of the solutions;
4. Prototyping;
5. Testing of the solutions.

The first phase, empathy, is in the authors' opinion one of the most meaningful for addressing engagement in museums based on their own experiences (Boiano and Gaia 2017b). The new emerging visitor-centered museum puts the relationship with the visitor at its core (Samis and Michelson 2016). No visitor relationship can exist without empathy. Understanding user needs requires museum staff to put themselves in the visitors' shoes, something which can be difficult to do but very fulfilling when it happens. InvisibleStudio used a variety of methods to achieve empathy, using methods that are typical of Design Thinking and that could be adapted to the specific museum environment. Two empathy methods typical of Design Thinking were applied in this project:

- Observation of teenagers in and out of museums;
- Deep conversations with individual teenagers regarding their museum experience.

In particular, the two methods offered some valuable insights on teenager attitudes towards the museum experience:

- teenagers love challenges and competition;
- they love to collaborate between themselves;
- they are fast and impatient;
- they love chatting between themselves using apps like *WhatsApp*;
- they are not willing to download museum apps, because they feel them as single-use and do not want to waste memory on their already overcrowded smartphones.

15.5.1 The Solution: A Chatbot Game

Drawing on the workshop insights, the InvisibleStudio production team decided that a chatbot game would be a close fit in terms of the empathetic qualities resulting from the field research. The decision was specifically based on the following reasons:

- As a smartphone-based application, a chatbot allows users to explore the museum while interacting with the software.
- A download of a museum app is avoided. Chatbot applications are usually lightweight on phone memory, and can be used on most smartphone platforms, even low-end or older versions.
- A chatbot can build on the natural tendency of teenagers to chat as observed during the Design Thinking Empathy phase.
- As a new technology, a chatbot can still offer a "wow-effect" and raise the interest of teenagers.

In this context it was also important to make the distinction between taking forward the development of a "virtual guide" chatbot or a chatbot game. Many of the museum chatbot examples explored in this chapter are digital tour guides which respond to a user's questions or provide hints and information on how to make the most of their visit to the museum. The virtual guide does not usually ask visitors to perform specific tasks; on the contrary they try to offer them the broadest possible freedom to choose their own subjects of interest and pathways.

The choice of a gamification approach in the design of the chatbot was based on the Design Thinking outcomes and separate research on what a suitable application might be for engaging teenage audiences. The opportunities afforded by gamification were reinforced by different assumptions and existing case studies, including earlier pilots in chatbot use in museums by the InvisibleStudio team (Boiano and Gaia 2017b; Cawston et al. 2017; Kelly and Russo 2008; Endo 2016; Fors 2016).

Research findings suggest that a combination of gamification and storytelling is more emotionally engaging for audiences not specifically interested in exploring the museum on their own or in a self-directed approach (Battaglino and Bickmore 2015). It builds on the interest in competition, challenge and collaboration. It brings teenagers' attention to the task to be performed, rather than on just the conversation. Limited conversational skills are the weakest point of today's chatbots; even AI intensive chatbots as the ones developed by Google or Apple are unable to understand all the nuances of human conversations (Hill et al. 2015).

Moreover, teenagers naturally tend to stress the conversational limits of chatbots when the conversation is the central activity. This is one of the drivers why the House Museum chatbot was more task oriented rather than conversationally focused: users tend to "forgive" more easily the limited conversational skills if they are engaging the chatbot to help them to solve something external to the conversation. A game focused on the collections can bring the user gaze away from the screen and on the actual objects inside the museum. One of the most significant challenges of museum digital tools should not be to distract users' attention from the content of the galleries; a game where the user must carefully watch the collection can be an effective tool to achieve this goal. Games can also encourage peer-to-peer collaboration.

With these lessons in hand, InvisibleStudio changed their approach when creating the chatbot for the House Museums project. The chatbot would only be used as a tool or "virtual companion" to help younger audiences solve a game set in the real physical environment of the museum. By engaging teenagers through gamification, it could shift the user's focus from the conversation with the chatbot to the actual exploration of the Museum collections (Boiano 2016; Cawston 2017). In this way it is not a guide to be followed, but a challenge to be solved.

The chatbot game for the House Museums was developed using Facebook Messenger and was intended mainly for young users and teenagers to engage them in exploring the four House Museums. The game takes the form of a treasure hunt inside the Museums, where users chat with an artificial character via Facebook Messenger on their own smartphones in order to find clues hidden in the Museum collections and to solve a mystery.

Aspects of storytelling were utilized with the chatbot platform to simulate a teenage girl asking visitors to help her in defeating the mysterious Ambrogio Varese da Rosate, a Renaissance physician, astronomer and magician at the court of Ludovico il Moro, the Duke of Milan in the 15th century. Ambrogio is a documented historical figure. Exploration is encouraged by users in looking for hidden clues that lead to a final discovery, which provides a further incentive to engage with the application.

Users can interact with the chatbot using the Facebook Messenger app or the Telegram Messenger app; the chatbot was developed in order to work with both messaging apps, although the Facebook Messenger continues to be the most popular of the two apps at the time of this case study.

The chatbot has two ways of interacting with the user, firstly by asking open-ended questions to which the user must respond. This is most effective in terms of emotional engagement, although it creates a complex interpretation problem because the chatbot developers must foresee all possible user's answers. For example, even if the user is to address a simple question like "how many jewels do you see in the painting?" and the correct answer is "zero", then the bot should be programmed to understand "0", "zero", "no one", "none", "I can't see any jewel" and so on. Otherwise the conversation can quickly become frustrating for users if they feel their answers are not correctly interpreted by the chatbot. This is by far the most difficult part in the implementation.

A second interaction is the approach of asking multiple-choices questions with pre-defined answers, visible by the users as a set of buttons (see Fig. 15.2). This is the best option to keep the game flow running and minimizing disruptions caused by chatbot and user misunderstandings, but it can make the user feel less flexible in the actions supported by the game and can limit the "serendipity".

At any time in the game, the user can send unsolicited messages to the chatbot. Depending on how the chatbot is programmed, it can try to understand the message or simply answer with a predetermined automated answer saying it does not understand the message. There is also an option for the user to choose to send commands to the chatbot like "pause", "stop", "restart", etc.

15.5.2 First Evaluations, Opportunities, and Challenges

Before operational release of the chatbot, it was piloted with teenagers aged 16–18 years. The pilot was conducted by InvisibleStudio with 80 teenage students from local high schools in Milan. The pilot resulted in the following findings:

90% of students managed to complete the game;
30% had connection problems;
34% were worried for their data traffic;
88% found the length of the game was right;
72% evaluated the game as highly entertaining;
66% found it a useful learning tool, especially if it was used with another student or in a small group (Fig. 15.3).

These results offered some clear directions for the final development stages. Especially interesting for the developers was the fact that students liked using the chatbot in small groups, rather than on their own, because the game triggered collaboration within the team and created a friendly competitive environment with other teams (Boiano and Gaia 2017b). At the same time, the pace and quality of the conversation emerged as a critical aspect for consideration, requiring a larger effort from the development team to create engaging and realistic non-linear narratives (Hill et al. 2015). For instance, key features which required considerable tweaking before publishing the application included: making conversations more realistic by studying real chats

Fig. 15.2 Example of multiple-choice question from the House-Museum Chatbot game. (© InvisibleStudio, 2017)

between users and guides, referencing objects which the user can see "here and now" in the galleries, and finding the perfect length for the game (Boiano and Gaia 2017a; 2017b). Levels of engagement need to be incorporated into the game, such as keeping points, tracking levels and mysteries solved, etc. Timing is a crucial aspect; the game should not be time-based, to discourage users from running around the galleries, and to reward precision rather than speed in solving the quizzes.

Another key challenge was the necessity of keeping open a continuous online connection between users and the chatbot. This can prove difficult in historical house museums, where the older infrastructure is comprised of complex layouts and thick walls which can prevent wireless connectivity or an even distribution of Wi-Fi con-

Fig. 15.3 Teenagers using the chatbot game in Milan. (© InvisibleStudio, 2017)

nections. Providing a reliable Wi-Fi connection to all users in the museum galleries was the practical way of addressing this issue.

Following these Phase 1 pilots, further testing was conducted in Phase 2 with another 120 teenage visitors. In this second phase, the production team derived some indications which could be useful for other museums and cultural institutions willing to experiment with chatbots.

The summative findings from the evaluation stages indicated that teenagers readily adopted the chatbot game as a way of exploring the museum. Some students pointed out that if they had not visited the museum before, playing the game on the first visit would have made them lose the overall context of the museum. There were three options in considering this issue:

- Propose the chatbot game to returning visitors only.
- Offer a short introductory tour to the museum before the game; this approach was tested with around 60 adult visitors in the Boschi Di Stefano museum in March 2018 and proved highly successful in giving them some context before the game.
- Try to tweak the game in order to give more context about the museum before playing it. This can be difficult due to time and playability constraints; it is clear from the test that only a certain amount of educational content can be delivered to the user without disrupting the pace and enjoyability of the game.

As in every digital product, keeping a low threshold for user adoption is essential. In the chatbot game, the fact that users tend to have the messaging app on their smartphone already is important in keeping a low threshold; they also do not have to learn how to use it. One difference in the chatbot application between normal conversations among humans and a conversation with the chatbot consists in the use of buttons with predetermined choices; these are used only by chatbots and not by humans. Apart from that, interacting with a chatbot through the text interface is exactly like text chatting with a human being.

Not least, user privacy is especially important as the chatbot game is aimed at minors. Chatbots do not need to acquire any substantial data about their users than summarily published on an individual's Facebook page. Hence, normal procedures aimed to protect Facebook page followers were deemed sufficiently safe by the House Museum developers. This approach was additionally considered in relation to the General Data Protection Regulation 2016/679 (GDPR) and privacy policy of the European Union (EU).

The varying perceptions about the extent or capacity of Facebook to fully protect users' privacy (e.g. the Cambridge Analytica data mining case) were acknowledged as a potential challenge which could drive users away from the Facebook Messenger app or make them less willing to use it in relation to a third party, even a trusted one like a public museum.

In this context, the development process brought to the foreground a degree of ethical transparency to engender trust among the stakeholders, and critically with the users. This consideration will become only more visible when autonomous decision-making and self-learning by chatbots have a directly negative impact on the engagement with museum audiences (IEEE 2017). The release of the Tay chatbot by Microsoft Corporation via Twitter in 2016 caused significant controversy when the chatbot began to post inflammatory and offensive tweets through its Twitter account. Microsoft was forced to shut down the service in less than 24 h after its launch. (Wakefield 2016). How can ethical transparency be achieved? A growing movement focusing on this issue and the future of AI systems is aiming to direct the control of chatbots to be intrinsically open, understandable and consistent (IEEE 2017). If sufficiently upheld, these approaches will ideally minimize privacy concerns and maximize accessibility, inclusiveness and trust (IEEE 2017).

Other potential obstacles arising from the House Museums pilot mainly relate to the Facebook Messenger platform itself, and the changing preferences of teenagers and audiences for different messaging services which may not have open APIs for chatbot development, such as the situation with the popular WhatsApp (Mool 2018). According to *Statista*, WhatsApp is the most used messaging app in 2018, with 1.5 billion users, followed by Facebook Messenger with 1.3 billion (Statista 2017). Since WhatsApp does not accommodate the building of chatbots (yet) on its platform, Facebook Messenger has become a default choice for most museums which have developed a chatbot application. Choosing which platform should be used for a chatbot application can inevitably affect the accessibility and extent of audience reach. The more popular messaging apps are likely to attract a larger user base and will lessen the risk of disengaging visitors who need to download another app that they might not usually use.

A concurrent problem is that Facebook as a social network is losing some ground with teenagers. According to a study by Pew Research Center, as of May 2018 only half of US teenagers use Facebook, and only 10% use it as their main social media platform (Anderson and Jiang 2018). This is down from 71 and 41% respectively in 2015. According to Hootsuite and We Are Social (2018), in Italy only 2% of teenagers aged 13–17 years use Facebook regularly. This clearly poses future challenges when deciding which chatbot platform to use for development, because the platform landscape is constantly evolving, both in terms of chatbot API capabilities and in market penetration regarding the target audiences.

From the case study presented here, a recommendation for prospective museums considering a chatbot application is to conduct research on their target audience before selecting a messaging platform of choice, and ideally to develop the application for more than one platform. For example, the House Museums chatbot can be used with both Facebook Messenger and Telegram Messenger to optimize accessibility by its known visitor groups. When messaging platforms, such as WhatsApp and Snapchat open their platforms to chatbots, an application extension using those platforms will likely be adopted by the House Museums team.

An important impetus in the decision to consider a chatbot game is the visible growth in chatbot-creating platforms on the Internet in which little coding knowledge is required. These platforms can potentially save time and core development costs, thus are becoming suitable choices for museums which have limited in-house resources. One drawback is the inevitable dependency on the reliability of the platform that hosts the chatbot application.

General guidance derived from the House Museums study is to select the platforms (1) with advice from known experts associated with previous chatbot development, (2) that have precedence in their use by trusted cultural organizations in similar contexts of use (e.g. digital guide, storytelling, gamification), and (3) that are widely used in the sector. These factors provide improved chances of sustainability in the Darwinian environment of a technology still in its infancy.

15.6 Thoughts on Future Directions of Chatbots and Museums

There is clear evidence of the potential of cultural heritage organizations to play a significant role in the use of chatbot technologies for visitor engagement and interaction. Developments suggest that the use of chatbot platforms will become increasingly more pervasive in museums, especially regarding chatbot guides. Thus far, comparable evaluations of visitor interactions with chatbots have not made their way into the published literature; however, from the case study of the House Museums of Milan, chatbots can be operationally successful in the short term at least, but much is dependent on the inclusion of chatbots in the overall museum communications strategy so they can be seen to be clearly aligned to the aims of the museum itself.

A second environmental factor contributing to the rise of the chatbot within the sector is that chatbot games have become simpler to build based on available platforms. One can draw on existing museum expertise in developing educational content, rather than a focus on the technology framework. Consequently, an audience pilot using chatbots can be more readily entertained by both larger and smaller museums.

The House Museums of Milan case study further illustrates that the convergence of chatbot and gamification can be a powerful tool in involving younger, digital savvy generations in novel and interesting ways to them. The combination of chatbot and gamification offers a future space for museums in layering new forms of interaction which can empower the participants as well as provide a visitor experience that promotes extended engagement. Particularly with the design and incorporation of interactive digital storytelling chatbots into a museum context, this presents new possibilities, enabling the development and creation of characters with feelings and personalities which can be empathetically tailored to different visitor interests and age groups.

As the use of more AI-intensive bots becomes a future consideration, the direction is set to establish broader and more contextual conversations with the museum visitor, and perhaps opening up the way for audience-led contributions to the design of museum chatbots themselves. The Akron Art Museum's personalized chatbot "Dot", funded by a grant from the Miami-based Knight Foundation, and the IBM Watson partnership with museums in Brazil, are among the next generation to offer insights for the future application of AI-enabled and deep learning chatbots in the cultural sector. Notwithstanding, challenges remain in achieving higher levels of sensitivity and contextual-awareness by chatbots—e.g., conversational interactions moving beyond one-to-one dialogues, and emotionally aware responses.

Above all, there remains a gap in the fuller understanding of the larger questions that such developments can entail; especially acute in the case where a chatbot agent embodies increased naturalness through deep learning and as a self-improving and/or self-learning entity through its participatory interactions with audiences. There is a critical and continuing need, therefore, to be able to address ethical responsibility, inclusivity, privacy and consent, and beneficial considerations in this transformational space. Why are we building this? –what are the benefits and what are the risks?

Future chatbots have the potential to truly impact on the visitor experience and create new paradigms of engagement in museums and cultural organizations, but the application of chatbots, as with any emergent technology, needs to directly and meaningfully support the higher aims of the museum as a trusted learning organization with respect to the public and in their participation as equal stakeholders in the process.

References

Alaieri F, Vellino A (2017) A decision making model for ethical (ro)bots. In: IEEE international symposium on robotics and intelligent sensors (IRIS), Ottawa, Canada, pp 203–207. https://doi.org/10.1109/iris.2017.8250122

Alarifi A, Alsaleh M, Al-Salman A (2016) Twitter Turing test: identifying social machines. Inf Sci 372:332–346

Altick R (1978) The shows of London. Cambridge, MA and London, Belknap

Anderson M. Jiang J (2018) Teens, social media & technology 2018. Pew Research Centre, 31 May 2018. http://www.pewinternet.org/2018/05/31/teens-social-media-technology-2018/. Accessed 5 Jan 2019

Anon (1846) The Euphonia, or speaking automaton. The Illustrated London News, 25 July 1846, p 59

Battaglino C, Bickmore T (2015) Increasing the engagement of conversational agents through co-constructed storytelling. In: Proceedings of AIIDE conference, pp 9–15

Best J (n.d.) IBM Watson: the inside story of how the Jeopardy-winning supercomputer was born, and what it wants to do next. TechRepublic. https://www.techrepublic.com/article/ibm-watson-the-inside-story-of-how-the-jeopardy-winning-supercomputer-was-born-and-what-it-wants-to-do-next/. Accessed 13 Mar 2018

Bickmore TW, Vardoulakis LMP, Schulman D (2013) Tinker: a relational agent museum guide. Auton Agent Multi-Agent Syst 27(2):254–276

Boiano S, Borda A, Gaia G, Rossi S, Cuomo P (2018) Chatbots and new audience opportunities for Museums and Heritage Organisations. In: Bowen JP, Weinel J, Diprose G, Lambert N (eds) EVA London 2018 conference proceedings. Electronic Workshops in Computing (eWiC), BCS, pp 164–171. https://doi.org/10.14236/ewic/eva2018.33

Boiano S, Cuomo P, Gaia G (2016) Real-time messaging platforms for storytelling and gamification in museums: a case history in Milan. In: Bowen JP, Diprose G, Lambert N (eds) EVA London 2016 conference proceedings, Electronic Workshops in Computing (eWiC), BCS, pp 291–293. https://doi.org/10.14236/ewic/eva2016.60

Boiano S, Gaia G, Caldarini M (2003) Make your museum talk: natural language interfaces for cultural institutions. Museums and the Web 2003. https://www.museumsandtheweb.com/mw2003/papers/gaia/gaia.html. Accessed 13 Mar 2018

Boiano S, Gaia G (2017a) 3 Lessons learnt from Building our first Museum Chatbot… 15 years ago! Invisible. (13 June 2017). https://medium.com/@invisiblestudio/3-lessons-learnt-from-building-our-first-museum-chatbot-15-years-ago-7189c8a8fe6. Accessed 13 Mar 2018

Boiano S, Gaia G (2017b) 5 tips for involving teenagers in your museum using a chatbot. InvisibleStudio. (27 June 2017). https://medium.com/@invisiblestudio/5-tips-for-involving-teenagers-in-your-museum-using-a-chatbot-bf88ff3ad568. Accessed 13 March 2018

Borda A, Bowen JP (2017) Smart cities and cultural heritage: a review of developments and future opportunities. In: Bowen JP, Diprose G, Lambert N (eds) EVA London 2017 conference proceedings, Electronic Workshops in Computing (eWiC), BCS, pp 9–18. https://doi.org/10.14236/ewic/eva2017.2

Bordoni L, Mele F, Sorgente A (eds) (2016) Artificial intelligence for cultural heritage. Cambridge Scholars, Newcastle

Cawston R, Efergan D, Green L (2017) It's in the game: can playful digital experiences help organisations connect with audiences in new ways? MW 2017: Museums and the Web. https://mw17.mwconf.org/paper/its-in-the-game-can-playful-digital-experiences-help-organisations-connect-with-audiences-in-new-ways/. Accessed 13 Mar 2018

Copeland BJ, Bowen JP, Sprevak M, Wilson R et al (2017) The Turing guide. Oxford University Press

Corti K, Gillespie A (2015) A truly human interface: interacting face-to-face with someone whose words are determined by a computer program. Frontiers in Psychology. https://doi.org/10.3389/fpsyg.2015.00634. (18 May 2015)

Dalakov G (2018) Joseph Faber's Euphonia. In: History of computers. http://history-computer.com/Dreamers/Faber.html. Accessed 28 Aug 2018

Dale R (2016) The return of the chatbots. Nat Lang Eng 22(5):811–817. https://doi.org/10.1017/S1351324916000243

Dennett D (2004) Can machines think? In: Teuscher C (ed) Alan Turing: life and legacy of a great thinker. Springer, Berlin, pp 295–316. https://doi.org/10.1007/978-3-662-05642-4_12

Endo T (2016) Teens use tech to talk art: amplifying teen voice and art interpretation. MW2016: Museums and the Web. http://mw2016.museumsandtheweb.com/paper/teens-use-tech-to-talk-art-amplifying-teen-voice-and-art-interpretation/. Accessed 13 Mar 2018

Fast E, Chen B, Mendelsohn, J, Bassen J, Bernstein M (2018) Iris: a conversational agent for complex tasks. In: Proceedings of the 2018 CHI conference on human factors in computing systems (CHI '18). ACM, New York. https://doi.org/10.1145/3173574.3174047

Ferrucci D et al (2010) Building Watson: an overview of the DeepQA project. AI Mag 36(3):59–79

Fors V (2016) Teenagers' multisensory routes for learning in the museum. The Senses Soc 8(3):268–289. https://doi.org/10.2752/174589313X13712175020479

Fuegi J, Francis J (2003) Lovelace & Babbage and the creation of the 1843 'Notes'. IEEE Ann Hist Comput 25:16–26. https://doi.org/10.1109/MAHC.2003.1253887

Gehl, R. W. (2014). Teaching to the Turing test with Cleverbot. Transform J Inclusive Sch Pedagogy, 24(1–2), pp. 56–66

Hill J, Ford WR, Farreras IG (2015) Real conversations with artificial intelligence: a comparison between human–human online conversations and human–chatbot conversations. Comput Hum Behav 49:245–250

Hoy MB (2018) Alexa, Siri, Cortana, and more: an introduction to voice assistants. Med Ref Serv Q 37(1):81–88

IBM (n.d.) IBM Shoebox, IBM archives exhibits IBM special products, vol 1. https://www-03.ibm.com/ibm/history/exhibits/specialprod1/specialprod1_7.html. Accessed 5 Jan 2019

IEEE (2017) Ethically aligned design: a vision for prioritizing human well-being with autonomous and intelligent systems, (EADv2). IEEE Global Initiative on Ethics of Autonomous and Intelligent Systems. https://ethicsinaction.ieee.org. Accessed 5 Jan 2019

Inglis K (2008) Becoming automatous: automata in the old curiosity shop and our mutual friend. Interdisc Stud Long Nineteenth Century 6. http://www.19.bbk.ac.uk. Accessed 5 Jan 2019

Kelly L, Russo A (2008) From ladders of participation to networks of participation: social media and the museum audiences. MW2008: Museum and the Web Conference, Montreal, Canada. 9–12 April

Kopp S, Gesellensetter L, Krämer NC, Wachsmuth I (2005) A conversational agent as museum guide–design and evaluation of a real-world application. In: International workshop on intelligent virtual agents. Springer, Berlin, pp 329–343

Litt S (2018) Dot, the new Akron Art Museum chatbot, wants to get you talking about art and life. Cleveland.com. (5 Aug 2018). https://www.cleveland.com/arts/index.ssf/2018/08/dot_the_new_akron_art_museum_c.html. Accessed 25 Aug 2018

Loebner H (2008) How to hold a Turing test contest. In Epstein R, Roberts G, Beber G (eds) Parsing the Turing test: philosophical and methodological issues in the quest for the thinking computer. Springer, New York, pp 173–179. https://doi.org/10.1007/978-1-4020-6710-5_12

Mauldin ML (2009) Going under cover: passing as human. In Epstein R, Roberts G, Beber G (eds) Parsing the Turing test. Springer, Dordrecht, pp 413–429. https://doi.org/10.1007/978-1-4020-6710-5_24

Merritt E (2018). Chat with AndyBot at AAM 2018. Center for the future of museums blog, American Alliance of Museums. 10 Apr 2018. https://www.aam-us.org/2018/04/10/chat-with-andybot-at-aam-2018/. Accessed 6 Jan 2019

Mills M (2012) Media and prosthesis: the vocoder, the artificial larynx, and the history of signal processing. Qui Parle 21(1):107–149

Mollica J (2017) Send Me SFMOMA. San Francisco Museum of Modern Art, USA, July 2017. https://www.sfmoma.org/read/send-me-sfmoma/. Accessed 13 Mar 2018

Mool T (2018) Chatbot trends: the year of the voicebot, WhatsApp Bots, MaaP. NativeMSG. https://nativemsg.com/blog/2018-chatbot-trends-the-year-of-the-voicebot-whatsapp-bots-maap. Accessed 13 Mar 2018

Morena D (2018) IRIS + part one: designing + Coding a museum AI. Center for the future of museums blog, American Alliance of Museums. 12 June 2018. https://www.aam-us.org/2018/06/12/iris-part-one-designing-coding-a-museum-ai/. Accessed 20 Jan 2019

Natividad A (2017) IBM Watson's New job as art museum guide could hint at lots of future roles with brands, Adweek, 19 April 2017. https://www.adweek.com/creativity/ibm-watsons-new-job-as-art-museum-guide-could-hint-at-lots-of-future-roles-with-brands/. Accessed 6 Jan 2019

O'Mallon F (2017) Museum of Australian Democracy uses facebook messenger chatbot to connect with Australia's past. Canberra Times. 26 May 2017. http://www.canberratimes.com.au/act-news/museum-of-australia-democracy-uses-facebook-messenger-chatbot-to-connect-with-australias-past-20170525-gwcvu5.html. Accessed 13 Mar 2018

Proudfoot D (2017) The Turing test—from every angle. In: Copeland BJ et al (2017), Chapter 27, pp 287–300

Robinson S, Traum DR, Ittycheriah M, Henderer J (2008) What would you ask a conversational agent? Observations of human-agent dialogues in a museum setting. In: Proceedings language resources and evaluation conference, Marrakech, May 2008. Accessed 13 Mar 2018

Rossbach S (2011) Mechanical conversation 1800, 1900, 2000—from von Kempelen's 'Speech Organ' to 'Alice the Chatterbot', Ars Semeiotica. 34(1–2):167–174

Samis P, Michelson M (2016) Creating the Visitor-centered Museum. Routledge

Shah H, Warwick K (2017) Machine humour: examples from Turing test experiments. AI & Soc 32:553–561. https://doi.org/10.1007/s00146-016-0669-0

Statista (2017) Reach of leading social media and networking sites used by teenagers and young adults in the United States as of Feb 2017. Statista. https://www.statista.com/statistics/199242/social-media-and-networking-sites-used-by-us-teenagers/. Accessed 13 Mar 2018

Swade D (2017) Turing, Lovelace and Babbage. In: Copeland BJ et al (2017), Chapter 24, pp 249–262

Swartout W et al (2010) Ada and grace: toward realistic and engaging virtual museum guides. International Conference on intelligent virtual agents. Springer, Berlin, pp 286–300

Turing AM (1950) Computing machinery and intelligence. Mind 59(236):433–460. https://doi.org/10.1093/mind/lix.236.433

Vassos S et al (2016) Art-Bots: toward chat-based conversational experiences in museums. In: Nack F, Gordon A (eds) Interactive Storytelling. ICIDS 2016, Lecture notes in computer science, vol 10045. Springer

Von Kempelen W (1791) Der Mechanismus der menschlichen Sprache. The Mechanism of Human Speech.: Kommentierte Transliteration & Übertragung ins Englische/Commented Transliteration & Translation into English. Herausgegeben von/ Edited by Fabian Brackhane, Richard Sproat & Jürgen Trouvain; Dresden 2017. http://www.coli.uni-saarland.de/~trouvain/Kempelen-Web_2017_07_31.pdf. Accessed 20 Jan 2019

Wakefield J (2016) Microsoft chatbot is taught to swear on Twitter. BBC. 24 Mar 2016. https://www.bbc.com/news/technology-35890188. Accessed 6 Jan 2019

Wallace R (2008) The anatomy of A.L.I.C.E. In: Epstein R, Roberts G, Beber G (eds) Parsing the Turing Test: philosophical and methodological issues in the quest for the thinking computer. Springer, New York, pp 181–210. https://doi.org/10.1007/978-1-4020-6710-5_13

Walter M (2016) Object phone: the continued evolution of a little chatbot. Cooper Hewitt Labs. 4 July 2016. https://labs.cooperhewitt.org/2016/object-phone-the-continued-evolution-of-a-little-chatbot/. Accessed 13 Mar 2018

Warwick K, Shah H (2016) The importance of a human viewpoint on computer natural language capabilities: a Turing test perspective. AI & Soc 31(2):207–221

We Are Social (2018) Digital Italia in 2018. SlideShare. 5 Feb 2018. https://www.slideshare.net/wearesocial/digital-in-italia-2018. Accessed 20 Jan 2019

Weizenbaum J (1966) ELIZA—a computer program for the study of natural language communication between man and machine. Commun ACM 9(1):36–45
You J (2015) Beyond the Turing test. Science 347(6218):116. https://doi.org/10.1126/science.347.6218.116

Chapter 16
Engagement at the Brooklyn Museum: A Case Study of Use Rate and Lessons Learned

Sara Devine

Abstract From interactives to apps, from labels to comment areas, museums spend a great deal of time and money planning a variety of digital and non-digital approaches for visitor engagement onsite. Best practice dictates that we offer a variety of ways for visitors to find relevance and make meaning and that we cater to different learning styles, abilities, and interest levels. However, not all these approaches garner the same amount of interest or use by our visitors. The Brooklyn Museum has a unique data set of use rate metrics from a variety of engagement projects, digital and non-digital, spanning ten years. When examining these use rate metrics, an interesting trend emerges. Certain engagement opportunities share an average use rate of 2%: our audio guide, our ASK app, question and answer kiosks in special exhibitions, a digital guestbook, and even guided tours. However, other projects have garnered much higher or lower use rates: an avatar interactive in *Vishnu: The Blue-Skinned Savior* (28%), a sticky-note activity outside of *Killer Heels: The Art of the High-Heeled Shoe* (11%), or a video response opportunity with *The Black List Project* (0.37%). Is there a reason for the shared use rate among certain opportunities and much different use rates among others? And if so, how might that inform engagement strategies and evaluation needs for the 21st-century museum? By examining the use rates of these engagement approaches in combination with anecdotal evidence, the author will examine lessons learned about digital and non-digital engagement opportunities including what these past projects can tell us about future planning and the limitations of quantitative data such as use rate in understanding visitor behavior.

16.1 Introduction: Engagement Projects at the Brooklyn Museum

The use of technology as a tool for providing information and engaging visitors is not new. As Tallon and Walker (2008) describes in the introduction of *Digital Technologies and the Museum Experience: Handheld Guides and Other Media*, the first

S. Devine (✉)
Brooklyn Museum, New York, USA
e-mail: sara.devine@gmail.com

T. Giannini and J. P. Bowen (eds.), *Museums and Digital Culture*,
Springer Series on Cultural Computing, https://doi.org/10.1007/978-3-319-97457-6_16

visitor technology deployed in a museum was the Stedelijik Museum's Short-Wave Ambulatory Lectures in 1952, an early radio-based audio guide. Since those early days, museums have been exploring uses of technology for providing information, and within the last 15–20 years, to provide an experience. In the early 20th century, Weil (1999) noted that American museums were undergoing a substantial shift from collecting-focused institutions to ones focused on educational services. This shift is attributable to several factors, which Weil (1999) describes, including the creation of many new museums in the post-World War II era, the need for museums to rely at least partially on admissions sales for funding, and the evolving professionalism of the museum field. The increasing influence of such professional organizations at the American Association of Museums (now the American Alliance of Museums) founded in 1906 and the International Council of Museums founded in 1946 along with other, more focused professional bodies have shaped the ideals, policies, and protocols of American museums. It is from this visitor-centered, service-based approach that the fields of museum education, interpretation, and visitor studies were born.

These visitor-centered approaches are where my training and professional interest lies. As Director of Visitor Experience and Engagement at the Brooklyn Museum, I am responsible for thinking holistically about a visitor's experience with us—from entry to exit, from online to onsite. My team is responsible for admissions and coat check, visitor metrics and evaluation, group tours and sales, and collaborating on in-gallery and online interpretation. I worked on all of the projects cited in this chapter that date from 2012 on, though my role at the time was either Manager of Interpretive Materials or Manager of Audience Engagement and Interpretive Materials (two previously held positions). Throughout my career, my goal has been to determine who the audiences are for a specific exhibition or installation and to develop strategies, both digital and non-digital, to engage, inform, and delight those audiences.

A primary goal of all forms of interpretation is engagement, that is, capturing and retaining someone's attention so that they can learn something new, find relevance, and participate in an active meaning-making process, which Ted Ansbacher (2013) describes as "experience-based learning". While engagement is subjective and difficult to measure, we can measure how many people use a specific engagement strategy, which can indicate something about its efficacy in engagement. After all, if visitors are not using a strategy or method, it cannot be engaging. When examining use rate across a variety of engagement approaches offered at the Brooklyn Museum, I noticed an interesting trend. 2% is the average percentage of visitors who elect to engage with us via several different opportunities: our audio guide, our ASK app, question and answer kiosks in special exhibitions, a digital guestbook, and even guided tours. However, some special exhibition projects have garnered much higher or lower use rates. Initial, cursory review found no immediate explanation, which warranted a deeper dive into the data, which this chapter presents.

Table 16.1 Summary of engagement projects

Date	Category	Project	Existing data for evaluation
2015	Labels	Collection gallery labels (Contemporary, European, Arts of the Americas, Ancient Egyptian, American, Arts of Africa)	Observation
2018	Labels	Special exhibition labels (*Ahmed Mater*, *Soulful Creatures*, *Auguste Rodin*)	Observation
2009	Comment areas	*The Black List* video response	Metrics
2014	Comment areas	*Killer Heels* sticky note activity	Metrics
2016	Comment areas	*This Place* index cards	Metrics
2017	Comment areas	*Legacy of Lynching* index cards	Metrics
2017	Guided tours	Collection and special exhibition	Metrics
2008–11	Audio guides	Collection areas (The Dinner Party, Ancient Egypt, American, Arts of Africa)	Metrics
2007–12	Audio guides	Special exhibitions (*Murakami*, *Votes for Women*, *Caillebotte*, *Who Shot Rock and Roll*, *Warhol*, *Youth and Beauty*, *Hide/Seek*, *Mickalene Thomas*, *Six Years*)	Metrics
2007–13	Kiosks	Digital comment kiosks	Metrics
2013	Kiosks	In conversation kiosks (*LaToya Ruby Frazier*, *John Singer Sargent*, *El Anatsui*, *War/Photography*)	Metrics and observation
2017	Kiosks	Digital guestbook	Metrics, observation, interviews
2011	Interactive digital	Vishnu exhibition interactive	Metrics, observation, interviews
2015–18	Interactive digital	ASK Brooklyn Museum app	Metrics, survey, focus group

16.2 Use Rate as a Metric to Capture Efficacy of Engagement

The Brooklyn Museum has a history of evaluating engagement projects, both non-digital and digital, which serves as a case study of one institution's approach. The data set spans time (2008–18), collection area, exhibition type, and engagement strategy for a total of six different project types and 16 individual studies. It includes evaluations on labels, audio guides, guided tours, comment areas, and digital interactives.

The data were gathered for a variety of reasons. In the case of audio guides, use rate data was gathered specifically to determine whether or not to cancel the program (we did). In the case of labels, data was gathered to learn how visitors were using labels in the galleries so that we might improve our approach. The focus was not on use rate, but rather if and how they were used. In the case of ASK Brooklyn Museum, data were fundamental to the development and evolution of the program as well a requirement of our grant. For other projects such as *The Black List* video response area, this case study was the reason for gathering and delving into the existing data. While each individual evaluation has a few caveats to bear in mind, when taken together, the data set allows for some interesting comparisons and insights (Table 16.1).

16.2.1 Labels

In 2015, the Associate Manager of Interpretive Materials at that time, Holly Harmon, embarked on a holistic evaluation of the Brooklyn Museum's approach to didactic labels. The entire process took over a year and included multiple individual studies completed by several interns and a great deal of research and oversight on Harmon's part. For this case study, the most relevant part of this holistic evaluation is a tracking and timing study of permanent collection labels completed by intern Yulun Huang. Over the course of a semester, Huang spent over 40 h in various portions of permanent collection galleries and observed 284 visitors. Since in most cases it was impossible to determine exactly where someone was looking, at the artwork or the explanatory label next to it, Huang treated each artwork and label pair as a single "display." For the purposes of observation, she noted the number of displays a visitor "attended to," that is, stopped and planted both feet to look (Serrell 1997). For this case study, a display is considered "used" if it was "attended to." (Fig. 16.1).

Since the holistic label evaluation focused only on permanent collection areas, I recreated Huang's tracking and timing study with a focus on three of the special exhibitions on view at the Museum in the beginning of 2018. With the help of several of my team members—Alexandra Harris, Dana Notine, Rachel Richardson, and Yasemin Yeldener—we spent over 12 h in three exhibitions observing 132 visitors. For these exhibitions, the label placement allowed us to better differentiate where someone was looking and focus on timing visitor attention with the labels especially. Using these two data sets, we can determine the use rate of permanent collection

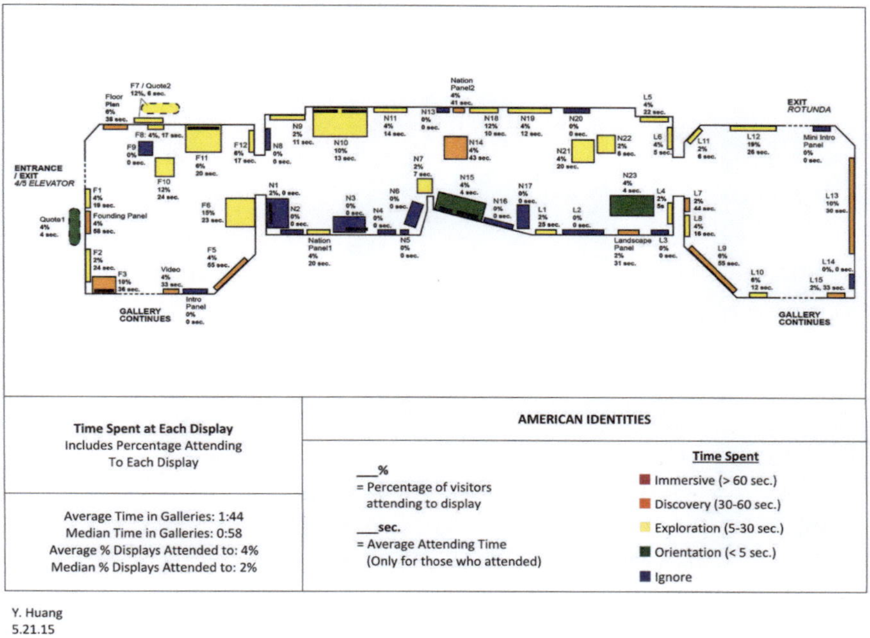

Fig. 16.1 Yulun Huang's tracking and timing worksheet for four of the American Art galleries

Table 16.2 Label evaluation

Collection area (2015 study)	Use rate (%)	Special exhibition (2018 study)	Use rate (%)
Contemporary art	13	Ahmed Mater: Mecca Journeys	32
European art	12	Soulful Creatures: Animal Mummies in Ancient Egypt	28
Arts of the Americas	14	Auguste Rodin: The Body in Bronze	12
Ancient Egyptian art	7	*Average use rate*	27
American art	4		
Arts of Africa	3		
Average use rate	8		
Average label use rate: 17%			

and special exhibition labels, which equals the average number of displays visitors attended to divided by the total number of displays in the space (Table 16.2).

Fig. 16.2 The "shoe closet" comment area outside the *Killer Heels* exhibition was well-used by visitors, who both left their own comments and spent time reading others'. (Photograph by Sara Devine)

16.2.2 Comment Areas

We often try to provide space in our exhibitions for visitors to participate, reflect, and share their thoughts about some aspect or idea in the show. Generally, this feedback/comment area is non-digital, though in 2009 as part of *The Black List* exhibition, we provided an opportunity to record a video response using YouTube and 482 visitors participated.

For *Killer Heels: The Art of the High-Heeled Shoe* (2014) we created a "shoe closet" at the end of the show where we posted Polaroids (70 in total by the end) of visitors who had rocked their killer heels for one of our scheduled photo-ops. The Polaroids had a word or short phrase describing how that person felt wearing those heels. We then invited visitors to write on a sticky note what they thought those heels said about that person and post it next to the photo. Like all activities of this kind, some visitors chose to "follow the directions" and participate in the specific way we set-up, while others just wanted to share their thoughts about the show, about heels, or just tell us they were there. The best data point we have around participation is the 10,000 red sticky notes that I had to purchase over the course of the show for visitors to use. While we cannot assume 10,000 notes equals 10,000 visitors, it can serve as an approximation for the purposes of this exercise (Fig. 16.2).

Similarly, with the exhibition *This Place* (2016), which the Brooklyn Museum website (2016) describes 'explored the complexity of Israel and the West Bank, as

Table 16.3 Comment area evaluation

Exhibition	Use rate (%)
Legacy of Lynching (2017) index cards	11
Killer Heels (2014) sticky notes	11
This Place (2016) index cards	3
The Black List (2009) videos	0.4
Average use rate: 6%	

place and metaphor, through the eyes of twelve internationally acclaimed photographers,' we provided a response area where visitors were encouraged to think about common themes running throughout the show. We posed the questions: What themes do you see in the photographs? Which spoke to you and why? We collected 1,629 response cards during the run of the exhibition.

More recently, for *Legacy of Lynching: Confronting Racial Terror in America* (2017), we offered a space for visitors to reflect on this personal and upsetting history by providing blank index cards and a space to write at the exit to the exhibition. We collected 3,099 cards by the end of the exhibition.

For all these comment areas, estimated use rate is calculated by dividing the number of cards/notes used (or purchased in the case of *Killer Heels*) or videos left by the number of visitors to the exhibition (Table 16.3).

16.2.3 Guided Tours

The Brooklyn Museum regularly offers free guided tours of the permanent collection and special exhibitions. The tours are traditional in nature. A tour guide escorts the participants around the museum, shares information, and answers questions.

During July–December 2017, the Museum offered 207 tours of the permanent collection and 86 tours of the special exhibitions, all free as part of regular offerings. With each tour, the guide records the number of attendees, which totaled 2,703 out of 133,075 visitors during that same period. Therefore, the use rate for guided tours, in this instance 2%, can be determined by dividing the total number of tour attendees by the number of visitors to the museum during that same period. One caveat here is that we do not track repeat tour attendees or repeat Museum visitors, so in practice we are dividing the number of tour attendances by the number of museum visitations. Additionally, popularity of tours may depend upon the exhibition schedule each season, so a bigger data set might yield different results.

Table 16.4 Audio guide evaluation for permanent collections and special exhibitions

Permanent collection (2008–11)	Use rate (%)	Special exhibitions (2007–12)	Use rate (%)
The Dinner Party	6	Caillebotte (2009)	24
Ancient Egyptian art	1	Murakami (2007–8)	14
American art	1	Who Shot Rock (2009–10)	8
Arts of Africa	0.2	Hide/Seek (2011–12)	6
Average use rate	2	Warhol (2010)	5
		Youth and Beauty (2011–12)	4
		Mickalene Thomas (2012–13)	2
		Six Years (2012–13)	1
		Votes for Women (2008)	0.40
		Average use rate	7
Average use rate: 3%			

16.2.4 Audio Tours

The Brooklyn Museum used the on-demand, dial-in audio tour service offered by Guide By Cell (GBC) from 2007–2012. GBC service included useful overall annual data such as unique visitors using the system, total number of prompts in the tours, average number of prompts listened to per visitor, average minutes listened to per visitor, and cost per prompt. The more granular data per audio tour included the total number of prompts listen to, the number of prompts in the tour, and the number of the days the tour was available. In addition to the annual data from 2007–2012, we have data on four permanent collection area tours and nine special exhibition tours. The primary, and important, caveat to this data is that the data on the individual tours does not include unique visitors or average number of prompt listened to per visitor. That has to be approximated by assuming each visitor only listened to a single prompt, which would not be true, of course. Using the data in this fashion however, we can determine the estimated use rate of the audio tours by dividing the number of prompts listened to by the number of visitors to that exhibition or gallery (Table 16.4).

When looking at the complete data set, however, we can get a more accurate picture of the use rate since GBC provided unique visitors (40,372 in total across all years) and average number of prompts in their dashboard. Interestingly, the averages are similar even with the data caveats (Table 16.5).

The average use rate of 3% aligns with that of the British Museum (and industry standard), and is influenced by factors such as available time, confidence, and aim for how visitors want to spend their time in the museum (Mannion et al. 2015).

Table 16.5 Audio guide museum-wide evaluation

Museum-wide (2007–12)	Use rate (%)
2012*	1
2011	1
2010	2
2009	4
2008	6
2007	1
Average use rate: 3%	

*Admission count is an average of FY11 and FY12 as 2012 annual data was unavailable

16.2.5 Comment Kiosks, In Conversation Kiosks and the Digital Guestbook

Starting in 2007, the Brooklyn Museum transitioned from traditional paper comment books to digital versions. These sat in every permanent collection and many special exhibition galleries and invited generic feedback (tell us what you think). Unfortunately, the total data set from these kiosks has been lost, but we do have a 2012 report on the average use rate by permanent collection (0.9%) or special exhibition (1.1%), which was calculated by number of comments divided by number of visitors. However, without the total data set, this information will not be included in the overall average use rate (Fig. 16.3).

In 2013, we experimented with ways to encourage deeper engagement in those kiosks by providing the opportunity to ask questions of artists and curators and by posing direct questions to visitors. We installed these In Conversation kiosks in four different special exhibitions in 2013. Each kiosk had a video prompt of a curator or artist speaking and posing a question or inviting questions. Most users viewed the video though not all left comments or questions. For these, we can calculate use rate by dividing the number of prompt video views to the number of visitors to the exhibition. The video views varied greatly across exhibition kiosk, from as low as 12 views for a prompt in *War/Photography* to as high as 1,783 in *John Singer Sargent Watercolors*.

In 2017, the Museum worked with C+G Partners design firm to install a digital guestbook in our lobby to capture contact information. Visitors could use the touchscreen to sign their name (or draw as some users did), type in their zip code that would appear on a map with others', leave a comment, and input their email address to sign-up for our newsletter. The guestbook was installed for about six months as a trial. Signing was the simplest form of engagement with the guestbook, so by dividing the number signatures (3,631) by the number of total visitors, we can calculate the use rate of the guestbook (Table 16.6).

Fig. 16.3 A video of artist LaToya Ruby Frazier invited visitors to ask questions using this iPad installed in the 2013 exhibition *A Haunted Capital*. (Photograph by Shelley Bernstein)

Table 16.6 Kiosk evaluation

In Conversation kiosks (2013)	Use rate (%)
John Singer Sargent Watercolors	1.8
LaToya Ruby Frazier: A Haunted Capital	2.2
Gravity and Grace: Monumental Works by El Anatsui	2.7
War/photography	3.7
Average use rate	*2.5*
Digital guestbook (2017)	2
Average kiosk use rate: 2%	

16.2.6 Interactive Digital

The majority of the Brooklyn Museum's ongoing digital interactives have consisted of the comment and In Conversation kiosks, with two notable exceptions included in this study: an avatar interactive as part of the special exhibition *Vishnu: Hinduism's Blue-Skinned Savior* (2011) and the ASK Brooklyn Museum app (launched 2015). This study does not take into account digital-embedded exhibition projects undertaken by Shelley Bernstein during her tenure at the Brooklyn Museum—*Click!: A*

Fig. 16.4 The interactive featured cartoon avatars by artist Sanjay Patel and a quiz inviting visitors to discover their avatar. (Photograph by Shelley Bernstein)

Crowd-Curated Exhibition, *Split Second: Indian Paintings*, and *GO*—which are outside the scope of this evaluation and worthy of devoted study on their own (Fig. 16.4).

Visitors to *Vishnu* could complete a quiz at the beginning of the exhibition to determine their avatar and use a series of iPads paired with artworks in the exhibition to find their avatar and learn more about it through close-looking of the artwork itself. 28% of visitors (8,629) to the exhibition completed the quiz (Fig. 16.4).

The ASK Brooklyn Museum app is modeled after iMessage and allows visitors to text in real time with a team of art historians and educators to get their questions answered during their museum visit. Launched on iOS in 2015 and later available via Android and SMS texting, we have held over 15,000 conversations about art with visitors. Over the course of two years, we have seen the monthly use rate (determined by number of chats divided by number of visitors) rise and fall between less than 1% to over 2%. This is based on a myriad of factors and we have written a great deal about the project on our Museum blog. An early trend we saw was higher use in the permanent collection than special exhibitions, but over time and with the help incentives and games like scavenger hunts that range all over the Museum, this has evened out so that in 2017, the average use rate was evenly split between the two. The average overall use rate for ASK since launch is 2% (Figs. 16.5 and 16.6).

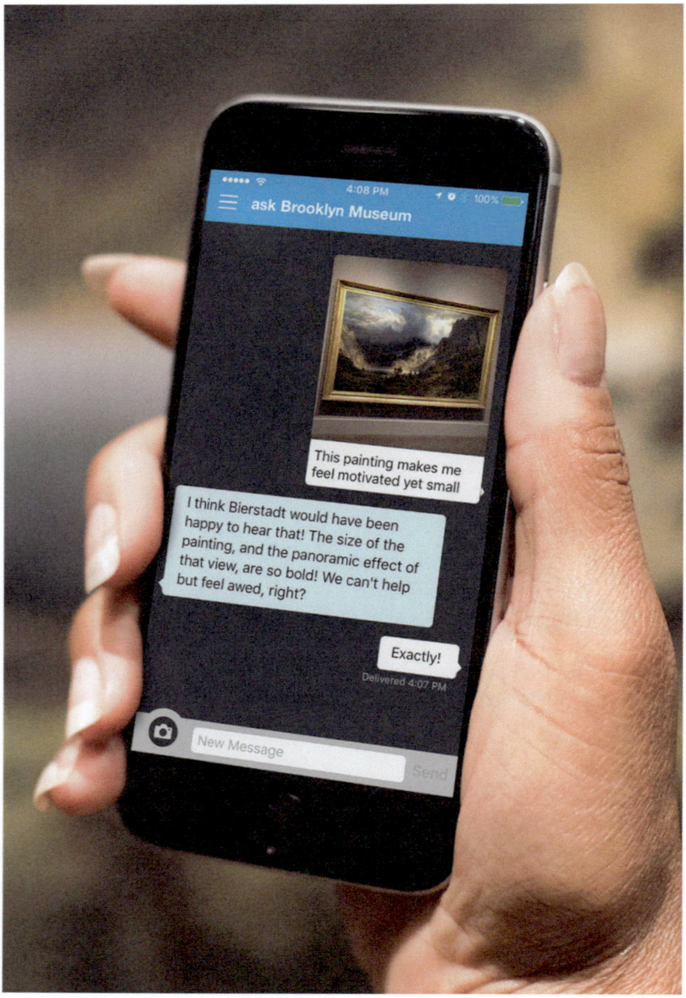

Fig. 16.5 Visitors can text and send photographs via the ASK Brooklyn Museum app. (Photograph by Jonathan Dorado, with permission of Brooklyn Museum)

16.2.7 Comparing Data Sets

A good aspect of this data, is that it can be processed in several ways, which can yield interesting insights. Below are four ways to compare the data to determine insights, patterns, or possible explanations for the use rates that we see: non-digital v. digital, permanent collection v. special exhibition, active v. passive behavior, and content-based v. comment-based opportunities. The use rates listed in the tables below are averages of the various project types (e.g. labels) except when there is a

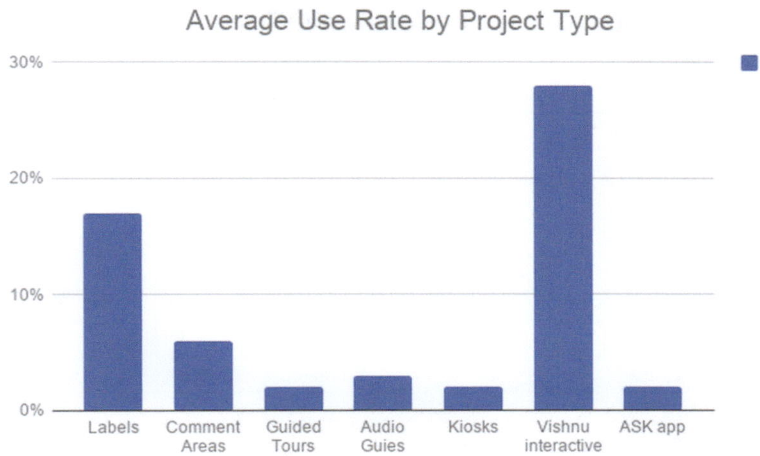

Fig. 16.6 Average use rate by project type

Table 16.7 Non-digital versus digital

Non-digital		Digital	
Engagement strategy	Average use rate (%)	Engagement strategy	Average use rate (%)
Labels	17	Vishnu interactive	28
Comment areas	10	Audio guide	3
Guided tours	2	Comment kiosks	2
		ASK app	2
Average use rate: 11%		Average use rate: 4%	

single example of the type (e.g., Vishnu interactive). The averages in bold are the overall average use rate delineated by the groupings of that chart calculated using the individual project use rates by type (Table 16.7).

This table indicates that many of the non-digital strategies see higher use rates than the digital ones, with the notable exception of the Vishnu interactive, which has the highest use rate of any engagement opportunity included in this study. The second highest use rate by engagement strategy is for labels, which is great news for curators and label writers everywhere. Even with the Vishnu interactive included in this data set, average use of digital strategies is 7% compared to 10% for non-digital (Table 16.8).

When comparing the data this way, special exhibition engagement strategies are two of the three top use rates, with the top two seeing a significantly higher use rate (around 28%) than the top permanent collection strategy (8%). When compared as overall groups, the different between use rates is 4% (Table 16.9).

Here passive opportunities see a higher use rate despite the inclusion of the *Vishnu* and *Killer Heels* activities in the "active" data set. It is important to note that Comment

Table 16.8 Permanent collection versus special exhibitions

Permanent collection		Special exhibitions	
Engagement strategy	Average use rate (%)	Engagement strategy	Average use rate (%)
Labels	8	Vishnu interactive	28
Audio guide	1	Labels	27
Comment kiosks	1	Comment areas	6
Guided tour	1	Audio guide	3
ASK app	1	Comment kiosks	2
		Guided tour	1
		ASK app	1
Average use rate: 2%		Average use rate: 6%	

Table 16.9 Active versus passive behavior

Active		Passive	
Engagement strategy	Average use rate (%)	Engagement strategy	Average use rate (%)
Vishnu interactive	28	Labels	17
Comment areas	6	Audio guide	3
Comment kiosks	2	Guided tour	2
ASK app	2		
Average use rate: 6%		Average use rate: 9%	

Areas, Comment Kiosks, and to certain extent guided tours can be both active and passive. We know from observation around the comment areas and kiosks (Devine 2014) that visitor behavior with these engagement strategies includes "lurking" (reading others' comments) as much as it does leaving a comment. However, since use rate is necessarily determined by those who left a note or watched the prompt video (not the least of which because one cannot easily measure lurking), they are listed as active behaviors. The guided tours, similarly, might include questions and answers or the guide might begin by ascertaining what the group would like to know more about and shape the tour accordingly, but in general, our tour approach is quite traditional, with the guide speaking and the group listening (Table 16.10).

This comparison mirrors the active/passive comparison in that most of the content-related projects are passives ones, while the comment-based are active. Perhaps it should not be surprising that passive and content-based opportunities have higher use rates. If participation is placed on a ladder (Arnstein 1969; Bovill and Bulley 2011) or stages (Simon 2010), the first rungs are passive. As one moves up the ladder, the activity becomes more active and participatory. In Simon's model the first of five stages is content consumption with the final stage is engaging with others and society.

ASK Brooklyn Museum is included as both content- and comment-based since the conversations we have with visitors often include information sharing as well as inviting personal opinions and insights. The ASK use rate was included in both

Table 16.10 Content-based versus comment-based opportunities

Content-based		Comment-based	
Engagement strategy	Average use rate (%)	Engagement strategy	Average use rate (%)
Vishnu interactive	28	Comment areas	6
Labels	17	Comment kiosks	2
Audio guide	3	Guided tour	2
Guided tour	2	ASK app	2
ASK app	2		
Average use rate: 9%		Average use rate: 4%	

averages because of this. The *Vishnu* interactive, while distinctly personal in nature, relied on a quiz that taught users about the many avatars of Vishnu and is therefore considered content-based.

By comparing data in these ways, a few trends emerge. The comparison of special exhibition and permanent collection strategies indicates that special exhibition projects see a higher use rate by 4%. This is not surprising, as special exhibitions are often a main reason people visit museums and visitors tend to be highly motivated to get all they can out their time in a special exhibition. This also helps to explain why the special exhibition labels in this case study saw triple the use rate of permanent collection labels and the special exhibition audio guides were more utilized.

No difference is noted between active and passive opportunities, which simply means people seek different ways to engage and this idea is supported by a litany of studies on meaning-making (Ansbacher 2013; Falk and Dierking 2000; Rounds 1999; Silverman 1995). People have different learning types, abilities, preferences, and attitudes. They seek different experiences, sometimes even within a single visit. Offering both passive and active opportunities caters to different visitor needs.

The greatest difference in use rate comparison is between content-based and comment-based opportunities. Perhaps this should not be surprising. After all, museums are educational institutions. Although while it is gratifying that content-based opportunities garnered a higher use rate, it is interesting to note that according to LaPlaca Cohen (2017), "fun" is the number one reason Americans visit arts and cultural organizations. If this study is any indication, the magic combination seems to be a content-based digital opportunity that is also fun and personal. The Vishnu interactive is a great example of this. It was thoughtfully executed and certainly fun, I remember doing it on my first visit to the Brooklyn Museum. The avatar designs were attractive, and it was possible to take a wristband tag with an avatar cartoon on it as a souvenir. It was a good combination of being both fun and informative.

While the Vishnu interactive had the highest use rate of all the projects included in this study, overall non-digital engagement opportunities had a 3% higher use rate than digital ones. This could be for any number of factors, but for most of these projects we are missing the information that could provide the answer: context.

16.3 Factors that Influence Engagement

The data set in this case study provides insight on the "what" without providing the "why." We have quantitative data without qualitative data, which means we can only guess at some of the reasons behind the behavior patterns hinted at in the data set. This is where anecdotal evidence combined with specific evaluation completed about certain projects can help fill in the gaps. The addition of this information indicates that certain factors affect the use rate of engagement projects: how the project fits into the landscape of available engagement strategies at the time, ease of use, and the physical location.

These data sets are not of concurrent projects, and this case study does not take into consideration the effect engagement projects might have on one another. However, a marketing study of the ASK app completed by ERm Research in the fall of 2017 provides some insight. The goal of this study was to determine why the use rate of the app remained at 1–2% despite our many efforts to increase it (Devine 2017). One memorable comment from a focus group participant was that if he got all the information he wanted from the label, he would not bother with the app. This serves as an important reminder that projects like those considered here do not happen in a vacuum; it stands to reason that the availability of multiple engagement opportunities simultaneously may affect use rates. In fact, we know this was the case for the Vishnu interactive. An evaluation completed at the time of the project reported that "users of the iPad kiosks were likely to have also used other interpretive materials, indicating that this was a supplementary experience to our labels and didactics." (Bernstein 2011).

Depending on the timespan of the project, labels and/or an audio guide were available simultaneously. Labels are a constant and consistent engagement strategy, available next to each artwork (sometimes with only identification information, sometimes with descriptive information) and with each gallery or new idea. When the audio guide was available, certain works had associated information ready for listening via a visitor's cell phone and the Guide by Cell phone number. What we do not know from the use rates in this study was if the availability of both an audio recording and a descriptive label with an artwork led to different use rates than the availability of one or the other only. The audio guides were no longer available when the label evaluation, from which the data in this case study was pulled, was completed.

The potential impact multiple engagement strategies have on use rate is one of the things I'm curious about with our ASK Brooklyn Museum app. We have held over 15,000 conversations with users since program launch in 2015. One of the early trends we noticed when testing the concept of ASK was what it could tell us about how people use the in-gallery interpretation (Bernstein 2014a, b). In our first concept testing session, two out of 10 people asked about the same artwork—out of hundreds on view in the gallery. When we looked into it, we discovered it was an artwork with only an identification label and no descriptive information. Right then we realized the possibility for what ASK could reveal about visitor behavior related to in-gallery interpretation. Over the course of the program, we have regularly shared with curators reports of visitor conversations, which informs curatorial thinking about the galleries including artwork juxtapositions, label placement, gallery design, and selection of stories (Bernstein 2015). We'd like to explore more about how ASK fits into a person's visit, if they use it in conjunction with labels (context clues in some conversations suggest this), and if they ask more often about works without labels. All of this context would give us a better idea of how our engagement strategies are working holistically.

The projects with the highest use rate are projects that are reasonably intuitive to use. For digital projects, this is called user experience design, or UX, and it includes everything from usability to content and visual design. The UX of a digital project is vital. As explained on the London Academy of IT blog, "If you fail to give a good user experience, customers are never going to return to your digital product, be it a website or a mobile app." This holds true for museum interactives as well. If users are frustrated or confused, they will simply walk away. I have watched it happen. We can point to UX as a successful component of the Vishnu interactive: 100% of user interviewed felt the iPads were easy and inviting to use (Bernstein 2011).

The *Killer Heels* sticky note activity was likewise intuitive, though many visitors did not participate in the way we intended them to. The activity was designed to invite visitors to consider not only the image they may try to convey when wearing heels, but how they view others in heels. While some visitors considered one or both of these ideas, many simply left a comment related to the exhibition or heels in general. Regardless, the basic concept of writing on a sticky note and putting in on the wall was very simple and easy to do.

Another factor influencing engagement is the physical location of the project. While labels are always present should visitors want them, that is not true of many of the other strategies described here, which often require more effort on the part of visitors to seek out. This is traditionally true of audio guides, tours, apps, and other interactives or comment areas, which often lie outside the main exhibition. We know the last matters from experimentation with the *In Conversation* kiosks in the *John Singer Sargent Watercolors* exhibition. Initially placed out of the line-of-sight of the main path through the exhibition, the kiosk was not garnering as many video prompt views as expected. After observing visitors in the space, we determined they were not seeing the kiosk and worked with the curator and designer to move it to a more prominent location. The video views immediately increased. This speaks to an ongoing challenge I have wrestled with as well as witnessed as the presence of technology in museums has grown, a challenge that Mann et al. (2013) best describe:

> Museum professionals—exhibition developers and educators in particular—are striving to define the space between engagement and distraction, where we can leverage technology to expand and enhance the visitor experience without overwhelming (or underwhelming) them with new digital tools.

While most, if not all, museum professionals today will readily admit that technology is here to stay—there is essentially nothing left to debate on that front—it is still often seen by some as a "distraction." I have particularly noticed this in an art museum context. This was even the focus of a *Museums and the Web* (MW) conference paper given by DiRienzo (2017), who makes a case for abandoning the Victoria and Albert Museum's "separate functions model" of exhibition design in favor of an integrated aesthetic approach, placing technology (in this case videos) in direct proximity with artworks. That said, some of the non-digital projects were also not in direct proximity, for example the *Killer Heels* sticky note activity and *Legacy of Lynching* comment area were located just outside the exhibition.

Taking these three factors into account, one could predict that any future engagement projects that hit that magic combination of working in tandem with the concurrent engagement opportunities, in a noticeable location, providing a smooth and easy user experience would have an extremely high use rate.

16.4 Conclusion: Towards a Holistic Approach of Engagement Evaluation

The examination of the data set available from the Brooklyn Museum provides unique insight on the use rate of a variety of digital and non-digital projects. Certain trends and shared factors can help in future project planning. Content-based, special exhibition focused projects tend to garner the highest use rate. Passive opportunities are utilized more than active ones. Non-digital projects, on average, saw a higher use rate than digital ones, though the project with the highest use rate was a digital one. This study, when combined with additional evidence, suggests the importance of certain factors on engagement. Location of the engagement opportunity, user experience, and consideration of how the project fits within the scope of available opportunities all influence the use rate.

This examination also sheds light on the need for holistic evaluation to truly begin to understand visitor engagement. Simon (2010) presents a useful model in measuring the impact of participatory projects that would translate well for various types of engagement projects. According to Simon, three main steps are required for evaluation: state goals, define behaviors and outcomes that reflect the goals, and assess the incidents of these outcomes as they relate to the goals. As Simon (2010) explains, the last "is often the most challenging part of evaluation design, and it requires thinking creatively about what behaviors or indicators are associated with desired outcomes." To measure engagement properly, we must be thoughtful as to what the goals of the project are and be creative in determining what behaviors we might see that indicate the goals are being met. We then have to put measurements in place to track those behaviors.

This does not mean that we abandon hard numbers like use rate, but it does mean use rate only provides part of the picture. It is the kind of quantitative data that allows for apples-to-apples comparison across project types, as done in this study. However, data like use rate also has limitations. Digital and non-digital engagement opportunities benefit from a more holistic understanding of the context of each project; factors such as location, content, user experience, and more. As indicated by individual evaluations for several of the projects included in this case study, these kinds of important factors come to light when a more holistic evaluation is undertaken. This kind of contextual information is important to understanding the reasons behind the use rates we see. Without this context, we can only begin to guess at the reasons behind metrics like use rate. Without it, we only see part of the picture.

References

Arnstein SR (1969) A ladder of citizen participation. J Am Plan Assoc 35(4):216–224
Ansbacher Ted (2013) Making sense of experience: a model for meaning-making. Exhibitionist 32(1):8–15
Bernstein S (2011) The Avatar and the iPad: lessons learned. Brooklyn Museum, USA, 12 Oct 2011. https://www.brooklynmuseum.org/community/blogosphere/2011/10/12/the-avatar-and-the-ipad-lessons-learned/. Accessed 9 Jan 2019
Bernstein S (2014) The Avatar and the iPad: lessons learned. Brooklyn Museum, USA, 17 Sept 2014
Bernstein S (2014) Leveraging technology for connection. Brooklyn Museum, USA, September 17, 2014. https://www.brooklynmuseum.org/community/blogosphere/2014/09/17/leveraging-technology-for-connection/. Accessed 9 Jan 2019
Bernstein S (2015) Sleuthing clues about the future from visitor interaction. Brooklyn Museum, USA, 2 Dec 2015. https://www.brooklynmuseum.org/community/blogosphere/2015/12/02/sleuthing-clues-about-the-future-from-visitor-interaction/. Accessed 9 Jan 2019
Bovill C, Bulley CJ (2011) A model of active student participation in curriculum design: exploring desirability and possibility. In: Rust C (ed) Improving student learning (ISL) 18: global theories and local practices: institutional, disciplinary and cultural variations. Oxford Centre for Staff and Learning Development, Oxford Brookes University, UK, pp 176–188
Brooklyn Museum (2016) This place. Brooklyn Museum, USA. https://www.brooklynmuseum.org/exhibitions/this_place. Accessed 10 Mar 2018
DiRienzo M (2017) No. It doesn't distract from the art. In: MW 2017: Museums and the Web, 13 Feb 2017. https://mw17.mwconf.org/paper/no-it-doesnt-distract-from-the-art/. Accessed 9 Jan 2019
Devine S (2014) Metrics tell (part of) the story. Brooklyn Museum, USA, 5 Nov 2014. https://www.brooklynmuseum.org/community/blogosphere/2014/11/05/metrics-tell-part-of-the-story/. Accessed 9 Jan 2019
Devine S (2017) Fresh eyes provide insight on ASK. Brooklyn Museum, USA, 8 Feb 2017. https://www.brooklynmuseum.org/community/blogosphere/2017/02/08/fresh-eyes-provide-insight-on-ask/. Accessed 9 Jan 2019
Falk JH, Dierking LD (2000) Learning from Museums: visitor experiences and the making of meaning. Alta Mira Press
LaPlaca Cohen (2017) Culture track '17—the evolution of culture. LaPlaca Cohen. http://2017study.culturetrack.com. Accessed 11 March 2018
Mann S, Moses J, Fisher M (2013) Catching our breath: assessing digital technologies for meaningful visitor engagement. Exhibitionist 31(1):15–19
Mannion S, Sabiescu A, Robinson W (2015) An audio state of mind: understanding behaviour around audio guides and visitor media. Retrieved from https://mw2015.museumsandtheweb.com/paper/an-audio-state-of-mind-understanding-behviour-around-audio-guides-and-visitor-media/. Accessed 9 Jan 2019
Rounds Jay T (1999) Meaning making: a new paradigm shift for museums? Exhibitionist 18(2):5–8

Serrell, Beverly (1997) Paying attention: the duration and allocation of visitors' time in Museum exhibitions. Curator Mus J 40(2):108–125

Silverman (1995) Visitor meaning-making in Museums for a new age

Simon N (2010) Evaluating participatory projects. The participatory museum, Chapter 10. http://www.participatorymuseum.org/chapter10/. Accessed 1 Feb 2019

Tallon L, Walker K (eds) (2008) Digital technologies and the museum experience: handheld guides and other media. Rowman & Littlefield

Weil SE (1999) From being about something to being for somebody: the ongoing transformation of the American Museum. Daedalus 128(3):229–258

Part VI
Digital Artists

Chapter 17
Morphogenetic Creations: Exhibiting and Collecting Digital Art

Andy Lomas

Abstract In 2016, the Victoria and Albert Museum (V&A) acquired a number of Andy Lomas' works from an exhibition held at the Watermans Art Centre (Watermans in Morphogenetic creations—Andy Lomas. New Media Arts Archive, 2016a) to add to its Computer Art Collection (V&A in The V&A's computer art collections, 2016). The exhibition, titled 'Morphogenetic Creations', explored how intricate complex structures, such as those found in nature, can be created emergently through computational simulation of growth processes. Following in a long-established tradition of art inspired by biology the work is at the intersection of art, science and computing. The artefacts collected by the V&A included prints, multi-screen video and stereoscopic works. This article looks at the works involved, as well as two works from the original exhibition that were not included in the acquisition, as a case study of providing digital works in a form suitable for preservation, and for display in the future when technology for playback of media is likely to have significantly changed.

17.1 Introduction to Morphogenetic Creations

Morphogenesis, the biological term for the creation of form through growth, is a theme that has been explored by a number of artists. In 1951 Richard Hamilton curated an exhibition at the Institute of Contemporary Art (Massey 1996) of work by a number of artists inspired by D'Arcy Thompson's seminal book 'On Growth and Form' (Thompson 1917). In more recent years, growth has been a subject explored by a number of computational artists including Yoichiro Kawaguchi's GROWTH Model (Wikipedia 2018h), William Latham's evolved forms (Todd and Latham 1992) and Daniel Brown's series of digitally generated flowers (Brown 2018). Interest by artists in morphogenesis, and D'Arcy Thompson specifically, has been sufficient for the University of Dundee to receive support from the Art Fund to create a collection of artwork dedicated to this subject (University of Dundee 2011).

The author is a practicing computational artist, whose work follows in this tradition by exploring how complex sculptural forms can be created through digital simulation

A. Lomas (✉)
Goldsmiths, University of London, London, UK

T. Giannini and J. P. Bowen (eds.), *Museums and Digital Culture*,
Springer Series on Cultural Computing, https://doi.org/10.1007/978-3-319-97457-6_17

of morphogenetic processes. Inspired by Alan Turing's use of simple equations to create rich self-organizing patterns (Turing 1952), the author's work focuses on creating simplified models of growth at the level of individual cells and exploring the emergent forms that can be created. In particular the work pushes detail and complexity, creating structures composed of many millions of cells and running simulations over tens of thousands of iterations (Lomas 2014). The author also uses a hybrid system that combines a number of techniques including genetic algorithms and lazy machine learning to explore the space of possibilities of the generative systems he creates, effectively working in collaboration with the computer to discover and fine tune parameter combinations that appear to create particularly interesting results (Lomas 2016).

His work has been exhibited internationally in a number of exhibitions, including the Centre Pompidou, V&A, The Royal Society, SIGGRAPH, Japan Media Arts Festival, Ars Electronica Festival, Los Angeles Municipal Art Gallery, Los Angeles Center for Digital Art, Centro Andaluz de Arte Contemporaneo, and the ZKM. In 2014 his work Cellular Forms won The Lumen Prize Gold Award, as well as Honorary Mention from the jury at the Ars Electronica Festival (Lomas 2018a). His artwork is in collections including the University of Dundee D'Arcy Thompson Collection (described above), the Computer Arts Society CAS50 collection (Computer Arts Society 2018), and in the Computer Art collection at the V&A.

17.2 Exhibition at Watermans

From 13 June to 21 July 2016, Watermans, a public art center in Brentford, west London, funded by the London Borough of Hounslow and Arts Council England, held a solo exhibition of the author's work entitled 'Morphogenetic Creations' (see Fig. 17.1). The exhibition was curated by Irini Papadimitriou, Head of New Media Arts at Watermans. As well as being responsible for the program of art exhibited in the gallery space at Watermans, Irini is also Digital Programmes Manager at the V&A.

Irini Papadimitriou had become aware of the author's artwork through involvement in the Computer Arts Society. The potential for holding an exhibition at the art center had been discussed informally following a talk that the author gave to the Computer Arts Society on 4th December 2014 (Computer Arts Society 2014). In April 2016 Irini contacted the author to let him know that the gallery space was available for a solo exhibition (personal communication, 2016), and asked him to make a proposal for how the space and equipment available at Watermans could be used to present his work.

Equipment available for the exhibition included six large wall mountable TVs, two matched high definition projectors, as well as the availability of the services of a carpenter for one day to fabricate necessary items. The author proposed an exhibition covering three different phases of his Cellular Forms work (e.g., see Fig. 17.2).

Fig. 17.1 Morphogenetic creations exhibition at Watermans

The following is from the exhibition proposal document sent to Irini Padadimitriou (personal communication, 2016):

> What I will be presenting in the exhibition is work from three different phases of exploration with this cellular growth system: 'Cellular Forms', 'Plantlike Forms' and 'Hybrid Forms'. The work is designed to show both the rich emergent variety that can be produced by growth processes as well as how simple changes to the system can produce dramatically different results.
>
> **Cellular Forms**
>
> These are the simplest structures. All the cells have identical properties, so in effect there's just one cell type. Cells grow through accumulating nutrient which is created by light rays coming in from a uniform light that illuminates the structures from all directions. Each photon of light hitting a cell generates some nutrient, and nutrient can also flow between adjacent cells. When a cell has accumulated enough nutrient, it splits into two.
>
> The Cellular Forms don't have any bias in any specific direction, and they grow into shapes which are roughly spherical. However, the surfaces of each form show different complex patterns of folding and stretching, with echoes that can range from pollen grain to reptile skin, fish scales, and internal organs such as brains or lungs.
>
> **Plantlike Forms**
>
> In these structures the light rays that create nutrient are restricted to only coming from above. This simple change causes the structures to grow into more complex plant or fungus-like forms as they grow upwards towards the light, with branching structures as well as complex surface patterns.

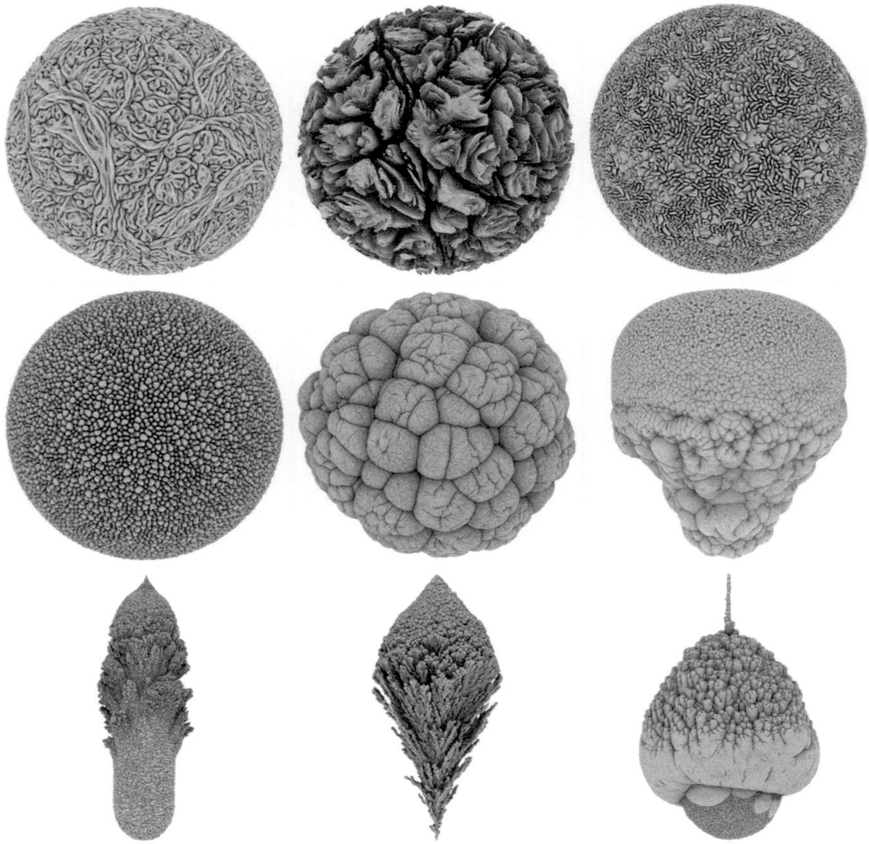

Fig. 17.2 Cellular Forms and Plantlike Forms shown as 2D prints in the Morphogenetic Creations exhibition at Waterma

Hybrid Forms

These introduce diversity by using two different cell types, with all the cells being given a blend between two extremes. When a new cell is born it inherits a proportion of the properties of its parent and a proportion of those of its immediate neighbors. This extremely simple form of cell differentiation results in much more complex structures, often reminiscent of early embryo growth, or multi-cellular organisms such as protozoa.

The proposal for the exhibition was to use a combination of methods to present the work, with a variety of different techniques being used to turn the original data from the morphogenetic simulations into exhibitable artefacts (personal communication, 2016):

Turning data into artefacts

The simulation process creates raw data that needs further work to realize it into visible form. Throughout these works I have been exploring a number of techniques, from different rendering techniques (such as to show the external shape through self-shadowing, or showing internal structures using a digital emulation of X-Rays) as well as presentation using techniques such as stereo vision, 3D printing and animated holographic imagery.

Each technique has different merits, often highlighting different aspects of the original data. High resolution 2D prints allow the highest resolution of detail. Animated videos show the progression through different intermediate states as the structures grow. Superimposing additional data from the simulations, such as to show different cell types or regions of recent growth, reveals additional facets that wouldn't be otherwise visible.

The final proposal for the exhibition at Watermans consisted of 14 different artworks using a variety of media:

- Five 90 cm × 90 cm framed archival prints of Cellular Forms.
- Four 90 cm × 90 cm framed archival prints of Plantlike Forms.
- 32 cm diameter 3D printed sculpture of a Cellular Form.
- Two 40″ TVs showing synchronized high definition playback of growing Cellular Forms. Screen 1: external structures (ambient occlusion), Screen 2: Internal structures (X-ray).
- Four 40″ TVs showing synchronized high definition playback of growing Plantlike Forms. Screen 1: External structures (ambient occlusion). Screen 2: Internal structures (X-Ray). Screen 3: Regions where food is being created by light ray. Screen 4: Regions of new growth.
- A LEIA 3D 40 mm × 40 mm holographic screen showing rotating 3D cellular forms.
- An installation with two front and rear projection screens showing animation of growth processes, with a viewer containing two front surface mirrors mounted between the screens to enable viewing of the animated structures in 3D using stereopsis.

The centerpiece of the exhibition was a stereoscopic installation of work from the Hybrid Forms series (see Figs. 17.3 and 17.4). This consisted of dual stream high definition video being projected onto two separate screens. These used a special projection screen material designed to have nearly identical luminance on both sides when projected on from one side, so working simultaneously for both front and rear projection (Gerriets 2018). The two streams of high definition video were designed to initially appear as if they are identical but are actually different images rendered from two separate camera positions so that they form a stereo pair consisting of left eye and right eye images. In the middle, between the two screens, an assembly of front surface mirrors was mounted on a pole. When looked into from the correct angle these mirrors function as a Wheatstone viewer (Wikipedia 2018g), fusing together the two projected images so that the viewer can perceive a three-dimensional version of the animated growing forms.

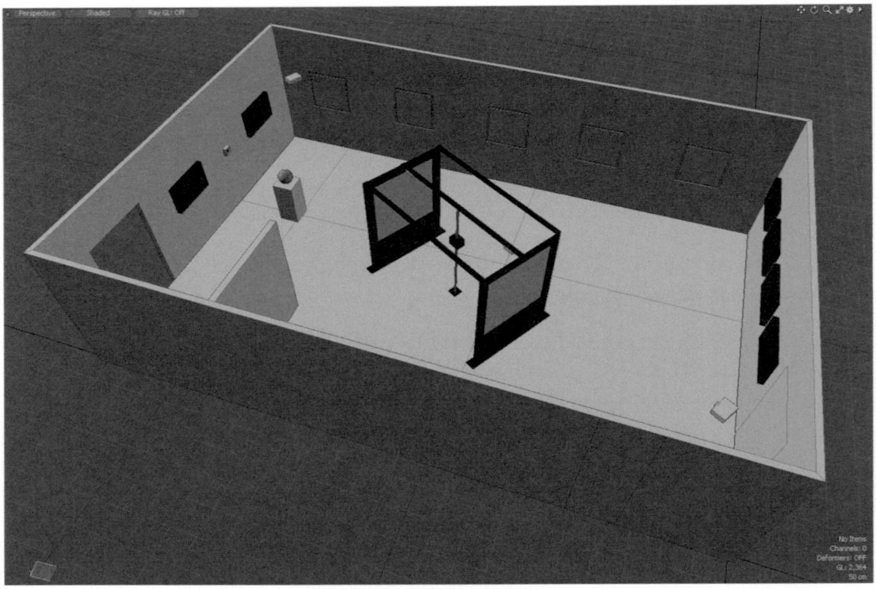

Fig. 17.3 3D model of the proposed exhibition in the Watermans gallery

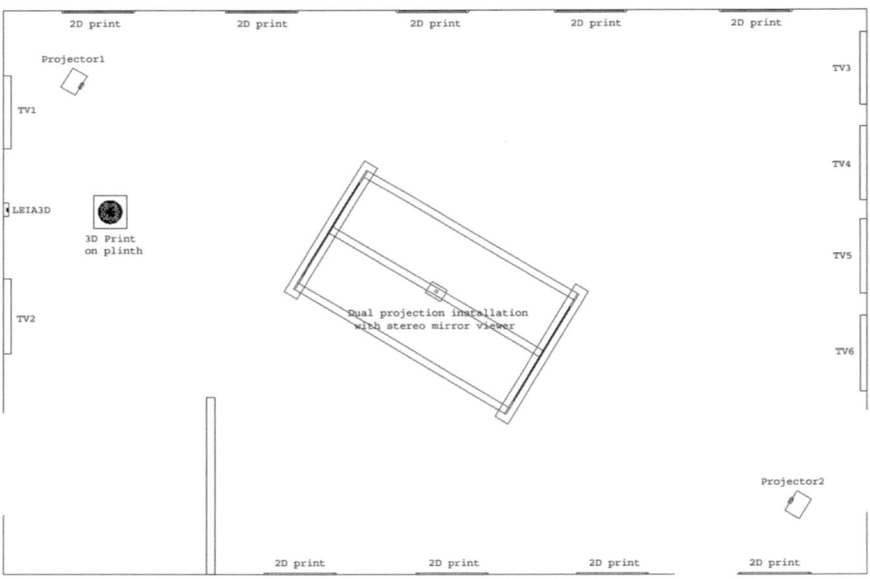

Fig. 17.4 Plan of exhibition in the Watermans gallery showing locations of different artworks

17.3 Acquisition of Works for the Computer Art Collection at the V&A

At Irini Papadimitriou's invitation, Douglas Dodds (see Chap. 10), Head of Digital Collections and Services at the V&A, and Melanie Lenz, Patric Prince Curator at the V&A, attended the exhibition at Watermans. Through his involvement with the Lumen Prize and the Computer Arts Society, Douglas Dodds was already aware of the author's work but commented he was pleasantly surprised at how the exhibition using different media worked together as a whole, providing what he considered to be new insight into the work.

Douglas Dodds subsequently expressed interest in acquiring artefacts from the exhibition as an integrated whole, and the author let Douglas know that he would be willing to donate any works from the exhibition they were interested in for the Computer Art Collection at the V&A. Following further discussion, the V&A decided to acquire 12 of the 14 artworks from the exhibition (Watermans 2016b).

17.3.1 2D Print Based Works

The V&A acquisition included all nine of the 90 cm × 90 cm archival prints, comprising five Cellular Forms and four Plantlike Forms. It is worth noting that all of the prints for the exhibition were created as unique originals of different generated forms, rather than being a limited edition as is more usual for digital prints. This was a feature that Douglas Dodds (personal communication, 2016) appeared to be interested in.

Prior to the acquisition the curators asked for information about the materials used to create the prints. All the physical prints were created using Epson K3 Ultrachrome ink (Epson 2018) on archival quality Hahnemühle photo rag cotton paper (Wikipedia 2018c), which appeared to satisfy their requirements.

As well as physical prints the author also supplied the original digital images used to create the prints in the form of TIFF (Wikipedia 2018e) format files. These provide lossless digital data that could be used to create reproductions of the original images in the future. In particular, the use of these files should allow higher quality results than could be achieved by photographic reproduction of the prints, and the author considers that reproduction directly from the digital files would be appropriate given how the works were computationally created.

17.3.2 Multi-screen Video Works

The physical hardware used to show the two multi-screen video works in the Watermans exhibition was owned by the center, so both of these works were given to the

Fig. 17.5 Image from Cellular Forms two-screen video file

Fig. 17.6 Image from Plantlike Forms four-screen video file

V&A in digital file form together with guidance for future display without any of the original equipment used to display them.

To allow for synchronized playback of multiple streams of high definition video, the digital files are formatted as several separate 1,920 × 1,080-pixel resolution images tiled together side by side into a single image. For the exhibition, these video files were played back on a Windows PC using VLC software. This was configured using the Video Wall output filter to split the video into the required number of separate output streams (VideoLAN 2013).

The files for the two-screen 'Cellular Forms' work were created at a resolution of 3,840 × 1,080 (2 HD video streams side by side, see Fig. 17.5), and the files for the four-screen 'Plantlike Forms' work were created at a resolution of 7,680 × 1,080 (4 HD video streams side by side, see Fig. 17.6).

As was communicated to Douglas Dodds and Melanie Lenz (personal communication, 2016), if higher quality equipment becomes available in future, that could provide improved quality playback than was possible using the equipment used at the Watermans exhibition, the author would prefer such equipment be used. To aid preservation, as well as to facilitate the use of new display technology that may become available in the future, both of these works were delivered using three different file formats.

- The M4V files that were used to playback the multi-stream high definition videos during the Watermans exhibition. These files use the H.264 codec, the same codec as is commonly used for DVD and Blu-ray Disk playback (Wikipedia 2018b). This format uses lossy compression, sacrificing some image quality to allow for fast playback.
- Apple ProRes HQ MOV files, which were used to edit the videos displayed in the exhibition before conversion to M4V format. Apple ProRes HQ uses lossy

compression but provides significantly higher image quality than the M4V files (Wikipedia 2018a). These files are not designed for playback on current video hardware but using these files it should be possible to create higher quality playable video files to match the capabilities of future equipment than would be possible with the M4V files used at the Watermans exhibition.
– Sequences of individual image files for each frame of the videos in TIFF format. These image files do not have any loss due to compression, so could be used in future to create even higher quality playback than from the Apple ProRes HQ files. These files should also have the advantage for preservation that TIFF file format is one of the most common standards for image files that has already been around for many years, improving the likelihood that it will still be readable when video codecs such as H.264 and Apple ProRes HQ have fallen into disuse.

The original files that the author used to render out images from his simulations were in the OpenEXR format (OpenEXR 2017). Originally developed by Industrial Light and Magic, this is a high-quality format capable of representing high dynamic range image data, and is a standard mainly used by the visual effects industry for computer generated work. The author decided not to supply image sequences in this format as he considered that it would probably not help preservation. OpenEXR is a much less commonly used format than TIFF files, and since the videos do not actively use high dynamic range image data the TIFF files that were supplied capture the full range of required luminance.

17.3.3 Stereoscopic Installation Work

The stereoscopic installation presented some additional challenges since the installation itself, consisting of two front/rear projection screens and an assembly of mirrors to fuse the two images, was a temporary installation custom built for the exhibition.

For the V&A collection is was decided to submit video files in the same manner as for the two multi-screen video works, with the left eye and right eye images tiled together side by side into a 3,840 × 1,080 resolution file. To enable the work to be viewed stereoscopically, the author also donated a simple 3D printed stereoscopic viewer (see Fig. 17.7), which internally mounts a Nexus 5 Android mobile phone. This can be used to playback a side by side video of Hybrid Forms, although at a lower resolution than the original playback where both eyes had a full 1,920 × 1,080 resolution.

17.3.4 Audio Files

The two-screen Cellular Forms video work and the stereoscopic Hybrid Forms installation were presented in the Watermans exhibition with accompanying sound tracks.

Fig. 17.7 3D printed stereoscopic viewer as supplied to the V&A for viewing Hybrid Forms

These use music that was created by the experimental electronic musician Max Cooper and composer Tom Hodge. The V&A requested and received appropriate permission through a copyright agreement for the music to be included with the acquired video works.

The audio for the works was included directly in the H.264 M4 V and Apple ProRes HQ MOV video files for these works, as well as being provided as separate Waveform Audio File Format (WAV) files (Wikipedia 2018f). This format was chosen as being one of the most common industry standards that uses uncompressed data, so should have a good longevity.

17.3.5 Works Not Included in the Acquisition

The two remaining artworks from the exhibition were not acquired by the V&A.

The LEIA 3D holographic screen showing rotating 3D cellular forms was not acquired as there were concerns about its preservation, given that it was based on experimental technology. The display used in the exhibition was a development kit of a light-field display (LEIA 2018; Wikipedia 2018d) that consists of a small very high-resolution screen (1,600 × 1,600 pixels in a 40 mm × 40 mm form factor) behind a diffraction grating. The development kit runs quite hot, so the author had to add a custom heat sink and a fan-based cooling system for exhibition. After discussions between the author and Douglas Dodds it was agreed that this piece would be difficult to maintain, as well as probably not being a critical part of the exhibition.

The 32 cm diameter 3D printed sculpture of a Cellular Form was also not acquired for the collection. Although the curators expressed interest in this work there was a concern about whether it should be considered a sculpture instead of as a digital work and how it would fit within the collections at the V&A (personal communication, 2016).

17.4 Conclusion

The use of computers in art has a history of over fifty years. Early works were generally algorithmically generated using code to produce final exhibitable artefacts using technology such as pen plotters and line printers, or by using numerical output from programs to direct the artist to create paintings or drawing by hand. The results were artefacts that could be collected and preserved in a similar manner to traditional non-computationally created drawings and paintings.

In more recent years, there has been increasing use of different standards for creation, exchange and archiving of digital data, such as for image and video files. A large number of different organizations define and develop these standards, such as the American National Standards Institute (ANSI 2018), the IEEE Standards Association (IEEE 2018), the Joint Photographic Experts Group (JPEG 2018) and the Motion Picture Academy of Arts and Sciences (ACES 2018).

Digital data formats have the potential to allow perfect duplication but can also suffer problems including data becoming unreadable as data standards change and software becomes obsolete. Formats used for display, such as video codecs designed for fast playback, are often particularly at risk of becoming obsolete and unreadable. The author's approach was to consider both ease of presentation using currently available equipment, as well as how to maximize the potential for preservation. This led the author to use multiple formats and media when submitting his work to the collection at the V&A. For print based works he submitted both physical prints and TIFF files. For the video-based works he submitted work in three formats: currently playable MP4 (MPEG-4) video files, higher quality Apple ProRes HQ files, and uncompressed sequences of TIFF files designed to facilitate preservation and future presentation. For the audio accompanying the video images he provided audio both embedded in video files and as separate WAV audio files. The delivery of assets using multiple file formats appears to have the support of the curators at the V&A and they are considering using this as a template for future acquisitions (personal communication, 2016).

The relationship between art and computers is continuously changing, in a manner that can be argued as going from one where computers are seen purely as another artistic medium, to one that, through advances in artificial intelligence, machine learning and computational creativity, the computer becomes an active collaborator with human artists (Agüera y Arcas 2016; Lomas 2018b) or as an artist in its own right (Smith and Leymarie 2017). This raises even more questions about what the nature of artefacts to be included in museum collections should be. In particular, if the computer is active participant in the creation of art, should we be considering not only collecting the artefacts produced, but the artificial creators of the artwork as well?

References

Agüera y Arcas B (2016) Art in the age of machine intelligence. Medium. https://medium.com/artists-and-machine-intelligence/what-is-ami-ccd936394a83. Accessed 2 Oct 2018

ACES (2018) ACES Documentation. https://www.oscars.org/science-technology/aces/aces-documentation. Accessed 5 Oct 2018

ANSI (2018) American National Standards Institute. https://www.ansi.org. Accessed 5 Oct 2018

Brown D (2018) Daniel Browns. http://danielbrowns.com. Accessed 19 June 2018

Computer Arts Society (2014) Morphogenetic creations. Talk by Andy Lomas, 4 Dec 2014. Computer Arts Society Programme Archive. http://computer-arts-society.com/event/96283. Accessed 5 Mar 2018

Computer Arts Society (2018) CAS50 Collection. http://computer-arts-society.com/cas50-collection. Accessed 19 June 2018

Epson (2018) Ink fact sheet. http://assets.epson-europe.com/eu/Label_Expo_2013/assets/downloads/Fact-Sheet-Aqueous-Ink.pdf. Accessed 6 Mar 2018

Gerriets (2018) Front and rear projection screen EVEN. https://www.gerriets.com/uk/products/screens/projection-screens/front-and-rear-projection/front-and-rear-projection-screen-br-even. Accessed 5 Mar 2018

IEEE (2018) IEEE Standards Association. https://standards.ieee.org/standard/. Accessed 5 Oct 2018

JPEG (2018) Joint photographic experts group. https://jpeg.org/about.html. Accessed 5 Oct 2018

LEIA (2018) Light up life: LEIA Inc. https://www.leiainc.com. Accessed 6 Mar 2018

Lomas A (2014) Cellular forms: an artistic exploration of morphogenesis. AISB-50, London, UK, 1–4 Apr 2014. Goldsmiths, University of London, UK

Lomas A (2016) Species explorer: an interface for artistic exploration of multi-dimensional parameter spaces. In: Bowen JP, Diprose G, Lambert N (eds) EVA London 2016 conference proceedings, Electronic Workshops in Computing (eWiC), BCS, pp 95–102. https://doi.org/10.14236/ewic/eva2016.23

Lomas A (2018a) Andy Lomas: morphogenetic creations. http://www.andylomas.com. Accessed 7 Mar 2018

Lomas A (2018b) On hybrid creativity. Arts 7(3):25. Multidisciplinary Digital Publishing Institute. https://www.mdpi.com/2076-0752/7/3/25. Accessed 2 Oct 2018

Massey A (1996) The independent group: modernism and mass culture in Britain, 1949–59. Manchester University Press, pp 42–45

OpenEXR (2017) About OpenEXR. http://www.openexr.com/about.html. Accessed 6 Mar 2018

Smith GW, Leymarie FF (2017) The machine as artist: an introduction. Arts 6(2):5. Multidisciplinary Digital Publishing Institute

Thompson DW (1917) On growth and form. Cambridge University Press

Todd S, Latham W (1992) Evolutionary art and computers. Academic Press, London

Turing AM (1952) The chemical basis of morphogenesis. Philos Trans Roy Soc London B: Biol Sci 237(641):37–72. https://doi.org/10.1098/rstb.1952.0012

University of Dundee (2011) D'Arcy Thompson zoology museum art collection. University of Dundee, Scotland. https://www.dundee.ac.uk/museum/collections/zoology/art. Accessed 19 June 2018

V&A (2016) The V&A's computer art collections. http://www.vam.ac.uk/content/articles/t/v-and-a-computer-art-collections. Accessed 5 Mar 2018

VideoLAN (2013) Documentation: modules/wall. https://wiki.videolan.org/Documentation:Modules/wall. Accessed 5 Mar 2018

Watermans (2016a) Morphogenetic creations—Andy Lomas. New Media Arts Archive. https://www.watermans.org.uk/new-media-arts-archive/morphogenetic-creations-andy-lomas. Accessed 5 Mar 2018

Watermans (2016b) V&A acquires suite of work from exhibition curated by Watermans with artist Andy Lomas. Press Release. https://s3-eu-west-1.amazonaws.com/watermans/wp-content/uploads/2015/12/27120044/VA-acquires-Andy-Lomas-work-from-Watermans-curated-exhibition-Sept-2016.pdf. Accessed 5 Mar 2018

Wikipedia (2018a) Apple ProRes. https://en.wikipedia.org/wiki/Apple_ProRes. Accessed 5 Mar 2018

Wikipedia (2018b) H.264/MPEG-4 AVC. https://en.wikipedia.org/wiki/H.264/MPEG-4_AVC. Accessed 5 Mar 2018

Wikipedia (2018c) Hahnemühle. https://en.wikipedia.org/wiki/Hahnem%C3%BChle. Accessed 6 Mar 2018

Wikipedia (2018d) LEIA Inc. https://en.wikipedia.org/wiki/LEIA_Inc. Accessed 6 Mar 2018

Wikipedia (2018e) TIFF. Available at: https://en.wikipedia.org/wiki/TIFF. Accessed 6 Mar 2018

Wikipedia (2018f) WAV. https://en.wikipedia.org/wiki/WAV. Accessed 6 Mar 2018

Wikipedia (2018g) Wheatstone stereoscope. https://en.wikipedia.org/wiki/Stereoscope#Wheatstone_stereoscope. Accessed 5 Mar 2018

Wikipedia (2018h) Yoichiro Kawaguchi. https://en.wikipedia.org/wiki/Yoichiro_Kawaguchi. Accessed 19 June 2018

Chapter 18
Evolving Installations: "Shaping Space"

Ernest Edmonds and Francesca Franco

Abstract Having been working on several projects together over the past nine years, the authors—an artist and a curator both specialized in computational and media art—discuss a range of issues that have arisen during the installation of Edmonds' generative interactive artwork *Shaping Space* in each of the six locations where it has been shown. The work arose in part from significant experiences by Edmonds in the work discussed in Chap. 6 by Deborah Turnbull Tillman, and by the collaborators Matthew Connell and Lizzie Muller. The installations of Shaping Space described range from its first at the Site Gallery in Sheffield, UK (2012), a contemporary art space specializing in moving image, new media and performance, to its latest at the Fondazione Bevilacqua La Masa in Venice (2017), a historical not-for-profit institution that supports more traditional and current developments in contemporary art practice. Technical and aesthetic questions arose, and pragmatics sometimes caused interesting unexpected innovation. What was the inspiration behind these works? Are they connected to each other, and if so, how? What were the major challenges in installing each iteration of the work? How did the different institutions involved in installing the work over the years approached and solved the technical issues around the installation? How did the various venues and surrounding environment influence the work?

18.1 Introduction

This chapter contains a conversation between Edmonds and Franco recorded in February 2018, discussing the challenges of installing *Shaping Space* and similar works (2000–2018) from an artist and curator's perspective. Works using data projection that predate *Shaping Space* discussed in the chapter include installations

E. Edmonds (✉)
De Montfort University, Leicester, UK
e-mail: ernest@ernestedmonds.com

F. Franco
University of Exeter, Exeter, UK
e-mail: iamfrafra@gmail.com

T. Giannini and J. P. Bowen (eds.), *Museums and Digital Culture*,
Springer Series on Cultural Computing, https://doi.org/10.1007/978-3-319-97457-6_18

featured in the following exhibitions: *Constructs & Reconstructions*, Loughborough University (2000); Kettles Yard House, Cambridge (2001); and *Algorithmic Signs* (including the specially commissioned work *Growth and Form*), Fondazione Bevilacqua La Masa, Venice (2017). The history of the exhibition of *Shaping Space* includes, in chronological order, the following shows: *Light Logic* (including the commission *Shaping Space*), Site Gallery, Sheffield, UK (2012/3); *PAF festival*, Olomouc, Czech Republic (2013); *Light Logic*, Conny Dietzschold Gallery, Sydney (2013); *Fields*, National Museum of Art, Riga, Latvia (2014); *Códigos Primordiais (Primary Codes)*, Oi Futuro Flamengo, Rio de Janeiro (2015); and *Algorithmic Signs*, Fondazione Bevilacqua La Masa, Venice (2017).

18.2 In Conversation: Ernest Edmonds and Francesca Franco

Francesca Franco: Since 2000, you have made several works using data projection. In particular, three works that have been intended for rear projection onto Perspex. The first two were each just shown once and the third one, *Shaping Space*, was shown quite a few times, although twice the installation didn't work out. Can you tell me more about these works? How were they installed? How did the installations change from one venue to the other? What unexpected results did they generate?

Ernest Edmonds: The first work dates back to my first retrospective, *Constructs & Reconstructions*, at Loughborough University in 2000. I had the idea of this notion of back projecting onto a sheet of Perspex for a work, which I did. It's quite interesting in the context of that discussion because I had a very powerful projector available and I went out and bought a sheet of Perspex, and tested it, and it worked! So, I drilled it, hung it, set it up myself with the help of one person, no great expertise and it all worked. It was successful. Then the next year I was part of an audiovisual art event at Kettles Yard in Cambridge held in the house. I did a few things there and, for one piece, I decided to use the very same piece of Perspex, so I knew that it worked quite straight forwardly. I think I was very fortunate with these two works because I didn't have any problems, it worked and seemed fine. The only thing I would say is that in both cases, I had quite a good distance between the projector and the Perspex so that a completely standard lens was fine. There the matter rested, until Site Gallery asked me to do an installation piece for the "Light Logic" exhibition, where I created *Shaping Space* for that purpose.

FF: In terms of technical requirements, especially for the Perspex (thickness, opacity, etc.), did you have any specific requirements from the very beginning?

EE: No, for the first one in Loughborough, looking back, I was just fortunate that the piece I bought worked and I did it without really investigating deeply. If it hadn't worked when I tested it, I'm sure I would have but I was just lucky with the first piece. It was very simple. I got into all those other concerns only for the Site Gallery's first installation of *Shaping Space*.

FF: Why did you choose Perspex for these works?

EE: To create the concept of an image floating in space.

FF: Could you have done it using other materials?

EE: Well, you couldn't because you had to back project onto something and I wanted something that had no frame, so that you didn't see the frame or support. I just used very thin wire through holes at the top of the Perspex which, more or less, could not be seen. If you projected carefully, the image goes to the very edges of the Perspex and then there is this appearance, in a slightly dark place, of an image floating in space. That was the visual concept.

FF: It's interesting that you mention the frame, because frames have been extremely important in your work from the very beginning. How did you see the difference in these two concepts?

EE: I've moved between two possibilities, from the very beginning. Either a very carefully determined frame, which was, more or less, part of the work, determined specifically by me for the work, or having no frame at all. I've used both of these strategies from very early on. In 2000, when I was looking at this idea, I started constructing frames for screens and in the same exhibition I had framed screens. But I also worked with the other alternative, which is no frame at all. Now you couldn't do that with a screen at that time, so the only way I could have no frame was by back projecting onto a sheet of translucent material and it needs to be rigid, so it didn't waive about. Perspex seemed to be the obvious choice.

FF: That must be quite liberating for an artist to work on an image without having the constrictions of a frame.

EE: I thought it was beautiful.

FF: This connects with the technical equipment that is now available and probably wasn't at the time you made the projected work in Loughborough. I'm thinking about the new screens you are using for *Shaping Forms*.

Note: Edmonds' *Shaping Form* series (2007 onwards), are individual works where images are constantly generated by a computer program that decides which colours, patterns and timing the work should display in any given moment. The movement in front of each work is detected by a small camera. This leads to continual changes in the program that generates the images and produces changes in the image, shape and duration, so that the environment, the active spectator and the work influence each other. A viewer can readily detect the immediate responses of the work to movement but the changes over time are only apparent when there is more prolonged, although not necessarily continuous, contact with it. A first viewing followed by one several months later will reveal noticeable developments in the colours and patterns. The work is made of a series of individual stand-alone rectangular screens framed so that the resulting image is square. The early frames were in white acrylic.

EE: In the early works, these works I was just talking about with the Perspex in 2000 and 2001 and the earlier piece *Nagoya* I used a rectangular screen, but then I became unhappy about this and wanted to move to square and I couldn't obtain squares screens so I had to use a frame in order to mask part of the monitor to make it square. The early Shaping Forms were all framed in one way or another, until I discovered square monitors. The one I chose is intended as a tile for a video wall and because it's a tile it is made with an almost zero frame, with an edge that is so very thin that it satisfied my need. So, I'm very happy using those screens raw, with no embellishments or additions. From the side it has an industrial aesthetic but from the front is just a square image and it's perfect. So, this idea of the image not having a frame is something that has grown in my preference and interest. A big step forward, before these screens came about was this piece *Shaping Space*.

FF: Talking about an image floating in space, did you have any inspirations, any artists you looked at?

EE: I didn't really get an inspiration from anyone specifically, but I think I might have got it from movies. If you go to see a movie with a very wide screen and you sit for example in the front row then sometimes you get scenes where a lot of the screen is dark and there is something, like a floating image, not something that I could copy but maybe an inspiration for this idea coming from that sensation I had sitting in the cinema.

FF: Talking about the way these works were installed for specific exhibitions in specific spaces, did you notice any major technical differences from one to another?

EE: Yes, very big differences. Most of these differences came because of the installation process and the availability of this or the other thing and the kind of people who were helping with the installation. So, of eight cases, two never worked and were never installed, three of them were different from my original plan, and three of them were exhibited as according to my original conception.

FF: I'd like to go through them. My direct experience was with the last installation for *Algorithmic Signs* in Venice in 2017, and I was totally taken by it and surprised by the overall experience of installing it, and how that iteration of the work was perceived by the audience.

EE: Yes, I'll go through in order and conclude with the *Algorithmic Signs* one, which was the most distinctive.

First, the original one was for Site Gallery (see Fig. 18.1). It was commissioned and supported by the Arts Council, the Henry Moore Foundation and Site Gallery itself. It received quite strong help in that respect. I had a clear conception of what I wanted and there was a single room into which it had to go. It was an existing space and was actually installed exactly as I had intended, but the process of getting from a to b was quite interesting. I wasn't entirely clear about the needs of the specifications of the Perspex. I said what I thought the Perspex had to do but I didn't specify it in the technical details. I just specified its function. The first sheets that were purchased by Site Gallery were too dense and the image didn't show through sufficiently well. We looked to all kinds of ways of coping with that including front projection which I rejected. In the end, Site Gallery bought different sheets of Perspex that did work. By the time they did that they had in any case hired an expert on data projection. He wasn't just someone who knew data projection. He was someone who earned his living setting up data projections at festivals etc., so was super expert, and in fact he's specified the projectors we bought. One of these projectors was taken to the Perspex supplier and used to check the back projection onto the Perspex and the correct Perspex was then selected, purchased and hung in the space according to how I wanted it. And then the expert data projection guy set the projectors up and it was

Fig. 18.1 Ernest Edmonds, *Shaping Space*, Site Gallery, Sheffield (2012). (Image courtesy of Francesca Franco)

very interesting observing him doing it with all his expertise. It wasn't just someone from audiovisual services, this was someone that knew very subtle things and how to get it really good. So that was the background to that one.

The second one was the piece installed as part of the "PAF festival", in Olomouc, Czech Republic (2013) where I was a special guest. Amongst several works dealing with film, they wanted to install *Shaping Space*. That ended up being a modified version because the space in which they wanted to put it was like a little old chapel, it was a strange and enormous and a very difficult space. They proposed not use the floating Perspex but to use two very large back projections screens, fitted to the floor. They were in frames, but they were certainly large that the frames seemed very small, almost not noticeable because of the scale of them, and I agreed to this as it seemed good for that space. So, this was a question of modifying the work as an installation to work well in a different space. They were very expert at projection also. It took two days' work but in that two days they successfully set it up and it was a very successful piece but modified in the way I just described.

The third was in Sydney in a commercial gallery. The gallery was small. They were showing my paintings and other work and really there was nowhere for *Shaping Space*, although they wanted to show it. There was no way to do it so in the end a version of it was displayed with front projection onto a wall but with only one screen. It was in an area where no one could walk so that no one moved between the projector and the image and we didn't have that problem of shadows on the image. It was only half of the work, so I felt this was more like an indication of *Shaping Space* rather than a real installation of the work so that was just like a side piece to an exhibition showing many other things.

FF: In terms of the algorithm of that work, you said that having one of the screens only (so half of the work) was like a *Shaping Form* piece. Does that mean that the algorithm is similar in that case?

EE: In fact, there are two very similar algorithms in *Shaping Space*: slightly different algorithms running in parallel on two different computers. In the case of the Sydney example, only one of those computers and only one of those algorithms was running, so it was literally only half of the work in terms of algorithms as well as images.

FF: and compared to *Shaping Form*?

EE: To be honest it was more like a *Shaping Form*. But that was because it was simply impossible in that small space to do what was needed. However, something interesting came out of this for Venice, which we might come to later.

The next one was in a large exhibition called "Fields" at the National Museum of Art, Riga, Latvia (see Fig. 18.2). It was an invited piece. I sent all the specifications, including the design of the room that it should be in. It was a large exhibition space, and, within that space, they built a room of the size that I specified and with the entrance as I specified (see Fig. 18.3). I sent all the projection and Perspex specifications we used in Sheffield. They copied that, and I had pretty much nothing to do with the installation except going and seeing it, and it all worked. But I think it was a lot of work, both building the space, painting it, obtaining the right Perspex, hanging it, and having the correct short throw projectors and setting that up. That was an exhibition which had quite a lot of electronic art in it, so I think they had hired people who were expert in projectors and computers. There was absolutely no problem.

I haven't mentioned the computer aspect yet so I'm going to wind back on that because the funny thing that happened in the Site Gallery show. I had used the computers in *Shaping Space* before, and set them up in the same way as for *Shaping Forms*. So the *Shaping Forms* set up and the *Shaping Space* set up for the computers was in the environment sense very similar. What I had been doing in the previous years was setting them up so that people could switch the work on and off at the wall. They didn't touch the computer in any sense, just treated it as if it was an electric kettle or a radio. We did have one trouble at Site Gallery when one of the technical staff there was competent in computers and didn't like the idea of switching a computer off by turning the power off at the wall. They did it the proper way and I hadn't allowed for that. That meant it didn't work properly and I had to adjust my computer set up to allow for the fact that someone turn the computer off "properly" rather than just from the wall—so that it worked both ways. By the time it got to Riga it didn't matter which way they did it, although I recommended they just used the power on the wall, which is I think what they did for the run of the exhibition. So that was fine.

FF: Did you see this modification as an evolution of the work? Like an improvement?

Fig. 18.2 Ernest Edmonds, *Shaping Space*, National Museum of Art, Riga, Latvia (2014). (Image courtesy of Ernest Edmonds)

EE: No. It didn't change the work at all, it was only a change to how you turned it on. It had no artistic or aesthetic influence on the work whatsoever.

FF: And in terms of installing the work, did that help others in the future installations of the work?

EE: Yes, it did. It meant that, whilst I still give instructions that people should turn it off by the power on the wall, if someone fails to follow that particular instruction, it still works. Whilst in my first version they really had to do what I asked, I realized that some people would not do what I ask and I made an adjustment to allow for that. So that was very good. I was very pleased with the way it was installed in "Fields", particularly the way they created the space for it.

The next installation was in "Códigos Primordiais (Primary Codes)", Oi Futuro Flamengo, in Rio de Janeiro. In this case a room was found that was slightly larger than my specifications but quite similar to the room size that I wanted. The piece was installed in the room that already existed. Unlike "Fields", there was no need to build a special room. It took some time to get it right. First of all, the Perspex was a story rather like Site Gallery. The Perspex had to be bought twice. The first time it was too thin, so this time it wasn't a question of the image being the problem but it bent in the heat. It was the right specification for the look of the work, but it was a bit too thin in that context. They had to replace it and buy some sheets that were a little bit thicker but still worked visually. The other point was that they had underestimated how much light got into that room and so the room was too light to start with and that had to be adjusted. Thirdly it took them about two days to set

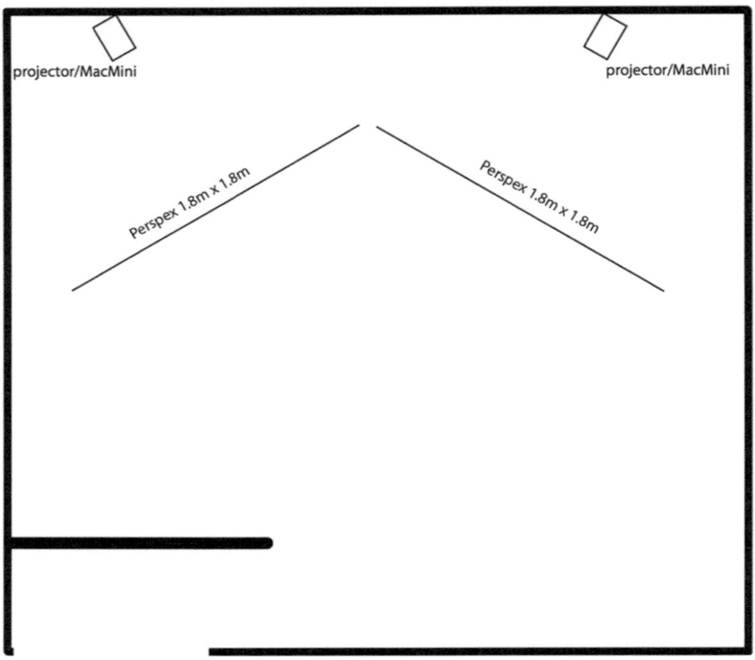

Fig. 18.3 Ernest Edmonds, *Shaping Space*, room plan for *Fields*, National Museum of Art, Riga, Latvia (2014). (Image courtesy of Ernest Edmonds)

up the projectors. They got the right projectors to do it and I'm not sure how expert they were or what problems they had but I know that it took a couple of days to do it. However, eventually it was all done successfully. We now had it three times in exhibitions precisely as I originally made the work for Sheffield.

The next two attempts didn't work. I don't know too much about all the details here but in an exhibition in Beijing, they tried to install it but somehow the data projection wasn't satisfactory. I don't speak any Chinese and the technical guys didn't speak any English, and in the timescale that we had available we couldn't come to a way of dealing with this. So I think this was a language problem really and probably nothing more. Maybe it could have been made to work if we haven't had that problem, so I don't think that's a real failure in terms of installation art and expertise. I had provided all the instructions in writing, but the writing was in English so maybe it wasn't clear enough to the guys who were doing the work. Then my show last year in Leicester, everything was set up, a room was built, everything seemed fine, but it was done rather close to the opening of the exhibition. Two things seemed not to be right, one is that the guys setting up the projectors couldn't get the projector settings correct. These were the same projectors that have been used in Sheffield so that should have been possible, but we never quite got to the bottom of that problem. Also, it seems that the Perspex was not quite the right. In these two cases, the two failures, the one

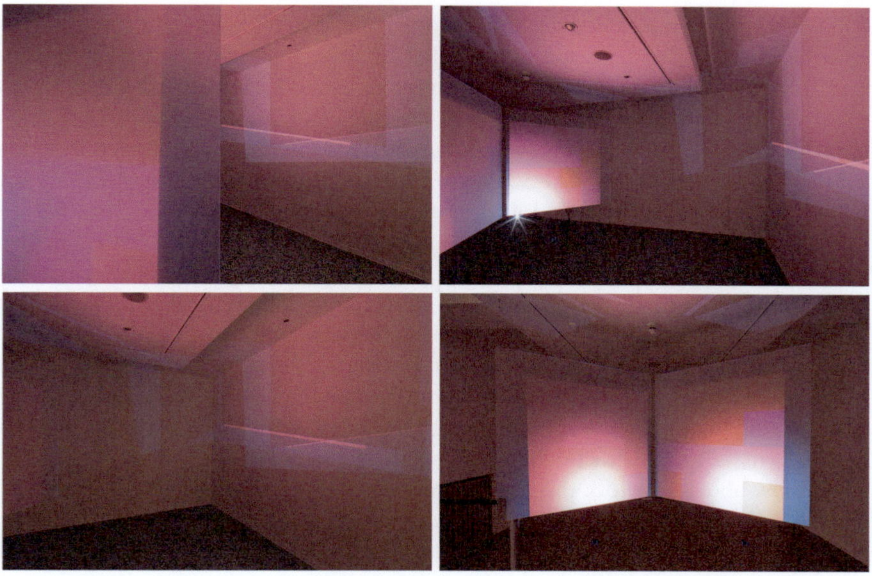

Fig. 18.4 Ernest Edmonds, *Shaping Space*, Fondazione Bevilacqua La Masa, Venice, Italy (2017). (Images courtesy of Giorgio Bombieri)

in Beijing in 2015 and 2017 in Leicester, technical complexities were such that, in the timescales and in the case of Beijing the language issues, they were not overcome in time.

FF: Were they supposed to be built in separate rooms in those two cases?

EE: Yes, in both cases. In the Beijing case, in a separate space demarcated in a big room, but separated so there was no light in there. In the case of Leicester in a constructed separate room. When this failed, we made the decision quite late in the day to use that space for a different purpose. We repurposed the space and so it wasn't all a waste.

Then the last one was the *Algorithmic Signs* exhibition in Venice (see Fig. 18.4). A lot of effort was put into the Perspex, which was correct. However, the projectors had the wrong lenses on them for the space that they were in and there was no way that anyone, no matter how expert or amateur, could fix it. The lenses had too narrow an angle. But what happened was, we played with it in various ways and out of the serendipity of the occasion something different happened. So actually *Shaping Space* in Venice wasn't *Shaping Space* exactly, it was some other thing, some other work, and it wasn't what I had intended, it did use the algorithms and the colors that I intended and it did interact as I had intended but the images, where the images were, how they were formed, was not what I had intended. These images were quite beautiful, so something very interesting happened, even if it wasn't *Shaping Space*.

FF: I remember watching the audience interacting with the work over the duration of the exhibition, and I noticed that when experiencing this installation, compared to the previous examples you described, some people initially thought that the work consisted in the image reflected to the wall created through the light passing underneath the Perspex sheets, and then, by moving around, they realized that it was actually an interactive piece that worked the other way round. So, it was interesting to see how people behaved then, and the surprise and fascination that this realization and the piece gave them was very nice to watch, and completely unexpected. How did that unexpected reaction feel, from the creator's point of view?

EE: It was quite attractive and interesting. It wasn't, as I said, what I had intended. Many of my works, like *Shaping Forms*, are not meant to have highly engaging interaction all the time, they have a whole different approach. Whereas *Shaping Space* has more of that engagement in the interaction. To my mind, the "cusp" between having interesting interaction and having a long-term interest is quite hard and different ways of dealing with this are something that I am very much working on and trying to develop. What I take away from this experience is some new ideas on how to make that interaction process engaging.

FF: how about the work that we commissioned for the entrance to *Algorithmic Signs*, the *Growth and Form* work? How did that relate to *Shaping Space*?

EE: Ah, well, that goes back to the installation of *Shaping Space* in Sydney that I talked about earlier. The title, by the way, was in celebration of the fact that 2017 was the 100th anniversary of the publication of D'Arcy Wentworth Thompson's book *On Growth and Form* that has influenced so many artists making generative and systems-based work. Anyway, the space in the entrance required front projection onto the end wall, but it was possible to mount a projector high on the ceiling and have a protected space, so that there were no shadows of the audience. It was also a single screen. So, although it was a new and quite different work, the installation came from what I had done in Sydney. It worked fine. In terms of the technical aspects, the specification issues were very similar to *Shaping Space*. It's only that no Perspex was used, and the light was reflected rather than transmitted.

FF: How did this unique location affect your choice of colors and the work in general when you conceived it? In other words, did the Venice environment have an effect on your creative process for this specific installation?

EE: Yes, the environment was quite influential on my choices. There were two aspects. First, the lighting conditions required stronger colors than I sometimes use, and I wanted at least some of those colors to relate to the physical environment, but just not too obviously. Second, this was a space where many people would move through, rather than stand and contemplate a work (although some did). I needed the work to grab people's attention more directly than, for example, the *Shaping Forms* shown in my room. So, things like the speed of response had to be more direct.

FF: In an ideal world, what would the optimal condition be for the installation of *Shaping Space*?

EE: I think the way that it was done in Riga was perfect. It was similar to the first installation in Sheffield. The room in Riga was constructed for the work, rather than the work having to fit into a given space. That point identifies the kind of installation it is. *Shaping Space* is not site specific in its intention. It was built for a room in Site Gallery of course but that was quite generic and the best way to tour it was to build its space. Of course, all the technical aspects, like the Perspex and projectors have to be correct, but that is standard stuff.

FF: So, what would the next step be, thinking about all the different variations this work has experienced?

EE: I'm working on two projects now. In one work I'm using augmented reality and I'm hoping to use augmented reality headsets to mix a real space with a virtual space in which people can move. And I think that the kind of experience people may have in this could be quite like the Venice example of *Shaping Space*. So that's one idea, and it's interesting because back in the 1980s I was working on virtual reality and I put it aside because technologically it wasn't good enough. It was interesting theoretically, but it wasn't technologically good enough to make art out of it.

The other project I'm working on is in the context of large domes and I'm working with a sound artist in Leicester, Pip Greasley. We are making an audio-visual experience in a large dome which would take this conceptual step further, being completely embracing. So, if you're in this space all you will have will be the color and the sound to interact with.

Both of these approaches are ones that lead on from that experience in Venice.

I'm still doing work with static images too, but in terms of what I'm taking forward from that experience, those two projects are the next direction. And they both are installation type pieces that are very different in kind, one is very specialized installation in a dome, and the other is using augmented reality and the environment that I'm adding and changing is, in fact, virtual.

FF: Has your relationship with sound changed now, compared to your previous interactive works involved with music and musicians? How is the relation with sound in your new work and how has that evolved, thinking about the advances in technology we are experiencing at present?

EE: The relationship is still quite similar. One does not mirror the other, but the visual and the sound parts are tightly linked. They always will be in anything I do. In the current project with Pip, I am having very little influence on the sound, except that he and I share an aesthetic position. That is true with Mark Fell, of course. In fact, after Mark and I recently performed some of our work at *Café OTO* in London, we definitely felt that we should make more together and I very much hope that we will. The key point with the current work with Pip is the use of a Dome in which the audience, the participants, are fully immersed. It is not like looking at a painting on a wall, in a room, or at a performance on a stage. There is nothing other than the artwork to experience. I guess the new augmented reality work will have something of that quality also. All this remains to be seen. I never really know how a work will be experienced until it is done.

18.3 Conclusion

This chapter has explored how the various installations of a generative interactive artwork using data projection onto Perspex created different reiterations of the work's original concept. Also, it has covered how the experience of installing the work in various locations posed distinctive pragmatic, physical, and technical questions, and challenges that affected, in one way or another, each iteration of the work. It is interesting to observe how the practical issues connected with installing the work in situ in very different locations, under different circumstances, created sometimes unexpected aesthetic results that inspired the artist in creating new work connected to his initial concept.

Further Reading

Boden MA, Edmonds E (2019) From fingers to digits: an artificial aesthetic (Leonardo). MIT Press
Candy L, Edmonds E (2002) Explorations in art and technology: intersections and correspondence. Springer
Candy L, Edmonds E, Poltronieri FA (eds) (2018) Explorations in art and technology. Springer Series on Cultural Computing. https://doi.org/10.1007/978-1-4471-7367-0
Edmonds E (2018a) The art of interaction: what HCI can learn from interactive art. Morgan and Claypool Publishers
Edmonds E (2018b) Structure in art practice. In: Candy L et al (2018), pp 51–57. https://doi.org/10.1007/978-1-4471-7367-0_4
Franco F (2017) Generative systems art: the work of Ernest Edmonds. Routledge, Abingdon
Franco F (2019) The algorithmic dimension: five artists in conversation. Springer Series on Cultural Computing

Ernest Edmonds has pioneered the field of computational art and contributed to the broader field of contemporary art from the late 1960s to the present. In 2017, he was awarded the SIGGRAPH Distinguished Artist Award for Lifetime Achievement in Digital Art. His innovative work has focused on the invention of new concepts, tools and forms over fifty years. His archives are collected by the Victoria and Albert Museum, as part of the National Archive of Computer-Based Art and Design. Edmonds' work represents one of the roots of generative art. His work not only acknowledges a historical connection, often overlooked, to the structural research undertaken by Constructivist artists in the 20th century; it also demonstrates that the points made by this past tradition could be taken further through the use of computation and logic. By applying color theory, computational logic and programmed systems to his work, Edmonds combined the structural research of Charles Biederman and the Constructivists with Matisse's use of color for the first time, and took them to a new level encompassing time, color and structure. The digital process gave generative art new possibilities and brought new opportunities for Edmonds, allowing him to create systems in which artworks have a life of their own.

Francesca Franco is a Venetian-born art historian and curator based in the UK. The central theme of her research is the history of art and technology and the pioneers of computer art. Increasingly it concerns issues of generative and interactive art and the connections between Constructivism and Systems art in early computational art. Her first solo authored book, *Generative Systems Art: the Work of Ernest Edmonds* (Franco 2017), explores the history of pioneering computer art and its contribution to art history by way of examining Edmonds' art from the late 1960s to the present day. One of Franco's most recent curatorial projects is *Algorithmic Signs*, an exhibition exploring the history of generative art featuring five of its most prominent pioneers Ernest Edmonds (b. 1942), Manfred Mohr (b. 1938), Vera Molnár (b. 1924), Frieder Nake (b. 1938), and Roman Verostko (b. 1929). The exhibition, fully documented in Franco's second monograph,

The Algorithmic Dimension: Five Artists in Conversation (Franco 2019), was held at the Fondazione Bevilacqua La Masa's historical gallery in St. Mark's square, Venice, between October and December 2017. The exhibition featured over 60 artworks, including early plotter drawings, four site-specific installations, two newly commissioned works, and an 8-hour video documentation showing how an algorithmic drawing is made. One of the site-specific generative interactive installations there was Edmonds' *Shaping Space*, first exhibited in Sheffield in 2012.

Chapter 19
Art, Life, and Technology, Through Time and Space

Carla Gannis and Tula Giannini

Abstract This chapter focuses on the work and life of digital artist Carla Gannis. Originally from North Carolina, Gannis received a BFA from UNC Greensboro, and an MFA in painting from Boston University. In 2005 she was awarded a New York Foundation for the Arts (NYFA) Grant in Computer Arts, and since then, she lives and works in Brooklyn, where she is a professor and assistant chairperson of The Department of Digital Arts at Pratt Institute. Conveying her journey from painter to digital artist and storyteller, we explore the evolution of her artistic expression from painting to digital art, a story that ties broadly to the development of the digital arts field from the 1990s to present. Presented both through images of her work, and by way of a face to face unrehearsed interview, this chapter touches upon many of the highly pertinent topics impacting artists and museums in the 21st-century digital age. Among these, of special interest to museums are her observations on audiences, and how working in digital media affords new opportunities and multiple ways of connecting to the viewer, and reaching vast numbers of people across the globe, traveling from the gallery to the public square, in particular, Times Square and the Internet, showing that the life of a digital work can have multiple states of being. Gannis emphasizes the cultural positioning of digital spaces in physical places where diverse large public audiences can experience the work and where the artist can feel the pulse of public reaction and interaction. A feature of her work is her expression of self and gender through digital manifestations of persona, being and social consciousness, that take very original shapes and forms, images, colors and animations that merge into digital interpretations of self and the surrounding world revealing her creative imagination and sense of poetry used to convey new narratives embedded in her work and life (Fig. 19.1).

C. Gannis
Pratt Institute, New York, USA

T. Giannini (✉)
School of Information, Pratt Institute, New York, USA
e-mail: giannini@pratt.edu

T. Giannini and J. P. Bowen (eds.), *Museums and Digital Culture*,
Springer Series on Cultural Computing, https://doi.org/10.1007/978-3-319-97457-6_19

Fig. 19.1 *Until the end of the world* by Carla Gannis, her solo exhibition at the DAM gallery, Berlin, Germany, November 2017, installation view. (Photograph by Carla Gannis, http://carlagannis.com/blog/prints/until-the-end-of-the-world/)

19.1 Introduction

19.1.1 When Digital Art Is Life—3D Models, Avatars and Selfies

Writing about her art, Gannis explains her thinking and process wrought from digital art and life using 3D models, avatars and selfies (Gannis 2017), while referencing 16th-century painting. Here, we glean the artist's perspectives firsthand:

> *Portraits in Landscape*, a single-channel video from my "After Arcimboldo" series, is a continuation of my focus on combining eccentric art-historical references with visual smartphone language. Through this process I reflect on the constructions and perceptions of identity in contemporary culture. Unlike the subjects of Arcimboldo's paintings, the portraits in this series are not of aristocrats and wealthy patrons. Instead they began as 3D models, the avatars of our age, that I digitally shaped into selfie poses. I then overlaid the models with hundreds of emoji, similar to Arcimboldo's process of using everyday objects to sculpt uncanny human likenesses. Bringing the portraits to life in a hyper landscape teeming with "digital nature" expresses my fascination with how virtual and physical embodiments intersect in our networked communication age. (Gannis 2018)

Gannis' *Lady Ava Interface*, an AI (Artificial Intelligence) assistant created for the Whitney Museum's Sunrise/Sunset project, draws inspiration from the work of the English mathematician, Lady Ada Lovelace, (1815–1852) recognized as the first computer programmer. Rather than providing practical assistance as does Siri and Alexa, Ava instills creative thinking and imagination, and similarly with her work, *Portraits in Landscape*, Gannis has applied techniques of Giuseppe Arcimboldo to create Lady Ava's persona using 3D-modeled emojis, and images of clouds and cookies, all symbolic of digital language.

Her works point to the smartphone selfie as a core element of digital culture (Klemperer 2018). Gannis has embraced the digital self and literally immerses her real and digital self in her art in highly original ways that capture the very essence

Fig. 19.2 *Lady Ava Interface*, by Carla Gannis, Lady Ava—Twitter, featured on the Whitney Museum website, part of the Sunrise/Sunset project organized by Christiane Paul, May 2018 (https://twitter.com/carlagannis/status/983861719687712769)

of being digital while her art blurs the boundaries between fine art and performance art, especially her intrinsic use of technology that can breathe new life into the works of master painters (see Figs. 19.2 and 19.3) and also in her 2016 tour de force, *The Garden of Emoji Delights*, based on the triptych *The Garden of Earthly Delights* by Hieronymus Bosh, which is reinvented through digital translation using animated emoji "GIF" images that she created to tell a story for the digital world (Giannini and Bowen 2016; http://carlagannis.com; Lorenzin 2016).

19.2 The Interview: Carla Gannis in Conversation with Tula Giannini

Tula Giannini: Today is August 20, 2018. I'm here with the famous Carla Gannis, star of the digital world!

Carla Gannis: I'm good with that!

TG: We have this wonderful opportunity to have a discussion. I gave you several questions beforehand but will restate each one as we go. The first is about how you think of your own work in terms of its relationship to the past because you have picked up certain artists of the past, going back to the Renaissance that you connect to and then re-interpret, remix, so please talk a little about that.

Fig. 19.3 *Lucile Tack Ball (LTB)*, by Carla Gannis (top left)—"is a work in progress… inspired by the portraits of the 16th Century mannerist painter Giuseppe Arcimboldo (top center) and the American comedy legend Lucille Ball (top right). I perform LTB by using facial tracking technologies and a computer-generated voice—an experiment in comedy through the perspective of a human who is trying to perform as a machine who is trying to entertain humans". Photograph courtesy of Carla Gannis, http://carlagannis.com/blog/prints/lucille-trackball/

CG: Sure. So, my background is traditional painting and oil painting. I studied oil painting as well as classical music and piano as a child and then I went on to pursue two degrees in painting and obviously in pursuing those degrees in painting I studied a lot of art history, and I suppose many images. I will say most of my references do tend to come from western art, however, and that has as much to do with being a western individual. But also, I was coming up a little earlier. I was in college in the late 1980s and early 1990s and I don't know if enough or as much attention was paid to, at the time, world history as it is today in art history programs. However, I don't want to digress too much on that topic.

In the digital work that I produce today, I do reference many artists from the canon and there are a few intentions behind that. Much of that work has been a source of inspiration since I was a small child, for example, "emojifying" Hieronymus Bosch. Some people have said I "DeBosched" a Bosch but that wasn't my intention because there was already enough "DeBoschery" in that piece. An intention in my piece was to pay tribute to the original work, but also to think about it within the context of our time. It is a piece that still resonates and reverberates, and a painting which at the time I had never actually seen, "The Garden of Earthly Delights". So I only knew it as a reproduction and that was appealing to, me and as well, it was a work that I would be appropriating from or basically translating with the new signs, symbols and iconography of our day—an iconography that isn't just part of high art but something that has to do with communication and that is used by everyone and so overlaying the emoji with the Bosch was important to me to find different connections between this 500-year-old iconography and iconography we use today often equated with just happiness or vacuity. What happens is if there's a different kind of gravitas or different interpretation possible in that mashup? (Rose 2017).

Now the other artists who I have quoted include Marcel Duchamp, Rene Magritte, and a quite a few of those quotations arose in a project that I worked on for about 2½ years and the project began as "the Selfie Drawing Project" and you're familiar with this and series of drawings I made, one a week for 52 weeks. I shared them on many social media networks and they were all selfies with augmented reality experiences. I also produced 4K video works, 3D prints, a longer form narrative—so all these works emerged out of this original idea. For the solo show that I produced to represent the translations I used the titled "a subject self-defined"—and that was based on a work of art that Joseph Kosuth made in 1966. The work was titled "a subject self-defined." I use this title for my show in 2016 as a means of reassessing the state of art now. In 1966, we were reading "The Death of the Author" and it was about expunging the texture of the artwork and it was what the viewer brought to it. There wasn't any relationship or emphasis, and this was a point that Kosuth and many artists of his time were making on identity or biography.

But 40 years later, we find ourselves in a heightened state of identity politics. And particularly as a woman producing these works where women historically have been the object of art and paintings to call oneself a subject and to self-define oneself in the age of selfies felt interesting to me and that's why I chose that title, so even the title of my work was a direct quotation from an earlier artist. Also instead of neon, I used glow in the dark letters for the title of my show so there was a direct reference quotation but then, as I was mentioning earlier, quite a few of the works referenced, was when I was referencing the Canon for these works, they're works that I admire, tremendous works, there's a Bernini, Saint Theresa in Ecstasy that—my gosh—that's the best orgasm face on a woman ever—right? (Sauerlaender 2016).

So, I wanted to incorporate that one but I'm also inserting myself into that canonical history. Not as an object but as the subject, as an author and that was important to me too, that there was an implicit critique to that. For centuries, we have elevated artists as the masters and the geniuses, but in those histories that we've written, many people were omitted. Many times, it didn't have to do with skill level or any of those aspects, when art was more about a skillset and now it's much more about concepts. Although I think the best artists and the ones that I love and the ones that I quote, always understood the marriage of form and content and their work is imbued with concept whether it was produced 500 years ago or 20 years ago, but there was something about inserting myself in that Canon and being an author who is like Sherrie Levine—re-photographing those photographs that's something where she's going into museums and she's looking at the masterworks in the male Canon and she's re-photographing them and then assigning her authorship to them so that was something I was consciously thinking about.

TG: Well that was beautifully spoken. It had many different ideas but one aspect I thought about, in your case, I think what stands out is that you might say the artist is art itself. The separation between the artist and the art is shrinking, because of the strength of identity, projection of image, but I also think the digital plays a role in this because whether you're there or not there, once your art is on the web or Internet, it's communicating…

CG: … and it's ubiquitous.

TG: This is totally new, relatively. And so, the position of the artist, when your art is out there in what I call the digital ecosystem is bumping up against all kinds of things it never would have otherwise. You're getting different juxtapositions that could jolt your way of seeing, your imagination, you might suddenly be seeing a work of art from 300 years ago that you weren't thinking about, but it's in the same mix when you're moving around on the Internet.

CG: Yes, and that's the point of the Bosch—was that I knew it as a work of art on the Internet. When I left painting, I was an abstract painter who wanted to work figuratively again. I was looking at quite a few photographers like Gregory Crewdson and was interested in telling a story in the moment where you must go into a piece instead of looking across like you do with a timeframe, like time-based media. And since then though over the past few years I've been getting back into kinetic work. I've done projection mapping, quite a bit of video work. *The Selfie Drawing Book* was my first experiment with augmented reality through its 52 augments. Halfway through, I've started expanding it to much more work that's 3D augmented reality. And since then I'm now working on a piece Lucille Trackball, that I presented at the EVA London 2018 Conference (Bowen et al. 2018) and Lucille's first instantiation was 2D and performed with facial tracking technologies (Salas 2016).

I've now modeled and rigged Lucille as a 3D entity and I have already produced my first, it's in progress but it's been published, an augmented reality version of

Lucille and then the next state for that is to bring Lucille into a VR space where—I want Lucille to be a VR comedian and it's actually a human, myself pretending to be an AI being who is trying to pretend to be human. So, there are many layers. But I'm also interested in that because I haven't done much in-depth research, but in cursory searches there doesn't seem to be a lot of comedy VR now. One person was telling me that a VR project with which they were they were familiar was misogynistic and Lucille is a big feminist. Many of the topics with which she grapples are topics that come up in her comedy and concern ageism, sexism, and classism, and some topics that in between her puns and her nerdy pun humor there are some biting satire too.

TG: I think part of what you felt was that you were not going to start painting representational as it was done in the past. But now you can bring realism in a form you might call digitalism into your work, but in a totally new way as all these new works you created in a digital structure that you now can work within, didn't exist before—and you are inside that digital space being creative. I think that is where you have been taking a leadership role from everything I've seen (Bowen et al. 2018).

TG: Do you think about this as being valid?

CG: Oh my gosh this is so valid because when I was in graduate school the big issue, and I must admit some of the people and professors with whom I was studying in graduate school were 4th or 5th generation abstract expressionism, but there was still this dichotomy where if you were a figurative painter, you were reactionary. And then if you were an abstract painter you were heroic, and you were dealing with the sublime and it was fractious. I remember when I first got to grad school, I was working figuratively and quite a few of the professors with whom I was working with, one was Alfred Leslie who had historically been an abstract expressionist. He moved into figuration, but he moved into very cool figurative work. The only acceptable figurative work was Alex Katz and Roy Lichtenstein figurative but pop, so it was either very cool and distant or pop.

I was angry and had all these ideas I wanted to resolve in my painting at that time, so figurative work didn't seem to be a vehicle for that expression at this point, if people were to take it seriously. So, I moved into abstraction although, interestingly, in most of the abstract works that I produced in the early and mid-1990s, had these kinds of hieroglyphs and symbols that I would use in figurative works, so they weren't nonobjective to me because that was also a big debate, nonobjective, abstraction, versus this content laden figurative work. With photography and film, one wonders why anybody would make a figurative representational work.

But once I started working digitally, I returned to working with figures and with overt narratives. Not narratives with a beginning, middle, end, because a lot of these were single images, static images and print works. And then I made some interactive works too that were nonlinear narratives but the idea of suggesting a narrative because that had also been something maligned when I was in grad school and in many academic circles. So, narratives were dead and "don't deal with allegory or metaphor by god" and with a new language. Once I threw away all my paintings from grad school which I did as my Baldessari act, it was liberating though—unfortunately, I spent a lot of money on oil paint and I threw all of those away, but it was liberating and so once I started working with Xerox machines, etc. I was trying anything, and I would throw away as much art as I created.

I was interested in Arte Povera—the Italians and conceptual art and I would combine photographs, Xerox and computer-generated images, collages, etc. I'd try these approaches and I was looking at many artists. And then finally through that process I found myself, found my interests and I began to develop my own language.

TG: So this is really revolutionary. Also the notion of thinking digitally. I listened to a lecture by Glenn Lowry and this was his big thing. Think digitally and people around him were not sure what he meant, but to me, it seemed that phrase very pertinent. He sees that as an inspiration for the whole redesign of the museum itself and the exhibits. Does that have any meaning to you? This idea of thinking digitally?—because you're in that space.

CG: It does and recently someone was doing an email interview with me and they were asking in terms of preparing students who would pursue a career working with digital tools or delving into intersections of art and technology. One aspect I mentioned that I thought was very important was it's not the programs you learn, it's learning to think and inhabit these digital spaces which requires you to be so much more elastic. You're straddling different worlds and with that I mean in terms of if you're thinking art market economics you're an artist who wants to have a successful career with a gallery, but you also make this work that can be shared ubiquitously. You're putting GIF images online, you're showing your 4 k videos with limited editions in a brick and mortar white cube and a select few see that and then a great deal more sees the GIFs you're putting online but you want to inhabit both of those spaces so that's one aspect of being a digital artist. That's thinking about it from the sense of your practice and economics, as if you know how you straddle those.

But more importantly, I think as an artist who enjoys my practice, no matter who is seeing it, a digital space requires you to be so much more adaptive so you have to be able to adapt the fact that your tools, your applications, your processes for delivery, your processes for output are constantly changing, updating, evolving and also you have to deal with them dying—with obsolescence of hardware and software and understanding migration and how you have to now adapt to that so you're a part of this living thing that is so dynamic, and both virtual and physical. I remember when I first stopped painting because I certainly identified as a "painter"—I would tell people "I'm not an artist I'm a painter" and I wore it—I had my jeans covered in paint, I had my arms and fingers covered in paint. I'd sleep in my studio, with turpentine and smoked my cigarettes. I bought into that as a trip and when I switched to digital at first, I felt "[gasp] my hands have been cut off!" I can't reach into the computer.

Because this is 20 years later, I've been working with these tools, now it is so intuitive it feels so real to me. I am in that space as much as I am in this physical space and I don't even like to use "in real life" (IRL) and "URL". We say "URL/IRL". They work for shorthand as distinctions between virtual and physical, but they're all real life now and that's something else about embracing the digital state of being is recognizing this is all real life now. These distinctions and these dichotomies it's all blending and so to be elastic and prismatic within that, I think, can contribute to the work you'll produce as an artist and we still use the nomenclature digital artist, new media artist, interdisciplinary artist but it's all art today. Even artists who are working with analog tools, their research and so much of what they are doing is informed either by the Internet or by using digital tools.

TG: Moving to the next question, it concerns the challenges for digital artists, but in the context of museums.

CG: So, within the contexts of museums, recently I was talking to somebody about participating in a show that takes place in a museum and I'm getting this augmented reality app ready for them and they were mentioning all the artists who were participating to make sure we show up for all the testing because the museum staff don't understand this and either they were intimidated by the technology or they haven't been trained, because generally they have been trained to deal with physical objects and making sure that they inhabit these spaces safely in these static non-touchable scenarios. So, that's one thing for artists who are working with new technologies, although interestingly, the second thing is that artists have always worked with technology.

Anyway, artists working with digital technologies or computer technologies—it's just that many museum staff haven't been trained on how to maintain these works and not even maintain them in terms of if they enter the collection, maintain them during an exhibition, such as turning them on and off or general maintenance. I think there is still some resistance to digital art—maybe it's not in museums that are well funded, or some private art collections who support new media, but they have resistance to buying works that are process driven, where in a few years you may have to migrate that work to a new operating system or it might require different hardware or software to even run it and that kind of maintenance intimidates certain museums.

But sometimes it's a matter for them now of funding and taking those risks because so many of these galleries that are still trying to operate on an antiquated system. Your artists don't get paid unless once a year you represent them, they have a solo show, and if they are lucky, they make a couple thousand bucks and the rest of the time they are represented but they don't have health benefits. Normally gallerists who are young gallerists don't have health benefits themselves. I've been working with Kelani Nicole at Transfer Gallery, and talk about a labor of love, and she has made a tremendous impact in the new media, digital arts world but also within mainstream arts because those things are finally colliding, and those barriers are collapsing but it has been a labor of love. She has worked full time, she runs a gallery, she puts on these laborious exhibitions trying out all sorts of new technology, ambitious projects but it's always "OK, where are we going to obtain screens? Where are we going to get projectors? Who can help us here?" because if you don't have some funding it is quite difficult. Much of the work with digital media used to just be sending files and playing it on a screen and that's still valid, but I think more artists are interested in instantiations in physical space, physical computing or what is it like to get screen-based Internet inspiration, "post-Internet" but then make physical works of art. There are these currents running between the virtual and physical and so all of that, those can be obstacles for people who want to support those projects but it's just like having the resources—because the commercial industry has the resources, but their content much of the time—it's just…crap.

TG: But do you think the museums should have a role in this—In other words, to be much more empathetic or much more prepared to support digital art. All their efforts have been going into having the perfect walls for the painting, but they haven't thought this through very carefully about how they are going to move towards the next step. I think MOMA especially is thinking about that with the new space that they are building now. They're rethinking the gallery so that has some promise.

CG: It seems as if so much has happened on the front end—and when I say front end, I mean "oh yes! Let's create tours where there's augmented reality or there are all these new technologies we're implementing but in the tour of one seeing the paintings and the sculptures" and so what I think will be radical when it's not only using this technology for tours or to access information or to learn about things or for school-age children but when you're now actually committed to nurturing and fostering the careers of artists working with these technologies. Investing in their works either in the programming and creating space that facilitates this more nonbinary, nonlinear work and also representing this work in your collections so you represent the time we live in now.

TG: That was brilliant, but I think personally we are at the tipping point for that. Because if museums don't do this, the perception will be dusty. Because people are coming in being digital people, and they can accommodate both, both can be there but if museums shut out digital art now, I think that's not going to be sustainable. That stance is a barrier. It's like another wall, and it won't hold—we are about at that point now. That's my sense of it. Embracing digital art will make museums much more exciting and will get more people coming. Visitors can take in both as they're living in this mixed reality world. It's not hard for them—maybe five or ten years ago, but not now.

CG: Not for generation Z.

TG: Exactly. They're going to be excited by this. They'll see themselves in it—their sensibilities—their aesthetics.

CG: Yea and now you mentioned something. It was funny when I used this term. I said work that's nonlinear and nonbinary. Now I know as digital practitioners, we're working with binary code, zeroes, and ones but I feel conceptually—Robert Rauschenberg said something about working between the gap of art and life and I feel as if the work of digital artists is between the ones and zeroes. They can find all that gray area between them to tease out these amazing expressions with binary code that is a result of nonbinary thinking and so to explain my usage of that terminology.

TG: So, looking ahead to the future, because you must always have this sense of the path you're moving on, the direction and how it resonates with the rest of the art world—how do you see yourself moving into the future and where does that resonate within the art world.

CG: This year, I've been fortunate to have two ephemeral exhibitions and opportunities, outside of the frameworks that we were talking about, the bounds of the gallery or museum walls—having my artworks on the Whitney museum's website but only at sunrise and sunset so at this very specific time you have this fleeting moment to experience the work of art. The work is also this artificial intelligence assistant who gives you nonsensical, nonlinear poetic advice instead of telling you to schedule your doctor's appointment and it's an embodied assistant who is comprised of emojis and again harking back like I always do, there's an art historical reference. I generally appreciate the more eccentric artists, like Giuseppe Arcimboldo, and so that was an exciting project to be commissioned for, and then also this year the Times Squares Art Project the Midnight Moment which is going on now.

The Whitney project is up—I don't know what you say—on view at sunrise and sunset and then I have midnight this year so I've covered everything except for—I have sunrise, sunset and midnight, I need someone to contact me about a lunchtime project and then I will have gotten all of these very important, monumental times and so again, the Time Square piece has been amazing in terms of seeing my art in this context for many reasons. I'm in this hypermediated space and we had talked about this before, how much of my work is hypermediated. Anyway, I call it "horror vacui" (fear of empty space) and consciously or not, I'm attracted, or I have this compulsion to fill up empty spaces in terms of aesthetics and art creation. I do think that's my response to visualizing "hypermediation", nonlinearity all these different kinds of frequencies occurring simultaneously. But it particularly fits well with the Times Square environment and it's been exciting to go up there I think 12 times now in this past month. I'm a little sleep deprived, traveling up there and back, but not only will I invite friends but also there are hundreds of thousands of people there every night from all walks of life, from all over the world, experiencing art for three minutes, some of them recognize it some of them don't.

I've engaged a few people in conversation but it's a totally different context and it's exciting to have your work in that environment. If you think again about some predecessors, if you think about someone like Beuys who thought "everyone's an artist." Warhol gave us all 15 min, but he was also very interested in the vernacular of his time, in advertising language, in the expressions of everyday people and not only lofty erudite "art language." Even someone like Giotto in the 13th century was interested in the vernacular and the vulgate, and these kinds of things, text and that the current that runs throughout history that I've always been very excited about and so this is that moment where I'm very enthusiastic.

Outside of the Internet, this is the largest audience I've ever had, outside of the Internet and so physical space—all these people from all over the world are seeing these works on these huge screens, now already I know I've reached millions of people with my artwork and that's not to sound arrogant, that's just true with my artwork, but generally on these small screens and so I've been able to reach people, I have sometimes people from high school who aren't studying art who will contact me. I really like that. It's not as if I'm only appealing to a sophisticated elite class, accessibility is another aspect of my work that is a conscious choice and so to have it in this context where I've had this much of a viewership every single night, almost reaching levels of the Internet but in a physical space. That is cool.

CG: I've been photographing many things associated with my work, just that juxtaposition with the other—and we were talking about James Rosenquist earlier. In Times Square my works become Rosenquist-like pictures in motion because there are all these different ads and things juxtaposed (since I don't get every advertising screen in Times Square). And to see that it's just become this huge montage and that's exciting!

TG: It makes the viewer suddenly see the other things differently. That's what's important.

CG: It's re-contextualizing.

TG: It's very big. I think it has much more impact.

CG: I agree.

TG: And they are in their environment. You see they're in their space. You're in their space.

CG: I'm in their space and it is a subversive act. With Times Squares Art and the Time Square Alliance, it's a delicate dance. It took a year for all of this to go through and there were layers and those kinds of things, but it's exciting that they have committed and stayed committed to a project like this because I think that is vital and you're correct, the art—and especially my art that has a pop quality to it shares certain aesthetics with contemporary advertising and so it re-contextualizes many of those commercial works and you see "oh wow there's cross-pollination here too and this is how an artist can parse all these messages, all these things that we're constantly bombarded with and that entertain us, that can be sensual experiences all that and again not denigrating it but this is how I have somewhat filtered it to create an expressive language that represents the age in which we exist.

TG: And now moving into the future—what do you see ahead?

CG: Yes, but I brought these works up because I feel like they both are events and have been events that are directing my vector for the future. However, I as a digital, thinker, responder, feeler who in the dynamic age we live in, I'm constantly in flux, and even though there are undercurrents that I think most people can, maybe now they are more familiar with my work, they think "oh yes, I can see that's Carla in there" but it is taking a different direction—I like to take different directions sometimes aesthetically but also challenging myself to learn new technology. So, for creating the Whitney piece, for this AI being, Lady Ava Interface was her name, and with Lady Ava Interface I was starting to approach topics about comedy but there's no audio, there's no voice and so that spawned the project Lucille Trackball that I'm now embarking on, now here Lucille is empowered with a voice. I'm doing the writing for it although I'm probably soon going to try to get some professional writers to collaborate with me on that and giving a voice to Lucille and thinking about that dark comedy has been infused in my work or I've infused in my work for several decades now, but I've never given a voice, a comedic voice to it.

Going forward, one of the things I've been thinking about is pushing myself in terms of the ambitiousness and scope of my projects. I would like to do this to the point of sometimes working with people who can bring it to culmination is also that level of detail or finesse because one of my good friends had told me "you're very Fluxist, constantly making things but it's this and it's this but sometimes they don't have refinement to the idea or the actual object". I think, oh OK, I've done that, I don't want to refine it, so that's something I've been thinking about in terms of scale, ambition and I'm becoming older, committing longer to—ah, OK, I've got the

Fig. 19.4 *Selfie Portrait 32* (2017), by Carla Gannis, American Digital Artist. This portrait is part of her selfie series of selfie portraits that was awarded the Lumen *Prize for Digital Art in 2017.* A brilliant and ground-breaking work that reveals the digital self in multiple facets of identity

confidence too because it was a self-esteem thing too. I'd think "I'll just dip my toe into that idea pool and see what I can come up with" and now I think after this year I'll have much more confidence.

TG: That's great.

CG: Yes, that's something, prior to the selfie project was another project I did where I collaborated with a poet first and then we invited all these people to participate, as performance artists, poets, artists collaborating we did performances in various locales and what was exciting about that project too was our publisher called it a Multi-tentacled Beast and so we started out with a text, this old text that he redacted and I created these drawings in response -you're familiar with this—we created an app, we created these projection mapping pieces, remix pieces with Mark Amerika's students in Colorado. We did other remix projects on Governors Island and taking these texts and finding ways to express it across all these different channels and in gallery channels and poetry houses all these things (Fig. 19.4).

TG: When you look ahead to the future do you see what you tied to the digital future in a sense, digital tools, digital thinking, technology, is going to evolve because it would be accepting change as a part of the whole thing, for some people extremely difficult, like you've said, but you don't have control over how it's going to evolve—what will be the tools. How the tools will change—that's an interesting thing although artists have dealt with that in the past but not at this speed.

CG: Not at this speed and I was talking about the joy in the studio, but it can be daunting. There are times when I feel overwhelmed to the point of exhaustion, particularly by having too many options. Because with proprietary software, they develop things that keep your productions within their parameters for one. So, you think “I’ll try this one of this one,” but at some point, you do need a stable platform that you can learn deeply and have ease in producing and making things on an intuitive level and so that sometimes can be daunting. When I’m adding plugins then I’m skipping to another program or I’m working in this program and those kinds of things and sometimes it’s just being capable of processing all of that and still thinking about what did I read that generated this idea or what drawing I made with a pen, on the subway, that got me started working in this application. I don’t want to lose touch with that stuff and sometimes when you get too much into a technical quagmire the poetry disappears and so it’s very important for me—it’s like music scales.

TG: So, keeping that poetic thread, which Gareth Polmeer puts forward in Chap. 3, seems critical.

CG: That’s so essential otherwise why are we doing this?

TG: It is a very good point, and regardless of the context or your tools—and the other thread is nature itself.

CG: Yes, and nature is a very important point especially regarding human nature and coming to terms with our culpability. At this point we’re developing technologies and other intelligences that we have to think about, albeit I’m excited about artificial intelligences but we’re responsible for encoding responsible data sets so these intelligences don’t propagate the worst in humanity. It’s not only about AI superseding us, it’s about things like perverse substantiations, their instantiation of “commands” in what we would deem perverse because we’re so biased.

TG: And it gets coded in.

CG: And how we fit into nature, the new nature we are building but the other nature that we have destroyed, and so there’s a lot of reconciliation going on and all of that certainly affects an artist’s practice if you’ve got your ear not to the ground but to the Internet to anything right? One other thing I said about my future trajectory was it’s not just the past year but the past couple of years I’ve been garnering more attention and more critical attention to my work and that’s been very exciting and, although an artist should have a healthy ego and believe in themselves, it certainly helps when other people start paying attention. So, I do have more confidence but this is also based on how long I’ve been making work, my years on the planet, and my years in New York. Something else in addition to just confidence is: I used to, because I was working in the tech industry, to support my “art habit”: before I got into teaching, I was sometimes terrified of not knowing a program or someone else saying “What? You don’t know how to do that?”

So, I would stay up night after night reading manuals so to make sure I would know technically how to “keep up with the boys,” as it was generally more boys. I’ve got to prove myself partially as a woman. I’ve got to prove twice that I’m smart enough or I can do the code and now I think no I’ve got things I want to say and a very limited amount of time and generally also considering “how can I say it”. It’s not as if I must use the most advanced system out there that costs tens of thousands of dollars. How can I be economical? Because that’s the other thing, artists are very good at being economical because historically we haven’t had funding. Thus, for example, Matthew Barney can produce a film for a million dollars that Hollywood takes 64 million dollars to produce and his is more stunning. So, economy is important to me too.

TG: Looking forward, do you think digital will become for the artists more intuitive, more natural in the connection? Do you think digital will get to the point that painting has reached, with an intuitive sense to it—as if a body extension and mind extension, so do you think it's moving in that way?

CG: I think it's already there—but I do see in terms of these technologies that they will disappear and what I mean by that, the Internet of Things (IoT) is going to become smaller and smaller and so all the things now that seem distinctive and artificial will become "natural." I think those distinctions will slowly disappear and blur again.

TG: But I think AI is particularly interesting, looking back to the 1940s with Claude Shannon and Alan Turing. They perceived AI as something artistic and something directly connected to humans as a mind-spirit state—not technical, and envisioned a thinking machine, which to them was the mind.

CG: Well if you think about that, there's been this obsession throughout human history. Automatons and bringing the inanimate to life from Pygmalion to a "golem" and the human fascination, not with the technology but infusing life or creating life and a mind but through a different portal.

TG: It's Lucille. Lucille is this person.

CG: Yes, so we'll see what happens.

TG: You've given Lucille life. Thank you, Carla—that is brilliant.

CG: Yes! Your questions were brilliant.

19.3 Conclusion

In this interview Carla Gannis touches upon many of the most pertinent topics impacting artists and museums in the digital age. Among these, of special importance to museums are her observations on audience and how working in digital media affords new opportunities and multiple ways of connecting to the viewer, and reaching vast numbers of people across the globe, a journey from the gallery to the public square, such as Times Square and the Internet. The life of a digital work can have several states of being (Bowen et al. 2018) and Gannis stresses the cultural positioning of digital spaces within physical locations where varied large public audiences can encounter the work and where the artist can sense the feeling of reaction from the public.

> It's not like I'm just appealing to a sophisticated elite class, accessibility is another aspect of my work that is a conscious choice and so to have it in this context [Times Square] where I've had this much of a viewership every single night, almost reaching levels of the Internet but in a physical space. That is cool.

Carla Gannis's observations of issues encountered when digital art is on exhibit in museums, provide important insights to some of the critical barriers that museums are experiencing, in terms of display, issues of preservation and conservation, and cost issues associated with digital artist's tools. Further, Gannis speaks to issues of gender discrimination that permeate computer science, which has meant that women need to prove themselves to a higher standard and be more facile than men. Still, most critically, contemporary art museums have been slow to recognize the importance of showing digital art, which more than any other art form ties museums to the present, to relevance and participation, and brings into harmony, the self of the digital visitor, the museum onsite and offsite, and the conversations between the museum and the visitor, and lest not forget, the voice of the artist living and working in today's digital landscape.

As Gannis notes, moving from painterly tools and methods, to digital tools and methods, changes the message, the meaning and connections to the viewer. If museums choose not to engage with digital art and artists, the more time that passes, the less relevant the contemporary art museum will become, and the dustier it will appear to the visitor. On the other hand, as museums form creative partnerships with digital artists, not only exhibiting and acquiring their work, but including them in the process of these activities, the more excited and engaged visitors will be as they connect art and contemporary life in the digital ecosystem—a place and space in in which they too can participate and create.

As an artist, Gannis's work lives in both physical and digital space connecting with a wide audience, from art aficionados and art lovers to the general public and straddling the domains of high, pop, and commercial art in a seamless flow of artistic energy and thought, harking back to the likes of Andy Warhol and Robert Rauchenberg. This mixed media, multifaceted approach to art and identity is emerging as a movement across cultural boundaries and differences. Talking to Gannis about her journey from the 1990s to present, as one of discovery of art and self, of consciousness and emotion, of thinking and feeling digitally and working intuitively, speaks to her work as a digital artist conveying original and authentic ways of expression, that inspire and engage her audience.

As we observe how digital culture is radically changing art and life in the 21st century, we can see how digital art sits at the heart of that transformation, situating culture in global contexts and new understandings of what it means to be human in a sea of diverse cultural narratives and artistic visions. These new relationships challenge museums to be more inclusive and to work more in partnership with artists and their diverse communities.

References

Bowen JP, Giannini T, Polmeer G, Gannis C, Gardiner J, Kearney J, Wands B, Weinel J (2018) States of being: art and identity in digital space and time. In Bowen JP, Weinel J, Diprose G, Lambert N (eds) EVA London 2018 conference proceedings, Electronic Workshops in Computing (eWiC), BCS, pp 1–7. https://doi.org/10.14236/ewic/eva2018.1

Gannis C (2017) The augmented selfie. In Bowen JP, Weinel J, Diprose G, Lambert N (eds) EVA London 2017 conference proceedings, Electronic Workshops in Computing (eWiC), BCS, pp 319–326. https://doi.org/10.14236/ewic/eva2017.66

Gannis C (2018) Portraits in landscape, August 1, 2018—August 31, 2018. Midnight Moment, Times Square Arts. http://arts.timessquarenyc.org/times-square-arts/projects/midnight-moment/portraits-in-landscape/index.aspx. Accessed 8 Jan 2019

Giannini T, Bowen JP (2016) Curating digital life and culture: art and information. In Bowen JP, Weinel J, Diprose G, Lambert N (eds) EVA London 2016 conference proceedings, Electronic Workshops in Computing (eWiC), BCS, pp 237–244. https://doi.org/10.14236/ewic/eva2016.46

Klemperer LV (2018) Contemporary artist Carla Gannis takes on the selfie. Art Report, Artist Interviews, 4 Apr, 2018. http://artreport.com/contemporary-artist-carla-gannis-takes-on-the-selfie/. Accessed 9 Jan 2019

Lorenzin F (2016) The emojification of reality: interview with Carla Gannis. Digitcult. http://digicult.it/news/the-emojification-of-reality-interview-with-carla-gannis/. Accessed 9 Jan 2019

Rose F (2017) Young digital artists, anxious about … technology. The New York Times, 24 July 2017. https://www.nytimes.com/2017/07/24/arts/design/sothebys-digital-artists-bunker.html. Accessed 9 Jan 2019)

Salas S (2016) Altarpieces for the digital age. Hyperallergic, 9 Mar 2016. https://hyperallergic.com/278335/altarpieces-for-the-digital-age/. Accessed 9 Jan 2019

Sauerlaender T (2016) The new narrative portrayal of women: artist Carla Gannis interviewed by curator Tina Sauerländer. Artefuse, 17 Mar 2016. https://artefuse.com/2016/03/17/artist-carla-gannis-interviewed-by-curator-tina-sauerlander-124445/. Accessed 9 Jan 2019

Chapter 20
A Conceptual Artist Programming for Social Change

Rachel Ara and Tula Giannini

Abstract Rachel Ara describes herself as a conceptual and data artist, whose work brings to light the trials and tribulations of women in a male dominated world. Through her art, she summons disparate elements from past to present, physical and digital, recalling histories of feminism and memories of women in an alien world. We see red neon lights and red-light districts, Florentine nuns in the shuttered silence of cloisters weaving cloth in codes. We are experiencing the artworks of Rachel Ara that conjure vivid feminist images and convey powerful messages about women's states of being and consciousness, and consider issues of gender and sexuality, a theme that runs through her work. By comparison, the 2017 exhibition at the Tate Britain, *Queer British Art, 1861–1967*, put on view mostly familiar works of women by male artists, and reframed them as works by queer artists living at a time when that identity seemed camouflaged. As gender and sexual identity have come to the fore, queer art and artists take more visible forms of gender expression. In this new and emerging approach, Ara takes a lead position for conveying, and putting before us, a female perspective where the artist and her art are one. Using the sophisticated means of production that she has mastered, from computing, technology, systems and data analytics, all part of her palette of artistic expression, her art takes its place at the intersection of the digital and physical worlds. She is not married to one mode of making art, as she considers what is possible and what is practical, but in either case, it is her passion for art as an expression of ideas that provoke the viewer to think critically about issues of contemporary life. You might say that Ara is a "postdigital" artist who delves deeply into these issues, and speaks with an authentic voice uniquely hers, and this is reflected in her aesthetic sense of hands-on highly skilled methods of working that meld computing and programming, woodworking and technology, for making art and making a difference.

R. Ara (✉)
London, UK

T. Giannini
School of Information, Pratt Institute, New York, USA
e-mail: giannini@pratt.edu

T. Giannini and J. P. Bowen (eds.), *Museums and Digital Culture*,
Springer Series on Cultural Computing, https://doi.org/10.1007/978-3-319-97457-6_20

20.1 Introduction

The centerpiece of this chapter is an interview between Rachel Ara (https://www.2ra.co) and Tula Giannini that took place at the Victoria and Albert Museum (V&A) in London on December 15, 2018. Drawing on the many facets of her early career as a programmer, analyst and computer system designer, her keen understanding of current socio-political issues is mixed with humor and irony, while exploring feminist and queer concerns. Her artwork, *This Much I'm Worth* (Ara 2017b), shown in Fig. 20.1, makes a statement about the social milieu of the art market, saying, "the idea of the work is to make people think about how works are valued", and with this work, the more time spent viewing it, the more the visible price rises, increasing from £37,418 in 2017, to £78,233 in June 2018. Speaking about the work, Ara points out that value also refers to human value, and the depreciating value construct around

Fig. 20.1 *This Much I'm Worth* (the self-evaluating artwork), featured on the cover of *FT Wealth* in summer 2018 (Pickford 2018). Interactive artwork by Rachel Ara, 2017, British data and conceptual artist. (Photograph © Anise Gallery, with permission of the artist)

women. A hybrid work, that merges physical and digital, exemplifies a mixed reality state, and points to an ascending genre of digital art that will no doubt take its place in museum galleries of the future (Fig. 20.1).

As an artist in residence at the V&A, Ara showcases her artistic vision with the work, *The Transubstantiation of Knowledge* (Ara 2018b), that was showcased in the London Design Festival 2018 (V&A 2018). It uses digital technology featuring holograms to retell the story of how Florentine nuns in the Renaissance became exploited laborers for the merchants and church. It also drew comparisons to the women workers at the museum today. Ara's artist profile (Ara 2018a) reflects broadly 21st-century trends in the arts, mainly artists that bring artistic vision to comment on key social and cultural issues, and which are also those that occupy the concerns of museums and other cultural institutions from equity, diversity and inclusion to women's rights and identity.

20.2 Artworks and Projects

Photographs and detailed information on each project are available online (https://www.2ra.co) (Figs. 20.2 and 20.3).

> Rachel Ara … explores the relationships between gender, technology and systems of power … *This Much I'm Worth* (The self-evaluating artwork) is part of a wider body of work that addresses feminist issues, conspiracies, of silence and misinformation. (It) has been made all

Fig. 20.2 The artist at the V&A directing a hologram of a nun in the work "The Transubstantiation of Knowledge". This image was taken through a Microsoft HoloLens. (Photograph © Rachel Ara/DoubleMe, with permission of the artist)

Fig. 20.3 *The Ancestor*, by Rachel Ara, 2017. **Left**: At the V&A *Friday Lates*, Victoria and Albert Museum, London, UK, 2018. (Photograph © Rachel Ara). **Right**: At the Arsenale, Venice, Italy, 2018. (Photograph © Rachel Ara)

the more complex by my own ambition to work with only women experts in fields dominated by men. (Ara 2017a, b)

20.3 Interview

Tula Giannini: It's wonderful to be here with you today, Rachel – being at the V&A where you've been an artist in residence – I hope that was a good experience for you.

Rachel Ara:Yes, very exciting. It's been a fantastic experience. After spending 30 years in the IT industry working predominately with men, coming to a museum with a demographic of 70% women has been an eye opener. Not only are the people engaging but they're interested in what you've got to say which creates a productive environment especially in research. It's been wonderful.

TG: That's great. So, I thought that we would begin with your critically acclaimed work, *This Much I'm Worth*, the self-evaluating artwork of 2017 – at once a physical and digital work of art – it would seem to embody key elements of the postdigital age, as it incorporates audience interaction and contemporary themes, meanings and messages from gender equity and identity to political messages, human states of being and questions of personal data, and surveillance. So, what I thought you might

Fig. 20.4 *This Much I'm Worth* (The self-evaluating artwork) with the artist Rachel Ara. (Photograph © Sculpted With Light, with permission of the artist)

talk about that work and how it brings together the digital and physical work. I think this is a very distinctive quality.

RA: That's interesting. As I said before, I don't distinguish digital from anything else.

TG: You're postdigital.

RA: It's just another material and tool. For this concept, I was looking at valuations of work especially by gender, how we value work and that's what I wanted to have the conversation about

TG: Was this work an expression of certain messages you had in mind?

RA: Many messages. I always think a work should have a multiplicity of meanings. There's got to be all these layers, so you're pulling people in and those people go on their own journey. There are messages in everything – the materials, even the weight – it's nearly half a ton. The fact that the work is hung has created technical challenges for me, but it had to be suspended from the wall to work conceptually. The frame was modeled on a sex shop sign I saw in Soho which used an arrow to point to where the action was. I used this format to reference the sex trade and how values are placed on women's' heads. The structure of the work mirrored the metal armature on the neon sign and then of course the orangy-red neon digit again referencing the sex trade – it also alludes to the hue of the original nixie lights, old calculator lights, that I used in the original prototype back in 2013 (Fig. 20.4).

TG: I didn't realize that. They didn't mention that in the *Financial Times* (Pickford 2018).

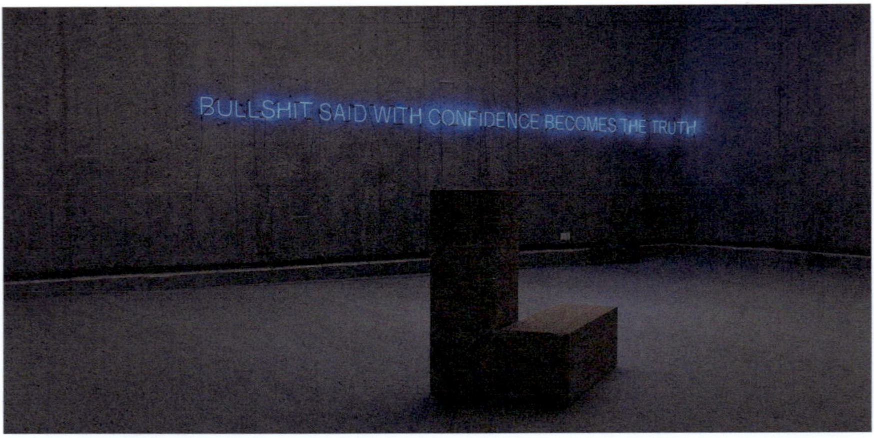

Fig. 20.5 *Cocksure (is anything ever what it seems), 2016*. CAD and Rendered Gallery with Neon Sign. (Image © Rachel Ara, http://www.2ra.co/cocksure-2016)

RA: No, they didn't. It's funny that the feminist aspects were ignored. Maybe that was a unconscious bias? The guy who was interviewing me was more focused on the technical aspects – surveillance, interaction and the endorsers – the calculating and valuing algorithms.

TG: So, this is very interesting – the red color, the Neon –

RA: Yes, the red-light districts, the model/sex worker signs in Soho. Women for sale. It's about how women are commodified and priced. As a woman, I've always found that disturbing and abhorrent.

TG: So, when you say *This Much I'm Worth*, it can also refer to the worth of the human being.

RG: Exactly.

TG: That's right, and here he's ignoring the states of being and human values.

RA: Because they're so linked in a sense, aren't they?

TG: Is it the role of the artist to convey their message in this type of work, which is a complex work. Do you see that within museums there could be better ways of communicating these messages? If the work is just there without messages, does each person conjure their own message. But I think it's so interesting and important hearing more specifically from the artist in the artist's words in a sense, or thoughts.

RA: That's why it's so important to utilize the correct materials and to consider the work from as many aspects as possible so you can subconsciously lead people down a path – but you can't control them. If the viewer sees red neon, there's a possibility they form an association in their mind to red-light districts or something similar. Saying that, nowadays there's a broader association with neon as a trope of the art world – there's so many artists using neon because it's quick. Artists with a budget can come up with inane sentences and then have it made up in neon, and then you've got your artwork (Fig. 20.5).

TG: I saw a few of those at the Royal Academy Summer Exhibition in 2017.

RA: Yes, they're everywhere.

TG: What some museums are doing now, is that you can see videos of the artist speaking about their work on their website or the museum site.

RA: I believe that certainly adds to the experience. I've seen that happen in a few museums and really enjoyed it. After spending time with the work and forming your own opinions, then it's great to watch the artist speak, then return to the work and you see it with different eyes – it opens it up. It's allowing you to look to access the work in different ways. I watched a film yesterday by Rachel Mclean which was excellent, but I didn't pick up on all the layers and connections. When I went home, I watched an interview with her talking – you'd be interested in her films – they're very much talking about digital in contemporary culture – the interview revealed more and more layers of meaning which opened up the work even further. During open studios at the V&A, I allowed visitors to look at all my notes and research for "The Transubstantiation of Knowledge" – which were quite extensive. It really blew their mind – exposing all the connections and depths – you could see they were really getting a lot out of it. Some even came back the next open studio and brought friends. What's interesting and new for me is the museum audience – unlike an art gallery audience – is very much engaged in the pursuit of knowledge and they love being taken down the rabbit hole. They are very different audiences.

I also think it's empowering for younger artists to understand how the more established ones approach their work, why they have made certain decisions, utilized certain materials … And for me the labor was so important in that piece because then you can create that narrative as you go along and have a degree of autonomy and independence. If you make the work, there are so many more layers in the stories you can tell.

Many artists who make digital works don't do the coding, they often don't even fabricate the physical work. Nowadays it's all about having the money to commission the making – which is about having a certain privilege – in the developing countries, you're not going to have neon signs all over walls. For me, especially *This Much I'm Worth*, the work was very much about the labor; it was very labor intensive, specifically female labor. So, it was making that point as well. But then you're talking about the digital in objects, nothing is devoid of digital anymore? That's because digital has touched everything.

TG: It does. That's why I refer to that as the digital ecosystem, and everyone is always connected to it – that's what I was thinking looking at that work. Can you talk about how you see your work developing from this? How it's been developing and how it will develop moving into the future.

RA: Practically, to make large work like *This Much I'm Worth* – you need a big studio and some funding. Previously I've funded myself through work and a fellowship but there are so few opportunities for funding this year. There's a possibility that I may have to let go my studio which will mean I won't be able to physically make largescale work anymore. It's been happening to other artists as well. My work will have to take a new form. I've been putting in proposals for film funding as this is something you can do from a smaller space– but I'm going to miss making in a workshop/studio, it keeps my sanity. Being at a computer all day can drive you a bit mad. Ideally, I'd like to do the two combined, working on computer projects and then physically working with something because that gives me the time to think as well. Thinking with my hands is very important – especially the way I work.

TG: And maybe that's interesting, because filmmaking and video have bubbled up.

RA: Definitely. If you look at what younger artists are doing – there's a huge increase in film and video. This change is probably being driven by people not being able to afford studios, people haven't got money, and there's no funding. The work adapts to the artists environment.

TG: You might be aware of the Turner Prize – and this year, 2018 they were all film and video.

RA: And this might stem from that. I was speaking to a sculptor last night and he said he's downgrading his studio, from 1,000 square foot to 350 square foot. I said you're not going to be able to continue making large work. He said he outsources the work anyway, so the process is becoming more like a conveyor belt – more commercialized. Well for me, being hands-on is so important because that's where the thinking happens and that's when things change – And now suddenly to have this very clinical idea that you might draw something in CAD and is output to fabrication. You've missed this whole in between aspect of looking, standing back, literally sculpting with the ideas and materials as they develop.

TG: Do you think of *This Much I'm Worth* as a sculpture?

RA: Yes. it's a sculpture. Although I planned and drew it in CAD, it changed as I went along because I didn't know how to do lots of the engineering parts and how things would fit together – it evolved as I learnt. Being hands on allowed me to consider the work throughout the build so if it isn't conveying the message that I want then you implement changes. I also like to consider and tweak the aesthetic as I progress. You also get to understand the materials as you delve more into the build so that may change your direction. If you do it in a clinical manner – CAD to finished product, then you're not going to get that. It loses a resonance (Fig. 20.6).

TG: You probably have a lot of the digital skills, is it a totally digital process when you're doing film and video now.

RA: It can be. You can still make digital mistakes – and this is what's interesting – this film I've recently proposed, is another CGI piece and very hyper-realistic. My working with new programs, part of the process is making mistakes – digital mistakes, spending time understating the program and its capabilities and exploiting them. If I had a budget and hired an animator – then there would be a limit to the amount of time spent animating and not the opportunity to revisit certain elements and change your mind over time. But if I'm doing it myself, I can spend time with it. I can tweak the facial expressions, I can sit back, I can be with it. And that again is the sculpting – so that can happen in the digital world. There's that time to think, to produce, to reflect, to change, and that's when the work is honed down to being something quite special.

TG: But I think this distinguishes you from many other artists who don't have a high level of digital ability.

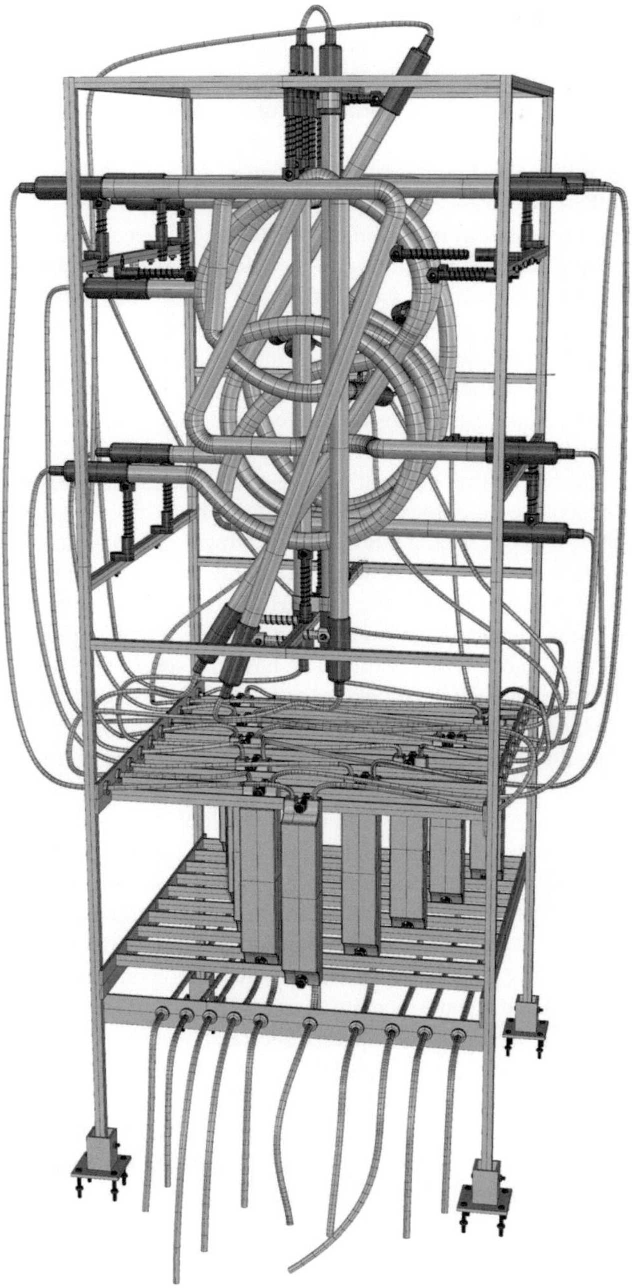

Fig. 20.6 CAD drawing by the artist Rachel Ara for a digit of *This Much I'm Worth*, 2017. (Image © Rachel Ara)

RA: Possibly, but I put some of that down to laziness and people wanting quick results. I know I'm sounding old fashioned. Maybe it's a time issue – no one seems to have spare time anymore? The resources are out there on the Internet for people to learn most skills for free. You go on YouTube, you watch a video … There's no excuse. I spend a lot of time learning skills to undertake the work. I guess in part it's because I'm ambitious and demand certain things of the work – and if I don't do it no one else will.

TG: Do you think that in the training of artists now, because if they're going to do digital art, there needs to be a lot more technical ability built into that?

RA: I guess they should get some of that at school and then if they need to learn something specific for a project then there are many free resources out there as I was saying. For example, I've been using YouTube to brush up on some of my programming skills because when I programmed, I used COBOL and mostly non-object orientated programming languages, so I'm having to catch up on more modern languages like Python.

TG: There are some things you can't do – because either the skillset is so specific, or it requires expensive equipment. In terms of my last work it was the blowing of the neon numbers. I work with a woman neon blower called Julia Bickerstaff who blows all my numbers. I provide her with 1:1 detailed CAD drawings and she blows them precisely to the millimeter so they fit perfectly into my structures. It takes great skill to get the accuracy and also neon blowing involves a very expensive piece of kit … but most things you can do yourself if you have the space. With digital, you don't need the space. You just need the mental space, which again, some people don't have because they're balancing a job, career or caring with the artwork.

TG: So, if you didn't have much ability in computational methods, that would need learning.

RA: Possibly, you would need some understanding or some reason to learn but that doesn't preclude people from making or having things made for them. I just think a deeper understanding resonates in the work… but you don't have to be an expert. I personally just don't like to have to rely on other people and like to do things in my own time – so having the skills is empowering and works for me.

TG: This leads to my next question, which is, what do you think characterizes the ways in which artists and you especially use computing, AI and machine learning and how this compares to that of companies such as Facebook, Twitter, and Google. Do these technologies hold great potential for art or is there a dark side?

RA: If you look at Facebook, Twitter and Google, they are writing real algorithms that must function in order for their business to survive. They are writing complex and functional systems that they can't afford to fail – probably with capitalist motivations. The role of the artist is not mimic this, it's to understand what these corporations are doing, the implications of these algorithms and question them. For example, if these corporations are being unethical – selling people's data or manipulating events, then artists need to respond to that, it doesn't even have to be a digital response. You don't need that high-end level of knowledge in terms of computing to respond –just an understanding or simply an opinion – it's a massive difference.

TG: So, what do you think when you see people using AI to create art?

RA: Is it real AI? Faked AI? Does it matter? What are the motivations? How is it working? What datasets has it been trained on? I guess we're beginning to explore the many questions around this type of art. What you must understand is that many of the curators don't fully understand computing or AI. The art world is in many ways lagging too far behind the science world. It's hard to distinguish the genuine questioning work from the work that applies the word AI to make it more appealing and current. *This Much I'm Worth* is not an AI piece – maybe it alludes to the potential of AI and creates a myth that it's sentient, but it is been curated into shows around AI. It utilizes very simple programs, in industrial terms. For anything that has a functioning algorithm, people think AI, AI, AI, because it's a buzzword. So, there's a cynical take on this, that people are associating the buzzwords such as VR, AR, mixed reality AI with their work to give it currency. Therefore, the artist is creating this myth themselves about what they are using in the process. Curators might be blindly picking up on this and marketing the work as groundbreaking or a first and not questioning the quality.

Artists can be cynical themselves and play into this game. Is it bad to say that? Well no it's not, because it's true and I think that's why sometimes you get very dead art. There are also many computational people who can do complex, clever things, but for me there must be more for it to be art.

AI creating art is to a degree sensational and the results potentially infinite. But is this art or science? There will always be artists perusing such routes, probably scientists as well.

TG: Well then you see the digital media screen type of art and then you see commercial art, and sometimes it's hard to distinguish them, so it blurs the lines.

RA: It's very much about who's doing the art and the context. Take for example Martin Creed's scrunched up bit of A4 paper, because of his provenance this work has value – well to the art world it does. If it had been done by some other unknown artist, with the same intention, it would be worthless. I believe the art world is frightened of being laughed at. If someone's got the right provenance then they'll feel bold enough to curate them, and I think in a sense that's happened with my work, because despite coming to practice art quite late, I have a track record in the tech industry, so I'll be taken seriously in those terms – especially as a woman. People are buying into myth in the art world.

TG: Interesting. I haven't thought about that. Do you think that the digital has come in with its own set of myths?

RA: Oh, absolutely, and that was partially reflected in the work, *This Much I'm Worth*. The aesthetic Heath Robinson over complicated look. Everything appears to be exposed – wires and guts, but essentially its controlled by a simple (in industrial terms) program, but people don't want to know that. They want to buy into this myth … (**TG**: I did) … well there you go – the whole point is that you do, because I'm selling you the myth – the myth is the work. Do you see what I mean, to enjoy it, and to explore? Artists are exploiting that.

TG: But do you see that what you did has a very strong physical presence, so that changes it totally. And it's the way the work is constructed, and has a certain look, a hand-crafted appearance – you can sense the artist's hand, which is something – so not as if it was just a little program.

RA: It's playing backwards and forwards between these dialogues as well. It can't be dismissed because of its size.

TG: I believe that that was very important about it – it has a Wizard of Oz feeling.

RA: Yes. And when you talk a lot about digital work, etc. I think I've spoken about this, artists tend to outsource the coding … Is that one of the questions you were asking?

TG: No, but that's an interesting one I hadn't thought about it.

RA: How much are artists really involved in their work? Does it matter, should it matter? Surely, you've got to understand the coding, to know the mistakes, to know the biases, to know all that, in order to create the work. I guess painters do outsource their paintings. For example, Damien Hirst has never painted a spot painting … you can feel that in the work – but is that relevant?

What's quite interesting is I often get asked by fellow artists, not curators, who makes my work. Who do I get to do the programming, who builds the structure? There's the assumption that you play little or no part in the making. It always surprises me how little involvement artists have nowadays in their own works. Due to lack of funding I've always had to do all the aspects of the build … from welding to coding … but I don't ever think I've considered it not as an option. It wouldn't suit the way my mind works. I have to get stuck in.

TG: It's almost a team or has almost an industrial model to a certain extent.

RA: Yes, art does now, and this is what you're competing with, artists who have studios and teams of people. And this is why the singular artist is going under. Because you cannot compete with that. For example, when I was installing my work in Venice last year for a show, some of the other artists had sent their assistants out to install their work – I guess that meant they could be in their studios in London or wherever and carrying on with their creative work and I'm in the gallery taking time out to install and deinstall – as well as transport the work myself. It was a learning experience. To be honest I would say that 80% of my waking time is on the non-creative aspects of the artwork – admin, applications, correspondence, transport, packaging, etc.

This Much I'm Worth will be going to big museums in Vienna and Korea in 2019. I'm spending lots of time talking to the galleries, writing texts, processing images, designing packaging, looking at parts getting made in the locations as its cheaper than transporting etc. – logistics really. It's interesting because that's the reality of my art world. It takes up so much time doing the behind the scenes stuff. Whereas if you are represented by one of the big galleries which is very rare – I assume all that is taken care of – so that the artist can focus on the creativity. I guess this is why you see the same artists in all the biennials and venues because the galleries have the money, time and connections to do this – they're throwing money at their artists.

TG: So how do you become one of those artists they're throwing money at?

RA: I've no idea. They want to see longevity and productivity, and maybe to have that longevity, you need money behind you – its very money driven.

TG: Yes, you can see that. So that's a very tough space to be in.

RA: It's tough, but it's easier when you're older because you can see it more objectively and understand what's happening. When I look at the young people in our studio, and you look at the painters who are doing relatively well currently, they fit into a particular stereotype. They're young, they're good looking. They're subject matter is often sexual – popular with the collectors. The menopause isn't as attractive!

TG: When you think about it, because I've been looking at some of these shows and festivals, you're right, except for some of the very established artists.

RA: And I understand it – in a way it fuels my work. This is partly what my work addresses. How we're evaluating work and placing values on it?

TG: And looking at this next question, – do you see your creative process continuing to combine physical sculpture with digital communication and interaction or do you see a different path?

RA: In terms of what I'm I going to work on next it's very much led by the idea – so I'm not thinking digital/physical – I'm thinking about the concept and how best to realize it.

I've got sketchbooks with hundreds of ideas. It's just what one can do currently, what position I'm in – physically with the space and financially. At the moment, my studio is crammed full of work, so I don't have much space to make. I also don't have any funding so that will dictate what I can and can't do. You don't necessarily need money to create work, but you need it to buy time. Time is money.

I guess physically making and digital form my natural toolset so will appear in most works at some point.

I've got two big shows coming up in Vienna and Korea and I'll be expanding on the work of *This Much I'm Worth* which will involve a lot of physical and programming work.

I also have another project on the go that's completely physical and non-digital. It's a smallish installation dealing with issues around this subject of FGM (Female Genital Mutilation). I've just finished reading a couple of books on FGM. I found it very moving and felt compelled to do some work around the subject.

I also have some screen-based ideas that I mentioned earlier.

TG: Another question I'd like to ask, coming out of our conversation about how you conceptualize yourself as an artist, it seems to me, you don't think you're a digital artist.

RA: No, I don't think of myself as a digital artist. For me an artist is someone trying to make sense of the world – initiating dialogues. Digital is just a tool – like a craft – I don't distinguish it from any other craft. I'm led by the concept not the tool.

To be honest – I guess initially I did emphasize my digital skills. After 30 years of hard labor in the tech industry, I had a lot of knowledge – and digital was/is trending in the art world. I only started practicing five years ago at aged 47 – and let's be honest – there's not a lot of interest in unestablished middle-aged women. Older women aren't cool – well they are – it's just nobody realizes it yet! Therefore, letting people know I knew what I was talking about made people take me more seriously.

I knew my work was good because on my art foundation course I was picked up by a dealer for work that's still being shown today and at Goldsmiths I received the

Neville Burston Award, for being the most outstanding student. But, it's having the confidence to say that. How do you market yourself – get people to notice?

Terminology – it's all about terminology – selling yourself. "IT" is dull. But when you change the "IT" to "Tech" it suddenly becomes more current and interesting – but it's the same thing. People don't "write programs" any more they "code algorithms" – same thing but cooler language. It's like the old days when you're at a party and someone asks what you do, and you say you're a COBOL programmer; everyone disappears. But it is about branding and rebranding and the art world has bought into this. And I guess that's what I picked-up on quite quickly. So, tech is cool, algorithms are cool, complex is cool, and AI is cool – menopause isn't but I'm working on that!

Coming back to terminology – I was having this conversation the other day with someone about AI and we were not understanding each other at all. When I got to the core of the misunderstanding – I thought we were having a conversation about Artificial Intelligence and they thought we were talking about Artificial Insemination. This crudely illustrates a lot of the confusion people are having around understanding terminology. We need to agree on the core words and common understandings. I often go to meetings in the art world about digital/computational subjects for example conservation, acquisitions, process, and people are just not understanding each other.

I do think people in the art/museum world need to open up more to the digital and embrace people who do know about these subjects, and get them into help and advise – there's not a wheel to be reinvented – these are all trodden paths – maybe not in the art world. I was recently at a meeting on digital conservation – it's a huge subject – and they were trying to implement a strategic approach without one person in the room having a tech background.

What is digital, what is the meaning of digital? (Fig. 20.7).

20.4 Conclusion

Rachel Ara thinks art is as much about concept, method and materials, as it is about message and moment in time and place. This combination of elements, that underscore her works afford them a highly original framework for creating art that sets her work apart and defines a style that is at once new and exciting as it is memorable and lasting. Ara writes in her artist's statement (Ara 2018a):

> My work starts with an initial concept that evolves through long periods of research and developmental processes; construction, deconstruction, intuition, experimentation even sporadic mishaps that require a hands-on approach. As I work I gain a deeper understanding of possible materials and methods which help to refine the idea. Prototyping each piece in the studio, by building maquettes, pilot tests or by computer-based 3D Modelling (CAD).

The interview reveals the challenges of producing large artworks requiring a spacious studio. An artist that can work to scale, her art comes in many sizes, shapes, and media, but often takes the form of sculpture à la Ara, as her iconic work, *This Much I'm Worth*. Ara demonstrates the depth and scope of her artistic vision. We see this with the project, *Transubstantiation of Knowledge*, that she created for the V&A

Fig. 20.7 The artist in her studio, 2017. (Photograph © Andrew Porter, with permission of the artist)

in 2018 as an artist in residence, for which the Museum's art galleries were intrinsic to the work, mixing real and virtual objects (Ara 2018b):

> Within the chapel the installation takes the form of an audio guide with a HoloLens. Using the HoloLens, the viewer will be able to see and interact with holographic nuns in the chapel. Behind the church are cases with "false" objects mixed into the real V&A collections that substantiate the story and add more intrigue.

Able to take risks, and venture into new territory, with each of her artworks, Ara brings new ideas and new ways of making and seeing. Nothing repeated, nothing assumed, with change and innovation feeding creativity while bringing forth new works that inspire women as they challenge conventions of the past, raising consciousness of self, having the self-confidence to be oneself, and finding new forms of self-expression. Ara's work has that type of power.

Further Reading

Aesthetica (2015) Rachel Ara: reactive systems. Aesthetica Magazine, 15 Aug 2015. http://www.aestheticamagazine.com/rachel-ara-reactive-systems/. Accessed 12 Jan 2019

Ara R (2017a) The making of a digital (master) piece. In Bowen JP, Diprose G, Lambert N (eds) EVA London 2017 conference proceedings. Electronic Workshops in Computing (eWiC), BCS, pp 327–334. https://doi.org/10.14236/ewic/eva2017.67

Ara R (2017b) This much I'm worth. http://www.2ra.co/tmiwfull. Accessed 12 Jan 2019
Ara R (2018a) About—Rachel Ara. https://www.2ra.co/about. Accessed 27 Jan 2019
Ara R (2018b) Transubstantiation of Knowledge. https://www.2ra.co/tok. Accessed 27 Jan 2019
Elgammal A (2018) When the line between machine and artist becomes blurred. The Conversation, 16 Oct 2018. http://theconversation.com/when-the-line-between-machine-and-artist-becomes-blurred-103149. Accessed 12 Jan 2019
Feldman R (2018) VARI Artist Rachel Ara introduces mixed reality nuns to the V&A. V&A Blog, Victoria and Albert Museum, UK, 15 Aug 2018. https://www.vam.ac.uk/blog/museum-life/vari-artist-rachel-ara-introduces-mixed-reality-nuns-to-the-va. Accessed 12 Jan 2019
Groys B (2017) Art, technology, and humanism. E-Flux, 82, May 2017. https://www.e-flux.com/journal/82/127763/art-technology-and-humanism/. Accessed 12 Jan 2019
Pes J (2018) As museums across Europe Grapple with new data protection regulations, one artist is pushing them to think differently. Artnet News, 5 July 2018. https://news.artnet.com/art-world/meet-artist-challenging-gender-bias-data-protection-1312727. Accessed 12 Jan 2019
Pickford J (2018) Artist Rachel Ara poses unsettling questions for the art world. Special report. FT Wealth, Financial Times, 17 June 2018. https://www.ft.com/content/61f4e1f8-5391-11e8-84f4-43d65af59d43. Accessed 12 Jan 2019
Schneider T, Rea N (2018) Has artificial intelligence given us the next great art movement? Experts say slow down, the 'Field Is in Its Infancy'. Artnet News, 25 Sept 2018. https://news.artnet.com/art-world/ai-art-comes-to-market-is-it-worth-the-hype-1352011. Accessed 12 Jan 2019
Solanas V (1968) Scum Manifesto. Olympia Press
Stinson E (2018) What artists can teach us about making technology more human. Wired, 5 May 2018. https://www.wired.com/story/bell-labs-eat-only-human-mana-contemporary/. Accessed 12 Jan 2019
Sussman AL (2019) The challenges female artists face mid-career. Artsy, 11 Jan 2019. https://www.artsy.net/article/artsy-editorial-women-artists-survive-challenges-mid-career-stagnation. Accessed 14 Jan 2019
V&A (2018) 'The Transubstantiation of Knowledge' by Rachel Ara. London Design Festival 2018, Victoria and Albert Museum, UK, 15–23 Sept 2018. https://www.vam.ac.uk/articles/the-transubstantiation-of-knowledge-by-rachel-ara. Accessed 27 Jan 2019
Whitechapel Gallery (2018) The London open catalogue. Whitechapel Gallery, UK
WIA (2018) WIA artist profile: Rachel Ara. WIA, 7 Dec 2018. https://wearewia.com/wia-artist-profile-rachel-ara/. Accessed 27 Jan 2019
Widewalls (2017) The serious relationship of art and technology. Editorial, Widewalls, 25 July 2017. https://www.widewalls.ch/the-serious-relationship-of-art-and-technology/. Accessed 12 Jan 2019
Zhexi G (2018) Art versus Silicon Valley: are artists losing the conceptual advantage? Frieze, 25 Sept 2018. https://frieze.com/article/art-versus-silicon-valley-are-artists-losing-conceptual-advantage. Accessed 12 Jan 2019

Part VII
Education

Chapter 21
The Education of a Digital Fine Artist

Bruce Wands

Abstract While early experiments in digital and technological art began in the 1960s, degree programs that focused on it did not emerge until the 1980s. Most digital art pioneers were self-taught and created their work at research centers and universities. Emerging digital artists were primarily fine art students who supplemented their education with courses in computer science, graphics and programming. The first MFA in Computer Arts was established at the School of Visual Arts in 1986. The goal of the program was to provide an academic and studio environment in which artists would learn about the theory, history and practice of digital art. Several MFA degree programs followed and continue to be established. While museums were resistant to this type of art early on, international organizations and a small group of galleries embraced it. Museum curators who had experience and an interest in digital art were few and far between. As digital artists began to redefine the contemporary art landscape, museums and galleries began to take an interest in exhibiting this creative work. The development of the World Wide Web in the mid-1990s radically changed both the museum and contemporary art world, and as well the education of artists. This chapter explores the parallel developments of digital art education; changes in how art is created, experienced and exhibited; new forms of contemporary art and the approaches modern curators are using to showcase this art.

21.1 Introduction

Early experiments in digital and technological art began in the 1960s. There was some early work done with photographing mathematical images from oscilloscopes in the 1950s by Ben F. Laposky, which he named "Oscillons." These images were analog in nature, yet they established the groundwork for the mathematical images used in early digital art. Most digital art pioneers were self-taught and created their work at research centers like Bell Labs and universities, such as MIT and the University of Utah. Emerging digital artists were mostly fine art students who supplemented their education with courses in Computer Science that taught graphics and programming.

B. Wands (✉)
MFA Computer Arts, School of Visual Arts, New York, USA

T. Giannini and J. P. Bowen (eds.), *Museums and Digital Culture*,
Springer Series on Cultural Computing, https://doi.org/10.1007/978-3-319-97457-6_21

The first MFA in Computer Arts in the United States was established at the School of Visual Arts in 1986. The goal of the program was to provide an academic and studio environment in which artists would learn about the theory, history and practice of digital art. Early graduates went on to careers as fine artists, animators, programmers, multimedia producers and teachers. While museums were resistant to this type of art early on, international organizations and a small group of galleries embraced it.

The resistance was based on the lack of digital art to fit into the traditional fine art categories of painting, drawing and sculpture. Digital art was also difficult to archive. Most prints were not made using archival inks and papers. Digital technology was also changing rapidly and quickly became outdated. Without ongoing technical support, a great deal of early digital art became inoperable, also adding to the non-archival criticisms. Museum curators who had experience and an interest in digital art were few and far between. International organizations, such as ACM SIGGRAPH, ISEA International, Ars Electronica, V2_ and ZKM, celebrated this new form of creativity and helped to nurture its development through festivals, exhibitions, artist residencies and the establishment of digital archives. As digital artists began to redefine the contemporary art landscape, museums and galleries began to take a deeper interest and exhibited this creative work.

The development of the World Wide Web in the mid-1990s radically changed both the museum and contemporary art world and art education. Museum collections began to appear online, and interactive exhibits proliferated in fine art, science, and other museums, as a new way to engage their audiences. Websites allowed artists to sidestep the traditional museum/gallery hierarchy and provide global access to their creative work. New forms of art, such as "net art" emerged using the Internet global network as their creative medium and platform. What follows is a look at how the art education process has changed under the influence of digital software and technology. It will also include descriptions of new forms of contemporary art that are emerging and how they are being integrated into art education. How curriculum is developed for digital art education will be contrasted with traditional methods of art education curriculum development. We will end with a discussion of how emerging artists are becoming a part of the contemporary art world and how museums and galleries are exhibiting these new forms of art.

21.2 Traditional Art Education

Before we discuss the education of digital fine artists, it will be helpful to review the elements of a traditional fine art education. There are four main pillars that support the education of an artist: Art History, Theory, Practice and Critique. Without a thorough knowledge of art history, it is difficult for an artist to put their work in context of the artists who have preceded them. While history and research are academic pursuits, they are vital to artistic development. The wealth of written and visual information on art history is immense and narrowing down those areas that an individual artist finds interesting and relevant to their unique form of creative expression allows them to refine their approach to their work.

There are differing opinions on the amount of research and writing that should be undertaken as part of the artist's education. The author believes that one day in a typical five-day week is appropriate. Two days a week represents 40% of their time and the other aspects of studio work and critique will then suffer. Art theory is a vital part of an artist's development. Learning how theorists and philosophers view art and the place it occupies in traditional and contemporary culture and society are extremely relevant. Also, what is the individual artist trying to communicate and how does their practical work achieve this end? Many artists take an intuitive approach to art making, and it is often helpful for them to understand the sources of this intuition and creative impulses that drive their work This helps them to incorporate more meaning into their work, rather than making it a simple or complex technical exercise.

Art practice is the actual time spent making art. Teaching an artist how to transform their creative ideas into form and experience is one of the most important elements of an art education. While the traditional metaphor of the isolated artist in their top floor studio with a skylight spending their time painting, drawing and sculpting from a model, still life constructs or from their imagination is still a very valid behavioral model, today's artists now also have a computer as an active creative partner in this endeavor. This can range from using the computer to help test sketch ideas, color palettes, working from reference photo images or building sculptural prototypes to altering the creative environment into a darkened room with the artist intently staring at the screen as they create their work. The final element of an artist's education is critique, whether it is self-criticism, individual critiques with their teacher or group critiques from their classmates. Critique provides a forum for discussion and the exchange of ideas, reactions to their creative work and suggestions to improve it or take it in new directions. Critique is, in and of itself, an art. From the artist's point of view, it is a way for them to present, explain and defend their work.

As an artist and a teacher, the author always asks the artist how far the critique should go. It is a delicate and sensitive area and the role of the critic is not to tell the artist what they should be doing or dismantle or discourage their ideas and inspiration. An artist should always walk away from a critique with a deeper understanding of their work and ideas on how to refine and improve it.

21.3 Digital Art Education

Now that we have reviewed the foundation of an art education, it is relevant to discuss how things have evolved, now that we are in the digital era. Some of the elements have remained the same and others have changed drastically, and new ones continue to emerge. One primary example is courses in programming, which allow the artist to create images and animation through algorithms and mathematics, rather than by hand. Looking at them in the same order as above, art theory and history, especially contemporary art history, continue to evolve, although at a much more rapid pace. One of the key factors in this is the ubiquity of the Internet and growing number of art history resources that exist online. While there continues to be a large-scale migration of imagery from museum collections to the Internet, digital art organizations are also focusing on developing historical archives of art, photography, video, interactive art, etc. European organizations became involved early in this process and there has been a positive change in the United States to encourage grant-funded opportunities for digital archiving and publishing that did not exist before.

The author has created a website (http://artofthedigitalage.com), which is a waypoint for digital art, new forms of contemporary art, and creative self-expression (Wands 2017). It contains links to digital art organizations, archives, academic resources, lists of digital artists, videos and extensive bibliographies, as well as research tools, assembled by the author and experts in the field. It is an evolving resource and continues to grow and develop over time, keeping track of recent developments in the field and emerging artists. Two helpful research links exist this website. The first is EPI-Search (http://isce-library.net/epi.aspx), a search engine that allows you to search blocks of text from 50–10,000 words. It is a very useful tool, since you can input artist statements, articles, chapters, lists of key words, etc. One major strength is that it often gives results that would not have otherwise been received through a standard search engine. For those involved with date-based searches on the Internet, the Internet Archive (http://archive.org), is a diverse archive that contains, at the time of this writing, 279 billion web pages, 1 million books and texts, 4 million audio recordings (including 160,000 live concerts), 3 million videos (including 1 million television news programs), 1 million images, and 100,000 software programs. One of the best features is the Wayback Machine, which allows you to trace the history of URLs over time and see what they looked like weeks, months and years ago. This is particularly helpful with net art, which came to prominence during the mid-1990s and was created using web browsers that changed and were updated frequently, often making the art inoperable.

21.4 Digital Art Practice

The process of art making has been changed by technology and software, yet also remains somewhat the same. Most artists begin a creative project with small sketches and writing down their ideas first. This is normally done with a sketchpad and handwritten notes. More and more, artists are utilizing smart phones and laptops to do the writing and sketching. As their ideas develop, the final form of the work begins to take shape. Painting, drawing and sculpture have been in existence for thousands of years and will continue to remain a vital part of fine art, and it is important to note that digital media and techniques do not replace traditional media, but augment them. Many painters have embraced digital tools, and some painters are also shifting their media from oil and water-based paint to digital media and printing methods, either in the conceptual or final stages. Technologies, such as the Wacom Cintiq tablet and the new Wacom Intuos Pro Paper, which can also work with paper and a pen, provide artist friendly interfaces to more closely mimic the sketchpad, canvas and pencil or brush. While these technologies assist the artist on the front end of the creative process, printing technology has also evolved to become more archival and diverse. Early digital prints were crude dot matrix prints with non-archival inks and papers. The development of digital photography has driven advances in printing to the point where now, pigment-based inks are available and archival paper is commonly used for digital fine art printmaking and archival photographs.

21.4.1 Digital Sculpture

While the changes in drawing and painting have been largely evolutionary in step with the advances in software technology, the field of sculpture has undergone revolutionary changes with the development of 3D modeling software and the ability to output these forms using 3D printing and the subtractive process of CNC milling. The traditional process of sculpture involved sketching and building small-scale models first to work out the specific details of the object. Once these had been made and materials had been chosen, the sculpture was either carved or cast into the final form. The new digital toolset has revolutionized the way in which sculpture is conceived and created. While the initial transfer of the creative idea continues to be sketches and small-scale models, modern sculptors often use 3D software to assist them in their work.

This does not have to be an exclusive approach, as many sculptors use 3D software to conceive their work and traditional methods to make it. However, increasing numbers of young sculptors are exclusively using digital tools to help refine the creative concept and to build the final version. There are many advantages to this. While the creation of small-scale models does allow the sculptor to handle and view the object in a tactile way, 3D software enables them to see it from any perspective, apply different materials and textures and even place the sculpture in a location through placing it in a digital photograph or 3D environment. Making scale models is time consuming and being able to see a software model of the sculpture and scale it into various sizes is a huge advantage in its design, as is viewing it in stone, metal, wood, etc., before even making a physical model. 3D software is also incredibly precise down to a few thousands of an inch, which allows more creative freedom when making a sculpture that has many interlocking parts. One additional advantage is that by using 3D printing and CNC sculpting, the precision and options available in the software give the artist amazing flexibility when conceiving the final work and, if desired, producing multiple editions. This does not eliminate the tactile element. Many sculptors will hand finish a 3D printed or CNC carved sculpture or use it as a cast for another material of their choosing (Fig. 21.1).

The software used in digital sculpture classes is either 3D solid modeling-based software or mesh/surface-based such as Autodesk Maya, Fusion 360, SOLIDWORKS 3D and others. There are a wide variety of 3D printers and CNC machines

Fig. 21.1 *Solar–Sailer,* Hwayong Jung, 2011, Kinetic sculpture and interactive installation. Constructed using digital fabrication techniques, this sculpture uses a microcontroller to transform weather data into wave motion of the component parts. The goal of the piece is to have people experience the invisible data around them in new ways and create a unique experience of our natural surroundings. A documentation video can be viewed online (http://vimeo.com/25466139)

on the market. CNC machines are widely used by industry and can range in price from under $1,000 to many thousands of dollars depending on the sophistication of the machine, the number of axes it can carve, etc. ShopBot is a popular entry-level CNC machine. The same parameters exist for 3D printers. Entry-level machines such as the MakerBot are popular and high-end machines include Stratasys and others. Fortunately, there are many service bureaus that will make 3D prints and CNC objects for artists. Very often, a digital sculpture lab will have entry-level machines and students with large-scale projects or specialized needs can use these service bureaus.

21.4.2 3D Animation, Motion Graphics and Video Art

Another fertile area for digital fine artists is 3D animation, motion graphics, and digital video. There is a long history of experimental animation and video art and the use of these media in digital fine art, either as films or videos. Incorporating them into installations or interactive artwork is relatively new territory. Pioneers in the field who used analog techniques that set the stage for this form of creative expression include Oskar Fischinger, Thomas Wilfred, Norman McClaren and John Whitney, Sr. While 3D animation involves the use of three-dimensional objects and space, it can also visualize natural phenomena such as fire, water, clouds and other abstract visual effects. Motion graphics is widely used in television commercials and one of the key features is the ability to combine layers of 3D animation, 2D animation, stop motion animation, 2D graphics and live video.

Naturally, motion graphics offers great potential to digital fine artists looking to work in a time-based medium. Both 3D/2D animation and motion graphic elements can also be incorporated into video art. Software used for teaching digital artists includes Autodesk Maya and Cinema 4D for 3D animation. Autodesk Maya is the software commonly used by Hollywood studios to produce 3D animated feature films. It is a complicated piece of software with a steep learning curve, but also provides superior control over all aspects of 3D animation. Cinema 4D is used more by television commercial production houses, as it is less complicated than Maya and the production cycle to complete animation is more in line with the tight deadlines demanded by commercial production.

The most popular software used for motion graphics is Adobe After Effects. Adobe Premiere, Apple Final Cut Pro and Avid Media Composer are popular with video editors. The software mentioned here is a small fraction of what professionals use in practice. In terms of computing power, high-end laptops will run most of this software, although more powerful desktop workstations are preferred by large commercial studios. Educational computer labs range from students who provide their own laptops and software to networked environments that use servers and a combination of Macintosh and Windows computers. The sophistication of these labs is dependent on the budget available to support them, which usually involves leasing equipment so that it dos not go out of date and hiring systems administrators to keep

Fig. 21.2 Daniel Sierra, *Oscillate,* 2013, 4:27, Abstract animation. Daniel Sierra composed the music and used Houdini software's VFX language "to visualize waveform patterns that evolve from the fundamental sine wave to more complex patterns, creating a mesmerizing audio-visual experience in which sight and sound work in unison." In 2014, *Oscillate* won the Student Academy Award in the Alternative category. The video can be viewed online (http://vimeo.com/65475425)

all the equipment running and assist students with questions regarding the appropriate software and hardware to use (Fig. 21.2).

21.4.3 Metaforms or Polyforms

Before we discuss additional new forms of contemporary art, it is important to mention what other possibilities exists with digital imaging and digital sculpture. The terms "polyforms" and "metaforms" refer to the ability of the computer to output a work of art in different media. This is often done using computer animation techniques, but also with objects and images. Once an object or image has been created in digital form, the data used to create it can be used in a variety of ways. For example, a 3D environment of objects can comprise the set of an animated movie, a 3D model of a digital sculpture can be output as a print and 2D images can be brought into an animation program and become animated characters or output as a print image. By being able to manipulate the digital data contained within a creative work, the potential to use this data in a variety of ways greatly expands the creative options for the artist and encourages a multidisciplinary approach to contemporary art making.

21.5 New Forms of Digital Fine Art

While painting, drawing, sculpture and video art are well established within the traditional art community, many new forms of fine art have emerged through the creative uses of technology. In addition to the ones mentioned below, the continual invention of new forms of technology also enables new creative opportunities. For example, locative art grew out of smartphones and GPS technology. When looking at the education of a digital fine artist, it is important to expose them to all of these new forms of creative expression and to encourage them to be inventive.

21.5.1 Interactive and Networked Media

Interactive art and networked media art have been in existence since the establishment of the Internet and even before. This type of art is defined not only by the way in which it is experienced and created, but also because they are not "object-based" like drawings, paintings and sculpture. Early interactive art appears somewhat primitive when compared to work produced with modern computers and software due to the limitations of the software and hardware. There are many organizations dedicated to archiving this work and migrating it to more modern equipment and software. This in no way diminishes the value of the concepts and aesthetics, as early work was experimental and helped to define what interactive and networked media art

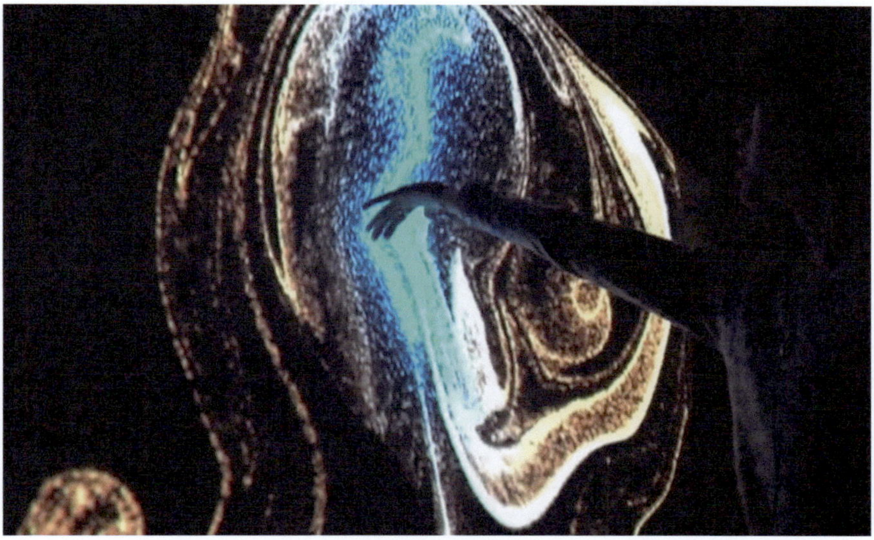

Fig. 21.3 Biwei Niu, *Evolution of Rhythm,* 2017, Haptic, interactive installation. Participants create generative, abstract graphics by touching and making gestures on a flexible fabric. Biwei Niu explores the philosophical concept of Chi to "make the connection between Chinese culture and Western technology." A documentation video can be viewed online (https://vimeo.com/219926017)

were and have evolved into. Artists who create this type of work need facility with programming or access to a programmer to define the interactive experience, as well as how the work is translated into a networked environment. Many of these works are collaborations, as not all artists are expert programmers. However, some introductory classes in programming are recommended for artists, so that even if they cannot do the programming themselves, they are able to communicate their ideas to a programmer in order to get the desired results (Fig. 21.3).

21.5.2 Digital Installation Art

Digital installation art ranges from an installation using digital media to ones that also have interactive elements. The dividing line between interactive art and installation art is a vague one. More often than not, interactive art is art where the interaction between the viewer/participant is critical to the meaning and experience of the work. Installation art generally has a subtler component of interaction and is more concerned with the environment that the art creates and what is experienced.

21.5.3 Programming and Software Art

Programming is a way to create digital art, animations and images from a fundamental mathematical level. Early pioneers did not have the portfolio of computer graphics applications we have today and had to write their own code to produce graphics. While off-the-shelf software gives artists incredible options for creative self-expression, artist/programmers can also create their work through original code. Many computer art academic programs require courses in programming for artists. There are two main reasons for this. Programming allows the artist to go beyond the options provided in off-the-shelf software and opens new possibilities. Also, artists who work collaboratively can do so more effectively with knowledge of how programming is done. The Processing programming language, created by Casey Reas and Ben Fry is a language of choice for artists (http://processing.org) (Fig. 21.4).

21.5.4 Virtual Reality

While the history of virtual reality traces back decades, the early technology was expensive and creative uses of the technology were rare. Two of the most notable works were *Osmose* and *Ephémère* created in the 1990s by Char Davies. Since the installation of the works required complex hardware and software, only a small number of people were able to experience these works. Since 2002, *Ephémère* has been ported to the PC. Given the huge increase is computer performance over the past several years, virtual reality is once again gaining popularity as a artistic medium and also shows tremendous promise for education. While there is still no single software package for producing virtual reality from concept to completion, artists and game producers are now combining 3D modeling and animation software with game engines to make creative work. In 2014, Google introduced Cardboard, which is a virtual reality platform that is used with a head-mounted cardboard viewer along with a smartphone. Other manufacturers are also introducing low-priced headsets intended for widespread use. The movie industry is also exploring virtual reality as an advance over stereo 3D movies, which have never become a standard for flat screen projection. The educational promise of a low-priced technology like Google Cardboard is that it can be used to provide virtual tours of recreated cultural environments, allowing students to virtually visit museums, the pyramids of Egypt and other historical locations (past and present) recreated with 3D modeling and animation software. Artists have embraced virtual reality and it is one of the new frontiers of creative self-expression.

Fig. 21.4 John F. Simon Jr., *Endless Bounty,* 2005, Custom software, Apple PowerBook G4, acrylic plastic 23 × 17 1/2 × 3 1/4 inches. The artist uses the term “art appliances” to describe these works. Using a deconstructed laptop, the screen is animated with original code. John F. Simon, Jr. describes his programming as a form of creative writing and also maintains a daily drawing practice

21.6 Curriculum Development for Digital Fine Art Education

Now that we have seen the various forms and media of digital fine art and the ways that artists use them, it will be helpful to address the development of curriculum for teaching it. Traditional curriculum development generally involved committees and is a time-consuming process. The traditional master/apprentice model used for hundreds of years still applies to the education of an artist, but the university model has supplanted it due to the large number of people wanting to become artists and the complexity of the knowledge required. The MFA in Computer Arts, established in 1986 at the School of Visual Arts (SVA) in New York City was the first graduate program to address the creative use of computers and technology in a graduate school setting. While there were MS and Ph.D. programs in Computer Graphics, they were focused on computer science and not art. The author was Chair of the MFA Computer Arts program at SVA during 1998–2017, founder of the BFA Computer Art program in 1994 and was primarily responsible for curriculum development in both programs.

One of the most important factors in developing curriculum for digital fine art is that it must be an ongoing and dynamic process. This is quite different from traditional art disciplines, where the tools, techniques and media have remained relatively the same. As software and technology continue to advance, new creative uses for them are constantly emerging. Curriculum needs to be reviewed and created on at least an annual basis and preferably on a per-semester basis. One technique used at SVA is to build courses starting with guest lectures by professional, practicing artists. This is a good way to gauge student interest. Fine art education is a two-way street and, while neither technology nor the students drive the curriculum, it is important to have courses that are created enroll and become vital parts of the curriculum. The responsibility for these decisions rests on the academic administration and faculty. While a new class may seem to be a good idea, if no one enrolls, it is a failure. Also, new opportunities for creative self-expression and digital art making are often new and not embraced by students right away. In this case, it often makes sense to run a class for a few semesters at low enrollment until students become aware of what this course is about and the creative potential it holds.

21.7 General Principles of Digital Fine Art Curriculum Development

When looking at a digital fine art curriculum holistically, there are a few general principles that need to be applied. The goal of an MFA degree program is to create a body of work that will launch the student on a professional career as an artist. When looking at the allocation of classes at SVA, the studio component takes prominence. This includes courses in art making with various digital media, e.g., 3D design and fabrication, interactive and installation art, interface design, etc.

Since the MFA is a two-year degree program, required first year classes include one year of digital art history, one year of programming, a systems class intended for students to learn the technology inside and out, and the Digital Art Seminar, which is a guest lecture series exposing students to professionals in the field from a wide variety of disciplines. This education is also supplemented by additional guest lectures, workshops, field trips and studio visits. Multidisciplinary study is encouraged. The only second year requirement is the thesis class, in which they produce their creative work. It also includes a research and writing component to assist in them in placing their work in context, learning about artists who have preceded them and putting together an artist statement, research paper, website and résumé. Students also enroll in elective classes to support their thesis process. The second year ends with an exhibition and public presentation of their work.

21.7.1 Alternatives to Digital Art Programs

While many programs have been established that focus exclusively on making digital fine art, there are other ways that this curriculum can be addressed. In the past several years, many traditional MFA programs are incorporating digital techniques into their curriculum or encouraging students to take electives in these areas. This eliminates the need for radical changes to the program, but also places increased responsibility on the department administration and advisors to provide proper guidance for students about which electives to take. Another approach is for students to enroll in a Computer Science program and take electives in the arts.

The establishment of interdisciplinary programs has become a popular new method that allows students to take courses in various departments after conferring with an advisor. The Royal College of Art in London uses this model in their MRes graduate program, which is taught across the four Schools of Communication, Design, Fine Art and Humanities and offers courses in practice and theory-led research for critical studies in art and design.

21.7.2 Fine Art Teaching Facilities

Teaching fine art has evolved from the mater/apprentice model to the more formal educational institutions of today. Traditional fine art facilities generally include painting and drawing studios, lecture/critique classrooms and individual studios for the art students. There are usually additional studios that focus on sculpture, woodworking, metal fabrication, etc. Digital art studios generally revolve around classrooms with 10–20 computers with a student at each workstation, lecture/critique classrooms and individual studios. There are generally specialized studios and equipment for 3D fabrication, photography, video, virtual reality and other digital media.

One important factor in digital fine art education is the expense of leasing and maintaining the computer laboratories and equipment. Traditional art facilities require no specialized equipment or staff to maintain them, other than the sculpture, metal fabrication and woodworking studios. Digital art studios are far more difficult to establish and maintain. Equipment and software need to be kept current and upgraded continually. Much of this expense is either shared among different departments, for example with computer science departments, or funded through student fees. For small institutions, there is generally a single multipurpose classroom with a faculty member whose role is also to maintain and upgrade the equipment. As a department grows in scale, systems administrators are hired and student lab assistants are also added to help maintain the equipment and answer student questions. In colleges where students are given their own studios, they are generally required to supply their own laptops and other digital equipment they need. While this does cut down on expenses, it also has an added benefit. Students should be encouraged to create works for which they can supply all the equipment needed to install it in a gallery or museum after graduation.

21.7.3 Exhibiting Student Digital Fine Art

The outcome of most MFA and BFA programs is for the artist to create a body of creative work to earn their degree. There are usually student exhibition opportunities during their studies and the great majority of graduates end their academic studies with a Thesis Exhibition. This exhibition is their entre to the professional art world. Early on, the exhibitions and photographic/video documentation served this purpose. In recent years, digital fine artists are increasing being expected to create their own website, which includes documentation of their creative work, an artist statement, résumé and press release for their final exhibition. As the art world evolves, galleries and museums often require artists interested in exhibiting their work to have an artist website. As the artist develops their career, has more exhibitions and evolves their artistic approach, the website becomes a living document of their ongoing creative self-expression.

Most degree programs make a point of inviting guest artists, gallerists and museum professionals to speak with and meet students to critique and refine their creative work and guide them to potential venues. Since the MFA Computer Arts program at SVA is in New York City, generally acknowledged as the "art capital" of the USA, we have many students who would like to start their fine art careers here. Having met with these students over the years, the author has developed a generic strategic plan for students who wish to do so. The plan is based on conversations with art professionals, gallerists and museum curators. The first stage of developing a career is to have a website, preferable with their name as the URL. On this site are the elements mentioned above: images, video documentation, artist statement, résumé, etc. While it is important to have their creative work stand on its own, the highly competitive environment for exhibitions also behooves emerging artists to mount a self-promotional campaign. This involves the easy first step of having a business card. We also encourage them to develop an email/mailing list and create postcards to promote their exhibitions. While having a generic postcard is helpful, having an exhibition listed on it helps to legitimize this self-promotional vehicle. The next step, which is vitally important, is for the artist to become a part of the art scene in New York, or as the author phrases it—"being on the set."

There are many websites that promote art openings at galleries to art-related events, websites and press publications. Attending openings, meeting gallerists, fellow artists and potential collectors is key to developing a career as a fine artist. The next piece of advice is to locate galleries that exhibit work that is like theirs or have the potential to do so. They should attend a few openings, meet the artists and gallerists and see if this is a gallery that is appropriate for them. Only then should they approach a gallery about an exhibition or representation. Walking into a gallery for the first time and requesting an exhibition is a recipe for disaster. Once you get to know the gallerist and they know you, that task is considerably easier and often much more successful.

One other option is for digital fine art graduates to enter their work in competitions and group shows. This can very often be the "foot in the door" that they need. International digital organizations like ACM SIGGRAPH, the Lumen Prize, ISEA International, Ars Electronica and others sponsor annual competitions and events. Being recognized on an international level is an important introduction into some venues. Many of these organizations also offer artist residencies that can end with an exhibition of the work they created as a visiting artist.

The goal of all of these efforts is to eventually gain gallery representation. Once this has been achieved, a contemporary artist has a solid base to build upon. Students should be reminded that galleries are business endeavors. Galleries exist to sell artwork, and this is an important factor in gaining this status. It also implies that there is an ongoing expectation for the creation of work for shows in the galleries or commissions from contacts they make through the gallery.

21.7.4 Digital Fine Art in Museums and Galleries

It would be helpful to review the current state of digital fine art in museums and galleries. As mentioned above, early digital art was viewed as Outsider Art and had little exposure in traditional art institutions. Things have changed considerably over the past few decades and will continue to do so. The new generation of contemporary artists has never known a world without computers, using technology and software to make art is not viewed as unusual anymore. Museums and galleries are also changing. In the early days of digital art, there were very few curators and gallerists familiar with this form of creative self-expression. What compounded the problem was that the "white cube" model was not easily transformed into a digital art space. Even the simplest of challenges like having enough and properly placed electrical outlets to power the equipment was a concern. Internet access and WiFi was also a considerable challenge. Museums and galleries did not have the equipment needed to exhibit the work, either. Digital art frequently uses computers, video projectors and audio. The sheer cost of mounting and maintaining these exhibitions was high, as was the lack of museum professionals to keep the equipment running, turn it on and off daily and troubleshooting problems. This challenge still exists and is slowly changing, as museum budgets and public funding adapt. Since contemporary art is becoming increasingly digital, it is now mandatory for these venues to update their facilities and keep them current.

Above and beyond the ability to exhibit this kind of work, museum acquisition of digital work is also an evolving process. Since digital work can be duplicated exactly, what determines what the original work is? Also, the ability to change and update the work can result in the work evolving and changing from the original acquisition to the final exhibited piece. Archival issues further complicate this. A large proportion of early digital art has been lost due to the obsolescence of the equipment used to create it. There is also an aesthetic issue that arises with early work. Early computers were limited in terms of resolution, the amount of colors they were capable of reproducing and operated at much slower speeds than the machines of today. While this does not discount the aesthetic value of the work, modern viewers often use the current technological environment to evaluate it. This brings the issue of migration and emulation to the forefront. Two precedents are photography and video art. While early photography was a chemical process, high-resolution scanners are now being used to preserve the prints and negatives.

The same process is happening with video art. Early videotapes are being digitized into HD and higher resolutions. Work that was done using videotape machines as part of the installation often have a DVD player concealed in the pedestal, so that there is no risk of destroying or wearing out the original videotape. While these are adequate solutions, we must also realize that technology will continue to advance. What is currently HD video will eventually be looked at as a low-resolution format. Artists are already working with 8K resolution and virtual reality is rapidly becoming more photorealistic.

Above and beyond media-based solutions, there are many initiatives that emulate operating systems and preserve digital art in its original form. One clear example is Net Art, which emerged in the mid-1990s when browser technology, the World Wide Web and graphics, sound and video became available on the Internet. Browser software was changing about every six months, and much of the early Net Art became inaccessible quickly. So, where does this leave us? The merging of contemporary art with digital art is an ongoing process. It is now being widely addressed by museums, galleries, international digital art organizations, and individual artists. The simplicity of a drawing, oil painting and sculpture that lasts hundreds of years has made contemporary art exhibitions, archiving and the collecting of art not as simple as it used to be. This is something that reinforces the adage that the only constant is change. The exciting part is that new forms of creative self-expression will continue to evolve and augment, not replace, the traditional forms of art.

21.8 Conclusion

The education of a digital fine artist is radically different from the traditional model of educating fine artists. There are many factors at play. Over the past several decades, digital art has proliferated and become an important component of contemporary art. The young artists of today have never known a non-digital world and software and technology have crept into every aspect of modern daily life. They have changed the way in which we experience the world, communicate with each other, define and creatively express ourselves. The changes have been so rapid that society is grappling with issues of instantaneous global communication, the interaction of diverse cultures and the powerful influence of social media. An important consideration for educators is that this educational process is still relatively new.

While the School of Visual Arts established the first MFA in Computer Arts in the United States over thirty years ago, tremendous changes have occurred since then and will continue to do so. Technology and facile access to information will not stop developing. The online archives of digital art history will require educators to provide guided access for students. New technology will also create the potential for new forms of art and courses will need to be written to take advantage of them. The model of guest lectures and workshops, which evolve into courses has proven to be an effective approach in developing digital fine art education. Another aspect educators should take into consideration is the choice of elective courses students should take. Not only is art education changing rapidly, but all other aspects of higher education are being affected. A few examples are how the ownership and development of intellectual property is being redefined. The changing nature of the design field has also radically changed. Graphic design used to consist solely of print. Now, graphic designers need to develop their work to be accessible and easily transferable between print, websites, broadcast media, video, interactive media, and other forms now used for communication.

In the art world, museums and galleries are no longer the sole domain within which to experience art. The art experience is omnipresent in public media and our smartphones, and contemporary art is exerting a strong influence on visual culture, particularly in advertising. While fine artists have a defined agenda, the realms and venues of creative self-expression extend beyond traditional ones and the art audience is ever-expanding. The dilemma for educators is how to continue to develop creativity and to nurture fine art in its purest form. While the traditional fine art educational model still includes art theory, history, studio practice and critique, new methods and subjects to teach are continually being invented. The Internet now allows teachers and students alike instant access to a global audience and information resources. While artists can sidestep the traditional museum and gallery models with their online presence, they still need to define themselves as artists through creative self-expression, the development of a unique individual style and the discipline of a dedicated devotion to their art practice.

For the educator, the process of educating digital fine artists is becoming increasingly difficult. Teachers can no longer be specialists in all forms of digital art and software. Digital art, as well as contemporary art, continues to define itself. Art historians, curators and educators alike are charged with the difficult task of navigating these changes and helping to form what contemporary art is and where it is going. The author defines contemporary art as a creative reflection of modern society. Each artist needs to be taught and learn how to make their own individual imprint on the development of visual culture and contemporary art. While a formidable task, we have not seen a time in recent history where the options for creative self-expression and the opportunity to redefine contemporary art have been so available to artists.

Further Reading

Archive of Digital Art. http://www.digitalartarchive.at/database/database-info/archive.html. Accessed 22 July 2018

Ars Electronica, Linz, Austria. http://www.aec.at/news. Accessed 22 July 2018

Barfield O (2010) Poetic diction: a study in meaning. Barfield Press, Oxford

Beddard H (2016) Computer art at the V&A. V&A Online J 2, Autumn. http://www.vam.ac.uk/content/journals/research-journal/issue-02/computer-art-at-the-v-and-a/. Accessed 22 July 2018

College Art Association and the Society of Architectural Historians (2016) Guidelines for evaluating digital scholarship in art and architectural history. http://www.collegeart.org/pdf/evaluating-digital-scholarship-in-art-and-architectural-history.pdf. Accessed 22 July 2018

Computer Arts Society, London, England. http://computer-arts-society.com. Accessed 22 July 2018

Grau O (2003) Virtual art: from illusion to immersion. MIT Press, Cambridge, MA

Paul C (2015) Digital art, Thames & Hudson, 3rd edn. London

Popper F (2007) From technological to virtual art. MIT Press, Cambridge, MA

SIGGRAPH Digital Arts Community. http://siggrapharts.ning.com. Accessed 22 July 2018

Wands B (2006) Art of the digital age, Thames & Hudson. London

Wands B (2017) Art of the digital age. http://artofthedigitalage.com. Accessed 22 July 2018

ZKM, Karlsruhe, Germany. http://zkm.de/en. Accessed 22 July 2018

Chapter 22
Breaking Silos: New Modes of Art, Education, and Technology Training in Museums

Rosanna Flouty

Abstract This chapter looks at the trajectory of an online training project called The Broad Museum's Online Learning Management System (LMS) Training Tool developed and launched for the museum's opening in 2015. The online platform was designed to train a new breed of front-line, part-time visitor services museum staff, empowering them to be conversant about the art and exhibitions on view, as well as safety procedures. The online training platform included basic safety training, management policies and operation materials for general museum facilities, and have been since extended for use with retail, restaurant and special events staff training after its initial launch. While the online platform was originally built to support robust, core training environments to support part-time staff with diverse backgrounds and experiences in service, hospitality, and contemporary art education, this chapter traces future potential to nourish museum talent across many digital platforms. Some of the larger questions that museums struggle with include how to help people connect and learn in museums, and how best to help staff engage with visitors to facilitate optimal museum experiences. Ultimately, this chapter looks at ways to form collaborations across many other contemporary art museums to support radical growth for supporting museum talent, across departments and across many kinds of museums.

22.1 Introduction

Despite vast advancements in ever-smarter digital tools for visitor engagement and interpretation, human interaction is central to the museum experience in contemporary art museums. Yet some of the questions with which museums struggle include how to help people connect and learn in museums, and how best to facilitate learning in partnership between museum staff and the visitor. Far from automating the connection between staff in a museum setting, a new type of learning platform that utilizes hybrid (or "blended") models for collaborative learning that engage museum

---

R. Flouty (✉)
New York University, New York, USA
e-mail: rosanna.flouty@nyu.edu

T. Giannini and J. P. Bowen (eds.), *Museums and Digital Culture*,
Springer Series on Cultural Computing, https://doi.org/10.1007/978-3-319-97457-6_22

educators, visitor services personnel and other front-line staff has recently been introduced by the visitor engagement staff at the Broad Museum in Los Angeles. Their new model for learning carries implications for online/offline sharing across the nation and holds the capacity for added and scalable digital platforms through white-labeled, out-of-the-box Learning Management System (LMS) software that can be further customized to align with an organization's brand identity.

This new model potentially could inspire museums across the USA to leverage such a platform in order to easily share resources and collaborate on research and exhibitions that include similar artworks, artists, or themes. Key to the development of such a platform requires a systematic call to action by museums to share resources across contemporary arts organizations; as one issue in the field of museum education is the duplication of research efforts across multiple departments which creates a siloed effect of "best practices" and the latest advances in the field. As the use and practices of distributed digital platforms are expanding to incorporate shared correspondence, shared research, and shared in-gallery solutions, all in real time, new ways of engaging front-line staff are moving to digital platforms with greatly improved effect.

Decades of museum visitor research starting as early as the 1980s point to a deep desire for visitors to gain more information about the works they are seeing on museum walls. In one of the earliest multi-year national studies conducted by the Getty Institute, called *Insights: Museums, Visitors, Attitudes and Expectations: A Focus Group Experiment* (Samis and Michaelson 2017, pp. 14–15), visitors reported feeling a deeper connection to what they were seeing when they were provided with more information that leads to deeper appreciation of the objects they are viewing. Anecdotally, a common question that visitors often ask is, "What makes this art?" (Pugliese 2018). On the contrary, viewers that do not feel welcomed by museum staff during their visit often feel alienated by contemporary art, and often feel alienated by contemporary art museums, in general. In a worst-case scenario, a negative experience or interaction with staff in one museum may result in a negative perception of *all* museums. But a human-based conversation with a focus toward visitor experience and connection in the context of a museum can open a door wide toward many future museum visits over a single lifetime.

The following pages outline how an online training platform in support of human interaction in museum galleries not only support current visitors but can support future visitors to come. This chapter outlines the trajectory of the Broad's online training platform in 2014–2015 with input from Broad museum staff and three consultants, including its design, implementation and launch before the museum's opening in September 2015. It covers an examination of some of the quandaries for supporting non-salaried, front-line museum staff—including gallery guides, docents, security guards, tour guides, and volunteers, as well as some opportunities for supporting talent that interacts with museum visitors on a daily basis. The chapter looks briefly at the platform's subsequent adoption at a second Los Angeles-based contemporary art organization, called the Marciano Arts Foundation, and its use to support education programs with a local partnership to support STEAM-based community programs. And finally, the chapter offers ways in which such an online training platform may be utilized to create internal change to support a larger turn towards placing visitor experience at the center in future museum practice.

22.2 Duplication of Efforts: The Xerox Machine as Albatross

Is there something about the field of contemporary art museum education that has kept it inextricably attached to the Xerox machine? In the spring of 2015, just as the Whitney Museum planned to open its doors to the public, I was briefly engaged in a series of conversations with staff about a forthcoming presentation of its collection, *America is Hard to See*. The inaugural show in the museum's stunning new home by the waterfront in the Meatpacking section of Manhattan already enjoyed an image of innovation and creativity that even in New York seemed unprecedented: much of the collection had never been on public view simultaneously, and the Whitney's new building designed by Renzo Piano became an instant draw. In a closet located next to my desk lay a stack of three-inch binders, each containing roughly 300 pages of Xeroxed materials for docents and tour guides to check out and read, in preparation for their critical role in leading tours throughout the exhibition. From this experience, it seemed clear that despite the active efforts of some museum educators to create an infrastructure that includes shared drives, password-protected research portals, and digitally-accessible file drives for staff training purposes, the phenomenon of Xeroxing study packets for front-line staff, volunteers and docents seems to still be common throughout museum education departments nationally.

One of several "critical" moments in preparing for a new exhibition is the request for original research about the upcoming exhibition, which is usually conducted by an intern (or team of interns) over many weeks to gather, collate, and disseminate packets with exhibition research results and materials to give to staff, docents and tour guides. In the case of the Whitney exhibition, *America Is Hard To See*, staff took extra care to spiral-bind and laminate the covers of the packets, so that many hands could handle the materials over time without damage to the hard copies. The release of the binders signaled a "moment," that it was time to prepare and study, digest and reflect—and most importantly of all, time to prepare tour scripts and strategies for engaging the public in meaningful ways. By no means did preparation for audience engagement end there, as additional unmarked hours of looking in the galleries still lay ahead, along with in-depth curatorial tours, audio tour content review, and development of tour materials to support differently-abled audiences, all conducted after the show was installed and just before the show opened to the public (Fig. 22.1).

Fig. 22.1 Training materials and associated binders that were developed for the exhibition, *America Is Hard To See*, at the Whitney Museum, New York City. Photographs by Rosanna Flouty

Xeroxed binders in the museum profession are integral to the exhibition process. Having been an employee in several education departments across the country, I have witnessed my colleagues standing over Xerox machines for countless hours as they prepared docent and tour guide training materials. Stacks of Xeroxed packets of paper and 3″ binders traverse staff hands across many types of museums, large and small. Ironically, similar Xerox marathons occur for shows that travel between organizations, resulting in a duplication of efforts that repeat across multiple institutions. Sometimes, the act of Xeroxing training packets for the same show also occurs across multiple departments within the *same* institution. The magnitude of the problem is compounded when paper-based Xeroxed packets are read and then discarded, only to be reconstructed from scratch at another institution in advance of the next venue and location.

The trajectory of the Broad Museum's online training platform began in late 2014 with a charge to look at the ways in which other museums currently conducted training for their docents, tour guides, and visitor services staff, while casting a critical eye to how current systems of training might be improved by adopting a digital platform to onboard staff for the museum's brand-new building, set to open in downtown Los Angeles in fall of 2015. The project's internal museum team included Richard Cherry, Deputy Director of the Broad Museum (2012–2017), Alex Capriotti, Director of Marketing and Communications (2013–2017), Lauren Girard, Manager of Visitor Services and later, Director of Visitor Services (2015–2018). The three outside consultants hired to build the training platform were Colleen Brogan, a specialist in online learning platforms who had worked with digital education platforms at the Museum of Modern Art, Ashley Weinard, a museum educator with a background in developing art-based content, and Rosanna Flouty as project director. Despite the lack of an existing training model to use as a basis for the project's development and a tight timeframe in which to develop the project, the Broad Museum launched a full-fledged LMS training program with roughly 12 hours of online content, designed to support an additional in-person training of roughly 40 hours of that was conducted during the week before the museum's opening.

The Broad Museum is a 120,000 ft^2 contemporary art museum (The Broad 2015). The collection features over 2,000 works owned by Eli and Edythe Broad, two of Los Angeles's leading philanthropists, and is housed in a $140 million, three-story building that was designed by architecture team of Diller Scofidio + Renfro in downtown Los Angeles (Cotter 2015). General admission is free to view most of the collection located on the third floor of the museum, but the museum generally charges for special exhibitions and public program events (https://ticketing.thebroad.org). Tickets are required and must be reserved online in advance of the museum visit, and the museum provides a free app with audio tour content. In its inaugural year, The Broad museum far exceeded all internal and external attendance projections, welcoming over 820,000 visitors through its doors (The Broad 2015). There is no front desk at the Broad, and visitors are welcomed by Visitor Service Associates, also known as VSAs (Fig. 22.2).

Fig. 22.2 The Broad Museum on its opening day, during a preview viewing on September 19, 2015. Photographs by Rosanna Flouty

Fig. 22.3 Broad Museum visitor service associates (VSAs) talking to museum visitors in the museum's third floor gallery during its inaugural preview viewing on September 19, 2015. Photographs by Rosanna Flouty

22.3 Digital Implementation of Training Standards, by Design—A Case Study

When the Broad Museum first approached our team to build an online training platform, their proposal featured the development of a digital platform focusing on the content of a still-nascent permanent collection, an introduction to the building's architecture, as well as safety and evacuation training, and core competencies in customer services. The project was greatly expanded before launch to include a video-based hiring platform that served to pre-screen candidates. Initial discussions within the project team focused on the varied ways in which docent training traditionally has been conducted at other museums, and in what ways the Broad team sought to innovate. Anecdotally, an expectation was upheld that by canvassing colleagues working across multiple contemporary art museums, our team would create a master resource of shared training resources that would be mined to form a knowledge base for the most effective practices. We assumed that we could locate multiple manuals and training materials to support in part-time staff training, in addition to security training and customer service materials, as well as use our research as a way to examine and cross-reference training manuals across institutions.

It turned out that easily identifiable training standards did not exist, nor could they be easily shared, as they relied heavily on the uniqueness of each organization's mission, history, and staff expectations. We also quickly learned that few organizations had a training manual that could be easily shared in 2014, as much of the material used in training staff existed in multiple places and formats and was conducted in-person to onboard new staff on an ad hoc basis. During our search, we received multiple requests to gain access to the materials we collected, pointing to a deep need in the field of museum education and visitor services for shared and accessible resources. In order to create a unique platform that could facilitate casual conversations between visitor services staff and visitor education on contemporary art throughout the museum galleries, it was clear we would need to create new content that was appropriate for the Broad's visitor-centric approach and could be developed to live in a format that also be shared with other museums upon request.

As the design project for the Broad Museum's platform evolved, our scope introduced strategies to support personalization and new adaption needs to support the new building. Our team was formally hired in February 2015 to create the content for the training and make it live and available for staff use in training before the museum opened to the public on September 19, 2015. Our consultant team, in partnership with Broad staff, knew that being able to see learner data on task completion rates and time allocation was essential to the usability of the platform design, and the ability of the Visitor Services site manager to determine the amount of new content that would be added to the platform. In the end, the platform selected we selected, called Litmos, supported a robust and embedded facilitation that allows for impromptu ways to share learning content and experiences in a co-created environment, as well as a legible dashboard to track user progress. Additionally, we designed the scope of work to phase out our team from the process of creating content, so that we could encourage visitor services attendants to 'ascend' through the ranks and move towards creating more content for their peers to use (Fig. 22.3).

22.3.1 A Progression Model for the Platform

The platform's training progression was co-designed by consultant Ashley Weinard to support three levels of training, designed to correspond to increasing levels of hourly pay (see Fig. 22.4). The first level, 'Level 1: Floor Ready,' was designed to support all basic requirements for training to support a Visitor Associate to be ready to work on the museum floor. This training level included Safety Expertise, Visitor Services Expertise, and Gallery Experience expertise. Safety Expertise focused on all of the elements of the VA role pertaining to visitor safety and guarding the works on view, such as what to do in the event of fire, earthquakes, active shooter situations, power outages, and protocols for lost items and damage to artwork. Level 1 also included Visitor Services Expertise, such as customer service language in welcoming museum visitors, and Broad museum protocols.

Also at Level 1 was Gallery Experience Expertise, which included engagement strategies for casual conversations between Visitor Associates and museum visitors, and six to eight conversational bullet points about each artist included in the inaugural

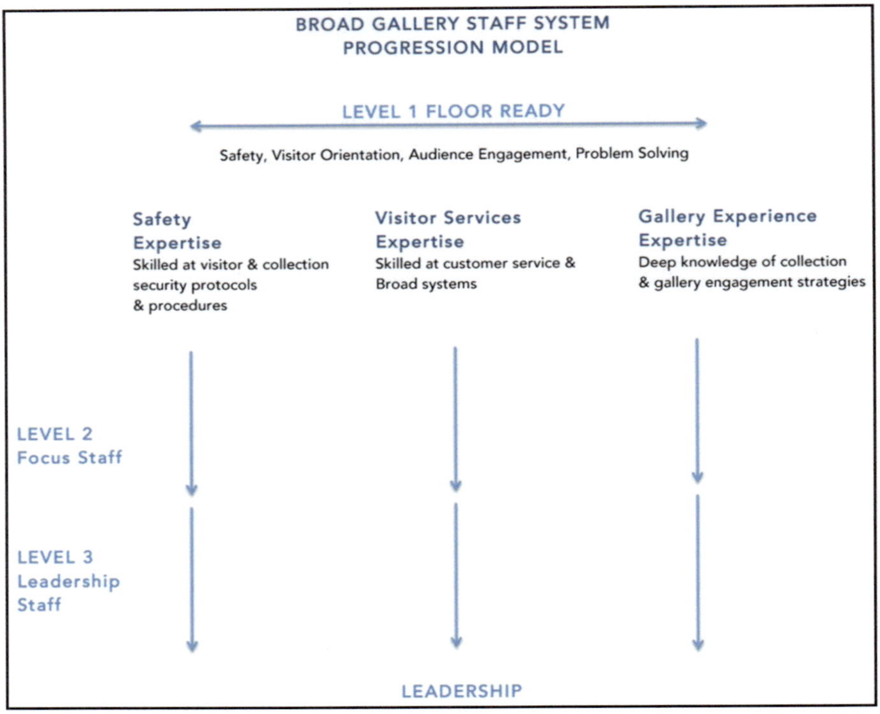

Fig. 22.4 The "Broad's gallery staff system progression model," designed by Ashley Weinard, March 2015. Screengrab: Courtesy of Ashley Weinard

exhibition to be placed on view for the Broad's opening. Later, our team added correct pronunciations for each artist's name, as well as biographical information about each artist's training and place of birth and work. We also decided to embed two videos that featured each artist talking about his or her own work, rather than reliance on curatorial texts or other supplementary material that used thematic interpretation or an art historical lens to shed light. We were also interested in featuring and embedding video footage that included the artist talking about inspiration for the work or process about how the work was made, and in his or her own words, rather than using material that did not have the artist voice present in the footage. We believed that it was likely that the artists featured in the exhibition were likely to walk into the Broad's galleries at any moment, especially since the Broads had close and personal connections to many of the artists that they collected. We wanted Visitor Associates to be able to recognize the artists by face, as well as feel confident in talking to the artist directly about quotes they might have once said about the creation of their own work.

22.3.2 Use of the Platform for Applicant Pre-screening

The challenge of developing and deploying a platform in such a compressed timeline gave rise to a new challenge: how to make sure that trainees would be comfortable with the platform in time to hit the ground running in just four short weeks, which was the time estimated between the announcement of the position openings at the Broad and the launch date of the platform. Meanwhile, Broad Museum staff pre-printed cards to carry around with them to actively recruit individuals from other types of retail and restaurant experiences throughout the greater Los Angeles area. Position openings were also announced on the museum's Facebook page, and on more traditional online job listing sites (Fig. 22.5).

Co-consultant Colleen Brogan then created a video-based design requirement that prompted potential staffing applicants to complete an initial training module and complete online assessment tests. This action of uploading application materials triggered an automatic invitation to the platform, and a pre-assessment that was required for the job application to be complete. Our team knew that the skills and requirements of the position of front-line staff at the Broad were qualities that were often overlooked or not adequately conveyed in a cover letter or on a resume, and a video assessment, coupled with writing prompt questions and more traditional assessment tools, could help a potential applicant without direct museum experience but excellent customer service skills land an interview (Fig. 22.6).

Fig. 22.5 The Broad created cards that could be used to encourage customer-service professionals in other sectors to apply to potential job openings at the museum. With permission from Alice Chung, The Broad

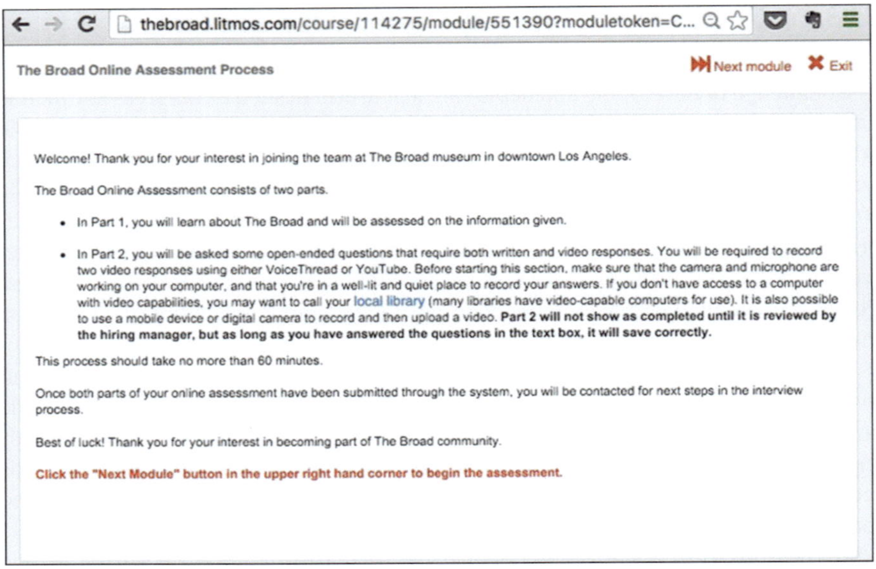

Fig. 22.6 The Broad's online learning platform pre-screening page. Screengrab: Courtesy of The Broad and Rosanna Flouty

This adoption meant that beyond merely uploading a resume and a cover letter, potential applicants were also asked to then go through a roughly one-hour online training and assessment through Litmos before they were considered to move forwards in the screening process for the part-time position (Fig. 22.7).

Applicants were asked to upload video of themselves talking about the reason why they wanted to work at the Broad, as well as a prompt to create a video as if the potential applicant was addressing a visitor to "please keep two feet away from the artwork at all times" (see Fig. 22.8). Brogan also created a series of mock scenarios that played various key attributes or skillsets that the Broad was looking to attract in their hiring base. A key design innovation in our project was to ask potential applicants to use different types of media to describe why interested in working at the Broad and what attracted them to apply in the first place, and to share a contemporary artist that they admired and why. The ability to speak or write about their favorite contemporary artwork or artist had far more bearing on the importance as to whether or not a potential applicant could work well with diverse audiences in the museum galleries, and we noted that these were additional skillsets that were often not reflected in the cover letter or resume.

Applicants that were successful with the completion of the first stage of the process, including completion of all of the assessments and had uploaded videos were then invited into the museum offices for a group interview. Since the museum needed to hire nearly 85 staff members in barely two short weeks dedicated to recruitment for the position hires, it was helpful for the museum's Director of Visitor Services to

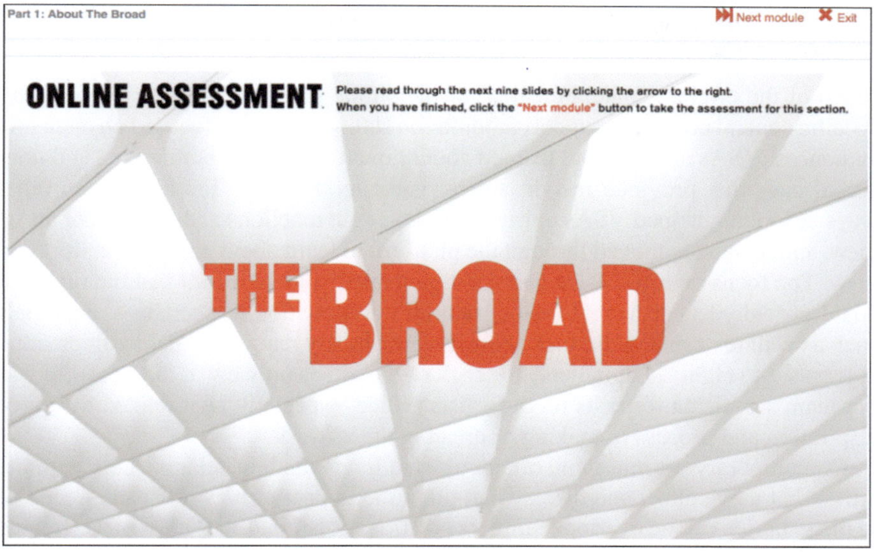

Fig. 22.7 The Broad's online learning platform video assessment. Screengrab: Courtesy of The Broad and Rosanna Flouty

have already become familiar with each of the candidates through their pre-recorded video responses and online text materials that were submitted through the platform.

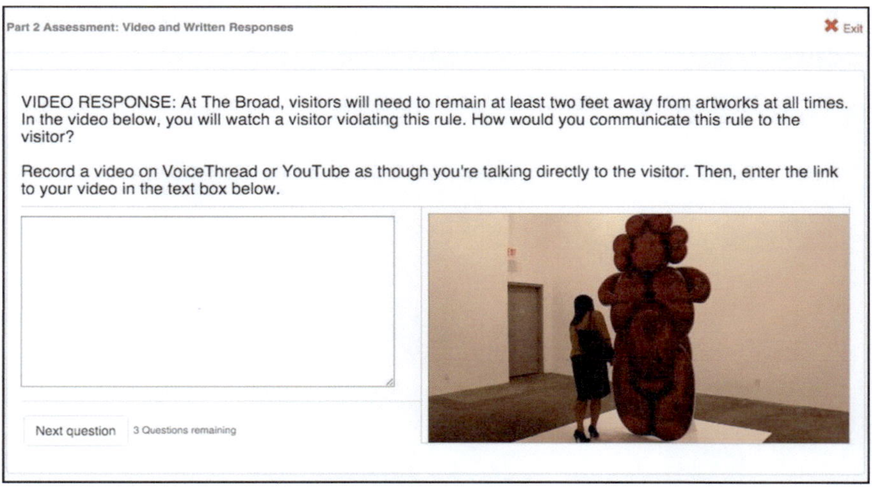

Fig. 22.8 A sample video for a potential recruit to watch, in which a mock "visitor" is seen walking up to a sculpture from the Broad's collection. Screengrab: Courtesy of Rosanna Flouty

22.3.3 Training Content: A Focus on Artists' Voices

Much of the original content created for the online training platform, beyond site-specific content created to support modules on safety protocols, focused on engaging audiences. VSAs at the Broad learned about how to recognize both verbal and non-verbal cues that provided insight about visitor motivations. Journaling and other ways of looking helped VSAs to trust their inner gut reactions about works of art on view, and then were moved through the platform to learn about each of the artists on view. The focus on artist voice and artist-generated content meant that the platform could provide deeper insight than curatorial interpretation, especially as materials such as wall texts and audio tour content were already readily available. In creating at least six to eight "chat bullets" for each of the artists on view at the Broad, it was our team's decision to focus on the artists' voice, especially as it related to source inspiration and process in making or creating the artwork.

Contemporary art museums often cultivate long-standing relationships with the artists that they collect and display, but often the impact of how artists are received in the galleries can be overlooked. In an NPR (National Public Radio) piece created about the success of the Broad's visitor associates, one memorable story emerged, through the telling of the museum's director, Joanne Heyler. She recounted how Glenn Ligon walked through the galleries feeling like he was being received like a rock star by museum staff who were knowledgeable about his work (Stanberg 2016). This anecdotal exchange between an artist and front-line gallery staff pointed to larger ways in which part-time museum staff felt comfortable approaching an artist directly to discuss that artist's works on view, an exchange that is usually strictly reserved for curators and artists to have privately. The platform was diligently created to support

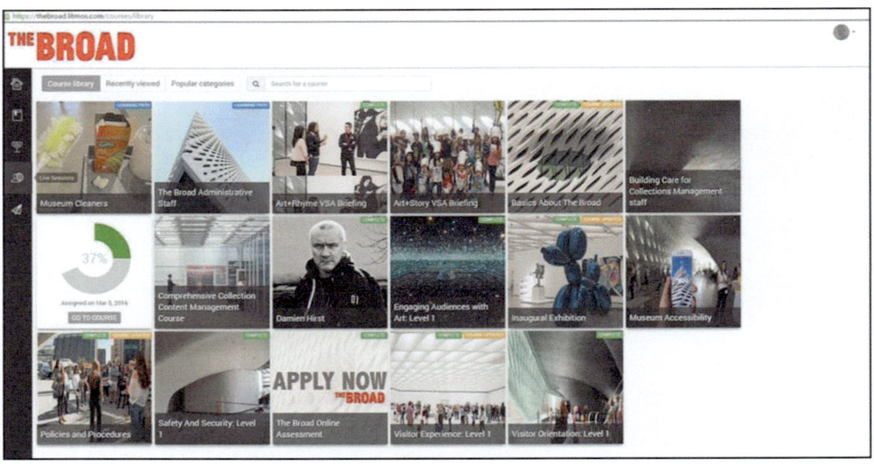

Fig. 22.9 A view of the complete course library in Litmos, administrator view. Courtesy of The Broad and Rosanna Flouty

Fig. 22.10 User assessments and engagement dashboard from the Broad's online learning platform, administrator view. Courtesy of The Broad and Rosanna Flouty

engagement with each artist's words and direct quotes, through video footage of the artist speaking in his or her own voice. The online platform did not include nor rely on text that merely included curatorial interpretation, and instead we placed reliance on content generated living artists' own voices and words to generate training modules for front line gallery staff to use (Figs. 22.9 and 22.10).

As the bulk of the content was generated in the days leading up to the museum's opening, it was very useful to be able to see how users were progressing through each of the modules. If there were areas within the content that were unclear, it was clear where the trainees were having trouble within the platform, based on the number of failed attempts in the user assessments.

22.3.4 *Upending Silos: 'I Don't Know' Is Not an Option*

The impetus for the creation of an online training platform stemmed directly from an experience recounted to staff by the museum's director, Joanne Heyler, while on another museum visit. Heyler, as director of the Broad Foundation, and later as founding director of the Broad Museum, related to her staff at a key point in the development of the museum's overall mission that she had visited another museum, and had asked the front desk staff person who had built the building. The response was simple and to no fault of the individual, but the front desk attendant did not know the name of the architect. According to Richard Cherry, then deputy director of the Broad, she then gently prodded to find out whether the staff person had any knowledge about the artist or the architecture, and "it seemed as if they did not—or if they did, it was disjointed." (Flouty and Cherry 2018). Heyler believed that if public-facing staff did not "know" an answer," they should be empowered to find out by any means that made sense, and that the result would be that much better for the visitor. Heyler believed that such a role would shape the visitor services role to be more like a 'concierge,' and that they should be able to help with anything, and any request. She believed that all of the Broad's new staff should need to know about the architecture of the building, the story behind founders of the museum and their personal history in building the Broad collection, and possess knowledge about the art on the walls. But even more so, they should also be able to know what was else going on in the surrounding Los Angeles area of downtown. According to Cherry, he saw firsthand how Eli Broad was not merely interested in developing downtown Los Angeles, but he also "was interested in place-making, and you cannot be part of something while also existing aside from it" (Flouty and Cherry 2018). This charge for the online platform's development, that "'I don't know' is not an option," was later echoed in some of the experiences related by the museum's first Visitor Services manager, Lauren Girard.

22.3.5 *'Not My Role' Is Not an Option*

As head of Visitor Services, Girard believed that the existence of silos within museums, and specifically siloed functions across departments resulted in an unbalanced expectation on behalf of the visitor to understand how a museum functioned. As a direct consequence of internal organization, an undue burden is then placed on the visitor to attempt to find or locate the 'right' person to answer the 'right' question. For many visitors, a museum staff person represents the entire museum, and therefore should know as much about the collection or the exhibitions on view as anybody else working at the museum. As Girard rightly pointed out, it was not really "fair" to expect a museum visitor to understand or grasp all of the nuances behind who works behind which desk, and why:

> I can share a story that also inspired me to think through the training platform. While visiting a museum on a recent trip, I recalled asking the person who had just sold me a ticket if they could tell me a little about the show I was about to see. And the reply shocked me. The person said, that actually they were not allowed to tell me because that was not their job. My perception was that the person was told that they were infringing on someone else's role. The guest relations associate seated behind the front desk could give me a ticket or give me directions, but no more. Worse, they were told they should not share information about the exhibitions on view. And I kept thinking about how demoralizing is it for the people who had to work in those positions, to not be empowered to help visitors beyond their role or function. When I went to work at the Broad [in 2015], I knew that there had to be a way to run this differently. (Flouty and Girard 2018)

As a museum professional who had also worked in the retail sector, Girard's orientation towards training museum personnel for public-facing roles such as Visitor Service Associates and security guards used a customer-comes-first model. She realized that in retail, the "Not My Job" concept does not exist, and that the jobs become customer-focused, because the customer always comes first. She saw the opportunity to help the visitor as an opportunity to also help the staff member grow and extend beyond their immediate training. By using a digital training method, she was able to use her customer service training background to also shape and inform how she structured training materials to form a deep knowledge base about contemporary art. Girard recounts, "I borrowed and appropriated a lot of retail training techniques when I came to The Broad. It was based on entry level sales training, just without the pushiness to close a sale" (Flouty and Girard 2018).

22.4 Upending Silos Online Training Across Departments

Prior to the incorporation of digital training platforms, in-gallery museum training unfolded much like classroom training occurs: a lecture by a curator or assistant curator, followed by a curatorial walk-through, copious notes are taken, and the experience was usually video-recorded for further access. These types of traditionally-driven training platforms did not allow for any type of extensive access after the day of training passed. Once the exhibition opened and the staff take their places, rarely were conversations in the galleries between staff and visitor become part of the exhibition, because they happen in "thin air," meaning once they happen, rarely were they charted or preserved or traced or even kept, besides in the minds and memory of the gallery guide, docent, or Visitor Services attendant. As multiple Xeroxed training packets became actively copied and disseminated throughout the ranks of docents and tour guides, they did not support a method to track or trace conversations with museum visitors, or even further research that occurred after the show opened. As analog training devices, the copies did not support any other method of training besides analog reading. Nor did they support digital resources. Any video-based materials such as recorded artist talks or digital presentation methods such as PowerPoint needed to reside in a separate place, usually password-protected, and usually managed by a full-time educator with limited resources and free time to continually update or expand the training materials once the show opened.

Rethinking training models for the staff mentioned in this chapter is critical for many reasons, but two rise as particularly pressing for the field of museum education. First, gallery attendants, visitor service personnel, docents, tour guides, security guards, cafe or restaurant servers are likely the only museum staff that a visitor will encounter during their museum visit. The exchange between museum visitor and a part-time staff member is an opportunity to provide a long-term impression about an individual museum. If the exchange is positive, the visitor is left with impressions that stay for a very long time. Second, the ways that Girard hired her staff remained located in her vision that they were being considered for their very first museum staff job as a stepping stone to a much bigger future role in a museum (Flouty and Girard 2018). She believed that she could train staff so that each individual could go on to a meaningful museum career, and the skills she designed within the Broad's digital learning platform supported hierarchies of scaled learning in transferable skills in customer service, problem solving, and other attributes. It was also this quality of training that inspired a neighboring arts organization called the Marciano Art Foundation, also based in Los Angeles, to further adopt the same online LMS for their opening and extended its use for onboarding outside education staff to support partnerships with other arts organizations.

22.5 Marciano Art Foundation—A Second Case Study

The discussion of digital implementation strategies became more fully realized when a second contemporary art museum based in Los Angeles called the Marciano Art Foundation ('MAF') planned to open their doors to the public in May of 2017. The collection is housed in a 100,000 ft^2 former Freemasonic temple with 55,000 square feet of dedicated exhibition space. Founders Maurice and Paul Marciano often "chafed" at the use of the word "museum" to describe the MAF, as the "designation was too institutional, too formal" to capture their vision (Schneider 2017). Like the Broad, a small staff meant there was interest in having an online training platform in place of an education department or fully-fledged visitor services department to support and train front-line staff.

Liza Hamalian was hired as MAF's Visitor Services Manager soon after the decision was made by the organization to use Litmos in their training program for their new contemporary art space. She believed that the success of MAF's readiness to engage with visitors stemmed from the fact that the Broad agreed to give her access to their training materials while she and her team were still in development, so that she could examine what they had already built and put in place prior to their opening, adding that: "Our willingness to engage with visitors stems from our mission to ensure that the collection is accessible to the public. This is the central reason why we educate our front-house staff. The Broad museum was instrumental in sharing their resources and providing a foundation which we used to expand on." (Flouty and Hamalian 2018). The MAF training platform also was designed using a similar organizational and personnel structure as The Broad, with no dedicated or formal education department. MAF also has no intention to build an education department after a successful launch to welcome its new public in May of 2017. The department of Visitor Services was designed to embrace an educational mission, and MAF wished to similarly incorporate visitor engagement techniques by training their part-time visitor associates. Hamalian envisioned a staffing plan that included a roster of smart and visitor associates that could be trained to engage in conversations about contemporary art, without creating a disconnect between an educational mission. "While other institutions usually had separated two departments to support education and visitor services," noted Hamalian, she saw "the strength to combine a more traditional gallery attendant into the role of an educator which fulfills the needs to engage audiences with thought-provoking and dynamic conversations." (Flouty and Hamalian 2018).

Litmos is the online training software program that she uses to support 13 full-time staff, and 70 part-time staff members. Like the Broad, she has doubled the initial pool of VSAs; when MAF first opened in May 2017, the organization initially had hired only 40 VSAs, and needed to nearly double that number after the opening (Flouty and Hamalian 2018). Staffing with part-time support has been critical for the museum. MAF does not have the same extensive opening hours nor capacity for large daily group numbers such as the Broad. When MAF first opened its doors, the organization was averaging to 600 to 800 visitors daily, and the space was limited to both timed ticketing and restricted parking opportunities due to the organization's proximity within a residential neighborhood in Los Angeles. When MAF opened an exhibition of Olafur Eliasson's work in fall of 2017, nearly all of the available viewing times were fully booked, and the organization saw some of its highest visitation numbers of around 1,200 visitors per day (Flouty and Hamalian 2018).

But a more innovative use of the MAF's online platform includes the ability to give immediate access to all of the organization's training materials about the collection with a simple click. MAF is a small organization and often partners with outside non-profits to expand their educational offerings. Hamalian noted that MAF had partnered with Genesis starting in 2017, a cultural non-profit based in Los Angeles that "reaches beyond the traditional classroom to provide underserved students with access to cutting-edge science, technology, engineering, art and mathematics (STEAM) education through hands-on, project-based learning experiences designed to inspire, develop 21st century skills, and motivate sustained STEAM learning" (Genesis 2018).

> When the partnership with Genesis launched [in 2017], many of Genesis' educators wanted to know 'where can we find more information about the works on display?' All I needed to do was input the educator's email address and instantly, they had access! It was wonderful, because they went through the courses, and they didn't need to ask for additional information from me. They structured their children's tours based on the content that we have on the platform. It is an effective tool that allows us to share information that is consistent across all departments. (Flouty and Hamalian 2018)

With the click of a single button, she can quickly help outside educators involved in her community partnerships fast access to the same rich training materials that she uses with her part-time, front-of-house staff. She also acknowledges that it was helpful to share the content she uses directly. She believes that many of the museums share similar agendas to make art accessible for museum visitors. She especially believes that it is helpful to share resources between new organizations that are just learning how to engage visitors in conversations about contemporary art. In her mind, the platform still leaves room for improvement, such as how to supplement evergreen content with more timely announcements, such as an upcoming artist talk that would be pertinent to a forthcoming show for an artist in the permanent collection (Flouty and Hamalian 2018).

22.6 Project Limitations

Both projects presented above held vast limitations that were not limited to time or budget but connected to the ways in which online platforms function. One of the greatest challenges to this project was that circa 2015, most out-of-the-box LMS primarily fell into two types or categories that possessed structural limitations that proved inappropriate for deployment in a museum context. The first type of LMS aligned with traditional, academic-based systems of learning. The school-based type of LMS (such as CANVAS, Coursly, etc.) traced classroom-based language, and included prompts to assign grades as a "teacher." School-based LMS systems were further limited to facilitate module-based learning to fall in a regimented manner across a semester-based schedule, instead of asynchronously. Learners needed to be manually entered and there were few ways in which they could engage with one another online besides peer critique on assignments. The second type of LMS considered was embraced by Human Resources, and as HR-based in focus, was traditionally used for compliance training and onboarding new staff. Neither type was appropriate for Visitor Services museum staff, and it was difficult to locate a platform that contained neutral language as well as a white-label, non-branded look that a museum could embrace and make its own.

Both Girard and Hamalian are also hopeful that Litmos will someday create an easy chat feature within the platform that would allow real-time and active sharing of resources and links. Rather than reading through an email chain and copying and pasting relevant information to an upcoming show or artist talk, Hamalian would like to have communication to come through the Litmos platform directly, in order to make sure that other people can see this communication, especially as it relates to artworks and discussions in the galleries. She believes that creating an ability to attach a link directly to a module, as well as an instant chat feature to capture some of the conversations that occur in the gallery, would be key to growing the platform (Flouty and Hamalian 2018).

And lastly, this project is limited by the types of connections that are supported within the Litmos platform across different types of media files. The platform can support and embed .MP3, .PPT, .PDF and just about any other type of SCORM-compliant content. Museums often are working in multiple formats, and so the platform can support most media types. But the platform does not allow for an easy way to connect content across multiple modules. If a painting or a work of art appears in multiple exhibitions over time, one can search for older content in prior modules, but Litmos does not allow for direct linkages across modules, often resulting in an unwieldy duplication of content.

22.7 Conclusion

To radicalize museum teaching and learning as conversations unfold in the galleries between Visitor Services staff and visitors, the field of contemporary art museum education needs fewer corporate platforms, and more input around lived experiences that can be shared actively and in real-time. Litmos, as a platform and as a corporate entity, may not, in fact, be an appropriate LMS platform to house museum training content in the future, despite its ease in sharing and adding new users. The company offers a small, 10% discount for licenses that are operated by non-profit entities, but the cost for any further design customization falls to an outside designer or other vendor, often without any discounted rates. Furthermore, in order to easily share materials from within the platform, one must first secure an access account from the host institution, which is ideal for assuaging general privacy concerns, but is less than ideal for sharing between other platforms beyond Litmos. And finally, the Litmos site is not as mobile-compatible as one would like, as the need for more collaborative models remains.

Collaborative models of online shared resources now hold the potential to provide extendable and scalable learning environments across education and visitor services departments and across many types of contemporary art collections. Such platforms may be used to share resources, strategies and training plans—and such initiatives such as at the Broad and at MAF have already moved museum practice towards a conversational visitor engagement strategy. The potential to connect with community organizations and educators to share critical resources also helps to connect people in the larger museum community back to the organization, ultimately creating an easy portal to share effective practices as they constantly evolve. Many other museums have taken the step to train part-time personnel to serve as both security guards and audience engagement ambassadors, including the Solomon R. Guggenheim Museum, the Whitney Museum, and many more, albeit minus the support of an institution-wide online training model that could facilitate such sharing.

Most importantly, the Broad online training platform could not have launched without direct and active input from field practitioners within contemporary art museum education. An expanded sense of collegiality between practitioners to improve upon our work with docents, gallery guides, and visitor services personnel resulted in charged conversations about ways in which digitally-distributed training materials could radicalize the museum education profession, including ways in which new possibilities for in-gallery assessments could further enrich the exchange between museum visitors and museum staff. As so many in-gallery museum staff are also part-time, at-will employees, the opportunity to build deeper connections to both new training content and to the organization also surfaced as an early ambition for this project.

New ways in which implementation for online training platforms need to be developed and deployed also demand internal organizational change, and ones that are designed to support new thinking about museum visitors that extend far beyond the digital realm. How best to facilitate learning in partnership between museum staff and the visitor often relies heavily on technology-driven solutions, yet one of the most powerful outcomes of the online platform's implementation has been facilitated conversation in the galleries about contemporary art, and between humans. Samis and Michaelson urge readers to think about the consequences of siloed practices across many museums they examined in their book, *Creating The Visitor-Centered Museum* (2017). The authors call for a visitor-centered approach in which each working group within museums thinks far beyond its own territory and domain in serving museum visitors, ultimately requiring for an impactful new way for museums to operate in the future (2017, pp. 5–7). They found in their extensive study across multiple global sites that a visitor-centered approach in museums also demands a fully new way to enact organizational change from deep within the museum, and new modalities of working with visitors cannot be extracted from new ways of working. Central and paramount to such a radical change requires the placement of museum collections and exhibitions on equal footing as the needs of museum visitors (p. 7), and digital training platforms help facilitate this change.

Organizational change in museum practice requires a fundamental shift toward customer service and visitor advocacy that extends far beyond the digital realm, despite a reliance on digital training to deploy new content to support such endeavors. These changes toward a visitor-focused museum will also need to rely on more ways in which part-time staff can co-create the content that their peers will use, allowing for more visibility and prestige and pride in the work they are later conducting during interactions with visitors out on gallery floors. Most importantly of all, the ways in which a younger generation trained using an online platform to support and even co-create new ways of engaging and interacting with visitors will impact the field in untold, myriad ways, with new and as-of-yet unrealized opportunities to share and extend practices across silos within a single organization, and across multiple organizations. What if a single conversation with a visitor in Los Angeles about an artwork could be documented, uploaded and shared into the training platform in 2020, only to be accessed when that same work is on loan to another organization in 2030? In its current iteration, the platform does not allow front-line museum staff to document in-gallery conversations in real time, and tracking conversation in ways that do not transgress privacy remains an issue. Yet an opportunity for tracking anonymous conversations about contemporary art, and the subsequent creation of an archive of anecdotes about each artwork, could allow for semantic entry-points in which visitors make connections with art objects and their everyday lives evolve over time, and would help future museum-based front-line staff to have even more real and authentic conversations with visitors someday.

References

Cotter H (2015) Review: the broad is an old-fashioned museum for a new gilded age. The New York Times, 13 Sept 2015. https://www.nytimes.com/2015/09/13/arts/design/review-broad-museum-los-angeles.html. Accessed 12 Mar 2018

Flouty R, Cherry R (2018) Conversation with Richard Cherry, phone interview conducted on 15 Mar 2018
Flouty R, Girard L (2018) Conversation with Lauren Girard, phone interview conducted on 15 Mar 2018
Flouty R, Hamalian L (2018) Conversation with Liza Hamalian, interview conducted on 8 June 2018
Genesis (2018) GENESIS Opens New Innovation Lab at the Marciano Art Foundation in Los Angeles. Genesis, USA. https://genesissteam.org/genesis-opens-new-innovation-lab-at-the-marciano-art-foundation-in-los-angeles/. Accessed 9 Jan 2019
Pugliese J (2018) Meet the people keeping MOCA's art fingerprint free. Los Angeles Magazine, 14 Feb 2018. http://www.lamag.com/culturefiles/moca-security/. Accessed 13 Jan 2018
Samis PS, Michaelson M (2017) Creating the visitor-centered museum. Routledge, New York
Schneider T (2017) Why the Marciano Foundation Embodies an Existential Art-World Crisis. Artnet News. https://news.artnet.com/market/new-marciano-foundation-existential-crisis-private-museums-everywhere-971639 (accessed January 9, 2019)
Stanberg S (2016) Avant Guard: At LA's Broad Museum, a new approach to protecting art. National Public Radio (NPR), USA, 23 Feb 2016. https://www.npr.org/2016/02/23/467681344/avant-guard-at-las-broad-museum-a-new-approach-to-protecting-art. Accessed 8 Jan 2019
The Broad (2015) Architectural fact sheet. The Broad, Los Angeles, California, USA. https://www.thebroad.org/sites/default/files/pressroom/the_broad_architectural_fact_sheet_1.pdf. Accessed 8 Jan 2018

Chapter 23
Transforming Education for Museum Professionals in the Digital Age

Tula Giannini and Jonathan P. Bowen

Abstract As the digital revolution accelerates, one of the most significant impacts that museums are experiencing, is how digital development is changing the very nature of work across the professions and disciplines from art and humanities to computer science and technology. Simply put—work and life are merging and becoming increasingly digital and cross-disciplinary, as they are absorbed into the digital ecosystem. Museums are recognizing that the digital shift is causing them to rethink the skills and knowledge their professional staff needs and are challenged to find effective strategies to respond to changes brought about by digital culture and related social and cultural issues, while graduate education for museum professionals is similarly challenged. As a case study, we consider Pratt Institute's Master of Science in *Museums and Digital Culture*, introduced in 2015 by Giannini. Representing the first master's degree of its kind, it offers a program set in a digital framework that encompasses the full range of museum activities and functions in contrast to the prevalent museum studies model taking a more traditional collection-centered approach. Over the past few years, the work of museum professionals behind the scenes has become increasingly carried out using digital tools and technologies, from collection management including digitization and access, to museum websites and social media, while using digital in galleries and exhibitions is an emerging area of critical focus aimed at developing digital strategies and methods for visitor engagement and experience and that expand the roles and responsibilities of museum professionals. Among digital advances, augmented and virtual reality, digital storytelling and artificial intelligence, are entering the mainstream of museum life, more fully immersing museums in the digital culture ecosystem. This chapter explores how education for museum professionals is transforming, as it responds to the need for graduates to possess digital skills and a deep knowledge and understanding of the social and cultural contexts in which museums are evolving.

T. Giannini (✉)
School of Information, Pratt Institute, New York, USA
e-mail: giannini@pratt.edu

J. P. Bowen
School of Engineering, London South Bank University, London, UK
e-mail: jonathan.bowen@lsbu.ac.uk

Southwest University, Chongqing, China

T. Giannini and J. P. Bowen (eds.), *Museums and Digital Culture*,
Springer Series on Cultural Computing, https://doi.org/10.1007/978-3-319-97457-6_23

23.1 Introduction

Graduate education for museum professionals traces its roots to the fields of art history and curatorial studies, and we see from recent research that although these foundational fields still hold sway, the rapid rise digital culture in the 21st century is causing museums to rethink their identity, their roles, responsibilities and relationships with their communities. This in turn, calls for new ways of thinking about what knowledge and skills graduates will need to acquire to be prepared to lead museums into the future. In a world where people across the globe are connected via our digital ecosystem, a digital world open 24/7 delivering a 360-degree view of life and culture, museum professional must learn to think digitally in a new 3D multi-dimensional, non-linear complex manner. New ways of thinking, seeing, and doing research are embedded in the digital evolution that encompasses learning, communication, human identity and behavior. Students entering the museum profession will be challenged not only by digital culture increasingly driven by artificial intelligence and machine leaning, but equally by digital art and the context of social and cultural change and interaction on a global stage.

Emanating from the digital revolution, the digital evolution of human states of being (Bowen et al. 2018) and consciousness is driving a continuous cycle of change in academe that has become common across all disciplines and professions. Those fields that hold tight to old ideas and old ways of thinking and doing to define our past and present, will get left behind, having missed the wave of awe-inspiring digital opportunities that lie before us to be creative and innovative so that we may make a more inclusive and diverse society, working together in digital and virtual reality. For the past several years, humanities departments have experienced deep declines in enrollments and humanists are truly concerned (Hayot 2018). On the other hand, the digital humanities field, which aligns with museums, digital culture and digital art history, is thriving and growing alongside the field's integration with emerging technologies. Thus, interdisciplinary approaches to learning and research conceptualized for the digital world are well-positioned to move into the future in ways that prospective students will recognize as part of their future (Fig 23.1).

Thinking Digitally by Tula Giannini (2018)

Traveling on the Internet
in digital space and time
From present
to past
and into the future
on my computer

Present and past
are clicks away
with digital display
The die is cast
connections fast
Linking data
A simple matter
makes sense
no expense

Exploring history
solving mysteries
finding answers
to unsolved questions
Make suggestions -
read e-books
have new looks
at old works
find documents
visit museums and monuments

Digitized collections
deep reflections
of times past
this should last
stories untold
of a research sleuth
looking for truth
don't delete
still incomplete

Fig. 23.1 'Mary's room'—an illustration of the thought experiment devised by the philosopher Frank Jackson in his article *Epiphenomenal Qualia* (Jackson 1982) and extended in *What Mary Didn't Know* (Jackson 1986)—Physicalism. Wikimedia Commons, https://commons.wikimedia.org/wiki/File:Mary_colour_scientist.png

23.2 What Museum Leaders and Researchers Are Saying

23.2.1 Research Report on 21st-Century Skills for Museum Professionals

A 2016 project report by the Museum Sector Alliance (Mu.SA, http://www.project-musa.eu) looks at the museum of the future from the perspective of "Insights and reflections from 10 international museums." It is one of several EU Mu.SA projects that are focusing on skills for museum professionals in the digital world that "aims to address the increasing disconnection between formal education and training and the world of work, because of the emergence of new job roles due to the quickening pace of the adoption of ICT in the museum sector." Is it not surprising that Mu.SA sees an "increasing disconnection" between education for museum professionals and their work in the real world in which digital reality is rapidly advancing as the new cultural frontier. The project poses a series of questions to museum leaders on how new digital skills should be defined to "assist cultural professionals to deepen their knowledge and skills for the digital transformation of the museum sector" (Sturabotti and Surace 2016) and strive to keep pace with digital developments while being consonant and integral with the digital culture ecosystem. Ten museum leaders representing the international museums being studied responded to questions related to six topic areas of which the final one focused on museum education, "6. Skills and profiles that facilitate the digital transformation of the museum" (Sturabotti and Surace 2016). The report's introduction ends by stating:

> Today a key figure is emerging in the promotion of a digital culture and the acquisition of digital skills necessary to modernize the museum: the Cultural ICT Consultant, who is responsible for the museum's digital strategy and the financial planning of technological resources. This profile is strategic for all the museums that want to take up the challenges of the digital transformation. [adding that] they also play a mediating role between the museum and the outside world, being able to talk to the different stakeholders, whether they are partners to work with, or different online and offline communities.

Pedro Gadanho, Director of the Museum of Art, Architecture and Technology (MAAT) in Lisbon, which opened in October of 2017, emphasizes the use digital technologies such as augmented reality, pointing out that rather than "reading the few explanatory phrases next to an art work, it is now possible to receive much more information, in a more immersive mode, for an immediate understanding of the object being exhibited."

Javier Pantoja, Chief Digital Officer, Head of technology at the Prado Museum in Madrid, stands out among leaders for his insightful and holistic vision of the future pointing out that, "in a changing world the worst mistake is to stand still and digitalization is the only way to go." When asked, "What is your ideal candidate?—he responded:

> Our ideal candidate must have a comprehensive approach of the world, also from the digital point of view. It is important that they know where they live as much as they know our collections, our history and our activities. Because the role they will have is that of mediator between two worlds: the Prado and the outside world. Then they have to be able to use the digital tools available today, like, a few years ago, it was essential to know how to write reports and other documentation.

When asked, "What is the most important emerging job profiles related to the digital aspect of a museum?" Pantoja responded, "Considering what I said so far, I believe that the emerging professional figure is that of the digital curator." In a similar sense, the authors recognized the key roles that digital art and digital curators will play in the transformation of museum practice.

> Looking to the future, inevitably, more galleries and museums will feature digital art, so that digital artists and digital curators will begin to hold sway in museum hierarchy, enabling them to take the lead in reimagining traditional gallery framework. This in turn, will introduce a new digital gallery concept designed for digital art and experience. Ideas and technical innovation growing out this creative digital arts partnership will no doubt influence exhibitions and gallery shows generally. (Bowen et al. 2017)

Art critic Bryan Boucher's article for *Artnet News* poses a key question in the title, "What's the Best Path to a Top Museum Job? We Analyzed the Training of 100 Curators to Find Out." He follows this with a simple answer, "There is no one path to success as a curator of contemporary art—but that doesn't prevent many top experts from having strong opinions" (Boucher 2018). For this study, Boucher examined the educational histories of 100 curators who specialize in contemporary art at 69 fine art museums in 32 US states. Although no one path to becoming a curator is delineated, the education and training identified by the museum curators interviewed points to a well-trodden educational path consisting of a degree program in art history and experience working with a museum curator, which generally takes the form of an internship, practicum or fellowship in a museum. Over the past decade a handful of degree programs in curatorial studies have emerged that are offering a more hands-on learning experience focusing on the making of exhibitions which is gaining traction. However, this staid educational path in light of the central role curators play in the life of the museum, would appear to signal a disconnect to the digital shift in museums and the requisite transformation of the museum as an audience-centered institution, able to absorb and respond to social and cultural change around for example, social justice, democratic ideals, gender and identify, and other relevant issues.

An apparent lack of this dimensionality in education programs that would prepare curators to meet 21st-century challenges, is already showing cracks in its foundations, both inside and outside the museum walls. We see examples of these fissures playing out in a slew of museum protests around social causes. Some, discussed in other chapters, focus on gender, sexual abuse such as the MeToo movement and others around corporate sponsorships. Protests by Brooklyn community activists, germane to this discussion of the education and roles of museum curators, took on the emotional draw of performance art being staged at the Brooklyn Museum in opposition to the Museum's appointment of a curator for African art (Neuendorf 2018a). The protests quickly attracted global attention in the press and social media bringing scrutiny to curatorial appointments which surprised the Museum, as it specifically raised questions over what should be the qualifications for this curator position. Other protests by Brooklyn activists were around (de)colonization, gentrification, displacement and race, themes that resonate with museum protests generally and speak to questions of museum leadership and communication.

The primary reason for these dramatic changes in audience behaviors, attitudes and expectations in general stems from audiences entering the museum being immersed in digital life and culture. Connected and communicating, participating and interacting as part of everyday digital life, they are unbounded by geography and diverse cultures. What they see and hear inside the museum is being tweeted, posted on Instagram, emailed, blogged, and messaged as the world watches and reacts.

This connected digital ecosystem across which the world communicates and acts, is recasting the curatorial role so that even what should be curated is in questions, for example, curating the visitor experience (Giannini and Bowen 2016).

Thus, the range of responsibilities covered by curatorial departments represents a diverse body of knowledge that extends well beyond art history, collections and content curation. Most notably, the use of digital tools and technology not only for collection management and other work activities are of growing importance to museum innovation, creativity in exhibitions, communication of content and message, digital scholarship and research. Thus, there is a need for broader community discussion among museum professionals in conversation with visitors and professionals in other fields such as digital art and design, information, computing, communication, social science and psychology, that can be marshalled to reassess academic preparation for curators. Should art history continue to be privileged above all other knowledge sets?

According to the US Bureau of Labor Statistics (2018), the career outlook for curators shows a trend of strong growth which provides further impetus to more strategically align museum education with the broader trends of society, the arts and digital culture:

> There are now more than 12,400 full-time curators in America. The bureau has estimated that the number of people practicing in the profession will increase by 14 percent between 2016 and 2026—twice the average growth rate for jobs in the US. (Bureau of Labor Statistics 2018)

Statistics from a 2015 Mellon Foundation study (Schonfeld et al. 2015) shows that 84% of curators at US museums are white (Boucher 2015). This and other statistics make clear that education, although a key factor, is not the only one that determines a curator's professional path, which can be complex. Efforts in the recruitment and admissions of minority students to graduate programs in art and museums have seen some results, but success will only come when museums recruit and hire these graduates and broaden their cultural perspectives, while considering the changes brought about by digital culture (Bowen and Giannini 2014; Giannini and Bowen 2016) to see the role of curator more broadly, and to be more inclusive and diverse. This brings new challenges and issues to the forefront such as social movements and political activism organized via social media and reflected in new media that are impacting museums such as the MeToo movement, and issues around cultural identity and ownership, all part of the digital culture ecosystem connecting museums onsite in physical space to museums online in cyberspace.

23.2.2 Rethinking the Role of Curator—Responding to Digital Culture and Social Change

The 2018 policy paper, *Culture is Digital* (DCMS 2018), by the UK government in consultation with leaders of the UK technology sector and some 150 cultural institutions solicited feedback on pertinent questions and topics through online interaction using the hashtag #cultureisdititital. The report, is based on the Digital Culture Project initiated by the UK's Secretary of State for Digital, Culture, Media and Sport, Rt Hon. Matt Hancock. In his forward to the Executive Summary, he brings insightful observations about digital culture creating new relationships across disciplines with exciting results that are engaging new audiences (DCMS 2018).

> Digital technology is breaking down the silos between the cultural sectors, blurring the lines between disciplines–theatre blends with film; computer programming merges with sculpture. We have virtual reality curatorship, animated artworks, video games scored by classical music composers…. Tech companies are collaborating with cultural organisations and practitioners to create new experiences for audiences, often exploring the boundaries of new technology at the same time. The Royal Shakespeare Company's groundbreaking production of The Tempest brought digital avatars to life in real-time as part of a collaboration with Intel and Imaginarium.

The policy paper, for which the UK government seeks support, is organized around three key themes each of which contain specific policy proposals tied to the Arts Council England and the Heritage Lottery Fund in support of digital culture policy that brings the tech and cultural sectors together under the concept that "culture is digital".

> Audiences – Using digital technology to engage audiences
>
> Skills and the digital capability of cultural organisations
>
> Future Strategy: Unleashing the creative potential of technology

The three priorities of the Digital Culture Project are: (1) Digital infrastructure for culture, (e.g., the National Archives have digitized and put online over 80 million historic documents); (2) Innovation (e.g., support research and development of UK creative industries such as immersive reality with a projected work of 100 million by 2020); (3) Collaborations and partnerships (e.g., Watershed in Bristol working with University of Bristol and industrial partners to prototype and showcase new public facing applications of 5G). The executive summary of *Culture is Digital* opens by saying, "The UK has a dual competitive advantage in creative and technological skills4 and our future prosperity will be driven by this particular combination of strengths." It goes on to describe these "strengths" in terms of the billions of pounds culture and tech are earning and is expected to grow.

A key point is that museum professionals need digital skills and an understanding of the relationship between physical and digital objects. Curating a physical collection requires knowing how to digitize it and provide for its access and use. Curators communicate a collection's meaning and history and can create the stories that it tells through research and analysis, onsite and online. The physical and digital aspects of museum work are integrated and can no longer be teased apart as digital information flows across all aspects of the life of museum object in both physical and digital states. This evolution of curatorial and professional museum work constitutes a paradigm shift to a new conceptual model that takes center stage as museums reframe their roles, responsibilities, identify and relationships to their communities and the digital culture ecosystem.

When 20 curators were interviewed by *Artsy* critics Surya Tuback and Casey Lessey, new ideas and trends in museum curating emerged, not only about changes in the nature of their work, but as well shed light on new areas of knowledge and skills for museum education that speak to the field's growing complexity from its starting point of subject expertise to "inspiring work [that] ranges from harnessing virtual reality technology and promoting accessibility, to revisiting age-old collections through a 21st-century lens." We present here a condensed version of several of these interviews of leading curators engaged in critical and creative exhibition projects (Tubach and Lesser 2018).

Gloria Groom, Chair of European Painting and Sculpture, Art Institute of Chicago is thinking about how museum technology continues to evolve from problematic audio tours to more successful digital applications. The authors note that Groom is excited "by the increasing flexibility curators have with their exhibitions," that Groom sees in the "incorporation of high art with the physical objects that inspired them," and an increased exploration of how the creative process "can enrich our understanding of the work and also the artist." Imma Ramos, Curator of the South Asia Collections, British Museum, London is concerned about social issues, such as calls to decolonize collections, that are impacting museums. For an exhibition she co-organized the symposium, "Exhibiting the Experience of Empire," in which "speakers stressed the need for alternative perspectives on European imperialism and transparent approaches to collecting histories." Ramos "hopes to work with colleagues at the British Museum to develop an exhibition wherein the institution will reflect on Britain's imperial past though its objects."

Hiromi Kinoshita, Associate Curator of Chinese Art, Philadelphia Museum of Art, at the Philadelphia Museum of Art, reimagined the permanent gallery of Song dynasty ceramics by hanging along site them "large-scale monochromatic photographs by Eric Zetterquist that zoomed in on specific details of them." Kinoshito notes, "I wanted to draw attention to the simple and elegant forms of the ceramics, as during this period, the aesthetic was form over decoration," She also used an interactive screen so the visitors could see details of a 15th-century Chinese Buddhist temple ceiling and understand, "how much time and effort was put into creating a work that, in effect, was never meant to be seen up close." Working with a team including interpreters, educators, designers, conservators, she is re-doing the Chinese galleries scheduled to open in 2019. In the words of Kinoshita, "We have an amazing collection, and the aim is to make it more accessible to a diverse audience by engaging their senses in attractive, meaningful thematic displays that highlight narratives important to Chinese art and culture." "Museums are integrated throughout society and those who work in them have the responsibility to address all audiences,"

Carlos G. Navarro said. Curators have the responsibility, he added, to confront museum-goers with new, unfamiliar questions, but also to "show them realities they do not know, excite their imagination, and finally, make them enjoy." Carlos G. Navarro, Junior Curator of 19th-century Paintings, Museo Nacional del Prado, Madrid, wants to express, "contemporary sensibilities through classical art that resonates with current events and issues." Co-curating the exhibition at the Prado, "The

Other's Gaze. Spaces of Difference," he brought attention to works from their collections by Caravaggio, Rubens and Ribera through the lens of homosexuality.

Ilona Katzew, Curator and Department Head of Latin American Art, Los Angeles County Museum of Art, believes that for large encyclopedic museums to remain current and relevant, they need "to strike the right balance between preserving history, being more inclusive, communicating new ideas, and reinvigorating display strategies. As curator of the Met's 2018 exhibition, *Painted in Mexico: 1700–1790: Pinxit Mexici*, an expansive look at 18th-century New Spanish (Mexican) painting, not formerly exhibited, "Katzew traveled to more than 30 cities in Mexico, the U.S., and Europe over the course of six years, examining over 2,000 artworks."

James Bradburne, Director General, Pinacoteca di Brera and Biblioteca Nazionale Braidense, Milan, as a recent museum manager, still draws on this expertise on late Renaissance natural philosophy and the court of Rudolph II while concentrating on project as the interactive exhibition "Brera Listens," that will engage, "Milan's citizens in the Pinacoteca di Brera's reinstallation of 20th-century Italian art from its permanent collection," aligned with his philosophy, "that it's not blockbuster traveling exhibitions that will push museums forward today, but rather a return to 'smaller and more focused exhibitions closely linked to museums' permanent collections.'"

Thinking about how these interviews apply to new curatorial perspectives and skills that are significant for museum education, and what stands out can be seen in the context of critical and innovative thinking and are: greater emphasis on being relevant and connected to trends in society, expanding the cultural diversity of museum collections and exhibitions, having a deep understanding of digital culture and its influence on audience behavior and expectations, the desire to convey ideas to visitors in meaningful ways, and finding ways to interact with the public and take seriously their lives and perspectives. Although a tall order for museum professionals, it is a necessary one.

The 2017 UK Art Fund study, carried-out by The Museums Consultancy under the title, *The 21st Century Curator*, poses the research question, "Who is the 21st Century Curator?" Data for the survey was gathered using an online survey of some 520 people "working in, or supporting people working in, curatorial roles," as well as phone interviews with 20 people working in curatorial or senior management roles (Art Fund 2017). Those interviewed were at various stages of their museum careers. When curators were asked, "What are the top development priorities for today's curator's?" they identified "communication, storytelling, and digital skills as the most important development priorities for curators and museum professionals." The study shows that:

> Digital technology has transformed relationships and new technologies and social media have changed the dynamic between curator and visitor. Curators can now share knowledge more easily and quickly, both with the public and between colleagues and institutions. Survey respondents note that the expansion in digital encourages innovation, and that social media and the internet allow the opportunity to highlight and improve access to collections.

This establishes that exhibitions dominate the work of a museum, and thus are at the heart of a curator's work.

> 44% of survey respondents say they are spending up to 25-50% of their time on exhibition-related work, and 45% identify exhibition development as the biggest driver for curatorial work in their organisation – which reflects the movement towards a greater and deeper engagement with audiences. Relatively little time is spent on fundraising, capital planning or Continuing Professional Development.

23.2.3 Lucas Museum of Narrative Art Focuses on Visual Storytelling

Looking at new ways of thinking digitally, the filmmaker, George Lucas, gives us new thinking about museums and about what is art, with his creation of the Lucas Museum of Narrative Art (https://lucasmuseum.org), defined as "visual art that tells a story." Construction of the museum began March 2018 and is scheduled to open sometime in 2021. Conceived as a feature attraction and part of the general revisioning and remaking of Exposition Park in Los Angeles, CA, it is planned as "a one-of-a-kind gathering place to experience collections, films and exhibitions dedicated to the power of visual storytelling and the evolution of art and moving images," and "will present original work by world renowned and emerging artists, cutting-edge digital technologies, and daily film screenings in state-of-the-art theaters, as well as extraordinary educational opportunities for students of all ages" (Cascone 2018). The museum's collections are drawn from Lucas' 40 years of filmmaking that have introduced groundbreaking film techniques through digital technology seen in his iconic film, *Star Wars* (1977), that sparked a type of digital revolution in film and cultural trend-setter in life, winning of six Academy Awards. His films, *The Empire Strikes Back* (1980) and *Return of the Jedi* (1983) reached further into this type of digital innovation for which the Pixar company he founded in 1979 became known.

Entering the museum world with bigger than life plans for the facilities and eleven landscaped acres estimated to cost one billion dollars, Lucas is applying his creative digital thinking to bringing together the Lucas Museum's foundational collections that place fine art and popular culture art on an equal footing and significantly draw on a wide range of materials representing all media, physical and digital, drawn from objects and materials made for his film productions by artists including costumes, fashion, set designs, props, musical scores, drawings, manuscripts, photography, comics, and other ephemera—all brought together to bring stories to life while creating a new type of museum experience (Vankin 2018). It seems clear, that these collections require a wide range of curatorial expertise and visual storytelling skills interpreted through the physical and digital objects of these diverse materials in ways that make for an engaging and exciting user experience and show. Quoting Lucas, "Narrative is one of the oldest and most important impulses in art. It is also the most popular form of art. Tracing the arc of narrative art reveals how culture is created, reinforced, and then compelled to evolve" (McLean 2017). The museum plans to develop its collections around three themes: history of narrative art, the art of cinema, and digital art, and it is inspiring to see their commitment continue to build on their digital art collections being one of the first museum to do so. Art as narrative, narrative as art, as a form of human expression that threads through our lives across the digital culture ecosystem where increasingly video and sound dominant the digital landscape.

23.2.4 Key Issues in Museum Education

We point to two concurrent issues for graduate programs for museum professionals:

1. Traditional museum studies programs lack curriculum that give students digital skills and the knowledge they require to carry-out a wide range of digital work at the heart of museum activities constituting the digital life of the museum, for example, collections digitization and management, preservation and conservation, exhibitions, museum websites, the virtual museum, social media, communications and public programs; and
2. An integrated physical and digital environment has yet to become mainstream as museums hold to a 19th-century organizational model by which departments are siloed within a hierarchical administrative structure so that digital departments tend to be ghettoized, leaving museum staff and administration wondering what the digital team is doing and why.

Addressing these issues, Pratt Institute's Master of Science in *Museums and Digital Culture* is designed to prepare museum professionals as leaders, having cutting-edge digital skills and future-forward thinking to create a diverse and socially aware environment where physical and digital ways of doing and states of being are integrated across the museum seamlessly as they connect to the omnipresent digital ecosystem. Glen Lowry provided thoughts on museums in the future at the 2018 Art Leaders Network conference in Berlin (Art Leaders Network 2018; New York Times Conferences 2018a):

> I think the real issue for all of us in the museum world is to learn to think digitally so that what we're talking about is not simply the transformation of certain kinds of stories into different formats or the use of new technologies to deliver those stories, but to fundamentally rethink how we think, to move away from the kind of analog art history that we were all taught, hierarchical, sequential, to a more networked reconsidered manner of actually presenting works of art, The way in which we display art actually is no longer so analog and I think one of the great advents of digital technology is that it has begun to teach us how to imagine different relationships between objects and between viewers and objects, and technology is simply the glue or the conduit by which those relationships can be developed, but we have to actually start thinking about the kinds of exhibitions we're doing in new and different ways.

23.2.5 A Case Study: A New Museum Master's for the Digital World

The quickening pace of digital adoption by individual users and business is causing major disconnects, or lack of fit between what graduate museum programs are teaching to prepare museum professionals, and what knowledge and skills museums need from their professionals to be successful in the digital world. Over the past few years, this has topic has been explored at museum conferences and meeting, in journals and professional literature, and only recently have some new perspectives and programs been introduced, and which continue to develop. What some call the digital shift, is in fact much more extensive and represents a paradigm shift in the mission and goals of the museum enterprise, which has been discussed in detail in parts 1 and 2, such as questions of museum identity, social responsibility, roles, visitor participation and interaction, and growing expectations for building museum visitor partnerships in a digitally managed environment onside and online. In this context, it becomes clear that the traditional graduate museum studies programs only peripherally account for these study areas, as generally, programs focus on established curatorial and administrative work as carried out in a pre-digital world

In fall 2015, Pratt School of Information led by Dean, Tula Giannini, introduced the Master of Science in *Museums and Digital Culture* (MS MDC). Located in on Manhattan on 14th and Seventh Avenue, between Chelsea and Greenwich Village, Pratt's program is greatly advantaged by its proximity to many museums and other cultural institutions, especially galleries, libraries, and archives. The MS MDC, responds to the paradigm shift in museums from a curatorial-centric focus on collection-building to a visitor/user-centered focus, and moves from past to present and into the museum digital future. The aim of the program, is that graduates will gain the knowledge and digital skill sets that align with museums living in our 21st century digital ecosystem. Importantly, the program merges the physical and digital life of the museum, to educate students for the postdigital world where curatorial departments work with collections and collection management, exhibitions, and user experience, onsite and online, while being framed in the context of current social and cultural issues and movements, and their communities.

As a program that brings focus to the use of digital technology and media in museums from physical to virtual and on the Web, it is grounded in information and communication theory and related fields of computing and digital cultural heritage. As such, it finds commonalities of theory and practice with galleries, libraries, and archives. Through the MDC curriculum, which draws upon the School of Information's longstanding programmatic focus on cultural informatics introduced to the curriculum in 1998 by Giannini, students understand how museums can integrate digital technology into museum functions and activities, how visitors' digital information behavior is advancing participation and interaction with museums, and how museums are developing new roles and relationships with their communities, local and global, onsite and online, which is transforming their social and cultural identities as they connect with the digital ecosystem Through experiential learning, research and projects, students acquire up-to-date knowledge and skills sets and build broad cultural competencies essential for museum professionals working in our diverse cultural landscape. Importantly, students need to able to think digitally and critically about museums and their audiences.

The Pratt program is organized into five study areas: (I) Theory and Practice; (II) Museum Collections and Services; Digital Preservation and Curation; (III) Digital Tools and Technology; (IV) User Experience, Education and Information Design; and (V) Field Research and Practicum. Building on our partnerships and grant projects with New York City's leading museums, students gain experience and mentoring to undertake professional work. Students have use of high-tech learning labs designed around curriculum goals and outcomes: (1) The iLab for Digital Culture, (2) Research Seminar Lab, (3) Information Experience Lab, (4) Cultural Informatics Lab and, four seminar/lab classrooms supporting participatory learning. Over the past several years through IMLS (Institute of Museum and Library Services) project grants in partnerships with Brooklyn Museum, Brooklyn Historical Society, Brooklyn Public Library, Frick Art Reference Library, the Watson Library, the Metropolitan Museum of Art, and the Museum of Modern Art (Giannini and Bowen 2014; 2015), we developed curriculum and advanced certificate programs in: Archives, Museum Libraries, User Experience, Digital Conservation and Curation, and Museum Studies with the Department of History of Art and Design. Students pursue these certificates within their master's program.

Among museum master's programs, Pratt's is distinguished by its interdisciplinary approach set in the context of art and culture making connections with digital humanities and art history. In 2013, Giannini introduced a fellowship program in partnership with New York City museums and libraries such as the Metropolitan Museum of Art, the Frick Art Reference Library, Brooklyn Museum, MoMA, Guggenheim Museum, and the Whitney Museum of American Art, supporting two-semester internships. Participating students can work on projects in best practice institutions and with leading professionals. They learn to apply user-centric principles for visitor experience to create narratives and tell stories, digitize to describe collections for access and use, apply digital strategies for audience communication, engagement and participation, and gain skills for programming, web design, information management, curatorial research, and creating exhibitions. Many of these skill sets are also applicable to galleries, libraries and archives, especially as archival materials are more regularly used exhibitions. The program emphasizes the social and cultural contexts of art, and especially understanding contemporary, conceptual and digital art, their connections to activism, politics and protests, and how museums will need to respond to the digital information behavior and digital identity of their audiences, and their life in the digital world.

23.2.6 Picturing the Student Experience

See Figs 23.2, 23.3 and 23.4.

Fig. 23.2 **Left**: A Pratt student at the Andy Warhol Exhibition working on the course project featuring digital capture and curation at several New York museums. (Photograph by Tula Giannini, December 2018). **Right**: Pratt students at the Frick Art Reference Library visiting the archives digitization center, seeing the curator demonstrate how photographs are digitized and made available on the Frick's website. (Photograph by Tula Giannini)

Fig. 23.3 Neighborhood Gallery—An exhibition of international fashion designers at Fashion Institute of Technology's Gallery on Seventh Avenue and 27th St. Museum students compared this display of designer dresses, to the ones at the Met's exhibition, *Heavenly Bodies: Fashion and the Catholic Imagination*. (Photograph by Tula Giannini)

Fig. 23.4 Pratt students participating in the London Summer School on *The Arts and Digital Culture* with the Department of Digital Humanities, King's College London, having lunch at the Wellcome Collection café on Euston Road, London, after spending the morning at the British Library for a curator presentation on Hebrew manuscripts and librarian talks on digital projects. (Photograph by Tula Giannini)

23.2.7 Reports from the Field

The report *Museum Professionals in the Digital Era—Agents of Change and Innovation* by the Museum Sector Alliance (Mu.SA) with the European Erasmus Programme and the Sector Skills Alliance presents findings of this study focused on identifying the key competencies for museum professionals and identifying the challenges they face (Silvaggi 2017a, b). Section 5 of the report gives an "overview of key findings." Janice Lane of the National Museum of Wales observes:

> One of the biggest challenges of the sector is seeing digital as an integral way of working. Regardless of where you may fit in the museum range of disciplines and areas of work, there will be a requirement for a set of digital skills and competencies that are taken for granted. (Silvaggi 2017b, p. 31)

An article in the journal, *Midas*, takes up the Report's question of, "skills for digital transformation in museums". The Mu.SA Project brings focus to the impacts of digital culture on museums:

> Technology is changing faster than ever and impacts not only on what we do but how we think about what we do. This document addresses the fact that institutions and arts organizations

> (public and private), set up to carry out a public purpose, now find that through the impact of digitization and internet tools, they are, in many cases, lagging behind… There is a growing sense, confirmed through the research carried out for this report, that there needs to be a recalibration within organizations and institutions. Previous assumptions about knowledge, power, trust and authority within our cultural ecosystems need to be rethought; also, the repository of these values may no longer be within the traditional hierarchies. In order to deliver the public purpose efficiently and effectively, things need to change. (Carvalho et al. 2018)

The Mu.SA Project, which spans 2016–2019, "aims to address the increasing disconnection between formal education and training and the world of work because of the emergence of new job roles due to the quickening pace of the adoption of ICT in the museum sector… and to assist cultural professionals to deepen their knowledge and skills for the digital transformation of the museum sector." The project raises some key questions about the future of museums, to be considered by ten world recognized European museums. The results of this process are published in the 2016 report, *Museum of the Future: Insights and reflections from 10 international museums. Mu.SA*. The introduction to the report poses four key question about the digital future of museums (Sturabotti and Surace 2016):

> What will happen to museums when digital technology shows its full potential? What features will the museum of the future have? How will it seize the opportunities offered by digital innovation? What competencies does this industry need to keep museums relevant from the 20th century to the present? To understand what role the digital driver is playing in the modernization of the industry, we asked these questions to ten internationally renowned European museums, where varying types and sizes of collections are conserved.

Here we quote from the responses of responses of museum leaders with special attention to the question on competencies.

Javier Pantoja, Chief Digital Officer, Head of Technology at The Prado Museum in Madrid, responded with both questions and ideas that were at once insightful and inspiring, taking a broad view of the museum in a global digital context. Importantly, he identifies the role of "digital curator" as a top museum professional:

> How do you recruit staff in your museum? What is your ideal candidate? Our ideal candidate must have a comprehensive approach of the world, also from the digital point of view. It is important that they know where they live as much as they know our collections, our history and our activities. Because the role they will have is that of mediator between two worlds: the Prado and the outside world. Then they have to be able to use the digital tools available today, like, a few years ago, it was essential to know how to write reports and other documentation. What are the most important emerging job profiles related to the digital aspect of a museum? Considering what I said so far, I believe that the emerging professional figure is that of the digital curator.

Other telling quotes consider the impact of digital culture bring insight into the importance of new vision for museums:

> In a changing world the worst mistake is to stand still and digitalization is the only way to go.
>
> Despite the difficulty of prediction what is certain is that the museum of the future must be a digital museum, able to seize the opportunities associated with sharing its collections online.

> Today museums live a very interesting phase, characterized by the transformation of their visitors from physical to virtual. To understand the extent of this change, one need only to think that the number of our website visitors is double the number of people that visit our rooms: 6 million in the first case, three in the second. And every year the number of visitors continues to grow.
>
> The digital is the means to realize the museum institution's mission, is not a goal itself. It is part of the museum strategic plan and, therefore, covers all aspects of a museum life.

Pantoja calls for the digital transformation of the museum which at the Prado began with communication:

> In fact, the information concerning the works of the collection are the backbone of the structure and design of our new website.
>
> More than a matter of skills and abilities it is a matter of mentality and will. The new museum professionals must have the digital world as one of their primary objectives.
>
> The sector needs a mix of skills, a good mixture of art history, computer science, history, communication, online marketing, and cultural management. My ideal staff should know how to use a computer writing code such as HTML and other specific applications, but also must have a degree in art subjects, because we need people who know how to produce content. Today the team I work with has 8–9 people with this type of expertise.

Linda Volkers, Marketing Manager at the Rijksmuseum, emphasizes sharing collections online, partnerships, and shared networks and not being siloed:

> If you stay in your silo, think only of your primary goals strictly, you won't have success. That's why is so important to work with partners: they can give you different ideas and expertise and working with them it's much more funny.

23.2.8 The Need for a Broad Range of Skills

Museum skills for curators and directors that are gaining traction are those embedded in digital culture including communication and conversation with audiences and outreach to communities, are increasingly included in positions, especially as museums become porous with local and global communities. Just as the museum has shifted from a collection-based model to a visitor/user/community model, these roles must too evolve along with the educational programs for museum leaders and professionals, so that students graduate prepared with to meet emerging social, cultural and digital challenges. Exhibitions present the public face of the museum and the place where the public enters with heightened expectations to engage and participate. As museums strive to navigate this challenging and the complex landscape effectively, they increasingly will need curators and leaders that understand how digital tools and technology used in innovative ways to create context, convey meaning and create relationships between objects and ideas, evoke critical thinking and immerse visitors in works displayed with awareness and sensitivity to diverse ways of living and working in our global digital ecosystem connecting us all.

AI is being used more often for museum projects, "possibly leading to a profound transformation of the profession of museum educators and mediators." The aim is to improve learning experiences, participation and content creation, while it can also be "considered as a threat to traditional jobs and not appropriated to treat delicate subjects or to replace human interaction." During a panel discussion at the ECSITE 2018 Conference in Geneva, Diane Drubay, founder of *We Are Museums* addressed the question, "how do we apply artificial intelligence to cultural mediation?" She presented three categories of for AI mediation: virtual companion, history-storyteller and digital replicas builder, all of which we already see in use and being developed (We Are Museums 2018).

23.2.9 Museum Leaders—Connecting Learning and Technology

The #FutureMuseum Project, *What will museums be like in the future?*, sponsored by Museum-ID, solicits thoughts and observations from leading museum professional on what trends and changes they see in the future of the 21st-century museum. To date, some 50 leaders have responded among them, here we quote Kaywin Feldman, Director and President, Minneapolis Institute of Arts, for the way she considers human behavior in the context of their digital lives and the dark-side of digital leaving open the question of how the two can be reconciled:

> I'm one of those people who believe that museums have become increasingly important in our chaotic, stress- and distraction-filled world. Since museums offer experiences, memories, and the self-directed exploration of content, they will beckon as a necessary respite from our often isolated, digital and virtual lives. Besides, in a world where we can fake anything, from art, to the news, to genetically manufactured food, the need to experience the real thing will only become greater.
>
> Ultimately, museums matter because they are filled with wondrous things that remind us of what it is to be human. Our shared experience is expressed in so many interesting, exciting, and impactful ways. As the philosopher Alan Watts said, "the meaning of life is life itself". Museums are full of life: past, present, and future.

Some leaders note the increasing integration of physical and digital in service of visitor experience, as we see in the comments of Jenny Kidd, Senior Lecturer, Cardiff University:

> Immersive media allow us to diversify the stories we tell, to layer meaning and to embrace ambiguity. They can work seamlessly at the interstices of the physical and digital, and offer experiences that move creatively between the individual and the collective. They are performative, embodied, unruly and increasingly ambitious.

Education programs in museums prepare young students to be engaged future museum visitors. Amy McDowall, Primary Learning Coordinator, Manchester Museum brings fresh ideas to standard practice and looks to the use of digital media to interact with young people in creative and participatory ways. She writes:

> Our best ideas and most inclusive practice rarely reach our day-to-day learning programmes. Does the average day-long school visitor get to co-produce an exhibition, pursue their per-

> sonal interests, or engage in dialogue with curators? Do they debate, collaborate, create, or feel a sense of ownership of their local museum?
>
> One barrier for us is, I imagine, the fear that that this type of visit wouldn't fit with the curriculum-focused demands of the customer here – namely, the teacher. But the wider education sector is now changing too. Heavily content-based curricula – much like the idea of 'museums as knowledge-keepers' – are looking increasingly archaic in the digital age. Education in the future will be about what is done with all this knowledge … though the debates we'll be having will be as old as humanity itself: How do we apply knowledge and technological advances to improve our world? How do we understand cultural difference? What makes a good life, or a just society? What is 'truth'?

These comments demonstrate the central role that digital technology studied in contemporary social and cultural contexts will play in the education of museum professionals. They indicate new directions for teaching methodologies that move our programs into the future successfully and holistically, so that we connect past and present values and creative practices for a digital world, as we move into an exciting future, where digital is infused with artificial intelligence, augmented and virtual reality, and 3D imaging and printing. This means that new directions in graduate museum education that once looked futuristic, become realistic and necessary to remain relevant and connected to real people and communities, and their social and cultural lives and issues.

Equally important, museums need museum professionals who are diverse, and see the world of art and culture through diverse perspectives and lenses. A Mellon Foundation study (Schonfeld et al. 2015) found that white people held 84% of professional positions in museums. In 2018, community protests relating to this issue at museums and galleries caught the attention of the art world and the concern of museums, most prominently, at the Brooklyn Museum where protests focused on the hiring of a white woman to serve as curator of African Art. Hearing the call to address this challenge, in 2018, Michael Govan, Director of the Los Angeles County Museum of Art (LACMA), turned to Arizona State University to form a partnership program "to establish a new master's program aimed at bringing more curators of color into the profession" (Neuendorf 2018b).

The key features of the program are work experience with salary at top museums in the western US and tuition scholarships. Both institutions are cognizant of changing US demographics showing that in 1960, 90% of babies born were of European decent, while in 2018, that number will decline to about 50%. Govan notes, "That is a metamorphic scale change like no one has ever seen in history, and our institutions are lagging behind in addressing it." Adding, "If you're looking to change the leadership positions you have to start at the bottom." Addressing this issue will also diversify cultural heritage collections and the stories they tell. The partnership program recruits a group of students as "fellows" who earn their master's degree in art history and are supported by both LACMA's staff and faculty of Herberger Institute for design and the Arts (Neuendorf 2018b).

In a similar fashion, the museum master's Giannini introduced in 2015, offers student fellowships that support students for a two-semester museum internship. The program also addresses the need to diversify the museum profession, but not only in terms of staff, but equally the knowledge and skills that students acquire, moving from a laser focus on curatorial skills and art history, to an amalgamation of content, curation, communication in the context of the digital ecosystem of 21st-century culture. Thus, the Master's in *Museums and Digital Culture* forges new directions for the museum profession.

Research remains at the core of museum work, both object and subject based research, and although this is reflected in the program, we feature research using new digital methodologies that incorporate Internet research, digital humanities and art research, data analytics and visualization. These tie to critical thinking and analysis, featuring non-linear thinking that speak to the complexity of the digital ecosystem that requires us to "think digitally." Students create exhibitions from permanent collections around a theme with each art work an expression of the them as if a theme and variations, showing the different states of being that make-up the whole where the theme is the thread that connects or links them. Importantly, students are learning to rethink the narratives and stories exhibitions tell so that they are relevant to museum audiences.

23.3 Conclusion

Once focused on collection building, conservation, and being keepers of cultural heritage, the museum has grown into a complex social and cultural institution taking on multi-faceted roles in society. No longer bound by their walls, museums take their place among their cultural and educational peers, in our vast digital ecosystem that connects us to global culture, the platform where museums share collections, ideas, exhibitions, and much more. Distancing themselves from an identity born out of an elitist culture that once symbolized the arts and museum world, museums now see themselves as major players in the cultural life of urban and suburban communities whose support they depend on for survival. In light of this radical shift in positioning, museum education is obliged to respond with new directions consonant with contemporary museum purposes and sharing their commitment to digital transformation. More than ever, museums and academic partnerships are essential for the education and training of the next generation of museum professionals. Connected to digital life and art, they already think digitally and are experiencing the nature of digital manifestations and effects on states of being human in a digital world.

As we move past social and cultural hierarchies into a world of complex relationships across time and space, where our goals reflect the values of equality, democracy, inclusion and participation expressed and advanced through digital life and art, it is critical that academic programs embrace and empower these values, central to digital culture.

When in 2018, the New York Times and the Art Leaders Network joined forces in Berlin to discuss the key issues and trends for the art world and the museum of the future (Art Leaders Network 2018), the closing keynote by Ai Wei Wei, *Art in a World of Disruption* (New York Times Conferences 2018b), focused on the importance of

Fig. 23.5 A toy panda stuffed with state secrets. Ai Wei Wei and Jacob Applebaum, 2015. "Hidden inside this Panda are Shredded government documents and a memory card with information leaked by whistle-blower Edward Snowden. A number of these toys were sent to political dissidents around the world." On display at the V&A museum exhibition, *The Future Starts Here*, 2018. (Photograph by Tula Giannini, July 2018)

redefining the canon to broaden the scope of collecting, and to democratize the art world around freedom of expression. He noted that:

> Museums are recognizing the gaps in their collections and acquiring works in traditionally underrepresented categories. What are institutions and collectors doing to think about art in a broader way and to redefine the historic canon? (Art Leaders Network 2018)

In an article for *Incollect* by Michael Connors (2018), summing up the conference, he highlights Berlin Bureau Chief, Katrin Bennhold's interview with Ai Wei Wei who "spoke about his immigration to Germany after being held prisoner under house arrest for four years in China. He emphatically argued that good art is always political and must have 'strong content.' Connors notes that: "a perception of elitism prevailed throughout the two days," an "ism" the museum world is committed to dispelling, as observed in the discussions among attendees who spoke of the need for greater diversity and inclusion—the desire to see "people of color get into the curatorial pipeline" (Connors 2018).

Importantly, speakers at the conference broadly represented the many facets of the art world including directors of museums, galleries and auction houses, art critics, academics, artists and dealers, engaged in conversations that questioned many critical aspects of their community (Fig 23.5).

Looking ahead, it will be important to open these conversations to a broader audience, and to reach-out to students who wish to enter the museum field and related industries to build mutual understandings of the roles and responsibilities of the museum professional. Equally important, will be sharing ideas and perspectives across all constituencies as museum move forward in the postdigital age, were the role of curator is linked to that of audience and visitor participants, while acknowledging the interdependent nature of these relationships while sharing our day-to-day existence living life in the digital ecosystem.

Museums and museum education can be more effective than ever in a digitally connected world of communication, conversation and sharing buoyed by information abundance, digital expression and aesthetics, all intrinsic to the nature of computational culture (Giannini and Bowen 2016; 2017). Our goal for museum education is to give students the knowledge and skills they will need be leaders in the museum field, and to evolve in tandem with museum professionals, audiences, and the public, as we move into the future together.

References

Art Fund (2017) The 21st Century Curator, A report into the evolving role of the UK museum curator, and their needs for the future. Art insights, Art Fund, UK, November 2017. https://www.artfund.org/assets/supporting-museums/curators/art-fund-21st-century-curator.pdf. Accessed 16 Jan 2019

Art Leaders Network (2018). A Summit for innovators and networks. Art Leaders Network, The New York Times. 2–3 May 2018. https://www.nytartleadersnetwork.com/aln2018/. Accessed 16 Jan 2019

Boucher B (2015). Mellon foundation study reveals uncomfortable lack of diversity in American. Artnet News, 4 Aug 2015. https://news.artnet.com/art-world/mellon-foundation-museum-diversity-study-322299. Accessed 16 Jan 2019

Boucher B (2018) What's the best path to a top museum job? We analyzed the training of 100 curators to find out. Artnet News, 2 Apr 2018. https://news.artnet.com/art-world/curator-schools-contemporary-art-1257305. Accessed 16 Jan 2019)

Bowen JP, Giannini T (2014) Digitalism: the new realism. In: Ng K, Bowen JP, McDaid S (eds) EVA London 2014 conference proceedings, Electronic Workshops in Computing (eWiC), BCS, pp 324–331. https://doi.org/10.14236/ewic/eva2014.38

Bowen JP, Giannini T, Polmeer G (2017) Coded communication: digital senses and aesthetics, merging art and life. In: Bowen JP, Diprose G, Lambert N (eds) EVA London 2017 conference proceedings, Electronic Workshops in Computing (eWiC), BCS, pp 1–8. https://doi.org/10.14236/ewic/eva2017.1

Bowen JP, Giannini T, Polmeer G, Gannis C, Gardiner J, Kearney J, Wands B, Weinel, J (2018) States of being: art and identity in digital space and time. In: Bowen JP, Weinel J, Diprose G, Lambert N (eds) EVA London 2018 conference proceedings, Electronic Workshops in Computing (eWiC), BCS, pp 1–7. https://doi.org/10.14236/ewic/eva2018.1

Bureau of Labor Statistics (2018). archivists, curators, and museum workers. occupational outlook handbook. Bureau of Labor Statistics, United States Department of Labor, USA. 2 July 2018. https://www.bls.gov/ooh/education-training-and-library/curators-museum-technicians-and-conservators.htm. Accessed 16 Jan 2019

Carvalho A, Matos A, Sarmento Pizarro MM (2018) Skills for digital transformation in museums: the Mu.Sa project. Midas. 9 2018. https://journals.openedition.org/midas/1463. Accessed Jan 16 Jan 2019

Cascone S (2018) What is a 'narrative art museum'? 6 Things to Expect from George Lucas's New LA Museum. Artnet News. 17 Apr 2018. https://news.artnet.com/art-world/what-is-a-narrative-art-museum-george-lucas-1258994. Accessed 16 Jan 2019

Connors M (2018) The New York Times Art Leaders Network Conference Recap. Incollect. 25–26 Apr 2018. https://www.incollect.com/articles/the-new-york-times-art-leaders-network-conference-recap. Accessed 16 Jan 2019

DCMS (2018). Culture is digital—executive summary. Department for digital, culture, media & sport, UK. https://assets.publishing.service.gov.uk/government/uploads/system/uploads/attachment_data/file/686725/Culture_is_Digital_Executive_summary__1_.pdf. Accessed 17 Jan 2019

Giannini T, Bowen JP (2014) The Brooklyn visual heritage website: brooklyn's museums and libraries collaborate for project CHART. MW2014: Museums and the Web 2014, Baltimore, USA, 2–5 April 2014. https://mw2014.museumsandtheweb.com/paper/the-brooklyn-visual-heritage-website/. Accessed 26 Jan 2019

Giannini T, Bowen JP (2015) A New York Museums and Pratt partnership: building web collections and preparing museum professionals for the digital world. MW2015: Museums and the Web 2015, Chicago, USA. 8–11 Apr 2015. https://mw2015.museumsandtheweb.com/paper/a-new-york-museums-and-pratt-partnership-building-web-collections-and-preparing-museum-professionals-for-the-digital-world/. Accessed 26 Jan 2019

Giannini T, Bowen JP (2016) Curating digital life and culture: art and information. In: Bowen JP, Diprose G, Lambert N (eds) EVA London 2016 conference proceedings, Electronic Workshops in Computing (eWiC), BCS, pp 237–244. https://doi.org/10.14236/ewic/eva2016.46

Giannini T, Bowen JP (2017) Life in code and digits: when Shannon met Turing. In: Bowen JP, Diprose G, Lambert N (eds) EVA London 2017 conference proceedings, Electronic Workshops in Computing (eWiC), BCS, pp 51–58. https://doi.org/10.14236/ewic/eva2017.9

Hayot E (2018) The humanities as we know them are doomed. Now What? The Chronicle of Higher Education. 1 July 2018. https://www.chronicle.com/article/The-Humanities-as-We-Know-Them/243769. Accessed 16 Jan 2019

Jackson F (1982) Epiphenomenal qualia. Philos Q 32(127):127–136. 1 Apr 1982. https://doi.org/10.2307/2960077

Jackson F (1986) What Mary Didn't Know. J Philos 83(5):291–295. May 1986. https://doi.org/10.2307/2026143

McLean S (2017) A New LA Landmark: The Lucas Museum of Narrative Art. Dunne-Edwards. 12 Jan 2017. https://www.dunnedwards.com/colors/specs/posts/a-new-la-landmark-the-lucas-museum-of-narrative-art Accessed 16 Jan 2019

Museum-ID (n.d.). The #FutureMuseum Project: what will museums be like in the future? Museum Identity Ltd. http://museum-id.com/the-futuremuseum-project-what-will-museums-be-like-in-the-future-essay-collection/. Accessed 16 Jan 2019

Neuendorf, H. (2018a) 'Simply Not a Good Look': Activists Criticize the Brooklyn Museum's Hiring of a White African Art Curator. Artnet News, April 5, 2018. https://news.artnet.com/art-world/brooklyn-museum-white-african-art-curator-1260662 (accessed January 16, 2019)

Neuendorf H (2018b) LACMA and Arizona State University Team Up for a New Grad Program Aimed at Diversifying Museum Leadership. Artnet News. 9 May 2018. https://news.artnet.com/art-world/lacma-asu-museum-graduate-program-1282433. Accessed 26 Jan 2019

New York Times Conferences (2018a) The future of art museums. Art Leaders Network 2018, The New York Times Conferences. YouTube. 27 Apr 2018. https://www.youtube.com/watch?v=IXwKjQJN2PU. Accessed 26 Jan 2018

New York Times Conferences (2018b) Closing keynote—art in a world of disruption. art leaders network 2018, The New York Times Conferences. YouTube. 27 Apr 2018. https://www.youtube.com/watch?v=mBACVJDRv6M. Accessed 26 Jan 2018

Schonfeld R, Westermann M, Sweeney L (2015) The Andrew W. Mellon Foundation Art Museum Staff Demographic Survey. The Andrew W. Mellon Foundation, USA. 28 July 2015. https://mellon.org/media/filer_public/ba/99/ba99e53a-48d5-4038-80e1-66f9ba1c020e/awmf_museum_diversity_report_aamd_7-28-15.pdf. Accessed 17 Jan 2019

Silvaggi A (2017a) Museum professionals in the digital era—agents of change and innovation. Mu.SA Project MOOC, Museum Sector Alliance. 23 June 2017. http://www.project-musa.eu/blog/2017/06/23/museum-professionals-in-the-digital-era-agents-of-change-and-innovation/. Accessed 16 Jan 2019

Silvaggi A (ed) (2017b) In: Museum professionals in the digital era—agents of change and innovation. Mu.SA Project MOOC, Museum Sector Alliance. Sept 2017. http://www.project-musa.eu/wp-content/uploads/2017/03/MuSA-Museum-professionals-in-the-digital-era-full-version.pdf (accessed January 17, 2019)

Sturabotti D, Surace R (eds) (2016) In: Museum of the future: insights and reflections from 10 international museums. Mu.SA Project MOOC, Museum Sector Alliance. http://www.project-musa.eu/wp-content/uploads/2017/03/MuSA-Museum-of-the-future.pdf. Accessed 17 Jan 2019

Tubach S, Lesser C (2018) In: New ways of curating—educators *take note*—20 curators taking a cutting-edge approach to art history. Artnet News. 20 June 2018. https://www.artsy.net/article/artsy-editorial-20-curators-cutting-edge-approach-art-history. Accessed 17 Jan 2019

Vankin D (2018) Los Angeles will be home to George Lucas' $1-billion museum. Los Angeles Times. 10 Jan 2018. http://www.latimes.com/entertainment/arts/la-et-cm-la-wins-lucas-museum-20170110-htmlstory.html. Accessed 17 Jan 2019

We Are Museums (2018) Humans versus machines: who is the better museum mediator? In: ECSITE Conference 2018, Geneva, Switzerland. Medium, 12 June 2018. https://medium.com/@WeAreMuseums/humans-versus-machines-who-is-the-better-museum-mediator-8be6938fe89d. Accessed 17 Jan 2019

Part VIII
Libraries and Archives

Chapter 24
Museum Libraries and Archives in the Digital 21st Century

Stephen J. Bury

Abstract Libraries and archives in museums have evolved from creating online catalogues and finding aids to digitization projects, which often involve social media interventions and other engagements with the wider public, including crowdsourcing. Beyond collecting or giving access to PDF files and e-books, fewer museum libraries and archives have grappled with the more challenging problems of born-digital art-rich websites. Even fewer museum libraries and archives have begun to exploit the possibilities of digital art history, including visualization, geospatial analysis or computer vision. Museum libraries (and art libraries more generally) have reached a pivot point, where their responsibility will be to explain the possibilities of the digital world to those rooted in the physical, and what can be learned from the physicality of items or collections of items (such as an archive) to the digital native.

24.1 Introduction

In the USA, there are some 35,000 cultural institutions. Many have a library and/or an archive of some sort, but their status and staffing vary widely. There are small collections run by volunteers, one-person run museum libraries or archives, libraries serving a curatorial department with a remit to support the study of objects in a collection or for an exhibition, more adequately staffed museum libraries and archives, to what are effectively research institutes based around a museum library, e.g., the Frick Art Reference Library, Getty Research Institute or the Yale Center for British Art. How all of these relate to the digital largely correlates with their access to resources and their influence on or how they synchronize with the strategic priorities of their respective institutions. But it also depends on their willingness to collaborate internally—with curatorial, IT, external relationships and development departments—with other libraries and archives locally, e.g., New York Art Resources Consortium (NYARC) (Fig. 24.1) or the Philadelphia Area Consortium of Special Col-

S. J. Bury (✉)
The Frick Collection, New York, USA
e-mail: bury@frick.org

T. Giannini and J. P. Bowen (eds.), *Museums and Digital Culture*,
Springer Series on Cultural Computing, https://doi.org/10.1007/978-3-319-97457-6_24

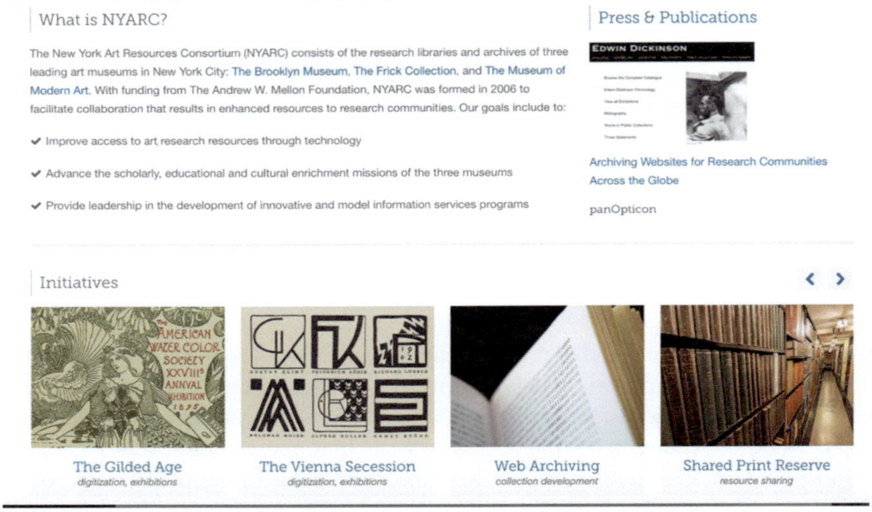

Fig. 24.1 What is NYAC, home page of NYARC website (New York Art Resources Consortium, http://www.nyarc.org)

lections Libraries (PACSCL), with technological and funding partners (Bury 2015; Decker 2015).

24.2 Beyond the Library Catalog

Libraries—of all varieties—were often pioneers in the use of computing, including developing the MARC (MAchine-Readable Cataloging) standards for bibliographic records in machine-readable form. Museum libraries often struggled financially to move their catalogs to the Web: it took a grant from the Andrew W. Mellon Foundation to enable the New York Art Consortium partners, Brooklyn Museum, Frick Art Reference Library and the Museum of Modern Art to create ARCADE, a consortial Integrated Library System (ILS) that also allows segmented views for each institution—BROOKMUSE, FRESCO, and DADABASE. Additional features allow searches for specific types of art and art historical materials. Some museum libraries have added discovery layers given access to full-text periodicals and other database resources (NYARC, Getty).

In 2014 Artlibraries.net worked with OCLC (and the Kress Foundation and Getty Research Institute) to produce an art view of WorldCat, allowing many museums to share their holdings (http://artdiscovery.net).

The holy grail of museum libraries is the integration of the library/archives catalog with the museum collections. There have been small-scale experiments, often more for collection management purposes. MOMA attempted a more public facing integration but this, as from 2018, is no longer available publicly, but Brooklyn's integration of Library Special Collections and Archives materials in the Collection search still remains. There are technical reasons that make the integration of integrated library catalogs with The Museum System (TMS), the most widespread US collection management system, difficult, but the problems are often more political—ranging from curators not wanting to surrender control of the selection of bibliographic information about their collection items, to institutions, despite their promotion of research, for marketing reasons, relegating library search off their website homepages.

24.3 Databases

Libraries were often pioneers in creating databases. The Getty Provenance Index provides 1.7 million searchable records for the study of collecting and provenance (http://www.getty.edu/research/tools/provenance/search.html). A project from 2016 aims to make available the contents as linked open data, and, meanwhile, some subsets; e.g., the Knoedler Gallery stock books are available on GitHub.

The Center for the History of Collecting at the Frick Art Reference Library has produced a database of collectors and dealers archives (http://research.frick.org/directoryweb/home.php). This also provides an interactive time-line and there is a project to enable chronological and geospatial visualizations.

24.4 Digitization

Largely because of perceived issues of copyright in images, museum libraries were slow to digitize their holdings. The New York Art Consortium has helped with the development of Elizabeth Townsend Gard's Durationator tool and now with the collaboration between Tulane Law School and the Internet Archive on using the 108 h provision of the Copyright Act to make accessible some items published between 1923 and 1941.

With limited resources, libraries have tried to avoid duplication: the Getty Portal (http://portal.getty.edu) allows art libraries to share digitized content and create a critical mass of digitized content. The Frick Art Reference Library entered into Public Private Partnerships (PPP) to fund digitization of auction catalogs for Brill's *Art Sales Catalogues Online*: these items are quarantined for five years after which the library can make them freely available online.

Other museums have digitized their own exhibition catalogs (Metropolitan Museum, MoMA), exhibition press releases (MoMA) or membership magazines (Frick Art Reference Library). Besides making these available in their own catalogs, many museum libraries have contributed their metadata and sometimes digital copies to the Getty Portal, the Internet Archive and other aggregators: one day they may also appear in the Digital Library of America. Conversely some libraries link to digital

Fig. 24.2 The Frick digital collections—books from the opening page of the digital collection site which is arranged in three section: Photoarchive, Books, and Archives (http://digitalcollections.frick.org)

versions of items they possess but have not digitized through the HAITI Trust App: this can lead to the erroneous view that the Library's copy is identical to the one digitized.

Digitization is not enough. Some libraries have added value to what they have digitized. In 2014, the New York Art Resources Consortium worked in conjunction with the Carnegie Hall Vienna, Capital of Culture theme on *"The Kiss to the Whole World": Klimt and the Vienna Secession* (http://secession.nyarc.org) to digitize their collection of Secession catalogs, related postcards of the installations and add explanatory materials and also recreate the 18th Secession (1903) of the Klimt exhibition.

The Frick Art Reference Library digitized the Art Collecting Files of Henry Clay Frick, 1881–1925 (Frick, n.d.). This melds the online archival finding aid with full text but also has a crowd-sourced transcription module, using Scripto (http://transcribe.frick.org). In addition, Wikipedia entries were amended or created on dealers and galleries associated with his purchases (Fig. 24.2).

24.5 Web Archiving

Web archiving is probably the most expensive form of collection development and it is not surprising that few museum libraries have developed a web archiving program, depending rather on the Internet Archive or national legal-deposit schemes. Unfortunately, the quality of capture by the Internet Archive is not of sufficient quality, whilst national libraries have to make their harvest of the national domain available to researchers physically visiting a reading room.

In 2011, The Frick Art Reference Library started an experiment to harvest smaller auction house websites on a permissions basis. After a scoping grant and then a full-implementation grant from the Andrew W. Mellon Foundation, the New York Art Resources Consortium established a program to document the websites of New York galleries and dealers, auction catalogs, online catalogues raisonnés and cultural restitution sites. These are made discoverable and available through a Discovery Layer (Primo) as well as WorldCat. The consortium is now working on a national scheme.

24.6 Digital Art History

Digital art history (DAH) is the use of computational tools and analysis to answer art-historical questions (Keramidas and Prokop 2018). Museum libraries have struggled to get curatorial departments, predominantly based on connoisseurship, interested in digital art history (Zorich 2012). Thus far, the Digital Art History Lab at the Frick Art Reference Library is the only such one in a museum (https://www.frick.org/research/DAHL). The Digital Art History Lab (DAHL) seeks to provide art historians with the digital tools and data necessary to explore new methodologies. It also aims to stimulate collaborations between art historians and specialists from a variety of fields, from computer science to historical Geographic Information Systems (GIS). It provides workshops on such subjects as OpenRefine and Omekha, demonstrations, lectures, datasets and supports developmental projects such as computer vision and ARIES.

24.7 ARIES (Art Image Exploration Space)

ARIES is a digital initiative begun by members of the Frick's Digital Art History Lab (DAHL) in concert with the department of computer science at New York University's Tandon School of Engineering. It stemmed from a frustration regarding the inability of currently available software to manipulate images in a way that was intuitive and useful for art historians. Traditionally, art historians had used light boxes or tables on which they placed slides or other reproductive images. In the physical world, they were able to move these around at will, organizing and reorganizing images as desired. In this way, images from multiple sources were brought together and compared to identify similarities, differences, stylistic links, and relationships for further research. The transition from analog photographs and transparencies to digital image files has rendered this workflow obsolescent, yet art historians still lack

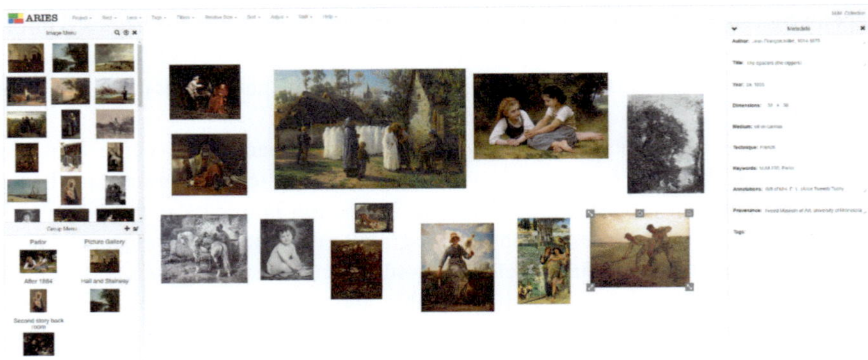

Fig. 24.3 Screenshot in 3 sections: 1. image menu, 2. images, 3. Metadata—of the ARIES system, "an intuitive web-based software platform now free for all to try at ARtImageExplorationSpace.com. The new tool simplifies the exploration, analysis, and organization of digital collections by allowing experts to easily manipulate images." (From: The Frick Collection Brings Art History Research Into The Digital Age—Unexpected Collaborators Offer Their New Open-Source Software to Help Museums and Others to Analyze, Curate, and Share Art. Press Release, August 27, 2018, Tandon School, NYU)

well-designed, unified computational tools that are able to replace what can be done in the analog world.

Working with Dr. Lhaylla Crissaff at New York University, two members of DAHL designed a prototype for an interactive image manipulation system that allows for the exploration and organization of fine art images (of paintings, drawings, prints, sculpture, etc.) taken from multiple sources (e.g. websites, digital photographs, scans) in a virtual space. ARIES provides a novel, intuitive interface to explore, annotate, rearrange, and group art images freely in a single workspace environment, using organizational ontologies (collections, etc.) drawn from existing best practices in art history. The system allows for multiple ways to compare images, from using dynamic overlays analogous to a physical light box to advanced image analysis and feature–matching functions available only through computational image processing. Additionally, users may import and export data to and from ARIES. Thanks to an anonymous donor, ARIES now has funding for further development that will result in an open-source BETA version by June 2018 (Fig. 24.3).

24.8 PHAROS

The Frick Collection has partnered with thirteen art institutions to establish the PHAROS Art Research Consortium (http://www.pharosartresearch.org), a digital research platform that could revolutionize access to photo archives around the world. This long-term initiative will bring together photo archive materials relating to more than 25 million works of art. These collections of images are also rich in previously unpublished related art historical documentation. Seven million images from the original partners are expected to be digitized and available by 2020. Eventually, PHAROS will expand to include records from additional photo archives worldwide. PHAROS currently includes the following museum libraries/archives: Courtauld Institute (London), Getty Research Institute (Los Angeles), I Tatti (Florence), National Gallery of Art (Washington, D.C.), Yale Center for British Art (New Haven), and the Frick Art Reference Library (New York).

Photo archives were first established in the late 19th century, capitalizing on photography—a cutting-edge technology of the time—to reproduce images that would supplant scholars' reliance on text descriptions, sketches, prints, and travel to study works in person. Photo archives capture multiple images of a single work over time, as well as related documentation compiled from scholarly research, making them treasured resources of unpublished knowledge. Over the course of her career, Helen Clay Frick, daughter of The Frick Collection's founder, purchased hundreds of thousands of images from major American and European suppliers and commissioned photographers to capture more than 55,000 pictures of artworks to create the first-ever photo archive in the United States, which has grown to encompass more than 1.2 million images. In many cases, they document works of art that have been subsequently altered or destroyed by war or natural disaster, providing critical information for art historians and conservators that would have otherwise been lost forever. The PHAROS platform, which will link the fourteen collections together for the first time, will allow integrated online access to images and data that may reveal clues to help illuminate investigations in attribution and provenance research, as well as conservation.

Now, with only a few key strokes, a scholar, student, conservator, or member of the public trying to identify, locate, or better understand the history of a work of art will be able to delve into the collections of fourteen institutions worldwide without having to travel to and search through separate archives on-site. Never before have researchers of all kinds had such comprehensive and easy access to the trove of materials held in these collections.

24.9 Innovative Image-Recognition Technology

PHAROS includes enhanced features and applications such as software that enables searching by image instead of by text, of great benefit because text from the multiple institutions can differ in both content and language. Using the proprietary image-recognition technology developed for PHAROS by John Resig, supported by grants from the Samuel H. Kress Foundation, those interested in Italian art are already able to find and compile multiple images and the related documentation as recorded by the different photo archives in different languages in seconds. Researchers are instantly rewarded with new insights into a work's attribution and provenance, exhibition and bibliographic histories, and can track previous conservation efforts or any physical modifications (images.pharosartresearch.org). Additionally, users can upload their own images to identify matching and related artworks held in the PHAROS database. This functionality will soon extend to include works of art of all national schools included in member archives.

24.10 Conclusion

In the digital 21st-century, museum libraries are often perceived as a drain on museum resources, whereas they support the research of staff and thus underpin the research quality of exhibitions and publications, preserve the institutional memory and reach out to local, national, and international communities. Museum libraries also have a pivotal role in explaining what real books and archives mean to the digital native, who may assume that everything is digitized and that the digital record cannot be falsified, and to the print/manuscript-based researcher who may not be aware of the creative possibilities of digital technology. But it is important to work collaboratively with other institutions, including universities, research organizations and technology companies. No museum library or archive can thrive without sharing resources and expertise.

In his study of Tolstoy, the ex-formalist literary critic, Victor Shklovsky, discussed Tolstoy's pursuit of perfection in the novel and the plot in terms of "the energy of delusion": without the delusion that one can attain the ultimate, one would never attain its approximate, the great (Shklovsky 2011). Likewise, museum libraries and archives should try for the best in their digital activities in support of their strategies: there will be failures along the way but they themselves can be useful learning experiences. The energy is all.

References

Bury SJ (2015) Embedding a culture of innovation at the Frick Art Reference Library. In: Decker J (ed) Technology and digital initiatives: innovative approaches for museums. Rowman & Littlefield, Lanham, pp 35–43

Decker J (ed) (2015) Technology and digital initiatives: innovative approaches for Museums. Rowman & Littlefield, Lanham

Frick (n.d.). Art collecting files of Henry Clay Frick, series i: purchases. frick digital collections, The Frick, New York, USA. http://digitalcollections.frick.org. Accessed 29 Dec 2018

Keramidas K, Prokop E (2018) Introduction: re-viewing digital technologies and art history. J Interact Technol Pedagogy (JITP), 12 City University of New York, USA. https://jitp.commons.gc.cuny.edu/introduction-re-viewing-digital-technologies-and-art-history. Accessed 29 Dec 2018

Shklovsky V (2011) The energy of delusion: a book on plot. Dalkey Archive Press, Champaign

Zorich D (2012) Transitioning to a digital world: art history, its research centers, and digital scholarship. Samuel H. Kress Foundation. http://kressfoundation.org/research/transitioning_to_a_digital_world. Accessed 29 Dec 2018

Chapter 25
Democratizing Discovery: The Impact of Digital Culture on the Research Library

Judith Siefring

Abstract This chapter will consider the changing nature of the work of research libraries such as the Bodleian Libraries in response to the digital shift, and the requirement to refresh, extend, and enhance our skills beyond traditional librarianship. It will consider the importance of an integrated approach to physical and digital collections and curation, and the key importance of collaboration for future digital development. The Bodleian Libraries form part of the GLAM (Gardens, Libraries, and Museums) division of the University of Oxford, and we are encouraged to work collaboratively with our museum colleagues to meet the challenge of engaging the public with our world-class collections while at the same time serving our 'traditional' constituency of researchers and scholars of the University. This changing focus has required the Bodleian Libraries to reassess user needs and audience expectations as part of our digital strategy, and feeds into our thinking on search and discovery, metadata management, digitization, preservation, and many other areas.

25.1 Introduction

The Bodleian Library was founded by the English diplomat and scholar Thomas Bodley, officially opening on 8 November 1602 with over two thousand volumes on its shelves. There were many early benefactors, including Sir Walter Raleigh, Sir William Knollys, and the deans and chapters of Exeter and Windsor, who donated many manuscript volumes, and in addition Bodley raised money for the purchase of volumes in a variety of languages and subjects. In 1610, Bodley reached an agreement with the Worshipful Company of Stationers (commonly referred to as the Stationers' Company) that the Bodleian should receive a copy of each work published under the Company's auspices without charge. While the library was intended to serve the members of the University of Oxford, Bodley recognized the need to serve a wider community:

J. Siefring (✉)
Bodleian Libraries, University of Oxford, Oxford, UK
e-mail: judith.siefring@bodleian.ox.ac.uk

T. Giannini and J. P. Bowen (eds.), *Museums and Digital Culture*,
Springer Series on Cultural Computing, https://doi.org/10.1007/978-3-319-97457-6_25

> Thomas Bodley wanted his library to be a resource not only for his own university, but also for the scholarly world at large. In early discussions with the university about who should be entitled to use it, he agreed that there would have to be some restrictions on access [...] [b]ut he insisted that bona fide scholars from outside Oxford should be allowed to study in the library[.]. (Clapinson 2015, p. 20)

Four centuries later, the Bodleian Libraries' current Strategy, covering the years 2017–2022, places significant emphasis on a commitment to sharing its collections more widely with the broader community—and is less concerned about whether users are 'bona fide scholars'. The Bodleian is at heart a library for researchers—the general public cannot, for the most part, walk in and study the treasures of the collections. The opening of the Weston Library in 2015 has opened up collections to the public through custom-built exhibition spaces and an ambitious exhibitions programme but visitor experience is, of necessity, mediated and so the average person cannot easily access physical special collections that are of interest to them. The Bodleian's Strategy makes central, therefore, the role of digital technology and development in making collections more discoverable—through metadata creation, digitization, application development, and collaborative partnerships. Many of the Bodleian's extensive special collections materials are not described at all; some are described only in legacy hardcopy catalogs. The Bodleian has committed to making such inaccessible collections available and is seeking to develop a programme of work covering both fresh cataloguing and analogue to digital conversion. However, the scale of the challenge—and its cost—cannot be underestimated.

The Bodleian Libraries' stated mission—*advancing learning, research and innovation from the heart of the University of Oxford through curating, collecting and unlocking the world's information*—emphasizes the Bodleian's role and responsibility as custodian of collections that represent our global cultural heritage. It recognizes the Bodleian's responsibility to make the collections that we hold as far as possible open to all. This unlocking of access cannot truly be done in the physical realm. It must, therefore, primarily be through digital methods, platforms, and tools that we democratize discovery for all our varied audiences, from undergraduate to professor, schoolchild to 'silver surfer'.

The Bodleian Libraries sit within the Gardens, Libraries and Museums (GLAM) division of the University of Oxford. This structure reflects the diversity of collections held by the University—the Botanic Garden and Arboretum, the Ashmolean Museum of Art and Archaeology, the Museum of Natural History, the Museum of the History of Science, and the Pitt Rivers Museum, which holds collections related to anthropology and ethnography. This expansion of the acronym GLAM to mean Gardens, Libraries and Museums at the University of Oxford is unusual; GLAM is widely used in the Heritage sector to refer to Galleries, Libraries, Archives and Museums. At Oxford in 2016, GLAM replaced the previous divisional name and acronym ASUC—Academic Services and University Collections. The GLAM division published an ambitious digital strategy for the years 2017–2020, which itself promotes a democratizing impulse. The vision of the GLAM digital strategy is

> To embrace the opportunities offered by digital to democratise access to the collections, eliminating geographic, cultural and economic boundaries.

This vision seeds the ambition

> To create full machine-readable metadata and digital surrogates of our unique collections and make them available and discoverable online, and to preserve and safeguard them for future generations.
>
> To fulfil this ambition, we will deliver the following:
>
> - Ensure that all collections are discoverable online through the provision of high-quality metadata.
> - Create digital surrogates of all unique collections.
> - Acquire and create born-digital material and digitise existing material.
> - Optimise access to the collections for digital teaching and research.
> - Utilise the collections to enhance public participation and engage new audiences – locally, nationally and internationally.
> - Create an efficient and sustainable model for preserving and managing the collections.
> - Develop commercial strategies and partnerships, where appropriate, to grow income streams and ensure the financial sustainability of our operations.
>
> Fulfilling the ambitions set out in the Digital Strategy will enable GLAM to facilitate further research, teaching, lifelong learning and public engagement, and encourage new collaborations and experimentation. (University of Oxford 2017)

Such laudable intent, which as a member of GLAM the Bodleian shares, illustrates not only the scale but the variety of the challenge. In order to achieve these stated aims, the Bodleian and its partners in GLAM have been and will be required to grapple with shifting requirements in terms of staff skills, technical capacity, funding, and priorities.

This chapter will unpick just a few of the various challenges facing research libraries in the 21st century and will seek to identify potential approaches which will help us meet those challenges realistically. Firstly, we will focus in more detail on the changing nature of the work of research libraries in response to the new audiences and raised user expectations that have resulted from the digital shift. Secondly, we will look at the increasingly GLAM-focused work of the Bodleian, and how it has encouraged us to think in terms of 'cultural heritage' rather than traditional library work. Thirdly, we will consider the in many ways unhelpful division between the physical and digital curation of library collections, while finally we will look at how collaboration and partnership can offer new models and methods for successful digital development, engagement, and impact.

25.2 'Personae' and 'Segments': Audience Analysis and User Needs

Traditionally, the Bodleian Libraries have served a core user group—students and academics affiliated to the University of Oxford, and Oxford-based independent researchers. We might see this reflected in the previous collective name for the various libraries that make up the Bodleian—Oxford University Library Services (OULS). OULS was rebranded as 'Bodleian Libraries' in 2010. Of course, a great many researchers from other institutions worldwide were also accommodated by—and continue to visit—the Bodleian, but a primary focus tended to be the University's own members. With the advent of the digital shift, the Libraries have been required to continue to meet the needs of this traditional constituency, while at the same time catering to a larger, more diverse, and less easily defined online audience.

For over 20 years, the Bodleian, like its comparable institutions internationally, has worked hard to keep pace with the rapid momentum of technological change and the accompanying digitally-driven shift in research methods. The Libraries must now curate and provide access to an enormous variety of databases, electronic journals, e-Books and other digital resources while maintaining its print collections. Early digitization projects focusing on Oxford's collections included the Toyota City Imaging Project, which ran from 1993 to 1996, and focused on motoring-related material in the John Johnson Collection of printed ephemera, and the Celtic and Medieval Manuscripts or 'Early Manuscripts at Oxford University', which ran from 1995 to 2000, and focused on major 'treasures' of various Oxford libraries, including those of the Bodleian and Balliol, Corpus Christi, Jesus, Magdalen, Merton, and St John's colleges. In 2018, the websites for these early projects remained available online (http://www.bodley.ox.ac.uk/toyota/openpage.html; http://image.ox.ac.uk). A variety of online catalogs and finding aids for Bodleian holdings were also developed. We are now faced with the challenge of how to migrate and sustain such early forays into online delivery of digital collections because the technologies with which they were built are now aging and no longer fit for purpose. How to sustain and preserve content delivered online has created a fresh challenge for research library staff and has led to new and significant work in the fields of Digital Preservation and Web Archiving. Alongside the need to preserve legacy content, the challenge of making Special Collections materials discoverable online remains huge—most Bodleian Special Collections, for example, are not discoverable online, while many have not even been cataloged at all.

The digital shift has therefore created new challenges around the management of *legacy* systems and content alongside the creation of *new* systems and content. But it has also significantly widened the potential audience for the resources that we create. Most obviously, before the invention of the Internet and the World Wide Web, those who wanted to use and study collections held in libraries like the Bodleian had to make physical visits—the possibilities for the work that researchers could do were in some ways limited by what they could achieve in the reading rooms. Expensive research trips would have been beyond many researchers. Largely, then, in pre-Internet days, those working with Bodleian collections would have been academic researchers either resident in Oxford or having made a special trip to work with particular materials. In a post-Internet world, research practice has been transformed. Scholars can access collections from institutions all around the world without leaving their home institution, or indeed the comfort of their study. If the materials that they are researching are available online—not a given—researchers can do substantial and significant work without having to make expensive research trips. Online finding aids can also help researchers decide whether a research trip is worthwhile or whether their limited resources would be better spent elsewhere. For researchers, then, online resources and digital collections have allowed them to carry out (and indeed disseminate) their research faster and more widely than was ever possible before.

Arguably, though, an even more fundamental shift has been the democratizing of access to knowledge—for everyone—that has been made possible by the invention of the Internet and the World Wide Web. Anyone with access to a computer and an Internet connection can view treasures held by libraries and museums around the world. In the academic year 2016–2017, there were 2,145,349 physical visits to various libraries that make up the Bodleian Libraries, but in the same period there was also 2,634,614 website sessions and 563,843 views of a digitized book or manuscript. The Web has therefore allowed us a new (and vast) potential audience for information about Bodleian collections, research, and expertise—and has required us to think quite differently about our users.

Users now have raised expectations about what is, or should be, available online. The need and ability to access information about any topic at any time, immediately, has become a fact of life for many of us in the age of Google and smartphones—and perhaps most especially for the generation that has grown up with the Internet, the famed 'digital natives'. However, the work of content creation required to facilitate such expectation is vast—and indeed too vast to be achieved quickly for institutions like the Bodleian Libraries. We must therefore prioritize—which collections should we try to surface? What technologies should we use to do so? What sort of cataloguing information should be the minimum for a record to be delivered online? Which collections should we create digital surrogates for? Are high-resolution images required, or should we use lower-resolution (and cheaper to create) images? Increasingly the Bodleian, together with colleagues in GLAM, are focusing on audience to help us with this prioritization work—if we can identify who our target audience is, what their motivations and behaviors are, we can focus our time and resources in the most effective way. But in doing so, we have had to think about users in new and non-traditional ways.

The practice of audience segmentation—assessing and dividing one's audience into categories—is an established one for cultural organizations who seek to engage the general public. Understanding audience groups is vital when planning a visitor or entertainment program that hopes to appeal to a range of people—for example, children and adults, knowledge-seekers and entertainment-seekers. Several different methods of categorization have emerged, although as Walsh et al. (2016) note in their survey of user categories, it can be hard to define useful categories:

> Increasingly, cultural heritage services are being tailored to individuals and groups […] and therefore require some kind of differentiation between user groups. However, despite the wealth of studies carried out to identify and characterise users, many of the categories appear general (e.g., historian vs. student; novice vs. expert), often without definition and therefore making comparisons between studies difficult.
>
> An examination of the literature suggests a lack of agreement on the appropriate terminology for categorising users of digital cultural heritage and their characteristics and needs (e.g.,

> exactly who are the "general public"?). Also, within groups users and their characteristics may vary widely and types of user are often abstract and generic. (Walsh et al. 2016, p. 1)

A more nuanced approach is therefore required, and one that focuses on what users want or how they behave rather than who they are is often more useful.

One segmentation method gaining currency is 'Culture Segments', described by the cultural strategy and research agency Morris Hargreaves McIntyre as "the international standard segmentation system for arts, culture and heritage organisations". The system is designed to provide:

> […] a compelling, shared language and deep insight to understand audiences. It can help you to target people more accurately, engage them more deeply and build lasting relationships.
>
> Culture Segments is more powerful than other systems because it's sector-specific and because it's based on people's deep-seated cultural values and their beliefs about the role that culture plays in their lives. It gets to the heart of what motivates them. (Morris Hargreaves McIntyre 2019)

Another example of a segmentation model is The Audience Agency's 'Audience Spectrum', which "segments the whole UK population by their attitudes towards culture, and by what they like to see and do" (http://www.theaudienceagency.org/audience-spectrum). Such segmentation models encourage organizations to take a fresh look at their audience(s) and to design their services and systems with users in mind.

The Bodleian Libraries are increasingly working with colleagues from GLAM institutions—Oxford's museums and gardens—and audience has been a key focus for our digital strategy implementation. Working in this context has encouraged us to examine where the Bodleian is 'museum-like' and where distinct research library services and structures mark us out as different. Engagement with the general public has become much more of a focus for the Libraries in recent years, and the opening of the Weston Library has provided an opportunity to engage local residents, tourists, and University staff members with the work and collections of the Libraries. The Weston has publicly accessible exhibition spaces (see Fig. 25.1), a café and shop, and an ambitious program of exhibitions and public talks and tours.

In 2018, the major exhibition in the Weston Library was 'Tolkien: Maker of Middle-earth', an excellent example of a topic with general appeal that can generate wide press coverage highlighting an event about which many potential visitors could otherwise be unaware. The Libraries' ability to bring in new audiences has been greatly enhanced by these new facilities (around 700,000 people per year have visited the Weston's public spaces since its opening in 2015) and has created greater synergies with the University museums and gardens, whose spaces are of their nature open and attractive to the general public. However, there are significant differences. A visitor to the Ashmolean museum can wander freely throughout the museum and can appreciate the enormous variety of material on display. A visitor to the Weston Library can only view those items on public display in the exhibition spaces—the great majority of the collections are closed to them unless they have a Bodleian reader's card, and they are using the Library for research and study. Considering this, nuanced thinking about our target audiences is particularly helpful as we plan

Fig. 25.1 Blackwell Hall, The Weston Library. (Image credit: Bodleian Libraries, University of Oxford)

our digital offering—access to our physical collections are of necessity restricted and so digital platforms become particularly valuable in allowing people to learn about the materials we hold.

Audience-focused work within the GLAM framework has allowed us to identify an evolving set of 'segments' or 'personae' and we can use these to help plan our digital projects and services. A range of GLAM user behavior types—such as browsers, followers, searchers, researchers—can be modeled to help institutions understand their audience profile. For the Libraries, this can create a tension between attempts to cater for our traditional core audience of students and academic researchers and the need to engage more widely with those who want to find out more about our collections purely for personal interest and in their spare time. Putting the needs of users first—and therefore understanding who our users are for a specific service or tool—when planning projects and services has forced the Libraries to think about audience in new ways. Clarity about what we are seeking to achieve and who we are seeking to reach helps us to bridge the gap between the Bodleian's role as a University research library but also as the custodian of world-class collections that are part of our common cultural heritage.

25.3 Custodianship and Cultural Heritage

From its foundation in 1602, the Bodleian Library has been dedicated to collecting and preserving artefacts of intellectual and cultural importance. As mentioned in the introduction, in 1610, Sir Thomas Bodley obtained from the Stationers' Company the right to claim a copy of each publication printed under royal license. This was the origin of the Bodleian Library's privileged status as a library of legal deposit—the University libraries of Oxford and Cambridge are the only universities in the United Kingdom to have this status, sitting alongside the British Library, the National Libraries of Scotland and Wales, and Trinity College, Dublin—allowing the Bodleian to receive material published in the United Kingdom and Ireland. Over the centuries, the library has amassed an enormous collection of print materials; in November 2015 it celebrated the acquisition of its 12 millionth printed item, a previously unseen copy of Percy Bysshe Shelley's *Poetical Essay on the Existing State of Things* (1811, http://poeticalessay.bodleian.ox.ac.uk). Alongside its print collections, the Bodleian has acquired manuscripts, maps, music, printed ephemera, and archival materials such as literary and political papers. Treasures of the library include the 16th-century Codex Mendoza, Shakespeare's First Folio, the medieval Gough Map, Mary Shelley's manuscript drafts of *Frankenstein*, and Jane Austen's original draft of *The Watsons*.

The collections held by the Bodleian Libraries are, therefore, of worldwide value and importance. The Bodleian must preserve and make available these collections for future generations—this custodianship is a core part of the Libraries mission. The emergence of digital culture has forced institutions to look afresh at what access and custodianship mean in the age of the Internet. Collections held by research libraries are not just collections of manuscripts, archives, and books—they are collections of artefacts that are part of the shared cultural heritage of all of humanity. The World Wide Web was developed in a spirit of openness—and this openness has resulted in new issues and challenges for research libraries like the Bodleian.

The benefit and necessity of openness in digital culture is reflected in the new and increasing responsibilities that research libraries have to meet in the areas of Open Access and Research Data Management. Significant investment has been made in the creation of fit-for-purpose institutional repositories where researchers can deposit research outputs—often a requirement mandated by funders. In Oxford, the Oxford University Research Archive (ORA, http://ora.ox.ac.uk) is developed, hosted, and maintained by the Bodleian Libraries, and includes within it the ORA-Data service, for archiving, preserving, and sharing Oxford's research data. The open-source software movement has also had a significant impact—as research libraries wrestle with the need to be able to manage and sustain digital tools and services beyond the period of their active development and with limited resources, open source tools and their user communities offer a cost-effective and collaborative option when choosing technologies to invest in.

However, an open approach can be challenging when planning digital developments for our cultural heritage collections. As Gill Hamilton and Fred Saunderson outline in their persuasive call for openness, *Open Licensing for Cultural Heritage* (2017):

> At the core of any cultural heritage or information sector strategy is likely to be access and use. Access to material and the onward use of that material is central to the organisational *raison d'être* of most institutions. In the analogue world 'access' often means visiting galleries or reading rooms, while 'using' means observing, consulting, noting, and sketching. Access and use are also key considerations for digital strategies and plans. In fact, in many respects the consideration and development required here is greater than for other aspects of digital collection management. This is not because digital access and use require greater investment (far from it), but because digital access – and, by extension, use – present possibly a great paradigm shift for the culture and information sector compared with 'traditional' access and reuse approaches. (Hamilton and Saunderson 2017, p. 68)

The paradigm shift referred to above requires library staff to engage with evolving legislative frameworks and communities of practice around copyright, intellectual property, and licensing. Curatorial, digital library, and imaging studio staff must keep abreast of legal regulations, as well as monitoring and developing policies for the distribution and download of materials, such as digital image surrogates of special collections. Reading room staff encounter most directly the change in reader behavior around special collections materials. The ubiquity of the smartphone means that DIY reader photography of material is commonplace. However, reading room invigilators must enforce rules designed to ensure that collections are not damaged in the process of being photographed and are not photographed at all when there are restrictions in place (e.g., by the terms of their deposit). The practice of DIY photography in reading rooms is done mostly for the purposes of private research.

As part of a project investigating DIY digitization funded by the University of Oxford's John Fell Fund, the present author interviewed 21 researchers who confirmed that they took their own photographs of special collections materials in reading rooms. 21 out of 21 stated that they used the photographs for their own private study and research, and 15 out of 21 also used them in teaching. However, the resulting photographs also give rise to policy decision-making requirements—should redistribution of such photographs be permitted, e.g., via social media? Should they be permissible in print publication? Even if a policy of restriction were in force, how and when would infringement be pursued? Researchers interviewed for the DIY digitization project noted with frustration the variation in policies that occur at different libraries and reading rooms. The ever-increasing opportunities to distribute material related to collections on the Internet mean that the amount of copyright triage and licensing decision-making that library staff must engage in is similarly ever-increasing. Indeed, it is Hamilton and Saunderson's argument that it may cost organizations more to enforce restrictions on content than the income that is generated from selling and licensing images (lack of protection for income streams is often perceived as a risk of open licensing)—"an organization seeking to restrict [...] content for the purposes of generating income needs first to consider what costs it has to introduce to generate that income and second whether it can recover in charges more than it bears in fresh costs." (Hamilton and Saunderson 2017, p. 84).

The immediacy of taking photographs of research objects with a smartphone and the desire to share them with others through social media channels such as Twitter is a neat illustration of how transformative digital culture has been in allowing people to engage much more informally with cultural heritage collections. This has encouraged institutions themselves to be more informal in how they disseminate information about their collections. The British Library's excellent Medieval Manuscripts blog, for example, covers a whole range of topics, from the Gospels of Tsar Ivan Alexander (British Library 2018c), a discussion of medieval rainbows in honor of Pride month celebrations (British Library 2018a), or even a Cotton Manuscripts Quiz (British Library 2018b). Similarly, the Bodleian's own blog for a collaborative digitization project undertaken in partnership with the Biblioteca Apostolica Vaticana has posts discussing such things as digital technologies facilitating the viewing of two Ashkenazi Pentateuch's side by side (Polonsky Foundation 2017a) alongside more lighthearted posts on, for example, marginal 'doodles' of animals in a 15th-century manuscript (Polonsky Foundation 2017b). Such informality is even more apparent on Twitter, where institutions like the Bodleian Libraries, the British Library, and Cambridge University Library seek to engage their followers in a deliberately unstuffy, enjoyable way. These approaches can only help position such institutions to appear more approachable, open, and willing to engage with a general audience.

The rise of social media and DIY digitization both illustrate how embedded digital culture has become in the everyday life of a research library. These activities occur in reading rooms and for marketing campaigns, by readers sharing a fun discovery with their friends or by library staff who want to show the less serious side of their library. Such informal activities are not happening only (or even mainly) in a designated 'digital' section of the library. The digital shift has happened across all aspects of the work of research libraries like the Bodleian—any assessment of its impact cannot therefore assume that there is a clear distinction between 'traditional' library staff and 'digital' library staff. Indeed, it is vital that such a perceived division is bridged for the successful implementation of digital strategies.

25.4 Reintegrating the Physical and the Digital

It is often the case that research libraries or similar institutions have digital departments which focus on digital projects, tools, and services—and that these departments are separate (often physically as well as organizationally) from the departments managing physical collections and library spaces. Indeed, this is the case for the Bodleian Libraries. The Bodleian Digital Library Systems and Services (BDLSS) department is housed in a building about a mile away from the iconic Bodleian buildings of the Radcliffe Camera, Old Bodleian and Weston Library which are situated in the center of Oxford. The need for organizationally separate digital departments reflects the need for spaces that can accommodate the systems, hardware, and people that are required to build digital tools and run digital services. However, such organizational separation can no longer—if it ever was—be assumed to mean that digital work is done by 'digital' staff, while the rest of the library's staff get on with 'traditional' librarianship. The use of technology in learning spaces, for teaching, for research, and in leisure time is now so pervasive across society, that all library staff have to engage with it. Digital skills are required by everyone, not just those directly involved in creating digital tools and services.

The most successful digital initiatives are often those that are developed in partnership. Specialist curators have extraordinarily rich knowledge of collections and are in close contact with users and researchers. This specialist knowledge is essential when planning, for example, online resource discovery. A solid understanding of the nature of our content is essential in order to know how best to make it available online. On the flip side, technical staff understand whether particular technologies are fit for a particular purpose, if and how software packages can be customized, how they should be implemented, supported, and maintained in the long term. It is crucial, then, that library staff members with such complementary expertise are able to collaborate on digital projects and initiatives, especially those which focus on collections.

Furthermore, curators and archivists have themselves often gained significant specialist expertise in digital technologies. For example, at the Bodleian Libraries born-digital archives are cared for and curated within the same Special Collections department—Modern Archives and Manuscripts—as post-medieval manuscripts and paper-based archives. Increasingly, archival collections held or acquired by the Library are themselves a mix of physical and digital material. The archive of the Labour Party politician Barbara Castle, for example, contains physical diaries, notebooks, and photographs but also digital files and correspondence. The archive of the international development charity Oxfam contains a huge number of paper documents alongside film, video, and audio material. Digital archives present new and specialized challenges for archivists as technical formats and media become obsolete and must be converted or migrated to new formats. Digital preservation—another area of activity best carried out collaboratively between curatorial/archivist and technical staff—is now recognized as a major challenge for cultural heritage organizations, and one that requires significant investment in policy development, skills training, and technical development. In recognition of this challenge, the Bodleian Libraries and Cambridge University Library undertook a collaborative project—Digital Preservation at Oxford and Cambridge (http://www.dpoc.ac.uk)—to enhance and improve digital preservation infrastructure, policy and training, and to begin the necessary work of embedding good digital preservation practice at Oxford and Cambridge.

It no longer makes sense to consider physical and digital collections, or analogue and digital behavior, as distinct and separate. All of us are used to accessing and sending information from a variety of sources and in different formats—we read newspapers online and in print, we read paperbacks and e-books, we listen to the radio, watch television, read Twitter, send an email, scribble a Post-it Note for a colleague. When we do these things, we aren't dividing our behavior into digital and analogue. The same is true for library collections and services—we must plan, develop, and deliver collections in an integrated way—the physical and digital must be considered in the round, core to the successful implementation of organizational strategy.

This integrated approach to analogue and digital library work facilitates the necessary collaborative work between library departments and individual staff members. Resource discovery is a good example of why such collaboration is necessary. As noted above, the special collections holdings of the Bodleian Libraries are extensive and of worldwide importance. However, a huge amount of these holdings has not yet been cataloged, due to the sheer scale of the work involved. Some materials are described only in print catalogs and have no online presence. Some catalog records are available online, but the underlying technical solutions are beginning to date and need to be replaced. Alongside these, new digital resources are being developed. In order to maximize impact and service to users, and to design and maintain tools that are fit for purpose, it is vital that curatorial and technical colleagues work in partnership. Only through collaborative working can we hope to implement the best approach to surfacing uncatalogued or print-only materials, and to create a resource discovery environment that gives the best experience for our users.

Such local collaboration is vital for the implementation of successful library services, but wider collaborative working is just as important for successful digital development. Shared strategies and approaches are key, and institutions must ensure that engagement with external institutions and communities is a core part of their digital development strategy.

25.5 Collaboration and Community

External collaboration and participation in community-based digital initiatives are important in many areas of library work. Cataloguing and metadata standards are an obvious and long-standing area that require connection with other institutions and organizations. For example, in recent years, the Bodleian Libraries have developed several Text Encoding Initiative (TEI) catalogs for our Western and Oriental manuscript collections. The TEI Consortium is an international organization that has as its members scholars, projects, and academic institutions, and members pay annual fees to support its work. Established in 1987, the TEI provides guidelines for the encoding of texts and a community of support and advice for those undertaking encoding work. The TEI guidelines evolve—currently they are in their fifth iteration, known as TEI P5 (TEI Consortium 2018)—in response to needs and input from the user community. The TEI has discussion lists, special interest groups, and an annual conference, providing many opportunities for members to gain support or to disseminate their work. The TEI guidelines have a manuscript description (msDesc) module which the Bodleian, together with many other institutions including Cambridge University Library, have used for cataloguing some manuscript collections. Participation in communities like the TEI has many benefits—it allows users to feel supported and to be able to sense-check their implementation of the guidelines, it gives organizations the opportunity to feed into future iterations of the guidelines, it offers avenues for outreach and engagement, and it fosters collaborative working and cross-institutional partnerships.

The development of the Bodleian's recently launched Western medieval manuscripts catalog (http://medieval.bodleian.ox.ac.uk), included close collaboration with colleagues at Cambridge University Library. Similarly, Fihrist, a Union Catalog of manuscripts from the Islamicate world hosted by the Bodleian Libraries and originally launched in 2011, is a collaboration between several holding institutions—Bodleian Libraries, Cambridge University Library, SOAS at the University of London, the British Library, the Universities of Birmingham and Manchester, the Royal Asiatic Society, and the Wellcome Library. The Fihrist catalog was recently (May 2018) relaunched as part of a Bodleian project to consolidate eight separate TEI catalogs into the same schema and technical infrastructure, with the aim of making the catalogs more sustainable and easier to support in the long term (http://www.fihrist.org.uk). The Fihrist initiative is an excellent example of just how far the digital shift has opened up the possibilities for cross-institutional collaboration.

Another exemplar for how collaboration and community create momentum for digital development can be found in the work of the International Image Interoperability Framework (IIIF). The IIIF is a community of cultural heritage institutions who have come together to create a shared set of standards and tools for delivery of image-based content on the web. As the IIIF website (https://iiif.io) explains:

> Access to image-based resources is fundamental to research, scholarship and the transmission of cultural knowledge. Digital images are a container for much of the information content in the Web-based delivery of images, books, newspapers, manuscripts, maps, scrolls, single sheet collections, and archival materials. Yet much of the Internet's image-based resources are locked up in silos, with access restricted to bespoke, locally built applications.
>
> A growing community of the world's leading research libraries and image repositories have embarked on an effort to collaboratively produce an interoperable technology and community framework for image delivery.

IIIF (International Image Interoperability Framework) has the following goals:

- To give scholars an unprecedented level of uniform and rich access to image-based resources hosted around the world.

- To define a set of common application programming interfaces that support interoperability between image repositories.
- To develop, cultivate and document shared technologies, such as image servers and web clients, that provide a world-class user experience in viewing, comparing, manipulating and annotating images.

In 2018, the IIIF had around 120 participating institutions and has grown rapidly. It is governed by the IIIF Consortium, a group of over 40 founding members, which was formed in June 2015 in Oxford.

The IIIF recognized the need for shared standards and technologies, and its continued success demonstrates the value of collaborative community-based endeavor for the delivery of digital content. In its early stages, membership was heavily represented by universities and university libraries—such as Harvard, Stanford, and Yale in the USA, as well as Oxford—and state or national libraries, such as the British Library, the Bayerische Staatsbibliothek, the Bibliothèque nationale de France, and the national libraries of Norway, Scotland, Wales, and Israel. Digitized manuscripts of the kind delivered by libraries like these (see Fig. 25.2) were an early use case for IIIF. However, IIIF actively seeks to encourage greater participation in the museum community—in recognition of the benefits of shared approaches across the cultural heritage sector. Some museums—including the Art Institute of Chicago, the Yale Centre for British Art, and the Smithsonian Institution (Robson 2017)—have already

Fig. 25.2 Digitization at the Bodleian Libraries. (Image credit: Bodleian Libraries, University of Oxford)

joined the IIIF. There is a Museums Community Group (IIIF n.d.) and a guide to help museums implement IIIF.

The interoperable software being created through projects and initiatives based on IIIF includes many open source options which again encourages community-driven collaboration and support. These include the Bodleian Libraries' own Digital Manuscripts Toolkit (http://dmt.bodleian.ox.ac.uk), which developed a set of open-source tools for creating, remixing, and sharing digitized manuscripts, funded by The Andrew W. Mellon Foundation. Open source technologies are often a good strategic choice for research libraries and other cultural heritage organizations because they offer a cost-effective and sustainable solution for content delivery, providing that the community support that surrounds them is maintained. It is to an organization's benefit, then, to actively collaborate and participate in the communities that surround the technologies in which they have invested time and resources.

25.6 Conclusion

The 'digital shift' has been so complete and pervasive that it no longer makes sense for institutions like the Bodleian Libraries to consider the management of their 'traditional' activities and their digital work separately. Closely integrated planning and collaboration and support between departments and staff members with different expertise and skills is essential if the aim is to deliver content, services, and library spaces that meet the expectations of the 21st-century user. Expectations for the delivery of content online are only going to increase—ambitious targets for scaling up digital activity within research libraries are necessary if that demand is to be met. The GLAM Digital Strategy of the University of Oxford has set an ambitious agenda, but the GLAM framework recognizes that such ambition can only be achieved in a spirit of partnership, in this case between the gardens, libraries, and museums of the University of Oxford. The GLAM framework also encourages us to consider how the advent of the digital can encourage us to consider where a research library might be like a museum or where differences lie, and to think of ourselves as a cultural heritage organization rather than 'just' a research library.

The seemingly boundless potential and popularity of the Internet and the World Wide Web for the dissemination of knowledge mean that all research library staff need digital skills, not just those that work in digital libraries or other technical departments. But those skills are often extensions of skills and expertise that are core to 'traditional' librarianship—conservation, preservation, cataloguing, archiving, resource discovery, and information skills training. Library staff, therefore, are well placed to embrace all of the potential that the digital age affords.

When planning and developing digital tools and initiatives, research library staff should take care to consult widely—talk to curatorial colleagues, seek out users of different types, engage directly with online audiences—to ensure that they are thinking in the round about what they are trying to achieve. They should look beyond their own institution to identify how others are making progress and reaching new audiences, as well as developing partnerships and collaborations, which will make their own digital resources more sustainable in the longer term. The Internet and the World Wide Web make many initiatives possible, but we must make sure that the initiatives that we prioritize are realistic and of genuine benefit to the end user. There is much that we *could* do but it is harder to be sure about what we *should* do—a greater awareness of our audiences and a pooling of collective knowledge in the field make it more likely that the tools and resources that we develop will be fit-for-purpose, effective, and above all well-used.

References

British Library (2018a) A medieval rainbow. Medieval manuscripts blog, British Library, UK, 8 June 2018. http://blogs.bl.uk/digitisedmanuscripts/2018/06/a-medieval-rainbow.html. Accessed 18 Sept 2018

British Library (2018b) Cotton manuscripts quiz. Medieval manuscripts blog, British Library, UK, 16 June 2018. http://blogs.bl.uk/digitisedmanuscripts/2018/06/cotton-manuscripts-quiz.html. Accessed 18 Sept 2018

British Library (2018c) The gospels of Tsar Ivan Alexander. Medieval manuscripts blog, British Library, UK, 19 June 2018. http://blogs.bl.uk/digitisedmanuscripts/2018/06/the-gospels-of-tsar-ivan-alexander.html. Accessed 18 Sept 2018

Clapinson M (2015) A brief history of the Bodleian library. Bodleian Library Publishing, Oxford

Hamilton G, Saunderson F (2017) Open licensing for cultural heritage. Facet Publishing, London

IIIF (n.d.) IIIF museums community group. International image interoperability framework. https://iiif.io/community/groups/museums/. Accessed 18 Sept 2018

Morris Hargreaves McIntyre (2019) Culture segments. Morris Hargreaves McIntyre, UK. https://mhminsight.com/culture-segments. Accessed 20 Jan 2019

Polonsky Foundation (2017a) Two Ashkenazi Pentateuchs side by side. Polonsky Foundation Digitization Project, Bodleian Libraries, UK, 3 Feb 2017. http://bav.bodleian.ox.ac.uk/news/two-ashkenazi-pentateuchs-side-by-side. Accessed 18 Sept 2018

Polonsky Foundation (2017b) Deer and other marginal creatures. Polonsky Foundation Digitization Project, Bodleian Libraries, 19 Apr 2017. http://bav.bodleian.ox.ac.uk/news/deer-and-other-marginal-creatures. Accessed 18 Sept 2018

Robson G (2017) IIIF consulting: American art collaborative. International image interoperability framework, 1 Nov 2017. https://iiif.io/news/2017/11/01/aac-collaboration/. Accessed 18 Sept 2018

TEI Consortium (2018) TEI P 5: guidelines for electronic text encoding and interchange. TEI: Text Encoding Initiative, 23 June 2018. http://www.tei-c.org/release/doc/tei-p5-doc/en/Guidelines.pdf. Accessed 18 Sept 2018

University of Oxford (2017) GLAM digital strategy. Gardens, Libraries & Museums, University of Oxford, UK. https://www.glam.ox.ac.uk/digital-strategy. Accessed 18 Sept 2018

Walsh D, Clough P, Foster J (2016) User categories for digital cultural heritage. In: First international workshop on accessing cultural heritage at scale, Newark, USA, 22 June 2016, pp 3–9

Part IX
Digital Future

Chapter 26
Digital Culture Leaders Visioning the Postdigital Museum

Seb Chan, Courtney Johnston and Tula Giannini

Abstract This chapter features an interview two senior museum leaders with a long history in digital product development and open access who discuss how their museums are evolving. A wide-ranging conversation explores the challenges and opportunities small to medium sized museums face, and what it means for leaders who emerge from 'digital culture' to be shaping museums. It is an important exploration, too, of the changing context in which museums now operate and how the slow shift to a "postdigital" museum cannot be abstracted from broader shifts in culture and politics.

26.1 Introducing Seb Chan and Courtney Johnston

Seb Chan is the chief experience officer at the Australian Centre for the Moving Image (ACMI, https://www.acmi.net.au) in Melbourne. Formerly, he worked at the Cooper Hewitt Smithsonian Design Museum in New York City as the director of digital and emerging media where he played a key role in creating a new digital visitor experience (Chan and Cope 2015) that represented a major step forward, and a milestone in museum experience design evidenced by the enthusiastic user response. To accomplish this, Chan drew on his innovative work at the Powerhouse Museum in Sydney as Head of Digital, Social and Emerging Technologies, where he worked just prior to his position at the Cooper Hewitt (Fig. 26.1).

Courtney Johnston formerly Director of The Dowse Art Museum (Edwards 2012) and the Petone Settlers Museum, since 2018 serves at the Director of Audience +

S. Chan (✉)
Australian Centre for the Moving Image, Melbourne, Australia
e-mail: seb.chan@acmi.net.au

C. Johnston
Museum of New Zealand Te Papa Tongarewa, Wellington, New Zealand
e-mail: auchmill@gmail.com

T. Giannini
School of Information, Pratt Institute, New York, USA
e-mail: giannini@pratt.edu

T. Giannini and J. P. Bowen (eds.), *Museums and Digital Culture*,
Springer Series on Cultural Computing, https://doi.org/10.1007/978-3-319-97457-6_26

Fig. 26.1 The Australian Museum of the Moving Image, located in Melbourne, is the national museum of film, tv, videogames, digital culture and art. ACMI has two cinemas, three exhibition galleries, a co-working and business accelerator for the creative sector, and in 2019 is undergoing a major redevelopment and expansion. ACMI's exhibition descriptions sync with what Seb Chan speaks about in the interview, namely, the importance of museums living at the intersection of local and global communities, offering visitors immersive experiences built around a digital framework. Wikimedia Commons, https://commons.wikimedia.org/wiki/File:Australian_Centre_for_the_Moving_Image_(6476609969).jpg

Insight at Te Papa Wellington and Wairarapa, New Zealand Museums and Institutions (Te Papa 2018). Courtney's extensive experience in the art world, past and present, digital and physical, with a focus on audience experience and engagement perfectly expresses Te Papa's strategic priority that "all aspects of the museum work together to deliver a richer experience" (Fig. 26.2).

26.2 The Conversation

Seb Chan: I remember when you were working at the National Library and later doing UX (User eXperience) for an agency. I'm curious as to how this experience changes how you operate as museum director and also as one New Zealand's cultural commentators… People of roughly our age are beginning to take up senior leadership roles in cultural institutions. We are certainly the last generation, at least until the dystopian climate/water/nuclear future arrives at all encompassing scale, to have straddled the pre and post Internet world. Expanded connectivity has brought with it

Fig. 26.2 The Te Papa Wellington and Wairarapa, New Zealand Museums and Institutions. View of front side with entrance. (Photograph by Ulrich Lange, Bochum, Germany. Wikimedia Commons, https://commons.wikimedia.org/wiki/File:Museum_of_New_Zealand_Te_Papa_Tongarewa.jpg)

great opportunity perhaps more so in New Zealand and Australia, who have always felt burdened by geographical isolation from UK/US/European cultural power—but also this now seems to have pushed us more towards pressing local concerns and local identity. Your work at the Dowse has straddled this elegantly.

Courtney Johnston: In 2012, I made the jump from being the general manager of a small web development and design agency to running a contemporary art museum. Going into the interview process, I had to frame up—for myself, before I could even begin to argue it to an interview panel—how my previous six years of working on the web equipped me to run an art gallery.

It surprised me what I came up with. There were obvious things: budgets, stakeholder relationships, HR, strategy and planning. There were also less obvious things. Six years spent advocating for engagement, sharing, openness, prioritization, experimentation, customer focus, both to colleagues and to clients.

I came of age professionally over this period. I joined the National Library at the start of 2006 as a communications advisor. That year, the *Time Magazine* 'Person of the Year' was 'You', an acknowledgement of the rise of Web 2.0 self-publishing, blogs, Wikipedia, and the new dominance of user-generated content. I started my blog in December of that year—with an incredibly geeky premise, that every day I would learn something new about the web and write about it.

When I reflect on it, my timing was incredibly lucky. In 2007, I was seconded from the communications team to work on a massive overhaul of the Library's website. The National Library was already committed to digitization, but there was a new excitement about openness and sharing and connection with people online as well as on-site, driven by all these new tools. A group of us coalesced at the Library around the opportunities that the new web was offering—reinforced by our Chief Executive, Penny Carnaby, but also by this new boom in online publishing and sharing.

With the National Digital Forum and Webstock conferences locally, the *Museums and the Web* conference and the publishing people like you at the Powerhouse and Shelley Bernstein at the Brooklyn Museum and George Oates at Flickr, looking at what we were doing, and the endless free guidance appearing on people's individual blogs and sites like *A List Apart* (https://alistapart.com) and *Boxes and Arrows* (http://boxesandarrows.com), there was just this incredible amount of knowledge and guidance being given away freely and generously, and I think it set an inspiring example for everyone in the GLAM sector to experiment, document, and reinforce this collective skill and knowledge building.

Coming of age on the web in this way shaped my value and practice. It's led me to place high value on collaboration, experimentation and sharing. It's meant that listening to data and new ideas about engagement comes naturally. Having been through Agile evangelism and emerged from the other side, those principles of iteration, prioritization, fast decision-making, teamwork, minimum viable product (MVP), and putting the customer at the center of decision-making still strongly informs my approach as a director. And I think being steeped in user experience design shaped the way I view my work—I'm just as interested in the venue hire experience as the exhibition experience, I think clean bathrooms are as important as good information architecture and sound roofs. (Actually, sound roofs are probably the most important thing in a museum.)

Being online has been, as you've observed, given our generation a new level of connectedness. And this goes both ways—for us Moana-nui-a-kiwa, these islands in the Pacific, to learn from the rest of the world, but also for the rest of the world to learn from us. As you've noted, there's a distinctiveness to identity in this place. As a Pākehā New Zealander, my worldview and my attitude towards being a citizen, an employer, a decision-maker and a contributor is shaped by what it means to be living and working as a non-indigenous person in a colonized country. When I travel, in the United States in particular, which is where we draw so much of our inspiration and direction from, I think there is a lot we have to offer from our Pacific countries that could still be heard more loudly.

SC: What I'm hearing, then, is that your background in digital has meant that you've become more sensitized to the notion of 'user needs' in operating your museum. While digital product development has brought these practices to the fore, the business models behind the web as well as the mindsets of those building the technologies of the web, have too heavily prioritized quantitative measures of success, often by quarterly reporting, too. How have you balanced this in your practice, especially as a director of a museum whose impact is, arguably, most felt qualitatively?

CJ: It feels like in the last 20 years or so museums—and art museums is what I'm most familiar with, of course—have looked for all kinds of 'objective' measures for the value they're creating, from hotel nights associated with blockbuster exhibitions to job creation. What we're not measuring are things like: are we advancing cultural conversations? Are we developing artists and their careers? Are we connecting people with creativity in ways that enrich their lives?

I'm persuaded by the analysis of Seph Rodney (2015) concerning the shifts in Western museology the end of the 19th century through to around World War II, museums were largely about collecting, cataloguing, and organizing to create knowledge, with side-benefits for the visitors. From the mid-20th century on, the educational benefits of museums were the chief focus and public-facing argument for their value. Over the past 25 years, political and economic changes have ushered in the understanding of the visitor as a consumer, to be targeted with personalization and to be seen increasingly in terms of economic value. This is the framework in which we now must perform and communicate our work and its value. Like all directors, I gather data and information that I find to be quite empty at times and use data to make arguments for continued funding. I guess the balance I try to strike is making sure that our programming is focused on advancing artists' careers and areas of the arts that need more attention given to them. To ensuring that what we do is as distinctive as possible, and with integrity that's recognized by our artist and museum peers. And to do that in a way that is fiscally responsible, meeting the agreement we have with our funders—who are at the end of the day our city's ratepayers—to provide museums that benefit the city. But at the same time, deliver on those qualitative things—not just the good that we bring to visitors' lives, but the good we do for the visual arts.

SC: As a Pākehā New Zealander too, I've become increasingly aware that a lot of the work that both you and I were doing in the 2000s around open access and digitization is now being critiqued by First Nations people. This criticism is long overdue and while we both lived through the early skirmishes with Wikipedia, I'm very interested in how institutions steer a path towards the affordances of networked society while also acknowledging the privilege that enables their usual core constituencies to avoid the inherent violence of networked society.

CJ: I feel fortunate to have studied art history at a time when post-colonial thinking was strong in academia, and in New Zealand at a time when biculturalism was a prominent topic. That gave me a strong basis for understanding the power, and inequities, of representation.

I remember in the first flush of my excitement around Flickr Commons, I was disappointed that I was only able to post the most neutral of images (lots of landscapes and ships) because of the National Library of New Zealand's internal guidelines around depictions of people, and especially of Māori. But it's meant that my understanding of 'openness' has always been tempered by an understanding of ideas of ownership and "kaitiakitanga" (caretaking or custodianship) that go beyond legal understandings of copyright and public domain. Two separate pieces of writing have driven this home for me. One was how enraged I was by Tiffany Jenkins' argument about repatriation and cultural appropriation of taonga (treasures) in the book *Keeping Their Marbles: How the Treasures of the Past Ended up in Museums—And Why They Should Stay There* (Jenkins 2016). Her approach privileges the Western Enlightenment values of freedom of information and the assumed availability of all things as part of knowledge creation above all other values. However, if you've had some exposure to First Nations' and indigenous thinking, you better understand that this is just one perspective: in others, knowledge and access has boundaries, and for good reasons.

The second aspect was how much I learned from reading a piece written by Tara Robertson (2018) about the digitization of *On Our Backs*, a lesbian porn magazine published during the 1960s–1980s. Correct copyright procedures had been followed to digitize the collection. You could see its digitization as bringing to light an under-represented community in our collections and placing value on the publication and the community by selecting it for digitization. Both a librarian and a lesbian, Robertson argues that while the people featured in On Our Backs assented to their reproduction and distribution, this was for a smaller and more boundaried community. The idea that one day anyone with an Internet connection and the right search term could find them.

You mention Wikipedia. I've found it interesting that when I've worked on art edit-a-thons with Māori and Pacific people, they often feel wrong just editing a page about a figure who they know personally, or who holds "mana" (prestige) in their community. They would prefer to talk with the person and create a shared understanding of what they're doing—to gain their consent. It's interesting how that sits with Wikipedia's blanket guidelines about neutrality and conflict of interest, which assume that objective distance between a contributor and their subject is optimal, necessary for independence, and central to creating a quality information tool.

SC: In terms of 'advancing artists careers', I've always been struck by the argument that museums should stay out of the art market—when obviously in terms of artist careers these are inextricably linked with the art market. When the contemporary art market—as Hito Steyerl (2017) describes in her essays on freeport art storage—has become a tax haven for oligarchs… not to mention the current interest of artists in cryptocurrency and blockchain. What are the implications for an art museum?

CJ: I think the implications are huge—but maybe not always the ones we leap to in terms of conflict of interest, or mega-galleries and mega-artists. To be honest, I'm not interested in the 1% of international art that functions as a kind of currency—whether of capital or status. I'm interested in the careers of Aotearoa's artists, and I'm interested in what New Zealand audiences (including artists) would benefit from seeing in terms of international artists. I'm interested in helping artists secure the income needed to have time to make art—be that through paying artist fees, buying works for the collection, helping with grant applications, or staging shows that will hopefully have a good effect on an artist's market or opportunity to make a living in the future. So long as you're not being disingenuous or duplicitous about your reason for doing a show (and I have resisted pressure to mount exhibitions based on collectors' desires to see 'their' artists getting a good public showing) there is no harm in considering what a beneficial market outcome might be for an artist.

This is certainly easier to say in Wellington than in New York, but it's one of the blessings of being in a largely publicly-funded system. If I don't have to source the funds to make a show from collectors, donors or dealers, I can bring focus to artists who don't, for whatever reason (age, lack of fashionability, historical bias, happenchance) have those financial backers. It creates a far more even playing field and much more opportunity for a diverse exhibition environment (Fig. 26.3).

Fig. 26.3 *Black Bridge over the Waiohini [sic] River*, "near Greytown, Wairarapa, New Zealand. From the album: New Zealand scenery: Wellington to the Wairarapa. Photograph by James Bragge, mid 1870s. A British photographer, he established a photography studio in New Zealand in 1865. This image is from his Wellington black-and-white silver albumen paper prints, from Te Papa Museum Collections online. No copyright claimed. https://collections.tepapa.govt.nz/object/982671

SC: I love the example from Tara Robertson and it reminds me of discussions I used to have in the office with Aaron Cope about his Parallel Flickr project—which intended to make a functional backup of your own Flickr photos but preserving their comments and social interactions as long as the original commenter was still public. Constant negotiation of privacy and an understanding of original context and consent seem like they will be the big issues for preservation, digitization, and born digital preservation into the future. As you've pointed out, we have a lot to learn from First Nations approaches to community knowledge. At what point do the boundaries of 'boundaried communities' need to be broached? I remember you telling me about some of the collections in the National Library that were, by donor decree, not to be widely available (Fig. 26.4).

CJ: In my 20s, I was frustrated by these boundaries. Like—what's the point of putting an oral history recording into an archive if you're going to put incredibly restrictive boundaries on access and re-use? And I think that was predicated on a perspective that information is always beneficial, and that the discovery of new

Fig. 26.4 Digital Cultural Heritage symposium at the Brooklyn Historical Society in 2013. Left to right: Seb Chan, Digital Media Director, Cooper Hewitt, 2011–2015; Aaron Straup Cope, Head of Engineering, Cooper Hewitt, 2011–2015; and Tula Giannini, Dean and Professor, Pratt School of Information, 2004–2017, Project Director, CHART project funded by the IMLS (Cultural Heritage Access, Research and Technology)—produced the Brooklyn Visual Heritage website (http://www.brooklynvisualheritage.org). (Photograph by Jonathan Bowen, May 17, 2013)

information is always exciting (based on my university study) and that 'information wants to be free' (based on my introduction to Web 2.0 philosophies). But do you know that whole quote? It's attributed to Stewart Brand, the Whole Earth Catalog founder and counterculture figure, who is documented as saying to Steve Wozniak (the Apple co-founder) at the first Hacker Conference in the States in 1984:

> On the one hand information wants to be expensive, because it's so valuable. The right information in the right place just changes your life. On the other hand, information wants to be free, because the cost of getting it out is getting lower and lower all the time. So you have these two fighting against each other.

And I love that idea of information wanting to be expensive, because it's so valuable. Not in a Western perspective, that's not how our educational and civic and media systems work (or should). But in other cultures' and perspectives, where information is not valued just on utilitarian value, but has community or spiritual value. There are cases where it should be expensive—not commercially, but in terms of the effort you must put in in terms of relationship and knowledge building before you are entitled to encounter it.

Having said this, I think there's an important addendum. We need to be clear on our mandates as *public institutions*. Based on my resources and remit at The Dowse, for example, I would be highly unlikely to add to the collection an artwork that could not be shown. We're primarily a working gallery, where art comes to be shown to people. But an institution like the National Library—I think it's totally suitable that they have the mandate and resource to take on material that is there for safekeeping on behalf of a community, rather than be public-facing. It's crucial that we build institutions like that, and systems of support for community memory institutions and projects, into our ecosystem.

SC: Changing tack, your museum is decidedly non-technological. Sure, there's a retail and ticketing system, but you've also been very committed to creating a space that allows for anonymity and privacy by rejecting some of the Wi-Fi tracking systems deployed by the local council around the exterior of the museum. Other museum directors would love to get that technology in their museums—tell me a bit about how you came to this choice.

CJ: I'm not adverse to clean data—we're constantly analyzing visitor numbers, retail and donations info, as well as voluntary visitor surveys and the resident surveys conducted by my Council. A couple of years ago I had a Winston Churchill Memorial Trust scholarship to travel around the US and visit art museums, looking at things including digitally-driven visitor experiences, like the Pen at Cooper Hewitt and the Ask app at Brooklyn Museum and the DMA Friends project. All three of these instances—lead by yourself at Cooper Hewitt, Shelley Bernstein at Brooklyn Museum and Rob Stein at the DMA—used data in a way that I found to be good hearted and applicable, often to direct marketing efforts to low-visiting areas or improve label copy or placement of works—things like that. But the collection of data like cellphone identifiers, from people who don't know they're being tracked, for ends from which they don't benefit from; that makes me feel uncomfortable. And then I do worry about the long term storage and use of that data, because the world's an unpredictable place I hew pretty closely to what technologist and commentator Ceglowski (2015) says on this topic: don't collect it ("your problems with data disappear if you stop collecting it"), if you do collect it, don't store it longer than you need to, and if you do store it, don't keep it any longer than it's useful to you.

I'm aware time is probably going to prove me wrong on this one. But right at this moment, my sense that we'd be infringing on people's privacy and creating future problems for ourselves outweighs the benefits of knowing how many times a certain cellphone walks through my doors, or how long it spends in a certain gallery. I can ask those questions face to face and keep the personal balance that makes me feel like I'm upholding my responsibilities.

CJ: Speaking of support for your maker/producer community: ACMI X is a co-working space hosted by ACMI that brings businesses and practitioners from the moving image field into the building alongside your own staff. How is that going? Have the original motivations/objectives changed because of the learning that's coming from running the space?

SC: "Bringing businesses into the museum" is something that other museums continue to try. Be it science museums working closely with R&D like Ars Electronica's FutureLab, or Science Gallery's positioning between academia and industry, or Cooper Hewitt's now prestigious National Design Awards which began as a strategy to engage with the top tier of professional designers along with the awards' inherent 'earned media' outcomes.

The concept came from our director, Katrina Sedgwick, who had run a similar co-working space in a previous role as a commissioner and director of the Adelaide Film Festival. Inside the museum's new offices, though, the co-working space (now also running a formal accelerator program) has been very successful. In standard terms it has set out what it intended to do – foster new connections between makers and the museum, but more interestingly it has also influenced internal work culture by modelling open office transparency along with encouraging serendipitous collaboration. The co-opting of 'serendipity' is critiqued usefully by Olma (2016). We quickly learned that what ACMI X offers is worth a lot more than a desk—and has been a valuable pathway for ACMI to create a new sense of public value and purpose in relation to the media industries. The next phase of ACMI will be about integrating this into the public face of the museum itself, as the co-working space and staff offices are located a ten-minute walk from the public galleries on the other side of the Yarra River.

CJ: What's your take on tech start-up incubators inside museums?

SC: The growth of start-up incubators inside museums—instead of artist residencies and artist studios—seems to reflect the cultural shift from "artist as hero" to "entrepreneur as hero". I find that narrative terribly problematic—more so than the "artist as hero"—Eno's notion of 'scenius' (Eno 1996) is more my experience of art, music and the culture industries. Technology incubators inside museums feels like a strange fit because the museum "market" is incredibly conservative, limited in size, and bound by a challenging procurement environment. With those limitations it seems odd to be encouraging start-ups inside such a difficult marketplace— especially when the traditional measures of start-up success—buy outs and scale—are next to impossible. Equally what the museum-field needs are long term strategic technology infrastructure, not short-term marketing apps.

That said, I do believe there is great value in having technologists working closer with and inside institutions. The British Council's *Geek In Residence* scheme, also replicated in Australia in the 2000s, was very valuable in embedding technologists inside small to medium arts organizations mostly because it encouraged a type of "border dissolution" between fields and began to make new conversations possible (as well as, at the time, quite a few websites).

CJ: Do you think the tertiary education sector (focus on Australia if it makes the answer more targeted) is equipping students for contemporary museums? Is there more we could be contributing to future arts worker's early development (not just skills, but ethics and the philosophical underpinnings of museum work)? Are there alternatives to the degree > volunteer > internship > paid role model?

SC: I'm suspicious of tying tertiary education too closely to the short term needs of the job market. If I look back over my career at the roles that for which I've hired or sat on interview panels in museums, I cannot think of anyone who has been successful with solely a traditional museum studies or curatorial studies background, and points out that, "Everyone has been able to prove their suitability for a role by having worked outside the museum sector, often in an adjacent field, and largely through independent projects which they have been able to successfully execute outside of an institutional structure." Museums need to take observations seriously, to progress from ingrained ways of doing, to move into the digital future.

I am very aware that the opportunities for people to have prior experience, or to be able to contextualize their prior experience in other fields, is part of what fuels the lack of diversity amongst our workforce. In some ways, education was supposed to be the great equalizer, but it hasn't turned out that way—especially as the skills that staff need now are about having the confidence and ability to pursue ideas, concepts and methods, very independently.

26.3 Seeking Relevance and Engaged Experience

Museums and art in a "postdigital" world, one in which the digital and physical are integrated and inseparable, faces complex challenges that flow across boundaries from inside to outside the museum walls, crossing cultures, geographies and identities in art and education while questioning the values, roles and responsibilities of museums. Chan and Johnston not only discuss these challenges but point to new ways of thinking about them, and of solving some of the longstanding issues that impede progress towards a new vision for the 21st-century museum, at the heart of which is thinking critically, digitally, creatively—non-linear and non-hierarchical. As life becomes integral to the digital culture ecosphere, it impinges upon museums' traditional and formal states of being. We see both physical and digital place becoming contested space where competing and diverse visions of art and culture, human expectations for equality, participation and voice, require that museums reinvent their organizing principles, values and priorities. Human life is evolving in an increasingly people-centered world, where new digital tools and technologies are in the hands of individuals and holdout the promise of participation and a seat at the table.

Chan was interviewed by a writer Tim Grey for *Broadsheet* published in Melbourne when he was appointed as the Chief Information Experience Designer for the Australian Centre for the Moving Image (ACMI). The article quotes Chan on his groundbreaking work at the Cooper Hewitt featuring the concept design for the "pen" (Grey 2015):

> Every visitor who comes to the museum gets given an interactive pen," Chan says. "With that pen you can create things, and save everything in the museum – all of the objects and videos, you can go through the exhibits, collect them, and take them away later to do whatever you want with them. It's this sense of the museum being a space where you can collect and take away stuff, but also create things while you're there.

The article ends with Chan making a prediction for the future about the role of information experience designers:

> How I'd describe it is that it's a post-digital role," he says. "It's the sort of role you're going to start seeing in a lot of places and organizations over the next decade as we start to realize that digital is not special anymore. In terms of good experiences, digital is just part of it. (Fig. 26.5).

Fig. 26.5 Display case showing the original "pen" for the Cooper Hewitt Museum designed by Chan, Sistelnetworks, Local Projects, GE, Undercurrent and MakeSimply. Standing next to the case, Tula Giannini, and Allen Shieh from MakeSimply, a company that oversaw the manufacturing of the "pen". At the Cooper Hewitt's opening party in 2014, celebrating its redesign and renovation, which Seb Chan led in his position of Director of Digital and Emerging Media. A brilliant success, his work set a new bar for visitor experience design. (Photograph by Tula Giannini, December 12, 2014)

26.4 Conclusion

Leading museums into the postdigital age, as is the case with Seb Chan and Courtney Johnston, Chan points out that coming from outside the walls, simply with a graduate education in museums or curatorial studies is inadequate to meet contemporary museum needs, especially in terms of digital skills. Chan notes, "I cannot think of anyone who has been successful with solely traditional museum studies or curatorial studies background, and points out that, "Everyone has been able to prove their suitability for a role by having worked outside the museum sector…" He speaks to the need for cross fertilization, inclusion, and breaking down silos, while Courtney speaks to the role of the artist as a creative force and authentic voice in the life of the museum, "ensuring that what we do is as distinctive as possible, and with integrity that's recognized by our artist and museum peers". These are critical insights into the issues museums face moving forward, especially at a time when digital tends to be more behind the scene, and graduates entering the museum field have little understanding of how digital culture affects museum culture, and few have digital work experience. Significantly, Seb questions the notion of entrepreneurial labs in museums, and sees that the real need is for having a solid digital infrastructure as opposed to designing apps.

The interview reveals that Seb Chan and Courtney Johnston, serving in their leadership roles in museums located in Australia and New Zealand respectively, both stress the importance of engaging the local community and the participation of indigenous people while recognizing the need to balance local and global knowledge to create exhibitions and programs that are relevant to both communities. Taking advantage of the growing opportunities presented by online exhibitions, small and medium museums can share community knowledge with the world and gain international relevance by juxtaposing local and global perspectives and commonalities.

References

Ceglowski M (2015) Haunted by Data. In: Presented at Strata + Hadoop World, New York City. http://idlewords.com/talks/haunted_by_data.htm. Accessed on 5 July 2018

Chan S, Cope A (2015) Strategies against architecture: interactive media and transformative technology at the Cooper Hewitt, Smithsonian Design Museum. Curator—The Museum J 58(3):52–368, July 2015. https://doi.org/10.1111/cura.12118

Edwards D (2012) Courtney Johnston can't wait to start at Dowse. Dominion Post, 11 Sept 2012. http://www.stuff.co.nz/dominion-post/news/local-papers/hutt-news/7649567/Courtney-Johnston-can-t-wait-to-start-at-Dowse. Accessed on 20 Jan 2019

Eno B (1996) A year with swollen appendices: brian eno's diary. Faber & Faber, London

Grey T (2015) What's a 'chief experience officer'?—it's not a title that crops up in the job ads much. Broadsheet, 9 Nov 2015. https://www.broadsheet.com.au/melbourne/entertainment/engineering-better-experiences. Accessed on 20 Jan 2019

Jenkins T (2016) Keeping their marbles: how the treasures of the past ended up in museums—and why they should stay there. Oxford University Press, Oxford

Olma S (2016) In defence of serendipity: for a radical politics of innovation. Repeater Books, London

Robertson T (2018) Not all information wants to be free: the case study of on our backs. In: Applying library values to emerging technology: decision-making in the age of open access, maker spaces, and the ever-changing library. Publications in Librarianship, 72. American Library Association, pp 225–239

Rodney S (2015) How museum visitors became consumers. Culturecom, France. https://culture-communication.fr/en/how-museum-visitors-became-consumers/. Accessed on 6 July 2018

Steyerl H (2017) Duty free art: art in the age of planetary civil war. Verso, London

Te Papa (2018) Leadership appointments bring new expertise to Te Papa. Scoop Business, 24 July 2018. http://www.scoop.co.nz/stories/BU1807/S00581/leadership-appointments-bring-new-expertise-to-te-papa.htm. Accessed on 7 Jan 2019

Chapter 27
Smart Cities and Digital Culture: Models of Innovation

Ann Borda and Jonathan P. Bowen

Abstract A smart city is an urban area that broadly refers to a collective model in which technological advancements are used to enhance systemic capabilities aiming to enhance competitiveness, effectiveness, quality of life and sustainability. A major focus of the chapter is a review of smart city platforms and participatory-centric approaches and their potential translation to innovations across digital culture and smart city developments. The results provide a landscape view and further scope for identifying models of innovation and future opportunities in developing smart digital culture services and evolving directions, particularly within the museum sector.

27.1 Introduction

In 2018, more than 54% of the world's population lives in urban areas. The United Nations projects that this number will increase to 68% by 2050 (United Nations 2018). As our cities become more populated and expansive, an increasingly uneven strain is placed on resources and infrastructure. Soja and Kanai (2006) use the terms "global city region" to refer to "a new metropolitan form characterized by sprawling polycentric networks of urban centres ..." Such networks are becoming identified with both the potential and the reality of 'smart' city infrastructures of connected transportation, financial, energy, health, information and cultural systems.

There are numerous definitions of a "smart city" across the literature with little consensus (Angelidou 2015) and there are many acknowledged technical issues involved (Palomar et al. 2016). For the purposes of this paper, the definition provided by the (ISO/IEC 2014) is considered an appropriately inclusive one, that is:

A. Borda (✉)
The University of Melbourne, Melbourne, Australia
e-mail: aborda@unimelb.edu.au

J. P. Bowen
School of Engineering, London South Bank University, London, UK
e-mail: jonathan.bowen@lsbu.ac.uk

Southwest University, Chongqing, China

T. Giannini and J. P. Bowen (eds.), *Museums and Digital Culture*,
Springer Series on Cultural Computing, https://doi.org/10.1007/978-3-319-97457-6_27

> The "smartness" of a city describes its ability to bring together all its resources, to effectively and seamlessly achieve the goals and fulfil the purposes it has set itself…[It] enables the integration and interoperability of city systems in order to provide value, both to the city as a whole, and to the individual citizen. This integration further enables potential synergies to be exploited and the city to function holistically, and to facilitate innovation and growth.

In the context of such values and goals, there is a global movement in the implementation of smart cities which was catalyzed in the Global Forum World Foundation for Smart Communities in 1997. Specifically, coordinated strategies and standards for smart city implementation are increasingly pervasive and being adopted at national and industry levels. For example, the UK Department of Business, Innovation and Skills commissioned BSI in 2012 to develop a standards strategy for smart cities in order to accelerate and minimize risks in the implementation of smart cities in the UK. In 2011, the European Commission (EC) initiated the European Innovation Partnership on Smart Cities and Communities (European Commission 2015). In China, comparable initiatives have been established, such as the China Strategic Alliance of Smart City Industrial Technology Innovation. In the United States, the Federal Smart Cities and Communities Task Force is seeking to embed new digital technologies into city and community infrastructures and services. The Australian Government has similarly launched a national *Smart Cities Plan* aimed at positioning Australian cities to succeed in the digital economy (Australian Government 2016).

Among individual cities themselves, there are examples of smart city plans that are being developed at local and municipal government level. One of the acknowledged "smartest cities" is the city nation of Singapore which has a comprehensive initiative called The Smart Nation (http://www.smartnation.sg). Singapore's Smart Nation goals focus on driving transformation across the economy, Government, and society guided by a Digital Economy Framework for Action and Digital Readiness Blueprint. In 2018, the City of London released *The Smarter London Together roadmap* with a comparable goal "to transform London into the smartest city in the world".

One example of a collective city initiative is GrowSmarter (2015). This initiative is a collaborative EU funded smart city project, focusing on sustainable solutions to economic, social and environmental issues. The project involves what are termed "Lighthouse Cities" of Stockholm, Cologne and Barcelona. It aims to integrate and demonstrate twelve smart solutions to energy, mobility and infrastructure in collaboration with twenty industrial partners, and importantly the project is intended to create a platform for sharing knowledge and experience. Industry involvement in smart city developments is especially key to such partnerships, and in supporting the technological enablers and connected platforms that underpin smart city infrastructures. Multinational communications and IT companies, Cisco and Nokia are among the industry players who are developing strategic White Papers about the platform components of a successful smart city, and partnering with cities on pilot implementations (Cisco 2014; Nokia 2017). The Internet of Things (IoT) is almost universally the global infrastructure that underpins smart city platforms interconnecting both physical and virtual objects (e.g., sensors, devices, people) based on evolving technologies and allowing them to transmit and receive data.

Across these standards and strategies is a shared vision to position communities at all scales to have equitable access to connected smart services that can enhance the sustainability and quality of life, improved health and safety, and economic prosperity. The path to this goes through the initiation of standards of development that are also culturally adaptable and can motivate communities and ignite change. Inevitably such a route requires an evolution from a technology-led smart city—"Smart City 1.0" to one which is technology-enabled and city-led "Smart City 2.0", to a participatory model empowering citizen cocreation aka "Smart City 3.0" (Cohen 2015).

Within the framework of this paper, the citizens of a smart city are potential participants in its governance and in the evolution of smarter services, including those related to future opportunities related to digital cultural heritage. Indeed, there are an increasing number of visible examples of digital cultural initiatives integrated with participatory innovation and smart city strategies. The rise of open innovation models and living labs, as tangible manifestations, are among the landscape of developments which are assessed further in this chapter.

27.2 Characterizing Innovation Platforms

Innovation platforms can be characterized, firstly, by a high level of citizen involvement in cocreating services and solutions, such as Internet-based applications applicable to different sectors of the economy and society; and secondly, by the emergence of new forms of collaboration among local governments, research institutes, universities, cultural organizations, and industry (Eskilinen et al. 2015). Such strategies and the resulting "innovation ecosystems" are becoming increasingly relevant in relation to the growing economic and social issues and opportunities that smart cities are facing.

27.2.1 Enabling Platforms

In the context of both smart cities and digital culture, the *smartness* requirements of each are equally aligned to new intelligent and contextualized services. Across the literature, these services are generally made possible by a common set of enabling platforms that are becoming ubiquitous and inseparably identified with the realization of innovation and participatory systems (Borda and Bowen 2017). Specifically, the innovation systems concept has been applied to smart cities only recently to be closely linked to national and regional levels, as an application to open innovation platforms and for public policies, such as open data policies, for example. According to the European Commission (EC), open innovation can only be realized within smart cities, if the prerequisites of innovation are considered and if open knowledge, data, access and connectivity are implemented in the cities (European Commission 2016). As these different modes of interaction become more integrated with digital and virtual approaches, the benefit of connecting to visitors via enabling platforms is impactful in assisting these institutions to innovate with public participation and communities (Borda and Bowen 2011, 2017).

27.2.2 IoT Connectivity

IoT makes possible an entirely new level of information access, retrieval and interaction, as the physical world becomes connected to the Internet. IoT, as a nearly synonymous term with smart cities, remains an evolving technology in digital culture initiatives. As yet, there are no published standards specific to digital culture projects as for smart cities, such as those developed by ISO/IEC or the IEEE Smart Cities Initiative (IEEE 2017). However, there are some advances towards developing platforms for smart cultural heritage utilizing enabling platforms that underline smart city implementation. There is the potential for IoT, for example, to underpin various smart cultural services (Chianese and Piccialli 2014; Jara et al. 2015). The EU-funded DATABENC (2014) initiative piloted an IoT service-oriented framework for an art exhibition of sculptures within the Maschio Angioino castle in Naples (Amato et al. 2013; Chianese and Piccialli 2014). An IoT platform has been recently architected for Gallery One of the Cleveland Museum of Art in which *The Collection Wall* and *ArtLens* mobile app are key features supporting participatory approaches through sensor-based technologies among others (Alexander 2014; Alexander et al. 2017).

27.2.3 Wireless Sensor Networks (WSN)

IoT initiatives are generally reliant on a form of Wireless Sensor Network (WSN), consisting of spatially distributed autonomous devices using sensors. The innovation of WSN is that it acts as a virtual layer where data about the physical world can be accessed by any computing system. Short-range wireless is becoming a preferred technology platform for the development of smart and location-aware environments.

Two emerging technologies in short range are: Bluetooth Low Energy (BLE)—a subset of Bluetooth wireless technology—it allows physical objects to exchange data wirelessly and is being applied in beacon technologies, for example. Near-Field Communication (NFC) enables short range wireless communication between devices or objects, e.g., a portable device, such as a mobile, iPad or smartphone, when they are touched together, or brought within a few centimeters of the other.

Digital culture applications of NFC technology can provide a more fine-grained context-awareness that allows users to receive customized information and a more realistic experience in close proximity, e.g., users can read or listen to museum guides, while watching animations or playing games. *The Pen* at Cooper Hewitt builds on NFC reading technology to enable personalized and individual interaction (Chan and Cope 2015; Cooper Hewitt n.d.).

Among the enabling platforms, mobile broadband is the most pervasive across digital culture initiatives. The cultural heritage sector has been an early adopter of mobile technologies in user engagement and the visitor experience in the development of mobile apps. It is also the most accessible and available of the technologies to the broadest spectrum of users, irrespective of their location (Roffia et al. 2005; Casella and Coelho 2013; Yovcheva et al. 2012, 2014). With the socio-technical rise of the mobile phone, museums and galleries worldwide developed mobile apps that visitors could download onto their own device and create self-guided tours (Petrelli and O'Brien 2018). The National Gallery in London was one of the first museums to develop *LoveArt*—an iPhone app launched in 2009 (Lagoudi and Sexton 2010).

27.2.4 Application Programming Interfaces (APIs)

Smart city services are increasingly being built using open or publicly available APIs. Finland has six of its largest cities using inter-city cooperation to disclose their data and interfaces since 2014 (Forum Virium Helsinki 2016). Building API-driven services have enabled Finnish cities to become more open and participatory urban centers that underpin strategic policies for smart city implementation.

In the cultural sector, APIs have provided developers with programmatic access to software applications and web services largely related to museum and cultural collections. For example, the Canadiana Discovery Portal (CDP) is a free web service allowing users to search the digital collections of Canadian libraries, archives, and museums. The CDP open API allows developers to programmatically query these collections by source, media type, language, record type, date range, among other fields (http://search.canadiana.ca/support/api). The Cooper Hewitt Smithsonian Design Collection in New York (USA), the British Museum and the Science Museum in London (UK), and the Auckland Museum in Auckland (New Zealand) are among a growing number of museums and cultural organizations that allow open access to collection data amounting to millions of artefacts.

One of the largest open cultural data services are available through the online *Europeana* cultural heritage platform (http://pro.europeana.eu) which provides access to collections containing over 50 million cultural heritage items, representing over 3,500 cultural institutions across Europe (Europeana 2015).

27.2.5 Machine Learning and Artificial Intelligence (AI)

The increasing deployment of sensors and hand-held electronics combined with the big data generated by these and other smart city infrastructure is allowing for new approaches in how we can participate within smart cities. In the built environment, for instance, Artificial Intelligence (AI) enabled systems using machine learning, can adjust to various inputs which allow them to perform tasks that are more human-like, such as self-driving cars and digital assistants. For instance, the City of Vienna has developed the 'Wienbot'—a chatbot assistant that answers questions about the city's most popular services. With 1.2 million hits on the official city website every month, this text-based computer program relies on natural language processing and machine learning to respond to questions via mobile devices or on the web (http://smartcity.wien.gv.at/site/en/wienbot/). The transformation of cities through AI, networked sensors, and the way we design and interact with them is being addressed through projects led by the Senseable City Laboratory (http://senseable.mit.edu), at the Massachusetts Institute of Technology (MIT) under the directorship of urban innovator, Professor Carlo Ratti. In museum settings, the adoption of AI is taking hold in the case of chatbots deployed as virtual guides, such as the chatbot game developed for the House Museums of Milan (Boiano et al. 2018). An overview of chatbots in museums is provided in Chap. 15.

27.2.6 Open Innovation

Smart city strategies are based on a new understanding of innovation platforms, grounded in the concept of open innovation ecosystems, and on citizens' empowerment for shaping innovation and urban development. For example, Amsterdam has established an innovation platform for its smart city developments that allows for an open collective of ideas and exchanges and resources to be made publicly available and codesigned by the citizens of Amsterdam (http://amsterdamsmartcity.com). This ecosystem aligns with the concept of open innovation which is most often defined as '…the use of purposive inflows and outflows of knowledge to accelerate internal innovation, and expand the markets for external use of innovation, respectively' (Chesbrough et al. 2006). It can further involve different stakeholder perspectives (Gassmann et al. 2010), such as that of the user perspective, the institutional perspective and the cultural perspective (Chesbrough et al. 2006; Dawson et al. 2017).

In relation to cultural heritage, Haitham Eid (2016) discusses a theoretical framework for an innovation model for museums based on three interconnected concepts of (1) open innovation, (2) social enterprise, and (3) social innovation, each of which are growing trends in the museum sector. Together they can present a formula for innovation in that museums which "adopt a social enterprise business model and utilize open innovation strategies are capable of achieving social innovation." In this way, museums can be open to many forms of innovation, not just involving their traditional visitors or users, but stakeholders, such as academia, industry, government, and other cultural organizations (Turnbull and Connell 2011).

In the Smart Nation plan for Singapore (see Fig. 27.1), enabling "a Culture of Innovation and Experimentation" is a pillar in its mission in which the government aims to put in place appropriate policies and legislations to facilitate innovations by the public and the private sector, and to encourage adoption of new ideas (http://www.smartnation.sg).

Fig. 27.1 Singapore's Smart Nation super tree grove and OCBC Skyway. By Jan, Wikimedia Commons, https://commons.wikimedia.org/wiki/File:OCBC_Skyway,_Gardens_By_The_Bay,_Singapore_-_20140809.jpg

Similarly, the *Smarter London Together* roadmap directly acknowledges the role of cultural institutions in engaging citizens, and aims to explore how museums, such as the new Museum of London being built at Smithfield Market, can promote greater understanding of Londoners about smart technologies and the data shaping their lives (Greater London Authority 2019). An early goal in the London smart city roadmap is the further establishment of a London Office of Technology and Innovation (LOTI) to support common capabilities and standards for future innovation (Greater London Authority 2019).

The city of Bristol in the UK has named itself as an 'Open Programmable City' making available new testing environments to address urban challenges. *Bristol is Open* (http://www.bristolisopen.com, see Fig. 27.2) is a smart city platform that offers local companies, communities, other international technology and ICT companies City Experimentation as a Service, using digital infrastructure across Bristol as a research and development laboratory for urban change (http://www.bristolisopen.com/platform/).

Fig. 27.2 *Bristol is Open* includes a smart data visualization facility. Housed in the Bristol Planetarium in Millennium Square, the 98-seat Bristol Data Dome, has a stereo 3D hemispherical screen with 4K resolution. Flickr, public domain, https://www.flickr.com/photos/126337928@N05/34252041972/

27.3 Living Labs

There is a global movement in the implementation of smart cities to initiate living labs as a key model for the fostering of open innovation (Leminen et al. 2012; Eskilinen et al. 2015). One of the most significant characteristics of living labs is that they are also open-innovation networks and collaborative development platforms that bring together relevant stakeholders: developers, public sector agencies, researchers, and end-users of new technologies and smart services (Leminen et al. 2012). The living labs model has a presence around the world, for example, RLabs in CapeTown, South Africa, was initiated in 2008, and has since supported the participation of more than 100,000 community members who have directly accessed RLabs skills training and economic empowerment opportunities (http://www.rlabs.org).

Living Labs were developed as a concept around the 1990s and pioneered by the Massachusetts Institute of Technology (MIT) and Georgia Tech in the USA to bring "together interdisciplinary experts to develop, deploy, and test—in actual living environments—new technologies and strategies for design that respond to this changing world" (Leminen et al. 2012; Lepik et al. 2010; Mulder 2012; Eskilinen et al. 2015). The Beta_space (see Chap. 6) of the Museum of Applied Arts and Sciences (now the Powerhouse) in Sydney, Australia, is an example of an early cultural-led living lab established in 2004 (Muller et al. 2006; Turnbull and Connell 2011).

The development of Living Labs in Europe accelerated over the past decade due to specific national and European Policy and Innovation initiatives (e.g., the 2020 Policy Frameworks and Digital Agenda) that prioritized placing the user at the center of the innovation lifecycle within real-life settings. For example, the European Network of Living Labs (ENoLL) is the largest formalized entity of Living Labs worldwide. ENoLL defines Living Labs as user-centered, open innovation ecosystems based on systematic user cocreation approach, integrating research and innovation processes in real life communities and settings. Since its inception in the 2006 Helsinki Manifesto, ENoLL has launched "waves" of several hundred accepted living labs hosted on all continents. Among relevant areas of thematic work of ENoLL is "Culture and creativity" which is tasked with overcoming societal challenges by using citizen and design driven cocreation processes. Main focus areas of this thematic area are as follows:

1. Cocreation of products and services;
2. Design driven market creation;
3. New educational technologies and methodologies, (e.g., Practice-based Experiential Learning).

Museums have been implementing participatory approaches and methods to engage visitors through various living labs. Common across these is to provide an arena of experimentation and prototyping where products and services are cocreated with private and public sectors. Examples of museum partnerships that are part of the ENoLL network include:

- *Living Lab Tokyo* (LLT) is based at the National Museum of Emerging Science and Innovation (Miraikan), one of Japan's major science centers dedicated to expanding the field of science communication. Visitors at this museum will be the early adopters for the development of LLT activities, which includes research on consumer behavior and emotions, in order to explore customized products and living spaces user needs.
- Barcelona City's *Barcelona Laboratori* is working within the wider context of culture, including science, technology and arts, in promoting and activating "Creativity and Innovation" in the city. One of the main research and innovation strands focuses on finding synergies between high-level research and innovation infrastructures (both scientific and technological), the cultural and creative sector and its citizens.
- *SAT Montreal* in Canada was founded in 1996 as the Society for Arts and Technology (SAT). SAT is a hybrid cultural institution, combining venue, artist residencies, research laboratories and a training centre. Internationally renowned for its active and leading role in the development of immersive and virtual reality technologies, and for the creative use of high-speed networks, the SAT was created to support a new generation of creators and researchers in the digital age. Created in 2010, Urban Hub is the SAT's Living Lab and the first in North America to be recognized by ENoLL.

Fig. 27.3 The Cité des Sciences et de l'Industrie, Paris. By Jean-Pierre Dalbéra, Flickr, CC BY 2.0, http://www.flickr.com/photos/dalbera/16500564162

- Based in Turkey, the *Eliminating Barriers* Living Lab is leading on a project called "Building Intercultural Dialogue of City Museums". Begun in 2012 with the Den Haag Historisch Museum and the Eskişehir Metropolitan Municipality, the aim is to increase the interest of people to interact with museums and in relation to the history of the city. The outcome involves designing a museum that adopts the idea of oral history studies accessible through touch screens and recorded voices specific to residents and visitors to Eskişehir.
- *Universcience* Living Lab in Paris brings together two science museum centers, the Cité des Sciences et de l'Industrie (see Fig. 27.3) and the Palais de la découverte, to develop an extensive network of partnerships (e.g., industrial partners and research bodies), both at the national and European level and with other science centers. Universcience is a catalyst for scientific discussion and creativity through its web portal which receives 8 million Internet visitors per year and its web TV channel (http://www.universcience.tv) that has tallied over 1.5 million downloads of published podcasts.

27.4 Participatory Innovation

Open innovation is closely linked with participatory innovation in which smart cities and/or organizations are open to the meaningful participation of their stakeholders, such as inviting open dialogue, similar to open dialogue as applied to open government frameworks. Participatory innovation generally takes on the form of an integrated approach that can cut across different research disciplines about how organizations can involve users and other stakeholders in innovation (Dawson et al. 2017). The *Participatory Museum* (Simon 2010) outlines approaches for museums to become more open to participation, involving users to inform and innovate projects and programs, as well as providing platforms for users to construct their own meanings with the institution.

Smart digital culture focuses on adopting more participatory and collaborative approaches, making cultural data freely available and open (as in the case of open APIs, for example), and consequently increasing the opportunities for interpretation, digital curation, and innovation. This offers potential and unprecedented access to cultural artefacts and experiences across distances, in which cultural consumers are no longer passive recipients (Amato et al. 2013; Angelaccio et al. 2012; Chianese et al. 2015; Roffia et al. 2005). As described in the Europeana White Paper on smart cities, "cultural heritage defines our identity and our communities. Sharing our past in smart city initiatives has the potential to promote social cohesion and increase innovation and tourism (Europeana 2015).

In this way, smart digital culture is strongly associated with the identity of place and communities through enabling technologies, knowledge and participation. It is not surprising that the cultural heritage sector has been working within smart requirements for many years due to the inseparable association with location and identity (Borda and Bowen 2017).

The development of context-aware services has been pervasive in demonstrator applications in the cultural heritage areas, not least focused on forms of digital data and user defined interactions (Chianese et al. 2015; Roffia et al. 2005; Borda and Bowen 2017). Barcelona City Council (Ajuntament de Barcelona), for example, has developed an application *Paisatge* (http://paisatge.bcn.cat/en) meaning 'landscape' in Catalan. *Paisatge* is an interactive web app that provides a digital trail around the City of Barcelona to discover the city's architectural and landscape features. The App allows for real-time discovery of landmarks in the proximity of the visitor and sends alerts of events in the vicinity. Visitors can share, recommend, and save information ("bookmarking") for a post-visit experience.

The Google Cultural Institute recently released the Arts and Culture app (http://artsandculture.google.com) which draws on a collaboration with over 1,200 international museums, galleries and institutions from 70 countries which allows participants to virtually visit museums and to immerse in virtual exhibitions and/or specific artworks. The Art Recognizer feature, for instance, provides information about nearby museums and cultural events, based on one's geographical location, and can also use the computer vision technology in one's device to overlay information about a specific artwork when the device is pointed at the work. A popular feature of the app is the Search with your selfie which uses facial recognition to match the selfie to a portrait from the Arts and Culture database. Still in an experimental stage, this feature is available in Australia, Brazil, Canada, India, Japan, Korea, New Zealand, Singapore, and parts of the USA.

With the widespread use of mobile devices, place-making can now be understood to include such digital spaces and increasingly those shaped and inhabited by social media and its participants. Within the framework of place-making, there are growing connections between museum audiences and their Instagram activity, and the contribution this makes to our notion of the museum or cultural experience. The rise of so-called "Pop-up Museums"—a short-term temporary exhibition set-up in a public space, is making appearances in major cities, like the Museum of Ice Cream in New York City and San Francisco (Walhimer 2018). These spaces are often associated with forms of experiential marketing that engage participants to share their visit and their stories using social media and selfie publishing (Pardes 2017).

The role of citizens in actively engaging in place-making has the potential to contribute to the social and cultural presence of museums, and in turn, their place in the evolution of creative smart cities. Most smart cities have developed web apps that provides cultural information but there remains a gap in advanced contextual services as these may be applied to existing and future planning, particularly supporting the evolution of participatory architectural and cultural heritage design in a city. A group of architects, planners and cultural historians have constructed what they term "4D Hyperlocal", that is a set of tools to foster dynamic relational spatial analysis and enabling a new 'hyperlocal' mode of design. This can be made possible by geolocation technologies and GPS-enabled mobile devices that support connectivity through open-source applications and real-time analysis of environments and individuals' input in order to bring about an immediacy and responsiveness (Bullivant et al. 2017).

27.4.1 Crowdsourcing

Crowdsourcing is a form of collective interaction and participation. The term crowdsourcing was coined by Jeff Howe (2006) and expanded in his book *Crowdsourcing: Why the Power of the Crowd is Driving the Future of Business* (2008). Various definitions have been applied to crowdsourcing since the inception of the concept. In the context of this chapter, the following definition provides suitable scope in relation to the diversity to be found in the Galleries, Libraries, Archives, and Museum (GLAM) sector:

> Crowdsourcing is an umbrella term for a variety of approaches that harness the potential of large crowds of people by issuing open calls for contribution to particular tasks (Geiger et al. 2012)

As smart cities evolve from more technology-centered approaches via government-led strategies to a more people-centric focus, the question is how a city can draw on the collective intelligence of its citizens through crowdsourcing approaches. The City of London (UK) *Smart City Challenge* held in 2015 was an example of a collaborative programme to accelerate its smart city development and to leverage existing platforms and open City data. The *Smart City Challenge*, backed by the Mayor's Office, City of London government, technology company IBM, and Tech London (http://tech.london, providing support for technology entrepreneurs in London), was effectively a crowdsourcing programme designed to bring together developers and startups to come up with technology applications to solve specific challenges identified by the City. An example of a finalist is *Blubel*, a smart bicycle device that guides cyclists around the City using IBM Bluemix® (http://blubel.co) and prioritizes safer cycle-friendly routes based on community feedback.

Crowdsourcing has been a visible form of participation also within the cultural sector (Ridge 2014). Crowdsourcing projects in digital cultural and humanities, for example, can be seen as novel paths of collaboration between institutions and their audiences helping to augment collections or to build digital assets through the aggregation of dispersed resources (Ridge 2014). Libraries have initiated crowdsourcing programs to support major transcription and annotation projects of large and culturally significant collections (Holley 2010). In 2006–2008, the National Library of Australia (NLA, see Fig. 27.4) launched two large-scale projects: *Picture Australia* and *Australian Historic Newspapers*. In the latter project, the NLA asked the Australian public to identify and proofread newspapers (from the years 1803–1954) scanned with OCR technology. The project was launched in 2008, and two years later more than 12 million lines of text had been corrected. The New York Public Library unveiled a project called Emigrant City (http://emigrantcity.nypl.org) built around the premise that important currents of New York City history are buried in a trove of bond and mortgage records from The Emigrant Savings Bank during the years 1841–1933. In order to make sense of these newly digitized collections, the Library set up a microsite to solicit citizen volunteers to provide identification, transcription, and tagging assistance of this vast data.

Tate was the first art gallery to collaborate with the Zooniverse citizen science platform team, led by the University of Oxford, to crowdsource text transcriptions of handwritten documents from artist's archives including Barbara Hepworth, Walter Sickert, Francis Bacon, Duncan Grant, Ian Breakwell and Donald Rodney. Begun in 2015, participants in the AnnoTate project (http://anno.tate.org.uk) can browse the collections and type up anything from Francis Bacon's letters to his art dealer, to the notes in British artist Donald Rodney's sketchbooks, and in doing so may be amongst the first to encounter the details contained therein. Once the resulting annotated texts have been verified by Tate's archivists, the official transcripts are published on Tate's website, alongside the original materials, making them internationally available.

Crowdsourcing can also be a means to gather resources that are 'owned' by the public to enrich collections, or building new ones (e.g., personal narratives, personal memorabilia, and information). *1001 Stories of Denmark* (http://www.kulturarv.dk/1001fortaellinger/en_GB), curated by the Danish Agency for Culture, displays stories about places, cultural heritage and history. The website is user-driven, so participants can contribute photographs, stories, and recommendations, creating additional visiting routes.

An example of an international crowdsourcing research project in which the public has contributed data relates to the destruction of the Mosul Museum in Iraq which led to the formation of Project Mosul, later renamed as *Rekrei*. Rekrei (http://rekrei.org) is a crowdsourced project to reconstruct lost heritage by bringing together

Fig. 27.4 National Library of Australia. Australia in Pictures (formerly PictureAustralia). Postcard of Elizabeth St. looking north from Collins St, circa 1900. Hobart, Tasmania, Australia. Flickr, public domain, http://www.flickr.com/photos/29903115@N06/44900130281/in/pool-pictureaustralia_ppe/

photographs of monuments, museums, and artefacts damaged by natural disasters or human intervention, and to use this data to create 3D representations to help preserve a global, shared, human heritage. Thousands of photographs uploaded to Project Mosul by local residents, tourists, and American soldiers deployed in the region during the Iraq war resulted in a collective reconstruction supported by the Economist, entitled RecoVR Mosul.

*The Rekre*i initiative highlights that the protection of heritage and culture must remain a high priority for all cultures. These online collections of 3D reconstructions representing endangered or destroyed artefacts, cultural landmarks and monuments bring new resonance to the role that "virtual museums" can play in terms of knowledge and wider accessibility of cultural heritage (Styliani et al. 2009). The worldwide engagement of thousands of users supporting *Rekrei*'s mission, in particular, also profiles the potential role of citizens in collectively protecting global cultural heritage, and that we do not need to be physically in the same place to participate in this goal.

This also brings to the foreground a related and larger question of accessibility in smart cultural contexts, and providing relatively low barriers to access content by a distributed audience. There is a means to directly contribute content as in the case of *Rekrei*. Of note, Rekrei is largely community-sourced and falls outside of more established cultural heritage organizations. Community engagement in the codesign of smart and open services is a characteristic of participatory planning that is starting to gain traction in smart city agendas (Saunders and Baeck 2015).

A feasibility study by researchers from Eindhoven University of Technology has further explored the role of paid crowdsourcing as a viable approach in the design of a museum app—*BrainChain*—from concept to the development of a working prototype, and the subsequent creation of scalable content (van der Lans et al. 2016). Using the platform Crowdflower (now renamed Figure Eight, http://www.figure-eight.com), members of the public were invited to help design a museum app, which upon completion, had elements of location-based gamification, content creation, communication and evaluation (e.g., curatorial thinking). Instead of giving the control to a curator solely, the cocreation of BrainChain enabled an understanding of the opportunities in the involvement of connected museum visitors at every stage of development, and the use of public voting on different kinds of rewards and functionalities (van der Lans et al. 2016).

27.5 Innovation at Scale

27.5.1 Fab Labs and Makerspaces

The rise of open fabrication and prototyping spaces is an international phenomenon that are advancing invention among different stakeholders and are becoming recognized as sites of civic and social innovation. Fab labs are generally equipped with resources to enable the development of intellectual and physical materials using digital tools (e.g., computers and circuit boards, design software, 3D and additive printers, laser cutters, and non-digital resources, such as milling and soldering tools). The movement has been principally led by Massachusetts Institute of Technology (MIT) Center for Bits and Atoms and its educational outreach component known as fab labs. The Fab Foundation (http://fabfoundation.org) is the worldwide network that facilitates and supports fab lab members in an open, creative community approach to education and enterprise. There are fab lab members on every continent that are innovating at a local and wider context. The Wanger Family Fab Lab @ Madatech science museum in Haifa, Israel, features 350 m^2 of fab space, and is one of the largest 3D printing fab labs in the world.

Fab Lab Barcelona, based at the Institute for Advanced Architecture of Catalonia, is the headquarters of the global coordination of the Fab Academy program and its own programming supports different educational and research programs related to the multiple scales of the human habitat. A key project is Organicity (http://organicity.eu)—a multi-city program involving European partners in London, Barcelona, Santander, and Aarhus, and Melbourne in Australia, to create and test new tools for next generation smart cities, especially focused on citizen engagement and cocreation. Barcelona is further leading on new production models for cities with the Fab

Fig. 27.5 The first Fab City experts summit in Amsterdam in 2016. By EU2016 NL, Wikimedia Commons, https://commons.wikimedia.org/wiki/File:160622_Closing_FabCity_Amsterdam_(27808415856).jpg

City project (http://fabcity.cc, see: Fig. 27.5) that encompasses 16 participating city regions in Europe, Asia, the USA and South America.

On a similarly ubiquitous scale, the rise of makerspaces, has been closely associated with the GLAM sector. Makerspaces, like fab labs, are dedicated physical locations providing a means for people to build, cocreate, share resources and knowledge, work collaboratively on projects, and network (Burke 2014). Makerspaces are often equipped with 3D printers, computers, audio/video editing tools, and arts and crafts resources.

Public libraries were among the first cultural organizations to incorporate makerspaces across geographies in the USA, Canada, the UK, and other parts of the world. The Fayetteville Free Library in New York State (USA), for example, established a makerspace in 2011 which now includes an expanded fab lab (Fallows 2016). In the 2015 NMC *Horizon Report* the increasing adoption of makerspaces by libraries has allowed for such publicly accessible creative spaces to "further position libraries as gateways to new skills, in addition to new knowledge" (Johnson et al. 2015, p. 1). In the UK, there was a recorded 97 makerspaces included in libraries, museums, and schools in a Nesta report published in 2015 (Sleigh et al. 2015). Makerspaces in libraries also featured prominently in the UK government's Digital Strategy in recognition of their value and impact (DCMS 2017) and further guidance on access and location of facilities is provided by the Department for Digital, Culture, Media and Sport (DCMS 2018).

In the USA, the Institute of Museum and Library Services (IMLS) has invested in a national makerspace programme in libraries and museums, partnering with the

Children's Museum of Pittsburgh and San Francisco's Exploratorium to support hands-on, mentor-led learning and STEM upskilling environments (IMLS 2018). The program underpins the national priorities of digital capability and capacity building:

> Museums and libraries are leveraging their content expertise and role as trusted community organizations to support the development of 21st century skills, such as creativity, critical thinking, and collaboration, which are essential for the development of a competitive workforce and engaged citizenry. (IMLS 2018).

27.6 Innovation Districts

Innovation districts are newer concepts in smart city developments, focusing around geographic areas where leading-edge anchor institutions and companies can cluster and connect with start-ups, business incubators and accelerators (Katz and Wagner 2014). Innovation districts (e.g., see Fig. 27.6) can be considered subsets of smart cities containing *economic, physical, and networking assets*. The combination of these three assets have the potential to create a regional *innovation ecosystem.*

Fig. 27.6 Cambridge, Mass—Innovation District. Aerial view of part of MIT's main campus. By DrKenneth, Wikimedia Commons, https://commons.wikimedia.org/wiki/File:MIT_Main_Campus_Aerial.jpg

Globally, Barcelona, Berlin, London, Montreal, Seoul, Stockholm, and Toronto, contain examples of evolving districts. Toronto, for instance, is the home of Sidewalk Toronto (https://sidewalktoronto.ca), a joint partnership between Waterfront Toronto and Alphabet's Sidewalk Labs to create people-centred neighbourhoods on Toronto's Eastern Waterfront using forward-thinking urban design and new digital technology (Etherington 2017).

In the USA, districts are emerging near so-called "anchor" institutions in the city centers and midtowns of cities such as Atlanta, Boston Cambridge, Cleveland, Detroit, Houston, Portland, and San Diego. In Boston, Portland, San Francisco, and Seattle, for instance, underutilized areas (particularly older industrial areas) are being re-imagined and regenerated. Digital culture has a particularly inclusive role in districts and in the support of localized service innovations, for instance.

Startup or seed accelerators have become an integral part of the regional or district innovation economy of evolving smart cities. In this way, innovation platforms have enormous potential to move cultural institutions from the margins of smart city life into the center of participatory innovation. An early prototype is the EmcArts Innovation Labs in the USA (http://emcarts.org/programs/innovation-labs) which has been described as "a deep dive program for museums, performing arts organizations, and arts development agencies experimenting with new practices." According to the EmcArts website, EmcArts has worked alongside 2,500 practitioners, 250 organizations and over a dozen communities since its establishment in 2005.

In this way, museums have the potential to become important partners in local initiatives to share in the revitalization of smart city economies and enhance the quality of life. The potential risks and costs of technology can also make these partnerships cost-effective solutions for museums and cultural organizations. Beyond the coworking model, museums investing in startups is a paradigm shift and very experimental. Of those museums that are developing a presence, NEW INC in New York (http://www.newinc.org) is an experimental initiative of the New Museum. NEW INC is a shared workspace and professional development program that brings together over a hundred cultural practitioners and creative entrepreneurs, including anchor tenants Rhizome and Columbia University's GSAPP Incubator.

In 2016, the Australian Centre for the Moving Image (ACMI) in Melbourne, Australia, launched ACMI X (http://www.acmi.net.au/acmi-x/) as a new coworking space that assembles a mix of filmmakers, digital and visual artists, digital producers, web developers, screenwriters and designers. ACMI Labs (http://labs.acmi.net.au) intends to foster experiments in media, technology, and user experience. In the same year, Te Papa (https://www.tepapa.govt.nz), the national Museum of New Zealand (2016), launched Mahuki (http://www.mahuki.org) to accelerate local startups focused on developing world-leading digital businesses for the GLAM sector. Ten creative teams were initially selected to take part in the museum's first-ever accelerator program.

> "Te Papa has always been a creative powerhouse, and working with these exciting companies will bring new ideas into the mix. We have done our homework and we know there is a need to support innovations for the cultural sector, both globally and locally," proclaimed the

museum's CEO, Rick Ellis in his statements around the launch of the accelerator. (Clecko 2016)

The Museum of the City of New York's Future City Lab (http://www.mcny.org/exhibitions/core/future-city) is an example of an interactive space exploring key challenges and opportunities that New York will face in coming generations, such as housing, urban nature, and mobility. The Future City Lab gives participants the opportunity to interact with these issues, to imagine the city's future by designing a street, a building, and a park, and to discover ways of addressing the challenges. In 2017, the Lab supported a 12-month professional development program geared towards creating technology that can encourage museum attendance and interest.

A hybrid of the innovation district, living lab and fab lab concepts, the *Laboratorio para la Ciudad* (Laboratory for the City/LabCDMX) is Mexico City's experimental office for civic innovation and urban creativity, and the first city government department of its kind in Latin America. Established in 2013 by the then newly elected Mayor Miguel Ángel Mancera, a key agenda was to create an experimental area within the new city government that could reimagine the way government and civil society could collaborate, by implementing public policy and projects that promote citizen participation, creativity and skills (Lu 2017).

The model for LabCDMX was informed by the City of Boston's New Urban Mechanics, comprising a civic research and development team who pilot experiments that aim to improve the quality of life for Boston's residents (http://www.boston.gov/departments/new-urban-mechanics). One of the more recent such innovation city

Fig. 27.7 Queen Elizabeth Olympic Park—London Legacy Development Corporation, 2013. By Londres Heritage, Flickr, CC BY-ND 2.0, http://www.flickr.com/photos/129867853@N06/15960115591

labs is Catapult UK (http://futurecities.catapult.org.uk) which is headquartered in the Urban Innovation Centre in London. Catapult UK specializes in urban strategies, connected cities and urban data science around three core themes of integrated urban infrastructure, healthy cities and urban mobility. A large development outlined in the recent *Smarter London* roadmap is planned for The Queen Elizabeth Olympic Park (see Fig. 27.7) situated in east London (Greater London Authority 2019). The ambition is to use the Park as a test-bed for new international standards in smart data, sustainability and community-building. The London's civic government invested in digital engagement tools to capture Londoners' say on its design. The Queen Elizabeth Olympic Park site will house a satellite campus of the London University of the Arts, new BBC studios, a satellite of the Victoria and Albert Museum (V&A) and Sadler's Wells.

27.7 Challenges

A key challenge centers on the idea of the smart city itself which is often perceived as a technology-centric vision of urban life and urban governance more generally. Consequently, it has become the subject of significant critique—particularly in the context of monolithic and smart technology intensive developments such as Songdo City, a $20–40 billion development for a 500,000-person city built on reclaimed land by the Yellow Sea in South Korea, the planned eco-city of Masdar in Abu Dhabi (see Fig. 27.8), and the proof-of concept PlanIT Valley, a $10 billion collaboration in Portugal, which has yet to be built. In view of these mixed outcomes of partnerships with multinational companies building smart cities 'from scratch' (Greenfield 2013), the question that has come to the foreground in public debate is whether the notion of smart cities have lived up to expectations in terms of the extent of citizen participation in the process. Arup Associate Director, Dan Hill, in his blog *City of Sound* expresses the central issues to this debate:

> Instead of the smart city, perhaps we should be more preoccupied with smart citizens. The smart city vision tends to focus on infrastructure, buildings, vehicles, looking for a client amidst the city governments that procure or plan such things. But the city is something else. The city is its people. We don't make cities in order to make buildings and infrastructure. We make cities in order to come together, to create wealth, culture, more people. (Hill 2013)

The dichotomy between the vision of the smart city on the one hand, and that of the smart citizen on the other calls for a shift in discourse and interventions to be more citizen-centric in order to achieve meaningful change (Hill 2013). If citizens are a core constituent of the smart city, they must also be supported and empowered to engage and participate in this way (Forlano 2016). Digital literacy and variable access to technology platforms, for example, are critical elements in both equity terms and in understanding what smart cities are (Morrison 2018).

What, therefore, are the conditions that must exist for a progressive future involving smart citizens as empowered participants in digital culture and smart innovation?

Fig. 27.8 Model of the Masdar City project by Foster + Partners (2006 onwards) in The Future Starts Here exhibition at the Victoria and Albert Museum, London (V&A, 2018). (Photograph by Jonathan Bowen, 2018)

The technology-oriented pathways of smart cities offer many unexplored opportunities for experimenting and cocreation with members of the public. So how does a city evolve into a Smart City 3.0?—Barcelona, London, Amsterdam, New York, and Singapore, are among the most advanced participatory smart cities due to targeted investments and policy strategies directed towards this evolution (Cohen 2015; Cowley et al. 2018).

The routes of less evolved cities may seem unclear, but some may argue that it is the "humble urban communities" who are leading the way in showing how smart open platforms can more widely impact a city's social and innovation fabric (Greenfield 2014). The *digital matatus* project in Nairobi (http://www.digitalmatatus.com/) is an example of leveraging ubiquitous mobile phone technology to capture transit data to develop mobile routing applications for a new transit map of the city. The data, maps and apps are available free to the public to allow them to transform the ways they can interact with transportation systems, and other city services. In Taiwan, the launch of the digital democracy platform, vTaiwan (http://info.vtaiwan.tw) has progressed from experiment to a successful open consultation process for smart citizens. Taiwan aims to develop the use of smart technology creatively to facilitate a more transparent, responsive, and participatory deliberation process for all its citizens.

Ethical transparency is also critical in order to engender trust among smart citizens and stakeholders in relation to city services and in the development of smart cultural heritage (IEEE 2017). Sidewalk Toronto is initiating an independent Civic Data Trust to ensure appropriate stewardship of smart urban data generated within the bounds of the Sidewalk precinct (Dawson 2018). This consideration will become only more visible when ubiquitous data collecting sensors and autonomous decision-making (e.g. AI-enabled) services adversely impact on the privacy, security, and trust of citizens. In the museum community, there is a steady adoption of AI, for instance, in the use of chatbot technologies to interact with museum audiences, but there is not yet a fuller understanding of both the benefits and the risks (Boiano et al. 2018). This is a transformational space which will require inclusive representation to address the challenges. See also Chap. 15 on chatbots.

Consequently, smart cultural activities are perhaps to be fostered which are oriented towards finding solutions to problems defined by citizens themselves and which can be accommodated within service-user models. An identified challenge is not simply to coopt museums and cultural organizations into an existing problem or model. They must ideally be empowered stakeholders within the smart city ecosystem so that the risk of neutralizing innovative potential and meaningful dialogue are lessened (Cowley et al. 2018). This equally relates to a reciprocity in the participation of members of the public and in identifying a shared social value in each other's roles (Ferronato and Ruecker 2018; Forlano 2016).

27.8 Future Opportunities

There is clear evidence of the potential of cultural heritage and GLAM organizations through innovation platforms to play a significant role in the development of the fabric of smart cities and in smart citizenship. The sector already has a strong provenance with decades long experience in piloting emerging and embedded technologies relevant to smart city services, and in its understanding of user-centric interaction characterized by context-awareness, personalization and adaptation (Borda and Bowen 2017).

The near future is further pointing to the possibility of connecting across geographies of place and accessing cultural and citizen centric services made possible through cultural organizations which has resonance with the idea of "a distributed museum" (Bautista and Balsamo 2011). No longer located in a particular physical space, the museum can now also extend its presence through virtual spaces on the web as well as in the transient spaces created through the diverse practices and technologies of mobility. This reinforces the importance of mobility in our thinking of future opportunities.

To this we can add that open innovation platforms still need to be part of the discussion in which we cannot lose sight that "smartness" is critically about citizen centric methodologies. A smart citizenship approach is associated with a systemic approach, including bottom-up initiatives, as well as more transparent and open participatory practices, that can overcome social exclusion, such as differences in technology access. The growing pervasiveness of localized models of innovation, like living labs, makerspaces, and fab labs, for example, illustrate the need for both physical and virtual places to incubate and facilitate transference of skills and equitable sharing of knowledge among a community.

In this sense, the smart city is less about technology and more about improving and fostering interactions leading to increased social capital and strengthening social networks. It is the complexity and multiplicity of different interactions that comprises the smart city ecosystem, of which smart citizens are an integral part to its realization and direction. Museums and cultural organizations are ideally placed to contribute to the interactions, if not to create new ways of interaction, in the process.

Generally, there is still much opportunity for the transformation of smart digital culture through the engagement of participants who themselves can directly influence the smart cities they inhabit. Further research is likely necessary to better understand this transformation in practice, and an applied understanding of models of innovation at localized, distributed, and scaled levels, and the extent of their potential impact and reciprocity.

The future for cultural heritage and the GLAM sector in the smart city agenda is evolving at a fast pace. There are many precedents as outlined in this chapter and by others in the book, and the future will most likely continue to be dynamically shaped, not only by models of innovation, but specifically by participant empowerment, open adaptation, and forms of sustainable engagement.

References

Alexander J (2014) Gallery one, the first year: sustainability, evaluation process, and a new smart phone app. MW2014: Museums and the Web. http://mw2014.museumsandtheweb.com/paper/gallery-one-the-first-year-sustainability-evaluation-process-and-a-new-smart-phone-app/. Accessed 30 Mar 2017

Alexander J, Wienke L, Tiongson P (2017) Removing the barriers of gallery one: a new approach to integrating art, interpretation, and technology. MW17: Museums and the Web, 19–22 April 2017. http://mw17.mwconf.org/paper/removing-the-barriers-of-gallery-one-a-new-approach-to-integrating-art-interpretation-and-technology/. Accessed 6 July 2018

Amato F, Chianese A, Mazzeo A, Moscato V, Picariello A, Piccialli F (2013) The talking museum project. In: 4th international conference on emerging ubiquitous systems and pervasive networks (EUSPN-2013). Procedia Computer Science, 21, pp 114–121. https://doi.org/10.1016/j.procs.2013.09.017

Angelaccio M, Basili A, Buttarazzi B, Liguori W (2012) Smart and mobile access to cultural heritage resources: a case study on ancient Italian renaissance villas. In: IEEE 21st international WETICE. IEEE Computer Society, pp 310–314. https://doi.org/10.1109/wetice.2012.36

Angelidou M (2015) Smart cities: a conjuncture of four forces. Cities, 47, pp 95–106, Sept 2015. https://doi.org/10.1016/j.cities.2015.05.004

Australian Government (2016) Smart cities plan. Commonwealth of Australia. Canberra: Department of the Prime Minister and Cabinet. http://cities.dpmc.gov.au/smart-cities-plan. Accessed 5 Apr 2017

Bautista S, Balsamo A (2011) Understanding the distributed museum: mapping the spaces of museology in contemporary culture. In: Trant J, Bearman D (eds) MW 2011: Museums and the Web: proceedings. Toronto: Archives and Museum Informatics. https://www.museumsandtheweb.com/mw2011/papers/understanding_the_distributed_museum_mapping_t.html. Accessed 1 Feb 2019

Boiano S, Borda A, Gaia G, Rossi A, Cuomo P (2018) Chatbots and new audience opportunities for museums and heritage organisations. In: Bowen JP,Weinel J, Diprose G, Lambert N (eds) EVA London 2018 conference proceedings, Electronic Workshops in Computing (eWiC), BCS, pp 164–171. https://doi.org/10.14236/ewic/eva2018.33

Borda A, Bowen JP (2011) Virtual collaboration and community. In: Information Resources Management Association (ed), Virtual communities: concepts, methodologies, tools and applications. IGI Global, Chapter 8.9, pp 2600–2611

Borda A, Bowen JP (2017) Smart cities and cultural heritage: a review of developments and future opportunities. In: Bowen JP, Diprose G, Lambert N (eds) EVA London 2017 conference proceedings, Electronic Workshops in Computing (eWiC), BCS, pp 9–18. https://doi.org/10.14236/ewic/eva2017.2

Bullivant L, Greenfield A, Zaera A, Pasquero C, Poletto M (eds) (2017) 4D hyperlocal: a cultural toolkit for the open-source city. Wiley, Oxford

Burke JJ (2014) Makerspaces: a practical guide for librarians, vol 8. Rowman & Littlefield, Lanham, MD

Casella G, Coelho M (2013) Augmented heritage: situating augmented reality mobile apps in cultural heritage communication. In: Proceedings of the 2013 international conference on information systems and design of communication (ISDOC 13). ACM, New York, NY, USA, pp 138–140. https://doi.org/10.1145/2503859.2503883

Chan S, Cope A (2015) Strategies against architecture: interactive media and transformative technology at Cooper Hewitt. MW2015: Museums and the Web, 6 Apr 2015. http://mw2015.museumsandtheweb.com/paper/strategies-against-architecture-interactive-media-and-transformative-technology-at-cooper-hewitt/. Accessed 6 July 2018

Chesbrough H, Vanhaverbek W, West J (eds) (2006) Open innovation: researching a new paradigm. Oxford University Press, Oxford

Chianese A, Piccialli F (2014) SmaCH: a framework for smart cultural heritage spaces. In: Tenth international conference on signal-image technology and internet-based systems, pp 477–484

Chianese A, Piccialli F, Valente I (2015) Smart environments and cultural heritage: a novel approach to create intelligent cultural spaces. J Location Based Serv 9(3):209–234. https://doi.org/10.1080/17489725.2015.1099752

Cisco (2014) Smart city readiness: understand the issues to accelerate the journey. White Paper. Smart Cities Council. http://www.cisco.com/c/dam/m/en_in/innovation/smartcities/assets/white-paper-c11-732985.pdf. Accessed 5 Apr 2017

Clecko B (2016) Museums, startups and accelerators… oh, my! TechCrunch. https://techcrunch.com/2017/01/02/museums-startups-and-accelerators-oh-my/. Accessed 1 Feb 2019

Cohen B (2015) The 3 generations of smart cities. Fast Company, 8 Oct 2015. http://www.fastcompany.com/3047795/the-3-generations-of-smart-cities. Accessed 6 Oct 2018

Cooper Hewitt (n.d.) Designing the pen. Cooper Hewitt Smithsonian Design Museum, USA. http://www.cooperhewitt.org/new-experience/designing-pen/. Accessed 7 Jan 2019

Cowley R, Joss S, Dayot Y (2018) The smart city and its publics: insights from across six UK cities. Urban Res Pract 11(1):53–77. https://doi.org/10.1080/17535069.2017.129315

DATABENC (2014). Distretto ad Alta Tecnologia per i Beni Culturali. Italy. http://www.databenc.it/en/. Accessed 30 Mar 2017

Dawson AW (2018) An update on data governance for sidewalk Toronto. Side Walk Talk, Medium. https://medium.com/sidewalk-talk/an-update-on-data-governance-for-sidewalk-toronto-d810245f10f7. Accessed 7 Jan 2019

Dawson B, Smith Hale F, Corbeil S (2017) Open innovation: open movements and the role of a museum in the 21st century. MW2017: Museums and the Web, 16 Feb 2017. http://mw17.mwconf.org/paper/open-innovation-open-movements-and-the-role-of-a-museum-in-the-21st-century/. Accessed 18 Mar 2018

DCMS (2017). Policy paper—UK digital strategy 2017. Department for Digital, Culture, Media & Sport, HM Government, UK, 1 Mar 2017. http://www.gov.uk/government/publications/uk-digital-strategy/uk-digital-strategy. Accessed 7 Jan 2019

DCMS (2018) Libraries and makerspaces. Guidance. Department for Digital, Culture, Media & Sport, HM Government, UK, 15 Oct 2018. http://www.gov.uk/government/publications/libraries-and-makerspaces/libraries-and-makerspaces. Accessed 7 Jan 2019

Eid H (2016) The museum innovation model: a museum perspective on innovation. MW2016: Museums and the Web, 14 Jan 2016. http://mw2016.museumsandtheweb.com/paper/the-museum-innovation-model-a-museum-perspective-to-innovation/. Accessed 13 Mar 2018

Eskelinen J, Garcia Robles A, Lindy I, Marsh J, Muente-Kunigami A (2015) Citizen-driven innovation: a guidebook for city mayors and public administrators. World Bank, Washington, DC, and European Network of Living Labs. http://openknowledge.worldbank.org/handle/10986/21984. Accessed 7 Jan 2019

Etherington D (2017) Alphabet's sidewalk labs to turn Toronto area into a model smart city. Techcrunch, 17 Oct 2017. http://tcrn.ch/2yvckkj. Accessed 6 Oct 2018

European Commission (2015) Smart cities and communities: the european innovation partnership on smart cities and communities. European Community, 4 June 2015. http://ec.europa.eu/eip/smartcities/index_en.htm. Accessed 24 Apr 2017

European Commission (2016) Open innovation, open science, open to the world: a vision for Europe. European Commission, Brussels, Belgium

European Network of Living Labs (n.d.) European network of living labs. http://www.openlivinglabs.eu. Accessed 2 Feb 2019

Europeana (2015) Transforming the world with culture. White Paper, Europeana Foundation. September. http://pro.europeana.eu/files/Europeana_Professional/Publications/Europeana%20Presidencies%20White%20Paper.pdf. Accessed 30 Mar 2017

Fallows D (2016) How libraries are becoming modern makerspaces. The Atlantic, March 11, 2016, http://www.theatlantic.com/technology/archive/2016/03/everyone-is-a-maker/473286/. Accessed 2 Feb 2019

Ferronato P, Ruecker S (2018) Smart citizenship: designing the interaction between citizens and smart cities. Design Research Society 2018, University of Limerick, 25–28 June 2018. https://doi.org/10.21606/dma.2017.480

Forlano L (2016) Decentering the human in the design of collaborative cities. Des Issues 32(3):42–54

Forum Virium Helsinki (2016) Open API recommendations for cities. Helsinki: The 6Aika Open Data and Interfaces Spearhead Project, Forum Virium

Gassmann O, Enkel E, Chesbrough H (2010) The future of open innovation. R&D Management 40(3):213–221. https://doi.org/10.1111/j.1467-9310.2010.00605.x

Geiger D, Rosemann M, Fielt E, Schader M (2012) Crowdsourcing information systems: definition, typology and design. In: George JF (ed) Proceedings of the 33rd international conference on information systems, association for information systems/AIS Electronic Library (AISeL), Orlando, Florida

Greater London Authority (2019) Mayor of London, London Assembly, UK. https://www.london.gov.uk. Accessed 7 Jan 2019

Greenfield A (2013) Against the smart city (the city is here for you to use Book 1). Do Projects, New York

Greenfield A (2014) The smartest cities rely on citizen cunning and unglamorous technology. The Guardian, 22 Dec 2014. http://www.theguardian.com/cities/2014/dec/22/the-smartest-cities-rely-on-citizen-cunning-and-unglamorous-technology. Accessed 11 May 2018

GrowSmarter (2015) GrowSmarter: transforming cities for a smart, sustainable Europe. http://www.grow-smarter.eu. Accessed 7 Jan 2019

Hill D (2013) Essay: on the smart city; or, a 'manifesto' for smart citizens instead, City of Sound, 1 Feb 2013. http://www.cityofsound.com/blog/2013/02/on-the-smart-city-a-call-for-smart-citizens-instead.html. Accessed 2 Feb 2019

Holley R (2010) Crowdsourcing: how and why should libraries do it? D-Lib Magazine 16(3–4), March/April 2010. https://doi.org/10.1045/march2010-holley

Howe J (2006) Neo neologism, crowdsourcing: why the power of the crowd is driving the future of business. Weblog, 16 June 2006. http://www.crowdsourcing.com/cs/2006/06/neo_neologisms.html. Accessed 2 Feb 2019

IEEE (2017) IEEE Smart Cities. IEEE. http://smartcities.ieee.org. Accessed 30 Mar 2018

IMLS (2018) Making spaces. Institute of Museum and Library Services, USA. http://www.imls.gov/issues/national-issues/makerspaces. Accessed 1 July 2018

ISO/IEC (2014) Information technology: smart cities, preliminary report. ISO/IEC JTC 1. http://www.iso.org/iso/smart_cities_report-jtc1.pdf. Accessed 30 Mar 2017

Jara AJ, Sun Y, Song H, Bie R, Genooud D, Bocchi Y (2015) Internet of Things for cultural heritage of smart cities and smart regions. In: 29th international conference on advanced information networking and applications workshops. IEEE, pp 668–675. https://doi.org/10.1109/waina.2015.169

Johnson L, Adams Becker S, Estrada V, Freeman A (2015) NMC horizon report: 2015 library edition. Austin, Texas. The New Media Consortium (NMC). http://cdn.nmc.org/media/2015-nmc-horizon-report-library-EN.pdf. Accessed 2 Feb 2019

Katz B, Wagner J (2014) The rise of innovation districts: a new geography of innovation in America. Brookings Institute, May 2014. http://www.brookings.edu/essay/rise-of-innovation-districts/. Accessed 2 Feb 2019

Lagoudi E, Sexton C (2010) Old masters at your fingertips: the journey of creating a museum app for the iPhone and iTouch. In: Trant J, Bearman D (eds) MW 2010: Museums and the Web: proceedings. Archives and Museum Informatics. https://www.museumsandtheweb.com/mw2010/papers/lagoudi/lagoudi.html. Accessed 2 Feb 2019

Leminen S, Westerlund M, Nyström A-G (2012) Living labs as open-innovation networks. Technol Innov Manag Rev 2(9):6–11. https://doi.org/10.22215/timreview602

Lepik K-L, Krigul M, Terk E (2010) Introducing living lab's method as knowledge transfer from one socio-institutional context to another: evidence from Helsinki-Tallinn cross-border region. J Univers Comput Sci 16(8):1089–1101. https://doi.org/10.3217/jucs-016-08-1089

Lu C (2017) Laboratorio Para La Ciudad: re-imagining Mexico City through Civic Tech, with additional files by Aaron Wytze

Morrison J (2018) With the growth of smart cities, how do we build smart citizens to match? Calvium, March 1, 2018. http://calvium.com/growth-smart-cities-build-smart-citizens-match/. Accessed 2 Feb 2019

Mulder I (2012) Living labbing the rotterdam way: co-creation as an enabler for urban innovation. Technol Innov Manag Rev 2(9):39–43. https://doi.org/10.22215/timreview607

Muller L, Edmonds E, Connell M (2006) Living laboratories for interactive art. CoDesign Int J CoCreation Des Arts 2(4):195–207. https://doi.org/10.1080/15710880601008109

Museum of New Zealand (2016) Te Papa's Mahuki teams showcase the future of innovation in the culture sector. Museum of New Zealand Te Papa Tongarewa, 6 Dec 2016. http://www.tepapa.govt.nz/about/press-and-media/press-releases/2016-news-and-media-releases/te-papas-mahuki-teams-showcase. Accessed 2 Feb 2019

Nokia (2017) Enabling smart, safe and sustainable cities: strategic white paper. Nokia Corporation. http://resources.alcatel-lucent.com/asset/191721. Accessed 30 Mar 2017

Palomar E, Chen X, Liu Z, Maharjan S, Bowen JP (2016) Component-based modelling for scalable smart city systems interoperability: a case study on integrating energy demand response systems. Sensors 16(11):1810. https://doi.org/10.3390/s16111810

Pardes A (2017) Selfie factories: the rise of the made-for-instagram museum. Wired, 27 Sept 2017. http://www.wired.com/story/selfie-factories-instagram-museum/. Accessed 2 Feb 2019

Petrelli D, O'Brien S (2018) Phone versus tangible in museums: a comparative study. In: CHI'18 proceedings of the 2018 CHI conference on human factors in computing systems paper no. 112, Montreal, Quebec, Canada, 21–26 Apr 2018. https://doi.org/10.1145/3173574.3173686

Ridge M (ed) (2014) Crowdsourcing our cultural heritage. Ashgate, Farnham

Roffia L, Pettinari M, Raffa G, Gaviani G (2005) Context awareness in mobile cultural heritage applications. In: Smart Environments and their Applications to Cultural Heritage Workshop. 7th International Conference on Ubiquitous Computing (UBICOMP'05), Tokyo, Japan, pp 33–36

Saunders T, Baeck P (2015) Rethinking the smart cities from the ground up Nesta, London, June 2015

Simon N (2010) Read online. The participatory museum. http://www.participatorymuseum.org/read/. Accessed 13 Mar 2018

Sleigh A, Stewart H, Stokes K (2015) Open dataset of UK makerspaces: a user's guide. Nesta, Apr 2015

Soja E, Kanai E (2006) The urbanization of the world. In: Burdett R, Sudjic D (eds) The endless city. Phaidon Books, London

Styliani S, Fotis L, Kostas K, Petros P (2009) Virtual museums, a survey and some issues for consideration. J Cult Heritage 10(4):520–528. https://doi.org/10.1016/j.culher.2009.03.003

Turnbull D, Connell M (2011) Prototyping Places: The museum. In: Candy L, Edmonds E (eds) Interacting: art research and the creative practitioner. Libri Publications, Faringdon

United Nations (2018) 68% of the world population projected to live in urban areas by 2050, says UN. Department of Economic and Social Affairs, United Nations, New York, 16 May 2018. http://www.un.org/development/desa/en/news/population/2018-revision-of-world-urbanization-prospects.html. Accessed 7 Jan 2019

V&A (2018) The Future Starts Here. Victoria and Albert Museum, UK. https://www.vam.ac.uk/exhibitions/the-future-starts-here. Accessed 7 Jan 2019

van der Lans L, Ansems EL, Khan JV (2016) BrainChain app: a fully crowdsourced design process for museums. In: 34th Annual ACM CHI conference on human factors in computing systems (CHI 2016) ACM

Walhimer M (2018) Popup museum. Museum Planner, 8 Apr 2018. http://museumplanner.org/pop-up-museum. Accessed 2 Feb 2019

Yovcheva Z, Buhalis D, Gatzidis C (2012) Overview of smartphone augmented reality applications for tourism. e-Rev Tour Res (eRTR), 10(2): 63–66

Yovcheva Z, Buhalis D, Gatzidis C, van Elzakker C (2014) Empirical evaluation of smartphone augmented reality browsers in an urban tourism destination context. Int J Mobile Human Comput Interact 6(2):10–31. https://doi.org/10.4018/ijmhci.2014040102

Chapter 28
The Digital Future for Museums

Jonathan P. Bowen and Tula Giannini

Abstract We discuss possible directions that museums could take with respect to the rapidly developing digital culture in which they find themselves. Successful museums must be very adaptable to the changing nature of public expectations. Some of the important aspects to be considered have been covered in earlier chapters in this book. Here we take this knowledge and speculate how museums could adapt to survive in the digital environment that is increasingly integrated as part of the real environment, in what will rapidly become a postdigital world. The chapter summarizes the prospective directions for museums and related institutions in the context of changes in the digital landscape of the rest of society.

28.1 Introduction

> Computing is not about computers any more. It is about living. (Negroponte 1995, p. 6)

The use of the term "digital culture" has developed rapidly since the introduction of the web in 1989 (Berners-Lee 1999). This is illustrated by the increase in books including the term, as illustrated in Fig. 28.1. Over the same period, the use of the term "virtual museum" has also increased but not so dramatically. Indeed, the term "virtual" has been adopted from its previous use meaning of "almost" to its more common use now in a digital context as "not physically existing".

As museums systematically intensify their efforts and initiatives to broaden and deepen their community connections while prioritizing audience engagement over the past few years, we see concurrent increases in attendance at museums and other culture institutions and venues and this is reflected in a report by the US National

J. P. Bowen (✉)
School of Engineering, London South Bank University, London, UK
e-mail: jonathan.bowen@lsbu.ac.uk

Southwest University, Chongqing, China

T. Giannini
School of Information, Pratt Institute, New York, USA
e-mail: giannini@pratt.edu

T. Giannini and J. P. Bowen (eds.), *Museums and Digital Culture*,
Springer Series on Cultural Computing, https://doi.org/10.1007/978-3-319-97457-6_28

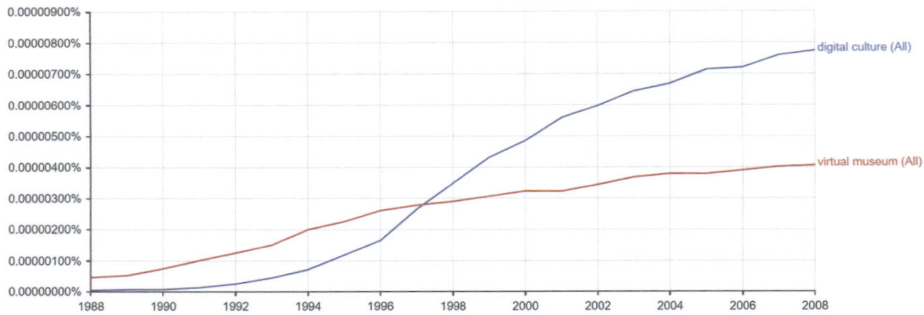

Fig. 28.1 Graph of books including "digital culture" and "virtual museum" during 1988–2008. (Generated by Jonathan Bowen, using Google Books Ngram Viewer, https://books.google.com/ngrams)

Endowment for the Arts working with the US Bureau of Economic Analysis (NEA 2018c). While the economic gains based on consumer spending and show that "The performing arts together with other arts and cultural industries contributed more than $760 billion to the nation's economy in 2015"—it is the growth of audience and its growing diversity which emerges as the key factor in sustaining the vitality and impact the museum as an institution in American culture. Looking at the report's breakdown of growth in attendance by gender and race we see substantial gains in attendance: women, up from 8% in 2012 to 14.5% in 2017, African Americans up 8.4% and Asian Americans up 7.8% between 2012 and 2017 and overall, during this period, visits to art museums or galleries by adults (18 years and older) grew by about 13% which means that a total of 57.5 million people visited museums in 2017.

In parallel with these increases in museum visits, are dramatic increases of visits to museum websites, and to arts events beyond the walls of the museum, all of which are connected to and served by the digital ecosystem that visitors and institutions share. With the average American spending 10–12 hours per day of screen time, competition for audience becomes intense, as time beyond work and screen time, the time one has to visit a museum, continues to shrink, a trend which calls for new digital strategies that in essence blur the lines between these states of being (Bowen et al. 2018), both real and digital. It was only a few years ago that museums forbid photography in their galleries and tried to separate visitors from their smartphones which alienated visitors rather than encouraging and using to advantage visitors' digital behavior. New survey findings from the National Endowment for the Arts (NEA) show gains in arts attendance totals, rates, and demographic groups plus sizeable growth in poetry-reading (NEA 2018a, b, c). In tandem with these trends, use of the Internet in the USA increased overall from 52% of the population in 2000, to 88% by 2016, although the use by people earning $50,000 or more was almost 100%, while Internet use for those earning less than $30,000 was at 76%, representing a steep increase from 30% in 2000. Global median Internet use in 2015 rose to 67% with several countries above %85 including the US, UK and Canada (Pew Research Center 2017). A report by the US Center for Media Justice demonstrates that use of the Internet has become a critical force for engagement in social justice movements, such as Black Lives Matter and MeToo, in achieving greater diversity and inclusion in what they call, "the culture shift," which now permeates the world of museums and digital culture. (Center for Media Justice 2015).

28.1.1 Learning from Visitors

Museums benefit when they encourage visitors to interact with their smart phones in galleries creating user generated content (UGC) as part of digital engagement planning. Among the many ways to obtain UGC, visitor photography is one of the most telling in terms of what visitors are doing, thinking and seeing in the museum.

> it is time, in 2018, to recognize that museums have an opportunity to leverage what their visitors do in their spaces. And more often than not, they take photos. This may be hard for some, but in my opinion, what our visitors do on their phones is more important than what we want them to do… what our visitors do on their phones is more important than what we want them to do. … By simply encouraging people to share their visiting experience, our visitors started to generate terabytes of valuable word of mouth content. Our attendance has increased by 10–20% year over year since 2012. (Dodge 2018)

From his study of 263,000 visitor photographs, Dodge draws three conclusions: "allow photography" for permanent collections and special exhibitions, "be reactive" to what your visitors do and think and "be mindful" and recognize that your visitors can contribute valuable insights and that the museums do not necessarily know best when it comes to engagement—listen to your visitors (Dodge 2018).

Similarly, museums can learn from website visits and from social media (Amichai-Hamburger 2013), gathering valuable data through applications such as Google Analytics, museum generated surveys and other online activities. And we see that museums are better linking the museum visit and exhibitions with relevant websites using a range of formats and media, such as videos of artists or curators talking about their work, museum gallery views, showing the objects on display, using 3D images of objects, and digital views of the exhibition catalog. Making meaningful connections between the onsite and online experience (Vermeeren et al. 2018a, b) has proven a strong incentive for museum attendance. Ultimately, it is these digital connections between the audience and museum that proffer communication of content from museum websites, social media, online publications, digital screens on the street as well as television and radio serving to bring awareness to the value and excitement of the arts experience that awaits the audience. A key challenge for the future, is how best to marshal these powerful forces of the digital world that now extend to artificial intelligence (Bostrom 2014; Papadimitriou et al. 2018), robots, augmented reality and 3D (Dodge 2018).

28.1.2 *Digital Art, Aesthetics and Interaction—Signposts of the Future*

Still, at this juncture in time, the unrecognized challenge museums face is that the journey of the arts between past and present and moving into the future brings to the fore the subject of digital art, aesthetics and seeing. One need only spend time visiting New York's museums to realize that digital art is rarely on view. Although it represents the most significant and new development in art, an iconic expression of digital culture, its presence and acceptance still seems illusive, although the V&A museum in London has made some steps in this regard (Beddard and Dodds 2009; see also Chap. 10), including organizing Digital Design Weekend events (Papadimitriou et al. 2016, 2017) and Digital Futures events (Papadimitriou and Bowen 2018). Why this disconnect from artistic practice continues to elude museum galleries and their curators calls for more conversation, lest we risk the progress museums are making towards being relevant and connected to the user. Digital tools and technology have empowered artists and users generally to be creative and innovative in new ways that point to the future and are in synch with global audiences, as they think digitally and critically and are finding new ways of expression and communicating meaning and message.

With the convergence of all media as digital, the number of participants in the arts who use digital tools intuitively, has enabled the creativity of thousands of people who have these tools in their hands daily, a phenomenon that is democratizing the arts. Their palette is digital, and they can communicate their art and artistic vision over global networks at little or no cost. The polemics around digital art seems to turn on which is better, traditional or digital art, when it is not an either-or matter. Each has its history and development and raison d'être in time and place. The subject of digital art, detailed in Part VI of this book, has a long history of development at the intersection of art, computing and technology driven by the luminaries of these disciplines, from Shannon and Turing (Giannini and Bowen 2017) to artists such as Joseph Albers and Nam June Paik, who have contributed new aesthetic and philosophical vision and consciousness that forms an intrinsic part of 20th-century art and the 21st century seeing in the digital age.

In terms of museum leadership for the future, the 2018 appointment of Max Hollein as Director of the Metropolitan Museum of Art sets an important signpost that seems predictive of the Met's digital future. In a two-part interview, Andrew Goldstein asks Hollein, in his introduction to the interview point out that, "one of the most vexing quandaries facing the Met: How can the venerable encyclopedic institution, with works stretching back to the earliest recorded human creations, meaningfully embrace contemporary art without giving off the vibe of a graying relative desperately trying to act cool?"—adding that, "Holistic" is a word for his path forward for the museum, and it's one Hollein uses frequently." A key question Goldstein poses is "What are the opportunities do you see for the Met in the digital sphere?" Hollein's response brings focus to the use of global platforms to reach beyond the walls of the museum, emphasizing storytelling, reaching out to audiences and the use of online "digital stories" on the Met's website to enhance visitors' exhibition experience onsite. His answer to what he sees as the three most important issues facing the Met, Hollein prioritizes (Goldstein 2018a):

1. "establishing the narrative of an encyclopedic museum for the future in regard to its representations of the cultures of the world and how they intersect… so that, "you evolve the narratives and that manifests itself in changes in the collection presentation and our exhibition programming."
2. "if you are a museum of the world and for the world, it's very clear that when you say the word 'museum,' you're not solely talking about the physical manifestation of an institution. I see 'museum' as a task that reaches way beyond the physical incarnation of the institution. There is so much responsibility and opportunity for us to be a conveyor of cultural understanding and art history. That means amplifying our work through digital media, through education, and through participating in complex, broader cultural debates."
3. "is the issue of contemporaneity at an encyclopedic institution… That would be another one of our priorities, but not just in terms of the collection. It's more about, what does "contemporary" mean at the Met? How do we define ourselves as a contemporary institution?"

Hollein's discussion of the "digital sphere" (Goldstein 2018b) seemed not to include the use of digital media in the Met's galleries nor of displaying digital art, while his comments on contemporary art are more about being a "contemporary institution" for which he focused on bringing greater attention to non-Western cultures and fresh interpretations of the permanent collections, an area which has fast become a top museum priority, in light of the persistence of old narratives that privilege Western culture, and challenges from contemporary social movements calling for de-colonization and repatriation. With profound change in the air, the question of whether digital art will be in the Met's future remains unclear. One wonders what it will it take major art museums to recognize digital artists as being in the mainstream of art in the 21st century that ties to digital aesthetics expression and seeing, and at the heart of the social and cultural content and contexts of art in the age of digital culture.

28.1.3 Digital Interactive Art

The Royal Academy of Arts, Summer Exhibition 2018 featured works that had decidedly strong social and political themes. This includes digital interactive works. James Burke's 2017 work, *The Constant Need for Approval* (see Fig. 28.2), which drew much attention and delight from visitors, presents commentary on the "like" rating Likert scale of the oft used thumbs up or down. The viewer touches one to five of the large silver stars to rate the work which is wired to a Samsung screen with a digital meter and the hash tag, #RATE THIS WORK. Stars turn yellow with touch, while the meter records the interaction. Climate change, sexual abuse and robots were some of the other topics interpreted.

Fig. 28.2 Installation view, *The Constant Need for Approval*, by James Burke, 2017. 250th Summer Exhibition, 2018, Royal Academy of Arts, London. (Photograph by Tula Giannini, July 17, 2018)

What's My Digital Future
by T. Giannini

What's my digital future
without digital expression
everyone's obsession
as well as depression
digital speak
texts and tweets
When I see digital art
I see digital can be
beautiful

What's my digital future
without being connected
Loneliness expected
I'd be so affected
Undetected

There's hope
for my digital future
Digital art speaks
to me
sets me free
a new materiality

I speak back
in conversation
with the realization
of the rising wave
of digitality
a future with
a new digital reality

Can't go back
to analog days
my digital ways
track to the future
as I ride the wave
of being digital
digital art
becomes pivotal
to being human
and smart

28.2 Predictions

Marshall Mcluhan is renowned for his late 20th-century predications of technological effects on culture and media, coining phrases such as "the global village" (McLuhan and Powers 1989). However, precise predictions are notoriously unreliable. Negroponte (1995) foresaw the digital future in his seminal book *Being Digital*. However, in the index, the Internet features extensively, but not the World Wide Web, even though it was widely available in academia by then. A year later, Wiener and Pescovitz (1996) considered possible year by year developments in the context of Wired magazine. For 2013, it was predicted that "the book goes digital" and for 2016, the "first large, public virtual library" was predicted. While Google Books (http://books.google.com) exists with scanned books, copyright issues have proved problematic. Amazon provides access to ebooks via Kindle, but sales of physical books are still significant. Further predicts for the digital age and its effect on the future from technological and social viewpoints have been made more recently (Schmidt and Cohen 2013; Susskind and Susskind 2017).

The Internet Archive (http://archive.org) does allow scanned books to be borrowed by one reader at a time. However, books are still largely physical in public libraries. Academic libraries are more electronic, although access to academic papers is often still restricted by commercial publishers behind pay walls, often charging around $30 US for access to an individual paper. Research-oriented universities are increasingly providing eprint servers with free access to papers produced by their own academics. A book genre that has remained print-centric is the art book, exhibition catalog, and artist book. These are typically now born-digital and then printed, which means they exist in the digital ecosphere, as digital objects that have a life of their own. This raises the question of printing born-digital objects.

At the turn of the millennium, a significant number of museums had their own websites, but there were still plenty of opportunities for the future (Bowen 2000a), including greater accessibility to databases. Bowen (2000b) predicted that access to museum collections could be provided using a universal web-based interface internationally, in a similar way to Google Books. While there have been initiatives such as Europeana in Europe (Petras et al. 2017), there is still no worldwide coordination of access to museum collections. Probably a large international Internet company like Google is needed to do this, since relevant international organizations such as ICOM (International Council of Museums) and UNESCO (United Nations Educational, Scientific and Cultural Organization) do not have the finances nor expertise to do this on their own. Google does provide some arts and cultural material (Google Arts and Culture, https://www.google.com/culturalinstitute), but this is not very extensive.

According to a survey, "from 2005 to 2015, the average amount of time Americans spent reading for personal interest on weekend days and holidays fell by six minutes to 21 minutes per day" (Humanities Indicators 2016). (See Fig. 28.3.) This includes print and digital, while "The average time American adults spent reading for personal interest has declined at every education level. The largest absolute decline occurred

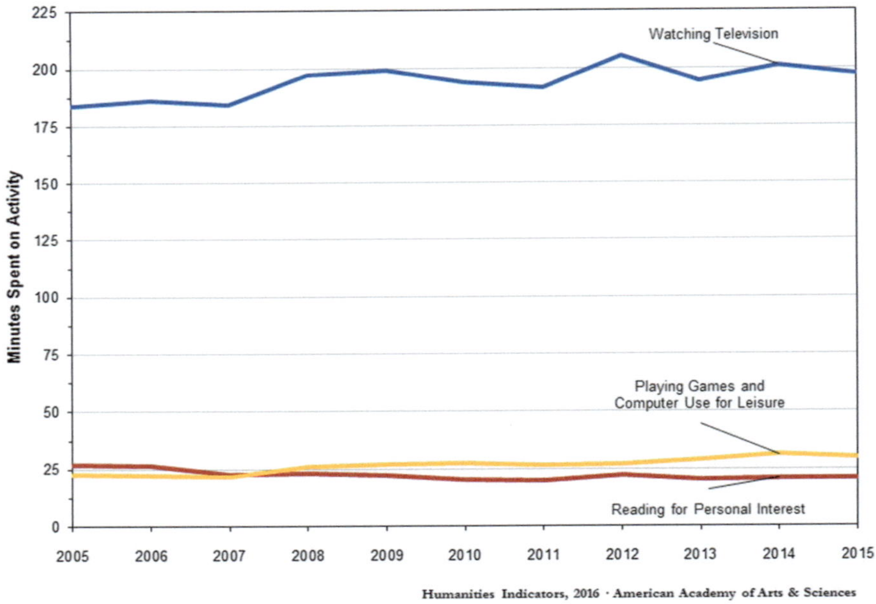

Fig. 28.3 Average number of minutes per weekend day or holiday spent engaged in selected leisure activities by Americans age 15 years and older, 2005–2015 (Humanities Indicators 2016) (Credit: American Academy of Arts and Sciences, *Humanities Indicators*, http://HumanitiesIndicators.org)

among those with college degrees, with the average falling from 45 minutes per day on weekends and holidays in 2005 to 30 min in 2014."

By 2018, the 21 minutes per day in 2015, had declined to 15 minutes per day. So, the real issue is not reading in print or online, but rather the steady upward trend of screen time, the rise of video and audio content, and search and browse online (Renaissance 2018). A Pew Research Center study on reading gives results in the percent of US adults who have read in the past 12 months, but this would seem to have minimal significance given that the amount of time spent per day adults spend reading as reported by the Renaissance study declined to 15 minutes per day—which raises the question of its significance compared to screen-time which is averaging 12 hours per day, including television (Perrin 2018).

How will these trends in leisure time use affect museum attendance in the future, and what might be some of the ways that museums will address these? The report, *Experimental Culture*, a horizon scan commissioned by Arts Council England presents a summary and data across four key areas of the arts and culture sector: (1) Audiences and participation; (2) Workforce and skills; (3) The changing funding environment and business models; (4) New technologies and the Conclusion—Charting a course to 2030. Here we focus on the section, "Provocations", quoting from leading experts in the arts who were interviewed to respond to the Report and talk about their vision for the future and some key issues cultural organizations might face as they move into the future (Armstrong 2018).

Jonathan Neelands, Academic Director for Cultural Partnerships, University of Warwick emphasizes:

> … the necessity for public investment in R&D, and the free flow of talent, technologies and investment across a vibrant ecosystem. Local communities look to the arts for a wide range of purposes- for entertainment, for social cohesion and identity making, for health and education, as a driver for economic growth and tourism. Are these wider purposes a distraction from or a return to the 'core' mission to deliver high quality arts for all? Are they the vital conduits towards new audiences, new aesthetics, new impact, new talent – providing a central role for artists and cultural organizations in their communities? Stresses diversity, local, place-based community arts.

Seb Chan, Chief Experience Officer, Australian Centre for the Moving Image, presents three key unresolved challenges based on his work with cultural heritage institutions over some twenty years—

> The first of these relates to the continued lack of institutional understanding of how audiences choose to spend their leisure time. The second, is how this is intertwined with issues of equity both in terms of audience and staff diversity. The third, of course, is how digital media and other technologies have been poorly understood – not just in terms of affordances and opportunities, but also in terms of competitors for this time.

Chan identifies "ambient media" as changing the way people choose to use their time and especially leisure time, which continues to decline as it competes with work and digital life. Deborah Bull, Assistant Principal, King's College London poses key questions focusing on inclusion and diversity.

> How can arts institutions and their funding be more inclusive of the public and the broader ecology of the arts they represent? "What is the role of the funded organizations in promoting and encouraging the cultural capabilities of everyone – in enabling all parts of the ecology to flourish in ways that are more empowering, more equitable and, in the end, more creative?"

Chris Michaels, Digital Director, National Gallery points a lack of change and sense of urgency in the way cultural and educational institutions are responding to the digital transformation of society, and rather hold tight past ways of doing and knowing.

> Too much of what the worlds of art and culture do is grounded in ideas that are old, breaking and desperate for renewal. Make comparisons between 'our' world and how people now behave in the digital-driven real-world, and the gap is painful.

He concludes by observing that:

> The underlying challenge is the same, everywhere: we need to align our behaviors to the new digital world around us. We need to let that world simplify what we do and how we do it. And we need, critically, to listen to the data and audience voices that new world makes easy to hear. We have the chance to renew and to rebuild. We need to take it.

Mark Robinson, founder of *Thinking Practice*, sees key challenges posed by the economic state of the arts as being underfunded and lacking diversity, which tends to discourage new talent and creativity and Pauline Tambling, Former Chief Executive, Creative and Cultural Skills also points to the economic issues facing the arts, "We could increase our sector's relevance, improve its productivity and gain wider credibility with the public if we could start to improve our sector's approach to employment."

The report's conclusions make recommendations defined in four areas: (1) Experimentation—the need to respond more quickly in adopting new technologies, and to create a research and development framework for the arts and cultural sector that feature experimentation; (2) Leveraging data—the need for a more systematic approach applied across the institution for decision making and to evaluate outcomes; (3) Shaping and sustaining partnerships for the goal of resource sharing and sustainability of projects; and (4) Reaching wider audiences through deepening relationships with local communities, great usage of technology to broaden institutional reach, and "by reimagining and renewing their relationship with audiences. This creativity will be vital in sustaining their relevance in future." Regarding "leveraging data", this was on view in the Glass Room exhibition space. A plaque about the exhibition poses thought-provoking questions about personal data and its collection.

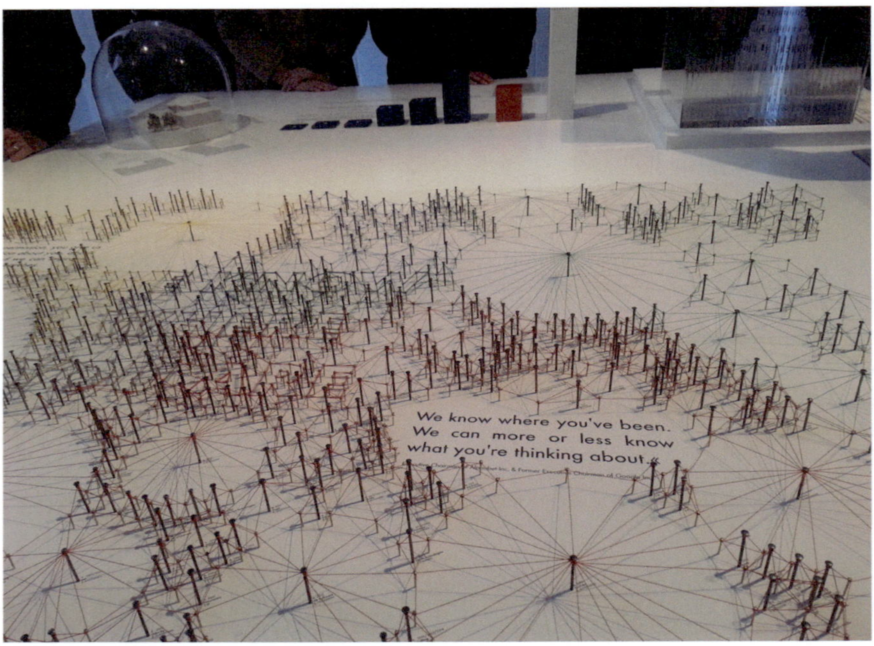

Fig. 28.4 *We know where you've been. We can more or less know what you're thinking about*—Text in center of work by Executive Chairman of Alphabet Inc. and former Executive Chairman of Google Inc. Data mapping work on display at the Glass Room Exhibition, London, 2017. (Photograph by Tula Giannini, November 11, 2017)

> What is personal data in an age where everything is but personal? The Glass Room is a space for reflection… What does your data say about you? What do you give up in the exchange? How are data and technology changing the personal, professional and social fabric of all of our lives? (Glass Room plaque text, November 2017) (Fig. 28.4)

These conclusions and the responses of experts presented above, show concordance in what is seen as the key issues and challenges for the arts and cultural sector: Being relevant, inclusive, diverse, operating locally and globally across platforms and via social media, building relationships and partnerships, new vision and strategies for economic equity in employment, and diversity in the workforce. Importantly, this will demand new ways of thinking about institution organization, moving from an old order to a new one that is non-linear and non-hierarchical to break down barriers to change allowing institutions to more rapidly transform into a postdigital world, in which the boundaries between physical and digital, real and virtual blur becoming integral, the separation between people and institutions, inside and outside the walls becomes porous allowing for collaboration, partnerships and sharing. With this institutional state of being comes new awareness and the ability to respond to social and cultural issues and movements, and most importantly, to adopt participatory and interactive models of a working community, insuring that public voices are heard and play a role in the life of the museum.

28.2.1 Postdigital Culture and Museums

Postdigital culture, defined by the integration of the physical and digital world, is moving with warp speed to encompass every aspect of human life with museum life mirroring this trend. From the perspective of the museum visitor, the integration of physical and digital is not quite apparent, as the digital work in the museum still remains behind the scenes, and rarely seen in the galleries. Although digitization of collections has been progressing for many years, it is only now that it is being done on a large scale, and with the latest technologies to create "coded digital objects" as opposed to images, to adopt open source and use APIs that support sharing and interoperability with other institutions, and with visitors, onsite or online. Museums such as the Art Institute of Chicago (AIC) in 2018, totally re-imagined their website within a user-centered framework, that transforms it into a postdigital space. Linked to the web redesign is a grand rollout of a new database of some 52,000 AIC public domain images made available through Creative Commons licensing, and with the expiration of Sonny Bono Copyright Term Extension Act on January 1, 2019, a large number of art works have now entered the public domain. (Fleishman 2019; Wexelman 2019). The images can be downloaded and viewed in high resolution, providing a great opportunity for researchers, students and the general public. From the homepage, the user clicks on "The Collection," and reads the following explanation and then choose, "Artworks, Writings or Resources." (Kinsella 2018):

> Explore thousands of artworks in the museum's wide-ranging collection – from our world-renowned icons to lesser-known gems from every corner of the globe – as well as our books, writings, reference materials, and other resources.

From the Writing section the user can read about the new web design.

> As part of a multiyear initiative to completely redesign our website, we've scrutinized every layer of the visitor's digital experience. With fresh insights in mind, we created a new site that highlights the full range of the museum's dynamic offerings – the collection, exhibitions, and public programming – and helps users connect more intimately with the stories behind the artwork. (Neault 2018)

Changes in users' digital behavior serve as a force for change in the way museums are developing their communication with users/visitors. For example, mobile devices are visitors first choice of access to a museum website which makes web collections and services available to them inside the museum. This holds great potential not only for visitors but for the museum itself—to communicate directly with visitors in the museum, and especially in the galleries. This opens the door to many new and exciting opportunities which draw upon the treasure trove of digital collections that can interact in advanced ways including artificial intelligence and machine learning (Papadimitriou et al. 2018). Looking to the future and given the vast collections of digitized coded materials and media, museum outreach to visitors in galleries will be able to connect art, information, communication and interaction. Text on walls will become a thing of the past, exhibition catalogs will go digital to be part of the learning experience, and new digital experiences using AI (Artificial Intelligence), AR (Augmented Reality), and VR (Virtual Reality) will enter the galleries to enhance seeing and experiencing art. The digital "behind the scene" will move to the forefront and integrate as part of a total experience that postdigital visitors expect and need. These developments will create a sense of transparency and greater understanding of the functioning and purpose of museums and allow them to participate and contribute.

28.2.2 Envisioning the Digital Future of Museums

We consider the growing forces competing with museums for audience: entertainment—global media—1.6 billion Facebook users—and the many hours people spend each day with digital media. Most importantly, artists across disciplines are using the Internet to create their own identities and communicate art works, and design exhibitions and shows that often occupy physical and digital space, whilst museums have long identified with their physical space as a specific place in time and space, they have now expanded to cyberspace, having a digital identity on the web. Thus, in the digital world, artists can tell their own story and create identity, bypassing the traditional gatekeepers. How should artists and museums relate to one another?

Times Square, New York City (see Fig. 28.5), captures an aspect of the museum digital dilemma, as museums find themselves trying to compete with digitally designed spaces including department stores, street art, digital media displays and

Fig. 28.5 *Window to the Heart*, by ArandaLasch + Marcelo Coelho, Duffy Square, Times Square at night, New York City, 2018. (Photograph by Tula Giannini, February 27, 2018)

public art and entertainment. Art or entertainment, Time Square is at the epicenter of digital New York, a place where millions of tourists can revel in its 24/7 light show and a gallery space for digital artists both fine art and commercial to reach millions of viewers.

> *Window to the Heart* places the world's largest lens in the center of Times Square. The 12 foot in diameter Fresnel lens was designed with 3D-printing manufacturer Formlabs to distort and capture the image of Times Square, optically bending light, and attention, to the heart-shaped window at its center. Visitors can look through the window or photograph themselves within it, completing the loop between the lens of the eye and the lens of the camera.

21st-century museums reside in the digital culture ecosystem and thus are in search of a new identity as they grapple with audience perceptions of the past and the promise of the future. Future challenges can be seen in:

- Balancing physical and digital reality of space and time.
- Beyond the walls—the impact of social and cultural trends and questions of human identity.
- Battle of museum insiders and outsiders.
- From protected spaces to common places—where will the museum reside?
- Is visitor experience enough—will museums be a new type of "Disneyland"?

- As museums strive to create a new model for the complex digital world, no one answer will be the solution.
- Baking a new museum cake—what will be the ingredients? (Fig. 28.6)

Museums are facing new challenges as new digital reality dominates human attention and existence. Looking out from within the museum, the insiders, the museum professionals, are thinking about what their museum should be or become. Outside, the world is speeding towards a dynamic synergy of physical and virtual life marked by rapid transformation and new states of being. This means that museums remaining the same, not changing, will fall behind, appearing old and dusty. Who will come to a quiet place of yesteryear? Central to finding a new sense of identity that seems relevant, contributes to social and cultural advancement, and enriches people's lives by being part of their future, is not a question at all, but a necessity and imperative. The new directions museums will take will be mostly determined by what is hap-

Fig. 28.6 Fashion display with neon light sculpture, Bloomingdales, Short Hills, New Jersey, USA, 2018. The use of pink neon is reminiscent of the British artist Tracy Emin (Santiago Cortés 2018) and is widely recognized for messages written in neon, and Eurostar passengers returning to London can enjoy seeing her sculpture, "I want my time with you.". (Photograph by Tula Giannini, November 23, 2018)

pening and developing outside—the social issues, how artists are seeing and making art, how people are responding to new cultural forms and expressions, and how they are living, communicating and working.

Museums have little choice but to embrace rapid change in order to maintain strong ties and connections to their audience, actual and potential, real and virtual. As computational culture causes radical change, it is creating a digital ecosystem where art and culture is everywhere and everyone—in every click in multiple forms across the Internet and social media. This complex, diverse digital ecosystem invites all participants to its democratic platform. Everyone who wishes to be, is a player, has a voice and speaks across digital media in an endless array of messages, blogs and websites, as they share stories, likes, opinions and ideas. How will museums assert a newly envisioned identity while being an integral part of daily digital happening and how will they position themselves in a growing network of cultural identities, find friends and collaborators and be in conversation with other cultural institutions and communities.

As museums evolve from being quiet, highly organized and predictable institutions, to complex cultural organizations entrenched in the life of diverse communities and connected to global platforms, they will need to adopt new ways of being and doing. Looking to the future, museums will need to communicate with diverse cultures, participate in public conversations, tell new stories and narratives, create visitor experiences, collaborate with other museums and with artists of all types, show process and pose questions, while relinquishing their long-standing role of unchallenged expertise, to one of sharing the stage with other actors, and address issues of an open museum that welcomes the digital future. For example, at the British Museum, half of the electronic guide usage is already in Mandarin.

28.2.3 The Digital Ecosystem Catalyzes Global Awareness of Cultural Heritage

Welcome to the postdigital world where the physical and digital come together on the Internet and web juxtaposing people and things across boundaries and cultural silos. This coming together produces new discoveries and relationships that are challenging long-held museum orthodoxy on the life and identity of collection objects, their history and message. (For example, see Chap. 12 on object itineraries using new digital techniques for special and geographical analysis.) New research methodologies used for digital art history and humanities meld archival resources and digital dialogues across the Internet resulting in new ways of interpreting objects and the stories they tell, and also allow scholars to garner new information regarding provenance. As the Internet developed during the 1990s, museums and libraries feared that having their collections online would reduce the number of visitors onsite and by extension their revenue.

Now in hindsight, we see that online collections are producing the opposite effect and are increasing visitor numbers, the cultural and monetary value of museum collections, and the public's interaction with them. The question as to whether 3D replicas of art works will replace the need to see originals is better framed around replicas allowing visitors to experience the object in places where it would not otherwise be possible. The V&A's cast collection galleries featuring plaster cast reproductions of great works of art including Michelangelo's David, Trajan's Column, and Ghiberti's Gates of Paradise offer an excellent example of a museum exhibiting copies of important works using plaster as well as electrotype, photography and digital media that is especially useful for students and scholars.

New 3D digital production techniques can serve museum visitors similarly. Further, using new digital techniques such as 3D scans, augmented and virtual reality, scholars, artists, researchers and the general public across the globe are enjoying enhanced digital access to museum collections. In the future, copies made with these new digital tools are increasing the desire to view originals when possible. The artist Thierry Oussou bemoans the riches of African art being in France, believes that these surrogates do not substitute for the originals saying that:

> "Africa is empty of its riches," the artist told *The Guardian* (Sawa 2018). "When young students wish to write about the treasures of their homeland, they have to travel to France to do their research. But when I was in Benin, I didn't have the money to buy a plane ticket like that." (Brown and Rea 2018)

28.2.4 Online Collection Databases

Looking ahead, we see that public access to online collections databases will grow exponentially as digital tools and technology for digitization and image search advance unabatedly. For example, new digital techniques using AI and machine learning are creating algorithms for programs such as *Aries* being developed by the Frick Collection (see Chap. 24) and Stanford University, designed to make visual search more accurate and responsive to user needs, bypassing labor-intensive methods and metadata schemas. Advances as these hold promise to uncover hidden images and collections, and to allow users to search vast numbers of images. Another exciting trend that advantages online users, is the vogue of the highly detailed collections databases as those being developed by the British Museum and Metropolitan Museum of art and that engender global awareness of art works by providing object history, description, images and conservation details, affording more transparency and access (British Museum 2015).

After much debate on the impact of online museum collections, there is consensus that collections on the web spur public recognition of the importance of cultural heritage to society, to cultural identity and to self. As users gain greater awareness of art and collections and see the vastness and scope of art in digital images which they can study with a click, these experiences are serving to strengthen user connections to cultural heritage, and unexpectedly, are also sparking interest in the emerging

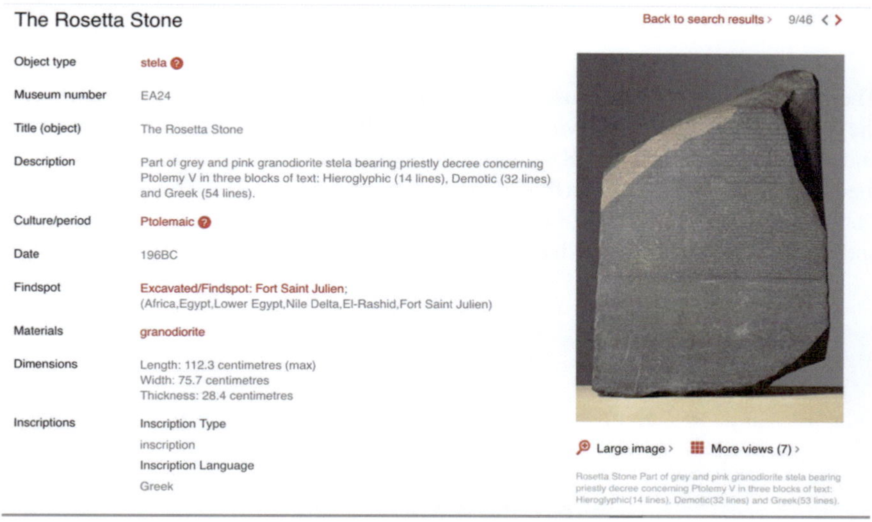

Fig. 28.7 *The Rosetta Stone*, 196 BCE, record from the British Museum Online Collection Database. (Screenshot by Tula Giannini, January 2018)

repatriation and restitution movements expressed by the flood of social media posts on Twitter, Instagram, and museums online.

The database record for the Rosetta Stone shown in Fig. 28.7 is an example of the level of detail provided. In addition to the information seen in this view, the record also provides extensive curator's comments, bibliography, location, exhibition history, condition, associated names, acquisition name and date, department and ID, and object reference number, and includes open data information, "British Museum collection data is also available in the W3C open data standard, RDF, allowing it to join and relate to a growing body of linked data published by organizations around the world." Links in red provide more information on the object. For years the Rosetta Stone has been an object of contention with new demands in 2018 for its return to the Grand Egyptian Museum.

> The ancient slab, which is engraved with three languages and unlocked the secret of Egyptian hieroglyphs, has been a long-running source of tension between Cairo and London. British soldiers captured the stone in 1801 after defeating Napoleon's army in Egypt and transferred it to the British Museum, where it has long been the most-visited object. Dr Tarek Tawfik, the director of the new Grand Egyptian Museum (GEM), said he was eager to see the Rosetta Stone back in Egypt. (Telegraph 2018)

28.2.5 Enter Popular Culture

The spectacular success of museum exhibitions featuring popular culture icons, from the V&A's exhibitions of David Bowie (also at the Brooklyn Museum), Pink Floyd, and Frida Kahlo (see Fig. 28.8), the Metropolitan's *Heavenly Bodies* juxtaposing medieval art and costume with that of famous fashion designers as Chanel, Dior, Saint Laurent and Versace, (Fig. 28.9) and the Louvre's new relationship with Beyoncé and Jay-Z (Pes 2019), have demonstrated the power of pop culture to attract new

Fig. 28.8 V&A front entrance with poster display of special exhibitions showing popular exhibition themes. Poster on right, *Frida Kahlo, Making Herself Up*, which moved to the Brooklyn Museum in 2019, with a new subtitle, *Appearances can be Deceiving*. (Photograph by Tula Giannini, July 16, 2018)

Fig. 28.9 Large crowds gather at the entrance to the Metropolitan Museum of Art on 5th Avenue in New York City. The featured exhibition in 2018 was *Heavenly Bodies: Fashion and the Catholic Imagination*, which drew record-breaking crowds estimated at 1.6 million people. *Note* the Heavenly Bodies poster in the upper right corner. (Photograph by Tula Giannini, July 31, 2018)

and larger audiences for art, and to push the boundaries between so-called high art and popular art. This subject was discussed in a 2018 two-part interview with Ann Pasternak, Director of the Brooklyn Museum in conversation with Goldstein (2018c, d). Pasternak noted (Goldstein 2018d):

> I think there are these paradigms within our field – like populist versus elitist, high versus low – that are very divisive, even destructive, to our institutions. In fact, I was a little concerned about taking on the David Bowie show because I know that one of the criticisms against the museum has been that we're populist.

Commenting on the public response to the Bowie exhibition, which attracted 180,000 people, Pasternak recalls that, "We saw people in tears in the exhibition every day, and people spent, on average, something like 96 min in the show—that's a long time to be in an exhibition." Some of the take-aways drawn from Pasternak's observations are, "people love an immersive experience. The sound system and the headphones were really additive to helping people connect with what they were seeing," adding that, "ultimately, people connect with biography, and they care about story. If you take a look at a lot of blockbusters, there's usually a great story behind them." (Goldstein 2018d). Pasternak sees her job as director, as "one of intervention—of questioning the orthodoxies of the past and creating a sustainable, relevant, exciting path forward." Her perspectives no doubt draw on the challenges she has faced at the Brooklyn Museum, from calls for de-colonize, to community objections on hiring a "white women" for the position of curator of the African collections, issues that brought large numbers of protesters into the museum. Speaking about her role as a museum director, Pasternak speaks clearly about the role of museums (Goldstein 2018d):

> We need to contribute to the diverse cultural vitality of our communities. We need to engage in the difficult conversations, not retreat from them. We need to be places of questioning and debate – not safe spaces – as we try as a society to plan for a greater future. Where else can you go today to have these kinds of conversations? College campuses? Well, then you have to be in college. Religious spaces? Maybe. There just aren't that many public spaces for these kinds of things today – so I think the role of the museum is critically important.

Fig. 28.10 Installation view from the V&A exhibition, *The Future Starts Now*, 2018. The text reads, "We are all connected, but do we feel lonely?" This illuminates the paradox and dichotomy between connection and isolation, part of the dark side of the Internet, where connection is not the same as a human relationship. (Photograph by Tula Giannini, June 13, 2018)

A key point Pasternak makes when asked about the museum's "unique selling proposition," she insightfully says, "So when you ask what the Brooklyn Museum offers that is unique, it's our ability to connect the past to this radical present—and also to engage in broad creativity." Here her emphasis on creativity and the connection of past to present flows seamlessly to the topic of connecting present to future, as we envision what that future might be moving forward into a postdigital age. As we look ahead, we can see that the trends of 2018 have set the course for change in the museum landscape of the digital future, and where digital culture becomes more pervasive and embedded in our physical environment, from smart homes to driverless cars, all part of the digital ecosystem where we're all connected (Fig. 28.10).

Over the past few years, we have witnessed many major museum expansions and new buildings, and this trend promises to continue. A leading example is MoMA's new building at 53W.53 (53 West 53rd Street, see Fig. 28.11) in New York City, a building that is the centerpiece of MoMA's new vision for the future which opens the museum's narrative to more diversity and new ways of thinking about their collections:

> … the museum is moving away from discipline-specific galleries that feature established artists – many of them white men – and toward more chronological and thematic approaches that include multiple formats as well as more minority and female artists. (Pogrebin 2017)

This ties to the redesign of their original building:

> The new design calls for more gallery space and a transformed main lobby, physical changes that, along with the re-examination of art collections and diversity, represent an effort to open up MoMA and break down the boundaries defined by its founder, Alfred Barr. (Pogrebin 2017)

The new MoMA building, a skyscraper that is more than a thousand feet tall, can be seen to symbolize museums entering a new era of an exciting and expanding universe of possibilities for the postdigital age, as we "think digitally", to quote Glen Lowry about what the museum of the future will look like and be like.

Fig. 28.11 Construction site for new MoMA building at 53W.53 in New York City. (Photograph by Tula Giannini, February 27, 2018)

28.3 Conclusion

We have entered the next wave of the digital revolution as all media has gone digital, a state of being that closely aligns with human creativity and innovation—mainly, art, culture and the humanities, the lifeblood of the museum. The convergence of media as digital, which makes all media equally usable, is fueling the rise of human expression through visual and sound media, as we shift to a post-text-dominated era to life on the Internet obsessed with YouTube, podcasts, video, and images, while new technology is introduced regularly such as Google Lens for smart phone visual recognition using AI. This trend reveals the power of visual and sound media as digital media language that enables museums to reach larger more diverse audiences.

Indeed, IT research has become the engine of change positioned at the heart of innovation and creativity while empowering interaction of individuals and institutions across the globe. Although the digital shift represents major challenges to the museum of the future (Bast et al. 2018), meeting these challenges will depend on how museums integrate into the digital ecosystem and use emerging technologies, while recognizing the power of digital culture to transform human identity, behavior, states of being, digital seeing, art and aesthetics. Museums too are transforming. With altered states being and a new sense of identity, they enter the digital future.

We are now only beginning to measure the impact of everyone being connected via the Internet, as the nature of this connection is being fueled by more pervasive and sophisticated social media empowered by AI and machine learning. There is no longer is a choice about whether museums should be on the web, joining the digital ecosystem is like saying we exist. And yet, in many ways, 2018 proves that museums were not fully prepared for the shared digital world that is overtaking real life. This new state of being is driving greater transparency, 24/7 news, and behind the scenes stories that at any moment can go viral and set alarms.

A central quality of digital culture, it that it has developed as a global culture without physical boundaries. It is a shared culture that allows us to see day to day activity across the globe, what people are doing and thinking. So, beyond everyone being connected, we are now thinking digitally, sharing thoughts and images, knowledge and resources, with a new transparency, a place where ways of doing and being are evolving in this shared space we call the digital ecosystem. A social and cultural space that is shaping human behavior and perceptions that validate the assumption that people seek the same basic things as they compare their lives to others via the Internet. They want the best there is, and at the top of everyone's list is freedom, democracy, and the right to life, liberty and the pursuit of happiness. In this digital infrastructure, museum collections (Knell 2017) are seen by a global audience of diverse cultural experiences. With digitization and born-digital, human knowledge held by cultural institutions in the arts, humanities and sciences are all packing their databases and moving to the web—it's the place to be! A new critical mass of digital information has emerged that is bigger than ever imagined—and is growing by leaps and bounds. What distinguishes digital culture from the culture of physical place, is that digital culture evolving over the last 70 years, grew out of a borderless global community around digital communication, sharing, working with digital tools in a world of flattened hierarchies, participation and unfettered conversations.

Although we are experiencing the growing integration of physical and digital place, at the same time, new tensions are arising as our ability of seeing on the net becomes super-real with 3D, VR, AR, and AI. We can visit virtual places, and even see and learn things that have not been revealed. Cyberspace continues to build its own infrastructure that now begins to control, influence and monitor the physical world. There is a cadre of things we can do on the Internet at the core of digital culture not possible in the real. As we move towards the coming together of these two worlds, we are experiencing culture clash of bounded physical places with borderless cyberspaces. The growing phenomenon of our omnipresent digital ecosystem is challenging our perceptions, our desires and goals.

The pace of the digital world is going into high gear with AI and machine learning at the forefront with realistic simulations of the physical world, while the physical world is dealing with old ways, structures and societal frameworks steeped in old regimes. We know little of what we cannot see and experience—while on the Internet, we see more, and digital experience becomes more real as the digital tools that we use to build cyberspace continue to advance. These developments tied to the impact of the digital ecosystem buoyed by a surge in global awareness of arts and culture, and human identity, has ignited activist movements (see Chap. 5) and a growing engagement in arts and culture. With the merging of physical and digital life set in relief by the fusion of high and popular culture, and digital arts and technology, there is a new synergy between these once disparate elements, all connected and communicating in cyberspace. This fusion is ushering in a new era of greater understanding, cultural diversity with new conversations across boundaries.

We see the gates of the arts and museum world opening to a new vision shared with audiences and the public. In 2019 alone, we will see the building or expansion of a slew of new museums across the globe set to transform their physical places. For example, in New York City, The Shed, under construction on the Highline, a new MoMA building expanding its presence in Midtown Manhattan, the Frick on 5th Avenue and American Museum of Natural on Manhattan's upper Westside being reimagined, and in the Middle East, there are new museums opening such the Grand Egyptian Museum and the National Museum of Qatar (Sutton 2019). These museum projects represent not only enormous financial investment, but as well, long-term commitment to our cultural future, and a predictor of a museum landscape that is ascending while engaging ever increasing audiences. The thoughts of the National Portrait Gallery Director, Nicolas Cullinan, who is leading the NGL's transformation, speak to his priorities for the museum's future, "It's very rare you get the chance to rethink an institution top to bottom… This is about making the whole institution more relevant, more open and more accessible," and clearly these are museum values integral to digital culture (Morris 2019).

Moving forward, museums will need new strategies for change and are challenged to embrace the unstoppable force of the digital ecosystem as they seek to integrate museums past and present and plan for the future. The new research and perspectives that this book presents responds to these questions and offer new vision for the 21st century. Set at the very moment we are arriving at an important juncture in time and space—the global crossroads of digital culture, digital life and art and the emerging postdigital world, we see that the museum of the digital future promises a burgeoning museum community, building new spaces and places, growing global culturally diverse audiences, welcoming participation, and fostering creative and innovative environments, a sure sign that museums are moving into a digital culture renaissance.

Acknowledgements A part of this chapter is based on material from Giannini and Bowen (2018).

References

Amichai-Hamburger Y (2013) The social net: understanding our online behavior. Oxford University Press

Armstrong H et al (2018) Experimental culture—a horizon scan commissioned by Arts Council England, Summary report and provocations, Mar 2018. Arts Council England Report 2018. https://www.artscouncil.org.uk/sites/default/files/download-file/Experimental_Culture_summary_150318.pdf. Accessed 18 Jan 2019

Bast G, Carayannis EG, Campbell DFJ (eds) (2018) The future of museums. Springer, Arts, Research, Innovation and Society Series

Beddard H, Dodds D (2009) Digital pioneers. V&A Pattern, V&A Publishing

Berners-Lee T (1999) Weaving the web: the past, present and future of the world wide web by its inventor. Orion Business Books

Bostrom N (2014) Superintelligence: paths, dangers, strategies. Oxford University Press

Bowen JP (2000a) Weaving the museum web: past, present and future. In: Proceedings of SSGRR 2000 computer & ebusiness conference, L'Aquila, Italy, 31 July–6 Aug 2000

Bowen JP (2000b) It's just a tool though: no it's not, it's an alien life form. Museum Comput Netw Spectra 27(1):19–20 (Summer)

Bowen JP, Giannini T, Polmeer G, Gannis C, Gardiner J, Kearney J, Wands B, Weinel J (2018) States of being: art and identity in digital space and time. In: Bowen JP, Weinel J, Diprose G, Lambert N (eds) EVA London 2018 conference proceedings, Electronic Workshops in Computing (eWiC), BCS, pp 1–7. https://doi.org/10.14236/ewic/eva2018.1

British Museum (2015) Towards 2020: the British Museum's strategy. The British Museum, UK. https://www.britishmuseum.org/pdf/Towards_2020-The_British_Museum_Strategy.pdf. Accessed 18 Jan 2019

Brown K, Rea N (2018) As the restitution debate rages on in Europe, could the solution lie in the art of the high-tech copy? Artnet News, 19 Dec 2018. https://news.artnet.com/art-world/restitution-and-technology-2018-1420246. Accessed 18 Jan 2019

Center for Media Justice (2015) The digital culture shift: from scale to power—how the internet shapes social change, and how social change is shaping the internet. Center for Media Justice, USA. https://centerformediajustice.org/wp-content/uploads/2015/08/digital_culture_shift_report.pdf. Accessed 18 Jan 2019

Dodge WR (2018) Unpacking 263,000 visitor photos at the Royal Ontario Museum. Noteworthy J Blog, 11 May 2018. https://blog.usejournal.com/https-medium-com-wrdodger-unpacking-260-000-visitor-photos-at-the-royal-ontario-museum-e35a51aa9f6b. Accessed 18 Jan 2019

Fleishman G (2019) For the first time in more than 20 years, copyrighted works will enter the public domain. Smithsonian Mag, Jan 2019. https://www.smithsonianmag.com/arts-culture/first-time-20-years-copyrighted-works-enter-public-domain-180971016/. Accessed 18 Jan 2019

Giannini T, Bowen JP (2017) Life in code and digits: when Shannon met Turing. In: Bowen JP, Diprose G, Lambert N (eds) EVA London 2017 conference proceedings, Electronic Workshops in Computing (eWiC), BCS, pp 51–58. https://doi.org/10.14236/ewic/eva2017.9

Giannini T, Bowen JP (2018) Of museums and digital culture: a landscape view. In: Bowen JP, Diprose G, Lambert N (eds) EVA London 2018 conference proceedings, Electronic Workshops in Computing (eWiC), BCS, pp 172–179. https://doi.org/10.14236/ewic/eva2018.34

Goldstein A (2018a) New met director max Hollein on how he plans to lead the museum into a more Egalitarian future—to mark the start of a new era. Artnet News, 24 Sept 2018. https://news.artnet.com/art-world/met-director-max-hollein-interview-1354600. Accessed 18 Jan 2019

Goldstein A (2018b) Max Hollein on how the met will redefine the entire way we think about contemporary art—the freshly installed met director spoke to Andrew Goldstein about his plans for new art, new technology, and new funding at the museum. Artnet News, 25 Sept 2018. https://news.artnet.com/art-world/met-director-max-hollein-interview-part-2-1355749

Goldstein A (2018c) Brooklyn museum director Anne Pasternak on how an encyclopedic institution can address entrenched racism and sexism. Artnet News, 3 Dec 2018. https://news.artnet.com/art-world/anne-pasternak-brooklyn-museum-interview-part-1-1408375. Accessed 18 Jan 2019

Goldstein G (2018d) The Brooklyn museum's Anne Pasternak on why 'protest is here to stay,' and how data (and David Bowie) show the way forward. Artnet News, 4 Dec 2018. https://news.artnet.com/art-world/anne-pasternak-brooklyn-museum-interview-part-2-1409434. Accessed 18 Jan 2019

Humanities Indicators (2016) Time spent reading. Humanities Indicators, American Academy of Arts & Science, Sept 2016. https://www.humanitiesindicators.org/content/indicatorDoc.aspx?i=11094. Accessed 19 Jan 2019

Kinsella E (2018) The Art Institute of Chicago is the latest museum to offer open access to thousands of images in its archive. Artnet News, 23 Oct 2018. https://news.artnet.com/art-world/art-institute-chicago-offers-open-access-44000-images-1377739. Accessed 18 Jan 2019

Knell SJ (ed) (2017) Museums and the future of collecting, 2nd edn. Routledge. https://doi.org/10.4324/9781315248561

McLuhan M, Powers BR (1989) The global village: transformations in world life and media in the 21st century. Oxford University Press

Morris J (2019) How Nicholas Cullinan is transforming London's national portrait gallery. Museum Network, Sotheby's, 23 Jan 2019. https://museumnetwork.sothebys.com/en/articles/portrait-of-the-director-how-nicholas-cullinan-is-transforming-londons-national-portrait-gallery. Accessed 24 Jan 2019

NEA (2018a) New report on arts attendance shows gains national endowment for the arts releases data from latest survey of public participation in the arts. National Endowment for the Arts, USA, 12 Sept 2018. https://www.arts.gov/news/2018/new-report-arts-attendance-shows-gains. Accessed 18 Jan 2019

NEA (2018b) The 2017 survey of public participation in the arts. National Endowment for the Arts, USA, Sept 2018. https://www.arts.gov/artistic-fields/research-analysis/arts-data-profiles/arts-data-profile-18. Accessed 18 Jan 2019

NEA (2018c) U.S. trends in arts attendance and literary reading: 2002–2017. National Endowment for the Arts, USA, Sept 2018. https://www.arts.gov/publications/us-trends-arts-attendance-and-literary-reading-2002-2017. Accessed 18 Jan 2019

Neault M (2018) Behind the scenes of the website redesign. Art Institute of Chicago, USA, 22 Oct 2018. https://www.artic.edu/articles/713/behind-the-scenes-of-the-website-redesign. Accessed 18 Jan 2019

Negroponte N (1995) Being digital. Alfred A. Knopf, Inc.

Papadimitriou I, Bowen JP (2018) Digital Futures: exhibits at EVA London 2018. In: Bowen JP, Diprose G, Lambert N (eds) EVA London 2018 conference proceedings, Electronic Workshops in Computing (eWiC), BCS, pp 41–42. https://doi.org/10.14236/ewic/eva2018.8

Papadimitriou I, Prescott A, Rogers J (eds) (2016) Engineering the future: as part of V&A Digital Design Weekend 2016. Uniform Communications Ltd

Papadimitriou I, Prescott A, Rogers J (eds) (2017) Bridging open borders: as part of V&A Digital Design Weekend 2017. Uniform Communications Ltd

Papadimitriou I, Prescott A, Rogers J (eds) (2018) Artificially intelligent. V&A Digital Design Weekend, Victoria and Albert Museum, UK

Perrin A (2018) Nearly one-in-five Americans now listen to audiobooks. Pew Research Center, 8 Mar 2018. http://www.pewresearch.org/fact-tank/2018/03/08/nearly-one-in-five-americans-now-listen-to-audiobooks/. Accessed 18 Jan 2019

Pes J (2019) The Louvre Shatters attendance records with 10 million visitors in 2018—with a little help from Beyoncé and Jay-Z. Artnet News, 3 Jan 2019. https://news.artnet.com/art-world/record-breaking-louvre-attendance-1430728. Accessed 18 Jan 2019

Petras V, Hill T, Stiller J, Gäde M (2017) Europeana—a search engine for digitised cultural heritage material. Datenbank Spektrum 17(1):41–46. https://doi.org/10.1007/s13222-016-0238-1

Pew Research Center (2017) The revolution is digital. Pew Research Center, Washington, DC, USA, 12 June 2017. https://trend.pewtrusts.org/en/archive/summer-2017/crunch-the-revolution-is-digital. Accessed 18 Jan 2019
Pogrebin R (2017) MoMA's makeover rethinks the presentation of art. The New York Times, 1 June 2017. https://www.nytimes.com/2017/06/01/arts/design/moma-redesign-art-expansion.html. Accessed 18 Jan 2019
Renaissance (2018) The magic of 15 minutes: reading practice and reading growth. Renaissance.com, 23 Jan 2018. https://www.renaissance.com/2018/01/23/blog-magic-15-minutes-reading-practice-reading-growth/. Accessed 18 Jan 2019
Santiago Cortés M (2018) 10 artists who made masterpieces with Neon. Michelle Santiago Cortés. Artsy, 10 Dec 2018. https://www.artsy.net/article/artsy-editorial-10-artists-who-work-with-neon. Accessed 18 Jan 2019
Sawa DB (2018) Watch the throne: why artist Thierry Oussou faked an archaeological dig. The Guardian, 9 July 2018. https://www.theguardian.com/artanddesign/2018/jul/09/thierry-oussou-faked-archaeological-dig-african-art-colonial-looting. Accessed 18 Jan 2019
Schmidt E, Cohen J (2013) The new digital age: reshaping the future of people, nations and business. John Murray
Susskind R, Susskind D (2017) The future of the professions: how technology will transform the work of human experts. Oxford University Press
Sutton B (2019) The buzziest and most beautiful museums opening in 2019. Artsy, 18 Jan 2019. https://www.artsy.net/article/artsy-editorial-buzziest-beautiful-museums-opening-2019. Accessed 24 Jan 2019
Telegraph (2018) Egyptian museum calls for Rosetta Stone to be returned from UK after 200 years. The Telegraph, UK, 6 Nov 2018. https://www.telegraph.co.uk/news/2018/11/06/egyptian-museum-calls-rosetta-stone-returned-uk-200-years/. Accessed 18 Jan 2019
Vermeeren A, Calvi L, Sabiescu A (2018a) Museum experience design: crowds, ecosystems and novel technologies. Springer Series on Cultural Computing. https://doi.org/10.1007/978-3-319-58550-5
Vermeeren A, Calvi L, Sabiescu A, Trocchianesi R, Stuedahl D, Giaccardi E, Radice S (2018b) Future museum experience design: crowds, ecosystems and novel technologies. In: Vermeeren A et al (2018a) Chapter 1, pp 1–16. https://doi.org/10.1007/978-3-319-58550-5_1
Wexelman A (2019) Works by Pablo Picasso, Marcel Duchamp, and others are now in the public domain. Artsy News, 2 Jan 2019. https://www.artsy.net/news/artsy-editorial-works-pablo-picasso-marcel-duchamp-public-domain. Accessed 18 Jan 2019
Wieners B, Pescovitz D (1996) Reality Check. Hardwired, p 161

Index

T. Giannini and J. P. Bowen (eds.), *Museums and Digital Culture*,
Springer Series on Cultural Computing, https://doi.org/10.1007/978-3-319-97457-6

MIX
Papier aus verantwortungsvollen Quellen
Paper from responsible sources
FSC® C105338

If you have any concerns about our products,
you can contact us on
ProductSafety@springernature.com

In case Publisher is established outside the EU,
the EU authorized representative is:
Springer Nature Customer Service Center GmbH
Europaplatz 3, 69115 Heidelberg, Germany

Printed by Libri Plureos GmbH
in Hamburg, Germany